Political Theory

AN ENCYCLOPEDIA OF CONTEMPORARY AND CLASSIC TERMS

SCOTT JOHN HAMMOND

GREENWOOD PRESS

Westport, Connecticut · London

Library of Congress Cataloging-in-Publication Data

Hammond, Scott J.
    Political theory : an encyclopedia of contemporary and classic terms / Scott John Hammond.
        p. cm.
    Includes bibliographical references and index.
    ISBN 978–0–313–33920–2 (alk. paper)
1. Political science—Encyclopedias. I. Title.
JA61.P66   2009
320.01—dc22   2008028516

British Library Cataloguing in Publication Data is available.

Library of Congress Catalog Card Number: 2008028516
ISBN: 978–0–313–33920–2

First published in 2009

Greenwood Press, 88 Post Road West, Westport, CT 06881
An imprint of Greenwood Publishing Group, Inc.
www.greenwood.com

Printed in the United States of America

The paper used in this book complies with the
Permanent Paper Standard issued by the National
Information Standards Organization (Z39.48–1984).

10 9 8 7 6 5 4 3 2 1

To my parents, Neil and Gilberdean Hammond, my wife Chereé,
and our children, Adriana and Neil Paul

CONTENTS

AUTHOR'S NOTE

By its very nature, this work will always remain somewhat unfinished. There are several reasons for this. No doubt the most prominent stems from the limited abilities of the author, but other factors must be conceded as well, among them the character of political ideas themselves. Reaching back to the ancient world, political theory and ideology range over a vast tradition, and thus to bind the whole of the tradition within the covers of any book, encyclopedic or otherwise, is a task that necessarily guarantees its own incompletion. On a tangible note, space limitations require abridgment of the number of topics covered, which is generally undesirable but preferable to alternatives such as the dilution of all entries. It goes without saying that this encyclopedia, while it is designed to be comprehensive, will no doubt omit entries some readers hope to find; the selection will appear puzzling to some and reasonable to others. In some cases a topic that appears to be omitted will in fact be covered elsewhere in the book, while in other cases the omission must unfortunately be acknowledged as a real shortcoming, the result of a deliberate decision or of space limitations, perhaps to be amended in a later effort. Having admitted these imperfections, it is hoped that the many entries, numbering over 250, will prove to be of some benefit to the overall instruction of students who are only now encountering political theory for the first time as well as to those who have engaged in political ideas throughout their lives and, in turning to these pages, find material sufficient to refresh memory and reignite interest. The entries are devoted to major thinkers, principal concepts and ideas, memorable phrases or maxims, and enduring ideological strains. Where appropriate, cross-references of related entries are provided, knowing all the while that by its very nature political concepts are prone to definitional overlap and ideational similarity. Modest bibliographical information is also provided to help spur further inquiry into the many issues and questions that naturally arise from within the human conversation regarding the nature of cities and citizenship. These entries will only wet the toe of those who test the waters, but they should provide enough exposure to prepare the more thorough investigator for endless explorations that always remain just ahead.

While it is the goal of this volume to supply readers with a sound and reliable introductory reference work, it is admitted that it will bear its own imperfections. Above all, may the reader find this reference book a serviceable gateway to a new and exciting field of study, sparking the more curious to explore ideas at greater length and in the spirit of open inquiry, with the hope of gaining a deeper understanding and a higher purpose.

PREFACE

Ideas matter. What we think, the values we embrace, and the principles we affirm all help to shape and reshape the contours of life within the human community, in ways that can either illuminate and ennoble the human spirit or drive us toward unspeakable and soulless inhumanity. Not every idea is so marked, not every ideal lies at the pole of a dichotomy between hope and despair. Without hesitation, one can suggest that many and perhaps even most ideas are for the most part neutral, their consequences benign and easily forgotten. But it only requires one great idea or one twisted design to elevate communities toward the realization of their highest potential or to ensnare the whole of humanity itself in a cruel and meaningless fate. Political ideas are capable of being so decisive, of inspiring us toward the realization of the truly good city or tempting us toward tyranny and death. Although the adage has become a cliché, the power of the pen indeed exceeds the power of the sword; the pen can turn the blade aside or tilt it back against ourselves. At the confluence of large ideas and visionary politics, we become aware of the importance of the principle, the necessity of values—of the right kind of love.

Therein lies the problem. To say that principles are important, values necessary, and some things more worthy of love than others is not, in itself, likely to provoke dispute. But to say that my principles are more important than yours, that your values are more reflective of what is necessary to human living than mine, or that love is more than a subjective response *is* provocative and will, more likely than not, stimulate dispute. Political life is marked by such distinctions at every turn, and it is here that ideas, great and small, come to influence and motivate. This is why, as Isaiah Berlin once admonished readers, referring to the German poet Heinrich Heine, we must be wary "not to underestimate the power of ideas: philosophical concepts nurtured in the stillness of a professor's study could destroy civilization." Ideas do have consequences, and this is why it becomes a matter of utmost concern which ideas and values we adopt and which ones we recognize as less worthy of our embrace. In many cases it is not a difficult decision, for there is an obvious, and one can say with confidence, *objective* preference for the "dedication to the proposition that all men are created equal" on the one hand over the assertion, on the other hand, that "the greater the lie, the greater the chance that it will be believed." For the most part, however, we seldom are afforded a choice between such clearly disparate alternatives. To understand what principles and values are important and why one may be good and the other bad usually comes with greater effort and may never be fully resolved even by the most penetrating of intellects. Perhaps this is why philosophers "love" wisdom, for under the spell of such a love, it might be possible to stumble upon the secret of what it really means to love the best things in the right way.

In a sense, such a stumbling through the love of wisdom constitutes the real distinction between political theory, characterized by its openness to transcendence and its affection for conversational inquiry, and ideology, crisply delivered to us as a set of conclusions that serve as the final word and the answer to all our questions. This is not to say that an ideological system is incapable of answering questions and, with the right kind of luck, arriving at some great truth. Yet it *is* to say that such good fortune is unlikely, and that the student of political theory who engages in the love of wisdom, politically directed, remains fully aware that, as Socrates once observed, "human knowledge is a poor thing." Theory does not abandon knowledge because of human limitations, but, on the contrary, courts wisdom in humility. With ideology, it is certainty that is courted, but not the certainty of the objectively right choice between freedom and totalitarianism, for such certainty is self-evident and in need of neither theory nor ideology. Rather, the certainty of the ideologue is shaped more by pride than recognition of self-evident truths. Whereas the theorist must always maintain an attitude of modesty in the pursuit of wisdom (which is itself a requirement that likely eludes all of us), the ideologue is the product of the marriage of conviction and pride. To stand by one's convictions on a personal level requires a steady soul, a character trait always to be recommended to the serious person. Ideology, however, tends toward the prideful, distorting a virtue into a vice and corrupting the rightful love of wisdom through a lower orientation that now directs one's love toward power. Whereas theory always remains aloof to power, as Plato observed long ago, ideology, even when reasonable, seeks power, and typically finds it through the compromise of the very certainty that it claims.

And yet our proclivity toward the comfort of ideological affirmation is something that we are unlikely to outgrow, if indeed it is something to be outgrown. The love of wisdom is always frustrated: hence the appeal of the ideological system that enables us to draw readily on the answers that we need and the programs for change that we instinctively know must be proposed, contested, and applied. Because ideology deals with ideas, it does not always steer us toward the wrong kind of life, but the element of pride and the closing of inquiry adds that risk, which in turn causes the theoretical approach to become even more vital in our times. If we are "spinning through cold space," as Nietzsche feared, then our desperation for certainty—*our* certainty provided by us on *our* terms—causes extremity of action, and at the extremes, the borderlines at which our humanity touches something more savage, violence becomes the only tangible certainty—that is, the only thing that is certain to follow. Ideas, those ideas that are better for human beings to hold, can pull us away from such extremes, but only if the ideas are held with humility, having been discovered through the pursuit of wisdom rather than spurred onward by the desire for power or the need for control.

Students of ideas already know this, and come to their studies in the recognition that even objective truth is not absolutely known. The love of wisdom is always partially unrequited, but never abandoned, and always ennobling. It is an arduous journey up and out of the cave that Plato described, but a journey that is to be eagerly undertaken in the full knowledge that one is always arriving without ever having arrived. This encyclopedia is meant to aid in the departure and hope for the arriving, but even should every word be read, memorized, and understood in a way that surpasses the author's poor powers, the reader will yet be far from having arrived. This volume is at best a first step, and perhaps not even that. From here all lovers of wisdom will quickly move on and up, and ultimately beyond this compendium of fragments and hopeful introductions to the world of ideas. If this text is to serve any useful purpose, it will be to provide a framework and reference from which longer and deeper adventures can begin. It is hoped that this text can provide auspicious beginnings and encourage all students of ideas to consider the possibility of values and principles that are worthy of the right kind of love.

ACKNOWLEDGMENTS

No book ever results from the work of just one person. Usually the better parts of a book are the product of many people, while the lesser parts may be attributed to the errors of one—the author. My appreciation is owed to a number of persons without whom this text would never have been brought into print.

First, thank you to the entire editorial and publishing staff at Greenwood Press. This is my second project with Greenwood, and as before, it has been my pleasure to work with professionals of high caliber. In particular, I thank Steven Vetrano, who, in his capacity as acquisitions editor, was the first to support the project in its initial stage. I also thank Sandy Towers, whose patient guidance and good-natured indulgence of my tendency to lace correspondence with Tolkien references helped ensure that the project remained enjoyable while keeping me focused on the task at hand. The Greenwood staff as a whole deserves credit for those parts of this book that are good, and none more than Sandy. Additionally, our project manager, Haylee Schwenk, helped to bring this project to completion; her diligence and smart suggestions in the finishing stages were gratefully received and much appreciated. Thanks also to Michael O'Connor for some important late-inning calls with the result of improving select passages. In sum, everyone at Greenwood has contributed in some important way in bringing this book to light.

Second, my colleagues and students at James Madison University have provided me with a stimulating and collegial environment, enabling me the privilege of doing nothing less than discussing the finest things with young and eager minds. The Department of Political Science and Public Administration at JMU is an association of friends, and it is my good fortune to be a member of their cohort.

Third, a deep intellectual debt is owed to my past teachers, all of whom played a significant role in inspiring and sustaining my love for political theory. Only what is good in this volume can be attributed to their enduring influence. No doubt some will inadvertently be left unmentioned, but the following professors—most of whom have likely forgotten me but who nonetheless have provided, in abundance, insight and direction for my own development as a student of political theory—all deserve my personal gratitude: Louis Morton, Morton Perry, William Prior, David Gross, John Searle, William Allen, Harry Jaffa, Sharon Snowiss, Theodore Waldman, Fr. Eleutherius Winance, Leonard Levy, Al Louch, T. Lindsay Moore, Jim Stewart, Paul Lowdenslager, Lee McDonald, and Scott Warren. Specifically, I leaned heavily on Lee McDonald's comprehensive work in drafting several of the entries in this book, and I still consider his three-volume survey of western political theory to be the best available. Lou Morton was the first instructor to formally introduce me to the serious study of political ideas in a rigorous, structured environment, and over the years he has remained a teacher, mentor, and close family friend. The late Paul Lowdenslager helped to rekindle my love of the ancients, thus returning me to the great classics that I had first encountered in my earliest exposure to the world of ideas, and he remains in my mind the epitome of what a college instructor should be for his students. Finally, more than anyone, Scott Warren has influenced my approach to the study and teaching of political theory and has guided me through the narrow way that marks the Great Conversation; he is in my eyes the best example of the life of the mind oriented toward the "discovery and creation of a world worthy of the human spirit to inhabit, as well as the discovery and creation of a human spirit worth of the world."

Above all, there is nothing without my family; my parents, Neil and Gilberdean Hammond, my wife Chereé, and my children, Adriana and Neil Paul. It is to them I dedicate this book, but it is really a poor exchange for all that they have given me.

LIST OF ENTRIES

A

absolutes (universals, objective principles, moral realism)

Absolutes are fundamental principles or values that are held to be true independently of cultural context, historical development, or human determination. An absolute value or principle is not a function of human will, judgment, or reason, nor is it true only within the context of a given time, situation, or social framework. Rather, an absolute is true in itself, whether it is held to be true or not, and whether it is applied within a given sociohistoric framework or not. Absolutes are essential concepts and normative ideas that exist objectively and are not considered true or correct situationally, but are discerned as true or correct because they are principles that exist beyond human enactment. In essence, to embrace absolutes amounts to a kind of "moral realism," or the notion that moral values are objectively real and are right or true independent of subjective judgment or exertion. For political theory, absolutes are particularly difficult to affirm or recognize. Mathematical absolutes, such as $7 + 5 = 12$, are not easily discovered in the social and political world. Nonetheless, the tradition of political theory includes just such an effort throughout the balance of its development.

Attempts at finding transcendent moral and political principles are as old as civilization itself, as evinced, for example, in the Babylonian Code of Hammurabi, the Egyptian principle of Ma'at, and the Hindu Law of Manu. The ancient Hebrew Scripture, or Tanakh (identical with the Old Testament of the Christian Bible), provides a timeless moral code of conduct that applies to social and political action as well as serving the faithful in their quest for a relationship with the Divine; this moral code is reaffirmed in its essence in the Christian New Testament. In Greek political philosophy—the conceptual foundation for Western political theory—we can see this same attempt at least as early as *Antigone,* part of the familiar *Oedipus* cycle of dramas composed by Sophocles (495 BC–406 BC). Antigone's appeal to a law that resides "even above Zeus" represents the pursuit of transcendent justice, a pursuit that reaches its philosophical apogee in Plato's theory of the Forms (*eidos;* consult his *Republic, Parmenides, Phaedo, Phaedrus*). For Plato (427 BC–347 BC) the Forms—including the Form of justice—are the eternal and essential reality behind all things, the things that *are* in contrast to the things that come to be and pass away. Thus, in Plato's political theory, it is clear that there are objective absolute principles that hold true across time and culture, and that what is just for an Athenian in his day is equally just for us in ours. While skeptical of Plato's theory of Forms, Aristotle (384 BC–322 BC) in his *Metaphysics* nonetheless recognized the existence of "first principles and basic reasons," which he describes as that which "is most intelligible" and "what is best in all nature" (*Metaphysics; Nicomachean Ethics*). Discovery of the first principles as a form of inquiry is "the only one of the sciences that is free, since it alone is for its own sake." First principles are expressed as primary factors that account for being, and are ultimately objective with regard to human understanding.

Stoic political thought affirmed natural law as an absolute repository of universal principle. Stoicism, particularly in its middle and late developments, grounded political and juristic thought on the premise that there is a justice and a law that is in itself and exists by nature. For the Stoic, this was often associated with divine wisdom, or "right reason" accessible to every sentient mind. "Law," the philosopher Cicero (usually associated with the Stoic movement) affirmed in *De Legibus,* "is the primal and ultimate Mind of God," and is thus ultimately only the transcendent and noncontextual principles of reason that are the ground of both law and justice. The ideas of both Aristotle and the Stoic philosophers were easily folded into the comprehensive philosophical and theological structure of St. Thomas Aquinas (1225–1274), who, along with his predecessor, St. Augustine (Aurelius Augustinus, 354–430), worked toward a synthesis of theological revelation with the universal affirmations of rational philosophy. For both St. Thomas Aquinas and St. Augustine before him, all moral values are established upon the eternal truths as promulgated by God. According to Aquinas, human beings are guided by the natural attribute of *synderesis,* which is a disposition toward the natural habit of following the moral principles of natural law in spite of the ongoing problem of Original Sin. As St. Augustine argued, even sin cannot obliterate our original nature, which is good as a result of our status as God's creatures. For Aquinas, all human beings retain the disposition toward goodness as grounded in the objective moral principles of both divine and natural law. In this way, it is possible for human beings to share common moral principles and engage in the same type of moral action regardless of their own situation. Additionally, thinkers such as the Islamic philosopher Alfarabi (c. 870–c. 950) recognized that political and moral values must be attuned to the First Principles of Being in order to establish the groundwork for the virtuous regime. Throughout the Middle Ages, thinkers of all faiths and philosophical persuasion assumed the fact of such principles, and affirmed their applicability to the actions of human beings in general, particularly emphasizing the need for political regimes to build upon principles and values that transcend any particular political order.

For classical and Medieval theory, natural law (along with divine law) provided the groundwork for a moral realism that informed the ethical choices faced by all human beings. The attempt to discover such principles continued into the development of early modern theory as well, often with a reduced emphasis on the religious dimensions of objective values. Natural law as a foundation for objective moral, political, and juristic action continued to draw the interest of political thinkers after the Renaissance. The Spanish neo-Thomists of the Salamanca School (such as Francesco de Vitoria and Francisco Suárez) carried forward the natural law traditions previously developed by the Stoics, following, above all, the principles discovered by St. Thomas Aquinas. As Christendom in the West fragmented, non-Catholic theories of natural law as the basis of an objective moral order were promoted by thinkers such as Hugo Grotius (1583–1645), Thomas Hobbes (1588–1679), John Locke (1632–1704) and Emerich Vattel (1714–1767), among others. As modern political thought grew increasingly distant from the theological aspects it had inherited from Medieval philosophers—to a large extent as a result of Enlightenment rationalism—natural law as objective moral ground diminished in importance. Yet moral realism remained a compelling conceptual framework well into the nineteenth century. Immanuel Kant (1724–1804), through his concepts of the thing in itself (*ding an sich*) and the categorical and practical imperatives, and his reflections on the moral will and the common human membership in a "Kingdom of Ends" (or realm of ends), provided a potent argument for the continued assertion of moral and political thought informed by objective values (*Groundwork for a Metaphysics of Morals*). Kant's influence on subsequent philosophy has proved nearly ubiquitous, and a good portion of philosophical developments after Kant were in direct answer to his overall project. It should be noted that while Kantian philosophy incorporates objectivist principles, certain elements of Kant (particularly his emphasis on the role of the will) can be construed as pointing toward systems of thought that challenge moral realism.

While Søren Kierkegaard (1813–1855) is arguably the first major modern thinker to challenge the assumptions of moral objectivism, it is only with Friedrich Nietzsche (1844–1900) that we encounter from a major intellectual figure an exhaustive and thoroughgoing rejection of absolutes. Moral realism would continue to be challenged by conventionalist/relativist views such as legalism, positivism, utilitarianism, pragmatism, existentialism, certain variants of Marxism (although Marxism can be said to adhere to its own version of objectivism), and postmodern constructivism throughout the twentieth century. Nonetheless, the writings of a diverse array of thinkers throughout the twentieth century continued to affirm the legitimacy of political and moral thought and action grounded in transcendent principles. Thomistic political theory experienced a revival through the writings of Pope Leo XIII (Vincenzo Pecci, 1810–1903) and Jacques Maritain (1882–1973). G.E.M. Anscombe (1919–2001), C.S. Lewis (1898–1963), Simone Weil (1909–1943), and Eric Voegelin (1901–1985) are just a few political and moral theorists who engaged in the reaffirmation of transcendent truth. More recently, scholars such as Alasdair MacIntyre (b. 1929) and Martha Nussbaum (b. 1947) have further carried moral realism forward, arguing for a return to classical first principles as a way to reinvigorate modern liberal democracy with moral purpose and meaning.

Even though moral absolutism is often regarded by public opinion as presumptuous at best and dangerous at worst, several scholars, critics, and prominent public figures alike persist in their attempts to forward first principles in opposition to moral and cultural subjectivism. A recent representation of such efforts, for example, has been offered by Pope Benedict XVI (Joseph Alois Ratzinger). In a homily delivered in April 2005, just prior to the conclave that elected him to the papacy, Cardinal Ratzinger spoke of a "dictatorship of relativism" that rejects all objective certainty and serves only the purposes of the independent ego. Later that year, in June 2005, during an address to the Ecclesial Diocesan Convention in Rome, His Holiness stated

> Today, a particularly insidious obstacle to the task of educating is the massive presence in our society and culture of that relativism which, recognizing nothing as definitive leaves as the ultimate criterion only the self with its desires. And under the semblance of freedom it becomes a prison for each one, for it separates people from one another, locking each person into his or her own 'ego.'

This position, while compatible with the teachings of the church and a continuation of the legacy of his predecessor, Pope John Paul II (Karol Wojtyla), nonetheless provoked a degree of controversy that established an ongoing tension between the Pope and the general public regarding moral issues and cultural sensitivities. This tension further illustrates the nature of the debate regarding the possibility of objective first principles and, more importantly, the implications of such a possibility.

Related Entries

Aquinas, Thomas; Aristotle; Augustine; Catholic social teaching; consequentialism; Plato; synderesis.

Suggested Reading

Aristotle. *Metaphysics,* trans. Richard Hope. 1952; repr. Ann Arbor: Univ. Mich. Press/Ann Arbor Paperbacks, 1960.

Germino, Dante. *Political Philosophy and the Open Society*. Baton Rouge: La. State Univ. Press, 1982.

Kant, Immanuel. *Groundwork for Metaphysics of Morals,* trans Mary Gregor. 1998; repr. New York: Cambridge Univ. Press, 2002.

Kreeft, Peter. *A Refutation of Moral Relativism: Interviews with an Absolutist*. San Francisco: Ignatius Press, 1999.

Plato. *Republic*. Translations by Cornford (1941; repr. Oxford, 1978), Griffith (Cambridge), Grube/Reeve (Hackett), Lee (1995; repr. Penguin Classics, 1985), Sachs (2007; R. Pullins Company), Shorey (1930; repr., 2 vols., Harvard Univ. Press/Loeb Classical Library, 1994), and Waterfield (1993; Oxford) are recommended, but other useful translations are available.

Voegelin, Eric. *The New Science of Politics*. 1952; repr. Chicago: Univ. Chicago Press, 1987.

Adams, John (1735–1826)

One of the most important theorists in the tradition of American political thought, John Adams in many ways embodies the aspirations of both liberal and conservative strains in American culture. By and large, Adams is regarded as a conservative thinker, yet it is nonetheless not lost on students of political inquiry that Adams was a major figure in the revolution against the British monarchy. As with most great minds, Adams is far more complex than either his champions or his detractors tend to acknowledge.

While the writings of John Adams are considerable and his role as a founder is inestimable, his basic political principles revolve around four concepts: a reading of human nature that emphasizes the role of pride and the "passion for distinction" in the quest for political power and social influence; a conservative respect of tradition; an ardent belief in constitutionalism and, in particular, in the notion of mixed government; and a notion of a natural aristocracy that can more capably serve republican government than a naïve reliance on the people as a whole.

Adams, like other political theorists (such as Thomas Hobbes, Jean-Jacques Rousseau, and Georg Wilhelm Friedrich Hegel), discerns in human motivation an abiding desire for distinction, that is, a love of public esteem. While this is a source of greed and conflict in society, with the correctly balanced institutions guided by the intelligent enactment and application of law, the passion for distinction can benefit public endeavors, bridling ambition for a common purpose. Hence, men of talent should be encouraged to engage in public life for the sake of duty and honor, and it can be expected that their thirst for acclaim will drive them to excellence. In autocratic regimes this impulse can easily (and inevitably will) turn tyrannical, but in a balanced republic abiding by the rule of law, it can be channeled in a way that promotes virtue rather than succumbing to vice.

Thus the best regime is one that mixes elements of monarchy, aristocracy, and democracy, as endorsed by classical theorists. For Adams, each of these elements is necessary for a healthy republic, particularly one that simultaneously checks ambition while drawing on its energy. Moderate governments are the only ones that can be fueled by ambitious men without risking immolation. To this end, a "natural" aristocracy (see also **Jefferson, Thomas**) provides the character and intelligence to guide popular government toward not only just rule, but also greatness. Like many of his contemporaries (such as James Madison and Alexander Hamilton), Adams believed that government based on the idea of popular sovereignty is preferable to the irrational hierarchies of the autocratic past, and yet the people as a whole are to be kept at an arm's length from the mechanisms of power. Because the people can act as tyrannically as any despot, institutions must be constructed that not only balance power among those who hold it but also prevent the inconstant and often irrational multitude from gaining too much influence. Good laws and time-tested traditions, dispersed power, and the fostering of a natural aristocracy are the necessary instruments to both solidify the principle of popular sovereignty while subduing its more dangerous inclinations.

Related Entries
conservatism; Jefferson, Thomas

Suggested Reading
Adams, John. *Political Writings of John Adams,* ed. George W. Carey Washington, DC: Regnery Publishing, 2000.

Adams, John. *Revolutionary Writings of John Adams,* ed. C. Bradley Thompson. Indianapolis: Liberty Fund, 2000.

administration of things

Writing in his *Anti-Dühring* (1878), part of which was later republished in 1880 as *Die Entwicklung des Sozialismus von der Utopie zur Wissenschaft* (*Socialism: Utopian and Scientific*), Friedrich Engels (1820–1895) indicted traditional politics—particularly in the form of the state and attendant legal and governmental institutions—as instruments of oppression stemming from deeper subjugation resulting from class conflict over the means of production. The state is but a tool of oppression, wielded on behalf of the ruling economic class and employed merely as an expression of power. Come the revolution, however, and the resolution of class conflict through the reconciliation of the ownership and the operation of the means of production, and the historical forces of power— namely, political things such as the state—will no longer be necessary and thus rendered obsolete. In reference to utopian socialist Claude Henri de St. Simon (1760–1825), Engels describes a postrevolutionary condition wherein "political rule over men" will be converted "into an administration of things," which amounts to, in Engels's view, the "abolition of the state." Later, in the same piece, he writes famously, "As soon as there is no longer any social class held in subjection.... State interference in social relations becomes...superfluous, and dies out of itself; the government of persons is replaced by the administration of things, and by the conduct of processes of production. The state is not 'abolished.' It dies out." This phrase is also referred to as the "withering away of the state," the state no longer provided with its coercive function, becomes a relic or "antique" of the past, for human beings will no longer need to be "governed;" all that will require our attention is the simple administration of the things that we need to gratify our material needs.

The St. Simonian connection is of interest here. St. Simon, an idiosyncratic figure who envisioned a reconstituted human society patterned after the industrial factory, was regarded by Engels in *Anti-Dühring* as an expansive thinker well ahead of his time, whose encyclopedic understanding of humanity exceeded that of his contemporaries, matching even Hegel's. With St. Simon, according to Engels, we encounter a forthright identification of politics with production, and the foretelling of a "complete absorption of politics by economics"—a state regarded by Engels to be the end of class antagonism. Engels's ssociation of his notion of the administration of things with St. Simon's techno-industrial collective reveals a decidedly different concept of social direction, one in which politics is not simply streamlined and rendered more efficient and responsive to the community, as in the case of public administration, but rather a notion of control that closely reflects the factory image. Such a vision is poised against the ancient notion, stemming from Plato and Aristotle, that political governance is a singular kind of rule, unlike and in most respects superior to direction and management in other endeavors (such as one finds in the household, market, or battlefield). For Engels, political rule is by necessity but an extension of and preservative for class oppression, and thus needs to "wither away" so that a more rational and mechanistic process of administration of resources will be brought forward. Thus, for Engels, the demise of the state and the various aspects of politics and government will usher a new age of rational direction, modeled after the organization of mass industry, and reconciling the production of things with their fair distribution. Hence, the administration of things, in Engels's estimation, will rightly provide a more intelligent and efficient reorganization of society along the lines of a new scientific socialism.

Related Entry
positivism

Suggested Reading
Engels, Friedrich. "Socialism: Utopian and Scientific," in Marx, Karl, and Friedrich Engels, *Basic*

Writings on Politics and Philosophy, ed. Lewis S. Feuer. 1959; repr. New York: Anchor Books, 1989.

advantage of the stronger

In the first book of Plato's *Republic,* Thrasymachus defines justice as "the advantage of the stronger," in rebuttal to Socrates's assertion that justice is a human virtue and that a just person when confronted with injustice does not respond in kind. That is, a person not only engages in just behavior (such as paying one's debts and telling the truth, as Cephalus had earlier stated), but even more importantly, a person *is* just, and thus will always act justly even when wronged, regardless of the case. In stating this, Socrates implies that justice is ultimately an objective principle, rooted in our being rather than provided for us by social or political convention. It is at this point, very early in the dialogue, that Thrasymachus strenuously objects, arguing with an intimidating confidence that justice has nothing to do with virtue, but rather is and should be a function of power (the advantage of the stronger). Hence, justice is situational and variable, and so it follows that one can even speak of "tyrannical laws" and hence tyrannical justice, as Thrasymachus does at *Republic I,* 338e. This notwithstanding, Thrasymachus does state that justice "is the same in all cities, the advantage of the established rule," thus even Thrasymachus's attempt at what we might call a relativist account relies on a general rule, that is, that justice is *always* a function of power.

Related Entries
Plato; *Republic,* The (*Politeia*)

Suggested Reading
Plato. *Republic,* in *Complete Works,* ed. John M. Cooper. Indianapolis: Hackett, 1997.

advice to princes

In Niccolò Machiavelli's *The Prince,* several points of advice are offered as reliable strategies for successful princes. While *The Prince* is much more than a "handbook for princes," the advice provided is nonetheless of interest to students of Machiavelli as well as to any reader interested in a close study of political skill. The substantive teaching in *The Prince* is conveyed through such principles as learning "how not to be good," the emphasis on appearance and reputation, the recognition of the need for both strength and cunning, and the willingness to use well-placed cruelty for the greater good. Nonetheless, a survey of the specific examples is informative, filling in to some extent the details of Machiavelli's murky intentions. These specific suggestions include the following: (1) In seizing new territory, the conquering prince must quickly win the support of the current inhabitants, but must be wary of potential enemies within. A prince who seizes territory where the inhabitants speak the same language and hold similar customs will find it easier to curry the favor of the populace, but if the case is otherwise, more stringent policies are in order. Machiavelli continues by suggesting that a new ruler reside in recently conquered territory, the better able to monitor the events, control lieutenants and ostensible allies, and familiarize himself with the population. (2) Additionally, a conquering prince is well-served by sending colonists from among his own people into the new territory, otherwise a "substantial army" will be necessary to "garrison your new territory." (3) A prince who governs a newly acquired territory where customs and language are heterogeneous to his own must be careful to strike an alliance with weaker neighbors for the sake of dominating them, and to devise ways to weaken more powerful neighbors, and in so doing, set himself up as the most important influence in the region. (4) A prince should not prefer disorder to war. (5) A prince must never allow another country to become more powerful than his own. (6) In governing, a prince must rely solely on his own servants for assistance or employ the aid of traditional barons. (7) For those who have earned their realms owing to their own skill (*virtu*), they should emulate the magnificent ancient founders, namely, Moses, Cyrus,

Romulus, Theseus, and so on, or a more contemporary example, Francesco Sforza. (8) Failing this, and given the difficulty of actually following these examples, a ruler who comes to power through good fortune must find other examples, specifically, Cesare Borgia. Borgia's swift and thorough elimination of his enemies through his lieutenant, Remiro d'Orco, who himself was gruesomely eliminated by Borgia after d'Orco had completed his atrocities, is praised by Machiavelli as an example of inflicting necessary cruelty all at once, to execute "all the crimes you have to commit at once." (9) Princes are better served by citizen armies than mercenaries, a subject to which Machiavelli devotes considerable enthusiasm. (10) The prince's first obligation is to learn the art of warfare. (11) A prince must avoid fomenting division among factions within areas under his control. (12) Having successfully led a rebellion, the wise prince does not trust other rebels once the rebellion is complete, even if they were allies in his cause. (13) The prince avoids hiding behind fortresses, for "the best fortress is to be found in the love of the people." (14) A prince understands the uses of religion for the ends of the state and appears to defer to religious observance. (15) The ruler must endeavor to keep his subjects either confused or amazed. (16) A prince should eschew alliances with those more powerful than he is, but also avoid neutrality. (17) A ruler should occupy his subjects with all manner of entertainment (what the Romans referred to as "bread and circuses"). (18) Without pandering, a prince should show himself to be a friend to craftsmen and the guild workers. (19) The prince must surround himself with intelligent advisors who are not disposed to idle flattery, but are nonetheless loyal beyond reproach. Finally, above all, (20) A successful ruler does not make a practice of always being good, but rather learns how not to be good so that he will not come to ruin among so many who are evil.

Some readers of Machiavelli regard these strategies as examples of his project to advance a *realpolitik,* in contrast to the more abstract philosophies of the past. Others, most famously Leo Strauss, consider Machiavelli's advice as illustrative of his pernicious doctrine, uprooting the Great Tradition of classical theory and its moral foundations, while others see a cynical attempt to regain patronage by giving to Lorenzo de Medici, to whom the book is dedicated, exactly the kind of advice that Lorenzo would approve—for the sole purpose of obtaining office for Machiavelli himself. Still others see only irony in Machiavelli's guidebook and mark it among the great works of satire. One interesting interpretation is offered by Mary Dietz, who, in her article "Trapping the Prince," argues that Machiavelli was being particularly "Machiavellian" by offering bad advice disguised as sincere in the hopes of actually undermining the Medici and thus stimulating a shift back to republican government, which, according to Dietz and other commentators, is the only true regime that Machiavelli admired. Machiavelli's motives will perhaps always remain hidden, but the advice is explicit for good or ill, even if the actual teaching may be less so.

Related Entries
Machiavelli, Niccolò

Suggested Reading
Dietz, Mary. "Trapping the Prince," *American Political Science Review,* Vol. 80, No. 3 (September 1986),
Machiavelli, Niccolò. *The Prince,* trans. Angelo M. Codevilla. New Haven: Yale Univ. Press, 1997.

Afrocentrism (afrocentricity)

A term coined by Molefi Asante (*né* Arthur Lee Smith, Jr., b. 1942) in 1988 to define a new approach to the study of Western culture and World history, Afrocentrism repositions academic inquiry from within an African perspective. While the term is new, the origins of this approach to scholarship can be traced to the early twentieth century, when scholars such as W.E.B. Du Bois (1868–1963) advocated a closer study of the true nature of African culture independent of European influence. According to this approach, the study of human culture at various levels has been shaped by the domination of European culture and its legacy in the United States, and thus excludes important contributions to human civilization from cultures distinct from the traditional "West," namely Africa and what has been referred to as the "Near East." Focusing on the contributions of ancient African cultures to the development of Western ideas as well as reexamining the nature and importance of the African diaspora in the shaping of Western civilization, Afrocentrism is both a critical reexamination of the moral and cultural foundations of the West and an attempt to restore the prominence of Africa in the unfolding of the human story. By shifting away from a Eurocentric view of history and focusing on the role of Africa, scholars who practice Afrocentricity hope to reclaim the lost legacy of a neglected continent. In so doing, they seek to provide alternative ways of thinking about culture and society, ways that are detached from what is perceived to be a cultural narrative premised in its foundations on the domination of one type of civilization over another. Hence the Afrocentric approach seeks to challenge "cultural hegemony" and political imperialism, and to offer an alternative review of history as well as a distinctive approach to understanding current global phenomena.

One element of Afrocentric history involves scholars in a reexamination of ancient Egypt and its influence on Mediterranean societies. Some argue that the legacy of ancient Greece, traditionally the crucible of Western civilization, is simply a by-product of earlier Nilotic/Egyptian accomplishments. This emphasis is accompanied by the assertion that the ancient Egyptians held more in common with Nubia, ancient Kush, and sub-Sahara Africa than with the various ancient cultures of the Near East, thus promoting a new understanding of the role of Africans in constructing the cultural foundations of the West. Ancient Egypt, in this view, is an

African civilization, and not Middle Eastern as it is traditionally depicted. Given this, the ancient Greeks were heavily influenced by Africa, receiving much of their cultural heritage from Africa through Egypt and Phoenicia. George G.M. James's *Stolen Legacy* (1954) was among the first attempts to reject the European nature of ancient Greek culture, arguing that Greek thought in general was simply a diluted summary of the thought of the ancient Egyptians. Senegalese historian Cheikh Anta Diop (1923–1986) was another early proponent of the view that the Nile culture of ancient Egypt was in fact predominantly Black African rather than Mediterranean. In his three-volume work *Black Athena* (1987–2006), Martin Bernal (b. 1937) focuses on what he argues are the Phoenician origins of ancient Greek language and culture, asserting that this lineage is a direct challenge to the traditional view that connects Greek civilization to northern (Aryan) peoples. This claim has proved controversial, with many scholars rebutting both Asante's and Bernal's claims regarding a cultural debt owed by ancient Greece to Africa. Mary Lefkowitz (b. 1935), in particular, has spearheaded a critical dismantling of the notion of an Afrocentric Greece, arguing that the African-Greek connection is based largely on poor scholarship and even fabrication. James's book in particular has not withstood critical examination, but the debate continues over the claims forwarded by Asante and Bernal, with Lefkowitz continuing as the leading critic of the Afrocentric depiction of the ancient Greek legacy.

An additional criticism of the Nilotic focus comes from within Afrocentrism itself, arguing that a fixation with Egypt undermines the diversity of African cultures and thus commits the same error of Eurocentrism, that is, devaluing other centers of African civilization while exaggerating the African character of Egypt, which has been proved to have been a complex, multiracial society.

Anthropological and cultural debates aside, Afrocentrist approaches have also been directed at an appreciation of Africa for its own sake, presumed Greco-Nilotic connections notwithstanding. The point is to recover African culture as such, regardless of its connections (or lack thereof) to the development of ancient Mediterranean societies such as that of the Greeks, or even the Egyptians. Africa bears its own legacy, ancient Egyptian civilization being, at best, just one element among many of Africa's contribution to the rest of the world. The focus here, therefore, is not so much on ancient civilizations and their interactions as on the African diaspora and what it has meant to the growth of civilization, both internally on the African continent and externally. African civilization is not homogenous, but owing to the diaspora, there is a connection among all African peoples, a connection that suggests a unique role for African traditions in the shaping of the West. Some argue that while this is a basically healthy approach to understanding the contributions of the real Africa to the greater world, discussion has nonetheless been dominated by a tendency to understand this diaspora in terms of the United States, neglecting the diversity of the African experience in places such as Brazil and the Caribbean.

Afrocentric approaches to history, philosophy, and culture have become visible perspectives in the academy. While criticism is still directed at certain aspects of Afrocentricity, by and large, the products of Afrocentric scholarship have proved beneficial to a broader understanding of ancient non-Nilotic African civilizations and of the global effects of the African diaspora. Shrill claims are still voiced on both extremes of the issue, but overall the African studies programs that have emerged have joined the family of credible academic disciplines. Afrocentric perspectives will likely gain more influence in political theory and ideology in the future, particularly among those thinkers who are concerned with the nature of erstwhile marginalized discourse and with perspectives that offer alternatives to more "traditional" ways of thinking.

Related Entry
ideology

Suggested Reading

Diop, Cheikh Anta. *The African Origin of Civilization: Myth or Reality?* Chicago: Lawrence Hill Books, 1989.
Henderson, Errol Anthony. *Afrocentrism and World Politics: Toward a New Paradigm.* Westport, CT: Praeger Publishers, 1995.
Lefkowitz, Mary. *Not Out of Africa: How "Afrocentrism" Became an Excuse to Teach Myth as History.* New York: Basic Books, 1997.

al-Afghani, Sayyid Jamal al-Din
(1837–1897)

A truly syncretic thinker, Sayyid al-Afghani promoted a vision of a universal Islamic community that would rival the influence and power of the West without wholly rejecting modernist ideas as would fundamentalist/traditionalist thinkers who came after him. Al-Afghani envisioned a pan-Islamic movement that would reconcile the Sunni and Shi'ite branches of Islam, weaving elements of both traditions into a new Muslim synthesis. For al-Afghani, the original principles of Islam must be revived, and done so in a way that recognizes the benefits of both Sunni and Shi'a interpretations. In this way, the intrusive and ever increasingly present influence of the West could be thwarted, and the glory of Islam asserted once again.

Unlike fundamentalists such as Sayyid Qutb, al-Afghani recognized benefits in different parts of Western culture. Modern science was a positive legacy of the West, and for al-Afghani, thoroughly compatible with the spirit of Islam. Islam is at once mystical and rational, simultaneously revelatory and philosophical. If one considers the grand history of Islamic culture, one is reminded of the intellectual tradition that characterized Islam at the apex of its political and cultural influence. Hence, Islam is not to be focused on tradition alone, but must incorporate the kind of philosophical and scientific inquiry that once accompanied Islamic scholarship, and can do so again in a fashion similar to the best of Western science. The spiritual heart and the inquisitive mind must be merged in the discovery of truth and the reaffirmation of Islamic faith. In a word, Western philosophy and science are to be emulated, Western politics and economic power defied.

Antony Black has noted al-Afghani's importance to and influence on both modernist tendencies within Islam (for example, in the vision of Turkey's founding hero, Mustafa Kemal Ataturk) as well as the initiating and growth of Islamic fundamentalism (as seen in the Muslim Brethren and Qutb, among others). As Black remarks,

> His [al-Afghani's] influence is everywhere. From Egypt to Afghanistan, he "has become almost a mythical hero." To the Muslim Brethren, al-Afghani was "the announcer." In [Muslim] India, where his works became popular from the 1880s, many regarded him with "something like worship"; the Caliphate movement of the 1920s and the poet-philosopher Muhammad Iqbal used his ideas. The special relationship between Shi-ite political theology and Western constitutionalism in Iran also reflected his approach.

Hence, through his blending of Sunni with Shi'a, Western science with Muslim devotion, and nationalism with a revival of Islam as a transnational political force, al-Afghani serves as a pivotal figure in the development of modern Islamic ideological attitudes and aspirations.

Related Entries
Muslim Brethren; Qutb, Sayyid

Suggested Reading
Black, Antony. *The History of Islamic Political Thought: From the Prophet to the Present*. New York: Routledge, 2001.

Alfarabi (al-Farabi, Abu Nasr al-Farabi; c. 870–c. 950)

Alfarabi's importance to political philosophy is demonstrated by the manner in which he continued Plato's inquiry into the nature of the ideal city (for Alfarabi, the "virtuous regime"),

as well as by his attempt to blend reason and faith, as St. Augustine and many of the church fathers had advocated before him and as Maimonides and St. Thomas Aquinas would do after him. For Alfarabi, a Muslim thinker, as for the Christian St. Augustine, reason and faith are fundamentally compatible, and thus in the discussion of political truths, the first principles upon which society rests are both open to the intellect and received by faith through divine revelation.

Knowledge of the First Principles of Being is the foundation of the virtuous regime. Like Plato's City of Speech, the virtuous regime is based on true justice (found in objective reality) and aimed at the creation of conditions wherein citizens can practice virtue. The virtuous regime, like Plato's Form of the *polis,* would be divided into three classes—those who know and thus rule, those who hold right opinions and thus rule and are ruled, and those (the many) who can only imitate (or accept "similitudes") the true beliefs and are thus ruled. As with Plato's hierarchy (philosopher-rulers, auxiliary-guardians, producers-distributors), the ideal state is placed in harmony for the greater good, one that is not arrived at by consensus or the exertion of power, but that is attuned to the nature of things as discerned by the wise. For Alfarabi, philosophy such as the kind practiced by Plato and Aristotle is a kind of revelation, and thus the prophet is also a philosopher of a sort.

Alfarabi's virtuous regime is comparable to Plato's City of Speech (which is the Form of the *polis*). In addition (and likewise similarly to Plato), Alfarabi comments on the various imperfect regimes within which human beings tend to live. There are three general types of imperfect regimes: (i) erring, or incorrect, regimes, which recognize that there are higher principles but are in error about their content or meaning; (ii) ignorant regimes, or regimes unaware of first principles or the possibility of transcendent ideals; and (iii) wicked regimes, which do recognize first principles for what they are but then willfully choose to ignore those principles, or perhaps distort them for their own lower purposes. Additionally, Alfarabi identifies six lower goals, or ends, of cities (the perfect city aims at virtue; the imperfect ones lower their sights: base regimes pursue pleasure; vile regimes, wealth). Following Plato, Alfarabi recognizes timocratic regimes motivated by the virtue of honor and despotic regimes concerned with power and domination. "Indispensable" regimes are simply cities that seek only to provide the necessities of life, a task that in itself concerns any political community. Corporate associations are, for Alfarabi, democratic cities, containing elements of all the other cities (including the virtuous city of the wise), and thus characterized by a kind of pluralism. All of these regimes are imperfect and fall short of the ideal, yet unlike Plato, Alfarabi is optimistic about building the virtuous city on earth, for democracy and the indispensable city are the most promising media from which virtue can be cultivated.

Related Entries
absolutes; Plato

Suggested Reading
Alfarabi. *The Political Writings, Selected Aphorisms and Other Texts,* trans. Charles E. Butterworth. Ithaca, NY.: Cornell Univ. Press, 2001.

al-Ghazali (Abu-Hamid Muhammad al-Ghazali, 1058–1111)
Al-Ghazali, like St. Augustine and Alfarabi before him, understood political questions to be best framed within the context of the religious community and the transcendent principles that inspire it. For al-Ghazali, however, this relationship is even more tightly drawn than for St. Augustine, who understood church and state to be decidedly separate. In al-Ghazali's view of politics, the state and religion are inseparable. It is the responsibility of the political regime to produce the temporal community that best serves the transcendent. Politics is not simply a means to ensure social order but is an important means toward attaining Paradise in the afterlife.

For al-Ghazali, the political community is based on the pursuit of fundamental human needs. Thus institutions must be structured in a way that most effectively satisfies those needs within the boundaries drawn by the law. This requires a division of functions along an organized hierarchy. Thus some level of authority is needed to properly administer the communal gratification of basic needs. Al-Ghazali emphasizes the economic dimensions of the state, recognizing their importance in the achievement of a just and ordered society. Production, commerce, and a sense of overall economic interaction is vital to the life of the community, and thus the economic dimensions of the state are understood in social terms rather than reserved to the gratification of private desires. This is not to recommend an expansion of the authority of political power into the economic realm; commerce should be free trade rather than centralized distribution. Nonetheless, for al-Ghazali, a relationship must exist between political community and economic associations, for they both provide the temporal order necessary to the acquisition of basic needs and requisite to the direction of souls toward eternal happiness.

Al-Ghazali's view of justice can be summarized as follows: " treat people in a way in which, if you were subject and another were sultan, you would deem right that you yourself be treated." This is strikingly like the Golden Rule, and a doctrine not in any sense foreign to the natural rights tradition of the West. Justice is a matter of balance for al-Ghazali, an attempt at equilibrium between individuals seeking a harmonious interaction based on equity in giving and receiving one's proper due.

For the most part, al-Ghazali seeks a kind of spiritual brotherhood within the community— a sentiment that he values above all else. The desire to place the interests of one's brother, or fellow member of the community, ahead of one's own interest, is what al-Ghazali regards as the essence of the political order. After all, it is the charge of the temporal government to prepare humanity for the eternal government of the Divine, and such a charge can only be fulfilled through a sense of mutual care and commitment to a greater good.

Related Entries
Alfarabi; Augustine; Averroes

Suggested Reading
al-Ghazali, Abu Hamid Muhammad *The Incoherence of the Philosophers,* trans. Michael E. Marmura. Provo, UT: Brigham Young Univ. Press, 2002.
Black, Antony. *The History of Islamic Political Thought: From the Prophet to the Present.* New York: Routledge, 2001.

alienation

Generally, alienation refers to an existential condition of estrangement from both the social and political order, one that is characterized by the person's disaffection, entrapment, and haunting realization of impotence owing to the oppressive and exploitative situation created and sustained by the established order of things. One feels as a stranger within one's own society—a sense of community and belonging is absent from human interaction. Such a condition either produces a social lassitude accompanied by political apathy within the society as a whole, or it can lead to a violent reaction to any perceived injustices of the state or the basic economic order.

More specifically, alienation is a prominent concept (and perhaps *the* central idea) in the Marxian critique of capitalism. Man in capitalist society is deprived of any connection to one's own productive capacity as well as any authentic relationship with society as a whole. Capitalism alienates human beings from their labor power, the product of their labor (through the fetishism of commodities and the exclusive pursuit of profit for its own sake), other human beings, and from their own "species-being" or awareness of their universal humanity. For Marx, we are free because we are universal beings, but under capitalism we are deluded into believing that our liberty is a function of our individuality. Marx insists that this is a

delusion primarily because any sense of the freedom of the self masks the hidden subjugation caused by the existential fact of alienation. To surmount this, society must be radically transformed, and the revolution that accomplishes this will change at the deepest level the relationship between human beings and their productive power as well as among human beings themselves. Only through the rehabilitation of the labor power of humanity through a classless society can the human community be free. Hence the only solution to alienation for Marx is communism.

Related Entries
Marx, Karl; socialism

Suggested Reading
Fromm, Erich. *Marx's Concept of Man.* 1961; repr. New York: Frederick Ungar Publishing, 1980.
Ollman, Bertell. *Alienation: Marx's Conception of Man in Capitalist Society.* 1971; repr. New York: Cambridge Univ. Press, 1977.
Schacht, Richard. *Alienation.* New York: Doubleday/Anchor Books, 1970.

allegory of the cave

The "allegory of the cave" stands at the heart of Plato's *Republic,* an undisputed masterpiece not only within the tradition of political theory and philosophy in general, but also as a triumph of literary artistry. The allegory opens Book VII of *Republic,* initially as an extended metaphor shedding light on Plato's theory of cognition as sketched at the end of Book VI through his divided line analogy. The allegory, however, while an epistemological exercise, is evidently far more than that. Full of meaning, the allegory is employed by Plato as a means to deliver his essential teachings not only on the nature of knowledge, but also on the very essence of being itself, while revealing in addition to these epistemological and ontological lessons the process of education, the need for the rule of wisdom in the *polis,* the difference between true (objective) justice and shadow justice, and the difference between the love of wisdom and the attachment to opinion.

The divided line analogy in the previous book demonstrated the levels of human knowledge and how they are related to the reality of being. *Eikasia* (image-making, imagery) represents the lowest stage of cognition, or sense-experience. The are but images of what is truly real; in other words, for Plato, that which is most accessible to our sense and thus our immediate experience of the world is that which is also least real, at best a reflection or shadow of the true reality remaining to be discovered. *Pistis* is a step above *eikasia,* representing perceptions that help us form opinions (*doxa*) about our experiences and yet remains an incomplete comprehension of the nature of things as it is still riveted to our own subjective perspective and framed by the visible and material phenomena. Through the efforts of increasing intellect, detached from experience and perception, we are able to ascend into the higher stages of cognition, namely *dianoia* and *noesis,* the former referring to reasoning of the intellect (such as logic, mathematics and geometry) while the latter, the highest stage of knowing wherein we come to discover the Forms (*eidos*) themselves, the essence of eternal reality that cannot be fully grasped through phenomenal perceptions nor completely communicated even through the language and formulas of the intellect. We can talk about a geometric shape, such as a triangle or circle, at the level of *dianoia,* and draw these shapes and make them visible to us, and yet neither the strict reasoning nor visual representation can reveal the true essence of the Forms of the triangle or circle. These are known only at the highest stage of cognition, and are entirely grasped only as pure concept.

The allegory of the cave further explains Plato's epistemological teaching. "Imagine a cave" Socrates muses at the beginning of Book VII, wherein the inhabitants are unwittingly bound by chains in such a way as to force them, without their awareness, to always face the wall at the far back of the cave. Unable to turn, they are fixed in a position wherein they can only face the cave wall. Behind them a fire burns,

casting a dim light on the wall that they perpetually face, but as far as the troglodytes know, this is the brightest kind of light possible within their experience. Unknown to the bound inhabitants, puppets and facsimiles of objects pass before the fire, casting shadows on the cave wall, and the noises of the mysterious puppeteers echo off the cave wall as the shadows pass before the constricted vision of the prisoners. Socrates states that these cave-dwellers are "just like us," our very own experiences of the world are but shadows of the ultimate reality—we are bound within a phenomenal trap that prevents us from widening our vision of things and seeing beyond shadows or hearing anything other than echoes. This is the stage of *eikasia,* wherein we mistake the appearance of things for the things themselves, the phenomenal for the essential. Those who manage to slip from their bonds and peer behind them, and then eventually move about the cave, are able to perceive (*pistis*) the cause of the shadows and echoes (the fire, puppets, and puppeteers), and thus have expanded their cognition of the cave world compared to their fellow troglodytes. The opinions held by these cave dwellers are sounder than those who think the shadows are the whole of reality, but nonetheless woefully incomplete.

These cave dwellers moving about the cave are becoming experts at perceiving the movement of shadows and sounds of echoes correlated with the procession of puppets. Should one, in noticing that there is another source of light and a path leading to another part of the cave, commence a journey away from the fire and puppets and toward the actual entrance of the cave itself, far from the inner wall, she/he will eventually discover the truth that the cave is but a minute part of a vast and boundless world, a mere pocket of air in the great expanse of the earth. The journey up and out of the cave is the upward journey of the soul, led by the intellect, discovering the intelligible reality beyond and above the visible reality, and drawing the soul closer to an awareness of what is truly real. For Plato the turning away from the cave shadows and toward at first the cave fire and then ultimately toward the light beyond the cave is in effect a turning of the soul away from appearance and toward what is real. Upon leaving the cave and now being exposed to the brilliance of daylight, the eyes need time to adjust, lingering in shaded areas and focused on reflections in water in order to adapt to the bright and endless world around it. This is the stage of *dianoia,* the exercise of the intellect independent of experience and perception (the visible, material realm of the cave). Eventually and with great effort, the eyes adjust and can step out of the shade and look at objects directly, not simply at their reflections. In so doing, the soul comes to know the Forms themselves, and ascends to the highest level of knowing, or *noesis.* At this level, the highest and most essential of all Forms, that which is "most prized" (even above justice) and both the "cause of and object of all knowledge," is the Good (*to agathon*), analogous to the resplendent sun that provides light and warmth to the entire world. It is the sun that enables the eye to see the world above the cave and all its forms; hence the sun is to the eye as the Good is to the soul, without which all knowledge and virtue would not be possible. At this level of cognition, the noetic discovery of the Forms and the revelation that it is the Good itself that is the foundation of all reality and purpose, the philosopher acquires the kind of wisdom that is the ground for truly just leadership in the *polis.* Reluctant to go back into the cave, the philosopher nonetheless again descends into the cave (in the same way that Socrates "goes down to the Piraeus" to open the *Republic*), compelled to apply wisdom to the just navigation of the ship of state.

And yet, the eyes of the philosopher must readjust to the darkness of the cave, an adjustment that causes the philosopher to stumble and grope about in the darkness, and appear foolish to those who have never left the cave and know no greater light than the fire they take to be real. The philosopher's wisdom is thus rejected by the people; and the philosopher is also reluctant to descend. Once the philosopher's eyes do adjust, it becomes clear that she/he is the only true ruler of city and soul, but few will accept this. It is more likely that the philosopher will be rejected, as Socrates was rejected by Athens. But the one who is rejected is the only one who knows justice, a knowledge that stems from the discovery of the nature of the Good.

The allegory of the cave illustrates many principles that are affirmed throughout Plato's overall philosophy. Knowledge (discerned in the intelligible realm) and opinion (held in the visible realm), being (the eternal realm of the immutable and immaterial Forms) and becoming (the transitory realm of mutable and material experience wherein everything is in flux), true justice (found as an eternal and transcendent Form) and interpretations of justice (the shadow justice familiar in the cave), the philosopher (lover of wisdom who knows of the Good) and the sophist (lovers of opinion who claim to possess wisdom and believe they can dispense it as a good), the educated (enlightened by the light of the Good or by those who have beheld the light of the Good) and the ignorant (who go about their lives thinking that what they experience through their immediate senses is all that there is to know), the truly happy (who know the nature of things) and the content (oblivious to the possibility of a richer life). One could go on with further examples, but for our purposes here, the political question of why the philosophers should rule in the ideal city, or in effect, why reason ideally should always guide power, is answered by Plato through Socrates in this stirring parable. The wise should govern because they recognize that the principles that must guide a just community are not of our construction, but rather transcend our narrow, shadowy perspective. And that best state is a state that, as closely as humanly possible, attempts to ground its laws upon principles that are not the product of our will or judgment and thus contingent upon our interests and desires, but rather are in fact based on the nature of being and the eternal principles that are independent of human determination and yet intimately and essentially present within the human soul.

Related Entry
Republic, The (*Politeia*)

Suggested Reading
Plato, *Republic,* in *Complete Works,* ed. John M. Cooper. Indianapolis: Hackett, 1997.
Weil, Simone. *Lectures on Philosophy.* New York: Cambridge Univ. Press, 2002.

all men and women are created equal

The Declaration of Rights and Sentiments was the product of an 1848 convention organized by Lucretia Mott and Elizabeth Cady Stanton advocating women's rights. The preamble of this document recapitulates the Declaration of Independence almost *verbatim,* and the phrase "we hold these truths to be self-evident, that all men and women are created equal" drew direct attention to the early women's movement and its expressed desire to advance equality between the sexes. The Seneca Falls Convention was initiated in response to male domination even among the reform movements that appeared during the Age of Jackson and developed throughout the antebellum period. This became painfully apparent at a world antislavery convention in 1840 when Lucretia Mott, an American delegate, was refused a seat on the main floor and was required to sit separately from her male counterparts. This revealed additional injustice to women involved in the antislavery movement as well as other reform movements and ignited at least for a time activists in behalf of their cause as well. By going back to Jefferson's text for the Declaration of Independence, Mott, Stanton, and their compatriots attempted to illuminate the cause of women within the conceptual language of American liberty and revolution.

Following the Jeffersonian preamble, the document enumerates several grievances before a "candid world" as did the original Declaration on Independence, addressing in this case examples of women's subjugation at the hands of a patriarchal society. The Declaration of Rights and Sentiments thus directly attacks the unjust position of political, social, and familial subordination thrust upon them by a male-dominated culture, and does so by effectively emulating a revered document in the political *mythos* of America.

In the short term, the Seneca Declaration had little impact. After the repeal of the Missouri Compromise, followed by the Kansas-Nebraska Act, the abolition of slavery almost exclusively dominated the American reformist mind. It was not until well after the Civil War and toward the end of Reconstruction that the women's movement began to gather its strength again, slowly building momentum in the later part of the nineteenth century and successfully enfranchising all American women voters with the 19th Amendment ratified in the summer of 1920.

Related Entries
all men are created equal; feminism

Suggested Reading
Commager, Henry Steele. *Documents of American History,* Vol. I. Englewood Cliffs, NJ: Prentice-Hall Publishers, 1973, pp. 315–317.
The Declaration of Sentiment, Seneca Falls Conference of 1848.

all men are created equal

"We hold these truths to be self-evident, that all men are created equal, that they are endowed by their Creator with certain unalienable Rights, that among these are Life, Liberty and the Pursuit of Happiness." This famous phrase from the American Declaration of Independence (1776) as originally written by Thomas Jefferson encapsulates the sentiment of a new era and illuminates the essential principles of the American founding.

The notion of natural equality among human beings was not new to the eighteenth century, the principle that human beings are essentially equal having been a part of Western culture since the emergence of Stoicism, Judaism, and Christianity. However, it is in the political ideas of the eighteenth century that equality became a viable political principle. With the American and French Revolutions, equality was moved to the foreground of political ideals, becoming a realistic aspiration attached to the promise of democracy. While the actualization of equality would still require generations of reform, revolution, and civil war throughout Western societies, the idea was now irresistible. It is in this passage in the Declaration of Independence that the hope of equality is not only expressed, but set firmly within the consciousness of the ongoing development of the liberal mind in the West.

Of particular interest to students of political thought is the deep connection between equality ("all men are created equal") to liberty ("endowed by their Creator with certain unalienable Rights, that among these are Life, *Liberty* and the pursuit of Happiness"). Equality and liberty are thus not only compatible but, according to the doctrine affirmed in the Declaration, inextricably bound together. One stems from the other—our natural liberty is the consequence of our natural equality as designed by a Creator and thus rooted in a transcendent principle. It is not human convention that defines and divides the notion and extent of equality and our liberties, but rather equality and liberty exist prior to the social and political order within the very structure of our nature. We come to the political sphere already established as possessing equal dignity, and the liberties that we thereby claim are inherent to all human beings antecedent to the origins of society, let alone the formal establishment of a particular political order. Hence equality and liberty are the ontological principles upon which self-government is founded, and are set as the dual principles animating political life itself. It is only through democracy that both of these principles can be simultaneously applied.

That said, the distance between principle and institutional practice has prevented the full realization of the ideals of the Declaration of Independence throughout American history.

This is not to say that the ideals themselves are unrealistic or that the American founding was an act of hypocrisy but only to recognize the tension between transcendent ideas and the limitations imposed on human beings by their conditions and circumstances. This was understood by the abolitionists of antebellum America in their efforts to fully realize the ideal of equality for an enslaved population. The early women's movement that emerged in the 1840s expressed the need to ensure its application to men and women alike. At Seneca Falls, a declaration and set of resolutions was to include the phrase "all men and women are created equal," thus drawing awareness to the problem of cultural bias against the interest of women. (It should be noted that the term "men" in fact and by definition denoted all human beings, not just male persons. The term "man," when applied generically, did imply men and women together. Whether or not this is what Thomas Jefferson and his colleagues were thinking at the time is open to debate, but at least in the linguistic sense, "men" was defined in general as including every person.)

Abraham Lincoln, perhaps more than any nineteenth-century statesmen, affirmed the notion that the American founding is fully expressed in Jefferson's 1776 declaration, and that liberty and equality are the essential ground for the practice of American democracy. This was fully understood by the Rev. Martin Luther King, Jr., who, like Lincoln before him, insisted on the realization of equality and liberty together as the only logical and just practice required by the American creed.

The history of the American polity, and, indeed, the development of Western political thought as a whole, is intimately related to the ideals expressed by the flawed human beings who drafted and endorsed the Declaration of Independence. And, along with the French Revolution, the American aspiration for a society of equal, free, and self-governing citizens initiated the great movement toward liberal democracy that continues to seek full realization today.

Related Entries
All men and women are created equal;
conservatism; equality; freedom; liberalism

Suggested Reading
The Declaration of Independence.
*The Declaration of Sentiment, Seneca Falls Conference of
1848.* (Both of these documents are easily found
in print and on the Internet.)

all other contentments

In Chapter 30 of *Leviathan,* Thomas Hobbes
(1588–1679) opens with a summary of the
"office of the sovereign," stating that "the end
for which [the sovereign] is trusted is the
"procuration of the safety of the people." This
trust binds the sovereign under the "law of
nature" and to "render an account therefore
to God, the author of that law, and none but
him." In this way, Hobbes recapitulates a good
portion of what has been said in previous chapters, that is, the sovereign duty is to be defined
in terms that involve the security of subjects.
However, Hobbes makes it clear that safety
and security, while necessary and foremost, are
not in themselves sufficient. Indeed, the term
safety encompasses more than mere security
or, as Hobbes phrases it, "bare preservation."
Rather, the safety of the people also implies,
for Hobbes, "all other contentments of life
which every man by lawful industry, without
danger or hurt to the commonwealth, shall
acquire to himself." Other "contentments," or
those things that make for a contented, felicitous life, are thus required for a stable political
order. This implies that Hobbes does not
understand sovereignty simply in terms of order
and protection, but also in terms of a public
good that includes more than the basic necessities. One cannot infer from this that Hobbes
advocated an activist state that would guarantee
or supply citizens with a certain standard of living, to do so would be anachronistic. Nonetheless, by taking care to draw our attention to the
nature of "safety," Hobbes does indicate that
the sovereign has a duty to somehow provide
basic support for his/her subjects in the pursuit
of a felicitous life, the elements of which are
already stated in Chapter 13 as those things that
would be absent a "common power to keep all
in awe."

Hobbes is often perceived as a political theorist more concerned about the use of power to
shelter human beings from the state of nature
(which is unequivocally defined as a "war of
all against all"), but such passages indicate that,
while protection against the state of nature
remains paramount, such protection does
involve more than the wielding of power in
the attainment of order. Hobbes understood
the pursuit of felicity to be an irresistible fact
of human activity, and thus appears to understand "safety" of the people at least in part as
the safety of the people to freely prosper in this
pursuit. This attitude is of some help in leading
us to a more thorough understanding of the
Hobbesian notion of the duties of sovereigns
and the purposes of sovereign power.

Related Entries
Hobbes, Thomas; Leviathan

Suggested Reading
Hobbes, Thomas. *Leviathan,* ed. Edwin Curley.
Indianapolis: Hackett, 1994.

Althusius, Johannes (1557–1638)

Somewhat overshadowed by such seventeenth-
century giants as Hobbes and Locke, Althusius
produced a political theory that in at least two
ways proved innovative with respect to the
political ideas of his time. First, Althusius proposed a theory of federalism that some regard as
more farsighted than both Hobbes and Locke,
and, second, his notion of popular sovereignty
stands as one of the more forthright expressions
of this doctrine in the seventeenth century as a
whole. Additionally, Althusius also contributed,
perhaps less innovatively, to theories of both
natural law and the social contract—the former
emphasizing the strong link between first principles and the Mosaic Decalogue (de-emphasizing
that part of natural law identified with "right
reason") and the latter more of a descriptive
account in comparison to other contract theorists who were interested in tracing the origin

of and need for government. For Althusius, the state of nature does not figure into his understanding of the social contract. Given this, the social contract is not so much a discourse on human nature and the possible condition of humanity outside politics, but rather a legal explanation of the inner mechanisms of the political community.

In at least one aspect of his political theory, his concept of the *consociatio symbiotica* (the natural consociation, or community living symbiotically), Althusius looked back toward the ancient theorists, and in particular Aristotle. For Althusius, as indicated earlier, politics and society are natural to human beings (the former was not natural in Locke's view, neither were natural to Hobbes). *Consociatio symbiotica* is the root form of human association, the basic pattern underlying all variations of community at all levels of size and sophistication. This root community contains two general kinds of law, the first producing the basic framework within which citizens interact and the other establishing and regulating authority within a given group (political or otherwise). In this sense Althusius breaks from Aristotle, as he discerns in the root community of the *consociatio symbiotica* the same basic principles of authority and interaction, whether the community is familial, corporate, or political. It is in the contract that we find the essential relationship within all levels of community; additionally, Althusius understands that contracts are formed between groups as well. Family, corporations (voluntary associations such as guilds, *collegia*), local political institutions, and communities, provinces, and states are all dependent on a contract understanding of mutual rights and obligations. Indeed, for Althusius, the most encompassing political association (the state) is in reality more of a contract between lesser groups than it is between individual members (as in Hobbes and Locke). Thus the grounding of federalism is the unifying notion of a series of interrelated contracts. In this way Althusius attempts to reconcile the reality of federalist decentralization with the desire for a binding political unity.

Thus, Althusius manages to combine the pluralistic aspects of federalism with the need for a strong unified sovereign.

Related Entries
natural law; Pufendorf, Samuel, Baron von

Suggested Reading
Althusius, Johannes. *Politica,* ed. and trans. Frederick S. Cerey. Indianapolis: Liberty Fund, 1995.

amor Dei/amor sui

"Two cities," St. Augustine affirmed in Book XIV of his monumental *City of God,* "have been formed by two loves; the earthly city by the love of self, even to the contempt of God; the heavenly by the love of God even to the contempt of self." With this statement, St. Augustine marks the distinction between concern for temporal affairs, which is always tainted by egotism, and the perfection of the eternal City of God, which is always drawn upward by the love of the divine. *Amor sui,* or love of self, is the spring of selfishness that leads to cupidity and violence, known to St. Augustine as the fruits of worldly interests. Hence the political will always "fall short of the glory of God," and it is incumbent on citizens to remind themselves of the limitations of ordinary politics. Only in the City of God, distinguished by *amor Dei,* which produces the fruits of charity and peace, can we find justice and goodness under the authority of Christ. Only by abandoning the love of self that results in the contempt of God and embracing the love of God even over the interests of the self can we begin to secure a just society. But for St. Augustine, no temporal regime will ever achieve such a state. Rather, the best that we can do is to recognize that the City of God is both transcendent and partially immanent, and, as such, we can approximate without fully acquiring the perfection of the City of God here on earth.

St. Augustine's two cities, born from two conflicted loves, is reminiscent of Plato's distinction between the perfect regime found in the form of the *polis* and the multitude of imperfect regimes that are found in temporal reality. For both Plato and St. Augustine, perfection in the phenomenal realm is ever elusive, but by looking toward the "heavenly patterns" of (for Plato) the form of the *polis* or (for St. Augustine) the City of God we can seek to govern human beings justly. Both thinkers understood such governance in terms of the proper orientation of one's love—the love of wisdom and the love of God, respectively.

Related Entry
Augustine

Suggested Reading
Augustine, *City of God,* ed. David Knowles, trans. Henry Bettenson. 1972; repr. New York: Penguin Classics, 1976.

amour de soi / amour propre

French philosopher Jean-Jacques Rousseau (1712–1778) employed two types of self-love to help clarify the distinction between the natural person and the inauthentic individual within society. *Amour de soi,* for Rousseau, describes a healthy love of self that is natural to all human beings and is the primary internal affect experienced in a "state of nature." A natural person is well-disposed to the self, needing only one's own self-judgment in measuring a person's worth and the value of one's actions. Natural self-love is independent of the conclusions of others, free from the demands of reputation before the public eye, and thus unfettered by the constraints of social conformity. *Amour de soi* is an indication of a radically free person, one who is not enchained by the expectations of others, one who is able to feel content within the limits of one's own comfortable sense of self. It is from the absence of dependence upon others to develop a sense of self that we see the beginnings of freedom, thus Rousseau finds the roots of true freedom within the ego of a natural innocent, indifferent to the external factors that would otherwise impinge upon us within the interdependencies of polite society.

Amour propre, or love of one's own, is contrasted to the more natural, innocent love of self that characterizes a free person. *Amour propre* is a vain self-absorption, a desire to consider the rest and to "wish to be considered in turn" that robs the natural person of their inwardly shaped identity and produces a dependency on the assessment of others for one's sense of self. Stemming from the intellect's tendency to compare, *amour propre* creates a condition wherein natural trivial differences are exaggerated in importance, ultimately causing human beings to not only accept, but actually to seek and embrace inequality. People compare and then compete, hoping to become the best at a variety of things, and in so doing, win a reputation for being faster, stronger, more agile, more beautiful—in a word, better—than others. But this sense of superiority depends on the recognition of that superiority by others; recognition needed and wanted in order to develop a sense of self-importance. Far from the healthy self-regard of natural *amour de soi, amour propre* initiates within individuals a reliance on others at the expense of a reliance on the self, deprives the person of the indifferent innocence of the state of nature, and ensnares the self within a net of social illusions and dissembling vanities. Rousseau considers the shift from *amour de soi* to *amour propre* as the origin of both social inequality and moral corruption, and thus the loss of the kind of freedom needed to ground a truly free person. Hope remains for Rousseau, however, as the right kinds of institutions formed by the social contract can restore human beings to a state of freedom in spite of the abiding presence of dependent and prideful inauthenticity and conceit. The desire for recognition that Rousseau connects to vain self-love is anticipated in Hobbes as well as further developed in Hegel, and it is not unreasonable to see similar conclusions drawn by Plato, Epictetus, and St. Augustine as well.

Related Entry
Rousseau, Jean-Jacques

Suggested Reading
Rousseau, Jean-Jacques. *On the Social Contract,* trans. Donald A. Cress. Indianapolis: Hackett, 1987.

analogy of the jars

In Plato's *Gorgias*, Socrates answers a challenge from Callicles by resorting to a metaphorical image of two jars. Earlier in the dialogue, Socrates asserts, when conversing with Polus, that it is better to suffer wrong than to commit it (although it is important to remember that one would hope to avoid doing either). When forced to choose, one cannot choose the commission of an immoral or unjust act, and then, if no other alternative is available in that situation, one must choose to suffer the wrong or the injustice. Callicles argues that such a position is ludicrous and unmanly. A superior person would never choose to suffer, and indeed, would ultimately remain indifferent to the suffering of another if it is for the correct purposes, that is, if it is in the correct interest of the superior person. A person of great soul, by nature, must command others, and the interests of the inferior must serve the interest of those who truly are superior. Additionally, Callicles argues that a superior person, knowing this, does not constrain the appetites, as Socrates prescribes, for to do so would be to turn oneself into a slave. Such statements by Socrates are tantamount to the use of social convention, framed by the mediocre, to restrain and suppress the urges and drives of the naturally superior. Law, in other words, is used by the mediocre to rule over the superior, and ensures that they do not become a law unto themselves and dominate society for their own purposes.

Rather than the self-mastery that Socrates endorses for the just soul, Callicles argues that the natural (and naturally superior) person should set his or her own standards and in practice "enlarge their appetites" in defiance of the common standards of the less capable masses. A person of great ability should not bear the same restrictions as the rest of us, but rather should live and love large, and accept no rule, even the rule of reason over the appetites as Socrates teaches.

To rebut this argument, Socrates speaks of "two jars," one jar that is "tightly closed" and one that leaks. One pours liquid into the tightly closed jar, fills it, seals it with its lid, the task being finished, and moves on to the next thing. Yet if one is trying to fill a leaking jar, the fluid constantly flows out; thus one is never able to seal it and move on, the leaking jar never reaching a point where it is full and the individual filling it never coming to a point when the task is finished. For Socrates, these two jars are analogous to two kinds of soul. The jars represent the appetites. In the case of the tightly closed jar, a person is able to fill their appetites with little effort, seal the jar, and move on to other things. Simplicity and self-control are represented by the sealed jar. One does not serve one's appetites, but rather addresses them and, once completed, is able to regard other things. But the intemperate person, the person of expansive and multiple appetites lacking any self-control or self-mastery, constantly serves the jar itself, that is, constantly serves one's own appetites. Thinking that they are a law unto themselves, always indulging in any pleasure that passes their way, they are in reality like the poor person attending to the task of filling a leaky jar, never finished, never satiate, always attending on the lower part of the soul without any rest or any chance of moving to other things. For Socrates, this is the fate of the intemperate, and even a "superior person" who thinks they are doing whatever they want, and indulging any appetite on their own terms, is in reality a slave to the basest part of the self.

This analogy is related, politically, to the depiction of the tyrannical soul in Plato's *Republic*. A tyrant is in fact a person driven by fear and lust—one whose appetites are so insatiable and restless that one's whole life is in slavish service to the worst kinds of pursuits. The tyrant, through fear of others and incessant lust, is the most slavish of all human beings, appearances notwithstanding. The tyrant and the tyrannical city are condemned to a life of perverse injustice. Thus in the tyrannical city, because of the conversion of persons into slaves—both the tyrant and the subjects of tyranny—the *polis* is lost and all that remains is the one master who is in truth a great slave, and the many slaves who serve the endless lust and who must suffer the consequence of the nagging fear of the tyrannical soul.

Related Entry
Plato

Suggested Reading
Plato. *Gorgias,* in *Complete Works,* ed. John M. Cooper. Indianapolis: Hackett, 1997.

anarchism

As with most terms and concepts in the political language and culture of the West, the words anarchy and anarchism stem from the ancient Greek, *an arkhe,* which means without ruling principle or without rule or authority. In essence, anarchy simply means a condition without formal authority or government leaders. It does not necessarily mean, as it is often construed, a chaotic and especially violent condition absent any authority whatsoever, although one could argue that certain (but not all) anarchistic methods do encourage social disruption. Anarchism certainly can involve violence as a revolutionary method, but it is not an elemental part of its essential definition. Anarchy only means the absence of institutional, formal, and fixed political rule, but it does not mean in every case a condition of lawless disorder. While anarchism certainly entails a critique of and at times a direct rejection of conventional law and politics, it is not in itself antipolitical, but it is what has been referred to as acephalous—literally without a head, or without a designated permanent leader.

As the term anarchy stems from the Greeks, there is a tendency among some students of political ideas to search for ancient examples of anarchistic theories. In the Western tradition, the ancient Greek Cynics (not to be confused with the modern usage of the word cynic or cynical) owing to their defiance of custom and their refusal to accept the political and legal norms of their times, are often described as early anarchists of a kind. Their focus on individual self-sufficiency and independence from political rule seems to anticipate modern libertarianism. Moreover, their indifference to

common worldly concerns is often viewed as a an example of active refusal to participate in public affairs, replacing such activity with a vague affiliation to the *cosmopolis,* or universal city, a concept of a stateless association of the free, wise and unattached. However, as the ideas of the Cynics are known mostly through fragments and secondhand accounts, the actual nature of the Cynics protoanarchist attitudes remains unclear and for the most part extrapolated.

Others regard the ancient writings of the Taoist sage, Lao-tse, as an example of antique and formative anarchism. Certainly Lao-tse and other Taoist writings can be so read, but in so doing other questions are raised. As Taoism is seen by some to be not only a philosophical approach but also properly numbered among the world's great religions, the suitability of assigning a political prescription becomes problematic. While one can certainly draw connections between religion and politics, it raises difficulties when a religious worldview is by necessity described in political terms alone. Hence it might be accurate to argue for a relationship between certain anarchistic strains and the *Tao te Ching,* but it may be inaccurate to regard early Taoism as programmatically and intentionally anarchistic. One could also advance the same argument for early Christians, as Christianity can also be read in ways that might encourage an anarchistic response to political and social order; but to do so would again risk an extrapolation that is possibly inaccurate and, in the end, misleading.

Hence anarchism, perhaps more than liberalism, conservatism, and socialism, owes its intellectual lineage to more modern thinkers, beginning in particular with the latter part of the eighteenth and early part of the nineteenth centuries. Additionally, it is necessary to recognize that there are at least two disparate strains of anarchistic thought, one that is decidedly libertarian in form and thus resembles classical liberalism, and a second that is strongly communitarian and thus, significantly, is closely identified with certain strains of socialism. Most modern variations of anarchism are included within one of these two main groups, that is, the libertarian or the communitarian. It should be noted that such a division is not the only, or even the best, method for categorizing anarchist thought. Andrew Vincent adeptly identifies five types of anarchism: individualist, collectivist, communist, mutualist, and anarcho-syndicalist. Additionally, Vincent identifies nihilist anarchism, eco-anarchism, and feminist anarchism as specific subcategories but does not regard them as wholly separate from the five principal types mentioned above. Whether we are looking at five or eight kinds of anarchism, such a more detailed classification can be helpful to those readers who seek to explore further. For our purposes, we will examine anarchism as falling under two apparently conflicting subtypes, to wit, libertarian (or radical individualism) and communitarian, while noting the inadequacy of any firm or fixed schematic.

To begin a focused history of anarchism, three thinkers draw our attention as representing "founding" influences in the initiation of anarchist thought: William Godwin (1756–1836), Pierre-Joseph Proudhon (1809–1865), and Mikhail Bakunin (1814–1876). Each of these figures has been identified as a "father of anarchism," even though in the case of both Godwin and Proudhon some difficulties are attached to that designation. In any event, these three figures, along with Josiah Warren (1798–1874), militant individualist Max Stirner (Johann Kaspar Schmidt, 1806–1856), American transcendentalists Ralph Waldo Emerson (1803–1882) and Henry David Thoreau (1817–1862), Lysander Spooner (1808–1887), Leo Tolstoy (1828–1910), and Petr Kropotkin (1842–1921), are of considerable historic and intellectual importance as among the earlier advocates of some type of anarchistic approach to politics. Later figures such as Errico Malatesta (1853–1932), Benjamin Tucker (1854–1939), Emma Goldman (1869–1940), Rudolf Rocker (1873–1958), Buenaventura Durrati (1896–1936), Murray Bookchin (1921–2006),

and Robert Paul Wolff (b. 1933) have all emerged as important contributors to the anarchist approach.

William Godwin, in his classic work *An Enquiry Concerning Political Justice* (1793), provided the first theoretical affirmation of libertarian anarchism, and thus he positioned himself philosophically as the first political thinker representing an anarchic view of politics and law. Indeed, Kramnick, in his introduction to the *Enquriy,* describes Godwin as anarchism's "prophet." For Godwin, there is a justice that transcends any political power and a higher rationality that is above the influence of convention and social conformity. In this sense, Godwin resembles both Socrates and the Cynics in his view that there are universal principles of justice and rational conduct that are independent of and superior to whatever laws and judgments are provided within a society or polity. Government, in Godwin's estimation, only impedes the development of individual judgment, which, if allowed to grow under the direction of sound education, is inherently superior to government, which, in the end, is more likely to corrupt than to civilize. As a child of the Enlightenment (and one particularly influenced by Claude Adrien Helvetius and Paul-Henri Thiry d'Holbach) Godwin firmly believed that through education and the cultivation of rational morality within each individual, government and politics would be replaced by self-regulation absent the coercion of state or society. This is not to be understood as a liberty reconfigured in terms of unrestricted license but rather a moral liberty that can be achieved through reason (under the proper guidance of education) and applied by individuals for the good of the whole. Godwin ardently believed in the Enlightenment vision of the inevitability of human progress and viewed the expansion of reason as the contraction of the state.

In Tom Bottomore's *A Dictionary of Marxist Thought,* Pierre-Joseph Proudhon "was the first person to use 'anarchy' in a nonpejorative sense to refer to his ideal of an ordered society without government." For this reason Proudhon is also a likely candidate for the appellation of "father of anarchism," even though his overall political thought is complex, and his later political writings somewhat idiosyncratically drew upon Hegel, a philosophical anathema to the anarchist worldview. Proudhon's anarchism is rooted primarily in two concepts: first, his belief that in order to overcome economic exploitation we must abolish political institutions and develop a purely economic culture of voluntary exchange absent the state and, second, that the new social organization that Proudhon envisaged, deemed "mutualism," would be built from the voluntary associations of local workers spontaneously directing their own production, managing without interference their property, and operating through natural exchange between mutually cooperating individuals. No centralized political or corporate organization would be involved. Proudhon believed that human beings could organize themselves naturally around a system that would reward needs according to one's own labor. "Property is theft," Proudhon famously declared, but he was only speaking in terms of property owned by the capitalist. If laborers were allowed to control their own property without interference from the state or from capitalist exploiters, then the conditions for a genuinely free exchange of needs and wants would be established.

Proudhon's ideas are described as both anarchist and socialist. Marx himself, in his early writings, praised Proudhon's economic observations, but later in *The Poverty of Philosophy* unequivocally disassociated himself from Proudhon's philosophical and bourgeois abstractions. It is of interest to note that while Proudhon insisted on abolishing political structures in favor of autonomous economic relations, he argued for the retention of other traditional social structures such as the family.

Bakunin, a noted opponent of Marx and champion of Slavic rebirth, is widely regarded as the most important anarchist thinker of the nineteenth century and perhaps the most important figure in the history of anarchist thought. Bakunin's conflict with Marx over the direction of the First International, with which Bakunin was for a time associated, marks the break between early socialism and anarchism, at least as organized political movements. Troubled by the centralizing tendencies of Marx's communism, Bakunin argued for a decentralized organization resembling a federal structure and stressing local autonomy. For this reason, Bakunin openly rejected the party organization and strategies of the communists, certain that the only result from any political system would be a new absolutism. Spontaneous organization from the people themselves was the only sure method of provoking the kind of revolution necessary to dissolve hierarchical structures and abolish absolutist tendencies. Any permanent political party would simply deprive the movement of that spontaneity. Additionally, while Marx, and particularly Engels advanced the concept of a postrevolutionary "dictatorship of the proletariat," Bakunin bristled at the suggestion, arguing that such a condition would guarantee the reinstitution of even more dangerous forms of power that would ultimately further oppress the workers.

Bakunin's anarchism was based on the belief that all traditional institutions—economic, political, religious—were essentially coercive, and that while they may have at one time served a beneficial purpose for earlier societies, they were now fundamentally obsolete. Every government, and every form of centralized direction, is inherently oppressive. Freedom and power are irreconcilable opposites in Bakunin's view, and even power democratically acquired and applied is basically against human freedom. For Bakunin, it was a scientific truth that humanity had evolved to a point wherein such coercion could be rejected, and a new enlightened and spontaneous mode of human association was near. Human beings are by nature free, and a higher level of freedom will be achieved if they are placed into harmony with the true laws of nature above and beyond the phony laws of society. In Bakunin's assessment, Marx's communism only impedes our ability to live as free, natural individuals.

Godwin, Proudhon, and Bakunin are typically offered as the principal founding anarchists, but several important thinkers could be numbered among the leading anarchist or quasi-anarchistic theorists. Kropotkin represents the communitarian strain of anarchism at its purest. Adopting a mutualist position, Kropotkin concluded that anarchism is the only natural organization, observing that all of nature is based on a subtle and pervasive mechanism of cooperation. Human society, if it is to be both free and just, must resolve to abandon its competitive, individualist habits and return to the way established by nature itself, a noncoercive social mutualism that will elevate at once society and individual. Max Stirner departs from Proudhon, Bakunin, and Kropotkin, while even exceeding the libertarian strains of Godwin and embodying the most strenuously radical type of individualist anarchism available. In his provocative *The Ego and Its Own,* Stirner rejects all ideas centered on principles or values above the raw individual. Politics, society, religion, God, for Stirner are all empty expressions of the "nothingness" of the self. The self is the "creative nothingness" from which all other concepts are produced. Only the ego can be explained as having any reality, beyond that is mere emptiness and illusion. The ego is the only determinant of what is true, of what can be certain. For Stirner, one should assert the ego without stint, for "all truths beneath me are to my liking; a truth above me, a truth that I should have to direct myself by, I am not acquainted with. For me there is no truth, for nothing is more than I." This fact, for Stirner, places the ego in a perpetual state of conflict with state and religion, a conflict that must be surmounted by the individual if one is to really live as a human being. Stirner's militant egoism is often contrasted to Hegel and Marx, and sometimes noted as a precursor to the egophilic elements of Nietzsche's philosophy.

Embracing a notion of the "sovereignty of the individual," Josiah Warren provides one of the earliest examples of anarchistic-libertarian arguments within the tradition of American political thought. Initially a follower of the collectivism of Welsh socialist Robert Owen (1771–1858), Warren broke from the communalism that characterized much of the nineteenth-century utopian movements in England and the United States, and asserted a theory of the absolute autonomy of the individual based on the natural state of human beings. By nature, only individuals, in Warren's view, are entitled to determine their own activities, and this includes command over one's own private property. Hence the communitarian elements of the Owenites and other socialist movements were, in Warren's estimation, contrary to the nature of things. Formal society of any kind is artificial, preventing individuals from their natural development, and thus necessarily unfair. Following from this, Warren conceived of an economic system, dubbed "cost as the limit of price," that would be based solely on the labor invested in the production of commodities, a system that he put into practice in his Cincinnati Time Store.

Two other American anarchists, Lysander Spooner and Benjamin Tucker, furthered the individualism promoted by their progenitor Warren. Spooner argued for a Natural Law that provides all individuals with the proper guide to individual action. Spooner is of particular interest owing to his fervent opposition to slavery. Interestingly enough, while Spooner is primarily known as an anarchist, he relied on political institutions to ground his argument against slavery. With Frederick Douglass, Spooner argued that slavery is incompatible with the principles of the Constitution, the Framers' intent notwithstanding. From this position, Spooner advocated militant resistance to the Peculiar Institution, expressing sympathy with the efforts of John Brown. Spooner's attack on slavery through the Constitution appears atypical of the anarchist vision, but ultimately Spooner remained consistent in his reference to Natural Law as the only foundation for true justice in any society.

Tucker's anarchism resembles Warren's in that both thinkers emphasized command over one's labor while rejecting the more collectivist tendencies of socialism. In Tucker's view, the only controls that can be legitimately placed on property would be restrictions imposed on the accumulation and use of land. To avoid land monopolies, one must use whatever land they have, subject to restrictions from the larger community. Beyond that, Tucker advocated free command of one's labor as well as an unfettered approach to personal and moral choices. In the end, Tucker embraced a radicalized form of individualism influenced by the egoistic anarchism of Max Stirner.

Additionally, American Transcendentalist thinkers Emerson and Thoreau both held ideas compatible with anarchism, although neither identified themselves as such. Emerson regarded the state with indifference, writing that traditional politics was superfluous. The state's primary function was to provide a structure wherein wise men would emerge and become educated, and once educated, the state would be rendered unnecessary and thus fade away. Emerson and other transcendentalists also saw in the established political system the foundations of injustice, most notably in the institutions that supported the practice of slavery. For Emerson, the poor beast that is the state can be fed clover and left alone so long as it doesn't turn its horns on you, but the moment it hooks you, one is justified in cutting its throat. Hence, while Emerson deems the state a superfluity and worthy of minimal involvement, a person can and should stand against it in the face of the injustices such as the political defense of enslavement.

Thoreau is even more insistently anarchistic in his views against the state. While acknowledging the need for minimal government, Thoreau, a radical individualist, ultimately considers the absence of governing power an ideal worthy of aspiration. "I heartily accept the motto," Thoreau states at the opening of his essay "On the Duty of Civil Disobedience, "'That government is best which governs least;' and I should like to see it acted up to more rapidly and systematically. Carried out, it finally amounts to this, which I also believe, —'That government is best which governs not at all;' and when men are prepared for it, that will be the kind of government they will have." As with Emerson, Thoreau celebrated the power of the individual intellect, and in the comparison, collective institutions such as the state and its attendant organizations are in every case inferior to the wisdom of an enlightened individual. The state's only advantage is raw force, intellectually and morally; the free individual is in every sense superior, and, therefore, the best society is a society wherein such individuals are left alone to their own direction. Human beings, for Thoreau, should consult the light of nature, and seek the higher principles of natural law rather than settle for the legalities of the state. The laws of governments do not make us just, Thoreau explains, but the laws of nature do guide us in accordance with the natural cycle of things and through the higher principles of reason alone. When the state and the individual are drawn into conflict based on such principles, the individual is a majority of one, affirming right over power, and acting on the principle of sacred autonomy. Slavery, for example, is the product of the kind of tyranny that is only possible in civil society, and thus the individual is not only justified in resisting it but required to do so in accordance with the just and natural principles of rationally discovered higher law.

Several other thinkers deserve our attention in discussing the principles of anarchism, but for our purposes we will focus on three: Emma Goldman, Leo Tolstoy, and Murray Bookchin. Goldman represents a resolute challenge to all systems of authority—political, religious, and familial. Goldman's anarchism combines a communitarian sensitivity, similar to Kropotkin's, with an ardent belief in the power of the individual. Additionally, Goldman is noteworthy for her emphasis on women's causes, attacking not only authoritarian institutions but patriarchy at the personal level. She was dedicated to the cause of women's suffrage and is often noted as an early apologist for women's reproductive rights. Her open resistance to America's participation in World War I led to her deportation.

Tolstoy is noteworthy for his fusion of Christianity with anarchist principles, although he never identified himself as an anarchist due to the militant connotations of that term. Tolstoy's *The Kingdom of God is within You* develops political principles based on the Christian teaching of universal love, which, if applied sincerely, Tolstoy believed would lead to social perfection. A pacifist, Tolstoy advocated a form of nonviolent resistance that would influence the methods of Mahatma Gandhi, with whom he shared a brief but profoundly important correspondence. Tolstoy also advocated communal sharing of property, and rejected the traditional notions of institutional marriage. Tolstoy's Christian anarchism is not singular in its attempt to meld religion with a new social vision. The Catholic Worker's Association, founded by Dorothy Day and Peter Maurin in 1933, based its sole purpose on developing a society wholly based on the "justice and charity of Jesus Christ," has been described as a kind of Christian anarchism. Another anarchist with similar views, Gary Snyder, has advocated a synthesis of the commitment to social revolution typified in Western democracies with inward enlightenment, which Snyder sees as an important element of Eastern philosophies. Snyder goes beyond the Christian tradition, and his work typifies certain writings by Buddhist anarchists that bear close similarities to the nonviolent, antiauthoritarian, and charitable methods of Tolstoy, Day, and Gandhi.

Bookchin is familiar within the environmental movement and is often identified as a leading figure in the promotion of a kind of communitarian anarchism known as social ecology or "eco-anarchism." All living things are equal members of the larger community of nature—a community that is radically antihierarchical. For Bookchin, nature is essentially anarchy, and human beings, as a part of nature, if we are to survive and flourish, must work to reconcile our social arrangements to this deep reality. While he was equally critical of Marxism for its tendency to promote new forms of exploitation disguised behind false claims of worker's revolution, Bookchin embraced a critique of capitalism—which he regards as a "social cancer"—and centralized political movements, promoted spontaneous grassroots movements, and is regarded as one of the founding influences in the emergence of green parties in the 1970s. However, his rejection of the more militant biocentric ideas such as "deep ecology" has led him to disassociate from the more deterministic strains of eco-anarchism.

While most variations of anarchism are not of necessity violent, it would be inaccurate to depict anarchism as thoroughly nonviolent. Bakunin did recognize the need for violent revolution where necessary, and some anarchists based their ideologies on what is called the "propaganda of the deed," a term coined by French anarchist Paul Brousse (1844–1912). That is to say, it is in acts, not words, that anarchistic goals are achieved—and the deed itself becomes the end that is sought. One must confront the state directly without regard to social and legal prohibitions. Hence, assassination, destruction of property, and theft are legitimate means in the war against oppression, and in a sense, become ends in themselves. But in the final analysis, anarchism, like any political ideology, contains its militant and less militant strains, and while violence and disorder are embraced by the extreme proponents of anarchism, for the most part, the philosophical principles of anarchism are not of necessity dependent on such tactics.

Related Entries
ideology; propaganda of the deed; socialism

Suggested Reading
Eltzbacher, P. and S. T. Byington. *The Great Anarchists: Ideas and Teachings of Seven Major Thinkers.* New York: Dover Publications, 2004.

Guerin, D., and P. Sharkey. *No Gods, No Masters: An Anthology of Anarchism.* Oakland, CA: AK Press, 2005.

Ward, Colin. *Anarchism: A Very Short Introduction.* New York: Oxford Univ. Press, 2004.

antifederalists

The antifederalists were a loose affiliation of thinkers and pamphleteers who, for various and at times disparate reasons, opposed the ratification of the proposed constitution for the United States that was the issue of the Philadelphia Convention of 1787. Among their cohort are numbered George Mason, Patrick Henry, Richard Henry Lee, Robert Yates, George Clinton, Samuel Bryan, and Melancthon Smith. Their abiding concern with the new innovation proposed at Philadelphia was the amount and nature of power inherent within the structure of the Constitution as it was drafted, a kind of power that was viewed by the antifederalists as incompatible with the principles of republican government and the virtues of a free citizenry. This power, the danger of which was further amplified by the absence of a proposed bill of rights, to the antifederalists promised centralization and tyranny, not federalism and democracy. Indeed, the antifederalists perceived only consolidation of power in the proposed Constitution, and regarded their own side of the issue as the truly "federal" voice in the debate.

By and large the antifederalists regarded a bill of rights as a premium element of any constitutional government. Without a bill of rights, the antifederalists were convinced that the principles of the Declaration of Independence would be seriously compromised, if not altogether jettisoned, as the new Constitution became more deeply entrenched. The vast powers of the new government—typified by the elastic clause and the supremacy clause as well as with a more comprehensive power of taxation—would wax as individual rights would disappear. Eventually the government would become so centralized and overweening that the states themselves would be rendered superfluous, and a new political hierarchy would emerge at the expense of popular sovereignty. The scheme of separated powers would either not be sufficient to check the expansion of the centralized state, or it would degenerate into a Byzantine structure remote to the petitions and the interests of the people.

As indicated above, the antifederalists did not cohere around the same principles as effectively as their federalist opponents, but they did embrace certain common values. The antifederalists valued the protection of the liberties won in the Revolutionary War, and saw themselves as the true party protecting the principles of the Declaration, namely, liberty, equality, popular government, and the consent of the governed. Additionally, to effectively advance self-government, the antifederalists preferred small government, and thus were inclined to guard state sovereignty with a degree of jealousy. The antifederalists were suspicious of executive power, and thus their response to the provisions of Article II of the proposed Constitution was often characterized by a sense of dread. The proposed Senate was equally suspicious, as it provided further proof of the convention's aristocratic designs. Additionally, the antifederalists raised concerns over the proportion of representatives relative to the general population, noting that, again, the proposed scheme would tilt heavily toward oligarchy rather than securing the practices of republicanism. Finally, the antifederalists believed firmly in cultivating the virtues of citizens rather than the erection of intricate governmental edifices. The institutions would only be as good as the citizens, who should be encouraged at all turns to become self-governing and self-reliant. But the proponents of the new Constitution seemed to distrust the people and invest all their faith in the institutions themselves, which was for the antifederalists discordant to the ancient principles connecting republican self-government directly with the virtues of the people and not with the efficiency of their institutions.

The Constitution was successfully ratified; thus the federalist faction emerged victorious.

Still, the general framework of the United States owes much to the legacy of the antifederalists. The insistence on a bill of rights was persuasive; hence the antifederalists achieved a significant victory of their own, evident in the inclusion of a bill of rights within the first ten amendments of the Constitution. Furthermore, the spirit of the antifederalists endures within the American distrust of big government, centralized power, political ambition, and vigilant regard for self-reliant liberty. We live under the constitution that they opposed, but it is in their impassioned opposition that the emotional ideal of personal liberty challenges the prudent realities of rational constitutionalism.

Related Entry
Federalist Papers

Suggested Reading
Allen, W. B., and Gordon Lloyd, eds. *The Essential Antifederalist.* Lanham, MD: Univ. Press of America, 1985.
Ketcham, Ralph. *The Anti-Federalist Papers and the Constitutional Debates.* New York: Mentor Books, 1986.

antifoundationalism

Antifoundationalism describes any theoretical approach or critique that rejects the possibility of discovering or discerning objective first principles underlying our understanding of politics, society, morality, and human nature. Antifoundationalism thus holds that there are no absolute, universal and transcendent principles. Instead, truth and knowledge, and by extension, moral norms, are produced only through social convention and culture. Antifoundationalism is purely contextualist in its approach to political inquiry, resisting at every turn any attempt to establish or uncover a principle or value that stands independently to the specific cases under examination. In essence it is a kind of relativism, for lack of a better term, meaning in this instance that ideas and values are not objectively found but rather that, in the final analysis, what we take to be higher ideals or the eternal verities are simply concepts that mask their contingent quality and subjectivist origins.

Antifoundational attitudes can be detected quite early in the history of ideas. The expression attributed to Protagoras that "man is the measure of all things" (sometimes referred to in Latin as the *homo mensura*) might serve as an example of an ancient strain of antifoundationalism, or at least it was for Plato in his *Laws* and *Theatetus* wherein he contrasted the *homo mensura* with his principle that it is ultimately "God who is the measure of all things." (*Laws* 716c-d). The Skeptics also provide an example of ancient philosophy openly critical of the search for objective principles or transcendent law. Some students of political theory in particular look to Machiavelli as the first antifoundationalist, given his apparent subordination of moral values as well as religious beliefs to the uses of politics. Some also detect precursors to antifoundationalism in the works of thinkers such as Thomas Hobbes, Bernard de Mandeville, and David Hume—although in each case enough evidence can be brought to offer a counterargument to that interpretation.

While earlier examples of or tendencies toward an antifoundationalist strain might be evident in a minority of classical and early modern theorists, the more explicit and intentional antifoundationalist critiques are fairly recent, not older than the nineteenth century. The more prominent nineteenth-century figures contributing to the ascent of antifoundationalism are Karl Marx (1818–1883) and Friedrich Nietzsche (1844–1900), although in Marx's case one can argue that he retains substantial foundationalist tendencies through his embrace of a modified Hegelian dialectic. That said, both Marx's proposition that the ruling ideas of any age are the ideas of the ruling class and Nietzsche's more sophisticated arguments against transcendent and objective principles are significant intellectual forces in the construction of an antifoundationalist strain. With the twentieth-century influence of Max Weber, Karl Mannheim, Carl Schmitt, John Dewey, Sigmund Freud, the Vienna Circle,

Martin Heidegger, and Jean-Paul Sartre, the ground was established for a variety of anti-foundationalist approaches to emerge. Hence an antifoundationalist impulse ranges through various schools of thought, from Freudian psychoanalysis through logical-positivism and American pragmatism to certain variants of existentialism. The rejection of transcendence and objective principles became almost *de rigueur* in these and other quarters. In the latter half of the twentieth century, and particularly from the mid-1970s onward, political theory has been influenced by the postmodern mood, preeminently represented by Jean-François Lyotard, Richard Rorty, and Michel Foucault. Postmodernism, a rather loose term to encompass a diverse array of thinkers, perhaps more than any other strain of contemporary political and social criticism is committed to the notion that there are no absolute truths, and no real certainty beyond the contextual frame that is generated by nonrational cultural forces. Today, the expressions "incredulity toward metanarratives" (Lyotard) and "power/knowledge" (Foucault) effectively summarize the postmodern rejection of foundations.

While some argue against the dangers of an antifoundationalist tendency to accept all values, even pernicious ones, as equals, and others claim that antifoundationalism is in itself a perverse kind of negative foundationalism, the critical voice challenging the objectivity of truth and first principles will continue, for good or ill, to captivate both scholarship and application of political theory and practice. This is particularly true as disparate cultures come into more intimate and complex interaction, for the quest for foundations, while certainly possible in a multicultural context, is one that must ever be made in sensitivity to the critics of universal truth. It is in this role that the best thinkers in the antifoundationalist strain will offer a service.

Related Entries

absolutes; dictatorship of relativism; Foucault, Michel; incredulity toward metanarratives; Nietzsche, Friedrich; Plato

Suggested Reading

Foucault, Michel. *The Foucault Reader,* ed. Paul Rabinow. New York: Pantheon Books, 1984.
Lyotard, Jean-François. *The Postmodern Condition.* Minneapolis: Univ. Minn. Press, 1984.
Nietzsche, Friedrich. *On the Genealogy of Morals.* Indianapolis: Hackett, 1988.
Rorty, Richard. *Contingency, Irony, and Solidarity.* 1989; repr. New York: Cambridge Univ. Press, 1996.

anti-Semitism

Anti-Semitism is a virulent form of bigotry directed against the faith of Judaism and the Jewish people as a whole. It can refer both to anti-Semitic (anti-Jewish) laws and policies formally supported by a regime (such as the Nuremburg Laws of Nazi Germany) or to more ambiguous but nonetheless pernicious social and cultural prejudices against Jews and Judaism. The actual term "anti-Semitism" can be traced to German journalist Wilhelm Marr, who first coined it in 1879, referring to any prejudice directed against Jews and Judaism as well as bigotry toward social, political, and cultural values advanced by Jewish communities or at least perceived to be associated with Jewish attitudes. Liberal political values that were in fact advanced by Christian and/or secular thinkers were often associated with Jews; hence throughout much of Europe, liberalism, cosmopolitanism, and both capitalism and socialism were associated with Jewish beliefs, often in a critical and negative manner. While many Jews did embrace liberalism, it is not accurate to say that liberalism is an outgrowth of Judaism. And yet antiliberal and antidemocratic forces in European society made that connection, and thus the divide between liberals and conservatives in nineteenth- and early twentieth-century European politics was colored by degrees of anti-Semitism, conservatives often adopting open anti-Semitic attitudes. These political-social patterns continued into the twentieth century and not only in the insanity of Hitlerian Germany.

The roots of anti-Semitism are ancient, reaching back to Biblical times well before the appearance of the first Christians who were themselves, at least initially, a community of devoutly observant Jews. Ancient Jews often found themselves under the subjugation of a great power, such as the Babylonians, the Greeks, or the Romans, and thus found themselves vulnerable to the whims of capricious leaders. While it is not the case that every conqueror attempted to suppress Judaism (some, such as the King Darius of Persia, practiced tolerance toward their Jewish subjects), nonetheless the pattern of subjugation against the Jewish people can be traced to the sufferings of the ancient Hebrews in their encounter with ambitious pagan empires.

In the earliest days of Christianity, as already mentioned, Christians remained within the Jewish community, even worshiping with non-Christian Jews in the Temple and synagogues. As Christianity drew adherents from the non-Jewish world (primarily Greek, Roman, Coptic, and Syrian), divisions formed between Jews and Christians, the latter the minority and at least initially persecuted by the established Jewish leadership. Saul of Tarsus was one such prosecutor of Christians before his conversion and spiritual rebirth as St. Paul. But with the destruction of the Temple by the Roman legion and the resulting diaspora, the Jewish community was grievously weakened and subject to new vulnerabilities. As Christianity gradually ascended as a growing faith within the Roman Empire, Judaism found itself in the minority. While the Roman Empire waned and dissolved, Christianity expanded and deepened as the universal and culturally unifying religion throughout Europe, Northern Africa, the Middle East, and Central Asia, remaining virtually unchallenged until the emergence of Islam in the sixth century. While it is not the case that Jewish populations were ubiquitously oppressed constantly throughout the Middle Ages, it is the case that variously and with greater frequency, Jewish communities became increasingly isolated, and on occasion targets of oppressive actions by both state and society. Jews at various times were often collectively and unjustly

blamed for the death of Christ, and perceived as stubbornly resistant to the cultural norms growing out of Christian religious and moral beliefs and practices. Furthermore, the scandal of blood libel, or the accusation that Jews secretly engaged in blood sacrifices of abducted Christian children, became lodged in the consciousness of Christians throughout various parts of Europe, even though evidence of such crimes was never presented. The "Christ killer" stigma and the "blood libel" lie became the twin truncheons against the Jewish community and provided the worst and most damaging ammunition against Jews by the dominant social group. (It should be noted that Christianity, as a faith, does not teach persecution of any group, and especially the Jews who are regarded as the Chosen People and the receptacle of the Incarnate Word. It is not Christianity that is anti-Semitic, but rather a cultural and social mind-set warping Christians against their Jewish neighbors, who are in reality their spiritual ancestors.)

While it is true that Jews and Christians coexisted in comparative harmony in certain times and places throughout the Middle Ages, Medieval Europe was marked by numerous instances of anti-Semitism, ranging from ghettoization and social exclusion to murderous mob violence savagely erupting at various times. During the Crusades, Jews were often victimized by Christian mobs even though these crimes were never endorsed by religious authorities. Pogroms were often declared against Jews, especially in Russia and Poland, throughout the Middle Ages. Millenarian movements (mob movements attempting to force God's hand to provoke the Millennium, or the thousand year reign of Christ on earth) often savagely victimized Jews. If not victims of murder and torture, Jews were increasingly excluded from the benefits of the larger society and the protections of the state. This was no more evident than in the Spanish Inquisition, which stands as one of the worst episodes of organized persecution against the Jews prior to the twentieth century. While the number of victims has sometimes been exaggerated, it is a historical fact that thousands of Jews were either killed or exiled owing to the cruelties of the Inquisition. The Inquisition in Spain was originally intended to ensure that converts to Christianity were sincere in their faith, and thus was only to be directed at dealing with Christian heretics (including those *conversos,* or converts to Christianity from Judaism, who did not genuinely accept church dogma) and was originally designed to militate against Muslim influence still pronounced in the Iberian Peninsula after the completion of the centuries old struggle known as the *reconquista,* but it was soon manipulated by political leaders into a full-blown persecution of all non-Christians, especially Jews. In its attempts to strengthen Christianity in Spain, non-Christians or heretical Christians were left with a choice: convert and be baptized or leave, failure to do so could result in death. The church never officially endorsed the actions of the Spanish Inquisition (Pope Sixtus IV protested its abuses from his authority in the Vatican, to no avail), and yet, Spanish clerics, with their civil counterparts, were directly involved in and responsible for the death and exile of thousands of their Jewish countrymen. Fueled by the pernicious forces of anti-Semitism virulent within the culture, the Spanish Inquisition rapidly transformed itself into a shameful and cruel persecution of Spanish Judaism that cost over 30,000 innocent lives, many of them Spanish Jews.

Anti-Semitism diminished for a time without altogether vanishing as the religious wars that roiled Europe began to subside, and by the eighteenth century overt attacks against Jews were less common (though not unheard of). However, in much of Christendom Jews remained marginalized, excluded from the political sphere either by law or through social pressure, and further driven into their own increasingly insular communities. Anti-Semitism began to regain its virulence in the latter half of the nineteenth century, particularly in France (as the infamous Dreyfus Affair attests) and Central Europe (particularly in various parts of the Germanic states). Additionally, conspiracy theories alleging a

Jewish plot to master the world, fueled by the lies contained within the spurious *Protocols of the Elders of Zion,* reinforced anti-Semitic bigotries normally hidden below the cultural surface. Anti-Semitism in the nineteenth century was also infused with the benighted racialist theories that were advanced as pseudoscience in the latter half of the century; the ancient prejudice was now further warped by the factor of race. The ideas and attitudes that led to the hate-mongering of Adolf Hitler and his Nazi murderers were already in percolation as Europe was thrown into war and depression during the first three decades of the twentieth century, and as the Nazi regime gained more power and confidence, the assault on the Jewish people became more aggressive, and ultimately, horrific. Atrocities against Jews in Germany and other parts of Europe, including Stalinist Russia, were committed on an unprecedented scale, driving Europe into the organized terror that would become the Holocaust, the systematic genocide of European Jews.

Today, with the Holocaust a recent memory, a basic awareness of the injustice against Jews throughout the world has mitigated somewhat anti-Semitic tendencies. Nonetheless, religious prejudice remains a problem even in more tolerant and liberal societies, reminding us of the importance of sustaining vigilance against the future reemergence of anti-Semitic attitudes and practices. The freedom to worship is as meaningful as it ever has been, and the need encourage tolerance is vital to the promotion of civilization.

Suggested Reading

Arendt, Hannah. *Antisemitism,* part one of *The Origins of Totalitarianism.* New York: Harcourt, Brace, Jovanovich, 1968.

Beller, Steven. *Antisemitism: A Very Short Introduction.* New York: Oxford Univ. Press, 2007.

Johnson, Paul M. *A History of the Jews.* New York: Harper Perennial, 1988.

apartheid (separate development)
Apartheid, or "apartness," is a term from the Afrikaans language that represents the political

enforcement of the social, cultural, and legal separation of races in Southern Africa that began in the mid-seventeenth century and continued in various forms until its abolition in 1994. The term originated in the 1930s and was eventually adopted as a slogan for the National Party. In 1948, what was primarily a social and cultural apartheid was formalized under law and fortified by official government policy and institutional support. Administrative policies that ensued would eventually come to be known as "separate development," but for most of the world the term apartheid was fixed in the consciousness of those who both opposed and supported the policy of keeping the races apart. In 1913 and again in 1936, legislation was enacted that began to formally segregate South Africans along racial lines as well as restrict the nonwhite ownership of land. The movement toward apartheid slowed during World War II (in which South Africa participated as a Commonwealth nation), but shortly after the end of the war the political and legal entrenchment of apartheid was increased.

Following the formal legalization of apartheid in 1948, the decade of the 1950s was marked by numerous legal acts directed at further racial separation to the severe disadvantage of the nonwhite majority. Under the Population Registration Act of 1950, all citizens of South Africa were labeled according to race, as follows: Bantu (or black African), Coloured (racially mixed), and White. Later a category labeled Asian (South Asian) was added to the system of racial classification. In the same year, the Group Areas Act designated specific urban areas for particular races. One's race determined where a person could reside, work, or conduct business. In the mid-1950s, the Land Act accomplished the same thing on a larger scale. The result of this was to create a near monopoly of land ownership held by a single privileged race—the white race—who represented a minority of the population but owned and controlled over 80 percent of the land in South Africa. Further insult was aimed at the nonwhite races through the segregation of

schools (accompanied by different kinds of education) and public facilities, legal assignment of specified jobs to nonwhites alone, regulations impairing the activities of nonwhite unions, and severe limitations on the ability of nonwhites to become involved in government at any level. The final blows were delivered at the beginning and the end of the decade through the enactment of the Bantu Authorities Act (1951) and the Promotion of Bantu Self-Government (1959). This legislation reserved delineated territories within South Africa as African (nonwhite African) homelands that were to enjoy a degree of governmental autonomy. While the idea appears to guarantee some political autonomy to nonwhites, it proved the reverse, resulting in the further exclusion of nonwhite representation in the political structure of the South African nation. The "homeland" territories themselves accorded little in the way of economic opportunity as they were resource poor and overcrowded. The homelands promoted economic disadvantage exacerbated by political fragmentation and cultural degradation. Thus, by 1970 with the formal separation of nonwhites from the white minority through legislation establishing citizenship in the "homelands" for nonwhites while retaining citizenship in the rest of South Africa for whites, the majority was utterly deprived of political influence, legal protection, and economic opportunity.

Through decades of internal resistance combined with international pressure, apartheid was eventually overcome. Domestically, several nonwhite dissident groups exhibiting various degrees of militancy became active, particularly in the 1970s and 1980s but actually traced back to the interwar period and perhaps earlier. As in the civil-rights movement in the United States, white sympathizers joined in support. Nelson Mandela, Stephen Biko, and Bishop Desmond Tutu emerged as the more visible leaders of the antiapartheid movement. Internationally, pressure was brought to bear on the minority government. In 1961 the United Kingdom forced South Africa from the Commonwealth of Nations and in 1985 the United Kingdom and the United States brought sanctions to bear against the government. By the late 1980s and early 1990s, the doom of apartheid became increasingly apparent. Reformist elements emerged in the once pro-apartheid National Party, and the illegal nonwhite African Congress was recognized. Imprisoned dissidents were eventually released from prison, and the government of F. W. de Klerk began a process of dismantling apartheid. By 1994, a new constitution was adopted reconfiguring the government of South Africa, now committed to the principle of majority rule. Former political prisoner Nelson Mandela served as the first non-white president of South Africa, governing over a peaceful transition of power that eliminated the remaining institutional residue of apartheid culture.

Suggested Reading

Clark, N.L., and W.H. Worger. *South Africa: The Rise and Fall of Apartheid.* New York: Longman, 2004.

Aquinas, Thomas (1225–1274)

St. Thomas Aquinas, known as the "Angelic Doctor," was the most important Christian theologian and philosopher since St. Augustine (354–430) and the preeminent political theorist of the Medieval period. Belonging to the Order of Preachers (Dominicans), Aquinas contributed more than any previous thinker except Augustine to the synthesis of philosophical inquiry and religious faith. One of the Doctors of the Church, Aquinas developed philosophical principles that have become central to Christianity, in particular to Catholicism, and his political thought has had a profound influence on the development of Western theory. In particular, his theories on law have helped to shape the Western mind-set, and he remains one of the more important proponents of a politics based on transcendent principles.

St. Thomas Aquinas lived and wrote during the High Middle Ages, which is noted as a period of philosophical revival in the West. Through his teacher, St. Albert the Great

(*Albertus Magnus;* 1206–1280)—who referred to this extraordinary student as the "Light of the Church" on receiving word of his unexpected death— Aquinas developed a strong grounding in the philosophy of Aristotle, which at that time was undergoing a revival in Western Europe. It was through this exposure to Aristotle that Aquinas would generate a complex and exhaustive philosophical system in service to the doctrine of the church, and in so doing, contribute more than any single thinker to the growth of that doctrine. His contribution is still prominent today.

With the meeting of Aristotlelian philosophy and Christian belief in the works of Albert the Great and Thomas Aquinas, a synthesis of reason and faith was accomplished that would promote a conceptual system grounded in two disparate traditions. Aquinas was not the first thinker to recognize the compatibility of faith and reason; this notion had been embraced by various thinkers for centuries. But more than anyone before him, Aquinas created a comprehensive and exhaustive system drawing on philosophy and religion, producing a voluminous written legacy. His Great Synthesis was grounded on the premise that reason and faith are at root wholly compatible, and that what is true to the rational mind is consistent with the truth of Divine revelation. Previous Christian theologians also embraced philosophy as an ally of the church—St. Augustine being the most notable but not the only example—and hence Aquinas's synthesis was not novel. However, his emphasis is on Aristotle rather than on Plato, whom the church Fathers had regarded as the greatest of the Greek philosophers and the one whose thought was most compatible with Christian revelation. In the writings of Aquinas, Aristotle is simply referred to as "the Philosopher," in the same way that St. Paul is called "the Apostle." Aquinas's own work illustrates a concerted attempt to fuse the rational principles and methods of Aristotle with the spiritual authority of St. Paul.

A writer of considerable depth and extensive learning, Aquinas was influenced by other thinkers as well. Along with his older contemporary Albert the Great, Aquinas drew heavily from the great thinkers of the past. Cicero ("Tully"), St. Augustine, St. Isidore of Seville, Plato, and—above all—Holy Scripture all supplied ample conceptual and spiritual substance to his ideas, but it is his reliance on Aristotle that distinguishes his achievement from that of his contemporaries and that would help to lend authority to his teachings throughout the progress of the Western tradition.

In the Thomistic system, faith and reason are the foundational pillars of all moral and political activity. For Aquinas, the goal of the state is to promote virtue among its citizens. The measure of this virtue can be found in Scripture, the teachings of the church, and the writings of the philosophers, especially Aristotle. Consistent with the teaching of the church, and similar to the ethical theories of Plato, Aristotle, and Cicero, Aquinas affirms four virtues that provide the basic structure for moral living: prudence, fortitude, temperance, and justice. Identified by the church as the cardinal virtues, these four constitute a close variation on Plato's virtues of wisdom, courage, temperance, and justice (see **Republic, The** (*Politeia*)). As Plato associates each cardinal virtue with an aspect of the soul, so Aquinas associates each virtue with a specific faculty. For both Plato and Aquinas, as with Aristotle, the cardinal virtues draw the various faculties toward improvement and, eventually, toward their perfection. Prudence, for Aquinas, is that virtue that lends perfection to the intellect. Fortitude provides the resolve needed to confront fear as well as to sacrifice oneself for a higher cause. The appetites are guided by temperance, which strengthens us against the temptations of excessive pleasure. Justice inspires the will to seek the good of others, and in particular to ensure that others are given what is justly due to them. For Aquinas, the cardinal virtues are natural to all human beings; we possess an inherent, prereflective disposition (*synderesis*) toward them and, if properly trained in the right habits and the correct way

of thinking, anyone can attain these virtues in their fullest sense.

Additionally, Aquinas follows the church in adding three theological or spiritual, virtues: faith, hope, and love (charity), based on the writings of St. Paul in the First Letter to the Corinthians. While the cardinal virtues are perfected through human effort, the theological virtues are available to us because of grace, and thus they depend on our connection to God. Together, these seven virtues are the elements of a moral life, and they are most fully affirmed within the human community.

Moral activity thus depends on these virtues and is measured by the manner in which the person acts as a free agent in the world. A person working toward perfection will engage the world as a moral agent, to the improvement of both self and society. To determine whether or not an act is moral, Aquinas rejects both consequentialism (as in Machiavelli and Bentham, for example) and deontological ethics—or nonconsequentialism (as in Kant). The former emphasizes the result or outcome of an act in judging its moral value; the latter stresses the intent of the agent, or the *a priori* purposes of what Kant calls the "good will." Aquinas does recognize and include the importance of both intent and consequence in the moral act, but neither one represents the whole of an ethical choice. For Aquinas, our moral actions are indicated by a combination of intent and consequence, further explained and discerned within the light of circumstances. Thus intent, consequences, and circumstances are all to be considered simultaneously if we are to assess the moral rectitude of the human agent engaged in the world. Human activity is far too complex to focus on just one factor. Rather, in the Thomistic system, we must regard three criteria for moral activity in the same way that we must look to seven principal virtues in the development of the ethical person.

As with both Aristotle and Plato, as well as in the teachings of the church, a person who cultivates virtue and endeavors to act as a moral agent will achieve true happiness and blessedness. The Aristotelian notion of *eudaimonia,* or flourishing (also happiness), is within the potential of all human beings, both by our nature and through the grace of God. St. Thomas Aquinas joins Aristotle in his belief that this flourishing is achieved through the *polis.* Indeed, like Aristotle (and unlike St. Augustine), Aquinas considers the *polis* as the "perfect community." In contrast to St. Augustine, with whom he generally agrees, he regards the political not simply as a necessity brought upon us as a consequence of sin, but rather as the complete community for human beings, one wherein we can achieve happiness (which is the goal of life in this world) and justice can be attained. The political life is a key to human completion, not merely a compulsory reality to be suffered in the quest to establish order. Justice, therefore, is reintroduced in Aquinas as a condition that is within our grasp, and one that can be realized politically, and not only in the City of God.

Given this, unlike St. Augustine, St. Thomas Aquinas reconsiders the question of the best regime. For Augustine, all regimes were irretrievably corrupt in various degrees. Aquinas, while not blind to the tendency of human beings toward corruption owing to original sin, nonetheless believed that with the proper regime the state can aspire toward a real justice that exceeds the expectations of Augustine. Investigating the nature of the best regime, Aquinas offers two examples for us to consider. In his work *On Kingship,* he asserts that monarchy is the best regime, for it follows both the cosmic order as created by God, the King of the Universe, and the example of nature, typified by the fact that gregarious creatures, from the beehive to the great empires of humanity, are governed by one leader. Nevertheless, while Aquinas praises monarchy in *On Kingship,* he embraces a different model of the best regime in his sweeping *Summa Theologica.* There he draws on both Aristotle and Holy Scripture to advance the notion that a mixed regime is the best regime. As he explains, "all should have a share in government. In this way peace is preserved among the people, and everyone loves and protects the constitution, as is stated in [Aristotle's] *Politics,* Book II." Aquinas continues by discussing how Aristotle advocates a regime that fuses the best elements of rule by the one, the few, and the many: "This is the best form of polity since it is a judicious combination of kingship—rule by one man; aristocracy—rule by many in accordance with virtue, and democracy, that is, popular rule in that the rulers are chosen from the people and the people have a right to choose their rulers."

Additionally, St. Thomas Aquinas demonstrates the desirability of mixed regimes by typically turning to revelation as well as reason. In so doing, he emphasizes the "form of government established by divine law" through the example of Moses and the Israelites as revealed through the books of Exodus and Deuteronomy. Moses himself acted as a kind of king or chieftain; noble elders, resembling an aristocracy, were selected from each tribe of Israel; and this selection occurred democratically, since it was the "people who chose them." In this way Aquinas draws on "the Philosopher" as well as the Revealed Word, again evincing the common ground that underlies both reason and faith.

Aquinas believed that all regimes, whether monarchial or mixed, were to be governed essentially by the rule of law. It is in the theory of law that we find his most sophisticated and influential work. Law is manifest in four dimensions, according to Aquinas: eternal, natural, divine, and human (positive, or civil). The eternal law is the law of God, the "rational governance of everything on the part of God, the ruler of the universe." The whole of creation is under the eternal law of God; that which is beyond time and that which entails the first principles of reality. This eternal law transcends our ability to understand it in its completion. Yet, owing to the twin sources of wisdom, reason and revelation, human beings are able to comprehend a part of the eternal law (while the whole of it remains beyond our full understanding) and therefore participate in it. Natural law is that part of the eternal law that is both discerned by our rational faculty and inherent within our dispositions. Divine law is eternal law that is revealed to us through Scripture and the dynamics of the Holy Spirit, and thus divine law is discovered in the Old and New Testaments as well as in the Magisterium of the Church. The highest principle of the natural law is to seek the good and avoid evil, a principle that is affirmed with equal force by the divine law that comes to us through revelation. Because both natural law and divine law are expressions of eternal law, they are thoroughly compatible. There is nothing in revelation that undercuts reason, and nothing that is arrived at through reason is inconsistent with revelation. Human law, if it is to be true law—and, by definition, just law—must be consonant with natural law (and, as such, divine law). Any law enacted by human beings that is contrary to reason and revelation (natural and divine law) is not properly law, and therefore not obligatory within the *polis*. In this sense, Aquinas follows the legacy of Plato, Aristotle, Cicero, and St. Augustine in affirming the need to orient civil legislation with the transcendent justice found in the natural law. If we fail at such an orientation, then we are no longer governed by law but by the caprice of men.

A law is only a law if it is just, that is, if it is in accord with the principles of natural and divine law. Otherwise, it is not considered a lawful decree and therefore is not binding on the citizens of a political community, particularly if it produces injustice or promotes defiance of God's commands. This position leads Aquinas to consider the nature of obligation to political authority. As the Apostle Paul teaches us, sedition, or resistance to or defiance of a government, is a mortal sin, and thus it is our duty to obey our political leaders, in spite of their foibles. If, however, a governing authority becomes tyrannical—which would entail a violation of justice according to the principles of natural and divine law—then the obligation to obey ceases. Indeed, for Aquinas,

a tyrant can be resisted, since it is actually the tyrant who has committed the sin of sedition against the community. Therefore, Aquinas does affirm the Christian duty willingly to submit to human authority, but he also insists that such submission is not to be extended to tyrants, who have already rebelled against the laws of God and the ends of the community.

After his theory of law, perhaps the most important element of Aquinas's political thought is found in this theory of just war, which is itself based on previous work by St. Augustine. As with St. Augustine before him, Aquinas asserts the Christian imperative to seek peace, and to respond to hate with love, violence with meekness. By and large, war is to be avoided, but given the worldly realities of politics, war may become the only option under dire circumstances. If such is the case, it is a moral imperative to fight a just war, discerned by following three criteria: legitimate political authority (no tyrant or usurper can wage a just war), just cause (for example, self-defense or avenging an unpunished wrong), and right intent (if chosen, belligerency must follow the first precept of natural law—to seek good and avoid evil—and must be designed to establish peace). The presence of one or two criteria is insufficient to the commission of a just war, for a war to be just, a belligerent nation must meet all three criteria.

St. Thomas Aquinas is also known for his views on private property and its relationship with the state. Knowing that property ownership may provoke covetousness and tempt greed, Aquinas sought to reconcile Christian injunctions against material attachments with the realities of worldly living. To do so, he again draws on both Aristotle and Scripture. Influenced by Aristotle, Aquinas argues that the ownership of private property is rational and to the benefit of both individuals and the community for three reasons: it is natural for people tend to care for what they own more than for what is owned collectively; laws governing private ownership of property lend a sense of order to the community; and, closely associated with the latter, private property clearly defined contributes to domestic peace. For these three reasons, the ownership of private property is legitimate and consistent with secondary principles of natural law. From Scripture, Aquinas admonishes against the use of private property for self-aggrandizement or for the accumulation of wealth for its own sake. He remarks that, "human beings...should not possess external goods as their own but as common possessions, namely, in such a way that they readily share the goods when others are in need. And so the Apostle [St. Paul] says in 1 Tim. 6-17–18: 'Teach the rich of this world to distribute and share readily.'" To punctuate this point, Aquinas also draws on church teaching: "And so St. Basil says ...'Why are you rich and others beggars, except that you gain the merit of dispensing your wealth well, and that others are rewarded with their patience?'"

Owing to his views on the compatibility of reason and faith; the reality of transcendent first principles discerned within a natural law that governs all human beings equally; his belief in limited government; his preference, at least in his greatest work, the *Summa,* for mixed government that requires a wider participation from its citizenry; and for his views on resistance to tyranny, just war, and property, St. Thomas Aquinas has been described as an early contributor to liberal political thought—the "first Whig," as Lord Acton would have it. But it is important to remember that Aquinas was a man of his times, a thirteenth-century friar writing on the cusp of the High Middle Ages and those developments that would soon initiate the Italian Renaissance. As such, his "liberalism" must be tempered with the realities of his culture. Following the two-swords doctrine of St. Gelasius, he accepted the distinction between church and state and their respective responsibilities. But in matters of heresy and apostasy, and even under threat of the impairment of faith, the power of the state can be employed as a buttress for the church. Therefore, while Aquinas believed in the

importance of tolerance and the voluntary acceptance of Christianity, when confronted with heresy and apostasy, he was willing to endorse coercive tactics to protect the true faith, which required the alliance of the state with church, at least in these matters.

For the most part, St. Thomas Aquinas was a thinker of endless depth and complexity. Not only does his intellectual legacy reach into the Catholic Church as it enters the twenty-first century, but he remains a major voice in the Great Conversation that is political theory. As this conversation becomes ever more diverse, Aquinas will offer numerous insights and points of inquiry that will continue to animate political dialogue, particularly for those who regard politics as a fragment of a still-greater vision and incomparably higher hope.

Related Entries
Aristotle; Augustine; Catholic social teaching; justice; just war theory; natural law; synderesis

Suggested Reading
Sigmund, Paul. *St. Thomas Aquinas on Politics and Ethics.* New York: W. W. Norton, 1988.

Arendt, Hannah (1906–1975)

Politics, for Hannah Arendt, is the only sphere of human effort that allows for the promotion and engagement in action. Her distinction between labor (those natural processes that provide necessities for human survival), work (through which we build our world even through the destruction of nature) and action (of which we are capable only insofar as we are free) correlate to the nonpolitical and political spheres within the larger scope of the human condition. We *act* as free human beings as political agents (not as individuals behaving according to stimuli from our environment) who are capable of doing great deeds and speaking noble words, and it is in the deed and the word that we are able to create a realm of freedom that is not determined by the forces of necessity that govern the economic (and thus private) sphere. Here Arendt embraces the ancient separation of private and public, the former involving the gratification of our needs, the latter enabling us to act on our will regardless of those needs. However, with the onset of modernity (with its technological, industrial, and commercial prowess) a new social sphere has emerged that transgresses both the private and the public and blends them together. With the rise of the social, the political sphere is no longer the realm of action, and the private sphere no longer the retreat from the gaze of the crowd. For Arendt, politics, which is about possibility and new birth, is increasingly pressured by the rise of the social, and thus misshapen by the expanding predominance of the realm of necessity. As politics is riveted to the necessary, the only sphere wherein the human free agent can truly act—to do great deeds and speak great works—becomes trivial, bureaucratic, and irrelevant. Owing to this, our very humanity is challenged by the anonymous forces of modern life.

Much of Arendt's writing is concerned with the origin and nature of totalitarianism; more than most authors, Arendt recognizes the radical difference between totalitarian systems and authoritarian regimes. For Arendt, totalitarianism is a senseless system of total domination established on fear and sustained by perpetual motion. No tradition, no institution, no sense of community can be found within totalitarianism—but rather the isolated and atomized individual completely and hopelessly vulnerable to the manipulative forces of the totalitarian movement. Arendt argues that totalitarianism is a thoroughgoing destruction of the political and the communal, a system of banal cogs operating not so much in tandem but in isolation through terror toward an irrational purpose. A totalitarian system is the death of man at the expense of blind power, a power that appears to be exerted by the centralized instruments of the state, but in reality possesses a life of its own that in actuality demolishes all elements and customs that constitute political life, especially the state and its legal and juridical system. In totalitarianism there is no sense of law, justice, right, or morality—or even of the nation (although totalitarian movements tend to mask themselves, at least initially, behind nationalism)—there is only the blindly irrational movement of power and the ubiquitous and relentless manipulation of the atomized, terrorized individual. The beast of Nuremburg is neither the absolute despotism of the state nor the collective wills of the *Volk,* but rather the very manifestation of an insidious evil that hides behind the crimes of otherwise ordinary men.

Totalitarianism is not the triumph of politics and collective will, but rather it is the abolition of politics and the illusion of collective unity. There is no political deliberation in totalitarianism, and no true unity of any kind. Totalitarianism is pure movement and domination exerted for irrational and ultimately evil designs. Indeed, as there is no real unity in totalitarianism, there can be no real power. Power, for Arendt, originates through the cooperative energies of free agents acting in the political sphere. Power occurs "in concert." According to Arendt, it cannot be exerted by one person or by one faction within society. Authoritarians and totalitarians master society through raw strength—a will to dominate—but power is created by citizens acting in concert, and not imposed upon subjects to force obedience. Power and will are one with Arendt, but only insofar as they are the energy through which the political arena of free citizens (not the subjects of authoritarians nor the cogs within the totalitarian pathology) can accomplish great things for the common good. This vision of political power as power in association rather than as pure domination provides a compelling lesson for citizens of all regimes following the horrors of two world wars.

Arendt's political theory involves more than can be covered here, but for our purposes her classical view of politics as free action markedly apart from the influence of private need, along with her insightful discussion of the perverse nature of totalitarian movements represents two prominent themes within her writings. And it is in these themes that her clearest contribution to contemporary thought can be appreciated. These, in addition to Arendt's crucial role in the revival of political theory in the mid-twentieth century, are the more valuable elements of her overall political project.

Related Entry
totalitarianism

Suggested Reading

Arendt, Hannah. *Between Past and Future*. 1961; repr. New York: Penguin Classics, 1976.

Arendt, Hannah. *The Human Condition*. Chicago: Univ. Chicago Press, 1958.

Arendt, Hannah. *The Life of the Mind*. New York: Harvest Books, 1981.

aristocracy (*aristos kratein*)

Aristocracy, derived from the Greek words *aristos,* meaning "the best," and *krateini,* usually translated as government or rule, is an ancient term that literally meant for Greek theorists such as Plato and Aristotle the rule by the few who are the best—the most intelligent and the most virtuous in the city. This definition held for centuries, reiterated in writings such as Polybius, Cicero, and much later, St. Thomas Aquinas. For these and other thinkers, an aristocracy was not rule by an arbitrarily fortunate minority who happened to hold political power owing to the control of land or the privileges of social status, but rather, the aristocrat in the true sense of the word was the most noble and able of rulers, a person of moral character and intellectual prowess. For Plato, the only real aristocracy would be the one governed by the wise philosopher-rulers and their spirited auxiliary warriors, for Aristotle, an aristocracy could only be populated by statesman of a mature disposition, men of prudence and moral integrity who were literally the most excellent (*arete*), the few best who are most fit to govern a free city. This notion of aristocracy may have been lost today, but it held throughout the classical world and influenced attitudes toward nobility well into the High Middle Ages. Whether or not the idea was in fact set into practice is a different issue, but the concept of aristocracy in the true sense of the word means rule by those who are the best in the sense of wisdom and moral virtue (which are themselves ultimately inseparable).

Aristocracy has also been associated with military valor and the ability to command troops in battle. Hegel, for example, recognized that the division between aristocrat (lord, master) and serf (bondsman, slave) was marked by the aristocrat's willingness to risk death—placing freedom as a value above even life. Hence the aristocrats were recognized as those who exerted their independent consciousness against necessity, defying even death in order to remain free. The serf, on the other hand, is of a mind to prefer life under the yolk to death in battle. Thus for Hegel, the origins of aristocracy are uncovered deep within the collective psychologies of social groups. Aristocrats may now enjoy their position owing to landed wealth and the legacy of a prestigious name and crest, but in the dim past their ancestors risked life and all worldly comfort so that they would remain free rather than submit to the commands of another. This contempt for death is, for Hegel and for Nietzsche after him, the justification for the aristocrats' authority over those who would rather live bound than die free.

Today aristocracy is often conflated with oligarchy, which for the modern reader connotes rule of the few who may or, more likely, may not be the best. From the vantage point of our modern democratic sensibilities, any aristocratic/oligarchic/plutocratic hierarchical political structure is determined by some arbitrary source of power, primarily but not exclusively wealth. Government of the few over the many is the rudimentary definition of both aristocracy and oligarchy in use today, the blending of the two terms concealing the ancient distinction between those few who rule for irrational or artificially justified reasons, and those few who really are the most fit to govern among human beings.

Related Entries
Aristotle; Hegel, Georg Wilhelm Friedrich; Plato

Suggested Reading
Aristotle, *Politics,* trans. H. Rackham. 1932. Cambridge, MA: Harvard Univ. Press/Loeb Classics, 1977.
Plato. *Republic* and *Statesman,* in *Complete Works,* ed. John M. Cooper. Indianapolis: Hackett, 1997.

Aristotle (384 BC–322 BC)

Aristotle's influence is so extensive throughout the development of the history of ideas as to be matched only by Plato's. Within the discipline of political theory, and the wider field of political science, Aristotle—known to St. Thomas Aquinas and other authors in the High Middle Ages simply as The Philosopher—is revered as one of the seminal figures in the canon. Aside from Plato, no student of politics and the human condition has shaped political and moral inquiry as much as Aristotle, and to this day he remains absolutely essential reading for anyone devoted to a fuller understanding of the nature of the human community.

Like Plato before him, Aristotle began his investigation of political and moral activity from the premise of the centrality of the good. In the opening book of the *Nicomachean Ethics,* which Aristotle regarded as a requisite text to the further examination of legislation and constitutions in his *Politics,* he observes that "Every art, and every investigation…aims at some good." But the good is not the Form of the Good embraced by Plato, but rather there are "as many ways of speaking of the good as there are ways of being." The good is not a single, universal concept that exists in itself and ultimately beyond our immediate experience, but rather, good is understood as those things or activities that are desired for their own sake, according to their own principle of intrinsic worth, and not only as a reflection of a singular conceptual Good lending meaning to all subordinate virtues. In other words, there is not, as Plato held, a singular Form of the Good that is the inward essence and highest purpose of all that exists. This is not to say that Aristotle regarded good as only subjectively understood, depending upon the case, for the intellect can make judgments affirming the intrinsic value of one thing or act in comparison to another, inferior thing or less worthwhile activity. But rather, that Aristotle appreciated the necessity of thinking of goodness in terms that lend accessibility to the object of investigation and its internally determined purpose. One must examine the nature of the subject before us with precision and care, and from there discern the character of the good toward which it aims, whether it is an object or an activity. Objective knowledge of the good inherent to any thing or activity can be discovered, but it is not through a study of the independent Form alone that such knowledge can be achieved. Instead, this objective knowledge is obtained through a conceptual dissection of the aspects and parts of the study at hand. Knowledge of *the* Good as Plato conceived it is simply beyond our reach, what is now needed is a practical catalog of goodness as it is manifested through the variety of being, the multifarious nature of our many activities as human beings in the world. But Aristotle still admits that there is a "final end," a chief good that we seek, but it endures as a principle beyond our full understanding. Aristotle does not rule out the possibility of such a good and even recognizes that "the chief good is evidently something final," but ultimately an ineffable principle that lends little to our knowledge of what is required to live a virtuous life within a community so dedicated.

Even though Aristotle states that we can speak of good in as many ways as we can speak of being in all its diversity, there are still only two basic types of good: directive or intrinsic (something that is good for its own sake) and secondary or subordinate goods (something that is good for a still further good, namely, a directive good). In his ethical writings, Aristotle grounds his observations of and prescriptions for humanity on the simple premise that the most directive intrinsic good for human beings is happiness. Happiness is always pursued for its own sake, and not for the sake of anything else. The acquisition of wealth, for example, if accumulated in moderation, is good, but it is a subordinate good to the higher end of happiness. A person seeks affluence as one ingredient for the achievement of happiness, but no one seeks happiness to become wealthy. This happiness of which Aristotle speaks is a rendering of the ancient Greek term *eudaemonia,* which he clearly distinguishes from pleasure—particularly the kind of pleasure that might spring to mind for the modern reader. *Eudaemonia* is more clearly understood as a comprehensive well-being, a state of "flourishing" within a person that leads to excellence. This sense of happiness requires a condition of *arete,* which can be translated as both virtue and excellence. As an activity, pleasure aims at a good, but it is a subordinate good to the higher good of happiness as flourishing. To reduce happiness to pleasure alone is to commit a vulgarity. Only the virtuous person, one who is "foursquare and blameless," flourishes, and thus only through the actualization of virtue in one's soul can a human being really find true happiness.

According to Aristotle, this virtue that constitutes true happiness as flourishing can only be found through habituation to the intermediate, to the mean between the extremes of excess and deficiency. Should one act in ways that are excessive (such as rash boldness without fear of anything) or deficient (such as cowardice in fear of everything) one would lead a vicious life. Virtue is found at the intermediate between the vice of excess and the vice of deficiency—not necessarily an equidistant mean (for rash boldness is closer to courage than cowardice, for example), but an approximation of some point between the extremes that promotes balance in one's inner self. Thus the virtues of courage, temperance, generosity—even justice—are inculcated by habits and states of mind that exhibit a moderate disposition in all things. Virtue is always found at the mean, but to always act consonant to such balance is an arduous commitment. It cannot be done in isolation; human beings need each other—human beings by their very nature need the life that is enjoyed only in the *polis.*

Just as all things and all activities aim at a good, so all forms of association, or partnership, aim at some good. That association which aims at the most complete good is the *polis,* for it is in the *polis* that human beings, the political animal, can live a life of goodness and nobility in common with each other. The good person is a person who is active, and as an active person, committed to a life of cooperation and friendship with others toward a common good. All associations enable human beings to realize this aspect of their nature, but the political sphere encompasses them all, and is thus aimed at the directive good—the flourishing of citizens in common purpose within the *polis.* The political begins from necessity, as Aristotle observes, but its aim is to go beyond necessity to a life of nobility, to live well rather than merely live. In the *polis,* we are accorded the only real opportunity to become excellent, and to perform virtuous deeds in devotion to the common advantage. Absent the *polis,* a human being is deprived of his or her humanity; thus our nature is implicated with the need for politics. Gods who are immortal and without care and beasts who are self-sufficient owing to the simplicity of their needs and wants do not need cities and are thus outside the *polis.* But the human being, who also seeks self-sufficiency but is incapable of achieving it in isolation, is by necessity a political creature. Indeed, it is in cities that human beings can live justly, for with justice, humanity is the perfection of nature, without justice, the most wicked and depraved of all brutes. Embraced within the constitutions, laws, practices, customs, and, above all, friendships that frame the political space, citizens governing together promote those habits that allow them to live well and to flourish— to find a virtuous happiness at the mean,

Justice is *the* political virtue for Aristotle, and as such, it is the most complete virtue. Aristotle devotes the entire scope of the fifth book of the *Nicomachean Ethics* to the virtue of justice, the only virtue to be so treated. In Book Five, Aristotle categorizes justice on two levels: the more general sense of justice and what he refers to as "special justice." Justice in the general sense is framed within the concepts of lawfulness and fairness. In this way Aristotle acknowledges the deep connection between justice and law while at the same time avoiding a legalistic identification of the two concepts. Justice involves law, and yet it must be more than law; it must also include an equally important element of fairness. In this way Aristotle joins Socrates and Plato before him in insisting on the translegal nature of justice. Additionally, Aristotle states that a general sense of justice is observed in its conduciveness to our happiness (*eudaemonia*), again illustrating the principle that happiness is the principal good for human beings, served even by the high-minded virtue of justice, and thus further lending a sense of nobility to the concept of happiness as flourishing. Finally, Aristotle remarks that justice is the most complete virtue in that it seeks the good of others, not just the good of the individual self. In this way the political content of justice is confirmed; it is only in the *polis* that persons as citizens can become completely virtuous for it is only in the *polis* that one can exercise justice.

Special justice is also divided into three parts: distributive (proportional) wherein social and political goods are apportioned in the city based upon a notion of merit, rectificatory (restorative, corrective) wherein wrongs committed between citizens are addressed and a fair remedy restores the balance of the relationship, and what he refers to as "political" justice. Proportional justice recognizes degrees of merit, and thus admits that justice to some extent involves inequality based on desert. Rectificatory justice attempts to rectify a wrong and thus to restore a state of initial fairness, respecting to an extent an equality before the law. This type of justice is further divided into what Aristotle refers to as "voluntary" and "involuntary" transactions, a concept that loosely resembles our modern notion of civil and criminal law, respectively.

Political justice is discussed in less detail. One dimension of political justice is "legal," defined in terms of the conventions of place and relative to a particular regime. What is just in Athens may not be just in Sparta, or what might be just in one way in one city may be just to a different degree in another. Here Aristotle again reminds us of the importance of law in the notion of justice. Yet again, Aristotle is convinced that justice involves much more than conventional legalistic concepts, for he also speaks of a natural justice that is the same for all human beings everywhere. Aristotle remains vague on precisely what this natural justice is, but he does not equivocate in his assertion that justice must be constituted by a translegal and universal principle. One aspect of natural justice might be available to us by returning to the doctrine of the mean. As justice is a virtue, it must also be intermediate between two extremes, but in this case it is not an intermediate between an excess and deficiency of justice (as you really can't have an excess of justice), but rather between the commission of injustice (a blameworthy vice) with impunity and the suffering of injustice (an unjust condition but not an unjust act and thus blameless) without recourse. Justice is always found where injustice is neither committed nor suffered; the manner in which this objective principle is understood or realized will itself vary according to context.

The discussion revolving around political justice exemplifies Aristotle's desire to convey the importance of actual cases and to acknowledge the diversity of custom and its importance for human happiness, while at the same time seeking a higher principle that leads us toward what is essentially human. There are many types of legal justice and therefore many kinds of cities can achieve a practical justice under the conventions that govern their particular case. But there is only one principle of justice—a first principle—that is natural and common to all human beings. And, there are many types of political systems or regimes, but as he claims in the *Ethics,* "only one system that is by nature the best everywhere."

It is in the *Politics* that Aristotle investigates the possibility of a best regime, but he does so by using a different approach than Plato. He is not interested in attempting to discover a paradigmatic "city of speech," as Socrates does in *Republic* or as the Athenian Stranger considers in his "second-best city" discussed in Plato's *Laws.* Aristotle does seek types and patterns, but they must have a stronger connection to the practicalities of public affairs, and therefore the best regime will more readily be set into practice. Indeed, Aristotle rejects Socrates's Form of the *polis* in Book Two of his own *Politics,* arguing that what Plato envisages through Socrates is in reality not a city at all. The political is marked by plurality, but Plato's paradigm is an extreme case of unity, one that when closely scrutinized resembles more a family, or even one individual, than it does a political community. For this and other reasons, we cannot turn to Plato's singular concept for the key to political justice and its practical limitations and frustrations, but rather we must begin anew by examining the various ways in which different kinds of cities can become just and right.

To forward this investigation, Aristotle develops a typology of regimes that closely resembles that which was provided by the Eleatic Stranger in Plato's *Statesman.* Based on determining whether or not a city is under the rule of the one, the few, or the many, this typology established by Plato and refined by Aristotle will provide the fundamental categories for the comparative study of regimes within the tradition of political theory, and fix the terminology in the lexicon of political inquiry that we still use today. For Aristotle (and for Plato in *Statesman*), there are six basic regimes, three correct or constitutional (the good regimes) and three deviant or lawless (perverse regimes). The good regimes are characterized by their ends; in this case, the end toward which they aim is the common advantage of the city as a whole. Good regimes rule lawfully and govern citizens (those who are equally capable of ruling and being ruled) rather than subjects (those who do not participate in ruling). Monarchy (or kingship) is the rule of one that is good or

correct, for in monarchy the king will rule lawfully for the benefit of the citizens first and foremost. Aristocracy literally means rule by the few who are the best (the most virtuous and the most intelligent), and is a regime that most closely resembles Plato's Form of the *polis* with significant modifications (for example, the aristocrats who would be wise and brave like Plato's guardians would nonetheless own property, and it is clear that women would not share power). Correct rule by the many would be what Aristotle calls a constitutional polity, or simply polity, as distinct from a democracy. Democracy is the least perverse of the incorrect regimes, but incorrect all the same as it would consist of government of the many who are poor, lawlessly ruling for their own private advantage rather than for the good of the whole city. Oligarchy (rule by the few who are not the best but whose power is solely attached to the possession of wealth) and tyranny, the latter being the worst possible regime, constitute the remaining deviant regimes.

While Aristotle does allow for three general types of good regimes, in the *Ethics* he clearly stated that there is one regime that is best everywhere. By definition, aristocracy would seem to be the best regime, for nothing could surpass government by those who are the wisest and the most virtuous (and again, indirectly recalling Plato's Form of the *polis* in its essence). But as stated before, Aristotle seeks not only the universal paradigm, but a model of a regime that can be realized by human beings, a regime within the grasp of the majority of humankind. Thus Aristotle seeks that regime which is not only best, but most practical, and it is in the constitutional polity, the lawful rule by the many for the common advantage, where Aristotle finds an ideal regime that ordinary human beings can achieve and sustain.

Like democracy, a polity is the rule of the many, but not the many poor for their own advantage, but rather the many who govern together as citizens dedicated to the common good. As it is a regime wherein most people can live a virtuous life, it stands at a mean between two vicious regimes: oligarchy and democracy. By mixing in elements of both, and by adhering to the lawful pursuit of goodness, the polity achieves the rule of the many without slipping into the selfish varieties of democracy that precipitate mob rule and encourage demagogues. Resting on an expanded and stable middle class that reduces the conflict between wealth and poverty and promotes a modest affluence, a polity attains a stability not enjoyed by a monarch or an aristocracy. While these latter two regimes are also good, and in their own way can be said to be best, they are difficult to obtain and even more difficult to sustain. A polity that governs an essentially middle-class society reduces faction and thereby stabilizes conflict. Moreover, under a polity, which Aristotle assumes will be guided by the kind of education that engenders virtue among the citizenry and is assisted by rule of law, the people as a whole will achieve a kind of wisdom that exceeds even the philosopher. This depends on the conditions of a free, educated, and moral body of citizens, but for Aristotle, this is within reach under the framework of a constitutional polity.

As stated above, the purpose of a good regime is to guide citizens toward a life of virtue, for while the political springs from the need to live, its final purpose is to live well, meaning to flourish in that happiness defined by a virtuous life. This prompts an inquiry into the relationship between the good citizen and the good man. Aristotle observes that it is possible to be good in terms established by a given regime, and thus act as a good citizen relative to the expectations of the city. It is clear that good citizenship does not make one a good person—which is an objective standard produced by a life habituated to the mean, regardless of circumstance. Hence the good citizen and the good man are not identical. Nonetheless, remembering the purpose of the political, which is to ensure a life worthy of human dignity, the best regime makes it possible, and perhaps more than likely, for a good person and a good citizen to become identical. Once again

Aristotle is sensitive to the particularities of the case while maintaining a firm conviction in the need to follow the principle. There are many kinds of good citizens, but only one kind of good person. In most regimes this is irrelevant, but in the better regimes the goal to reconcile the duties of citizens with the character of good persons is ever in view.

For these and other reasons, we cannot depend solely on the government of men, but rather, we must ultimately adhere to a government of laws. Aristotle admonishes that even a good person will abuse or distort power, and to rely solely upon the rule of men is as if one were to give oneself over to wild beasts. The law is "reason without passion," and as Plato also stated in his *Laws,* a thing divine. This is why, for Aristotle, it is always preferable to live under the rule of law than under the rule of men, for it is only through the rule of law that we can commit ourselves to the common interest in a fashion that hews closely to the principle of justice. It is here, in the just city lawfully directed, that human nobility and perfection are actualized to the widest possible extent.

While much of Aristotle's political thought has much to recommend even to the modern reader, his writings are not without controversy. Aristotle's praise of the contemplative life as the highest life is also seen as an indication of a lower regard for politics than the balance of his writing would otherwise indicate, and perhaps reveals an antipolitical side to this most important of political scientists. Notorious by our standards and unlike his predecessor Plato, he follows conventional mores in his insistence that women are not capable of sharing political power. Indeed, whereas Plato states that men and women share the same essential nature, Aristotle concludes that women are "incomplete men." This is not to say that women are less than human, and Aristotle does regard the role of women to be vital in the household. It also must be remembered that this position was in line with the attitudes of his times, and would have been received as uncontroversial. Additionally, not only were women incapable of acting justly within the *polis*, but also barbarians, or non-Greeks, whom Aristotle considered, consistent with the attitudes of his culture, bereft of civilization. "It is mete that Greeks should rule barbarians," according to Aristotle, not because they were less human, but because they lacked the benefits accorded the high civilization of Greek culture and language. Not only barbarians, but even those who engage in physical labor—including mechanics and craftsmen—possess a sensibility that prevents a fuller understanding of the subtleties of political life. Finally, slavery is another issue that, for the modern reader, impugns Aristotle's claim to enlightened political understanding. Aristotle describes two kinds of slavery, one artificial and thus unjust, but one natural and therefore acceptable, even necessary. Natural slaves are those human beings who are incapable of governing themselves, and thus are in need of the mastery of another. Again, this seems benighted by our standards, but Aristotle's conception of slavery in this instance was not conventional, and he was critical of slavery justified by any other standard.

There are many other facets to Aristotle's political thought, too many for us to consider here and the reader is encouraged to pursue her or his inquiries still further. Any genuine investigation of political theory requires some exposure to the principles developed by Aristotle, and the closer we read his texts and legacy for clues into the best life for human beings, the more we benefit from the many questions and issues raised therein.

Related Entries

Plato; Aquinas, Thomas; *Politcs*; Socrates

Suggested Reading

Aristotle, *The Complete Works of Aristotle (In Two Volumes)*, ed. Jonathan Barnes. Princeton, NJ: Princeton/Bollingen Series, 1984. In particular, the *Politics* and *Nicomachean Ethics* are recommended (in volume two)

auctor—*See auctoritas*

auctoritas

Auctoritas, a derivation of the word *auctor*, itself derived from *augeo*, or "to augment," is the Latin root for the English word "authority," as well as serving as the root of the word "author." Thus *auctor/auctoritas* bear two connotations that are relevant to the etymological development of English usage. *Auctor* refers to one who affirms and lends credibility, one who fulfills something, or makes things manifest. In this sense, the common understanding of authority is drawn out, for those in authority are those who are able to execute, to lead something toward its conclusion, to confirm and complete. Additionally, *auctor* also refers to that which originates or initiates, and is thus related to a sense of authorship. *Auctoritas* can be understood in both of these connotations, as that which originates or founds and therefore serves as a founder, and as that which fulfills or applies authority in the act of leading. Hannah Arendt wrote of the concept *auctoritas* in terms of "founding" as a contrast to power deviated by the emergence of absolutism. It should further be noted that *auctoritas*, while properly translated as "authority" or "authorship" is not easily translated, hence some ambiguity characterizes the origin and evolution of the word. Nonetheless, we can without risking inaccuracy refer to the roots of the words "authority and "authorship" to the ancient terms *auctor/auctoritas*.

In republican Rome, *auctoritas* was distinguished from *potestas* (power), and usually employed in reference to the Senate (*auctoritas* meaning in this context a resolution or a specific sanction) or the office of the praetor (and is thus connected to judicial authority and the concept of legal injunction). However, anyone who was able to exert influence through the force of their personality, or to claim authority over something owing to holding office or through recognition by others as an expert in a certain field or task was considered to possess *auctoritas*. Thus while *auctoritas* was generally associated with public figures, such as senators, praetors, and priests, influential private individuals would also bear authority in some cases. As such, *auctoritas* relies somewhat on the presence of *dignitas*. *Auctoritas* as a concept figured prominently in the political thought of Cicero, who writing in the last years of the republic, emphasized that while the senate possessed authority, power (*potestas*) remained in the people. As J.P.V.D. Balsdon once explained,

> "Auctoritas" was naturally one of Cicero's favorite concepts. In the ideal republic power lay with the people, *auctoritas* with the Senate. . . . Alternatively, in a balanced state, *potestas* would lie with the magistrates, *libertas* with the people, but still *auctoritas* would be the property of the Senate, "*in principium consilio.*"

"*Principium consilio*" here refers to the principle of deliberation in council.

In imperial Rome, the emperor was considered *auctoritas princes,* or as holding the authority of the "first citizen," (*princes*—or the Latin root for the term "prince"). *Auctoritas* also connotes legal ownership over property, with the origin of the concept reaching back to Rome's ancient Twelve Tablets (c. 450 BC). Additionally, as Balsdon has remarked, the authority of the Senate, as affirmed by Cicero, depended on free senatorial debate and deliberation. With the ascent of Julius Caesar and the establishment of the dictatorship for life that presaged the empire, the free discussion within the Senate was "...effectively abolished. The world of the dictator was one in which there was no more place for '*consilium*' and '*auctoritas.*'" In other words, as the republic faded and the empire emerged, authority shifted from Senate, praetors, and priests to the emperor.

The nature of authority and its relation to both power and obedience were thus fixed in the grammar of Western political thought from the classical era. Considerable discussion of these concepts and their interrelationship helped to frame political writing in the course of the history of political theory and remains an element of political inquiry to this day. Notions of legitimate authority, popular sovereignty,

representation, and the relationship between law and power can be traced, at least in part, to the manner in which the Romans conceived the term *auctoritas,* along with *potestas* and *dignitas.* This is perhaps most clearly seen in democratic theory, but not exclusively so. In any discussion of the dynamics that flow between ruler and ruled, state and citizen, the question of authority and its relation to power will be appropriately broached, the achievement of the ancient Romans, and in particular Cicero, remaining a viable starting point for any examination of these concepts and the manner in which they bear upon us today.

Related Entry
potestas

Suggested Reading
Balsdon, J.P.V.D. "Auctoritas, Dignitas, Otium, *Classical Quarterly,* Vol. X, No. 1 (May 1960).

Augustinus, Aurelius—*See* Augustine.

Augustine (Aurelius Augustinus; 354–430) St. Augustine of Hippo, one of the four eminent "Fathers of the Church" (also regarded as Doctors of the Church), and one of the most important theologians in the history of religion, is known within the history of Western political theory as the first major Christian philosopher to contribute substantively to the Great Conversation. While St. Augustine did not write treatises specifically on politics, his theological and philosophical writings contain ample discussions of the nature of politics, the need for government, and the relationship between earthly authority and purposes of the Divine. St. Augustine's thoughts on government and politics are provided primarily within his *City of God,* but some discussion of political affairs does emerge in other works. For St. Augustine, the world of politics is not as central to human life as it had been for Plato, Aristotle, and Cicero, but, nonetheless, it was a necessary element of the human condition and thus required some consideration in the context of the greater scheme of things.

To understand St. Augustine's political thought, one must first consider his views on human nature. Human beings, while created by God to be perfect, are now in a fallen and corrupt state owing to Original Sin, or the consequences of the sin of Adam. In rebelling against God and attempting to presume independence from God's design, human will, according to St. Augustine, was exerted by the ego in defiance of God, and thus placed the self over God, discord over harmony, rebellion over love. Even though we are under the influence of sin, our original nature as created by God remains, no human action is incapable of obliterating God's design. Through free will, we can reorient ourselves to God, and in so doing, recover that which is good within us from the beginning. Will and its corruption, therefore, are a pivotal theme in the Augustinian conception of the political. Whereas reason, by way of contrast, is the principal aspect of the soul in Plato and Aristotle, St. Augustine shifts to the primacy of the will. This is not to say that reason is unimportant, but rather to note that in St. Augustine's understanding of human nature, it is the will that governs our actions. Given this emphasis on the autonomy of will, the object of our various endeavors becomes paramount, and for St. Augustine, it is in an examination of the things that we love that we can measure the virtue of the will and thus properly sound the depths of our human nature. Whereas Plato discusses the virtues of wisdom, courage, temperance, and justice, St. Augustine, without abandoning these virtues or denying their value, draws out love as the preeminent aspect of the human soul. We must therefore work to orient our will with the proper kind of love, the love of God and neighbor being the correct orientation, the love of self and worldliness a deviation from the right way.

This has an important bearing on the development of St. Augustine's political theory. In the *City of God* he identifies two principle types of ruling authority, or more concisely, "two cities": the City of God (*civitas Dei*) and the city of the world, or the various earthly cities (*civitas terrena*). In so doing, St. Augustine significantly abandons reliance on the earlier typology of regimes variously described by Plato, Aristotle, Polybius, and Cicero and revises the categories of regimes along two axes, the one worldly and the other Divine. It is interesting to note, however, that there is a resemblance between Plato's perfect regime, or the Form of the polis, and St. Augustine's City of God, so in at least one sense, St. Augustine's new categories echo the typology of an earlier thinker.

The two cities are manifest through two distinct and disparate kinds of love that result in the production of two different "fruits." The City of God is inspired by the love of God, "even to the contempt of self," and thus is appropriately aligned with the reign of Christ, resulting in the "fruit" of *caritas,* which is love for humanity or charity in the broader sense of the word. Placing God over self, love of others over ego, the City of God is city of perfection, the one commonwealth that is governed by Christ and praised in the eighty-seventh psalm, "Glorious things are spoken of thee, O city of God." Earthly cities are motivated by the love of self, "even to the contempt of God," the consequences of which are the fruits of *cupiditas* (cupidity, greed, violent sin). Like Plato's many imperfect cities, the earthly cities of St. Augustine fall short of the perfection of the City of God (as Plato's imperfect regimes are deviations of the perfect city). In this vein, as St. Augustine observes, all earthly cities are to some degree unjust, true justice being found only in the Divine commonwealth under the reign of Christ. As with Plato, therefore, St. Augustine recognizes that all temporal regimes are somehow flawed, and can only at best approximate the City of God, and in most cases, fall well short of it. In a sense, the City of God *is* St. Augustine's version of Plato's Form of the polis, for nothing can exceed the justice and mercy of Christ, and it is in His reign as ruler of the City of God that we find the only real example of virtuous rule. However, St. Augustine argues that the City of God and the earthly cities are intermingled in a way that Plato's Form of the polis is not. Thus the City of God is partly visible and partly invisible, whereas Plato's Form is wholly intelligible—the imperfect cities can only approximate the pattern established by the Form. With St. Augustine, we will always "fall short of the glory of God," but through God's grace at least a portion of the City of God is among us, even though it is not always evident. Thus the City of God is more than a "heavenly pattern," it is a living community partially intermingled with the corrupt cities of the world.

As indicated above, earthly cities will ever be impure, some more vicious than others, but all corrupt. This is the legacy of sin, which is the one constant of the human condition in the world. Owing to sin, government is necessary, but because it is the result of sin and not a part of our original nature as created, it is inherently flawed. Human beings are created by God to live together in society, and as such, political association is an aspect of our nature. Nonetheless, because of our tendency to disorder and disobedience, we must submit to the authority and the ever imperfect rule of human beings, having already defied the perfect rule of God. Moreover, because of original sin, our freedom has been compromised. God intended human beings to be free, but that very freedom provided the opportunity to choose the wrong course, to succumb to the temptation to eat the fruit from the tree of knowledge of good and evil. Absolute freedom, or a freedom to do completely as one desires was enjoyed in Paradise, but once Adam made the wrong choice this kind of freedom was withdrawn from humanity. If we really do possess free will, the occasion for sin is in a sense inevitable. But in the state of Paradise, however brief, the freedom of choice was unlimited. There is a sense in St. Augustine that, because of this absolute freedom in our original state, the choice to obey God was as real and viable, and thus as possible, as the decision to disobey God. Paradoxically, the existence of all possible alternatives available to a limitless free will seems to make the Fall preordained. Nonetheless,

absolute freedom was a part of our original nature, but human free will is no longer unlimited. Sin draws our free will down, and orients us toward the commission of wrong acts and the holding of impure beliefs. We are in a state of abridged freedom, constantly plagued by the legacy and lure of sin. Unlike his theological opponents, the Pelagians, St. Augustine did not believe absolute freedom could be restored in this world. Nonetheless, fragments of our original freedom remain with us, and with the coercive support of government, we can carve out enough order in the world to promote peace, even if true justice remains elusive.

The City of God is thus intermingled with earthly cities for a purpose. It is here that true freedom, or *vere libero,* is found, not the absolute freedom of Paradise, but the freedom to follow God's laws in this world, in our post-Edenic state. As St. Augustine states, "...the first liberty of the will was to be able not to sin, the last will be much greater, not to be able to sin." This second freedom is now available to us through the redemptive act of God Incarnate, thus for St. Augustine, in the City of God as it is comingled with the earthly cities, we can discover through grace the true freedom on which all of our virtues now hinge. But the state cannot provide this for us. At best, the state can supply the temporal order requisite to the kind of peace and stability that will enable us to find this true freedom, but *vere libero* will always hover beyond the influence of human beings. Only through Christ are we able to achieve this state of freedom; the political is but a necessary and temporary instrument that will at best facilitate our freedom, but it can never really promote or secure it. This might explain why, for St. Augustine, the primary political question is peace, not justice. This is not to say that justice is wholly unimportant for St. Augustine, but only an admission by St. Augustine that all human attempts at justice will be inadequate. All kingdoms are only slightly removed from "bands of robbers," St. Augustine famously notes in following Cicero, thus the quest for justice will always carry a tinge of futility. True justice is only found in the pure city of God, but even the impure cities of the earth can work toward peace. Injustice is a product of sin, and as such, the state by itself cannot overcome it. Redemption depends on the Divine; the state can only at best support institutions, viz., the Holy Church, in any effort to assist sinners in the awareness of this. The state preserves the order in which the church can thrive, and the church teaches the virtues necessary for good citizens. For St. Augustine, the state can only preserve the peace; it cannot interfere with the theological, moral, and liturgical responsibilities of the church. Some scholars recognize in St. Augustine's understanding of the relationship between church and state a level of qualified separation that anticipates the two swords doctrine of St. Gelasius. The universal and eternal church was the deposit of faith, and thus would ever remain the only source of moral guidance and the only guide in understanding the redemptive nature of God's love. The state was by its nature bound in time and located in space, a very narrow space in comparison to the compass of the body of Christ. Its charge would always be more immediate but less important, more practical and less essential, useful in providing decent institutions but not in itself the source of decency. Thus obedience to the power of the state continues to be obligatory for all Christians; the church can survive even an immoral regime. An alliance with secular power can be useful provided the church itself is not manipulated by political power, but if such an alliance is not possible, the church will continue to survive.

Even so, because the church is the true deposit of faith, and thus the only sure moral guide for the human community, the actions and institutions of governments can be properly judged. A law which is "not just," according to St. Augustine, is in effect "no law at all." As the only true measure of what is just is in the City of God, and the commands of God that are revealed through that city, then we are able to recognize whether or not a human law is good

law by deferring to the authority of the church, which is the only sure guardian of the revealed Scripture. St. Augustine does not advocate collective or organized resistance to earthly power gone astray from this principle, but there is ample room in his political thought for dissent and even defiance of the secular power.

While St. Augustine's earlier writing evinces a view of church-state separation, particular with regard to the ability of the state to interfere with the church, the Augustinian notion of the relationship between church and state turned in a different direction in the early years of the fifth century. St. Augustine always insisted that faith was a personal matter, and that acceptance of Christ and the church must be voluntary. Nonetheless, in the years 406–418, St. Augustine shifted his position to allow for the use of state authority for the imposition of penalties against heretics. "[L]et kings of the earth serve Christ by making laws for Him and for His cause," St. Augustine states, affirming the ability and even the duty of Christian kings to join with the church in preserving the purity of the faith. In 418, St. Augustine asserted that heretics are not only to be silenced but also to be coerced into promoting the true faith. This can only mean that the power of the political authority is to be allied with the church in the fight against heresy, something that St. Augustine found to be an urgency throughout his service to the church. St. Augustine opposed the use of extreme force against heretics, and even interceded on behalf of an accused heretic who was in danger of being executed by the civil government. Nonetheless, he modified his earlier views regarding separate, coexisting sacred and civil spheres for a closer cooperation between civil authority and ecclesial authority, at least in addressing the problem of heresy.

Perhaps his most famous legacy, after the discussion of the two cities, is St. Augustine's commentary on just war. Consonant with the teachings of the church, St. Augustine regarded war with disdain, and consistent with the central purpose of his political theory, he considered the achievement of peace to be of paramount concern. Nonetheless, St. Augustine was not a strict pacifist. War, like all the vices and plagues that cause suffering, is the product of Original Sin, and is thus an inevitability among the earthly cities. It is to be avoided as far as possible, and both king and bishop, solider and layman, should ever work towards peace. Despite efforts to avoid it, war will come, and in that eventuality it is incumbent upon states and their leaders to conduct wars justly. That is to say, war is to be avoided, but secular authorities are bound by duty to protect their subjects, and thus will at times find themselves with no alternative than to take up the sword. But any belligerent action must be done according to the principles of justice; war cannot be fought for unjust purposes, nor executed through unjust methods. In Book XXII of his *Contra Faustum,* St. Augustine discerns two criteria requisite to the prosecution of a just war. First, for St. Augustine, it is always just to defend oneself. If attacked, a state is completely justified in the use of force to repel any belligerent. Second, a state can initiate a war, or go on the offensive, in order to correct a specific wrong inflicted by a hostile power on its citizens, or to restore the legitimate *status quo ante bellum* by seeking to "return what has been wrongfully appropriated." War cannot be waged for the sake of conquest or worldly ambition. If it is, then the action is unjust. Still further, a just war is just only in an incomplete sense, the true justice of Christ, found only in the City of God, is not the principle behind belligerency. War is completely worldly, and has no connection to the Divine will. Thus, St. Augustine's theory of just war would not allow for a war inspired by religious devotion, for true devotion to Christ would reveal the essential message of peace in the revealed word. Just wars establish earthly peace, but they do not guarantee "peace on earth, and good will to all men." That remains for God alone.

And yet, St. Augustine still regards a just war as not incompatible with the teachings of Jesus. He notes that even though Christ taught us to "love our enemies," "offer the other cheek," and "pray for those who persecute us," he never explicitly required the categorical abolition of war, nor did he criticize those who served within the military. Military duty stems from the need to "render unto Caesar," and St. Augustine notes that Christ received soldiers with compassion, not criticism. Thus, for St. Augustine, peace is a central value of Christian faith, and all are commanded to love their fellow human beings, and to treat them with mercy and compassion. Yet war can be waged if the reasons and the methods are just. Most wars are not just and cannot be defended, but the rare exception of a just war is, for St. Augustine, a reality of this world that cannot be avoided, and can be legitimate within limited bounds.

Just war theory can be traced to St. Augustine, but he left certain aspects somewhat unclear. It is with later thinkers, and in particular, St. Thomas Aquinas, that the concept of the just war would be further developed.

By and large, St. Augustine's political thought is best understood as a whole in the context of his otherworldliness. His notions on justice, peace, free will, and the proper relationship between sacred and civil are only really appreciated from within his theology, which is in its essence mystical. And yet he serves as a pivotal figure in the history of political thought, for in the resemblance of the City of God to Plato's Form of the polis we find the idealism of classical theory in its noblest expression, and in his candid view of human nature and the consequence of sin, we discern the adumbration of a political realism that would more fully emerge in the writings of Machiavelli and Hobbes. In St. Augustine both of these voices can be heard, and at his best we are brought into a deeper consideration of the human condition in both its limits and its possibilities.

Related Entries
Aquinas, Thomas; Catholic social teaching; Plato

Suggested Reading
Augustine. *City of God,* ed. David Knowles. 1972; repr. New York: Penguin Classics, 1976.

Augustine. *On Free Choice of the Will.* Indianapolis: Hackett, 1993.

Augustine. *Political Writings,* trans. Michael W. Tkacz and Douglas Kries, ed. Ernest L. Fortin and Douglas Kries with Roland Gunn. Indianapolis: Hackett, 1994.

autarky

From the Greek *autarkeia,* meaning self-sufficiency, autarky is a principle of domestic economic independence and self-reliance that promotes highly restricted trade and even the elimination of commercial interaction with external economies. Autarky is an economic species of isolationism, a principle that promotes public policies that are aimed at a thoroughgoing independence of a domestic economy from any foreign commercial or political interest. Autarky has usually been associated with closed societies, such as Cold War Albania or North Korea today, but it is not necessarily an exclusively totalitarian feature (although it is safe to say that true totalitarian systems are or aspire to be autarkic). Authoritarian Spain under Franco, postcolonial India, Burma during its attempt to combine socialism and inwardly focused nationalism during the 1960s–1980s, Japan prior to the encounter with Commodore Perry, and even the young American republic during the embargo under the Jefferson administration (1808–1809) exhibited autarkic tendencies.

Theories resembling autarky are as old as political theory. Both Plato and Aristotle endorsed the notion of self-sufficiency as a political ideal. For both thinkers, the ideal *polis* should be small enough to attain self-sufficiency and yet large enough for adequate self-defense. In modern political theory, Johann Fichte is perhaps the most notable proponent of economic autarky, having supported the policy in his 1800 treatise *The Closed Commercial State.* Autarky is a common feature in the nineteenth-century utopias envisioned by idealists such as Robert Owen and Charles Fourier, and, as implied above, there is a close affinity between autarky and fascist or quasi-fascistic ideologies.

Mussolini in particular aspired toward autarky, and yet he remained somewhat dependent on trade with Nazi Germany. The Nazis themselves were not particularly enamored with any single economic system or set of policies. For Hitler, economics was less important than the exertion of will—and whatever served to promote the triumph of the Teutonic will was deemed an acceptable course of action.

Today the best example of a deliberately autarkic system, or at least an attempt at such a system, can be found in the "juche" principle in totalitarian North Korea. In the pervasive global economy that characterizes the twenty-first century, such efforts at real autarky are less likely to be seriously promoted or implemented, and still more unlikely to succeed.

Related Entry
authoritarianism

authoritarianism

Authoritarianism is a generic term referring to any regime where power is largely concentrated in one person (for example, dictatorship, despotism) or a small group of elites (such as an oligarchy). For the most part, an authoritarian regime presumes to stand above the law (as contrasted to a monarchy, aristocracy, or democracy, which all defer to the rule of law) and is driven primarily by personality and charisma of a single leader, or by the will of a group of elites who seize power for their own purposes. Authoritarianism implies unlimited authority of the state and complete obedience among the subjects and in some cases can lead to totalitarianism (although it is important to note the distinction between the two). An authoritarian state does not, as in the case of totalitarianism, necessarily destroy the political order, nor is it characterized by the elimination of the private sphere (although, again, this can be a result of authoritarianism that precipitates a greater tyranny), for it is possible under an authoritarian state to sustain associations and relationships that enjoy some independence from the power of the state, so long as they are cooperative with the designs of the political leadership. Strictly speaking, a monarchy is not an authoritarian regime, if it is a monarchy in the true sense. Authoritarianism implies some illegitimate seizure of power, and presumption that the sovereign power is somehow above the law.

Related Entries
despot; despotism; dictator; fascism; *magister populi*; monarchy; totalitarianism; tyranny

autocracy

Literally rule by one person who has seized power on his own authority. An autocrat is any ruler who holds complete power within a political system, justified on the terms established by the autocrat alone. The term *autocrat* usually is interchangeable with *despot* or *dictator*. Monarchs are not autocrats; monarchs have institutional legitimacy and hold power and govern under the limitations of law. Autocracy is also distinct from totalitarianism, under which political power is actually destroyed.

Related Entries
authoritarianism; despot, despotism; monarchy; totalitarianism; tyranny

Suggested Reading
Altemeyer, Robert. *The Authoritarian Specter*. Cambridge, MA: Harvard Univ. Press, 1996.

Averroes (Ibn Roschd, Ibn Rusch, 1126–1198)

A significant contributor to the promotion of Aristotle during the High Middle Ages, Averroes is of interest in his assertion that while both faith and reason are compatible (as argued by several previous authors) philosophy is in the last analysis a higher path toward truth, or at least a more reliable one. This is not to say that religion and theology are to be rejected, but only to assert that the inquiry of the philosopher, and especially as epitomized by Plato and Aristotle, provides a greater clarity about the nature of divine things. Averroes argues that truth arrived at via reflection and the discipline of the intellect is fundamentally a divine

truth, and in actuality more coherent than that which is revealed. Revealed truth is important and necessary for most human beings, but the great insights of the philosophers, who arrive at truth through the power of the intellect, are divine in a still higher way.

Scripture, while bearing truth, must sometimes be read as allegory according to Averroes, but philosophy when practiced as it should be will always demonstrate truth, and in this sense it is more certain. Allegories are open to interpretation, but philosophical truths are not—they achieve a level of objective certainty that is in the end indisputable. It is not that theology and philosophy are in conflict, but rather that, for Averroes, philosophy is theology at its most rarified.

In his commentary on Plato's *Republic,* Averroes modifies Plato through his reading of Aristotle in an attempt to apply the synthesis of reason and faith to Islamic political communities. He regarded Plato's form of the *polis* as the real "second-best city," surpassed only by the community of Islam itself. In his discussion of imperfect regimes, Averroes again leans heavily on both Plato and Alfarabi, but he goes a step further by directly comparing examples of corrupt regimes to specific Islamic regimes that have fallen away from the shari'a (the law of Islam as perfectly revealed through the *Qur'ān* and Hadith). Averroes calls for a renewal of philosophical inquiry to help restore the purity of the Islamic community through a correct reading of shari'a, one that is not necessarily accessible to the entire community but nonetheless available to true lovers of wisdom.

A good part of Averroes's writing is in response to the Islamic scholars and his predecessor, al-Ghazali. However, Averroes himself, or at least his "Latin" interpreters, drew the attention of another great philosopher, St. Thomas Aquinas, who, while approaching Averroes with admiration, ultimately offers an alternative reading of the relationship between the reason of philosophy and the faith of religion. Thus the legacy of Averroes is intimately tied to the development of Medieval Scholasticism.

Related Entries
Alfarabi; Aquinas, Thomas; Plato

Suggested Reading

Averroes. *Averroes on Plato's Republic,* trans. Ralph Lerner. Ithaca, NY: Cornell Univ. Press, 2005.

Black, Antony. *The History of Islamic Political Thought: From the Prophet to the Present.* New York: Routledge, 2001.

B

the ballot or the bullet?

The title and most famous line of a 1964 speech by Malcolm X, the "ballot or the bullet?" frames the question regarding the possibilities for reform on behalf of African Americans during the civil-rights movement as it moved into the mid-1960s. Malcolm X, known for his unwillingness to renounce the possibilities of violence in the struggle against injustice and for a more substantive equality, is often contrasted against Martin Luther King, Jr. and the nonviolent methods he advocated.

In this speech, Malcolm X argued that the system had not only failed African Americans historically but also had not responded to the tactics of the nonviolent mainstream of the civil-rights movement to the benefit of the black minority. Arguing that the black community was actually more disadvantaged in 1964 than in 1954, he proposed the consideration of alternatives, and anticipated a "new deal coming in" led by a new generation of African Americans no longer willing to use gradualist methods and political compromise to promote full equality and justice. "And now you're facing," Malcolm X intoned,

> a situation where the young Negro's coming up. They don't want to hear that 'turn-the-other-cheek' stuff, no. In Jacksonville, those were teenagers, they were throwing Molotov cocktails. Negroes have never done that before. But it shows you there's a new deal coming in ...It'll be Molotov cocktails this month, hand

grenades next month, and something else next month. It will be ballots, or it'll be bullets. It'll be liberty, or it will be death.

For Malcolm X, the time for gradualist methods was drawing to a close. Decisive action on behalf of all oppressed minorities needed to be accepted. This does not mean that violence ("the bullet") is inevitable, only that it is no longer dismissed as unacceptable. If progress is to be achieved, it must be achieved by "any means necessary," and while the ballot is preferable, the bullet is not to be rejected out of hand. Malcolm X insisted that the ballot meant freedom for African Americans, and was a much more powerful instrument toward that freedom than economic opportunity. The strategy of the Black Nationalist was an economic one, and Malcolm X did not deny that fact, indeed, in his "Ballot or Bullet" speech he reasserted and explained the importance of economic power for African Americans. Still, the most important power was political power, and it could be won through peaceful democratic processes, or it could be won by other necessary means.

Malcolm X was particularly impatient with the Democratic Party under the leadership of the pro–civil rights President Lyndon Johnson, whom he saw as duplicitous in his public support for civil rights while remaining in a cozy relationship with segregationist politicians such as Senator Richard Russell. It would have been better for President Johnson to abandon the compromising posture toward the segregationist and immediately and openly "denounce the Southern branch of his party" that had been allowed to impair peaceful progress. If denial of the ballot continued, the only answer would be in the bullet. "...if I die in the morning," Malcolm X declared, "I'll die saying one thing: the ballot or the bullet, the ballot or the bullet." Concluding his speech with a reference to the efforts of President Johnson and others advocating civil-rights legislation, he invited the president to address the Senate against the interests of the segregationist, "Tell him [Johnson], Malcolm X recommends, don't wait until election time. If he waits too long, brothers and sisters, he will be responsible for letting a condition develop in this country which will create a climate that will bring seeds up out of the ground with vegetation on the end of them looking like something these people never dreamed of. In 1964, it's the ballot or the bullet.

Related Entries
black power; I have a dream

Suggested Reading
Conyers, James L., and Andrew P. Smallwood, eds., *Malcolm X: A Historical Reader.* Durham, NC: Carolina Academic Press, 2008.
Malcolm X, "The Ballot or the Bullet?" Address delivered April 12, 1964. Malcolm X. *A Malcolm X Reader,* ed. David Gallen. New York: Carroll & Graf, 1994.

Beccaria, Cesare (Marquis of Beccaria-Bonesana), 1738–1794

Beccaria is almost exclusively known for his writings on the punishment of crime, which are notable in that, influenced by utilitarian principles, he concluded that the only legitimate reason for punishing criminals is to improve society as a whole through deterrence rather than to exact revenge against malefactors. Beccaria's approach was closer to rehabilitation than retribution, as he believed that punishment would not only benefit society by deterring crime, but also improve those who commit the crimes. If the punishment is swift (thus punctuating the consequences of crime) without being severe (which leads over time to an inadvertent acclimation to severe punishments and thus the diminution of their effectiveness) it will serve as an effective preventative to future malfeasance.

More significantly, however, Beccaria advocated legal and penal reforms to address the problem of crime. Clear, concise laws that set appropriate punishments for different crimes with reasonable degrees of severity serve as the initial step. Some crimes or other practices that undermine social order and

civility could be more adequately addressed through legal reform rather than penal measures. For example, dueling (a problem in the eighteenth century) could be eradicated given new laws that allow individuals recourse to the courts when honor is insulted rather than leaving them to their own resources. Bounty hunting would be eradicated as it promotes immoral treatment of others. Such measures are in line with Beccaria's overall principle that the best way to treat crime is not so much through an elaborate system of punishments and fear of the scaffold, but rather through the promulgation of clear and simple laws that promote virtue, accompanied by education that encourages good citizenship.

Above all, Beccaria provides an influential critique of capital punishment unusual for his times. Beccaria does not agree that the state has power over life but rather that one's right to life is thoroughly inalienable. While it is important for the punishment to fit the crime, Beccaria does not see capital punishment as justifiable in any case. It is neither justifiable through the social contract (for the right to life cannot be surrendered) nor beneficial in practical terms. The historical record of crime and social disorder disproves the effectiveness of capital punishment as a deterrent. A more effective deterrent for the most dangerous crimes would be, in Becarria's view, perpetual slavery, or life in prison under compulsory labor. Indeed, Beccaria observes that capital punishment inures citizens to the problems of suffering and violence, and promotes underlying disorders in our attitudes toward the enforcement of law and preservation of order.

Related Entries
Bentham, Jeremy; Hobbes, Thomas; utilitarianism

Suggested Reading
Beccaria, Cesare. *On Crimes and Punishments and Other Writings,* ed. Richard Bellamy and trans. Richard Davies et al. New York: Cambridge Univ. Press, 1995.

behavioralism

Within the tradition of political inquiry, specifically the formalized study of political science as it has developed within the last 80 years, the term behavioralism loosely describes a methodological approach to political behavior that applies scientific and mathematical procedures and measures to the collection, measurement, and analysis of observable phenomena within a given universe of investigation. Empirical and descriptive, behavioralism is a more sophisticated and mathematically subtle variation of positivism; representing a procedurally systematic and structurally coherent examination of quantifiable observations of the political world and the way in which people conduct themselves in the public sphere. Political scientists schooled in the experiential and analytical methods of behavioralism seek to identify and understand patterns of behavior that interconnect the undercurrents of the social world with the more visible dynamics and institutions of the political realm. As with the natural sciences, observation, collection of data, application of statistical models, analysis of significant information offered through those models, and the identification of patterns that lead to the predictable trends are features of what Heinz Eulau once dubbed the "behavioral persuasion" of political science. In the end, behavioral political science aims at knowledge of politics experientially based, employing the rigorous scientific test of falsifiability and producing a level of certainty more reliable than nonquantitative subfields and their methods.

Behavioralism traces its conceptual lineage to positivism, but its more immediate influence comes from the behavioral school of psychology founded by John B. Watson and B. F. Skinner. Skinner's behavoralistic psychology itself turned prescriptive through his controversial *Walden Two,* a utopian effort to endorse the application of the new science of behavorialism toward the construction of a new social order, one that would inevitably lead to the abolition of politics and all other traditional forms of social direction. But Skinner's blueprints for social engineering are largely viewed as eccentric declensions of behavioralism, at least from the perspective of political inquiry. Within the discipline of political science, broadly conceived, behavioralism as a model for the scientific study of the human polity can be more directly (and perhaps properly) traced to the efforts and influence of Charles Merriam, a key innovator in the advocacy of a new and systematic kind of political investigation aimed at the improvement of society through the emulation of scientific rigor. Another early proponent of behavioralism in political science, Herbert A. Simon, whose expertise ranged beyond political inquiry into other areas of social science (particularly economics) and even into computer science, made his name through the analysis of decision-making and organizations within public administration. Harold Lasswell, perhaps more than anyone, represents the attempt to fashion political science into a "hard science" through his close study of the nature of power and its relationship to public communication, in particular, the uses of propaganda. Lasswell's famous dictum that politics is the study of "who gets what, when and how" epitomizes for some the behavioralist project.

Eugene Meehan, another principal contributor to the "behavioral persuasion," assumes a more aggressive stance in endorsing scientific methodology as the only meaningful path toward political knowledge. For Meehan, the classical tradition from Plato on is antiquated and thus irrelevant. He rejected the metaphysical, epistemological, and ethical dimensions of political theory and strenuously advocated a science of politics thoroughly quantifiable. Empirical political science is the sole method that can lead students of politics to any meaningful body of knowledge, and the emulation of the natural sciences, mathematics, and linguistic analysis has provided political science with a system of investigation so illuminating that "...[i]mmense piles of philosophic rubbish accumulated from over two millennia of speculation were speedily dissolved by its cauterizing touch." In Meehan's estimation, political inquiry prior to the twentieth century—with the important exceptions of David Hume and Auguste Comte—is at root theological. The new political science produces an authentic knowledge of the social world, not one that is colored by romantic metaphysical longing for the heavenly cities of the philosophers.

Not all behavioralists exude such confidence. Eulau, for example, while decidedly in the behavioral camp, claimed a connection to the classical theorists of the past, and mused that they would have employed modern methods in their attempts at certainty had they been available to them. Eulau's behaviorism is cautious and moderate, reminiscent of the more empirically angled ruminations of Aristotle or Machiavelli absent the precision of a modern scientific sensibility as in the case of Eulau and his contemporaries.

Behavioralist political inquiry would develop further through the efforts of social scientists such as Talcott Parsons, Robert Merton, David Easton, and Robert Dahl. One might also include other luminaries of modern political science, such as Karl Deutsch, but only at the risk of overstretching the type. By and large, the behavioral approach to political science has a long reach in the broader discipline and will continue to play an important and at times vital role in the further evolution of the study of the political dimension of the human condition.

Related Entry
positivism

Suggested Reading
Eulau, Heinz. *The Behavioral Persuasion*. New York: Random House 1963.
Germino, Dante. *Beyond Ideology*. 1967; repr. Chicago: Univ. of Chicago Press/Midway Reprint, 1976.

bellum omnium contra omnes

(Latin) "war of all against all," or the "war of everyone against everyone," "every man against every man," "every man for himself." From the Latin edition of *Leviathan* by Thomas Hobbes, it is employed as a phrase depicting the aggressive, egotistic, and even violent tendencies in human nature, or what could be called in shorthand, "man's inhumanity to man." A similar sentiment can be mined from a much earlier source, "*lupus est homo homini*" or "man is a wolf to man," penned long before Hobbes by Plautus in *Asinaria* in the third century BC. A variation, *homo homini lupus,* means essentially the same thing.

Related Entries
Hobbes, Thomas; war of all against all

Suggested Reading
Hobbes, Thomas. *Leviathan*. Indianapolis: Hackett, 1992. Chapter 13 is of particular relevance.

Bentham, Jeremy (1748–1832)

One of the more provocative thinkers in the nineteenth century, Jeremy Bentham's utilitarian philosophy has remained influential throughout much of the twentieth century, both throughout philosophy in general and political theory in particular. While Bentham's theories have been modified, his basic principles still remain the substantive ground of the utilitarian school of thought.

Bentham argues that the source of all human conduct, both as it is and as it ought to be, whether we are speaking of moral, political, or economic decisions, can be fully understood in terms of the expansion of pleasure and the reduction of pain aimed at the overall happiness of rational, individual agents. For Bentham, we cannot speak of any good beyond the interest of the individual—even a common good is but an aggregate of individuals measuring their own interest; thus the community itself is in effect a fiction wherein independent and self-reliant individuals operate. The only real measure of the value of an act is the degree to which it secures the happiness of an individual, and the only way to comprehend happiness is through the relationship between pleasure and pain. "Nature," according to Bentham,

> has placed mankind under the governance of two sovereign masters, "pain" and "pleasure." It is for them alone to point out what we ought to do, as

well as to determine what we shall do. On the one hand the standard of right and wrong, on the other the chain of causes and effects, are fastened to their throne. They govern us in all we do, in all we say, in all we think: every effort we can make to throw off their subjection, will serve but to demonstrate and confirm it.

Hence, not only is the pursuit of pleasure and the avoidance of pain *the* description of how human beings act—morally or otherwise—but it also prescribes the manner in which we should measure the value of all of our actions and alternatives.

For Bentham, the expansion of pleasure (and in the long term, happiness) is achieved by individuals through what can be called a felicific calculus (or hedonistic calculus). Seven circumstances are and should be weighed in the estimation of potential pleasure or pain before acting on any alternative: the intensity of a pleasure, its duration, its certainty (to what extent are one's actions certain to produce the desired result), propinquity (whether or not what is needed to induce a pleasure is proximate or remote), what Bentham calls "fecundity" (or the likelihood of the repetition of a pleasure), purity (some pleasures are less pure than others as they are accompanied by a degree of pain), and finally, extent—or the number of persons to which a pleasure will be experienced, or to which benefits will redound. It is this last circumstance, that is, extent, which allows political actors to determine the "greatest happiness for the greatest number." Pleasures is experienced by individuals, but those who enact laws and govern our institutions can use the principles of the calculus of felicity on a broader scale if the "extent" of the pleasures is taken into account.

Bentham's utilitarianism is strictly quantitative—all pleasures are equal in Bentham's assessment. Thus it is not the precise pleasure that is to be judged, but whether or not that given pleasure has succeeded in advancing a great amount of happiness for a larger number of people. "Pushpin is as good as poetry" in Bentham's calculus—the actual substance of the activity is a secondary consideration. Or, in more current terms, a video game would be

of equal value to reading Hamlet, in Bentham's assessment, if the pleasure of the individual is maximized and the pain minimized. It makes little difference which activity is to be sought as long as the seven circumstances of the felicific calculus are taken into account.

Democratic reform aimed at a more humane society was the ultimate goal for Bentham, who believed that his doctrine of utility provided the key to a more egalitarian and rational society. All policies and practices, regardless of how venerable, must be exposed to the "corrosive acids of utility." Those principles, practices, laws, and policies that prove valid based on the calculus of felicity in pursuit of the greatest happiness principle are to be applied or continued. Those that fail the test of utility should be abandoned forthwith. Thus Bentham believed that the whole of society could be improved through the intelligent maximization of pleasure. Politics, law, economics, even prison reform, exemplified by his panopticon, are inevitably improved under the guidance of utilitarianism. In the final analysis, Bentham's political theory is individualistic and reformist, seeking a society that is most conducive to the liberty of the person, and truly just in accord with that which results in a more expansive happiness for society as a whole. The community may indeed be a fiction for Bentham, but his egoistic ethic is directed at the improvement of the whole.

Related Entries
Mill, John Stuart; nonsense on stilts; utilitarianism

Suggested Reading
Bentham, Jeremy. *An Introduction to the Principles of Morals and Legislation,* ed. J.H. Burns and H.L.A. Hart, with an interpretive essay by Hart, H.L.A.. New York: Oxford Univ. Press 1996.

Big Brother
From George Orwell's famous dystopia, *1984,* "Big Brother" is the anonymous leader of the future totalitarian society that serves as the context for Orwell's story of protagonist Winston

Smith and his personal decline under the irrational and crushing weight of the system. Big Brother is never actually seen, and is in fact less a specific character and more the personification of the totalitarian regime. Always coldly monitoring the movements of every subject of the system. Big Brother is the symbol of the loss of the private sphere in the wake of the abolition of the political. The totalitarian state of Big Brother is not a state at all, but a collectivist perversion of control and intrusion. "Big Brother is watching you" is the slogan of the death of privacy and the birth of ubiquitous power. Orwell conceived of this dystopia as a warning against the siren temptations of revolutionary collectivism and the potential for the absolute corruption of mass movements by the abuses of power amplified to a paranoid pitch of absurd irrationality under the guise of order and security. Orwell's main target of criticism was the Soviet state, and the image of Big Brother evokes Josef Stalin, but in the larger view Orwell's achievement is a timeless caution against investing in grand visions of social engineering and centralized control. Indeed, given the surveillance capacities and ever expanding media of the twenty-first century, the slogan "Big Brother is watching" sustains its relevance even without the immediate threat of the iron-booted totalitarianism of Stalin's Soviet State.

Related Entry
doublespeak

Suggested Reading
Orwell, George. *Nineteen Eighty-Four, Centennial Edition, with a foreword by Thomas Pynchon and afterword by Erich Fromm.* New York: Plume 2003.

biopower

Michel Foucault's concept of power, in shedding the old conceptualization of sovereign power over life and death that stems from earlier political thought and practice, posits a notion of power in postindustrial (postmodern) society as ubiquitous and decentralized, applying pressure and control not so much through the threat of execution but through the control of our lives, through "biopower." The individual is coerced in numerous ways from multiple points of pressure throughout society, not simply from a localized visible sovereign (such as the Medieval king or baron or even Hobbes's "mortal god" Leviathan). This multidirectional pressure, or biopower, while not menacing our lives as did the older notion of sovereignty through the threat of violence and even death against malfeasance, is a disciplinary power that insidiously and for the most part imperceptibly forces us to conform to social and political norms. We are under the pressure of biopower in every facet of our lives, and as such we are subtly disciplined in ways that shape us according to the prejudices and habits of our culture and the expectations of the political and juridical system. Thus while the consequences of openly opposing the older sense of sovereignty are no longer dangerous to the person, the fact that our lives are manipulated anonymously and without deliberate reason causes Foucault to question the level of true freedom human beings can enjoy in contemporary society. Biopower, for Foucault, while not the terror that keeps "all in awe" as Hobbes would say, nonetheless is the pressure that holds all in the grip of normativity.

Related Entries
capillary power; carceral society; Foucault, Michel

Suggested Reading
Foucault, Michel. *The Foucault Reader,* ed. Paul Rabinow. New York: Pantheon Books, 1984.

black power

Coined in late 1966 by the firebrand activist Stokely Carmichael, the term "black power" represents a voice within the African American community directed not only at the injustices suffered within American society, but also aimed at the exertion of a new sense of black nationalism based on notions of black pride and uniqueness, and the refusal to compromise with a system guilty of racism and callous indifference to the problems of the black community. The concept behind the term stems from the Black Nationalism and pan-African movements of the early twentieth century. Rejecting the social inferiority imposed by the white-dominated status quo, these movements sought to invigorate the African American community with a sense of communal self-worth and racial cohesion. Black Nationalism offered a more radical alternative than the positions represented by W.E.B. Du Bois and Booker T. Washington, and provided a direct challenge to the dominant cultural assumptions supporting American political institutions and framing the social conventions of the white mainstream.

After World War II the voice of Black Nationalism receded as the more moderate NAACP and similar groups began to make inroads toward integration. As white majority resistance stiffened in the early 1960s, elements of the civil-rights movement began to follow a more militant turn; these radicalized alternatives began to gain renewed momentum. In this climate Carmichael promoted the challenge of black power to an increasingly frustrated African American community. Carmichael voiced suspicions regarding the motives of the established white majority, bluntly asserting that the black community must win their freedom on their own, no longer relying on the tender mercies of their white oppressors. Carmichael argued

> In order to understand white supremacy we must dismiss the fallacious notion that white people can give anybody their freedom. No man can give anybody his freedom. A man is born free. You may enslave a man after he is born free, and that is in fact what this country does. It enslaves black people after they're born, so that the only acts that white people can do is to stop denying black people their freedom; that is, they must stop denying freedom. They never give it to anyone.

Civil-rights legislation, in the end, served white people, as Carmichael understood it, and it is only through organizations populated solely by African Americans behind their own leadership that real social improvement can be won, and it must be won on the terms of the black community, not presumptuously given by the institutions that are governed by and serve only the white majority. The right to move freely through society at all levels, the power of the vote, all the freedoms enjoyed by white America are, as Carmichael affirmed, rights that belong to blacks as human beings, and not privileges now conceded through the largesse of white politicians. It is through this awareness that a new power must be aimed at the injustices of a racist establishment; black power, independent of the unreliable and, in the end, self-serving designs of purported white allies. The time to speak and act as black Americans for black Americans was at hand. "Now we are now engaged in a psychological struggle in this country," inveighed Carmichael,

> and that is whether or not black people will have the right to use the words they want to use without white people giving their sanction to it;...whether they like it or not, we gonna use the word "Black Power"—and let them address themselves to that; but that we are not going to wait for white people to sanction Black Power. We're tired of waiting; every time black people move in this country, they're forced to defend their position before they move. It's time that the people who are supposed to be defending their position do that. That's white people. They ought to start defending themselves as to why they have oppressed and exploited us.

While black power was initially both offered and received as a more militant strategy for liberation, the term soon became a prominent feature of the general cultural landscape of the late 1960s and early 1970s, and as such, the radical edge was somewhat blunted. Nonetheless, "black power," when considered in the context of the times from which it was voiced as well as from within any situation of social and political inequity, retains its symbolic force.

Related Entries
the ballot or the bullet; I have a dream

Suggested Reading
Carmichael, Stokely, and Charles V. Hamilton. *Black Power: The Politics of Liberation in America.* New York: Random House, 1967.

Bodin, Jean (1530–1596)

Jean Bodin is credited by many students of the history of political thought for establishing the foundations of the modern theory of sovereignty. Three principles within Bodin's theory of sovereignty are of particular interest to the emergence of modern political thought. First, Bodin, while favoring monarchy, recognized that sovereignty need not be posited by necessity in a king. This by itself is not an innovation, as nonautocratic sovereignty had already been prescribed and practiced since Cleisthenes. When combined with the second principle, the "absolute" nature of sovereign power, we witness the beginnings of a new understanding of sovereign power. Bodin argued that the sovereign possesses by definition absolute and perpetual power. The sovereign is absolutely "seized" of power, and yields to no other human authority.

Indeed, not only is the sovereign the sole source of the administration and adjudication of law, the sovereign concentrates within one body (or one person) the power of legislation— to make law and not only rule and adjudicate laws established by custom and the authority of precedent. In all instances, the authority of the sovereign is the final word in civil affairs, and the prince who bears this power is above all other authority, even above the civil law. Prior to Bodin, legitimate political power was always understood as somehow limited, but with Bodin, at least in relation to temporal power, the sovereign is alone the highest authority, regardless of whether sovereignty resides in one person or in the many. Hence sovereignty is abstracted from the person and expanded beyond law. Because of this, later readers of Bodin are thereby tempted to see in his notion of sovereignty the intellectual seeds

of the absolutism claimed by the Divine Right kings of the seventeenth and eighteenth centuries as well as a distant precursor to later and still more virulent forms of absolutism. However, Bodin can be exonerated from this charge by a close examination of the third principle shaping his theory of sovereignty, combined with his insistence that even though sovereignty is a power even above civil law, it remains subordinate to God.

The third principle clearly marks a distinction between three types of sovereignty: royal, despotic, and tyrannical. Royal and despotic power are both legitimate, the former governing free citizens under the laws of God, the latter governing conquered subjects with an authority that emulates that of a patriarch or master.

> Royal, or legitimate, monarchy is one in which the subject obeys the laws of the prince, the prince in his turn obeys the laws of God, and natural liberty and the natural right to property is secured to all. Despotic monarchy is one in which the prince is lord and master of both the possessions and the persons of his subjects by right of conquest in a just war; he governs his subjects as absolutely as the head of a household governs his slaves.

This distinction illustrates Bodin's recognition that royal sovereignty, which is "absolute" by definition, is not *absolute* in the connotation assigned to that term generations after Bodin. The royal sovereign does not rule with the unrestricted authority of a conquering despot, and is thus, compared to that despot, limited. Furthermore, the comparison is even more illustrative when considering tyranny, for as Bodin continues,

> Tyrannical monarchy is one in which the laws of nature are set at naught, free subjects oppressed as if they were slaves, and their property treated as if it belonged to the tyrant. Exactly the same diversity is to be found in aristocracies and popular states, for each in its turn can be either legitimate, despotic, or tyrannical in the way I have described

No royal sovereign or despotic sovereign can legitimately assume the kind of power exercised by tyrants. This alone indicates that Bodin's absolutism was not so "absolute." Rather, his notion of "absolute sovereignty" revives, as commentators have pointed out, a Roman conception of *absolutus,* which is related to the quality of *legibus solutus,* a notion closer to the prerogative power of government officials and deputies of the sovereign to act on the authority of their office, as in the case of the modern notion of implied powers. The fact that royal and despotic monarchs act in accord with natural law and only become tyrannical when they cease that practice demonstrates the complexities of Bodin's understanding of absolute sovereignty. Pursuant to this set of distinctions Bodin further declares

> A TRUE king is one who observes the laws of nature as punctiliously as he wishes his subjects to observe his own laws, thereby securing to them their liberty, and the enjoyment of their own property. I have added these last qualifications in order to distinguish kingship from despotism. A despot can be a just and virtuous prince, and an equitable governor of his people, but he is the master of their persons and their goods. If a despot who has overcome his enemies in a just war, restores to them their liberty, and permits them to dispose of themselves and their possessions as they wish, he ceases to be a despot and becomes a king.

Additionally, it must be remembered, as stated above, that Bodin is clear in this insistence on the deference of sovereignty to the authority of God and the law of nature. For a sixteenth-century author, such an irresistible check on the abuse of power held a genuine meaning that might be lost to the modern reader. A prince is the ultimate civil authority, but is himself governed by the law of nature, and must in the end answer to the law of God. That in itself, for Bodin, was a sufficient limitation set against the abuses of absolutism as we understand it. While Bodin was *not* a divine right theorists; kings nonetheless are duty-bound to God, and representatives of his will in the state.

Furthermore, Bodin did identify other limitations on royal sovereignty. A royal sovereign is duty bound to protect private property, and thus serves the public in this capacity. Kings could not confiscate public lands for their own purposes, and were obligated to protect and not abridge the property rights of their subjects. Therefore the "absolute" authority of the prince above all others is qualified by these traditions.

Bodin is also noteworthy for having anticipated Montesquieu's connection between climate and the development of national character. As the most prominent member of the *politiques,* he promoted religious tolerance during a period marked by severe sectarian conflict in France and throughout much of western and central Europe. While features of Bodin's political thought still look behind his time to both the Romans and the feudal states of the Middle Ages, much of his contribution to political thought stands as a pivot moving toward modernity, particularly the modernist ideas of Grotius, Hobbes, and Rousseau.

Related Entry
politiques

Suggested Reading
Bodin, Jean. *On Sovereignty, Four Chapters from the Six Books of the Commonwealth,* ed. and trans. Julian H. Franklin. 1992; repr. New York: Cambridge Univ. Press, 2007.

bread and peace

Shortly after seizing power in the October Revolution, V.I. Lenin, Bolshevik leader and founder of the Marxist state in what would become the Soviet Union, resolved to pull Russia out of the Great War (World War I) that was consuming the whole of Europe at the time of the storming of the Winter Palace. Lenin argued that the war served not the good of the people, but rather the moneyed interest of bankers and financiers, especially those in Britain and Germany. Soldiers dying on the front lines were, in Lenin's opinion, not sacrificing their lives for a noble cause such as love and defense of country or international justice, but rather were being killed to help fund the accounts of the wealthy few who controlled the investments and resources that drove the engine of war. Indeed, Lenin intoned, even should a truce between the capitalist countries be settled, it would only be a temporary calm that would eventually give way to a new round of slaughter to the profit of the capitalist class. Socialism, argued Lenin offered a true peace and a new prosperity—"bread and peace" rather than incessant war and misery. Thus it was necessary to pull the new socialist state that Russia was becoming out of the senseless money-driven war of the European financier.

Even so, the prosperity that the capitalist class enjoys at the expense of the war-shocked masses can only be short-lived, as the forces that are driving the war, as Lenin saw it, would be the same forces that would cause the very collapse of the capitalist world structure.

As Lenin wrote in late 1917 (for publication in May of the following year),

> Peace and bread are the basic demands of the workers and the exploited. The war has made these demands extremely urgent. The war has brought hunger to the most civilized countries, to those most culturally developed. On the other hand, the war, as a tremendous historical process, has accelerated social development to an unheard-of degree. Capitalism had developed into imperialism, i.e., into monopoly capitalism, and under the influence of the war it has become state monopoly capitalism. We have now reached the stage of world economy that is the immediate stepping stone to socialism.

Imperialism as the "final stage of capitalism" was an important theme in Lenin's interpretation of applied Marxism. The class struggle within nations was to be broadened and thrust onto the international stage in the form of imperialism. It would initially appear as the triumph of the capitalist system, but ultimately provide the platform from which the final revolution would be launched. Lenin continues, "The socialist revolution that has begun in Russia is, therefore, only the beginning of the world socialist revolution. Peace and bread, the overthrow of the bourgeoisie, revolutionary means for the healing of war wounds, the complete victory of socialism—such are the aims of the struggle."

Hence the term "bread and peace" is often associated with Lenin's initial promise to the Russian proletariat, a slogan of inspiration to his followers, a mask for treason to his detractors. In either case, the promise of peace and bread speaks well to the basic needs of human beings recently propelled into any kind of conflict, let alone one so massive as WWI, and thus the power of the slogan to move the populace toward support of any regime that holds this promise.

Related Entries
ideology; socialism

Suggested Reading
Lenin, Vladimir Ilich. *Collected Works,* ed. Y. Sdobnikov and G. Hanna, Vol. 26. Moscow: Progress Publishers, 1972.
Lenin, Vladimir Ilich. *Selected Works in Three Volumes*, Vol. 2, ed. Y.Sdobnikov and G. Hanna. Moscow: Progress Publishers, 1970–1971.

Buber, Martin (1878–1965)
The most prominent and influential Jewish voice within the loosely defined circle of existential theologians and philosophers, Martin Buber is also a thinker of significant import for the study of contemporary political theory. Buber's interest in different forms of human association and how they are related to the development of the human person places him well within the same tradition as Christian figures such as Jacques Maritain and Reinhold Niebuhr, a tradition that blends modern philosophical thought, current ideological concerns, and traditional religious values in order to promote a more just political realm. Buber was deeply stirred by the Hasidic movement within

Judaism, as well as being well-read in and influenced by modern philosophers such as Kant, Kierkegaard, and Nietzsche. Devoted to his Jewish faith, Buber was also open to non-Jewish religious influences such as the Christian mystic Meister Eckhart, and he collaborated closely with scholars from both the Catholic and Protestant wings of Christianity. Owing to this broad-minded approach, Buber's writings hold a wide appeal reaching across several religious traditions and philosophical schools. Additionally, Buber provided a major impetus for the Zionist movement in the first half of the twentieth century, and the long reach of his ideas can still be felt today both within and without the Jewish community.

Buber's earlier work is suffused with a mystical impulse, one that was somewhat tempered in his mature, more socially oriented writings, but it nonetheless continued to characterize much of his overall project. This mystical impulse can be discerned in the framework of his concept of the "I-Thou" as contrasted against the "I-It." The latter represents the purely unreflective, mundane and quotidian relations that human beings experience throughout the course of their ordinary lives. It is a relationship that lacks transcendence and fulfillment, and in the end, is a sort of truncated and dehumanized condition. We see ourselves and our fellow human beings as things, understood through the pronoun "it," distant and objectified, superficial and lost in the background of the environment around us. The I-It is encased in the material and causal realm of phenomenal being, and less open to the transcendent experiences that can become available to us in real dialogue with both God and with other human beings. This higher dialogue inspires the renewing and fully human relationship of the I-Thou, a dramatic break from and contrast against the banality of the I-It.

Within the I-Thou relationship, human beings are interconnected to the divine and to each other in a substantively radical way. Rather than sustaining the one-dimensionality and superficiality of the I-It, we are able to devote our whole being in a deeper and more meaningful way as we engage in dialogue as partners and fellow humans with each other and with God. Indeed, as we move more thoroughly into the I-Thou experience of our shared humanity, our personal relationships with other human beings become reflections of our authentic connection to God. While God remains ever remote, He becomes intimately known to us through the I-Thou openness to the divine and to that part of our common humanity that is created in the Divine image. By fostering the other-directed and spiritual I-Thou relationship, the I-It can be overcome, and a new social, political, and cultural vision can be advanced.

Buber's contribution to Zionism is thus best understood through close attention to his concept of the I-Thou. Less political than most Zionists, (such as Theodor Herzl), Buber envisioned a new political and social life primarily rooted in a cultural Zionism. Not denying the need for political action, Buber reminds his readers that it is the historical dialogue with God that defines Israel above all. God is the eternal Thou, and Israel is first and foremost a partner in the conversation between the sacred and profane. Therefore it is through a return to and revival of the piety of Israel that Zionism can effect a worthwhile change for Jews as well as for all humanity. From the Hasidic tradition, this joyful piety will promote a community of love for human beings distinguished by drawing closer to God. For this reason, Buber cast his Zionism not only in terms that promoted the promise of a Jewish homeland, but also in ways that conceived of a Palestinian state shared jointly by Arabs and Jews, working together as a community of partners (I-Thou) rather than as irreconcilable antagonists (I-It).

In the end, Buber realized that to speak of genuine humanity is also to discover God, and in knowing God we come to affirm the unique and transcendent character of humanity. Once this dialogue between I and Thou becomes the rule for humanity, our political and social values and practices will follow naturally and promote a dignity and harmony for human beings that will exceed the limitations of the ideological mind.

Related Entries
existentialism; Herzl, Theodor; Maritain, Jacques; Niebuhr, Reinhold

Suggested Reading
Buber, Martin. *I and Thou,* trans. Walter Kaufman. 1970; repr. New York: Touchstone Books, 1996.

Burke, Edmund (1729–1797)

As with most thinkers of the first rank, Sir Edmund Burke defies labels. Generally regarded as perhaps the greatest conservative philosopher, Burke's political ideas and actions could at times be accurately described as ''liberal'' in the broader sense of that term, although such a label is used at the risk of anachronism. Indeed, for three decades, Burke was associated with the Whig party, and served intermittently and yet effectively as a leading Whig Member of Parliament throughout much of his adult life. Burke's political career was marked by his unconventional approach to issues, and punctuated by an oratorical skill far above his peers. Toward the end of his life, his identification with the Whigs was jeopardized by his biting criticism of the French Revolution, but he remained firm in his loyalty to what he deemed the older values of the Whig party, and never completely renounced his political identity for an alternative faction. Lee McDonald has aptly described Burke as one committed to a ''principled avoidance of systemization,'' thereby reinforcing the perception of Burke as ideologically elusive. Furthermore, on certain controversial issues, Burke assumed positions that were decidedly nontraditional for his times, and by later standards reasonably described as more liberal in inclination. Burke's economic views, for example, were aligned with Adam Smith and free market policies, an essentially liberal orientation. Additionally, Burke was an adamant defender of the rights and interest of Britain's colonies, in particular, his native Ireland as well as America

and India. His insistence upon justice for these corners of the empire placed him at odds with Crown and Parliament on numerous occasions. As Russell Kirk wrote, ''Burke the conservative was also Burke the liberal—the foe of arbitrary power, in Britain, in America, in India.'' Furthermore, in criticizing the court of King George III for its efforts in transforming the Tory Party into the part of the King's Court, Burke called for a closer relationship between government and the ''sentiments and opinions of the people.'' This is not to say that Burke embraced populism, but only to recognize an affinity with this aspect of Burke's understanding of the accountability of government and liberalism in general. Additionally, Burke also argued forthrightly for freedom of speech, thus sounding a critical note against traditional views on political obedience to institutional authority. Finally, owing to his upbringing (a Catholic mother, an Anglican father, an education influenced by Quaker and Calvinist elements), Burke, who saw himself as a devoted Christian and a nominal Anglican throughout his life, sympathized with a variety of Christian sects—Catholicism in particular—and thus adopted views of religious and cultural tolerance against the conventional wisdom of the day. Among Burke's early writings can be found his *Tracts on Popery Laws,* in which the young Anglican indicted British oppression of Catholics, a criticism that would, over time, weaken his political influence. Conor Cruise O'Brien, in his introduction to the Penguin edition of Burke's *Reflections on the Revolution in France,* aptly reviews the significance of Burke's Irish-Catholic background, and notes Burke's apparent detachment to Protestantism, in general accompanied by his open support of Catholic interests.

Burke's quasi-liberalism as a statesman and orator aside, conservatism supplies a more fitting description for his political philosophy. Burke championed the preservation of the ancient British constitution, arguing that loyalty and adherence to the ancient political inheritance of an illustrious past is essential for the protection of liberty and the deliverance of justice. Liberty and justice are not metaphysical abstractions; rather they are the legacy of a lawful political order carefully and gradually developed through centuries of unremitting effort and patient discovery. Liberty is thus an "entailed inheritance, derived from our forefathers and transmitted to our posterity." In other words, the tested wisdom of antiquity is a potent ground for the defense and promotion of a practical liberty, defined by law and limited by the "prejudices"—or commonsense proclivities—of culture. (These "prejudices" of which Burke spoke are not to be confused with our current identification of prejudice as irrational discrimination based on an unfair "prejudgment" or, in the worst case, raw bigotry.) In adopting this view in his *Reflections,* Burke challenged the initial infatuation with the French Revolution experienced by many of his peers, contemporaries, and friends. In particular, Burke rebuked Thomas Paine for his endorsement of the French Revolution, and set himself against the vision of egalitarian democracy that inspired not only Paine but a large segment of the intelligentsia in Britain and America, including his own Whig Party. Liberty is not to be snatched out of the rarefied air of metaphysical notions of "the rights of man," but rather, liberty is formed and affirmed through the accretive processes of law, tradition, and habit. It is only through established institutions and the proven currents of custom that liberty can be preserved and enjoyed. Once institutions, customs, and laws are abandoned, then liberty is quickly lost, or malformed into an impulse toward the reckless accumulation of power for its own sake.

For Burke, the French Revolution raised the specter of social leveling and the senseless demolition of the priceless resource of ancient culture and its tested values. It was as clear to Burke as to any other critic that French society was in need of reform, but such reform could only be successful by drawing upon the principles and practices of French culture. While Burke generally regarded revolution with disdain, he recognized that sweeping reform of a revolutionary nature could be adopted if one relied not upon arrogant presumption of a universal vision of the perfectibility of man, but rather on the deeper foundations of a society's particular expression of civilization. Precedent could be found in the Glorious Revolution of 1689 or the American Revolution of the 1770s–1780s, revolutions that reaffirmed existing liberties without embracing contrived ideals appealing to groundless abstractions. This is not to say that Burke adopted a contextualist view of political culture—a view that regards all regimes as somehow legitimized by their historical experiences. Rather, Burke's understanding of liberty is one that recognizes the necessity of freedom circumscribed by prudent experience and framed within an ordered and civilized structure. Without such delimitations, liberty deteriorates into will, and will tends toward a fixation with mere power.

Free societies are defined largely through the liberty of citizens to command their property. All "men have equal rights, but not to equal things," Burke averred. One's right to property was not a universal entitlement, but rather earned through one's own merit and sanctioned by the custom of the political obligations and social privileges of the landed. Without regard for the ownership of property, liberty loses its connection to the person, and is rendered hollow, purposeless, ungrounded. As with both liberals and other conservatives, the right to property is essential to the promotion of civil liberty. Reforms proposing the deliberate restructuring of property arrangements in the name of equality for its own sake menace the liberty of citizens and the value of the social order. In the attempt to produce a broader economic equality, liberty itself is hollowed of its personal nature, and thus loses a critical element of its meaning.

Liberty and equality are decidedly important principles in the development of just societies and the affirmation of political rights. But, liberty, equality, justice, and right cannot be either understood or applied without locating them in the context of tradition and prudent usage. Burke thus regarded the question of right to be linked not to principled abstraction, but rather to historical and cultural birthright. There are no rights of "man" in the generalized sense, but rather there are rights of Englishmen, rights of Frenchmen, the rights of Indians; rights developed and expressed through the legal and institutional practices and customs of a culture and nation. Burke believed that all human beings are meant to enjoy liberty, and that right as a principle ought to be affirmed in all societies. But he insisted on a difference between real values and intangible generalizations. We cannot fully understand our rights without knowing the cultural preconditions and historical circumstances from which they in fact arise. Rights do not descend from the ether but are instead the natural outgrowth of civilized community, and not just a community of the present, but a community that involves both ancestral wisdom as well as a culture's posterity. Burke referred to this notion of right as "prescription," an idea that affirms the achievements of the past as the proven and prudent ground for political order. Our rights are thus based on what exists in time, and not upon a mere idea or theoretical claim. Innovation for its own sake, or for the sake of an applied abstraction, militates against the nobler liberties grounded in the wisdom of a cultured and mannered past. Thus every generation is legitimized by the fact that we are born into a polity already given, and thus the practices and prejudices of that community form the substance of our rights as citizens. The French Revolution, in its detachment of the individual from the ancient community, irrationally and pridefully resists the hallowed values of the ancestral community. "Liberty, equality and fraternity" are empty words without the context of culture to define not only their deeper meaning, but also their relevance to citizens devoted to a given regime.

The principle of equality in operation under the banner of the Revolution also provoked a dismayed Burke's dissent. Human beings are equal, Burke would argue, but only so as equal creatures of God. This affirmed, hierarchy is the proper order of society, one based on a natural aristocracy not unlike that which was advanced across the ocean by John Adams and Thomas Jefferson. Natural aristocracy ensured sober and able leadership in contrast with the often capricious whims of popular government on the one hand and the unfounded privilege and questionable competency of artificial aristocracy on the other. Both kinds of government tended toward arbitrary exercise of power absent deliberation and calm direction, guaranteeing irresponsibility as well as inability among those holding power.

This belief in a natural aristocracy further influences his views on representation. According to Burke, Parliament is not a "congress of ambassadors" or deputies serving at the people's pleasure. Rather, Parliament exists to deliberate as a forum representing one nation, holding one common interest, and reflecting the good of the whole. All members of Parliament represent the nation in all its parts. To only speak for a district or segment would be to reduce membership of that august body to that of mouthpiece for the masses. Hence, while representative government is a right rooted in British values and traditions, it must be of the "virtual" kind, and not merely a collective of delegates from disparate regions. There is but one interest, and the natural aristocracy must represent that interest ably and objectively on behalf of the entire realm. Burke's notion of representation is not compatible with the practice of the representative who primarily speaks for a specific constituency.

Above all, Burke's approach to just and rational political order rests on his belief in a transcendent reality, and the attendant notion that society is formed not by human convention or even through a merely natural proclivity, but rather as the design of ineffable Providence. God's will moves unseen through society—an unfolding of divine purpose that spans centuries and provides the ultimate foundation for a legitimate and, above all, truly civil social order. We are created by God for society, and as time builds and hones our institutions, mores and practices, normative prejudices are formed that provide us with a prudent understanding of the real foundation of rights and morals. According to conservative scholar Russell Kirk, "This Christian orthodoxy is the kernel of Burke's philosophy." Radical innovation in politics and claims to rights and liberties absent a sense of divine sanction were, for Burke, the greatest danger in the rise of the modern political mind. And while he did not live to see the more turbulent and violent stages of the French Revolution, his suspicions regarding the Revolution's rejection of traditional religion were confirmed. Such a rejection, for Burke, was the surest indication of the triumph of incivility and impiety.

Alliteratively, one could summarize (albeit inadequately) Burke's overall political theory as embracing prudence, prescription, prejudice, piety, and Providential design. These are the basic elements of an understanding of society and politics that definitely marks Burke's conservatism, a conservatism that is set toward the liberal end of a society of free and thoughtful citizens.

Related Entries
conservatism; equality; liberty

Suggested Reading
Burke, Edmund. *Reflections on the Revolution in France,* ed. Conor Cruise O'Brien. 1968; repr. New York: Penguin Classics, 1984.
Burke, Edmund. *A Vindication of Natural Society,* ed. Frank N. Pagano. Indianapolis: Liberty Fund, Inc., 1982.

the butcher, the brewer, or the baker
A famous phrase in Adam Smith's *Wealth of Nations* asserting the principle of the primacy of self-interest as the most effective way to secure, without intention, the overall public good. A person, in Smith's assessment of human behavior, does not make choices based on anything other than tangible and immediate need or want, Hence, as Smith intones,

> man has almost constant occasion for the help of his brethren, and it is in vain for him to expect it from their benevolence only. He will be more likely to prevail if he can interest their self-love in his favor, and show them that it is for their own advantage to do for him what he requires of them.

Put simply, Smith recognizes the power of *quid pro quo* in human interaction, a perception of "scratching each other's backs," as it were. Smith continues as he pens his famous phrase,

> Whoever offers to another a bargain of any kind, proposes to do this. Give me that which I want and you shall have this which you want, is the meaning of every offer; and it is in this manner that we obtain from one another the far greater part of those good offices which we stand in need of. It is not from the benevolence of the butcher, the brewer, or the baker, that we expect our dinner, but from their regard to their own interest. We address ourselves not to their humanity, but to their self-love, and never talk to them of our own necessities but of their advantages.

Smith's observation is well known among champions and critics of both utilitarianism and libertarianism. Perhaps more importantly for contemporary political inquiry and social science in general, it serves as an underlying characteristic of human agents in the study of rational actors and game theory. One could even connect this notion, admittedly anachronistically but conceptually so, to certain aspects of social contract theory (developed prior to Smith's life and work), particularly as understood by Thomas Hobbes. That is to say, by applying Smith's view of human choice, certain tendencies in Hobbes's mutual transference of right might become clearer to readers regardless of their sympathies. Suffice it to say that Adam Smith's candid assessment of human motivation and purpose has always provoked debate, and will continue to do so as long as human beings continue to critically examine their inward nature.

Related Entries
invisible hand; liberalism

Suggested Reading
Smith, Adam. *An Inquiry Into the Nature and Causes of the Wealth of Nations,* 2 vols., ed. W.B. Todd. Indianapolis: Liberty Classics, 1976.

C

capillary power

In his examination of the nature of power as it has developed within modernity, Michel Foucault concluded that the old model of political authority based on a centralized sovereign is no longer applicable. Rather, for Foucault, power today is ubiquitous, no longer permanently located in one place within the polity, but dispersed unevenly throughout a central network marked by power nodes. In a sense, the king's head has been "cut off," meaning that the image of sovereignty that goes back to at least the Middle Ages, and was limned in its most compelling form in the early modern theories of sovereignty, especially as analyzed by Hobbes, no longer provides a useful or accurate description of the nature of power. It is more beneficial to now study power at "the extremes," in the capillaries in which power circulates as it moves throughout the entire social network. Power flows everywhere, Foucault held, at all levels and within all corners of society. It is not diffused, necessarily, as we can still speak of asymmetrical power within the matrix, and yet it is definitely dispersed and in circulation, no longer centralized or localized as it had been under, for example, a Medieval king or even Hobbes's conception of that "mortal god" *Leviathan.*

Owing to the ubiquity and capillary nature of power, Foucault argues that we are constantly under pressure. Power, though anonymous, is relentless, and it compels us, imperceptibly and insidiously, ceaselessly running the gamut of our activities. Every person is under the stress of power, is in fact a nodule of power, and thus is ever vulnerable to control and manipulation. But power also runs in two directions, and it is possible for individuals to tap into power and exert their own interest against that of the power network. Thus, while Foucault is alarmed at the way in which ubiquitous capillary power causes docility, he also recognizes that given the circulation of power through all levels and nodes of society, it is possible for individuals and groups to exert themselves if they are aware of their condition and the possibility for change.

However, a strong strain of pessimism should be noted in Foucault's argument. Capillary power is not only structurally different from earlier models; it is also different in a qualitative sense. With capillary ubiquitous power comes power over one's daily life that is basically unprecedented. Earlier kinds of sovereignty were partially defined by the sovereign's power over death. The sovereign would not necessarily be involved in an individual's life beyond a few necessities (mainly taxes and war), and hence even though political power would be concentrated and might become arbitrary, for the most part the average subject did not feel the presence of sovereignty. Capillary power means power over life, or biopower, a constant pressure applied on individuals at every turn, thus remolding them to serve an anonymous and shapeless system. Biopower produces docility, and docility enervates the political will, and hence in decidedly striking ways the political forces of a modern technological society are even more repressive than the more obvious types of sovereignty and authority experienced in the past.

Capillary power offers a different framework within which we can study power. Not the distant "common power that keeps all in awe" as in Hobbes, nor entirely the sterile bureaucracy of Weber (although it is possible for it to be both and not necessary to be either), nor the economically determined state of the Marxist, power in a real sense assumes its own life, erupts through the different nodes of the social net to the advantage of a few and the detriment of many, and yet is within reach of any citizen who can tap into its ever circulating currents. Through Foucault's capillary power, democracy can find both a harsh criticism of its imbalanced equilibrium and a hope that individuals outside the normal institutions of authority will engage positively in political action and reform.

Related Entries
biopower; carceral society; Foucault, Michel

Suggested Reading
Foucault, Michel. *The Foucault Reader,* ed. Paul Rabinow. New York: Pantheon Books, 1984.

carceral society
A concept developed by postmodern critic Michel Foucault to describe the pervasive encroachment of anonymous power through all dimensions of human society. Foucault argues that modern surveillance power and administrative manipulation have implemented Jeremy Bentham's panopticon (a type of prison structure designed by Bentham that enables prison guards and wardens to view all prisoner cells from one vantage point without themselves being seen) on a social scale so that all areas of personal life are potentially monitored and controlled. The carceral society is related to Foucault's understanding of modern power as primarily disciplinary, transforming the whole of our culture into a penal system. The model of the modern prison is but a microcosm of society as a whole; we are all incarcerated in subtle ways. We are all subject to the discipline of the faceless and ubiquitous power of modernity; all individuals in modern life are under the "normalizing gaze" of technocracy. Even the social sciences are participants in this process through the aspiration to impose "scientificity" on human behavior, thus contributing in the construction of a disciplinary apparatus that transforms human society into a macro-prison, a "carceral archipelago" that insidiously shapes the individual according to an arbitrary norm.

Foucault's critique provides an important discussion of the nature of power. To think of power along the old terms of visible sovereign and consensual citizens, or even loyal subjects, may no longer provide an accurate account of the dynamics of power in a postindustrial society. In this sense, a closer examination of Foucault's concerns is of benefit to any student of political inquiry unsure about the new shapes and forces of power in an age of rapidly expanding and expansive technology and forms of control.

Related Entries
biopower; capillary power; Foucault, Michel; panopticon

Suggested Reading
Foucault, Michel, *The Foucault Reader,* ed. Paul Rabinow. New York: Pantheon Books, 1984.

Catholic League (Holy League)
Responding to the ascending power of the Huguenots in France, the Catholic League was assembled in 1576 buttressed by the leadership of Henri de Guise. Smaller forerunners of the league were formed within the middle class throughout France as early as 1563, but it is with the support of de Guise and other nobles that the Catholic, or Holy League grew in influence. Unlike the moderate *Politiques* who opposed them, the Catholic League aimed at altogether eliminating Calvinist influence in France. Among the intellectuals who supported the Catholic League, the impassioned Jean Boucher (1551–1646) serves as the most visible example. Boucher and others within the Catholic League argued for a notion of sovereignty detached from the office of the monarch, for the problem of succession to potential Protestant heirs was uppermost in their minds during the religious conflicts of the sixteenth century. Boucher, for example, asserted that the people were in fact the true font of kingship, thereby reserving the right to depose intransigent monarchs when it was deemed necessary. Additionally, Boucher accepted the notion that the Pope held the same authority and could depose and coronate kings under his own authority.

While the Catholic League did sustain considerable influence in the latter half of the sixteenth century, it was the *Politiques* who came to enjoy a more enduring voice in the exchange of ideas regarding the character of legitimate sovereign power in the formation of early modern political thought.

Related Entry
Politiques

Suggested Reading
Konnert, Mark W. *Local Politics in the French Wars of Religion: The Towns of Champagne, the Duc de Guise, and the Catholic League, 1560–95.* Burlington, VT: Ashgate, 2006

Catholic social teaching

Catholic social and political ideas are as old as Christianity; hence we could begin a study of Catholicism and political theory from the founding of the church. Stemming from the Biblical moral principles, shared with Judaism, to foster compassion and mercy; care for the poor, the orphan, and the widow; and seek peace and the promotion of universal love, Christian concern for the improvement of the community and the fostering of egalitarianism is as old as the church itself. In Catholicism, this has been evident both in the practices of the monastic tradition reaching back to the origins of Christianity as well as in the various doctrines of the church advocating peace, mercy, hospitality, love for all (even one's enemies), and care for the poor and the ill. In addition to Christ and the Apostles and the early martyrs, figures such as St. Francis and St. Clare of Assisi as well as St. Catherine of Sienna represent examples of prominent individuals engaged in fusing Christian piety with social action. Within the tradition of normative political theory, several thinkers from within the church have contributed important elements to its development, in particular, St. Augustine of Hippo, St. Gelasius I, John of Salisbury, St. Thomas Aquinas, and the efforts of the Salamanca School during the fourteenth through sixteenth centuries.

Modern social thought within the church, however, is usually traced directly to the 1891 Papal Encyclical issued by Pope Leo XIII, *Rerum Novarum.* This encyclical proved to be a pivotal document in Catholic political thought, reviving interest in the natural law theories of St. Thomas Aquinas as well as influencing a number of intellectuals and activists such as the great twentieth-century neo-Thomist Jacques Maritain; Emmanuel Mounier (who, along with Maritain, defined and promoted the doctrine of "personalism"); Catholic Worker Movement founders Dorothy Day and Peter Maurin; several recent popes such as Pope John XXIII, Pope Paul VI, and Pope John Paul II; author and activist monk Thomas Merton; and probably most notably Blessed Mother Teresa, among numerous others. Pope Leo XIII's teaching promotes an active attempt to apply Christian principles of love and peace in the social and political realm by encouraging a greater effort to improve the lives and opportunities of society's disadvantaged and disaffected. Concern for the poor is central to Catholic social teaching, and while it is not the only tenet advanced in this encyclical, it is a primary focus. Pope Leo XIII criticized modern society for the manner in which poverty had been allowed to continue, but he was equally suspicious of ideological solutions offered by both the left and the right. This critique of modern ideologies has been sustained throughout the church's social teaching, with popes and bishops condemning the excesses of capitalism, socialism, libertarianism, fascism, and other more militant or fanatical political worldviews. Social justice must be sought and realized, according to the church, but all simplistic and zealously held political solutions are incapable of promoting true justice for all. Indeed, as Pope Pius XI once wrote, capitalism and socialism are both dangerous when taken to their extremes, nothing less than the "twin rocks of shipwreck."

In addition to continuing focus on the plight of the poor, Catholic social teaching today includes a number of causes. Respect for the sanctity of human life is an essential principle—leading to a critique of what Pope John Paul II has referred to as the modern "culture of death." Abortion, capital punishment, and war (although just wars are still recognized) are all condemned as examples of this tendency to profane the value of human life. Social solidarity, economic justice that rejects both the collectivism of communism and socialism as well as the *laissez-faire* principles of capitalism, and the dignity of work are also key tenets of Catholic social teaching today. Popes and bishops have also challenged wealthy nations to take responsibility for improving the economic conditions and opportunities of poorer nations, exhorting responsibility among the more fortunate countries and their citizens.

Additionally, in more recent years Catholic bishops have condemned the proliferation of nuclear weapons and those military strategies that incorporate the threat of mass destruction as a deterrent. More recently still, Catholic bishops, along with a growing voice within the various Protestant denominations, have recommended a greater sense of stewardship for the environment, recognizing this as a charge for the care of Creation that has been held by human beings from the beginning. Finally, Catholic social teaching includes the political doctrine of subsidiarity, which encourages the value and practice of localized self-government. According to this teaching, democratic governance can only occur at the local level, and thus the more responsibility given to small communities the better. Hence, while the centralized and hierarchical ecclesial organization of the church relies on the authority of the Magisterium, the political organizations most consistent with Catholic social teaching tend toward decentralization.

Related Entries

Catholic Worker movement; Maritain, Jacques; personalism; subsidiarity

Suggested Reading

Hornsby-Smith, Michael P. *An Introduction to Catholic Social Thought*. New York: Cambridge Univ. Press, 2006.

O'Brien, David, and Thomas Shannon, eds., *Catholic Social Thought: The Documentary Heritage*. Maryknoll, NY: Orbis Books, 1992.

Schall, James V. *Roman Catholic Political Philosophy*. Lanham, MD: Lexington Books, 2004.

Catholic Worker movement

First established in 1933 during the Great Depression, The Catholic Worker movement was directed at affirming the primacy of human rights, promoting the interest of labor, initiating economic cooperatives at the local level, providing emergency care for the disaffected and unemployed (such as housing and provisions of food and clothing), and adhering to nonviolent social reform aimed at enduring peace. The movement was primarily led by Dorothy Day, a devout convert to Catholicism (1897–1980). Day, along with Peter Maurin (1877–1949), the radical inspiration for Day and a cofounder of the movement, attempted to blend religious devotion and moral imperative with social justice. Day saw the Catholic Church as the church of the poor and the immigrant, and devoted herself to putting the principles of Christian compassion into daily practice. The movement began in New York city, quickly expanded to over 30 Catholic Worker communities by mid-decade, and eventually grew to today number over 180 fully autonomous communities.

For Day, through mercy and nonviolence, religious piety can be directed to the improvement of the entire community, and especially of the disadvantaged (the workers, the poor, the homeless, and the unemployed). Hence Day and the Catholic Worker movement represent an important cohort within the greater imperative of social justice that has been a feature of Catholicism since its ancient birth and more formally adopted by the church hierarchy in the 19th and 20th centuries. The Catholic Worker movement is thus another example of that element within Christianity engaged in social and political reform. Given their spirit of autonomy, each Catholic Worker community is different, but in general they reflect the radicalism of their founders, Day and Maurin.

Related Entry
Catholic social teaching

Suggested Reading
Zwick, Mark, and Louise Zwick. *The Catholic Worker Movement: Intellectual and Spiritual Origins.* Mahwah, NJ: Paulist Press, 2005.

checks and balances

The political institution of "checks and balances" is essentially a governmental system designed to prevent the abuse of power by harnessing it through dispersal and equilibrium. Power is dispersed and shared within separated branches of government, with each branch holding enough power to check the ability of other branches to achieve predominance. The principle of dispersed power set in equilibrium through a system of mutual checks is a hallmark of constitutional government and republican institutions. "Power must be a check to power," penned the Baron de Montesquieu, the most celebrated proponent of checks and balances, and must be set in counterpoise as a guarantee against its corruption into tyranny. Before Montesquieu, Machiavelli employed the term "checks and balances" in his prescription for republican government in *The Discourses.* As a theoretical principle, the notion of separation of powers and checks and balances is not only ancient but widely endorsed, and as a practice the method of dispersed power for the sake of preventing its abuse is common throughout political history.

Checks and balances through the separation of powers is generally associated with modern political theory, and for good reason, as the more familiar features of this concept were for the most part developed in the seventeenth and eighteenth centuries. However, the practice of separated power precedes the writings of modern theorists, and one can even trace the conceptual heritage to classical political theory, long before the efforts of Montesquieu and James Madison. Plato's *Laws* is marked by

an intricate network of separated power, combining the dispersal of authority throughout the regime in various offices and governmental bodies as well as a broadly shared power across classes and tribes encompassed within the greater *polis.* Aristotle also features a scheme of divided power in his constitutional polity as described in his *Politics.* The example of republican Rome is often depicted as an ancient forerunner of the separation of power, with power divided and shared between the two major classes (patrician and plebian) and through a variety of distinct offices and administrative functions that grew increasingly more complex as the republic expanded and gained in influence throughout the Mediterranean. Polybius celebrated the prudential insight of this Roman institution in his discussion of mixed regimes, the embrace of which would be emulated by the great Roman statesman, orator, and philosopher of the late republic, Cicero. For both Polybius and Cicero, republican Rome had achieved perfection through the division and blending of power, ensuring its vigor while checking its excesses. It was only with the ascent of the empire that Roman checks and balances wavered, and some would argue that even under imperial Rome with its deification of emperors a tradition of checked power endured, somewhat attenuated, but occasionally reasserted. By the Middle Ages, the notion of checks and balances through the separation of mutually opposed power in the West was an ancient practice, however imperfectly conceived and still more imperfectly applied.

Medieval political institutions, while hierarchical by our standards, were less centralized and at various times more balanced than modern students of politics usually realize. Absolute monarchy was a greater reality in the ancient world and, ironically, in the post–Medieval world than it was during the Middle Ages. Kings held limited power, and were often regarded as *primus inter pares* among the nobility. Formal advisory bodies, such as the Anglo-Saxon Witan (Witenagemot) and the Norman

Curia Regis, the various courts that advised powerful nobles in Medieval Spain and culminated with the Cortes of the Kingdoms of Castile and Leon, and the gradual growth of the authority of the French parlements anticipated the sharing of power that would later emerge in full bloom in more modern legislative bodies led by the English Parliament. The Icelandic Althing, dating back to the tenth century, might also be included as an early example of dispersed power, although not technically a separation of powers as the Althing held both legislative and judicial functions. Perhaps the best example, as Montesquieu himself noted, of the separation of powers and checks and balances in the European tradition was the gradual division of power between Crown and Parliament within the English tradition. Often buffeted and even battered by the struggle for supremacy between the branches—a struggle that ultimately resulted in civil war—the English system settled into a working example of power dispersed and set into a system of mutual checks.

By the seventeenth century, English political theory was reflecting the legitimacy and desirability of this practice. English theorist James Harrington embraced the "mixed government" established by "the ancients, and their learned disciple [Machiavelli]," and the separated mutually checked power that this implies. John Locke in chapter twelve of his *Second Treatise* observed the need to disperse the legislative power and place it "into the hands of divers persons," owing to the "temptation of human frailty, apt to grasp at power." Furthermore, Locke remarks favorably on that tradition, already long established, to separate the legislative power and executive power. Scottish philosopher David Hume wrote, "The government which...receives the appellation of free, is that which admits of a partition of power among several members." Harrington, Locke, and Hume all recognized an existential connection between free government and the balanced dispersal of power. The great French thinker Montesquieu, however, is rightly known as the preeminent theorist

advocating the separation of powers and checks and balances, and it is from his *Spirit of the Laws* that all modern notions of dispersed power receive their intellectual legacy.

In the *Spirit of the Laws,* Montesquieu establishes the essential principles of the practice of checks and balances that would later be adopted in the American Constitution. It is evident, Montesquieu reflects, that "every man invested with power is apt to abuse it, and to carry his authority as far as it will go." Neither democracy nor aristocracy, both of which are pure types of regimes, are in themselves "free states by their nature." The tendency to abuse power is not checked in either form. For Montesquieu, "political liberty is found only in moderate governments. But it is not always in moderate states." Therefore a reliable and effective method of containing power and preventing its abuse must be imposed on any political society. The method that Montesquieu recognizes as the most efficacious is the setting of power against itself, "To prevent this abuse, it is necessary from the very nature of things that power should be a check to power." By using power against itself, liberty is preserved and virtue promoted within a balanced and moderate republic.

Montesquieu looked to the Constitution of England as his closest example of the theory of checks and balances put into practice. In so doing, he identified "in each state" three separated "sorts of powers: a bicameral legislative power, executive power over the things depending on the right of nations, and executive power over the things depending on civil right." The latter he calls the "power of judging," or judicial power, "exercised by persons drawn from the body of the people" independently of the legislature and distinguished from the executive power proper (which is the power to make "peace or war," guard against invasion, and to dispatch and receive ambassadors). This triad of power is the conceptual pattern developed by the American Founders, who knew the author of the *Spirit of the Laws* as nothing less than the "oracle Montesquieu."

As stated above, the Montesquieuian notion of checks and balances entered into the political grammar of the American founding. Founding authors such as John Adams and James Madison were firm in their conviction that republican government is the only medium to promote liberty, and, as such, the separation of power and checks and balances are essential parts of any free government. The framing of the United States Constitution embodies this ideal, and serves as evidence of the value placed on moderate government within the American political mind. Today the notion of power separated and limited through checks and balances is familiar throughout those nations that embrace liberal democracy and constitutionalism, a concept so firmly entrenched as to be a given in the formation of societies premised on the ideal of self-government.

Related Entries
Federalist Papers; Harrington, James; Hume, David; Machiavelli, Niccolò; Madison, James; Montesquieu, Charles-Louis de Secondat Baron de la Brede et de la

Suggested Reading
Hamilton, Alexander, James Madison, and John Jay. *The Federalist Papers,* ed. Clinton Rossiter and Charles Kessler. New York: Mentor Books, 1999.
Montesquieu, Charles-Louis de Secondat Baron de la Brede et de la, *The Spirit of the Laws,* trans. Thomas Nugent. New York: Hafner Press/Macmillan, 1975.

Cicero, Marcus Tullius (106 BC–43 BC)
Statesman, lawyer, orator, and philosopher, Cicero is the most important political theorist between Aristotle and St. Augustine, and the preeminent commentator on politics in the Stoic tradition. A student for a time of the Greek Stoic Poseidonius, Cicero has sometimes been described as not fully within the Stoic orbit. The influence of Plato is certainly pronounced as well, but it is a fair assessment of his overall worldview to place him in the compass of the Stoic tradition, particularly that period of

Stoicism referred to as "middle Stoicism" under the influence of the "Scipionic Circle" (which may or may not have actually existed). In any event, it is evident from Cicero's writings, particularly his views on natural law, that he was at least influenced by Stoic ideals, if not a purely Stoic sage himself. As a man of worldly affairs, philosophical purity was perhaps a luxury unavailable to him.

Natural law and the essence of justice is a principal theme in Cicero's more philosophical writings. In his *Republic* (or *On the Commonwealth,* a work that in many ways emulates Plato's *Republic*), Cicero orchestrated a dialogue between those who hold to a view of justice as conventional (through the voice of Philus), and those who discern in justice a universal and objective essence (Laelius). In the voice of Laelius, Cicero reveals his own beliefs,

> There is in fact a true law—namely, right reason—which is in accordance with nature, applies to all men, and is unchangeable and eternal....Its commands and prohibitions always influence good men, but are without effect upon the bad. To invalidate this law by human legislation is never morally right, nor is it permissible ever to restrict its operation, and to annul it wholly is impossible....It will not lay down one rule at Rome and another at Athens, nor will it be one rule today and another tomorrow. But there will be one law, eternal and unchangeable, binding at all times upon all peoples; and there will be, as it were, one common master and ruler of men, namely God, who is the author of this law, its interpreter, and its sponsor.

In the *Laws,* Cicero adds the following observation,

> Law is not a product of human thought, nor is It any enactment of peoples, but something eternal which rules the whole universe by its wisdom in command and prohibition. Law is the primal and ultimate mind of God, whose reason directs all things either by compulsion or restraint.

Hence for Cicero there is a natural justice that governs the world. It is implanted in all human beings by nature and is the only real standard to discern the difference between the just and the unjust. Indeed, as Cicero states in his *Laws,* "Justice does not exist at all if it does not exist in Nature." The skeptical doctrine of Carneades that rejects natural law and natural justice is, for Cicero, a monstrosity. All human beings are bound to universal and enduring principles of justice, and thus all human statutes and customs can only be legitimate if they are in harmony with justice itself. Justice is deeply rooted in our nature; it is not a mere product of judgment or will. In this sense, Cicero relies heavily on Stoic universalism, and echoes the more distant ideas of Plato and Aristotle.

A common theme among all Stoic philosophers is the essential moral equality of all human beings. As all things are interconnected through their participation in rational Nature, each person is fundamentally equal, even though certain social and political inequalities are to be tolerated with typical Stoic resignation. Still, there exist, according to Cicero, a basic element of equality in all human beings, their social status notwithstanding.

> [T]here is no difference in kind between man and man; for if there were, one definition could not be applicable to all men; and indeed reason, which alone raises us above the level of the beasts. . . [is] common to us all. . . . In fact, there is no human being of any race who, if he finds a guide, cannot attain to virtue.

As a Stoic thinker (or at least a philosopher influenced by Stoicism), Cicero's focus was also drawn to the nature of virtue. As justice is lodged deeply within our nature, human beings are inclined toward virtue, and need only the proper education and civil institutions to draw out their natural goodness. For Cicero, in addition to this natural tendency toward justice shared by all humanity, there are four kinds of moral goodness that apply to the human person as such: dignity, the contemplation of truth, a sense of order and self-restraint, and the awareness that one should despise what is false or insincere. These are the elements of character for Cicero, which, when carefully aligned, will ensure the development of a kind of citizen prepared to perform duty in the pursuit of the common good. Duty is a central Stoic virtue, and it is through the right instruction in character that one learns to recognize and follow one's duty.

The highest commitment to duty is in the life of public affairs. As indicated above, the contemplation of truth, which is the province of philosophy, is an aspect of moral goodness and always beneficial to building the character of the virtuous person and the dutiful citizen. Thus philosophy is a noble calling, one that is to be prized by the best kind of men. However, the life and work of the statesman is nobler still, and Cicero's model of virtue is not the philosopher of Plato, but the wise statesman who is schooled in philosophy; a man focused on performing his duty for the common good. Commitment to public service through participation in government and law, for Cicero, is the best kind of life for the most virtuous person.

Cicero's notion of the best regime is borrowed from the earlier writings of Polybius, which itself looks back to the influence of both Plato (especially *Statesman* and *Laws*) and Aristotle. Following Polybius, Cicero identifies three simple types of legitimate regimes: monarchy, aristocracy, and democracy. Through the voice of Scipio (in his *Republic*), Cicero remarks that of the simple types, monarchy that follows its "proper nature" is the best as it is able to establish more effectively "permanent authority, the sense of justice, and the wisdom of a single individual [who can] control the safety, the political equality, and the peace of the citizens." Nonetheless, even a monarchy for all its benefits can "deprive the people of many blessings" and, as with any simple type of regime, eventually expose its instability. Hence Scipio (Cicero) affirms the principle of the mixed regime, following the lead of Polybius before him, holding that "the best constituted state is one which is formed by the due combination of monarchy, aristocracy, and democracy." A combined regime is most in tune with the character of human beings, who are by nature political and thus need to engage in public affairs on wide scale, but are also better fit to do so with the right mixture of lawful authority to provide the necessary order. Cicero envisioned the political sphere as a "commonwealth" (*res publica,* or the things public) that was structured in such as way as to encourage civic participation balanced by a respect for the structure of authority.

> The commonwealth, then, is the people's affair; and the people is not every group of men, associated in any manner, but is the coming together of a considerable number of men who are united by a common agreement about law and rights and by the desire to participate in mutual advantages. The original cause of this coming together is not so much weakness as a kind of social instinct natural to man.

As with Polybius before him and Machiavelli long after him, Cicero adopts as his model the example of republican Rome as the best case for the rule of law and the balancing of interests, and because Rome is an actual city (in contrast with Plato's theoretical paradigm), a study of its history and institutions can provide for us the key to a just commonwealth. Cicero does not want to found a "city in speech" or even a "second-best city" that approximates it, for as a man of public affairs he naturally looks to his experiences and culture for the ideal that he seeks.

One other facet of Cicero's political thought may prove of interest to modern readers, and is certainly important in the development of political criticism. As with Aristotle before him and St. Augustine and St. Thomas Aquinas (both of whom acknowledged their debt to Cicero, or "Tully" as he was referred to by St. Thomas Aquinas), Cicero was concerned with the question of just war, and when a war could be waged according to reason rather than from the desire to conquer or out of revenge. As Cicero states,

> Wars are unlawful which are undertaken without a reason. For no war can be justly waged except for the purpose of redressing an injury or of driving out an invader. No war is to be held lawful unless it is officially announced, unless it is declared and unless a formal claim for satisfaction has been made.

Cicero insists that war should only be waged to secure a greater peace, and if waged at all, it should be done with a view toward mercy, especially to those enemies who have not been "blood-thirsty and barbarous" in the conduct of their aggression. Interestingly, Cicero does allow for a "superior people" to justly conduct aggression against those who are "inferior." His own Rome is an example of a "superior people" (due to their culture, institutions, and valor). Clearly on this point Cicero undercuts the consistency of his higher principles in an attempt to maintain the integrity of his model republic.

Cicero's political philosophy has been variously received. Some regard him as a secondary figure, more orator and lawmaker than philosopher. Others consider him a major figure, and while not as seminal as Plato or Aristotle, nonetheless an important thinker in his own right and one whose influence is underappreciated. One thing is certain: whether as statesman, orator, advocate, or theorists, Cicero's name has endured through the centuries, and he remains a compelling study, for good or ill, of the meeting of intellect and power.

Related Entries
justice; natural law; Seneca, Lucius Annaeus

Suggested Reading
Cicero, Marcus Tullius. *On the Commonwealth,* trans. G.H. Sabine and S.B. Smith. Indianapolis: Library of Liberal Arts/Bobbs-Merrill, 1977.
Cicero, Marcus Tullius. *De Re Publica, De Legibus,* trans. C.W. Keynes. Cambridge, MA: Harvard Univ. Press/Loeb Classical Library, 1977.

Circle of Power

The Circle of Power is an ancient Iranian concept incorporated into Islamic political theory during the ninth century, an innovation that was primarily the contribution of Ibn-Qutaiba (828–889) of Baghdad. Ibn-Qutaiba was a leader in the synthesis of the Arabic foundations of Islam with the cultural and philosophical legacy of ancient Persia. Drawing from this Persian tradition, Ibn-Qutaiba conceived of the political realm as a cycle of interdependency. Human beings as political and social creatures depend equally on four elements: property, cultivation, justice, and good government. To illustrate this and draw the connection between Islamic theology and the pre-Islamic ethics and folklore of Persia, Ibn-Qutaiba cited, as Antony Black instructs us, a *Hadith* (or Report—a teaching delivered by Muhammad independent of the *Qur'ān*) of Muhammad, to wit:

> The relation between Islam, the ruler and the people is like that between tent, poles, ropes and pegs. The tent is Islam, the pole the ruler, the ropes and pegs the people.

Hence the whole of society is interdependent, not unlike the notion of Medieval organicism that characterized European Christendom prior to the Renaissance. Political power, economic exchange, and religious leadership are all arcs on this circle, each one needing the other, finding its locus in the teachings of the faith.

The Circle of Power would continue as an important concept throughout the development of Islamic political thought, often bearing close resemblance to similar ideas in Christian polities such as the organicism mentioned above. For al-Ghazali (1058–1111), the Circle of Power was a Circle of Knowledge, and as Black cites, al-Ghazali described it as a tight relationship between all aspects of society. "[G]overnment educates the labourers; the prophets educate the *'ulama* [the Learned, the Religious Guides]; the *'ulama* educate the rulers; and the angels educate the prophets." In this and other ways, the notion of the Circle of Power would reappear frequently throughout the writings of students of politics within the Islamic tradition, particularly at its zenith during the Middle Ages. The Circle of Power evinces the nuanced approach to politics that characterized much of Islamic political scholarship during this era. As Black concludes,

The greatest number of [Islamic] original thinkers were active between about 800–1100, at a time when Islam was the most creative culture in the world. In its springtime, Islamic political thought and culture looked more promising than the West's. The idea of the Circle of Power suggests a sophisticated understanding of political society.

For Black, Islamic political thought accomplished its greatest achievements during this era through ideas such as the Circle of Power. In his view, "[Islamic] political thought has remained in many respects unaltered since the eleventh century."

Related Entries
al-Ghazali; organicism; two-swords doctrine

Suggested Reading
Black, Antony. *The History of Islamic Political Thought: From the Prophet to the Present.* New York: Routledge, 2001.

circulation of elites

Developed by Vilfredo Pareto (1848–1923), the concept of the circulation of elites describes a law-like tendency throughout any political or social system not only to generate and rely upon elites, but to replace them constantly, either gradually or through revolutionary disruption, within a cyclical pattern of ascent and decline. Pareto, as with other elite theorists, concluded that every social organization or human association naturally produces elites, the ideological conceptions or institutional structures that motivate and frame a political community notwithstanding.

For Pareto, regardless of the formal structure and principles that frame and animate any given regime, elites will be drawn toward small circles of leadership. Even democracies produce and depend on elites in spite of the genuine belief in the principles of popular sovereignty and self-government. Elites are a natural part of any human association, and particularly political associations, but they are not fixed and are vulnerable to social cycles that constantly adjust the basic hierarchies within any community.

Both governing and nongoverning are necessary, but the actual participants within these higher strata of society tend to change owing to a variety of social and political forces. Every ruling class will decline; it may occur slowly, over generations or, in more traditional societies, centuries, but the descent is unavoidable just as the ascent of new elites pushing upward is inexorable within any social or political system. According to Pareto,

> Aristocracies do not last. Whatever the causes, it is an incontestable fact that after a certain length of time they pass away. History is a graveyard of aristocracies....They decay not in numbers only. They decay also in quality in the sense that they lose their vigor...[and those qualities] that enabled them to win their power and hold it.

And Pareto continues,

> In virtue of class-circulation, the governing *elite* is always in a state of slow and continuous transformation. It flows on like a river, never being today what it was yesterday. From time to time sudden and violent disturbances occur. There is a flood—the river overflows its banks. Afterwards the new governing *elite* again resumes its slow transformation. The flood has subsided, the river is again flowing normally in its wonted bed.

Pareto conceives the cycles of society as tending toward what he calls "social equilibrium," a condition always characterized by the fact that minorities will hold power in various ways and exercise it to various degrees. While elites will always govern humanity as a general rule, the particular varieties are numerous and dependent on social circumstances and the needs that arise out of diverse situations. There will at times be a need for elites to be strong as lions, and other times when they must use the cunning of the fox. Now the speculator is needed, at another time the "*rentier*" (or land owner who controls the resources of a territory or population). The middle and lower classes will be subordinate only for a time. Eventually, the upper class will lose its will, competence, and ability to sustain its own legitimizing myths and hence its superiority, while energy and drive will shift to lower classes who no longer hold the old loyalties to the traditional leadership and renew ambition from within their segment of society, thus reconfiguring the structure of power in either a gradual evolution or through upheaval. Social change cannot be reduced to the consequence of "class struggle," the tendency of society toward rationalization, democratic enlightenment, or Providence. Rather, societies change and their political institutions along with them as elites change, a change that Pareto regards as certain in its basic pattern, but widely varied in its distinct manifestations.

Pareto, along with Robert Michels, Gaetano Mosca, and Guido Dorso, is a principal figure in the development of what is called elite theory. The circulation of elites is a fundamental rule adopted throughout this branch of political theory, and continues to remain compelling for social scientists today. Since the 1970s, many college freshmen and sophomores cut their first teeth as students of political science on the famous statement from Thomas Dye and Harmon Ziegler's *Irony of Democracy,* to wit—"It is the irony of democracy that the responsibility for the survival of liberal democratic values depends on elites, not masses." This statement typifies the spirit of elite theory, and effectively illustrates the patterns of power as described by Pareto in his concept of the circulation of elites.

Related Entries
circulation of elites; iron law of oligarchy

Suggested Reading

Curtis, Michael. *The Great Political Theories,* vol. II. New York: Avon Books, 1981.

Dye, Thomas R., and L. Harmon Zeigler, *The Irony of Democracy: An Uncommon Introduction to American Politics,* 3d ed. Belmont, CA: Duxbury/Wadsworth, 1971.

Pareto, Vilfredo. *The Mind and Society,* 4 vols., ed. Arthur Livingston and trans. A. Livingston and Andrew Bongiorno, 1935; repr. New York: AMS Press 1983.

city fit for pigs

The phrase "city fit for pigs" comes from Plato's *Republic,* Book. II, from the character of Glaucon, a young companion of Socrates and Plato's brother. Socrates discerns a city in theory in his attempt to answer the question of the nature of justice in city and soul, and, more importantly, to prove that living a life of justice is always preferable to one of injustice. Glaucon objects to what he perceives to be a spare city, one that secures nothing but provender for its citizens, and is in his view a city that is only "fit for pigs." Socrates does not agree with Glaucon's criticism, but concedes his young companion's point, realizing that by considering Glaucon's insistence on a "luxurious city," that is, a city that provides "unnecessary needs," we might be able to more fully understand injustice, and in the process, arrive at a stronger conception of justice and a better case for always choosing the life of genuine justice over injustice. It is Glaucon's dismissive "city of pigs" remark that initiates the discussion by Socrates of the guardians, their life, their education, and ultimately, the need for rule of reason in all cities.

Related Entries
Plato; *Republic,* The (*Politeia*)

Suggested Reading
Plato. *Complete Works,* ed. John M. Cooper. Indianapolis: Hackett, 1997.

city upon a hill

The phrase "city upon a hill" has come to be associated with the belief that America serves the ascendant role of a model nation for all humankind to emulate in some way, or to follow in the progress toward a civilized democracy. This attitude is traced to the earliest years of the British colonies in North America, specifically to a speech by Puritan eminence John Winthrop while on board the sailing ship *Arabella* just before landfall in what is now Massachusetts Bay. Lifting the phrase from Scripture (St. Matthew), Winthrop intoned

We must entertain each other in brotherly affection. We must be willing to abridge ourselves of our superfluities, for the supply of others' necessities. We must uphold a familiar commerce in all meekness, gentleness, patience and liberality. We must delight in each other; make others' conditions our own; rejoice together, mourn together, labor and suffer together, always having before our eyes our commission and community in the work, as members of the same bond of peace....For we must consider that we shall be made a city upon a hill. The eyes of all people are upon us.

Winthrop was specifically addressing the aspiration of his followers toward the realization of a true Christian community in the wilderness, one wherein the teachings of the Gospel were put into practice in every dimension of private and public life. Over the years the phrase has carried the additional meaning of the American polity as a model for freedom offered for the entire world, "an asylum for mankind" (Thomas Paine, 1776), "the last best hope " for the practice of self-government (Abraham Lincoln, 1861), and implied in the realizable dream of Martin Luther King Jr.'s stirring Lincoln Memorial Address in 1963. The theme of a city upon a hill was again explicitly evoked by Ronald Reagan in his 1974 Address before the Conservative Political Action Committee, wherein he quoted both Winthrop's phrase from his *Arabella* speech as well as referring to Lincoln's "last best hope" sentiment by way of conclusion. To further punctuate this notion, Reagan directly quoted Pope Pius XII, to wit, "The American people have a great genius for splendid and unselfish actions. Into the hands of America God has placed the destinies of an afflicted mankind."

These sentiments, ranging from thinkers as diverse as Thomas Paine and Pope Pius XII, reflect a frequently reappearing theme centered, rightly or wrongly, on the notion that America stands in a unique position in history and thus is somehow responsible for the common improvement of humankind. It is in this sense that America is still regarded by many as a "city upon a hill," perhaps no longer seen as exceptional and thus mandated by God for the promotion of democracy throughout the world, but nonetheless a nation charged with a singular responsibility for the cause of justice for all humankind.

Related Entry
Protestant Reformation and political thought

Suggested Reading
Morgan, Edmund S., ed. *Puritan Political Ideas, 1558–1794.* Indianapolis: Hackett, 2003.

civil disobedience

Civil disobedience is best summarized as a peaceful refusal to obey laws considered to be unjust; a direct and deliberate but nonviolent act in violation of the law risking punishment by the legal authorities. When one is required by the state to follow an unjust law, one is morally obligated to disobey that law, even if it means incurring a legal penalty such as a heavy fine or, more to the point, a term of imprisonment. It is better to openly and peacefully but firmly oppose a law and meet the jailer than it is to obey a law that is inherently immoral. This is, in short, the essence of civil disobedience as an act of civil resistance to oppression.

Civil disobedience is firmly rooted in the tradition of Western political theory, reaching back at least to the ancient Greeks as depicted in the play *Antigone,* written by Sophocles in the fifth century BC. The Stoic thinker Cicero remarked that laws passed by human legislators are morally bound to follow the universal principles of the natural law, and St. Augustine affirmed the principle that an unjust law is "no law at all," and thus does not require our obedience. Thus the notion that a law that is against the moral laws of God and nature, or an unjust law, is not in fact true law has been fully known since the beginnings of political theory. However, civil disobedience as a political strategy is more commonly associated with the growth of modern democratic protests, not confined to the West but rather practiced against perceived oppression throughout the world.

Perhaps the most instructive and simultaneously familiar proponents of civil disobedience are Henry David Thoreau, Mohandas K. Gandhi, Martin Luther King Jr., and Cesar Chavez. Thoreau's nineteenth-century essay, *On the Duty of Civil Disobedience,* identifies the nature of the act and sets the tone for subsequent advocates and activists well into the twenty-first century. Thoreau argues that one must always follow one's inward moral conscience, and never allow the power of the state nor the pressures of society to coerce one into committing or sanctioning injustice. Inveighing against the unjust laws and institutions of his times that supported or allowed slavery, Thoreau intones that if the government and its laws demand that you act against moral principle, " [T]hen I say break the law. Let your life be a counter friction to stop the machine." One must always act from principle, regardless of the opinions of the public or the degree of consensus supporting oppressive measures. "[A]ny man," Thoreau concludes, "more right than his neighbors, constitutes a majority of one.". Moreover, the truly just person will openly reject, personal consequences notwithstanding any society that is sustained by or invested in unjust laws or immoral policies. "Under a government which imprisons unjustly, the true place for a just man is also in prison."

These sentiments are also stirringly reaffirmed in the actions of twentieth-century activists such as Gandhi, King, and Chavez, among others. For King, in his prophetic "Letter from a Birmingham Jail," the entire Western tradition is drawn on to advance the cause of racial integration through the direct and public strategies of civil disobedience. Forthrightly, King writes to his fellow clergymen who are sympathetic with the cause of civil rights but troubled by the tactics of civil disobedience,

> You express a great deal of anxiety over our willingness to break laws. This is certainly a legitimate concern. Since we so diligently urge

people to obey the Supreme Court's decision of 1954 outlawing segregation in the public schools, at first glance it may seem rather paradoxical for us consciously to break laws. One may ask: "How can you advocate breaking some laws and obeying others?" The answer lies in the fact that there are two types of laws: just and unjust. I would be the first to advocate obeying just laws. One has not only a legal but a moral responsibility to obey just laws. Conversely, one has a moral responsibility to disobey unjust laws. I would agree with St. Augustine that "an unjust law is no law at all."

Thus, for King, to tolerate or obey an unjust law is an immoral act. Better to break the unjust law and face prison than abide it and allow others to suffer as you go free.

In Chavez's "Delano Statement," the principles of civil disobedience are expressed to equal effect, focusing on the personal dimensions of sacrifice that invites suffering for the liberation of one's fellow human beings.

When we are really honest with ourselves we must admit that our lives are all that really belong to us. So, it is how we use our lives that determines what kind of men we are. It is my deepest belief that only by giving our lives do we find life. I am convinced that the truest act of courage, the strongest act of manliness is to sacrifice ourselves for others in a totally nonviolent struggle for justice. To be a man is to suffer for others. God help us to be men.

Related Entry
satyagraha

Suggested Reading
King's "Letter from a Birmingham Jail" is available in *A Testament of Hope: The Essential Writings and Speeches of Martin Luther King, Jr.,* ed. James M. Washington. San Francisco: HarperSanFrancisco, 1991, among numerous other sources.
Thoreau, Henry David. *Collected Essays and Poems.* Library of America, 2001.

communism

Communism in the broad sense connotes any social arrangement wherein the interest of the community and those of individuals are deemed identical in every aspect, and in particular, wherein the property and all material resources are held in and cared for in common. Communism is thus an amplified form of communalism, one that regards the common as bearing supremacy over the private, and that fosters a strong sense of unity between the individual members of any given association. It is not, as is often interpreted, necessarily statist, for most communist theory envisions a form of association that is not guided by the formal political structures that are framed around a state. However, communism is also not necessarily anarchistic, for there is ample room for some kind of political direction, whether or not it stems from an actual regime.

Communism as a principle can be detected early in the tradition of political thought. In some ways, the ideal city in Plato's *Republic* resembles a kind of communism in that its aim is to fuse the interest of the guardians with that of the public good, and in so doing, abolish the ownership of private property among the guardian class. What the guardians own, in Plato's explanation of the ideal, is spare and only held in common. Another example of an early form of communism might be found throughout the Middle Ages in various religious communities that espoused a simple, communalistic lifestyle eschewing the ownership of private possessions. During the English Civil War in the mid-seventeenth century, radical religious communities such as the Levellers and Diggers embraced communist or quasi-communist views regarding the common ownership of property and the egalitarian nature of the community. In other words, the term communism in general can be fairly applied to ideas and movements antecedent to the image of communism that we are accustomed to today. That image invariably bears the visage of Marxism.

Communism in this sense of the term denotes a specific theory and practice of revolutionary thought and activity, couched in the language of dialectical materialism and aimed at the abolition of all private property and, ultimately, at the elimination of the need for political institutions such as the state. Although we rightly think of communism as attempted in the old Soviet Union and its satellites, Karl Marx's vision of communism is more vague, and not necessarily fully realized in the Soviet state (a fact that does not disqualify Soviet statism from being a type of communism in the more general, and what some would call, a more deviant form, but it does disqualify the Soviet state from serving as an example of pure Marxian theory in application). For Marx, there are basically two types of communism, the first, a "crude" and "vulgar" communism that depersonalizes the human individual and, rather than abolishing capital, simply universalizes it by making everyone a worker and servant of an overarching, dehumanizing system. Such a description from Marx (written in 1844) indeed reminds one of the types of communism that emerged in the twentieth century, particularly in places like the Soviet Union. But Marx also identified another type of communism that he referred to as "authentic" or "genuine" communism, which he comprehended as not only the abolition of all private property, and hence of all classes, but also as the reconciliation of all internal contradictions found within society as a whole, even contradictions that reach into the nature of being, thus resolving the tension between the subject and the object, essence and existence. This authentic communism, for Marx, is cryptically the "riddle of history and knows itself to be so."

Authentic communism remains a vague ideal for Marx. He attempts to clarify what it would be in *The German Ideology,* wherein he describes a kind of society that does not truncate the labor power of the individual by coercing her or him into one occupation, but a society that allows a person to be many things— hunter, fisher, poet, and critic. This is the ability to fully command one's own labor power, which for Marx is the essence of communism, the abolition of alienated labor within a community that defines freedom in the most universal terms. Marx's vision of communism is basically incompatible with the ideology as practiced by his epigones, one that requires a fundamental change in the nature of human association as we know it, and ultimately, in the nature of humanity itself.

Other theories of communism have also emerged, such as the anarcho-communism of theorists such as Petr Kropotkin and Mikhail Bakunin. For the most part, though, they are substantively approximate to the ends that Marx sought, a society that reconciles every human being to the universality of humankind and that ground the meaning of a free person on the requirements of a free humanity.

Related Entries
anarchism; Marx, Karl; *Republic,* The; socialism

Suggested Reading
Fried, Albert, and Ronald Sanders, eds. *Socialist Thought: A Documentary History.* New York: Doubleday/Anchor, 1964.
Marx, Karl, and Friedrich Engels. *The Marx-Engels Reader,* 2nd ed., ed. Robert C. Tucker. New York: Norton, 1978.
Vincent, Andrew. *Modern Political Ideologies.* Oxford: Blackwell, 1995.

complex equality

A principle that operates in Michael Walzer's concept of distinct spheres of justice, complex equality is his attempt at reconciling the notion of equality with the reality of a pluralistic society that pursues various goods, all of which are prized for different values. Every good is the focal point of a set of relations developed around how a certain good is valued, and these diverse sets of relations are configured along different conceptions of just distribution. What is a just distribution in one sphere (such as the sphere that is anchored by the good of wealth) would be an unjust distribution in another sphere (such as one that is anchored by power). The patterns of distribution in the sphere of wealth should have little to no bearing on the sphere of power, or the political sphere. In other words, inequalities that might occur fairly (within limits) in the sphere of wealth should not convert to inequalities in power, any more than differences in beauty or piety or athletic prowess should convert to advantages in other spheres. Different spheres will only be just according to different patterns of distribution, some tending toward full equality, others admitting some inequality. The pattern of any one sphere cannot convert to an unfair advantage or disadvantage in another sphere. In other words, equality is complex rather than a simple equality that attempts to equalize dominant goods across society in the same way, following a homogenous model of equal distribution. The disparate classes of goods that animate their separate spheres cannot be similarly treated if we are to achieve any real justice in a pluralistic society (and most democracies are pluralistic). Hence complex equality is just that, a notion of equality that allows life to remain complex, and the various distributions of the things we value to admit of this complexity.

Complex equality is explained within the context of the distinction Michael Walzer draws between dominance and monopoly, as well as in his concept of the open-ended distributive model.

Related Entries
dominance and monopoly; open-ended distributive principle

Suggested Reading
Walzer, Michael. *Spheres of Justice*. New York: Basic Books, 1983.

consequentialism

Consequentialism refers to a family of moral theories that measure moral acts primarily or exclusively on the consequences, or results, of the action in question. Simply put, if an act or series of acts produce a beneficial result or good consequence, the determination of whether or not said acts are moral is to be considered primarily or perhaps even solely in that light. This is contrasted with a view to moral action that examines other aspects, such as the intent of the agent or the intrinsic value of certain acts independent of human measure.

In political theory, the prototype for consequentialism as a serious approach to moral and political questions is generally regarded to be Machiavelli, who advocated judging actions by their outcomes (or according to some translations, "the end justifies the means"). Good intentions or the desire to always be good is insufficient in the political realm, but the only standard (in cases where there is no other appeal) of measuring the justification of an act is in the end achieved or the outcome produced. Whether or not this is a reasonable standard for practical politics or the legitimization of pernicious policies is a matter of debate, but all told, Machiavelli's political theory is essentially consequentialist.

Utilitarianism, or the principle that moral and political actions should seek to secure the "greatest happiness (or good) for the greatest number," is far and away the most prominent consequentialist approach within the tradition of political theory. This approach emphasizes the maximum expansion of pleasure and the contraction of pain as the best way to secure happiness for individuals, both privately and publicly. Thus moral principles and political policies are to be valuated based on the outcome of the greatest happiness for the greatest number, the actual act itself bears no intrinsic value nor is grounded in any principle independent of the actual result. So, if act x or policy y increases the overall happiness of an individual or group of individuals, it is deemed ethically valid and politically sound. The substantive content of the act is deemphasized in proportion to the efficacy of its application.

One might argue that this inevitably leads to at best a self-absorbed hedonism and at worst a dangerous relativism that can justify any means should the desired end be achieved. And, like many theories, under the manipulative direction of a tyrannical personage, such an admonition raises a genuine alarm. But a consequentialist theory like utilitarianism recognizes the value in avoiding such dire prospects, for happiness is measured in multiple ways, and not simply in an abstract outcome that could be used to justify pernicious acts. While consequentialism, like any theory, might contain imperfections and inconsistencies, the worst acts are not necessarily justified to produce an allegedly ideal end.

Related Entries
absolutes; advantage of the stronger; Machiavelli, Niccolò; utilitarianism

Suggested Reading
Darwell, Stephen, ed. *Consequentialism.* Oxford: Wiley-Blackwell, 2002.
Scheffler, Samuel. *Consequentialism and Its Critics.* New York: Oxford Univ. Press, 1988.

conservatism
Conservatism as a general category of political thought encompasses a variety of complex and often disparate schools of thought, social prescriptions, philosophical projects, and political movements. According to Andrew Vincent, the term conservative was coined in the 1820s by French Romantic François-René de Chateaubriand. Use of the term soon followed in Britain, supplanting Tory as the name designating the party of tradition. As with liberalism and other broadly described conceptual frameworks, conservatism eludes succinct definition and thus cannot easily be encapsulated. Unlike liberalism, though, conservatism is not as easily identifiable as a coherent historical development. For all its own diversity, the appearance and growth of liberal political theory is more readily traced. But conservative ideas and sentiments regarding the political world are not so easily charted. Conservative approaches to understanding society and politics seem to range further than liberalism within the history of ideas. As Lee McDonald has stated, "There will be 'conservatives' even in societies where the term 'liberalism' has no meaning."

Hence conservatism, whether it is viewed as an abstract political theory or as a purposive ideology, does not lend itself to easy analysis, let alone explication. In the popular use of the term, conservative connotes traditional values, cultural unity qualified by an appreciation of social heterogeneity, indifference to majority opinion, restrained but effective government, a political realism informed by the acceptance of human imperfection, and limited practical applications of public policies. And yet, while these elements represent themes common to conservatives of various types, they are not adequate to a fuller understanding of what Russell Kirk (1918–1994) called "the conservative mind," a mind that includes an array of thinkers ranging from the great Whig statesman Edmund Burke, often regarded as the intellectual grandfather of modern conservatism, to the likes of Chateaubriand, Sir Robert Filmer, John Adams, Joseph de Maistre, Lord Acton, Benjamin Disraeli, Otto von Bismarck, George Santayana, Henry Adams, Oswald Spengler, Walter Lippman, Herbert Hoover, Winston Churchill, Charles de Gaulle, William F. Buckley, Harry Jaffa, Ronald Reagan, Jeanne Kirkpatrick, George Will, and Jerry Falwell, among others. Each of these thinkers, while holding certain qualities in common, nonetheless stand apart from any generalized depiction of their own views and values.

Michael Oakeshott (1901–1990), in his 1956 essay "On Being Conservative," described conservatism as a "disposition" rather than a "creed or doctrine." "To be conservative," Oakeshott explains, "is to be disposed to think and behave in certain manners; it is to prefer certain kinds of conduct and certain conditions of human circumstances to others; it is to be disposed to make certain kinds of choices." As a disposition, conservatism, for Oakeshott, lends itself to the formation of certain characteristics that "centre upon a propensity to use and to enjoy what is available rather than to wish for or to look for something else; to delight in what is present rather than what was or what may be." In other words, for Oakeshott, the conservative disposition is neither nostalgic nor utopian, but a proclivity toward embracing what is, and patiently working through difficulties rather than investing in elusive promises for sudden and exhaustive social improvement. The conservative disposition, according to Oakeshott, thus is not a set of agendas or a grand plan defined by specific reforms, but rather "an appropriate gratefulness for what is available." In this sense, conservative thought is disinclined to cohere around a set of prescriptions for a better future but rather more likely to recognize the importance of drawing up the cultural and material resources that are here and now.

Kirk, in affirming the notion of "social conservatism" as fundamentally "the preservation of the ancient moral traditions of humanity," identifies in his work *The Conservative Mind* six principles that frame political thought for the balance of conservative thinkers. First, conservative thought for Kirk adheres to a "belief in a transcendent order." Thus "political problems...[ultimately] are religious and moral problems." Implicit in this understanding is the recognition of natural law and the principle of universal justice. But the existence of natural law is not to be construed as the imposition of cultural uniformity across the human race. Rather, as the second principle avers, one should resist such "logicalism," as Robert Graves called it, and embrace with affection the "proliferating variety and mystery of human existence." Belief in transcendent order and its laws cannot be translated into a desire to apply one principle or set of principles to deliberate improvement of the human condition. Third, as the universe is ordered, so is the social world; thus civilization rests on the fact of order and hierarchy. Society should reflect natural distinctions, and the attempt to eliminate them would be to risk control by unnatural and unjust oligarchies. All humans are equal before God alone; society depends upon a certain degree of inequality for the sake of maintaining civilized order.

The fourth principle stems from the third: given the requirements of order and the necessity of hierarchy, "economic leveling" produces artificial and illegitimate power structures that impair human freedom rather than ensure progress. For the conservative, according to Kirk, "freedom and property are closely linked," thus the proclivity to protect private interests when confronted by the designs of the state. Fifth, Kirk states that conservatism invests its "faith in prescription and distrust of 'sophisters, calculator, and economists,'" bent on redesigning society according to abstract theories. An adherence to tradition and cultural integrity provide a vital check against the "innovator's lust for power" and the fools gold of social engineering. Finally, Kirk recognizes that conservatives are not ossified in the past, but rather are open to "salutary reform" made not out of the passions of the moment, but through the prudent actions of statesmen who "take the [will of] Providence" into account. Hence conservatism, for Kirk, is not simply about reverence for the past at the expense of any beneficial changes, but rather, the conservative mind seeks to reform without dismantling the inherited wisdom and achievements foundational to civilized society.

Poised against the catalog of conservative principles, Kirk indicates a variety of disparate schools and movements, among them are numbered the rationalist *philosophes* of the French Enlightenment; the romantic impulse that reacted against Enlightenment rationalism, typified by Rousseau; "Benthamite" utilitarianism, positivism, collectivism, socialism—in particular Marxism; and Darwinism. For Kirk, each of these movements in some way erodes the conservative principles of tradition, reverence, and place and thus promotes a false progress that actually militates against the true flourishing of civilized society.

Kirk and other students of political theory characteristically point to the eighteenth-century philosopher-statesman Edmund Burke (1729–1797) as the greatest of conservative thinkers. A complex thinker, Burke's political philosophy does not lend itself to concise description. Nonetheless, to understand Burke one can begin with three basic values: prudence, prescription, and prejudice. Prudence, for Burke, is the exercise of practical wisdom, a kind of commonsense reasoning that rejects attachment to abstractions and generalized laws applicable to all human beings. Prescription describes Burke's belief that there are indeed political rights, but that they are not empty platitudes appearing *ex nihilo* in the same way for all humanity. Rights exist, but are the product of cultural experience and effort. Rights are based on truth, but truth as gradually discovered through tradition and trial, not through the proclamations of political or religious reformers and revolutionaries. Prejudice, for Burke, does not denote what it does for twenty-first century Americans. Rather, prejudice represents cultural proclivities that guide us toward the preservation of those manners and customs requisite to civilization. To overhaul such conventional attitudes can provoke barbarism, the opposite of what is intended by reformers of good will but unrealistic expectations for rapid improvement. Burke did not reject reform out of hand, but he insisted on political change based on tested institutions and historically rooted values. For Burke, radical revolutionary movements that abruptly promise the instantaneous construction of newer and more just societies guarantee barbarity rather than meaningful improvement.

Given the diversity within conservatism as both philosophy and political disposition, it is helpful to turn to Anthony Vincent's "fivefold classification" of conservative thought. According to Vincent, conservatism is divided into five basic branches: traditionalist, romantic, paternalistic, liberal, and New Right. Burke epitomizes the traditionalist branch, characterized by its fidelity to custom, ancient values, and tested institutions. Romantic conservatism, a branch populated by, among others, many German philosophers and British poets, celebrates rustic pastoral societies as its ideal while lamenting the loss of civility and a sense of the mystery of life as the cost of industrialization and the rise of a technologically driven society. Romantic conservatism regards the Medieval concept of chivalry as the standard for decency within society. Closely related to traditionalism and romanticism, Vincent identifies aristocratic paternalism as a third

branch, one that regards the state as duty-bound to promote a decent life for its citizens and thus is more inclined to propose moderated governmental activity toward that end. This branch of conservatism is critical of the excesses of unregulated free markets, and while defending the bedrock belief in the right to property and free commerce, nonetheless reacts with contempt to the more mercenary attitudes of unbridled capitalism. Unlike liberal movements that share similar concerns, paternalistic conservatism eschews democratic progressivism, preferring to entrust the fostering of the common good through the leadership of committed elites.

Vincent's "liberal conservatism" resembles in many ways what is sometimes called "classical liberalism," a revealing terminological quirk that is a consequence of the shifting nature of ideological development. Liberal conservatism/classical liberalism champions the primacy of the economic sphere, and in so doing, advances the ideals of minimal state regulation of the economy and the expansion of the private realm. The most efficient and fair means of distributing the material goods of society, for the liberal conservative, is through the private choices and activities of individuals freely engaged in expansive commerce. Much of what we call conservatism today is defined in this way, and for the modern student of politics, this concentration on uninhibited markets and the expansion of the free, economic person translates into "fiscal" free-market conservatism in today's political jargon. From liberal conservatism, according to Vincent, a fifth and more contemporary conservatism emerges, to wit, the New Right. Embracing the same belief in the minimal state and free markets, the New Right is equally defined by its resolute stand against totalitarianism. Hence the New Right is a hybrid of state minimalism regarding economic activity and vigorous state activism in response to the Cold War. Hence individual self-reliance and duty to one's country are equally valued by the New Right, the former insisting upon personal initiative and individualistic diversity, the latter requiring a shared, collective, and patriotic resolve.

Additionally, conservatism, particularly in the United States, has over the course of the past three to four decades been defined by two disparate attitudes regarding the role of government in the direction of social policy. "Fiscal" conservatism remains a compelling position among conservatives as a whole due to its commitment to a decentralized state and streamlined government. And yet, this conservative belief in a minimal state has been challenged since the early 1970s (and perhaps earlier as some would trace this disposition to the 1950s) by the equally conservative commitment to social and moral issues. "Social conservatism," by contrast, endorses state regulation that encourages or protects the moral fiber of society. In the view of social conservatives, controversies revolving around state-sanctioned abortion, the role of religion in the public sphere, and sexual mores justify a more vigilant and active role for government. Social conservatism is often, but not necessarily, identified with religious fundamentalism, particularly the activist fundamentalism of the last thirty years. It is not unusual to adopt both a minimalist approach to government when addressing economic policy and an activist approach to government when criticizing what is perceived by many conservatives as the erosion of traditional cultural norms and healthy social mores.

Both impulses, while appearing contradictory, do typify two important and consistent strains throughout the various types of conservatism: the necessity of culture and the value of a unified community (social conservatism) and the importance of individual responsibility and self-reliance (fiscal/economic conservatism).

Above all, conservative political philosophy and practice represents certain tendencies that are natural to human beings regardless of their ideological loyalties or particular interests. A need for rational order in the world, the longing for place, an appreciation of common sense, and the desire for cultural continuity are characteristics shared by humans as such, and thus

will ever rest as the foundation for and motivation toward conservative ideals.

Related Entries
aristocracy; Burke, Edmund; equality; *Federalist Papers*; liberalism; libertarianism; natural law; What is conservatism?

Suggested Reading
Kirk, Russell. *The Conservative Mind,* 7th ed. Lake Bluff, IL: Regnery Books, 1986.
Vincent, Andrew. *Modern Political Ideologies.* Oxford: Blackwell, 1995.

conspicuous consumption

A term coined by the idiosyncratic economist, philosopher, and social critic Thorstein Veblen, conspicuous consumption is a modern manifestation of what Veblen described as pecuniary emulation—which is in itself regarded as a means to amplify one's status and good repute within a given community. There was a time in history when a reputation was won through war, or when leisure was accorded to only the nobility and the clergy. Now, however, the "leisure class" is identical with those who are dominant in the accumulation of things pecuniary, and reputation and standing in society are signaled by the ability to great wealth without any purpose other than the mere spending of it. The greater the expense and the more frivolous the object consumed, the more conspicuously consumers assert their dominant status.

Conspicuous consumption is the mark of membership in the leisure class and thus evidence of a high level of accomplishment and status in society. One can demonstrate one's affiliation with the leisured and landed through openly consuming without need, thereby proving one's superiority within the socioeconomic matrix. If one only consumes what one needs, one cannot display one's pecuniary strength. Indeed, the purest mode of conspicuous consumption is to spend wastefully, to "burn money" on the most unnecessary and ephemeral products. In this way one achieves the greatest display of the inexhaustible resources that one might have in their command, and thus displaying his or her ultimate social worth.

In Veblen's assessment, pecuniary emulation and its more visible manifestations (conspicuous leisure) can be traced back to predatory aggression. Those with the strongest predatory instincts would eventually establish the warrior culture of primitive societies, and in so doing ensure their position on top of the ancient hierarchies. Warriors are now gone, but the wealthy bear the same impulse to dominate and control, and as with warriors who increased their reputation through victory, the rich ensure their status through an open, hedonistically unrestrained, and opulent style of life. More than the drive for profit or the industry of the work ethic and any attendant assurances, it is consumption without stint or reason that is the root of economic activity. Even Aristotle's distinction between acquisition of things for use and acquisition of things as an end in itself does not, for Veblen, fully explain the motivation for ever-expanding wealth. Acquisition for the sake of endless consumption is in Veblen's conclusion the only factor that really lubricates the economies of the most affluent industrial societies, a lubricant that at root is the residue of the most primitive of instincts for complete domination.

Veblen's theories are less well known than those of Aristotle, Adam Smith, or Karl Marx, but they continue to snap us back to a realization that human nature is in most cases far more complex than social scientists are often inclined to admit. Whether or not Veblen's conclusions are insightful and educative today is another issue, but in either case, Veblen's approach provides considerable stimulus for further consideration of the diverse emotions that motivate human beings.

Related Entries
Marx, Karl; *Politics*

Suggested Reading
Veblen, Thorstein. *The Theory of the Leisure Class,* ed. Martha Banta. Oxford: Oxford World Classics, 2007.

constructivism

Constructivism (not to be confused here with the educational theories of psychologist Jean Piaget) is a theory of knowledge that understands our truths and basic ideas of the world as the product of human thought and shared language, and not reflective of an objective reality. What is objectively real is not what human beings understand as real, for our reality is constructed by our activities as thinking agents. Truth is not discovered, meanings not found; rather, our truths and ideas and the meaning that we invest in them are functions generated contextually. There is no corresponding reality that is the ground of our truths. Knowledge does emerge from our encounter with the world, but not because we can discern objective truth in that world—only because as our minds interact with our environment and the conditions predetermined by our social life-world we produce our own mental and moral conceptions of what we take to be real. Thus constructivism is contrasted against correspondence theory, which posits a notion of truth as rooted in an objective structure.

Related Entries
conventionalism; correspondence theory

Suggested Reading
Berger, Peter L. and Thomas Luckmann. *The Social Construction of Reality: A Treatise in the Sociology of Knowledge.* Garden City, NY: Anchor Books, 1966.
Dewey, John. *The Philosophy of John Dewey,* ed. John J. McDermott. Chicago: Univ. Chicago Press, 1981.
Searle, John. *The Construction of Social Reality.* New York: Simon & Schuster, Inc, 1995.

content of their character

A now-familiar line from Martin Luther King Jr.'s famous "I Have a Dream" speech (Address before the Lincoln Memorial, August 29, 1963), this phrase has come to symbolize the highest aspirations of democracy, a society wherein a person is only assessed on who they are rather than how they appear to others. The notion reaches back at least as far as Socrates and Plato (see the second book of Plato's

Republic wherein Plato considers the importance of the essence of a person's soul rather than the superficial physical attributes with regard to the political abilities of women), runs through Stoicism, Christian political theory, and notions of meritocracy associated with American founders such as John Adams and Thomas Jefferson), and has been held as a central tenet of the democratic notion of political and social justice. The entire phrase was uttered by King as follows,

> I have a dream that my four little children will one day live in a nation where they will not be judged by the color of their skin but by the content of their character.

In a real sense, this brief affirmation encapsulates the personal dignity requisite of any civilized society, but one that is both particularly poignant and absolutely essential for the promotion of a democratic polity. King's phrase reminds the thoughtful of the necessity of abandoning stale prejudices and the irrational exclusion of minorities from the political, social and cultural benefits of society at large. The phrase promotes replacing them with a community that fosters a respect for all citizens from the assumption of equality, and encourages the further advancement of each member of the political community by an appeal to the ancient desire for a virtuous citizenry. Here we find the confluence of the egalitarian foundation of democracy and the ethical aspirations of the ancient *polis,* brilliantly delivered through one sentence contained within one of the most universally inspiring speeches in history. While King's legacy is far more significant and complex to be aptly summarized in one line of one speech, the ideal expressed through these words nonetheless not only represent the noblest ideals of the American civil-rights movement but also captures the highest hopes of the spirit of human community.

Related Entries
the ballot or the bullet; equality; I have a dream; justice

Suggested Reading
King's "I Have a Dream" speech is available in *A Testament of Hope: The Essential Writings and Speeches of Martin Luther King, Jr.,* ed. by James M. Washington. San Francisco: HarperSanFrancisco, 1991, among numerous other sources.

conventionalism (constructivism)
Conventionalism loosely describes those concepts that regard political principles and moral values as wholly depending upon the cultural norms or "conventions" of a given social order. There is no standard for truth, meaning, or the legitimacy of values beyond the internal structures, mores, and consensual agreements of society. Hence principles of justice, right, and the good are rooted in the legal and moral agreements of a given community, and not in an external standard that transcends a particular association. A political theory that adheres to this view understands political and moral values as contingent and evolutionary, a function of culture and the arrangements of institutions. An example of a conventionalist view would be Michael Walzer's statement that "justice is a human construction," or a "social construct," or something that is constructed by consensus within a particular community. For example, in a democracy, the maxim *vox populi, vox Dei* is the epitome of the conventional attitude.

Related Entries
advantage of the stronger; constructivism; correspondence theory; Machiavelli, Niccolò

Suggested Reading
Berger, Peter L. and Thomas Luckmann. *The Social Construction of Reality: A Treatise in the Sociology of Knowledge.* Garden City, NY: Anchor Books, 1966
Dewey, John. *The Philosophy of John Dewey,* ed. John J. McDermott. Chicago: Univ. Chicago Press, 1981.
Searle, John. *The Construction of Social Reality.* New York: Simon & Schuster, Inc, 1995.

correspondence theory
Related to moral realism, correspondence theory holds the view that for anything to be

true it must correspond to the facts of an external reality and is thus not a function of perspective alone. Correspondence theory embraces the notion of an objective ground for knowledge and values that is independent of human judgment and evaluation. Rooted in the classical tradition of Plato and Aristotle and forwarded by Medieval philosophers, the correspondence theory of truth rests on transcendent foundations and first principles antecedent to human judgment. However, correspondence theory is also descriptive of certain kinds of empiricism. Factual experience as the test of truth is also a type of correspondence theory, although one that departs dramatically from the order of reality as conceived by thinkers such as Plato and St. Thomas Aquinas. In this sense the quantitative methods of "hard" political science and the metaphysical systems of the classical theorists share a common belief that truth is not constructed, but rather corresponds to a reality that is not wholly constructed by human judgment or will.

Related Entry
absolutes

Suggested Reading
Alston, W.P. *A Realist Conception of Truth.* Ithaca, NY: Cornell Univ. Press, 1996.
Aristotle, *Metaphysics,* trans. Richard Hope. 1952; repr. Ann Arbor: Univ. Mich. Press/Ann Arbor Paperbacks, 1960.
Plato's *Cratylus,* in Plato, *Complete Works,* ed. John M. Cooper. Indianapolis: Hackett, 1997.
Searle, John. *The Construction of Social Reality.* New York: Simon & Schuster, 1995.

cost as the limit of price

Josiah Warren subscribed to a labor theory of value similar to John Locke and Adam Smith before him (and Marx after him). Warren's theory advocated a free and unfettered exchange of goods based solely on the value of labor invested in their production. Profits, or any other measures based on what price the market will bear, are inherently flawed, according to Warren. Ultimately, his vision was to

create an economy based on a kind of mutualism involving the exchange of labor as the index of value, and not goods. He instituted the Cincinnati Time Store, a retail store based on promises to perform labor in exchange for commodities. Hence, commodities were valued in terms of how much labor would be needed to produce a certain good. For example, one hour of labor might be equated with a certain quantity of corn or milled flour. The principle was to insure that no one's labor was exploited for the profit of another, but that goods and the real amount of labor that produced them were the only true basis of a fair economy.

Related Entry
anarchism

Suggested Reading
Warren, Josiah. *Equitable Commerce.* 1852; repr. New York: B. Franklin, 1967.

critical theory

While it is accurate to say that philosophy by its very nature is a critical endeavor and thus the method of sustained criticism of society can be identified at least as early as Protagoras and Socrates, "critical theory" in the formal sense as a school of analysis can be directly traced to Karl Marx's eleventh thesis on Feuerbach, which reads "Hitherto philosophers have only interpreted the world in various ways; the point, however, is to change it." This is the essence of the concept of *praxis,* or the fusion of philosophical inquiry and political commitment into the same activity. Critical theory is thus revolutionary, emancipatory, and subjectivist in its approach to both culture in general and politics in particular. It is an attempt to construct a radical analysis and critique of all established institutions and ideologies, and to move beyond them through the liberation of political and social life from the iron cage of domination, control, and instrumental reason.

Critical theory can be spoken of as having experienced two different waves within a larger movement. The first wave has its roots in Marx, but also combines ideas provided by Kant, Hegel, Nietzsche, Freud, Weber, phenomenology, and existentialism. Closely associated with the Frankfurt School, a group of continental philosophers who were critical of both the liberal-capitalist/imperialist West as well as the vulgar Marxism of the statist East (namely the Soviet Union), critical theory emerged in the 1920s and 1930s as an attempt to return radical philosophy to its humanistic roots. To do this, critical theory, even though it emerges to a large extent out of basic Marxian principles, must undergo a criticism of all philosophical and ideological perspectives, including the various strains of Marxism itself. This involves the exposure of "false consciousness" and a return to authentic philosophical activity through the suspension of assumptions. All institutions are potentially repressive—even those that are erected by the left, and especially those that are the product of the right (much of what we take to be the first wave of critical theory was written as fascism was on the ascent), and must be challenged by free and uncompromising criticism.

In his book *The Emergence of Dialectical Theory* (1984), political theorist Scott Warren delineates five basic elements of this wave of critical theory. First, critical theory is oriented toward practice, interested in the "practical transformation" of the social world and the general improvement of humanity as a whole. This occurs through the rehabilitation of the lost dialectical method (a legacy of Hegel and Marx), and the application of this method to uncover the inherent contradiction within modern society, both capitalist and state socialist. Second, critical theory rejects "disinterested or neutral research." It is impossible to undertake research without some investment in human improvement; hence there is no "value-neutral social science." Third, critical theory cannot investigate social or political phenomena in isolation, for "critical theory is concerned with the totality of all aspects of social life." Hence, a positive social science that isolates phenomena is incomplete. Fourth, critical theory is essentially historicist, thus no

understanding of current social forces can be achieved without a deeper inquiry into sociohistoric context, and, finally, "critical theory is radical *and* foundational. That is to say, we can discern basic elements at the foundations of society, but to do so requires a devotion to "get to the root," as Marx would say.

The second wave (or sense) of critical theory moves away from the Frankfurt School origins; adopting the deconstructionist methods of the postmodern thinkers (Derrida, Lyotard, and, above all, Foucault). This wave of critical theory rejects all foundationalism, finding even radical theory to be a contingent narrative. Nonetheless, in spite of its antifoundationalist claims, the postmodern wave of critical theory does embrace its own premises, beginning with the "incredulity toward metanarratives" and ending with a resistance to forms of dominance with which the Frankfurt critical theorists would definitely appreciate.

Related Entries
dialectical theory; Foucault, Michel; Habermas, Jürgen; incredulity toward metanarratives; Marx, Karl

Suggested Reading
Jay, Martin. *The Dialectical Imagination*. Boston: Little Brown and Company, 1973.
Warren, Scott. *The Emergence of Dialectical Theory: Philosophy and Political Inquiry*, 1984; repr. Chicago: Univ. Chicago Press, 2008.

culture of death

The "culture of death" was identified by His Holiness Pope John Paul II in his encyclical *Evangelium vitae* (1995) to describe those practices and moral issues that in his judgment and according to the moral principles of Catholic Christianity violate the sanctity of life. For the Pope, speaking in behalf of the Magisterium of the Church, practices such as abortion, euthanasia, poverty, capital punishment (although the church does recognize the qualified legitimacy of its rare use in the most extreme cases in accordance with practices of particular cultures), and wars waged for unjust reasons.

The "culture of death" is a principle compatible with the philosophy of personalism, advanced by thinkers such as Jacques Maritain and Emmanuel Mounier and embraced in the writings of the late Pope. The life of the person is of immeasurable value, and any policy or practice that reduces the dignity of the person or treats human beings as simply material individuals to be manipulated by power participates in the culture of death.

Related Entries

Aquinas, Thomas; Catholic social teaching

Suggested Reading

Pope John Paul II, *The Gospel of Life: Evangelium Vitae.* Boston: Pauline Books and Media, 1995.

***Cum potestas in populo auctoritas in senatu sit—See* While power resides in the people, authority rests with the Senate**

D

decision theory—*See* game theory

democracy

The term "democracy" encompasses a broad range of political concepts and connotations and is generally used in a loose rather than precise technical sense. Literally meaning the "rule of the people," such a political apparatus is in practice rare. This is not to say that democratic systems and processes are not real, but only to admit that "the people" seldom "rule" in the precise sense. Additionally, the term democracy means different things to different people. For some it is a procedural term requiring the fullest possible participation among the widest possible segment of the population. "Direct" democracy or "participatory" democracy connotes a nearly universally active citizenry, fully engaged politically and truly responsible for their own government. "Representative" or "indirect"

democracy allows for the placement of governmental responsibilities more firmly within elected officials, and thus the people "govern" primarily through the ballot box as well as through the sheer force of public opinion. "Representative democracy" is sometimes cast as a "republican" rather than "democratic" mode of government, but this too is an example of the broad nature of much of our political terminology. While the "representative" and "participatory" types are both standard and useful in the classification of democracies, they do not adequately convey the complex variety of democratic regimes, possible or actual. One might also speak of "elite" democracies (governments that embrace democratic principles and yet are basically controlled or guided by identifiable elites), corporate democracies (democracies that are structured along the lines of distinct groups and associations within the larger polity), and social democracy (democracies that attempt to combine politically democratic processes and institutions with centralized control of principal aspects of the economy). These are but a few examples of the diverse types of democracy that one can either conceive in principle or locate in practice, within varying degrees.

That said, a few institutions, traditions and procedural practices are requisite to democratic polities. The pervasive and frequent use of electoral processes to determine who will hold at least a sizeable portion of public offices stands as one of the more obvious requirements of democratic government. It is seldom possible and perhaps even undesirable that every office can be an elective one, but in the democratic form of government a good many officials must be directly or indirectly chosen by the broader electorate. The election of legislatures is a universal element of democratic government, and the election of at least a part of the executive branch (either directly or indirectly) is also typical. The judiciary can be a mixture of elected and nonelected judges, with the latter often being associated with higher courts. Bureaucracies exist, and by definition they are nonelective, but a bureaucratic administration is accountable to the electorate, usually indirectly through the oversight of both the legislative and executive branches.

In addition, democracies by and large are characterized by the following: they are universally grounded on the rule of law, offer a wide range of opportunities for citizens to participate in politics and government, have a political sphere independent of the formal institutions of government involving at least two distinct political parties, retain civil control over the military, promote an independent and free press, provide universal public education, and are usually framed by a constitution (either written or unwritten or a mixture of both). This constitution is treated as both a framework for government as well as the highest law of the land and furthermore includes articles protecting the rights and liberties of citizens as well as defining the powers of government offices, the accountability of leaders to the people (regardless of the means of their selection), and the dispersal of power (most democracies rely upon some kind of separation of power). In addition, there is at least some means through which the constitution or basic law can be altered or amended in response to social and cultural change. This is but a brief list providing examples of features that are commonly—and in some cases perhaps universally—found in democracies in the broader sense of the term; this is not meant to exclude the possibility that other common elements may also be identified across the various types of democracies.

As with so much of our political vocabulary currently in use, the term democracy comes from the Greek words *demos* (the people) and *kratia* (authority, rule, power), combined to form *demokratia*—*democratie* in the French (derived from the Latin). Fittingly, the first known democracy in recorded history emerged in ancient Athens through the efforts of the reformer Cleisthenes (570 BC–508 BC), although it is frequently noted that the still earlier reforms of Solon (638 BC–558 BC) established the institutional groundwork and mind-set that would eventually lead to the achievement of Cleisthenes after the fall of the Pisistradae tyranny. Solon broadened political participation within Athens and also initiated economic and moral reforms that appear compatible with democracy, but it is with Cleisthenes that we generally identify the initiation of a democratic government in the fuller sense. As is commonly noted, Athenian democracy is decidedly different from modern notions of democracy, the most obvious difference being in the kinds of social structures found in the ancient world, in particular, the ubiquity of social hierarchy, tribalism, and slavery. Citizenship in Athens excluded slaves, metics (foreign residents), and women. Hence citizenship in the *polis* was in truth a membership not available to all residents. Additionally, citizenship required at least some level of active participation within the government of the city, but this occurred throughout a wide range of commitment. Not every citizen participated to the same extent, but all participated in some way, and all (citizens) were accorded opportunities to become engaged in the affairs of the city in which they were active members.

In the renowned *Funeral Oration* of Pericles—the great Athenian leader who oversaw both the pinnacle of Athenian democracy as well as the beginning of her decline owing to the protracted war with Sparta—the ideals and sentiments of Athenian democracy are eloquently articulated. Throughout the speech, civic devotion and duty, requirements characteristic of the Athenian model of democracy, are emphasized. For Pericles, citizenship meant engagement in the polity, and those who are not so engaged are regarded as of no use to the common good. Democracy, in the Periclean Age, meant participation for the greater glory, and not simply the enjoyment of certain rights and privileges owing to the good fortune of simply residing in the right place. Citizens do more than vote and pay taxes, according to the Periclean vision; they are, in various degrees, expected to assume the mantle of public responsibility at some point in their lives and to see that their private interests are not set apart from the needs of the public weal.

The most extensive theoretical examination of democracy in the ancient world can be found in the writings of Plato and Aristotle, both of whom lived and taught in Athens, the former as a citizen and the latter as a metic. Plato's critique of democracy in *Republic* is well known for its candor. For Plato, democratic government is marked by instability, incontinence, the delusion that anyone can govern (for Plato, only a few are, by nature, suited to rule), and above all, by the tendency to regard all pleasures and all values as equal. These elements make democracy vulnerable to the caprice of mobs, which in itself is the breeding ground for the emergence of those demagogues who can manipulate the *demos* for their own purposes. Hence, in *Republic*, democracy is but a step above tyranny in Plato's estimation. Nonetheless, in both *Statesman* and *Laws*, Plato regards democracy less harshly. It is still prone to the same problems anticipated in *Republic*, but Plato does emphasize, especially in *Laws*, its positive attributes—namely the qualities of friendship and freedom that are engendered in democratic government and, if offset by sufficient authority and the rule of law, are the primary ingredients in the moderate regime of the "second-best city." Thus while Plato is critical of democracy, he recognizes the benefits enjoyed by a city that incorporates significant democratic elements.

Aristotle, following Plato, is critical of democracy, and he numbers it as one of his "deviant" regimes. For Aristotle, as for Plato, democracy means the rule of the many poor in pursuit of their interest in a manner adverse to the good of the whole. Democracy rules lawlessly and without regard for the common interest, but only with a view to the interest of the majority and/or individuals as they seek to satisfy their own personal needs and ambitions. Nonetheless, Aristotle does state that democracy is the "least deviant" or least imperfect regime, and actually recognizes certain virtues in an agrarian democracy. Furthermore,

Aristotle does recognize a legitimate or correct from of "rule by the many," which in important ways does resemble democracy in the broader sense, or at least contains features that we today would consider democratic. This correct form of "rule by the many," or the constitutional polity, is a mixture of oligarchy *and* democracy (hence containing democratic structures and practices mixed in with more authoritative institutions, not unlike Plato's "second-best city" of the *Laws*), relies on a strong and expanded middle class to reduce tension across the classes as well as to diminish the influence of factions, and is rooted in the rule of law understood to serve the common good rather than the interest of one group or segment of the *polis*. This is not technically a democracy in Aristotle's usage, but it does contain important democratic aspects; many of which are vaguely familiar to the modern reader who brings a certain preconception of democracy to Aristotle's text.

As political influence shifted to Rome, commentators tended to seek out ideal practices in the institutions of the great republic that had emerged on the Italic peninsula. Polybius, a Greek historian, saw in Rome elements of democracy that were important for its stability and enduring success. Following Polybius, the Roman statesman and philosopher Cicero recognized the importance of democracy in the same way—as a principal ingredient in the creation of mixed regimes. Democracy as a pure type was regarded by both Polybius and Cicero as a legitimate regime, although unstable (as any pure type would be); hence the importance of democratic practices was to provide balance within a regime that combined it with monarchial and aristocratic elements. Whereas Plato (in *Republic*) and Aristotle in his *Politics* both identified democracy as somehow deviant, Polybius and Cicero considered it to be a correct regime, but sharing the flaw of instability with other pure types. It is only through the mixed regime that the people can enjoy any lasting share in power, a pure democracy, as both Polybius and Cicero understood it (as well as Plato and Aristotle) would inevitably decay into mob rule (ochlocracy).

While it is an incontrovertible fact of history that most human communities in the historical record have not been democratic, democracy having only recently demonstrated widespread success, as an idea democracy has long been familiar to students and writers of political theory, and as stated above, democratic elements were present in certain ancient regimes in addition to the Athenian example. In the Middle Ages, political feudalism, far removed from democracy as such, nonetheless did contain hints of quasi-democratic elements. Autocracy and hierarchy shaped the basic structure of Medieval society, but over the broad span of Medieval history, certain institutions emerged that were receptive to a more "democratic" impulse. The English common law, for example, was an attempt to establish a law of the land equally applicable to all. This is not to say that the lower rungs of society were thus guaranteed equal rights—far from it—but it is this recognition of the desire to govern a community through the objective application of law that is a feature of democratic life. Baronial assemblies emerged in advisory capacities to regal courts, and over time, they were expanded to include a broader range of participants. Parliaments were established throughout various parts of Medieval Europe (particularly in Iceland, England, France and Spain with the appearance of the Cortes), eventually evolving into bodies of relative importance, and ultimately capable of (especially in the case of England) challenging royal sovereignty. The larger and more economically dynamic Medieval cities began to enjoy a degree of independence from king and baron, stimulating a desire for localized self-government. Renaissance Italy stands at the culmination of the reemergence of small republics, which where not democratic in the pure sense, but which did in their own way advance practices of local self-government removed from the ancient hierarchies of the older continental dynasties that dominated the great powers such as Britain, Spain, France, and Austria.

Political theorists continued to advance the notion that government needs to be in some way accountable to the people. While democracy still remained to be established as a working system, many Medieval commentators understood political rule to be legitimized by at least some degree of consent of the governed. John of Salisbury, whose political philosophy was fully in line with the hierarchies of his day, nonetheless understood kings to serve the people, even comparing them to ministers in the sense that they are to tend to the needs of the people in the same way that a priest tends to his flock, and thus are not charged with simply commanding the polity. Kings that allow themselves to become masters above the law, that is, tyrants (the "very likeness of the Devil" in John of Salisbury's description), are to be destroyed—not by collective resistance, but by reliance upon some other official authority working in behalf of the common good. William of Occam spoke of the assent of the people in the promulgation of laws and the selection of leaders—"what touches all must be done by all"—and even though this is not meant to affirm a strict democratic community, it is evidence of the idea that regimes should be responsive to the general needs of the people as a whole. Marsiglio of Padua and Nicholas of Cusa also anticipated in their writings the expanded role of the people in their self-government, and, while not properly democratic, they were nonetheless critical of unresponsive hierarchy. Perhaps even more telling is the attitude of the greatest philosopher of the Middle Ages, St. Thomas Aquinas, who in his *Summa Theologica,* affirmed the mixed regime as the best regime (even though in *On Kingship,* he speaks of monarchy in the same way, it is a reasonable argument to assert that his comments in the *Summa* are more indicative of his mature conclusions). Aquinas teaches that the best regime combines elements of monarchy, aristocracy, and—notable for a Medieval theorist—democracy. Typically, he bases his conclusion on the lessons of both reason and faith: the Philosopher Aristotle (in *Politics*) favored a mixed regime (his constitutional polity) according to St. Thomas, and in the Holy Scripture, the Israelites under Moses governed themselves by combining the rule of the one (Moses) the few (seventy-two elders) and the many (the people as a whole who selected the elders). For St. Thomas, the wisdom of mixed regimes that rely on democratic features is evident and compatible with both nature and revelation. Additionally, St. Thomas, as Marsiglio after him, affirmed the importance of the rule of law and the accountability of leaders to the community, and while they are not democratic in the strict sense they nonetheless are elements associative of the principles of democracy. Finally, certain quasi-democratic elements are evident in the Medieval church. While the popular image of the Medieval church that is held today is one that conceives of it as a strict hierarchy, the actual story is more complex. While the church was (and remains) hierarchical in structure, many practices emerged within the Medieval church that were quasi-democratic. Medieval feudalism was politically rigid, and it was impossible for a person to cross class barriers and ascend the social-political ladder, so to speak. However, within the church a person born of any class could succeed in a number of ways not accorded to most people in the political and economic spheres of Medieval life. Monastic life was essentially egalitarian, and it was possible for individuals born of any rank to enter the priesthood. Additionally, the church offered opportunities for women that were absent in society at large. Contrary to the popular image of women as oppressed by the Medieval church, many women became leaders within their local communities through the church. Cloistered women governed themselves; studied theology, philosophy, and law; and in some cases would hold political influence with local leaders both within and without the ecclesial community. To be sure, women were disadvantaged throughout Medieval society, and not all women living in religious cloisters were liberated, but there is evidence that where there was freedom for women, it was either in the political courts of powerful women such as the legendary Eleanor of Aquitaine or in the monastic life that enabled women a degree of autonomy that they could never experience in the larger world dominated by men.

The emergence and what some would say is the final triumph of democracy in modernity is a familiar story. Traditionally traced to the English Civil War and the political theories of the seventeenth century, modern theories of democracy supplanted the vague, quasi-democratic leanings in the writings and practices of the Middle Ages (again, this is not to say that the Middle Ages were democratic but rather to concede that the Medieval mind, and to some extent, even Medieval practices, were not unfamiliar with certain aspects of democracy). At best, only vague democratic adumbrations can be discerned in Medieval institutions, for political feudalism is inherently autocratic. But the ideas were there, and one can detect seeds of republicanism along with vague democratic tendencies in Medieval thought and practice. But it is with the great revolutions of the seventeenth and eighteenth centuries that democracy reappears for the first time since the decline of Athens, a reappearance far distant from the conceptions and applications of the ancient city. For the most part, what the ancients called "pure" democracy was not embraced as a political solution. Rather, as with Republican Rome, elements of democracy were deliberately established as a result of political turmoil. Legislative assemblies such as Parliament ascended at the expense of the monarchy, the "common" people enjoyed more influence, the common law became more expansive still, and bills of rights appeared guaranteeing certain protections for the people against arbitrary rule (although bills of rights were not always universal in application). In every case, democracy in itself was not a goal (a notable example is the American Founding, which wove elements of democracy into the Constitution while at the same time erecting barriers against its full practice and the dangers perceived as inherent therein). More radical political elements, such as the Levellers and Diggers in seventeenth-century England and the Jacobins during the French Terror, were democratic in a more strict sense, but their presence and practices actually worked against the acceptance of democracy across society at large. It was James Harrington and the Baron de Montesquieu, modern champions of mixed government, who persuaded statesmen and theorists alike, and not John Lilburne and Gerrard Winstanley. Nonetheless, one of the finest expressions of the democratic aspiration comes from a Leveller, Colonel Rainborough, in the famous Putney Debates of 1647. "For really, I think that the poorest he that is in England," Rainborough observed, "hath a life to live, as the greatest he; therefore . . . I think it's clear, that every man that is to live under a government ought first by his own consent put himself under that government." This notion echoes Occam's "what touches all must be done by all," and looks ahead to the principles of the American Declaration of Independence, wherein it is stated that as a self-evident truth all governments derive "their just powers from the consent of the governed." The Declaration of Independence is a thoroughgoing and unequivocal statement of democratic principles, the actual application of those principles notwithstanding. It is in the Declaration of Independence that we see the idea of democracy fully affirmed, no longer a vaguely developing set of tendencies and concepts, but now a completely democratic affirmation.

As an idea, democracy has been both a vibrant possibility as well as subject of controversy since the days of Solon and Cleisthenes, and continues to remain so today. As stated earlier, with the Declaration of Independence democracy is fully evident as an operating principle of government, but it is less so as a rule of practical politics. Democracy has always been received with mixed reactions, and it was no less for the American Founders, many of whom embraced democratic ideals (such as James Otis,

Samuel Adams, Thomas Paine, and Thomas Jefferson) while others sustained a tolerant skepticism. The birth of American democracy did not occur within the medium of social and economic equality, and in particular, the existence of chattel slavery militated against the progress of democratic politics in the young republic. This serves as just one illustration of the difficulties of full democratic application throughout any given social medium. As a political ideal, democracy today is nearly universally embraced—even authoritarian and in some cases totalitarian regimes have referred to themselves as "democratic"—and yet the practice of democracy is a continual experiment, the realization of which is a perpetual struggle. In the United States, by way of example, the civil-rights and women's rights movements demonstrate the ongoing battle for the universalization of democracy and democratic liberties even among one of the more democratic nations in the record of history. Such continuing social and political struggles toward the promotion of a more perfect democracy remind us of the divide between principle and practice—a divide that can be bridged and perhaps even closed, but one that requires continual effort to achieve and vigilance to preserve.

Perhaps the most astute student of democracy in modern political thought is the French liberal aristocrat Alexis de Tocqueville, who perceived in democracy both its many advantages and benefits as well as its more dangerous and socially corrosive tendencies. Democracy promotes a more meaningful sense of justice, enlightened self-interest, and a liberty of the spirit foreign to European society. On the other hand, democracy exposes humanity to new, subtler forms of tyranny—not just tyranny of the electoral majority, but the coercive tyranny of conformity, the leveling impulses of egalitarianism, and the tendency toward centralization that can ultimately thwart self-government. Nonetheless, while Tocqueville warns his readers (in particular his French readers) about the dangers of democracy and the need to control its strengths, he remains optimistic (but not naïve) regarding the ability of America to "mitigate the tyranny of the majority" and to counteract the effects of more insidious forms of subjugation (conformism, sterile centralization, the tendency of the human spirit to be truncated by mediocrity in egalitarian societies). Tocqueville's honest analysis and assessment of democracy, the good and the bad of it, remains a stunning achievement of political and social criticism and a reservoir of theoretical insight.

Democracy today is varied, both practically and theoretically. In practice, the range of democratic institutions and traditions run from the local town meetings of New England to the relationship between Prime Minister and Monarch in Great Britain. Democratic legislatures are found in all parts of the world, and both the presidential and the parliamentarian forms of democracy have proved their worth in promoting the ideals and methods of republicanism and democracy, broadly construed. Many countries guarantee individual rights against their diverse governments, and the rule of law prevails throughout many regimes across various regions of the world. Democratization as a sociopolitical movement can be seen in quarters as disparate as South Africa (with the end of apartheid) and, haltingly, in Eastern Europe (with the dissolution of the Soviet Union and the demise of its satellite regimes). While Francis Fukuyama's prediction that liberal democracy has emerged victorious in the battle of ideologies is premature, it is reasonable to say that throughout much of the world the democratic idea, in its myriad manifestations, has proven, as Tocqueville once wrote, "irresistible." There are important exceptions to this trend (e.g., in parts of the Islamic world), but generally the principles of democracy that can be traced back to the revolutions of the seventeenth and eighteenth century, then further through certain aspects of Medieval Europe, into the Roman republic, and ultimately to ancient Athens, are becoming more entrenched, albeit on terms preestablished by cultural preconceptions and influences.

The limits of space prevent a further exposition of the many forms in which democracy has developed since the eighteenth century, and it must again be noted that, save a few exceptions, democracy remained in the minority among the world's great nations until the latter half of the twentieth century. Democracy and republican government is only now achieving a wider acceptance across the human community, although some social and political critics on both sides of the traditional ideological spectrum would still argue that democracy remains far from any substantial realization, even in those countries that refer to themselves as democratic. Whether or not such analysis is fair remains to be considered, and whether or not democracy will continue to expand or experience a contraction, is ultimately unforeseeable. But the nature of democracy remains well conceived. This nature is perhaps best summarized in President Lincoln's succinct phrase (which was itself based on a phrase from Theodore Parker), "government of the people, by the people, for the people." A government that is of and by the people would be a government that not only rests on popular consent and guided by democratic processes, but also a government that is substantively for the people, advancing a notion of the common good that is truly universal, and thus essentially democratic. In Lincoln's phrase, democracy as both process and substance, as both dynamic and essence, is affirmed, a reminder that a truly democratic system must not only succeed in the erection of institutions and the promulgation of laws that promote and ensure democratic processes but also in the manifestation of the principles of justice and the establishment of the common good that is to the equal benefit of all citizens. This is the essence of democracy—its structures and processes all are directed toward these ends.

Related Entries
equality; equality of condition/equality of opportunity; freedom; negative and positive liberty

Suggested Reading

Dahl, Robert. *A Preface to Democratic Theory.* 1956; repr. Chicago: Univ. Chicago Press, 2007.

Gould, Carol C. *Rethinking Democracy.* 1988; repr. New York: Cambridge Univ. Press, 1988.

Tocqueville, Alexis de. *Democracy in America,* trans. and ed. Harvey C. Mansfield and Delba Winthrop. Chicago: Univ. Chicago Press, 2000.

despot, despotism (*despotes*)

Usually employed as a term interchangeable with tyranny, despotism sometimes simply connotes the strong rule of a single person, neither monarchial nor tyrannical. Hence, the term despot reflects a more neutral tone than tyrant, by and large, although the practice of despotism is regarded as a kind of arbitrary rule in the same genus as that of tyrants.

The difference between despot, tyrant, and monarch might be sorted out by appealing to Aristotle. Kings are constitutional leaders who govern free citizens under the rule of law. They do possess the highest political authority and the power requisite to governing a *polis,* but their power is limited, their authority defined by law and custom. Tyrants, for Aristotle (following the lead of Plato), are in every case lawless and vicious, commanding subjects as a master commands slaves, but only to the benefit of the tyrant. For Aristotle and Plato, tyranny is actually a regime that destroys the *polis* rather than directing it. A despot governs men as a master would slaves, but to the benefit of both, and thus a despot can hold authority over a state without destroying it. Hence the common phrase "benevolent despot" as a further distinction between the legitimate use of absolute power (an idea in itself requiring close scrutiny) and that kind of power that consumes a state from within. In Aristotle, there is an element of consent in the rule of the despot, whereas tyranny is always a question of force, and always to the eventual detriment of the *polis.* To the Greeks, the Persian and Egyptian models were examples of despotism, which may or may not be tyrannical.

Related Entries

monarchy; tyranny

Suggested Reading

Strauss, Leo. *On Tyranny.* 1961; repr. Chicago: Univ. Chicago Press, 2000.

Dewey, John (1859–1952)

A leading founder of pragmatism (along with his predecessor C. S. Peirce and older contemporary William James), John Dewey spans an intellectual development that parallels the emergence of the American century. Yet Dewey is not a typical American theorist; deeply influenced by both Hegel and Darwin, and yet never strictly an Hegelian or a Darwinian, Dewey carves a path all his own, one that has come to be appreciated by thinkers as diverse as Jürgen Habermas and Richard Rorty.

What struck Dewey about both Darwin and Hegel was the abiding theme of development. Indeed, for Dewey growth in itself is an important measure of the value of a society. However, Dewey resisted the egoistic interpretations of social Darwinism (as found in Herbert Spencer and William Graham Sumner) as well as the more Byzantine intoxications of the Hegelian system. With Peirce, Dewey embraced the pragmatic maxim, "Consider what effects, which might conceivably have practical bearings, we conceive the object of our conception to have. Then, our conception of these is the whole of our conception of the object." This is to say, both Dewey and Peirce (from whom this quote comes), seek to understand the potential consequences of ideas and theories. Rather than seek eternal verities or abstract "mind stuff," Dewey and the pragmatist school of thought are more interested in the applicability of ideas. It is in the consequence that the usefulness of an idea can be measured; it is in the suitability of a theory or program for the world that we can find its real value. Both Dewey and Peirce resist the identification of pragmatic with "practical," for the latter connotes expediency or the easiest means of achieving immediate goals. Pragmatism is that and more; it involves the willingness to struggle with an idea in the realm of the really possible, to employ experimentation and innovation to discover what works, not for the sake of expediency or reward, necessarily, but to resolve the many social problems confronted by humanity within the world on the world's own terms, rather than the terms set by detached ideas.

Hence, Dewey and the other pragmatists regard values and truths to be a function of the encounter between agent and environment. Rejecting the correspondence theory of truth (that there is an objective truth to be found independent of the knowing subject), Dewey believed that truth is discerned somewhere between the external world and the internal thinker. As with any value, the only way to know the truth of an idea or proposition is to logically anticipate all of its possible consequences. Should the idea under this kind of inquiry prove beneficial, it can be said to be valid. Therefore, in Dewey's philosophy (or antiphilosophy, as the case may be), there is no absolute truth or universal Good as in Plato or St. Thomas Aquinas (for example). Truth and value is entirely relative to context and situation, there being no one perception or line of thought that can said to be objectively true or meaningful to all engaged in inquiry. In this sense, Dewey agrees with Nietzsche writing before him and the postmoderns (such as Rorty) who come after him. Our values are contingent, our truths perspectival—of this we can be sure, according to Dewey, and little more than this. Moral principles are a response to our environment, not in the sense of Spencer's survival of the fittest, but rather in the spirit of pragmatic experimentalism. Again, the theme of growth and of thriving is important; it is through the healthy growth of individuals in community that we can detect values beneficial to human beings, and not in the transcendent principles of the great philosophies of the past.

Given these philosophical foundations, Dewey's political thought is community centered and characterized by an imperative to experiment, to test, to adapt, and to try anew. We should not be fixated on the abstract ideals of democracy (such as liberty, equality, and right), but rather on the means in which democracy can actually be manifested as a working process to the benefit of the community at large. Through education (a field in which he is also well known) and open communication, a democratic association can be truly communitarian, neither the unreflective populous feared by its critics nor the arena in which atomistic egos compete for social goods, but a cooperative sphere of citizens who are also neighbors in the best sense, sharing experiences and directing their own associations with a sense of common purpose. Democracy should be small and participatory, in Dewey's mind, and the citizens capable of engaging with one another as associates, not competitors. This involves a sense of responsibility for planning social improvement, and not simply responding to the events as they come. Dewey's theory of politics relies on the cooperative association and aims at the managed state. But this managed planning must not be directed from above in accordance with the dreams of the detached idealists. Social planning that inspires growth is the outcome—the consequence, as it were—of experimentation. The willingness to innovate and begin again is, for Dewey, an assurance of a truly flourishing democracy.

Related Entries
consequentialism; pragmatic maxim

Suggested Reading

Morris, Debra, and Ian Shapiro, eds. *John Dewey: The Political Writings*. Indianapolis: Hackett, 1993.
Ryan, Alan. *John Dewey and the High Tide of American Liberalism*. New York: Norton, 1995.

dhimmi (those of the covenant, care, custody, pact of protection)

The *dhimmi* is an institution in Muslim polities that establishes rules of protection for non-Muslim communities who are not under the full guidance of Islamic *shari'a,* or religious law. In exchange for offering both a tribute to the Islamic authorities and conceding Muslim supremacy, non-Muslim religious communities are granted a degree of autonomy wherein they can practice their faith as well as receive protection from uninvited encroachment on the customs of their particular communities. Originally, the concept was applied only to fellow People of the Book, i.e., to Jewish and Christian minorities under Muslim rule, but over time other faith traditions, such as Hindu and Zoroastrian, have fallen under the Islamic *dhimmi.*

Dhimmi has drawn both negative criticism as well as positive acceptance. In the case of the latter, *dhimmi* is set as an example of religious toleration, a benevolent respect for the religious identities of non-Muslim communities, especially their fellow monotheists. However, it has also been noted that those living under the *dhimmi* are by definition second-class citizens, unable to fully enjoy the opportunities accorded to those who declare for Islam. Often those under the *dhimmi* are heavily taxed, deprived of political office, susceptible to false accusations, restricted in their choice of housing and transportation, required to wear only certain kinds of apparel, exposed to humiliating treatment by public officials, and even left vulnerable to arbitrary violence committed by Muslims against them. Hence, the *dhimmi* is regarded as not unlike the anti-Catholic laws formerly enacted in England or laws restricting Protestantism in France, or even similar to the secular segregation and apartheid laws eventually abolished within the United States and South Africa. As a result, the term *dhimmitude* is an expression of contempt for a status of servitude imposed upon minorities by a religious majority. Indeed, a status of inferiority has in the past resulted from the application of *dhimmi,* but the actual degree and persistence of this social inferiority has varied greatly throughout the Islamic world.

Related Entry
shari'a

Suggested Reading

Black, Antony. *The History of Islamic Political Thought: From the Prophet to the Present.* New York: Routledge, 2001.

dialectical theory (the dialectic)
As with almost any enduring philosophical term, the concept "dialectic" can be traced directly back to Plato, who spoke of the dialectical method of critical inquiry undertaken without preconceptions as the true method to achieve *noesis,* or the highest level of cognition. Today, and more generally, dialectical theory refers to a method of philosophy that emerges out of German idealism, in particular Johann Gottlieb Fichte and Georg Wilhelm Friedrich Hegel. It is in Hegel that we receive the most sophisticated expression of the modern dialectic. For Hegel, the world is a totality of radically connected and interpenetrating contradictions. All phases of development and all manifestations of existence within the greater manifold of being are marked by a dynamic interaction of apparently disparate aspects of being concealing an overarching unity that is forwarded to higher stages of development by opposition and contradiction. This development occurs at all levels of being, blurring the lines between the universal and the particular, the subject and the object, spirit and matter, essence and existence. The nature of the progress of this dynamic totality of being occurs dialectically through innumerable triadic relations, beginning with what we call the affirmation (or thesis), which produces its own negation (antithesis). Diametrically opposed to each other, the conflict between affirmation and negation wants resolution, and in this resolution is produced the negation of the negation (or synthesis), which propels all facets of the triad into a higher stage of development, itself now becoming a new affirmation.

Karl Marx adopted the Hegelian dialectic, but he inverted it to reflect his own materialism. Hegel understood the dialectic in terms of idea and concept, of the rational purpose of spirit (*Geist*) unfolding itself into the world. For

Marx, this was an inversion of the true nature of the dialectic, which is in reality driven by the material relations of production. Hence, Marxian dialectics is sometimes referred to as "dialectical materialism." Marx posits the dialectic firmly in the material world; any ideational or conceptual principle is the product of humanity's material activity. Marx also understands the dialectic as thoroughly historic. History is not moved by spirit reconciling itself with matter, but rather, all of history is "the history of class struggle," the contest of the material means of production. The dialectic thus moves forward temporally, there being no aspect of the dialectic that exists outside time or beyond the perception of our material reality. With Marx, the dialectic becomes the central principle of the science of history, and the skeleton key to unlocking the hidden forces of historical development.

Related Entries
alienation; communism; critical theory; Hegel, Georg Wilhelm Friedrich; Marx, Karl; socialism

Suggested Reading
Jay, Martin. *The Dialectical Imagination.* Boston: Little Brown, 1973.
Warren, Scott. *The Emergence of Dialectical Theory.* 1984; repr. Chicago: Univ. Chicago Press, 2008.

dictator
Originally a Latin term describing the office of *magister populi,* a legal position temporarily granting extralegal powers to a strong leader during times of crisis, the term now refers to any single ruler holding absolute or nearly absolute power. Often but not necessarily associated with a coup d'état, a dictator's rule is the only substantive authority wherever they hold power. Dictators are typically abusive of their authority in various degrees, thus prompting the appellation of "tyrant" (particularly as understood by Plato and Aristotle). Modern dictators act as head of state and head of government, with or without the cooperation of legislatures (if the former, the legislature

serves as a rubber stamp), also acting as the head of the military in a way that exceeds the civilian direction of the armed forces as exemplified in a democratically elected president or prime minister. Dictators are almost universally oppressive and homicidal, the worst examples being Adolf Hitler, Josef Stalin, Mao tse-Tung, and Pol Pot. The type known as "benevolent dictator," like the "enlightened despot" of the eighteenth century, refers to a strong leader who nonetheless serves the public interest in ways that soften the authoritarian nature of the regime. By and large, the benevolent dictator is the exception to the case, as modern dictatorship is generally prone to the use of violence and in most cases terror to attain and sustain power.

Related Entries
despot, despotism; tyranny

Suggested Reading
Boesche, Roger. *Theories of Tyranny, from Plato to Arendt.* University Park, PA: Pa. State Univ. Press, 1996.
Maier, Hans, and Michael Schäfer, eds. *Concepts for the Comparison of Dictatorships,* vol. 2 of *Totalitarianism and Political Religions,* 3 vols., trans. Jodi Bruhn. New York: Routledge, 2007.

dictatorship of relativism
On April 19, 2005, Cardinal Joseph Alois Ratzinger was elected to the Holy See to succeed His Holiness Pope John Paul II, choosing for his papacy the name Pope Benedict XVI. On the morning of the 19th, just prior to the meeting of the conclave that would appoint him to the papacy, Cardinal Ratzinger identified relativism as one of the more dangerous problems facing the church in the world today. He spoke of a "dictatorship of relativism" that promoted egoistic subjectivism over the search for transcendent principles. Referring in his homily to the fourth chapter of St. Paul's Epistle to the Ephesians, the Cardinal reflected on the source, meaning, and power of contemporary relativism.

How many winds of doctrine we have known in recent decades, how many ideological currents, how many ways of thinking...The small boat of thought of many Christians has often been tossed about by these waves—thrown from one extreme to the other: from Marxism to liberalism, even to libertinism; from collectivism to radical individualism; from atheism to a vague religious mysticism; from agnosticism to syncretism, and so forth. Every day new sects are created and what Saint Paul says about human trickery comes true, with cunning which tries to draw those into error (cf Eph 4, 14). Having a clear faith, based on the Creed of the Church, is often labeled today as a fundamentalism. Whereas, relativism, which is letting oneself be tossed and "swept along by every wind of teaching," looks like the only attitude (acceptable) to today's standards. We are moving towards a dictatorship of relativism which does not recognize anything as for certain and which has as its highest goal one's own ego and one's own desires.

For many, this homily represents one of the key missions of Benedict XVI's papacy, that is, a new resolve to confront the pervasive assumption that truth is relative to one's subjective opinions, and as such, serves to promote the ends of the self even at the expense of those values that have been traditionally embraced as universal throughout history. In this homily, the Cardinal Ratzinger would affirm a belief central to all Christians and renew the discussion over the meaning of truth and its relation to cultural attitudes and personal needs.

Related Entries
absolutes; Catholic social teaching

Suggested Reading
"Homily of His Eminence, Joseph Ratzinger, Dean of the College of Cardinals, April 18, 2005." Available at the Vatican Web site, http://www.vatican.va/gpII/documents/homily-pro-eligendo-pontifice_20050418_en.html.

dictatorship of the proletariat

While coined by Karl Marx and a prominent concept in Marxian revolutionary theory, the actual term and idea was scarcely mentioned throughout the body of his work. As Robert Tucker illustrates in his useful and comprehensive anthology, the term was first used in a candid letter to Marx's friend and correspondent, Joseph Weydemeyer, dated March 5, 1852, to wit:

> No credit is due to me for discovering the existence of classes in modern society or the struggle between them....What I did that was new was to prove: 1.) that the existence of classes is only bound up with particular historical phases in the development of production, 2.) that the class struggle necessarily leads to the dictatorship of the proletariat, 3.) that this dictatorship itself only constitutes the transition to the abolition of all classes and to a classless society.

The phrase does not again find its way into Marx's writing until May 1875, in a passage within the *Critique of the Gotha Program,* wherein he once again states,

> Between capitalist and communist society lies the period of the revolutionary transformation of the one into the other. There corresponds to this also a political transition period in which the state can be nothing but *the revolutionary dictatorship of the proletariat.*

Marx raises this idea as a reminder of the limitations of certain socialist programs that fail to go beyond "the old democratic litany familiar to all: universal suffrage, direct legislation, popular rights, a people's militia, etc." For Marx, these were bourgeois reforms that are necessary to a point, but are now only "petty little gewgaws." What is really required for the advancement of the demise of capitalism is something more exhaustive and radical and can only be accomplished through the power of the proletariat.

In his editorial comments to Marx's 1871 pamphlet, *Civil War in France,* Friedrich Engels identified the Paris Commune as the "Dictatorship of the Proletariat," and in the body of his text Marx refers to the Commune as "essentially a working class government, the produce of the struggle of the producing against the appropriating class, the political form at last discovered under which to work out the economic emancipation of labor." This latter point, the "political form" of the "emancipation of labor" likely encapsulates what Marx had earlier meant by the phrase "dictatorship of the proletariat." He continues with the assertion that the Commune was the "true representative of all the healthy elements of French society,...as a working men's Government, as the bold champion of the emancipation of labour, emphatically international." He concludes the pamphlet with a revealing peroration, "Working man's Paris, with its Commune, will be for ever celebrated as the glorious harbinger of a new society. Its martyrs are enshrined in the great heart of the working class." In this way, Marx provides a concrete historical example of what he intends with the transitional worker's dictatorship, as well as a clue as to how Marx predicted communism would unfold in its initial stages once the revolution finally breaks capitalism.

Even though Marx's use of the term and the concept behind it are somewhat limited, particularly in comparison to other Marxian principles such as alienation, appropriation, surplus value, and class struggle, Marx's political followers drew heavily upon it. Lenin employed the concept in *State and Revolution* (1917), arguing that a class dictatorship was necessary to hasten the revolution, and associated the dictatorship of the proletariat with the soviet system. Indeed, the Soviet Union defined itself as a "dictatorship of the proletariat," the only true democracy that was advancing society toward "communist self-government," the actual achievement of which was still to be secured. This element of Soviet ideology achieved its most exhaustive, violent, and, in the judgment of history, virulent expression in the Stalinist programs of the 1930s.

Not all Marxists viewed the "dictatorship of the proletariat" as necessary, and those that did see it as a useful step toward the dream of classless society were not as militant as either Lenin or Stalin in their understanding and application. Eduard Bernstein preferred a series of parliamentary and policy reforms that would eventually lead to socialism without having to risk the possible violence of a class dictatorship. Rosa Luxemburg, while opposing the reformist view represented by Bernstein in favor of dramatic revolution, nonetheless understood the dictatorship of the proletariat differently, to wit:

> This dictatorship consists in the *manner of applying democracy,* not in its *elimination,* but in energetic, resolute attacks upon the well-entrenched rights and economic relationships of bourgeois society, without which a socialist transformation cannot be accomplished. This dictatorship must be the work of the class and not of a little leading minority in the name of the class—that is, it must proceed step by step out of the active participation of the masses; it must be under their direct influence, subjected to the control of complete public activity; it must arise out of the growing political training of the mass of the people.

The "little leading minority," is Luxemburg's direct reference to Lenin's "vanguard of the revolution," which is to say, the leadership of the Communist Party who, having accomplished revolution, thereafter direct the dictatorship on behalf of the proletariat. For Luxemburg, the dictatorship of the proletariat must be just that, the full participation of the working class in challenging capitalism and securing its own revolutionary destiny.

Marx's lack of emphasis notwithstanding, the dictatorship of the proletariat developed into a central tenet of radical socialism. While today it appears as an archaic notion, its importance in the ideological history of the twentieth century cannot be overlooked, and the effects of the initial impact of this idea on those nations inspired by the examples offered by Lenin or Stalin in Marx's name remains to this day.

Related Entry
Marx, Karl

Suggested Reading
Ehrenberg, John. *The Dictatorship of the Proletariat: Marx's Socialist Democracy.* New York: Routledge, 1992.
Marx, Karl, and Friedrich Engels. *The Marx-Engels Reader,* 2d ed., ed. Robert C. Tucker. New York: Norton, 1978.

difference principle

In his major opus, *A Theory of Justice,* John Rawls identified two principles of justice, the second of these, also known as the "difference principle," is defined as follows, "social and economic inequalities are to be arranged so that they are both (a) reasonably expected to be to everyone's advantage, and (b) attached to positions and offices open to all." Or, as he restated it elsewhere, "Social and economic inequalities are to be arranged so that they are both (a) to the greatest benefit of the least advantaged, consistent with the just saving principle, and (b) attached to offices and positions open to all under conditions of fair equality of opportunity." In other words, the difference principle is concerned with providing the best possible social arrangement for society's most disadvantaged individuals.

Rawls's difference principle, in essence, "insists that each person [within a given society] benefit from permissible inequalities in the basic structure," the basic structure being a "structure that we enter only by birth and exit only by death." Specifically, the basic structure is the sum of the social, economic, and political institutions and customs of a given society, as well as how they are interrelated. Through this basic structure, certain primary social goods, or the "chief primary goods at the disposition of society," viz., "rights and liberties, powers and opportunities, incomes and wealth," are distributed based on accepted principles of justice. (Primary natural goods are not at the disposition of society.) To arrive at a fair, which is to say just, distribution of social goods, or to understand if a society rationally and fairly distributes these goods, the difference principle "holds that social and economic inequalities,

for example inequalities of wealth and authority, are just only if they result in compensating benefits for the least advantaged members of society."

This principle, along with the first principle of justice, is arrived at through the hypothetical exercise offered by Rawls as the "original position," more specifically, through the conception of a "veil of ignorance" in an "original position of equality" from which members of a society can choose rational and just principles. For Rawls, given the opportunity to choose those principles that will govern the basic structure of society while reflecting on the alternatives hypothetically unaware of one's position in society (the veil of ignorance), a free and rational person would recognize the need to minimize the worst-case scenario to a point that, should one find oneself in such a position, some benefit will still be received. Hence, the difference principle enjoins us to ensure that the least advantaged will benefit even from inequalities in the basic structure, or what Rawls referred to as "permissible" inequalities. Not prepared to endorse a radical notion of equality in all the elements of the basic structure, Rawls recognized that some inequality is unavoidable, even in considering "social goods." Nonetheless, if universal equality cannot be achieved the distribution of social goods must only be unequal to the extent that they are fair, a measure that is discerned from behind the veil of ignorance. The key, for Rawls, is to minimize the degree of inequality by "maximizing the minimum," and in so doing, guaranteeing that those at the greatest disadvantage in society do enjoy the benefits secured by the principles of justice, which are essentially fair.

Rawls specifies his concept by stating that the difference principle "applies, in the first approximation, to the distribution of income and wealth and to the design of organizations that make use of difference in authority and responsibility, or chains of command." The distribution of income addresses economic disadvantages in the distribution of social goods, the "design of organizations" focuses on opportunities to advance one's position throughout society without suffering obstacles that would unfairly impede one's own initiative. In other words, for a political and juridical system to be fair for all its members, it must raise the benefits of the least advantaged as high as possible while remaining cognizant of the reality of some degree of inequality in the economic sphere of social goods. Additionally, the "just saving principle" recognizes the need to preserve some benefits for future generations, therefore any politically implemented corrective to the basic structure addressing an impermissible inequality must regard the effect of such correctives on the future. Overall, Rawls's second principle of justice, or the difference principle, has been compared to the liberal activism of the late nineteenth and twentieth centuries, associated with progressivism, the New Deal, and the Great Society. While Rawls does not explicitly identify his principles of justice with these movements and their policies, the social programs that were generated by these programs in effect apply, to an extent, the goal of distributing social goods under a rubric of permissible inequalities.

Rawls's difference principle has been compared to the Pareto optimal, and indeed, Rawls acknowledges a debt to Vilfredo Pareto in *A Theory of Justice*. Ultimately, however, Rawls argues that his hypothetical approach to a just distribution of social goods is akin to the "social contract" theories of the seventeenth and eighteenth centuries.

Related Entries
dominance and monopoly; justice; Rawls, John; Wilt Chamberlain argument

Suggested Reading
Rawls, John. *Theory of Justice*. Cambridge, MA: Harvard Univ. Press, 1971.

differend

A term employed by postmodern theorist Jean-François Lyotard, the "differend" refers to any example of conflict or contest between two or more agents that ultimately eludes resolution. As Lyotard explains,

> I would like to call a *differend* the case where the plaintiff is divested of the means to argue and becomes for that reason a victim. If the addressor, the addressee, and the sense of testimony are neutralized, everything takes place as if there were not damages....A case of differend between two parties takes place when the "regulation" of the conflict that opposes them is done in the idiom of one of the parties while the wrong suffered by the other is not signified in that idiom.

The differend is found in the absence of a "rule of judgment" that can assess all arguments expressed, implying a basic incommensurability between the different kinds of discourse under review. Should a rule be imposed, it would close debate at the expense of at least one voice, now a silenced voice that Lyotard refers to as the differend. This results in the domination of discourse by a particular "phrase regimen," or basic element of communication governed by a rule that excludes heterogeneity of meaning. That phrase regimen that cannot be voiced becomes a victim to the dominant discourse, or in political terms, a victim to an agent of repression. According to Lyotard, there is always something silenced that remains to be phrased; this is what we call the *differend*.

Examples of the differend in the political context would be that of Holocaust denial. As the victims of the death camps are no longer alive, their voices are silenced. Those who deny the Holocaust argue that no one is around to testify, hence the denial becomes the dominant voice, and the voice of the victim is silenced. There is no rule to appeal, and if there were, an appeal could not be made for the victims who are no longer living. Another example would be the repression of the voices of indigenous peoples in some cultures. The dominant discourse does not recognize the voice of the marginalized, thus producing a victimization of the differend that is unable to appeal to an objective rule of judgment.

The differend is an important concept in the postmodern lexicon, one that emphasizes the problems of cultural asymmetry within any pluralistic society that enables a single dominant phrase regimen. The use of the differend is an attempt at deconstruction of the dominant voice.

Related Entry
incredulity toward metanarratives

Suggested Readings
Haber, Honi Fern. *Beyond Postmodern Politics: Lyotard, Rorty, Foucault.* New York: Routledge, 1994.
Lyotard, Jean-François. *The Differend: Phrases in Dispute,* trans. George Van Den Abbeele. Minneapolis: Univ. Minn. Press, 1988.

dominance and monopoly

In his *Spheres of Justice,* political theorist Michael Walzer explained his notion of complex equality through a consideration of the distinction between "monopoly" on one hand and "domination" on the other. Walzer begins with the premise of pluralism of interests and the multiplicity of goods. Given a pluralism of interests and preferences, there is "no single set of primary or basic goods conceivable across all moral and material worlds," or at least, Walzer explained, if there are universal principles of good "they would be so abstract as to be of little use in thinking about particular distributions." Rather than one Good or one set of abstract universal goods, Walzer proposed a plurality of goods animating autonomous but not wholly discrete distributive spheres. "Every social good or set of goods constitutes, as it were, a distributive sphere within which only certain criteria and arrangements are appropriate." That is, there is no single good, and every good within the multiplicity of goods is defined by various meanings assigned to it by those who seek to acquire or share in those goods. Each good is thus encompassed within its own sphere of value, and the principles of distribution within that sphere will vary from other goods within their autonomous spheres.

A principle of distribution that would be just within one sphere encompassing the distribution of goods would be less just, or even unjust, regarding other goods and their spheres of distribution. "Money," Walzer offered as an example, "is inappropriate in the sphere of ecclesiastical office, it is an intrusion from another sphere. And piety should make for no advantage in the marketplace, as the marketplace is commonly understood." The good of the acquisition of wealth and the good of religious devotion are wholly autonomous; any attempt to convert one pattern of distribution from one sphere to the other is inappropriate. An inappropriate conversion of the pattern of distribution from one sphere to another is a violation, a usurpation of the one by the other (such as the case of money corrupting the assignment of ecclesial office.)

Monopolies may or may not occur within one distributive sphere, depending upon which good is the locus of that sphere and what that good means to the association that values it. One could possibly even monopolize some spheres without committing an injustice, for in some cases it is appropriate to allow "small inequalities." There will always be a few social goods that are monopolistically held. Not every good will be so distributed, but it will always be the case that a few "are in fact and always will be, barring any state intervention." Given this, Walzer argued that "we should focus on the reduction of dominance—not, or not primarily, on the break up or the constraint of monopoly." Should one convert a monopoly held in one distributive sphere to other goods, then a state of domination is established, and thus the complex equality enjoyed by the disparate pluralistic spheres is usurped by a tyranny. "To convert one good into another," Walzer explains,

> when there is no intrinsic connection between the two is to invade the sphere where another company of men and women properly rules. Monopoly is not inappropriate within the spheres. There is nothing wrong, for example, with the grip that persuasive and helpful men

and women (politicians) establish on political power. But the use of political power to gain access to other goods is a tyrannical use.

Thus the following formula is posited: "No social good x should be distributed to men and women who possess some other good y merely because they possess y and without regard to the meaning of x." This dictum captures in simple terms the meaning of complex equality, which is an equality that recognizes multiple goods and thus variegated measures of how those goods should be distributed and which is the most reliable defense against dominance and tyranny within the social world.

Related Entries
complex equality; entitlement theory; equality; justice; Rawls, John

Suggested Reading
Walzer, Michael. *Spheres of Justice: A Defense of Pluralism and Equality*. New York: Basic Books, 1983.

doublespeak

A term coined by George Orwell in his nightmarish *1984,* wherein language is manipulated in a dystopic society to subvert and distort reality in pursuit of the inscrutable purposes of Big Brother. "War is Peace" and "Slavery is Freedom" are examples of doublespeak, which in effect stands as an example of a demagogical dismissal of the ancient admonition, traced back to both Plato as well as the Old Testament prophet Isaiah, against calling the "good evil and the evil good." Any language that attempts to invert truth or subvert reality can be referred to as doublespeak. Additionally, the term doublespeak can be broadened to include any evasive or deliberately ambiguous language that attempts to obscure facts or deceive people into thinking a certain way about something that is in fact against the reality of things as they are. In a sense, doublespeak is an attempt at collective mind control, propaganda taken to such an extreme that what is real seems unreal and what is unreal is the only reality.

Given the power of technology and the ubiquity of instant communication conveyed through an ever-expanding array of media throughout our lives, the Orwellian warning against doublespeak is not to be dismissed. Big Brother may or may not be watching, but the symbols of control, Orwell would remind us, are easily worked on our habits of thought unless we are resolved to sustain vigilance. This is the basic message of Orwell's warning against the dangers of doublespeak.

Related Entry
Big Brother

Suggested Reading
Orwell, George. *Nineteen Eighty-Four, Centennial Edition, with a foreword by Thomas Pynchon and afterword by Erich Fromm.* New York: Plume 2003.

E

end justifies the means

Although Niccolò Machiavelli is commonly perceived as the embodiment of and responsible for this political maxim, the concept of the "end justifies the means" is actually of uncertain origins. Machiavelli's statement in the original Renaissance Italian is "*si guarda al fini,*" and it has been variously translated, including "the end justifies the means." Whether or not Machiavelli actually intended to say this or not, it is certain that he was not the first to say it, nor was he by any means the first to endorse such a policy. Those who lead and hold power have likely exhibited this attitude, or something similar to it, since the beginning of politics itself, although there is no way to trace its initial practice.

The Latin epigram, "exitus acta probat," attributed to Ovid (but probably older still) has been translated as "end justifies the means," "outcome justifies the deed," "result validates the deed," and "action produces results." A similar Italian proverb, "Il fine giustificia i mezzi," has also been translated as "end justifies the means." In any event, the concept itself endures, regardless of the extent to which Machiavelli himself intended to promote it.

The idea of the end justifying the means is essentially a consequentialist formula. That is to say, in examining the moral merit or political validity of a given action or program, we measure its value in terms of consequences, or results. Intent is not as important as outcome, thus in deciding upon a course of action, we look to the anticipated result as our guide, relying less, or not at all, on the motivation. For the most part, such an approach can be justifiable. If a good intent produces a bad result, then the morality of the act in question, or the wisdom of the policy applied, are suspect. Thus in terms of both moral action and political practice, the outcome is the governing factor in judging matters of principle.

One might argue that pragmatism is an example of the maxim of the ends justifying the means in action. In other words, whatever works to promote the public good is, in essence, deemed valuable, and even ethical in most circumstances. Hence, Alexander Pope observed that it is in the practice of proposed solutions that we can test what is to our benefit, the result being the best measure of the value of a decision or act. This idea was embraced by thinkers such as Alexander Hamilton and, to an extent, President Franklin Roosevelt during his New Deal experimentation epitomize the pragmatist consequentialist ethic. This is not to say the President Roosevelt and Alexander Hamilton were consequentialists in their thinking, always adopting an ends-means standard of conduct or policy, but it does serve as an example of the kind of ends-means consequentialism that Pope may have held in his own reflections.

However, the maxim that the end justifies the means has a controversial and even decidedly darker side. If a good end can justify any means, then any abuse of power, however terrifying, might be justified given a suitable outcome. Such a maxim might be a legitimate description of the kind of excesses undertaken by tyrants. Fratricide, regicide, and genocide, for example, might all be defended if one can claim a good end. This sense of the concept goes far beyond the pragmatic consequentialism that often inspires policy experimentalism, and is found far outside the sphere of political and moral activity in any common understanding. It is because of this danger that the proposal to justify means by ends attained raises alarm, at least within civilized political discourse and action. If the "end justifies the means" simply refers to the kind of nonideological attitude toward public policy offered by Pope, Hamilton, and Roosevelt, then such fears are perhaps examples of emotional overreaction. However, if the "end justifies the means" does entail "any means to a given end," then it must be admitted that those fears are not only valid but also thoroughly justifiable.

Related Entries
consequentialism; Machiavelli, Niccolò; *Si guarda al fini*

Suggested Reading
Machiavelli, Niccolò. *The Prince,* trans. and ed. Angelo M. Codevilla. New Haven: Yale Univ. Press, 1997.

entitlement theory

In *Anarchy, State and Utopia,* Robert Nozick forwards a theory of justice as entitlements in response to the notion of distributive justice as fairness asserted by John Rawls in his *Theory of Justice.* According to Nozick, "the minimal state is the most extensive state that can be justified. Any state more extensive violates people's rights." As Nozick states, there is no "person or group entitled to control" the distribution of social goods from a centralized point, but rather in a "free society, diverse persons control different resources, and new holdings arise out of the voluntary exchanges and actions of persons."

According to Nozick, any redistribution of social benefits following notions of distributive justice such as those advanced by Rawls would violate the autonomy of the individual and thus abridge a person's rights. Nozick prefers to dispense with a distributive justice model and advance in its place a theory based on justice in holdings. For Nozick, we can speak of just holdings under three categories: original acquisition, transfer, and rectification. Original acquisition is simply the "appropriation of unheld things" through a person's own labor. Voluntary exchanges, or transfers, are only just if they are the result of voluntary actions of the participants involved. Holdings that are transferred without consent, such as through theft or enslavement, are involuntary and thus cannot be regarded as just. Nozick asserts that "justice in holdings is historical; it depends upon what really happened." A Rawlesian prescription for just distribution is focused not on the historical events explaining why a certain distribution exists, but rather mistakenly considers only the current structure of things ahistorically, as if it were a "time-slice" removed from the sequence of acts and consequences. Only the historical background behind acquisition and exchange are relevant, according to Nozick, in determining why something is held justly or why someone is entitled to a specific holding. In contrast, a time-slice principle ignores the history behind entitlements and treats all holdings as the same.

Therefore, involuntary redistribution of resources for Nozick, whether it is fraud, theft, or taxation supported by state coercion, is a violation of the rights of individuals and consequently unjust. All principles of redistribution that attempt to fit just holdings to an ahistoric pattern (such as welfare redistributive policies in liberal democracies or command economy restructuring in socialism) are by their nature unjust. A third principle of justice as holdings, rectification addresses situations wherein involuntary and impermissible transfer of holdings occurs (such as theft, forced labor, or fraud); thus unjust distributions resulting from past injustices can and should be rectified. Nonetheless, according to Nozick, this can only be done to correct a historically unjust situation; no other consideration (such as the desire to fit a particular end result or preferred pattern of distribution) is valid.

Nozick employs the Wilt Chamberlain argument (see **Wilt Chamberlain argument**) to illustrate his point and to demonstrate how experience demonstrates the inability to adhere to time-slice patterns given the fact of individual liberty. Even if a reasonably fair and noble pattern of redistribution were discovered and effectively implemented, the liberty of persons engaged in voluntary activity would eventually alter the pattern regardless of its initial purpose or desirability.

Anarchy, State and Utopia and the entitlement theory that it introduced is regarded as the most effective response to the Rawlesian project, and hailed by libertarians as a credible challenge to the presumptions of state activism. Nozick himself, while critical of the activist state even to the point of referring to welfare distribution patterns as immoral, was uncomfortable with ideological labels. His political theory is strongly libertarian, but he was critical of those who interpreted his views as endorsing anarchism. Even in a society populated by individuals who enjoy a situation wherein they can transfer all holdings voluntarily, some political mechanism would emerge, even if it meant only to enforce the orderly acquisition and transference of entitlements. Nozick's primary concern remained focused on the choice of the person free of the intervention of wrongheaded and artificial (that is—ahistorical) policies aimed at an abstract end result.

Related Entries
difference principle; liberalism; Rawls, John; Wilt Chamberlain argument

Suggested Reading
Nozick, Robert. *Anarchy, State and Utopia*. 1974; repr. Malden. MA: Blackwell, 2003.
Rawls, John. *A Theory of Justice*. 1971; repr. Cambridge, MA: Harvard Univ. Press, 2005; new ed., Cambridge, MA: Harvard Univ. Press, 1999.

environmentalism

Any movement or set of principles centered around the main value of care and restoration of the environment above all other issues and policies can be regarded as an example of environmentalism. By and large, environmentalism is a movement located within the latter half twentieth century and the early years of the twenty-first century, although as with any movement precursors are evident. Both the nineteenth-century transcendentalism of Henry David Thoreau and the later conservation advocacy of Theodore Roosevelt are examples of an environmental consciousness predating the crises of the twentieth century. Environmental movements for the most part view the environment as valuable in itself, and thus question the primacy of the human person in the consideration of moral choices. Humanity is still valued, but as a part of a greater ecological web, a community of living beings belonging to the larger landscape of nature itself. The human race is one of many elements within a greater biotic order, and thus our ethical and political values must take into consideration not only the real needs of human beings but also our position within the environment itself. Everything is connected, and everything is part of a matrix of being. We are not placed in this world to merely exploit it beyond our basic needs, but rather to attune ourselves to its rhythms, to follow natural cycles rather than simply extract its resources at the expanse of ecological balance.

A familiar example of this way of thinking can be seen in Aldo Leopold's (1887–1948) concept of the "land ethic." Leopold argued that we must consider the consequences of all our actions on the environment around us, and not only the immediate environment but the whole ecosphere—a community of life and the water, soil, air, and topography in which they together exist. Human beings cannot claim nature for their own, but nature holds a real claim on our humanity. Without this sense of responsibility to the land and the life it sustains, the human race cannot act as moral beings consonant with the purposes of nature hidden behind the complexities of environmental interaction. Hence we must assume that all of our actions have some effect on our environment

and that we must therefore treat the land around us, the waters that flow through it, and the air that immerses all of us as a part of the community to which we are responsible.

The 1960s and the early 1970s were a time of environmental awakening. Books such as Rachel Carson's *Silent Spring* (1962) and E.F. Schumacher's *Small is Beautiful* (1973) helped to promote a newer awareness of the environment and the long-term degradation resulting from pollution and unabated extraction of resources. In the late 1970s, green parties and "Green Thought" appeared within the political sphere challenging a status quo they regarded as hostile to nature and oblivious to our true place within it. Today with the debate over global warming, environmental policy and bioethics are again in the foreground, increasingly influencing the attitudes of the general public in ways that are reminiscent of the late 1960s.

In addition to a genuine sense of connection to the environment and an anxiety over its evident destruction, most environmental movements are characterized by a strain of Romanticism, and thus critical of the Enlightenment rationalism that has produced the kind of instrumental reasoning that has led to the objectification of nature. Our science has been manipulated to produce technologies and industries that violate nature and deprive humankind of its authentic connection to the world. A deep mistrust of the institutions and customs wrought within the crucible of the Enlightenment are concurrent with environmentalism of nearly any variety. For this reason, environmentalism has an affinity with the protest movements of the left and has thus been rightly associated with any creed that challenges traditional society. However, in recent years, environmentalism has broadened its appeal, and is now being embraced by more moderate, and as in the case of certain evangelical Christians, political conservatives. Environmental degradation is a concern of many religious sects, and the ancient Judeo-Christian theme of stewardship is being reemphasized. Hence, environmentalism is fast becoming a movement of considerable sweep.

No longer confined to a Romantic critique of Enlightenment industrialism or associated with antiestablishment politics, it is now a way of thinking fully embraced within the political mainstream while still retaining its radical edge.

Related Entry
ideology

Suggested Readings

Carson, Rachel. *Silent Spring,* Fortieth anniversary ed., with an introduction by Linda Lear and an afterword by Edward O. Wilson. New York: Houghton Mifflin, 2002.

Leopold, Aldo. *Sand County Almanac,* with an introduction by Robert Finch. New York: Oxford Univ. Press, 1987.

Schumacher, E. F. *Small Is Beautiful,* 1973; repr., New York: Harper Perennial, 1989.

Thoreau, Henry David. *Walden.* New York: Mentor Books, 1960.

equality, egalitarianism

Equality has been an integral part of the study of political inquiry since the beginning of political discourse in the ancient world. The historian Herodotus (484 BC–425 BC) referred to a concept of equality under the law as early as c. 440 BC, and the idea is prominent in both the writings of the Stoics and ancient Judaism and Christianity. Stoic philosophers, in a manner atypical of the ancient world, asserted a notion that all human beings are in their essence equal, each possessing a divine spark of reason that dissolves all barriers of rank and social affiliation or membership. Judaism and Christianity both emphasized the equality of all human persons before God. Every person, created as a child of God, is of equal value and thus is loved equally by a just and merciful Creator.

The issue of equality is not confined to the Western tradition alone. Buddhism teaches that all differences separating human beings are in essence illusory, and that the cycle of birth can end within one lifetime, thus providing a theological ground critical of the ancient caste system. While these philosophical and religious principles did not always translate into equality in the political and power hierarchies of the ancient and Medieval world, their influence pervaded the development of civilization and marked humanity with an awareness of the inestimable worth shared by each person.

Hence, the sense that human beings share a moral equality is as old as social commentary itself. A moral point of view regards every human being as of equal worth, a common thread running through a variety of philosophical approaches and traditions. Indeed, the belief in the moral equality of all human beings, rooted in the religious principles of Judaism and Christianity as well as the philosophical ideals of Stoicism, is shard by otherwise disparate political and intellectual orientations. Thinkers as different as St. Thomas Aquinas and Jeremy Bentham would not dispute this basic premise. Several conflicting ideologies agree on this one point: conservatism, liberalism, socialism, feminism, and many others all operate on the assumption that each person bears the same dignity and worth.

Additionally, juridical principles that emerged within the West promoted, at least within the legal sphere, notions of an inherent equality between persons, social status notwithstanding. Legal equality is less universalistic than moral equality yet still aspires to a basic fairness within a given political community. The ancient ideas of the "law of the land" and the related concept of "due process of law" advances the ideal that within a given polity all are equal before the law and all are entitled to the same judicious proceedings in the prosecution of the law. Moreover, the very notion of law itself is essentially egalitarian. Law is generally held by the majority of major political philosophers (such as St. Thomas Aquinas, John Locke, and Jean-Jacques Rousseau, to name only a small segment) to apply to all equally. With Rousseau, for example, the law must come from all (the people as sovereign) and apply to all equally (individual citizens). To do otherwise would be to promote an arbitrary (and thus unjust) inequality.

Most students of political theory embrace both moral and legal equality as a given, although the actual manner in which this is done will vary from each thinker. Other forms of equality—namely, social and economic—are more controversial. A thinker such as Adam Smith, for example, would eagerly endorse moral and legal equality, but allow for inequalities in other spheres of society, mainly as a consequence of liberty. Karl Marx, as an opposing contrast, argued that moral equality is meaningless and political equality incomplete. Without a more pervasive equality, especially in the economic relations of society, there can be no political equality and definitely no real liberty. John Rawls, for example, argues that citizens should be guaranteed an equal right to liberty consistent with an equal liberty for others, but also allows what he calls "permissible inequalities," or a level of inequality that still benefits the least advantaged within the political community.

More recently, equality has been discussed in terms of groups in addition to the more traditional conception of equality as between individuals. Hence we must find ways to ensure that groups of people (such as a racial or religious minority, or women as a whole) are able to fully enjoy the same rights and opportunities as other more dominant groups within the social order. In this vein, equality addresses not only the value of each person, but also the realities of group situations and the dynamics of oppression. Hence, rather than being a static concept well covered by the tradition of political thought, the concept of equality continues to be reexamined and interpreted by new generations of political thinkers and within new expressions of political action.

Related Entries
conservatism; equality of condition, equality of opportunity; liberalism; socialism

Suggested Reading
Johnston, David, ed. *Equality*. Indianapolis: Hackett, 2000.

equality of condition, equality of opportunity

Imagine two races held in two adjacent stadiums. The first race brings all runners to the starting line. Great care is taken to ensure that no one runner is able to get even a split second head start. Additionally, the training of all runners prior to the race is constantly monitored so that no athlete is able to bring to the race any kind of aid that would result in an advantage over the other racers. The gun sounds, the race begins, and a winner crosses the line, with each racer finishing with his best possible time having scrupulously followed all the rules. Medals are allotted for the first place and the other close finishers, and each runner crosses the line in their own time content in knowing they have run a legitimate race. Even though they may not have finished first to win the big prize, they take pride in their ability to finish the race honestly through the best use of their talents and training.

In the next stadium over, a different kind of race is run. There is a clearly demarcated finish line but in this race the runners are not brought to the same starting point to begin the race. Some runners actually start closer to the finish line than others. It is apparent to the spectators that the participants in the race are considerably different in physical shape and mental preparedness. Most runners seem to be of average build and speed, at least as they warm up the majority of runners seem unremarkable. Some of those who are scheduled to race, however, don't seem to be in any kind of shape to run but the shortest distance, a number of them even appear disabled. There is, however, a small but visibly impressive minority among those athletes who appear to possess considerable athletic prowess. Furthermore, each of these exceedingly able runners has brought a retinue of supporters: coaches, trainers, doctors, water boys, agents, even their own cheerleaders. It also becomes apparent that an even tinier minority of the most physically imposing and lavishly supported runners have done everything that they can, including what might be considered by some to be the use of dangerous training methods and even the ingestion of certain questionable substances that further enhance already extremely strong and gifted athletes. But the judges don't seem to worry about that, as they place those athletes at the furthest possible point from the finish line—they are to begin the race practically outside the stadium. The rest of the runners are carefully assessed in various ways and placed at different points along the track, those who promise to be the poorest runners quite close to the finish line, and the rest interspersed between these and the strongest—allegedly chemically enhanced—athletes chomping at the bit near the edge of the stadium. The gun sounds, and all the runners begin the race. As the race unfolds, the spectators see the wisdom of the judges in placing the runners at various starting points. Everyone does their best, everyone runs to their fullest abilities, all cross the finish line at the same time in a well-orchestrated moment of synchronicity, and everyone shares the prize together. All have run the race according to their abilities, all are now provided with what they need.

The first race is an example of what political theorists often call "equality of opportunity." That is, society is responsible for ensuring that every citizen has the same opportunities as every other citizen, that all are given a chance to run a fair race without any advantage or disadvantage, to be given an equal chance to start at the same place as everyone else. From there, a person earns her or his place in society by their own wits and through their own abilities and discipline. The second race is analogous to what is usually called "equality of condition," wherein the goal is to ensure that a condition of full equality is achieved for all citizens, an egalitarian vision of a society that truly guarantees a good life for all, regardless of differences and any socially imposed and thus unfair disadvantages. Rather than place everyone at the same starting position and leaving them to their own devices, which would result in a situation of widely disparate inequalities, the runners are redistributed along the track in such a way that the inequalities of differently distributed starting points will result in a just equality in the outcome. The first race is one in which the judges are aimed at bringing everyone to the same starting line and then allowing them to rise or fall on their own talent and drive. The second race is one in which the judges are more interested in an outcome in which all cross the finish line at the same time, each one running as far and as fast as they can, thus contributing their full abilities to the exhibition, and finding comparable or even identical rewards in the end.

Libertarian and classical minimal-state liberalism approaches seek to design a race after the first example. More activist-state liberalism and socialism (in its various forms) prefer the second race as its model. In practice, most political theory recognizes the desirability of equality of opportunity and the inescapable need, in at least some cases, to seek a degree of equality of condition, thus indicating that opportunity and condition are ideals that are both difficult to reach in their purest sense, but necessary to pursue in a modified and more practical sense.

Related Entries
equality; freedom; justice

Suggested Reading
Johnston, David, ed. *Equality*. Indianapolis: Hackett, 2000.

ethic of care

The "ethic of care" is a concept, advanced by psychologist Carol Gilligan, that responds to what she perceived to be androcentric moral theories and schemas developed within the broad tradition of Western moral theory and the development of psychology in particular. Gilligan, in examining the nature of moral activity, formed a critique of the more conventional views typified by the efforts of her eminent teacher and mentor, Lawrence Kohlberg. Specifically, Gilligan took issue with Kohlberg's highly influential six-stage process of moral development, noting that Kohlberg's schema is not only male-centered but also sketched in such a way as to depict most women as incapable of ascending beyond the third stage (the "good boy–nice girl" phase centered around conformity and the desire for love and approval of one's peers). The higher stages in Kohlberg's schema are characterized by sophisticated legalistic, juridical, political, and moral concepts (decidedly Kantian in their character), which Gilligan saw as posited in a way that attaches these notions to men, thus promoting a notion that men are more inclined to think and act on abstract principle and out of a sense of duty to objective ethical and juridical norms. For Gilligan, what Kohlberg described is an "ethic of right" that stems from a male bias in Western thought that ignores or diminishes the moral qualities of women. Notions of justice, right, duty, principle, and the following of general rules are thus male gendered, and as such, represent only one aspect of human morality. That other aspect, for Gilligan, is a female-gendered ethic of care.

The ethic of care is the expression of a "different voice," a repressed feminine voice that focuses more on interpersonal responsibilities and relationships with others. It is not as concerned with abstract principles or adherence to objective rules as one finds in the ethic of right, but rather is oriented toward the needs and wants of others on a more personal level, a level that seeks mutual care and cooperation as a moral reference instead of the application of a universal standard or rule. Solidarity and community are the outgrowth of an ethic of care that is not thwarted by the more individualistic and objectivist aspirations of the ethic of right. Gilligan argued that the ethic of care is an expression of a deeper sense of benevolence than can be found in the ethic of right, which focuses more on doing what is right in accordance with a rule rather than doing what is needed in care for the benefit of the persons involved.

In identifying the ethic of right with the male and the ethic of care with the female, Gilligan did not mean to say that this is a necessarily innate distinction. The ethic of care is evident more in women owing to the tendency of our culture to stifle those emotions that are more conventionally, rightly or wrongly, associated with women, such as nurturing, sensitivity, patience, and open affection. Men are encouraged to compete, to assert themselves as autonomous individuals even to the point of aggression when necessary, and are discouraged by our cultural norms from exercising the more selfless qualities now associated with the feminine. Women are not as hampered, for they are more able to cross between the language of rights and the "different voice" of care, which is the voice that women speak in almost exclusively. However, Gilligan observed that this is only a function of the current structure of society, and the male can be brought to appreciate the more emotive and nurturing elements of moral conduct, and in so doing, deemphasize the more juridical and rule-focused notion of ethical activity.

Gilligan's ethic of care has received some criticism from different quarters, ranging from charges of an inverted sexism that depicts men as universally insensitive to the caution that an ethic of care attached to women will inadvertently place women into a position where they are expected to be nurturing, patient, sensitive. In this position, women will not be expected to stand up for "what is right" in the sense of the ethic of right that ostensibly is the province of men. In spite of her critics, the notion of a "different moral voice" has provided an important service in the discussion of the nature and sources of morality, reminding ethicists, psychologists, philosophers, political theorists, and their readers of the complexity of human virtue.

Related Entries
ethic of conviction and ethic of responsibility; ethic of right; justice

Suggested Reading
Gilligan, Carol. *In a Different Voice*. Cambridge, MA: Harvard Univ. Press, 1993.
Kohlberg, Lawrence, *Essays in Moral Development*. Cambridge, MA: Harvard Univ. Press, 1978.

ethic of conviction and ethic of responsibility

Toward the end of Max Weber's 1918 lecture on *Politics as a Vocation,* the great sociologist and political analyst drew a sharp distinction between two kinds of moral passion: the "ethic of conviction" and the "ethic of responsibility." The ethic of conviction, in Weber's definition, is formed by the idealistic passions of those dedicated to a grand, principled vision of the world. Driven by the belief that their "convictions" hold the truest prescription for the salvation of humankind, they tenaciously promote their ideals and commit their lives to their realization. To act otherwise, from the perspective of the ethic of conviction, would be inauthentic. To Weber, this is an "absolutist ethics" that seeks purity of principle, and then acts in the world accordingly. It is in the absolute rightness of the ideal and the true consistency of one's actions informed by that ideal that a person's acts are consonant with moral rectitude. "The man who embraces an ethics of conviction," Weber remarks, "is unable to tolerate the ethical irrationality of the world. He is a cosmic, ethical 'rationalist.'" The irrationality of the world can be corrected with the proper application of pure—that is truly moral—principles. It is in the purity of these principles and an unyielding devotion to their absolute realization that one can act with genuine commitment. Consequences, within the ethic of conviction, Weber notes, are an afterthought, a lesser consideration. As Weber observes,

> [T]here is a profound abyss between acting in accordance with the maxim governing an ethics of conviction and acting in tune with an ethics of responsibility. In the former case this means, to put it in religious terms: "A Christian does what is right and leaves the outcome to God," while in the latter you must answer for the (foreseeable) *consequences* of your actions.

Weber detects in this "profound abyss" a disturbing and potentially dangerous prospect for politics in the age of ideology. Those gripped by their convictions, while admirably impassioned and sincere in their desire for a better world, in the final analysis blind themselves to the realties around them and to the manner in which their inability to comprehend predictable consequences may in fact undercut the purposes behind their principles even to the point of producing the opposite result of what was initially desired or intended. Ultimately, the fault is not to be found in the principle, but in the corrupt ways of the world around us, in the society that stubbornly refuses to admit to the truth that confirms one's convictions. Weber continues,

> You may be able to prove to a syndicalist who is a convinced adherent of an ethics of conviction that in all likelihood the consequences of his actions will be to improve the prospects of the reactionaries, to increase the oppression of his own class and to hamper its rise. But however convincing your proofs may be, you will make no impression on him at all. Such a man believes that if an action performed out of pure conviction has evil consequences, then the responsibility must lie not with the agent but with the world, the stupidity of men—or the will of God who created them thus.

Weber explains that an ethic of responsibility is not only concerned with the question of foreseeable consequences and how one's actions will directly effect society, but also recognizes, and even assumes from the beginning, human flaws, the "average human failings" that are a fact of social and political life. The trouble is "not in the stars" as Shakespeare wrote in *Julius Caesar,* "but in ourselves;" this is the basic premise of the ethic of responsibility. It does not seek to change a decrepit or wicked system or to cast blame on the external world around us—"the stars" as it were—but rather to engage in political and social activity, whether reformist or otherwise, with a keen sense of caution regarding the long-term effects that any chosen policy might produce. To the person who holds an "ethic of responsibility," the man of conviction is a fanatic, one who is obsessed with the purity of his convictions more than with the benefits of his immediate actions, and who is more devoted to "ensuring that the flame of protest against the injustice of the social order should never be extinguished. To keep on reigniting is the purpose of his actions." For Weber, such an attitude risks the implementation of harmful means aimed at a purely just but abstract end. An ethic of responsibility, on the other hand, while less impassioned and perhaps overly cautious, nonetheless is more likely to avoid the excesses of ideological fanaticism.

In the final analysis, Weber concedes that conviction and responsibility are both necessary for a political commitment that is both concerned with social improvement and realistic in the assessment of possibilities, good and bad. Weber acknowledges that politics is an activity that involves both the "head" and the "heart," and in devotion to the latter, the ethics of conviction is spot on. After all, Weber elsewhere in his lecture on *Politics as Vocation* admires the charismatic side of political leadership, a side that is intimately related to the passions of conviction. A proper blending of ideals and prudence are healthy, and can encourage a mentality that is political in the best sense.

> [A]n ethics of conviction and an ethics of responsibility are not absolute antitheses but are mutually complementary, and only when taken together do they constitute the authentic human being who *is capable* of having a "vocation for politics."

In this way Weber admits the necessity of both impulses in the vocation of politics—a sense of responsibility that is fully aware of the effect ideas will have on the lives of ordinary citizens, while at the same time admitting the value of idealistic aspiration. In this way Weber adroitly and sensitively balances the need for both the practical realism of experience and concern for consequences as well as the meaningful purposive aspiration for the good and the right. Those who truly possess a vocation for politics will be known to the world as persons of responsible conviction.

Related Entries
ethic of care; ethic of right; iron cage of modernity

Suggested Reading
"Politics as a Vocation," in Weber, Max. *The Vocation Lectures,* ed. David Owen and Tracy Strong, trans. Rodney Livingston. Indianapolis: Hackett, 2004.

ethic of right

In Carol Gilligan's analysis of feminist ethics and its relationship to political thought and practice, she makes a distinction between an "ethic of care" and an "ethic of right." The latter refers to those principles, practices, laws, and institutions that revolve around a notion of individual rights objectively universal to human beings as such. The content of these principles are basically political, juridical, rationalist, and egocentric. An ethic of right is often cast in terms of individual claims against the state and society, and thus is interpreted as a factor in a theory of individualism that under certain circumstances provokes conflict between citizens and their political community or legal institutions. An ethic of right treats legal and moral claims formally, as the decisions of abstract individuals somehow linking their moral judgments to individual interests or as the generalized rules governing the duties and responsibilities of moral agents. In Gilligan's analysis, the individual is regarded as an abstraction easily universalized and detached from context and therefore from the particularities of the social world that constitute a person's qualities.

The notion of the "rights of man" is an example of the formalistic concept of the ethic of right that is defined in terms of right and wrong. The ethic of right involves the desire by rational individuals to follow a general rule or set of rules regarding right and wrong actions, asserting the priority of principled decisions over the context of relationships and situations. For Gilligan, this mode of ethics stems from a gendered worldview that shapes moral and political values in masculine terms, or at least in ways that have been influenced by an androcentric ethical culture. The emphasis on rational individuals making moral choices, political decisions, or legal enactments is essentially the consequence of a lopsided ethics that is the product of a culture that has historically associated such activities with men. In contrast, Gilligan proposes that a new approach to ethics and politics is possible by examining, as well as acknowledging, a "different voice: that also shapes our moral outlook, but is generally considered less seriously as it is associated with a more feminine attitude." This is what Gilligan calls the "ethic of care," and its recovery is necessary if the formalist, individualistic, and abstract notion of ethic of right is to be balanced against a more communally centered normativity.

Related Entries
ethic of care; ethic of conviction and ethic of responsibility

Suggested Reading
Gilligan, Carol. *In a Different Voice*. Cambridge, MA: Harvard Univ. Press, 1993.
Kohlberg, Lawrence, *Essays in Moral Development*. Cambridge, MA: Harvard Univ. Press, 1978.

existentialism

In a word, existentialism describes those ideas or attitudes that begin all ideational investigations and moral questions from the premise that "existence precedes essence." Existentialism is not so much a school of thought or even a coherent fixed set of propositions as a philosophical inclination or even a cultural trend. The term is so broadly employed that students of philosophy, if they so desire, can trace existentialist ideas and methods as far back as one can go in the history of ideas. The usual precursors to existentialism that are listed in historical introductions, however, are Søren Kierkegaard, Friedrich Nietzsche, Karl Jaspers, and Martin Heidegger, with the usual nod to the novelist Fyodor Dostoevsky and even earlier thinkers such as Blaise Pascal and René Descartes. Kierkegaard is most important for his rejection of Hegelian hyper-rationalism, his refusal to categorize immediate existence with abstract philosophical concepts and definitions, and his emphasis on the themes of subjectivity as the fount of knowing and freedom as the only authentic reaction to *angst*. (*Angst* is the objectless anguish evoked by the encounter with pure being). Nietzsche contributed his subjectivist perspectivism and critical revaluation of values, and Jaspers provided a humanistic sensibility critical of philosophical rigidity and affirming the dignity of an authentic self-examination that leads to a transformative freedom. Jaspers emphasized the moral necessity of embracing the concrete while simultaneously remaining aware of the "incomprehensible reality" above all things that eludes the scrutiny and definition of the intellect. In embracing the world before us and recognizing our responsibility for critical self-examination of one's purpose in the world, we can discover the basis of our freedom and initiate the changes needed to live authentically rather than behind the partial delusions of abstract categories and technical definitions.

Heidegger is a different breed of cat. As such, it is impossible to summarize him in a few short sentences. Suffice it to say that in Heidegger we are introduced to themes that emphasize the uncovering of being in the temporality of the world, the problem of death and nothingness, and the attempt to rediscover the authentic meaning of human life through a recovery of the lost tradition of ontology. For Heidegger, we are "thrown" into the world, beings destined for death and constructing meaning only out of a sense of care for one's existence in the foreknowledge of one's inevitable fate. We act authentically when the nature of reality flashes before us, a reality that is oriented to the future, a future that is already known as inevitably terminable. Being is care for the world in the awareness that our inexorable destination is an encounter with nothingness.

From Heidegger we move to Jean-Paul Sartre, the most famous of the existential thinkers and one of the few who explicitly accepted the term "existentialism" as an apt description. Following Jaspers and Heidegger, Sartre understood all meaning to emerge directly out of lived experiences. "Existence precedes essence," that is to say, what we take to be essential is really simply a product of the encounter between consciousness (*l'etre pour soi*—being for itself, which is nothingness) and being itself (*l'etre en soi*). Consciousness is for Sartre a nothingness, empty of content, absolutely alone in the world, without presuppositions, innate structures or predetermined meaning, and ultimately, without hope. Being in itself is the dense matrix of existence, the only thing that really "is," without justification, without reason, without meaning of its own, wholly alien to the emptiness of the world, the very fact of its indifference nausea inducing. There is no human nature, there is no transcendent meaning—there is only the nature that we make of ourselves in the sum of our choices and actions (or nonactions) and the meaning that we impose in order to make sense of the absurdity of our situation. Meaning emerges in the encounter between the nothingness of consciousness and the density of being, a meaning that can be riddled by anxiety, doubt, fear, denial, and inauthenticity. To overcome these reactions to the alien nature of being, we must realize that we are radically free to act and create without any preconceptions or predetermined conditions to limit our choices. We are radically free to act as we see fit, but with this freedom we must also accept radical responsibility for all that we do, and all that we have made of ourselves. It is not in God or nature or the social system that we are made, but only in our decisions to think, feel, and act in response to the contingency of life. From the exertion of our freedom, meaning can be identified, but on our terms, not on the acts of anyone else, or the foundations of anything external to us.

The concept of radical freedom is the primary contribution of existentialism to political thought. From here Sartre attempts to connect radical freedom and personal responsibility to social commitment. Unless we recognize our responsibility for our actions in the world, we are acting in bad faith, a self-delusion that we are not able to act in any other way, that our choices are made for us, and that our life is structured by forces beyond our control. We choose everything, according to Sartre, and to ignore our choices is a mere mask for our own anxieties, a pretense to hide from our own freedom. Sartre's commitment to social responsibility led him to embrace Marxism, a decision that required him to engage in some considerable ontological gymnastics in order to reconcile his earlier concept of radical existential atomism with the Marxian notion that "man is the ensemble of social relations." Sartre embraced Marxism as the only course of authentic action against oppression, whether that oppression comes through the Nazi storm trooper or disguised behind a liberal-capitalist façade of inauthentic liberty. Sartre went to great lengths to fuse the nothingness of consciousness with the Marxian claim that our ideas are products of our material relations of production, a project that consumed the last three decades of his intellectual career.

For thinkers such as Maurice Merleau-Ponty and Albert Camus, Sartre's decision to embrace Marxism (and especially a deterministic strain of Marxism) is an utter failure. For Merleau-Ponty in particular, the notion of radical freedom that Sartre espouses was an error to begin with; we are free, but our freedom is at least partially influenced by the context of the world around us. Merleau-Ponty's understanding of freedom is more evocative of Stoicism: it is in our response to contingency and absurdity that we are free, but we are not so free as to abolish contingency and absurdity. We are not empty consciousness alone in an alien world of impenetrable, meaningless being—rather, we are filled with being, wholly embodied and embedded in the world, we are *of* being, not against it. Meaning stems from the way in which we intend consciousness from our position as corporeal agents, thus we can never really separate the thought from the object of intention, nor can we discern a clear difference between the initiation of will and the reactions of our body as we move within the layers of our being. We are free, according to Merleau-Ponty, but our freedom is not so much a matter of radical indeterminacy as it is a participation in the lived world as a radical part of that world. For Sartre, everything is alien to us except our own acts; for Merleau-Ponty, nothing is alien to us except our refusal to live.

Existentialism reached the peak of its influence in the postwar period, particularly relevant from the late 1950s to the early 1970s. In fact; existentialism can be identified with the cultural changes of the 1960s. By the later 1970s its cachet was on the wane, although it was still relevant in the academy. Ten years later it would be displaced by postmodernism, its influence come and gone. Still, existentialism as a philosophical method will continue to contribute to the open inquiry of the nature and meaning of human existence, for many of the issues that drew the attention of the "existential approach" are as old as philosophy itself, perhaps as old as the Oracle of Delphi's injunction to "Know Thyself." It is in that injunction that existentialism is best comprehended; all the rest is an extrapolation.

Related Entry
Merleau-Ponty, Maurice

Suggested Reading

Heidegger, Martin. *Being and Time,* trans. J. Macquarrie and E. Robinson. New York: Harper and Row, 1962.

Jaspers, Karl. *Reason and Existing: Five Lectures,* trans. William Earle. New York: Farrar, Strauss and Giroux, 1955.

Merleau-Ponty, Maurice. *Sense and Non-Sense,* trans. H.L. Dreyfus and P.A.. Dreyfus. Chicago: Northwestern Univ. Press, 1964.

Sartre, Jean-Paul. *Being and Nothingness,* trans. Hazel Barnes. New York: Philosophical Library, 1966.

Exitus actor probat—See **end justifies the means**

F

faction

The *polis* or political community, as Aristotle observed in Book Two of his *Politics,* is a plurality, an association composed of a multiplicity of groups of various sizes and divergent allegiances. The tendency to gather in groups identified by common interests, backgrounds, loyalties, or responsibilities is thus a substantive feature of any polity. This is the basic origin of and even necessity for the existence of what we today call, within the discourse of politics, factions. Prior to Aristotle, Plato acknowledged the inevitability of plurality in his *Laws,* wherein his "second-best city" was to be composed of four classes and twelve tribes, all representing different segments of the *polis* within a configuration that would encourage a harmony of parts. But factions, while they can evince a healthy pluralism, are also sources of friction and division. Every major political theorist has understood this. For Plato and Aristotle, the conflict between the affluent and the poor is a constant within the life of any society, and if not checked by appropriate education, wise statesmanship and just institutions and laws (and in the case of Aristotle, the expansion of the middle class), these divisions, or factions, will precipitate a state of civil war between the contemptuous wealthy class and the envious impoverished class.

This concern over the power of factions to undercut social and political unity is common throughout the Great Conversation. Notably, within the modern element of that tradition, the Scottish thinker David Hume warned against attachments to parties, particularly what he deemed "parties of principle," which he contrasted against "parties of personal friendship" or allegiance. The former is what we would today call "ideological" affiliations, which Hume judged to be dangerous to the political community, especially if such parties emerged holding opposite views regarding "the essentials" of government. Hume asserts, "Factions subvert government, render laws impotent, and beget the fiercest animosities among men of the same nation, who ought to give mutual assistance and protection to each other." Parties of principle, a modern phenomenon for Hume, are at once divisive and dangerous. In other words, attachments to abstract ideas and their attendant approaches to governing are inimical to the sense of community and the common allegiances required of citizenship. Going even further with this admonition, French philosopher Jean-Jacques Rousseau, Hume's contemporary, inveighed against "partial associations," for they exert a strong particular will that in every way places antipathy between citizens and the general will, which is the common good of the entire polity. Rousseau argued that as long as these partial associations competed against the common good as established by the general will, the state would not be able to promote the rule of law and the conditions of equal citizenship vital to the restoration of freedom among true citizens.

Perhaps the most famous, at least to American students of political ideas, remarks concerning factions were made during the founding of the American republic. George Washington, Alexander Hamilton, John Adams, Thomas Jefferson, and, most effectively of all, James Madison, shared the view that factions produce a constant state of tension and precipitate political strife within republican societies. Yet, the American founders understood faction to be natural to human beings, and therefore never entirely insurmountable. Factions exist to the detriment of social and political community, but factions must exist if we are to live as free human beings. Factions are in every case, according to Madison, "adverse to the rights of other citizens, or to the permanent and aggregate interests of the community." But as Madison continues, faction springs from latent causes "sown in the nature of man," and cannot be eradicated without militating against human nature and, as it follows, human liberty itself. Or as Washington observed, faction, or "the Spirit of Party" along with all its "baneful effects...is inseparable from our nature, having its root in the strongest passions of the human Mind." Rousseau's vision toward the fullest triumph of the general will over partial societies violates the very essence of what it means to be human for statesmen-philosophers like

Washington and Madison. Factions are undesirable, to be sure, but unavoidable. Unavoidable, yes, but not irresistible, as certain prudent measures are available to us to reduce and check what Madison called the "violence of faction," it is this that ranks among the higher priorities given to republican government.

Thus if, as Aristotle taught, the polity is in its deepest nature a multiplicity of interests, students of political inquiry and participants in the act of citizenship must concede this fact while working toward a just harmonization of diverse interests. To a large extent, then, the art of politics is devoted to this balance between the partial and the general, the protection of diversity within the common space combined with that sense of community by which such a space cannot exist.

Related Entries
Federalist Papers; Madison, James; Rousseau, Jean-Jacques

Suggested Reading
Federalist Paper No. 10, by Madison, is the first place to look when considering the topic of the nature of factions. This essay can be found in all collections of the *Federalist Papers* as well as in nearly every anthology of American political theory, and even as an appendix to a sizeable number of American government textbooks. In particular, consult Hamilton, Alexander, James Madison, and John Jay. *The Federalist Papers,* ed. Clinton Rossiter, rev. Charles Kesler. New York: Mentor Books, 1999.
For contrast, consult Rousseau, Jean-Jacques. *On the Social Contract,* trans. Donald Cress. Indianapolis: Hackett, 1987.

fascism
Etymologically, the word "fascism" can be traced to the Latin *fasces,* an ancient image of rods bundled together surrounding an axe and symbolizing authority in Roman culture. The image itself is benign, and is commonly employed even in democracies to represent political order and the just rule of law in a variety of contexts. Ideologically, Fascism is anything but benign; a term frequently employed,

usually as a pejorative, and yet infrequently understood, often to the detriment of intelligent political discourse. This is not necessarily the result of intellectual dishonesty or laziness, but more likely the result of the concept's inner contradictions and slippery conceptual framework. Of all the ideological movements that have appeared in the past two centuries, fascism is the most difficult to accurately define and yet one of the more destructive social forces to emerge in history. Fascism is at minimum authoritarian and yet defiantly opposed to any genuine recognition of authority as such. It is primarily a populist movement, yet it is formed around an intense devotion to elites. While exhibiting this elitism, it nonetheless rejects any notion of a fixed elite and is thus antiaristocratic. It is anticommunist, anti-Bolshevik, anti-Marxist while openly trumpeting its own internal collectivism. It is anti-Enlightenment yet more than willing to take advantage of the Enlightenment's legacy of technological progress. It is antimaterialist yet often frames the progress of its programs in terms of prosperity, even to grotesque extremes as in the example of Hitler's attempt at building an opulent New Berlin. It is antireligious and yet aspires toward a kind of mysticism. It is antirationalist and yet unabashedly relies on science in service to its various forms of domination. It is antiindividualist and yet invests everything in the unique personality of the charismatic leader. It celebrates devotion to duty yet sardonically dismisses adherence to personal conviction. It is antibureaucratic yet depends on organization and regimentation of society at all levels. It is vigorously antimodern yet is more the product of modernity than any of its contemporary ideologies. It is critical of the decadence and cultural despair of modernity yet, in the end, has exhibited a pathological despair far more decadent than the worst excesses of industrial liberalism. In a word, as José Ortega y Gasset explained, it is "A and not A." A few common themes do emerge across the strains of fascistic ideology. Fascists are generally inclined to celebrate the irrational and the elemental, insist

on devotion to nation, and from this devotion, mix socialist collectivism with nationalist ardor defined in terms that reject class division, adore heroic and flamboyant leadership, adopt autarkic economic views, seek either cultural purity or racial purity, exclude political dissent, marginalize vulnerable groups within society, regard "truth" askance and appeal to it only in service to power, and, finally and perhaps more importantly, understand and act in the world from the premise that war is the natural order of things.

While it is problematic to do so and thus a point of debate among students of intellectual history, one can see a conceptual lineage reaching back to some of the ideas advanced by the nineteenth-century German philosopher, Friedrich Nietzsche (1844–1900). It is important to remember that Nietzsche himself was critical of the kind of herd mentality, vulgar aesthetics, and mass manipulation characteristic of fascistic movements, but even so, certain aspects of Nietzsche's thought do resemble, anticipate, and perhaps directly influence the antirationalism of fascism. Nietzsche's uncompromising critique of the "decadence" of Platonism, Christianity, and both liberal democracy and socialism and his insistence on the exertion of the will and the preeminence of the life instinct are at least intellectually compatible with the fascistic mentality. It is not an unreasonable jump from Nietzsche's assertion that "all life is will-to-power" to the obsession among fascist ideologues over the acquisition and use of power for its own sake as the defining quality of the superior man. Additionally, in the writings of Henri Bergson (1859–1941), Mark Neocleous identifies an inadvertently antirationalist strain that again, while not endorsing or causing fascism, nonetheless resembles attitudes that lead to the fascistic posture. As with Nietzsche before him, Bergson sought to reexamine the history of Western philosophy and culture in terms of nonrational forces. Philosophy in particular and Western culture in general are for Bergson not in fact the result of rational accretion of ideas and principles but rather the direct product of life instincts and precognitive forces. Bergson's notion of an *élan vital* (or vital force) explains the development of Western culture. It is in "life-philosophy" and the instincts and energies associated with nature that we find the foundation of ideas and values. Such an assertion rejects the rationalist legacy of Western philosophy from Socrates through John Locke and unintentionally opens the way for both a nonrationalist as well as an antirationalist approach to political thought and ideological activity, a necessary but not in itself sufficient or inevitable step toward generating the normative conditions for a fascistic movement.

In addition to Nietzsche and Bergson, a variety of other thinkers, rightly or wrongly, have been associated with, at least in part and in some cases unfairly, the development of concepts that would eventually stimulate the growth of a fascistic perspective. Elite theorists such as Vilfredo Pareto (1848–1923) and Gaetano Mosca (1858–1941), nationalists such as Joseph Mazzinni (1805–1872), German idealist such as Johann Gottlieb Fichte (1762–1814—also an ardent nationalist who has been seen by some as the true philosophical precursor to Nazism) and G. W. F. Hegel (1770–1831), prophet of doom Oswald Spengler (1880–1936—explicitly identified by Nazis as an intellectual inspiration, although he eventually incurred the wrath of the party after 1933 for his criticism of Nazi racialism and militarism), the idiosyncratic Georges Sorel (1847–1922), and even Jean-Jacques Rousseau (1712–1778) have appeared on the list of theoretical suspects. Sorel, who identified with Marxism and is associated with French syndicalism, is of particular interest in that he emphasized a thoroughgoing irrationalism in political action and promoted the use of myth and violence in the achievement of political ends. Carl Schmitt (1888–1985) is also numbered among those intellectuals who may have fueled Nazi ideology, in part due to his early cooperation with the Nazi regime, and in part due to his political views that emphasized a strong authoritarian state as well as the concepts of "friend" and "enemy" as central to the shaping of political engagement. Schmitt's legacy is somewhat muddied, though, by his falling out of favor with the Nazis in the mid-1930s (having been accused of inauthenticity in spite his public anti-Semitism and his support of the Führer), and for his apparent affinity with an older more conservative form of political autocracy more reminiscent of Bismarck than Hitler.

A more direct and explicitly established ideological lineage stems from the French counterrevolutionary movement *Action Française,* particularly the writings of Charles Maurras (1868–1952); an obscure anti-Semite and Beer Hall putsch conspirator, Dietrich Eckart (1868–1923); and the active intellectual support provided by Giovanni Gentile (1875–1944) in the development of Italian fascism under Benito Mussolini (1883–1945). Additionally, racialists such as France's Joseph Gobineau (1816–1882) and British-born Germanophile Houston Chamberlain (1855–1927) helped to provide a conceptual language through which virulent anti-Semitism and racism could find expression within fascistic movements. An intense nationalist and monarchist, Maurras blamed the French Revolution and subsequent republicanism for the decline of French civilization and the end of French glory. Both anti-Semitic and anti-Protestant, Maurras, an agnostic, promoted Catholicism as a state-sanctioned religion but only for political purposes and against the interest of the church itself—the Vatican officially condemned *Action Française* in 1926. Maurras was less critical of scientific methodology than other fascistic ideologues, but resembled the other ideologues in his attempt to advance a mystical unity with the historic destiny of the French nation.

Interestingly, Gentile's influence is explicitly drawn more deeply from Hegelian idealism than from the life philosophy or vitalism of Nietzsche or Bergson, adding Hegel's name to the ranks of fascism's unwitting precursors. Gentile, an erstwhile student of Benedetto Croce (who openly opposed Mussolini after

1924 and thus broke with Gentile) became a staunch apologist for Italian fascism and is believed to have penned as ghost writer Mussolini's *Doctrine of Fascism,* wherein older forms of conservative and autocratic thought are renounced and the totalitarian features of fascism are explicitly expressed. Gentile, more than any single thinker, is aptly titled the "philosopher of fascism." The young Hitler drew heavily on Eckart; Anton Drexler (1884–1942), a founder of the German Worker's Party (to be renamed the National Socialist German Worker's Party); and Gottfried Feder (1883–1941), a member of the occultist Thule Society that believed in Aryan supremacy and a lost landmass that was presumably the location of an advanced Aryan civilization. Drexler and Feder joined Hitler in drafting the "25 points" that would serve as a founding document of early National Socialism. Eckart's ideas would be easily dismissed were it not for their influence on Hitler, for it was to Eckart that the second volume of *Mein Kampf* was dedicated. And yet, as Ernst Nolte has remarked, it is not so much in the intellectual precursors and ideologues as it is through the speeches and actions of leaders that the symbols and myths of fascism are expressed. The basic patterns followed by fascistic politics "must be," Nolte states, "derived from the writings and speeches of Mussolini and Hitler." Fascism's open contempt for rational politics militates against any authentic reliance on an intellectual tradition. Owing to this varied and confusing ideological history of ideas that ambiguously and ambivalently points toward fascism, it becomes difficult to really identify key principles and to recognize major philosophical thinkers who can be confidently depicted as founders of fascist tenets. Only the deed bears meaning to the fascist believer. It is in the words and deeds of leaders—and not in any set doctrine or philosophical principles—that the patterns of fascistic movements unequivocally emerge. As Neocleous has incisively written, "For fascism, one should ask not which doctrine is true, but adopt whatever belief expresses the will most forcefully and is most likely to mobilize the masses. Action, not thought, will be the basis of individual and social transformation."

Given this succinct and yet illuminative observation, Neocleous provides further assistance in understanding the fascistic mentality through the discernment of three general and effective "central concepts" of fascistic ideology: war, nature, and nation. According to Neocleous, fascism is essentially an ideology that engages in universal "perpetual war." This aspect of fascism reflects the obsession with the exertion of will, and again raises an indictment against Nietzsche. It also recognizes, as do the Marxists, that struggle is a fact of history, but for the fascist, class struggle is an illusion and misdirection. Ultimately, the only struggle that is real is the one between peoples and nations. And only in warfare is the value of a people tested for its mettle. War for the fascist is the only reliable fact of life, and victory in war is the only true test of the value of a people or the will behind a culture. War is pure deed, and thus the only worthy test of the strength of a society. Hitler in particular focused on this element, convinced that German will would ultimately be the decisive factor in the triumph of the Aryan race. In the end, Hitler was prepared to stake the will of the German people against the encroaching armies moving upon them, for should the German people fail, it was better for them, in Hitler's mind, to die in flames than to survive, weak and defeated. War, for fascism, is the only way to determine who should gain and who should lose, the only principle that can justify itself, and the only real test from which we can judge the merit of any idea.

The notion of perpetual war as the fundamental value of fascism is closely intertwined with fascistic ideas regarding nature. Nature is the ground for struggle, a struggle to exert the will over and against all resistance. As Neocleous illustrates, there really is no historical sense behind fascistic politics. Neither the grandeur of ancient Rome for Mussolini nor the search for a historical Aryan culture for Hitler are the real foundation of their respective political visions. Rather, history is an academic exercise and of no real interest beyond that which serves to confirm the reality of underlying natural forces. It is in nature, the law of the strong and the dynamic of collective struggle through war, that the master race and a truly great culture are rooted. Nature is dynamic and ever changing and, more importantly, always looking toward the next conquest. History bears a sense of the past and a reverence for tradition that is incompatible with the unfettered will. Custom and tradition are only valuable in so far as they support the movement of will, and the movement of will is the dynamism of nature itself. Nature is force and motion, symbolized in the swastika and glorified in *Blitzkrieg,* and ultimately beyond moral judgment.

Nations are more than products of history and the development of traditions and tried institutions. In the fascist mind peoples and nations are generated by nature itself. Thus it is in the nation and its power that nature is fully affirmed. The individual is strengthened through this absorption into the energy of nations, and through such strength, is able to struggle against the flaccid comforts of petty self-gratification. Both Mussolini and Hitler understood the power of nationalism, and were repulsed by both the worker's internationalism of socialism and legalistic internationalism of liberalism in the post–World War I era. It is the nation, not class consciousness nor international order, to which we owe allegiance. Internationalism is either a weak delusion of bourgeois liberal-capitalism or a nefarious Bolshevik attempt at domination. Only in the nation can the individual find meaning. The nation goes beyond a record of commonly held experiences and shared customs; it is its own personality and its own end. It is important to keep in mind that this is more than the ardent nationalism of the latter nineteenth century, although some commentators have drawn connections between the nineteenth-century nationalists and fascism. For the fascist, the nation is more than the public realm common to a given people, more than the state and its attendant institutions, and more than the commonly held values that spring from cultural and religious traditions shared by a particular ethnic group. The nation is a spiritual dynamic within which the individual is absorbed and from which the individual is given purpose. Nations convey their own myths and exist as a spiritual alternative to religion. No religion, for the fascists, can equal the inspirational power of and devotion to the nation. The nation itself, the great *patria* or *Volk,* alone can sustain the individual in a meaningful way. And it does so because it is natural, it is the only true and pure source of value for individuals and their actions. Anything else, for the fascist mentality, is at best ancillary to the nation. There are no rivals in fascism. Religion, philosophy, democracy, science—all are either summarily repressed or somehow cynically absorbed in service to the fascist cause. Fascism knows but one law—the law of power exerted through universal, natural war. And the medium through which this natural war is executed must be the nation, for only a sense of national duty truly evokes the unequivocal devotion of the fascist individual.

Fascism reached its apex in the 1930s and early 1940s. Not only in Germany and Italy but also in France, Romania, Spain, Croatia, Japan, and Argentina, fascist or quasi-fascistic movements were able to gain considerable allegiance. As a major political movement, fascism no longer draws the same volume of allegiance, nor does it achieve the same type of influence that it held from the early 1920s to the end of World War II. By and large, fascism as a political force is a relic, and currently can be found only on the outer fringes of militant disaffection. Nonetheless, both populist movements and highly authoritarian and militaristic regimes remain vulnerable to the temptations of the fascistic impulse and act as reminders of the dangers inherent in antirationalist appeals to the triumph of the collective will.

Related Entries
authoritarianism; ideology; totalitarianism; tyranny

Suggested Reading

Neocleous, Mark. *Fascism.* Minneapolis: Univ. Minn. Press, 1997.

Nolte, Ernst. *Three Faces of Fascism: Action Française, Italian Fascism, National Socialism,* tr. Leila Vennewitz. New York: Holt, Rinehart, and Winston, 1965

Passmore, Kevin. *Fascism: A Very Short Introduction.* New York: Oxford Univ. Press, 2002.

Federalist Papers

Composed under the pseudonym "Publius" by Alexander Hamilton, James Madison, and John Jay (whose contribution was minimal owing to circumstances surrounding his health), 85 essays successfully championing the ratification of the newly proposed Constitution of the United States came to be collectively known and published as *The Federalist,* or the *Federalist Papers.* The *Federalist Papers* would ultimately become the most important contribution of American political thought to the general history of ideas. While the immediate purpose of these essays was to persuade the voters of the state of New York to endorse the proposed constitution, the essays combined together soon became a classic exercise in political theory. Thomas Jefferson, rival to Hamilton, friend and ally of Madison, observed in 1788 that the essays of Publius were "the best commentary on the principles of government, which ever was written." Jefferson's insight has sustained a degree of credibility throughout the generations since the essays were first published in two volumes in 1788.

Several themes run throughout the 85 essays, too many to cover in one encyclopedia entry. However, some themes are more prominent than others, and taken together, represent a coherent voice projected by the three authors behind the *nom de plume* of Publius. Among others, Publius (Hamilton, Madison, and Jay) promotes moderate republicanism ambitiously framed within a national scope of considerable extent, the dispersal of power directed by a vigorous administration, a distrust of both the raw power of the majority and the caprice of elites, a concern for the divisive tendencies of parochial regionalism, a realist view of the requirements of states in an essentially hostile international order, a sober assessment of human nature and its influence on political activity, a belief that the "true principles" of republican government can be prudently applied through sound institutions in spite of the many flaws of human character, and the necessity of a more intimate connection between citizen and state tempered by the protections of law. These, and others remaining unmentioned here for lack of space represent ongoing themes that interweave the 85 essays into a coherent whole.

Borrowing from Charles Kesler, these basic themes are examined and clarified according to the following outline: essays 1–14 review "the utility of the union" and its ability to promote "political prosperity," essays 15–22 examine the failure of the union under the Articles of Confederation, and essays 23–36 call for energetic and ambitious government for the promotion of liberty, prosperity, and security. For Kesler, these 36 essays constitute the first part of the *Federalist Papers,* buttressed by the overarching theme advocating a stronger union among the several states. The second part, in Kesler's assessment, explain the merits of the proposed constitution, as follows: essays 37–40 illuminate the new Constitution as both republican and federal in form and point out the delicacy of the balance between these two principles, essays 41–46 explain the question of power in the newly proposed structure and its bearing on the several states, essays 47–51 provide Madison's famous lesson on the doctrine of "separation of powers and checks and balances," essays 52–83 explain the various branches of government, how they operate, and how elections are to be conducted, and finally the last two essays (84 and 85) offer a response to additional objections (including Hamilton's reply to the concern over a lack of a Bill of Rights) while comparing the proposed federal structure to the states, asserting the efficacy of the new Constitution in securing liberty and the free enjoyment of property.

ain
er-
:on
14,
son
son
70,
. In
did
). 9
the
son
as a
lity
blic.
: of
the
ded
ides
rent
: for
iven
rates
tion
and
four

essays on the separation of powers, and No. 51 is especially prominent as Madison provides the strongest argument for the dispersal of power after Montesquieu. Madison No. 55 stands as a masterpiece in the literature on the nature of representation. In Nos. 67, 70, and 78, Hamilton discusses the nature of executive and judicial power and authority, and in Hamilton No. 84 he lucidly explains the absence of a bill of rights in the initial draft of the constitution as proposed. No doubt an alternative perspective would add essays not identified here and delete some of those that are, but it is safe to say that the majority of the essays in the aforementioned list are widely regarded as the more substantively compelling and historically enduring.

The *Federalist Papers* continue to serve as an important commentary illuminating the nature of constitutional government as many of the Founders understood it. And while they cannot be read without comparison to the less unified writings of the various antifederalists, the *Federalist Papers* continue to provide important theoretical insight into the relationship between political reflection and practical application. Martin Diamond once referred to the framing and ratification of the American Constitution as a "revolution in sober expectations," an observation easily confirmed by a close reading of the *Federalist Papers*.

Related Entries
antifederalists; Hamilton, Alexander; Madison, James

Suggested Reading
Hamilton, Alexander, James Madison, and John Jay. *The Federalist Papers*, ed. Clinton Rossiter, rev. Charles Kesler. New York: Mentor Books, 1999.

feminism

Feminism as a general concept represents a critique of society explaining the essential oppression suffered historically and currently by women within traditional societies that are inherently patriarchal and androcentric (male centered). It also represents a prescription for the advocacy and application of a new approach to social action and political activity that challenges patriarchy, promotes the liberation of women, advances a more pervasive sense of equality, and offers new dynamics of power no longer burdened by the desire to dominate and subdue. As with any ideology or school of thought, feminism is divided into different types, but for the most part all branches of feminist thought and activism support the realization of political and legal rights for women equal to men and address the continuing economic inequalities that have stifled equal opportunity for men and women alike throughout history. Political and legal rights, coupled with equal economic opportunity, are the defining issues of liberal feminism, which can be said to be the oldest type of feminist theory, dating back to at least the nineteenth century; although a careful reading of the history of ideas traces feminism further to the writings of Mary Wollstonecraft (1759–1797) and Mary Astell (1666–1731), and some might argue that Plato's conclusion that men and women are essentially the same represents a precursor to feminist theory. Liberal feminism focused primarily on political rights (universal suffrage, opportunities for women in the political sphere) and legal reform (advocating equality of women before the law, especially concerning the rights of property) and labor reform (equal pay for equal work). While all branches of feminism can be said to adopt these (liberal) positions, more recent types have attempted to carry feminism into a more penetrating criticism of society as a whole.

In addition to liberal feminism as described in the previous paragraph, one can discern four basic strains within current feminist theory: socialist, radical, cultural, and ecological (ecofeminism). Socialist feminism is an outgrowth of Marxian theory, which is in itself primarily informed by theories of class oppression. Socialist feminism is an attempt to combine the Marxian focus on class struggle, which remains a real phenomenon for the socialist feminist, with the challenge to patriarchy (which is a form of oppression not exclusive to capitalism). Socialist feminists agree that the class structure is oppressive, but they add that women are doubly subjugated. Not only are women exposed to the same economic injustices suffered by working men, but they are also victims of secondary status even within the labor class. Men dominate women across the classes, subordinating the interest of women to the ambitions of laboring men. Women are not only moral equals to men, but they are and should be economic equals and should thus share ownership of the means of production with their male counterparts. Hence, not only should the goal of revolution be to abolish class, but it should also work toward the abolition of gender as well. Men and women are equals in every sphere; this is the key to the socialist feminist critique of liberal feminism, which is viewed by the socialist feminist as at best only a half-measure.

Radical feminism also begins with a critique of liberal feminism but goes further still. The reformist methods of liberal feminist are insufficient to effect a true liberation of all women. The legislative and policy strategies aimed at a meliorist improvement of women's status is not enough. Furthermore, the socialist feminists, in spite of their rejection of patriarchy, are still too dependent on the old model of class struggle, which is in the end a distraction. For the radical feminist, the liberation of women means a complete liberation from the power of men, something that the socialist feminist is not willing to admit. Radical feminists argue that the source of oppression runs deeper than laws and political practices and runs right to the core of society, which is in every facet a patriarchy hostile to the interests of women. More than economic class struggle or political disenfranchisement, the radical position is one that seeks to reform society on deeper levels. A revolution against patriarchy is the key; a complete rejection of traditional society, which has evolved only to the advantage of men and at the direct expense of women. Some, like Shulamith Firestone, envision a society where men are abolished altogether, although radical feminism is not necessarily so militant. Extremist aside, the lessons of the radicals are important in revealing the deeper problems of oppression that are beyond the reach of ordinary political reform. Feminism for the radical is ultimately an ontological question— women are oppressed in the nature of things, the structure of which has always been shaped by the power of the male.

What can be called cultural feminism represents a branch of feminist reform that takes a different approach. Unlike the universalism of liberal and social feminism, or the ontological rebellion of radical feminism, cultural feminism seeks to both emphasize and promote the differences between the sexes. Women are by nature more nurturing and communitarian than men, who are by their nature more aggressive and individualistic. Where men seek to conquer, women seek resolution through peace, tolerance, and interdependency. Hence a new ethic, one that is other-directed and based on the principles of care, should be forwarded in the hopes that the male-dominated and juridical ethic of right can be replaced, or at least significantly altered, by a more feminine way of operating in the world. For the cultural feminist, there is some truth to the old (but misrepresented and even distorted) attributes associated with women. These attributes are not weaknesses but strengths, and should women gain more influence and power, the world would itself be transformed toward peace and cooperation, mitigating or even replacing the militaristic and competitive values of men.

More recently, an ecological strain of feminism has emerged, one that insists that the degradation of the natural environment has been an extension of an oppressive androcentric tendency to seek domination over not only other human beings, but over nature itself. Men seek to subdue and develop wilderness, and are thus disconnected from the cycles of the natural process. Women hold a deeper connection to the natural world—to Mother Earth—and thus know nature in a way that men cannot appreciate. Hence, the only way the environmental movement can achieve any success is to abandon male-defined and male-driven policies and emulate the naturalism of women, and in so doing, foster a new stewardship of nature that is guided by the intuitive connection of women to the natural world. Eco-feminism proposes a new way to regard nature and seeks solutions to the destruction of the natural world that are not misshapen by the masculine impulse to dominate nature, bending it to the will of humanity.

Feminism is both an ideology and a critical strain within philosophy. While some of the more fanatical proposals like Firestone's are easily dismissed by the more impatient critics of feminism, on the whole feminism offers an honest appraisal of the nature of power within any given ideological system or political regime, and an alternate perspective on the cultural undercurrents that are often invisible to those engaged in action on the political level.

For political theory to obtain a more comprehensive understanding of the currents of power in modernity, the voice of the feminist must be carefully examined.

Related Entries
ethic of care; ideology; liberalism; socialism

Suggested Reading
Kolmar, Wendy, and Frances Bartkowski, eds. *Feminist Theory: A Reader.* New York: McGraw Hill, 2003.

Schneir, Miriam. *Feminism: The Essential Historical Writings.* New York, Vintage Press, 1994.

Vincent, Andrew. *Modern Political Ideologies.* Oxford: Blackwell, 1995.

first principle of justice (Rawls)
In *Theory of Justice,* political theorist John Rawls argued that two principles of justice would naturally emerge from within an original position of equality among rational self-interested actors. The first principle that rational actors would agree upon from this original position is, according to Rawls, as follows:

> Each person is to have an equal right to the most extensive total system of equal basic liberties compatible with a similar system of liberty for all.

Rawls states that this is a principle of justice as fairness that can be embodied within institutions for the sake of achieving a just distribution of social goods. Any rational actor deliberating with other rational actors from within an original position of equality would arrive at this essential principle of justice. Every human being would desire as much liberty as possible while at the same time recognizing that it would be in one's interest to acknowledge the need for compatible liberties among all participants within a given polity. The first principle of justice is associated with what Rawls considers to be a thin theory of the good, wherein any rational agent would desire a basic respect for liberty and would seek a fair chance at the opportunities available to persons in society. Additionally, the first principle of justice is related to Rawls's first priority, which affirms the priority of liberty as the first social good necessary to a fair society, even over the desirable value of equality.

Rawls's first principle, which stresses liberty, is accompanied by a second principle regarding the distribution of social goods in such a way as to guarantee the improvement of even the least advantaged. This is the difference principle, which is a fair limitation on both liberty and equality. This difference principle advances the notion that our liberties must be enjoyed within a system that still benefits the least advantaged (and hence is limited by responsibility) and that for the sake of liberty, some inequalities are to be permitted so long as they remain beneficial to all. This second principle of justice is discussed separately under the entry on the **difference principle**, but it is important to bear in mind in consideration of Rawls's deeper understanding in the mutual respect of liberty as evinced in his first principle of justice.

Related Entries
difference principle; entitlement theory; liberalism; veil of ignorance

Suggested Reading
Rawls, John. *Theory of Justice.* Cambridge, MA: Harvard Univ. Press, 1971.

first principles
In metaphysics, first principles refer to those principles that are objectively real and prior to any subjective judgment. They serve as both the foundation of particular human moral activity as well as the framework wherein human inquiry can discern universal verities. To speak of a first principle is to ground both knowledge and ethics in a transcendent source, such as Plato's Forms or the natural law as understood by St. Thomas Aquinas. Moral realism assumes the independent existence of general truths and values and is premised on the notion that these truths and values are discernable through the application of human reason. Hence there is an objective moral order that enables certainty in our actions and

provides a reliable test of the rectitude of our societies. For the moral realist, this is vital to the affirmation of real values, for without these higher principles, all of our judgments are exposed to the uncertainty of subjectivism and thus vulnerable to the exertions of human will. A principle guides us to moral action, not by our invention, but by the inner truth contained within the principle itself. It should be noted that theoretical schemes can rest on first principles that are not necessarily transcendent. For example, Kant's categorical imperative and Rawls's first and second principles of justice—or even Rousseau's notion of the general will—might all serve in different ways as species of first principles that are not metaphysically grounded. St. Thomas Aquinas's First Precept of the Natural Law—to do good and shun evil—is an example of a more traditional understanding of first principles.

Classical political theory for the most part embraces the premise of first principles in various ways. It is only fairly recently in the history of ideas, scarcely 150 years or so that widespread criticism of moral objectivism has emerged. Throughout the balance of the history of political theory, first principles of some type were assumed as given.

Related Entries
absolutes; Aquinas, Thomas; Aristotle; Plato; *Republic,* The (*Politeia*)

Suggested Reading
Aristotle, *Metaphysics,* trans. Richard Hope. Ann Arbor: Univ. Mich. Press, 1960.
Kreeft, Peter. *A Refutation of Moral Relativism: Interviews with an Absolutist.* San Francisco: Ignatius Press, 1999.
Lewis, C.S. *The Abolition of Man.* New York: Macmillan, 1947.
Plato. *Complete Works,* ed. John M. Cooper. Indianapolis: Hackett, 1997.

Foucault, Michel (1926–1984)
A driving force in the postmodern movements of the second half of the twentieth century, Michel Foucault is a singular figure. Not a philosopher, political theorist, or even ideologue

in the traditional sense, Foucault's academic training was in psychology and the history of science. Nonetheless, his intellectual bent was toward the analysis of politics and culture, and it is here that Foucault left his style and imprint upon contemporary theory. Only Jean-François Lyotard, Jacques Derrida, and Richard Rorty can be said to match his stature as principal figures in the "postmodern movement," and his remains a compelling voice in the candid critique of established modes and dynamics of power.

Four themes can be said to represent Foucault's attitude toward the political: inquiry as genealogy, the ubiquity of power and its inseparability from knowledge, the panopticon as a model of the carceral society, and the nature of and need for oppositional politics. There are other important elements to Foucault's thought as well, but for the purposes of examining his attitude toward politics, we will confine ourselves to these four themes.

Genealogy is a term deliberately employed by Foucault to draw a connection to the antifoundational perspectivism of Friedrich Nietzsche (1844–1900). The genealogical analysis of ideas and movements depicts the manner in which concepts and values are outgrowths of nonrational and contingent influences and social forces. In other words, concepts such as justice, right, power, and the Good are not discerned by rationality, but rather are constructed from a complex of prerational factors. Nothing is really essential; rather, the norms and ideas that we value are elements of an idiom wholly contingent on aspects of culture and society antecedent to formalized thought. Additionally, history is not correctly understood in terms of the inevitability of reason and continual progress. Rather, discontinuity and random occurrence are the factors that reveal historical currents and their effects on contemporary cultures and institutions. Moral, political and juridical norms are by-products of social and cultural developments—not in the Marxist sense grounding ideas and values in an inevitable conflict with the realm of material production but rather with a keen sensitivity to the lack of inevitability in the formation of values and institutions. All is contingent, yet everything is somehow traceable to concealed stories. As with Nietzsche before him, Foucault found the Enlightenment apotheosis of reason and inevitable progress, like the search for first principles in the classical and Medieval worlds, to be simply one contingent discourse out of many, and a discourse that in presuming universality and objective rationality ultimately produces domination. From here Foucault entered into a second theme, what can be called the power/knowledge inseparability thesis.

Foucault concludes that power is "ubiquitous," moving throughout the entire social body from every direction. Power in premodern and even early modern societies visibly flowed from the sovereign to the subjects, but modernity has decapitated power, severing the king's head as it were, reconfiguring the flow of power so that it originates from multiple sources. "Power is exercised from innumerable points," argues Foucault, and we are all enmeshed in a matrix of power with no center or visible head. Power is "capillary," penetrating every aspect of human life and dissolving the ancient distinction between the public and the private. No longer are we confronted with the older understanding of the power of a single, identifiable sovereign who commands the power over death. Instead, we are shaped and pressured by a less visible but more insidious power over life, or what Foucault calls "biopower." We have moved from a juridical notion of law and power to its ubiquity as the determining factor in our lives. Whereas under past notions of sovereignty those in power seldom affected us directly, capillary power means that we are constantly under the direct pressure of power in some way.

Accordingly, Foucault introduces the famous couplet of power/knowledge. What we understand to be knowledge is particularly shaped by power. Hence, as with Nietzsche, concepts such as knowledge, truth, belief, and principle are really manifestations of power. Every truth that we determine is really an outgrowth of power. The Baconian dictum "knowledge is power" is, for Foucault, drawn to its logical conclusion. Knowledge is evidence of a power relationship, and truth therefore is an exertion of dominance over other possibilities. Once power determines truth, alternative viewpoints are marginalized or abolished.

Concomitant to the marginalization of difference, Foucault describes the formation of the carceral society, a political and social structure realizing Bentham's panopticon at the most general level. Because of the ubiquity of power and the tendency of power to dominate, coerce, and punish, society itself is transformed from association to incarceration, and the model of the prison becomes the norm for the community. Power is primarily disciplinary and manipulative and produces uniformity and docility within the members of the social body. As with a prison, we are molded and coerced into submission, accepting externally imposed routine as the only norm available to us and responding passively to the multiple sources of pressure that discipline us to behave in uniform ways. Hence, for Foucault, what was once the type of life reserved for the prisoner under the traditional sovereign now is the way of life for everyone in the omnidirectional network of knowledge/power.

For Foucault, this life as a prisoner can be resisted, but it requires a commitment to opposition, a decision to refuse the univocal structure of power/knowledge within postindustrial societies and an embrace of multiplicity and alterity. If power is capillary as Foucault asserts, then it can be seized at any moment by anyone and at any point within the knowledge/power matrix. What is needed is an oppositional politics that challenges uniformity and normativity with heterogeneity and the decentering of knowledge and self. Power must be exposed for what it is and resisted by what it is not. This involves the refusal to accept contingent norms and a promotion of difference for its own sake. This commands us toward not only an acceptance of multiplicity, but the actual creation of it. Power is capillary, but it

operates from nodal points, what is needed is the elimination of the fixed nodes and a reconfiguration of power in such a way as to prevent marginalization and univocality. Knowledge/power must be deconstructed and replaced by demarginalized pluralism undefined by a dominant voice or perspective masking itself behind a false universality. Margins are dissolved through the decentering of society—no single "head" or "voice" capable of governing from the top or controlling discourse from the center is to be allowed. Such a decentering reaches even into the individual self. The self is no longer to be constructed as a discrete individual with an ego as its nucleus. Rather, the self is to be understood in terms of the specific eruptions of discourse, desire, gesture, and, above all, power. There is no objective self, but rather effects of the social and cultural pressures that lead us toward, or away, from normativity.

Foucault's critique of knowledge/power has had a broad effect within contemporary political theory, particularly since the mid-1970s. Whether or not Foucault will continue to inspire the next generation of theorists remains to be seen, but regardless of his future influence, his ideas and arguments will always rouse interest and stimulate the consideration of alternative points of view. In this Foucault, for all his controversy, has provided an important service to the meeting of ideas.

Related Entries
biopower; carceral society; differend; incredulity toward metanarratives; Nietzsche, Friedrich

Suggested Reading
Foucault, Michel. *The Foucault Reader,* ed. Paul Rabinow. New York: Pantheon Books, 1984.

Four Freedoms

On January 6, 1941, toward the end of his Annual Address to Congress with America's full entry into World War II a growing inevitability, President Franklin Roosevelt affirmed four principles of freedom upon which, in his estimation, the balance of civilization relied. The first two freedoms, regarding free speech and religion, echoed rights traditionally embraced by Americans and protected in the First Amendment. Additionally, President Roosevelt affirmed two principles that speak to economic justice and international security: freedom from want and freedom from fear. However, even the first two freedoms are linked by Roosevelt to all human beings, for in adding the phrase "anywhere in the world," the Anglo-American tradition of right is expanded to a universal principle of freedom shared by all humanity and set firmly against the horrific tyranny that was at the time menacing all civilization and decency. In so doing, President Roosevelt's speech linked the older tradition of civil liberties with a growing awareness for the need to develop freedoms in other aspects of human life in order to ensure both justice and security as well as promote basic liberties. The text of President Roosevelt's declaration is as follows:

> In the future days, which we seek to make secure, we look forward to a world founded upon four essential human freedoms. The first is freedom of speech and expression—everywhere in the world. The second is freedom of every person to worship God in his own way—everywhere in the world. The third is freedom from want—which, translated into world terms, means economic understandings which will secure to every nation a healthy peacetime life for its inhabitants—everywhere in the world. The fourth is freedom from fear—which, translated into world terms, means a world-wide reduction of armaments to such a point and in such a thorough fashion that no nation will be in a position to commit an act of physical aggression against any neighbor—anywhere in the world. That is no vision of a distant millennium. It is a definite basis for a kind of world attainable in our own time and generation. That kind of world is the very antithesis of the so-called new order of tyranny which the dictators seek to create with the crash of a bomb. To that new order we oppose the greater conception—the moral order. A good society is able to face schemes of world domination and foreign revolutions alike without fear.

> Since the beginning of our American history, we have been engaged in change—in a perpetual peaceful revolution—a revolution which goes on steadily, quietly adjusting itself to changing conditions—without the concentration camp or the quick-lime in the ditch. The world order which we seek is the cooperation of free countries, working together in a friendly, civilized society. This nation has placed its destiny in the hands and heads and hearts of its millions of free men and women; and its faith in freedom under the guidance of God. Freedom means the supremacy of human rights everywhere. Our support goes to those who struggle to gain those rights or keep them. Our strength is our unity of purpose. To that high concept there can be no end save victory.

Shortly after Roosevelt's speech, the American artist Norman Rockwell produced a set of four paintings respectively depicting each of the four freedoms so averred.

Related Entries
freedom; justice; liberalism

Suggested Reading
Roosevelt, Franklin D. "State of the Union Address before Congress," Jan. 6, 1941.

free development of each is the condition for the free development of all

Concluding part two of *The Communist Manifesto*, Karl Marx and Friedrich Engels, in almost anthemic phrasing, reaffirmed the socialist commitment to the realization of a notion of social equality that rests on the foundations of complete universality of benefits. "In place of the old bourgeois society," the authors asserted, "with its classes and class antagonisms, we shall have an association, in which the free development of each is the condition for the free development of all." In a real sense, this statement encapsulates not only the Marxian vision but also the defining goal of most communitarian movements and related theories. Nonetheless, as it comes from the pen of the nineteenth century's most famous radical (or pair of radicals, as the case may be), it is rightly associated with Marxist revolutionary politics and served as an elemental maxim of twentieth-century communist movements.

Related Entries
communism; from each according to his ability, to each according to his need; Marx, Karl; socialism

Suggested Reading
Marx, Karl, and Friedrich Engels. *The Marx-Engels Reader,* 2nd ed., ed. Robert C. Tucker. New York: Norton, 1978.

freedom (liberty)

One of the central concepts in political inquiry, freedom is nonetheless variously interpreted and applied. The question as to the extent of our freedom, or perhaps even the illusion of it, is basic to the concerns of political thought and action. Indeed, political action itself is impossible without the premise of freedom to some degree, for only the free person can act as moral and political agent. Should determinism be proved, then the possibility of political activity is substantively reconfigured.

For Plato, to be free is to be capable of self-mastery—the governance of the self under the rule of reason. It is inaccurate to claim that the ancients did not possess a concept of individual freedom owing to their emphasis on communal obligation. While it is the case that thinkers such as Plato, Aristotle, and the Stoics did not conceive freedom in terms with which we are today familiar or comfortable, it is an error to cast the ancient theorists as ignoring the requirements of what it means to be a free person. It is not the individual liberty from external interference that we often speak of today that was uppermost in the minds of thinkers such as Plato (although it is clear from Plato's critique of ancient democracy that he was well aware of this kind of freedom and its implications), but rather one's ability to apply self-discipline within one's own soul. In the view of both Plato and Aristotle, freedom was ultimately in service to the Good, however vaguely understood. A rational person is only truly free (in terms of self-mastery) if his or her actions are directed at the Good or in pursuit of goodness. Moreover, what applies for the person also applies for the *polis;* hence a political association worthy of the name is composed of free citizens intending virtue. Anything less is not a true polity, but rather a regime of rulers and subjects rather than governors and citizens, or in the worst case, one master (the tyrant) and a slavish multitude.

The Stoics connected freedom to fate, and thus understood the concept as primarily the response of the inward self to a predetermined necessity. "Some things are up to us and some are not up to us," the Stoic philosopher Epictetus once wrote, a sentiment representative of the Stoic conflation of freedom and necessity. Epictetus elaborates,

> Our opinions are up to us, and our impulses, desires, aversions—in short, whatever is our own doing. Our bodies are not up to us, nor are our possessions, reputations, or our public offices. The things that are up to us are by nature free, unhindered, and unimpeded; the things that are not up to us are weak, enslaved, hindered, not our own.

Epictetus and the Stoics in general embraced a fatalistic notion to the effect that there is little a person can really do to change external circumstances. We are unable to impose our will upon the world, but we can learn how to discipline ourselves, and in particular our thoughts and emotions, in order to respond with dignity to the circumstances and events around us. Freedom is thus a sort of quietism defined in terms of how we respond to those things and events that are really beyond our control. Even more than Plato and Aristotle, freedom is an inward state of mind involving the self alone. Beyond that, the world around us and even our role in it is determined by the forces of necessity. Interestingly, in Machiavelli's *The Prince,* he states that half our actions are owing to our free will and half to fortune, or fate—a view reminiscent of Stoicism.

With the emergence of Christianity, freedom of the will became a vital element of the acting person. To be created in the image of God means, among other things, to be a person possessing freedom of the will, and thus to be able to act upon the world according to one's own lights. For a human being to discern and follow the moral law of God and to be responsible for all actions toward or away from that purpose, free will is an essential premise and fundamental aspect of human nature. The very choice to disobey the Creator in the Edenic paradise illustrates the manner in which human beings both possess freedom and thus can act on their own choices, for good or ill. Significantly, St. Augustine taught without equivocation that human beings possess free will while at the same time held firm to the notion that God is the true sovereign of all things, and thus that the grace of God is necessary for salvation. God's omnipotence and omniscience would seem to place the possibility of free will in doubt, but for St. Augustine and the Magisterium of the Roman Catholic Church, freedom is still requisite to the moral conduct of the human person. Hence it is inaccurate (albeit understandable) to interpret St. Augustine as teaching a strict doctrine of predestination, for St. Augustine, while confessing the necessity of grace, nonetheless adheres to a position that regards freedom to be an ontological quality of our humanity. We are free to orient our will toward the love of God or the love of the self alone, to embrace the City of God or the city of the earth. An omniscient God knows in advance the choice that is to be made, but the choice is there in St. Augustine's view, otherwise we cannot properly speak of human beings as free agents.

This is also the foundation of the views of St. Thomas Aquinas. Free will is the power to elect a life of blessedness in its various forms. Will, according to Aquinas, is a "rational appetite" for both temporal happiness and spiritual beatitude, and thus is a desire of the human soul that is established because of the basic goodness in human beings as creatures of God. Our freedom is founded on the reality of universal goodness, and it is only because we are created to be good and remain, in spite of the stain of Original Sin, capable of being good, that we are known to be free. The problem of God's foreknowledge of our acts is explained by Aquinas through the realization that God does not exist as we exist, and that our perception of time—of the order and duration of things as they come into being—makes us unable to grasp the eternity that is known only by the Godhead. We are of necessity free creatures, for this is a primary characteristic of our essential nature. However, our freedom is not absolute, nor are we able to fully comprehend it when juxtaposed to the omnipotence and omniscience of God. As souls created in the image of God, we must be free, rational, and capable of love, but as creatures of God, there is nothing that we can conceal from God. For St. Thomas Aquinas and St. Augustine, freedom remains a mystery of faith.

With the emergence of Protestantism, the apparent tension between free will and grace was reconsidered, leading to the development of a theory of predestination that militates against free will. This is particularly evident in Calvin, although the idea is present in Luther as well. God's omniscience and omnipotence in this case is interpreted as eliminating the freedom of the will. No good act can be performed, under the doctrine of predestination, absent the preordained dictates of God. Hence a free person is, in reality, according to this view free insofar as God has determined such a person to lead a righteous life, thus judgment regarding this person is already passed. With the Council of Trent (1545–1563) these views were condemned, opening another rift between Protestant (particularly the Calvinist wing) and Catholic Christians. Catholicism hewed to a view that free will allows human persons to cooperate with God's divine plan and thus to prepare to receive the grace of God, which for the Calvinist is irresistible. Under Trent, God's grace can be resisted, but, following St. Thomas Aquinas and St. Augustine, we are disposed to goodness, and thus inclined toward following God's design. As Protestantism further divided, many Protestants modified or dropped the doctrine of irresistible grace; hence Christianity's position on the freedom of the will is rendered complex as a result. In particular, Anglican and Anabaptist views, while considerably disparate, both in their own way resemble the Catholic view on free will more than they do the Calvinist position, thus serving as an example of the manifold diversity within the many branches of Christian theology.

Modern views of freedom are most easily traced to Thomas Hobbes, more than any other thinker. With precision Hobbes defined liberty (or freedom) "properly signified" as "the absence of external impediments," or the "absence of opposition." Fundamentally, human beings are "bodies in motion," the ability to "move" without impairment being the only reliable measure of one's degree of liberty. Hence liberty, with Hobbes, is conceived with regard to external variables and conditions within the environment. The will, for Hobbes, becomes the "last appetite in deliberation," a notion that accomplishes a conflation of free agency and desire. Hence the notion of liberty now becomes attached to both the free movements of individuals in pursuit of their appetites and in reaction to their aversions, and to their deliberation of their private interests. Freedom is, with Hobbes, no longer conceived as a state or quality of being but rather as an environmental condition. In spite of Hobbes's influence, John Locke's notion of free agency returns the moral will to the equation. Locke agrees with Hobbes that we are by nature free, but that freedom as Locke interprets it resembles the older notion of freedom to choose to follow the moral law of nature more than mere appetitive impulse, as in Hobbes. Both Locke and Montesquieu distinguish freedom or liberty from license (or, as Sir Robert Filmer defined it, "to do as one lists") and attach true liberty to the rational obedience to moral and political law. Hence the threads of free will that can be traced back to the ancients remain in both Locke and Montesquieu, although somewhat refracted through a more individualistic medium, particularly in the case of Locke.

Utilitarianism, by and large, follows the Hobbesian template in its conception of individual liberty, although with varying degrees of sophistication. The Benthamite understanding of individual choice as "chained" to the sovereign "thrones" of pain and pleasure is closely aligned with Hobbesian materialism and conceptions of human nature framed by individual self-interest. But not all utilitarianism is strictly Benthamite (J.S. Mill representing the most notable exception); thus the utilitarian conception of liberty is not identical to the Hobbesian, although Hobbes's influence remains pervasive.

Rousseau and Kant forward the Lockean-Montesquieuian notion in a way that draws the relationship between freedom and law even more tightly. "To be driven by appetite alone is slavery," Rousseau asserts, "and obedience to the law one has prescribed for oneself is liberty." By fusing our interest to that of the "general will," which is manifest through law as issued by the people in their capacity as sovereign, the human agent can exert a moral freedom superior to the liberty associated with our natural impulses and appetites. This notion is reaffirmed at a more complex level in Kant's categorical and practical imperatives; grounding free will in the commitment to follow a self-prescribed principle. With Kant and Rousseau, the concept of human freedom is attached to moral obligation without reference to a transcendent source of principle beyond the sovereign will of the collective legislator exerting its interest in the "kingdom of ends." Thus, the Hobbesian-utilitarian conception of freedom (and for some, this would also include, arguably, the Lockean view) represent an individualistic "negative" conception of freedom while the Rousseauian-Kantian (and by extension Hegelian-Marxian) conception represents a "positive" notion of freedom.

Related Entries
conservatism; equality; justice; liberalism; negative and positive liberty; socialism; utilitarianism

Suggested Reading
Augustine, *On Free Choice of the Will,* trans. Thomas Williams. Indianapolis: Hackett, 1993.
Bauman, Zygmunt. *Freedom.* Minneapolis: Univ. Minn. Press, 1988.
Flathman, Richard E. *The Philosophy and Politics of Freedom.* Chicago: Univ. Chicago Press, 1987.
Mill, John Stuart. *On Liberty,* ed. Michael B. Mathias. New York: Pearson and Longman, 2007.
Morgan, Michael. *Classics in Moral and Political Theory,* 4th ed. Indianapolis: Hackett, 2005.
Patterson, Orlando. *Freedom in the Making of Western Culture.* New York: Basic Books, 1991.

from each according to his ability, to each according to his need

A seminal tenet of Marxian theory, the familiar phrase was first coined by Marx in 1875 in his *Critique of the Gotha Program,* as follows:

> In a higher phase of communist society, after the enslaving subordination of the individual to the division of labour, and therewith also the antithesis between mental and physical labor, has vanished; after labour has become not only a means of life but life's prime want; after the productive forces have also increased with the all-round development of the individual, and all the springs of cooperative wealth flow more abundantly—only then can the narrow horizon of bourgeois right be crossed in its entirety and society inscribe on its banner: from each according to his ability, to each according to his needs.

Here Marx effectively summarized his social ethic. Society, according to Marx, should aim at an arrangement wherein persons will freely and creatively contribute in ways that reflect their talents and aspirations. Labor will not be coerced, but becomes the activity that is desired above all else, the merger of one's authentic skills and genuine aspirations. This amounts to the emancipation of labor, returning labor to its natural state wherein it is both an expression of life as well as the only certain guarantee of the gratification of true needs. As labor is no longer coerced and controlled by capital, according to Marx, its collective power will finally be realized in its fullest capacity, and "cooperative wealth"

will achieve a degree of unprecedented abundance. With the reconciliation of the ownership and the operation of the means of production, the fruits of this abundance are no longer commanded by a specific class, but are now freely available to all who need. One gives what they can, and takes what they need (needs now also being more authentic, not created by the engines of commerce or the habits of society). This is the communist ideal, a society wherein all needs are easily gratified, regardless of one's natural abilities to contribute in a particular way. Through the full emancipation (and in Marx's eyes, rehabilitation) of human labor power combined with an awareness of genuine needs that will be more compatible with the human spirit, motivation to engage in work will be defined by one's talents and inner desires, and what is really needed will be realistically understood and easily obtained.

Related Entries
anarchism; communism; from each according to his ability, to each according to his work; Marx, Karl; socialism

Suggested Reading
Marx, Karl, and Friedrich Engels. *The Marx-Engels Reader,* 2d ed., ed. Robert C. Tucker. New York: Norton, 1978.

from each according to his ability, to each according to his work (or, from each…to each according to his contribution)

The Marxian principle that one should give what one is able and take what one needs (see **from each according to his ability, to each according to his need**) is often modified within Marxian literature through the emphasis on one's contribution. One should give what one can, and in return one is entitled to receive rewards due to the fact that one has somehow contributed to the collective good. Whereas the original phrase that encourages one to take what one needs appears unconditional, this modification of the maxim that draws attention to work (or contribution) reintroduces a condition that rests on some vague notion of merit. In other words, one should be able to receive what one needs, but one must also, if a claim is to be made to any of the fruits of collective production, contribute substantively in some way. This phrase is found in the Stalinist constitution of 1936 and is regarded for the most part as recognition that there will be a transitional period between capitalism and communism that will still employ a degree of incentive in order to spur production. "From each according to his work" concedes the need for this incentive at least until the authentic communist person emerges, and in so doing, transcends the notion of incentive as we now know it.

While the emphasis on work and attendant merit is readily associated with followers of Marx (particularly those who actually gained power), the idea can be traced to Karl Marx himself in his *Critique of the Gotha Program*. It is here that Marx at first states that one should freely take what is needed (unconditionally as explained in from each according to his ability, to each according to his need), but before doing so, Marx reminds his readers that communism grows dialectically from the foundations already established by capitalism, and in its early manifestation is "in every respect, economically, morally and intellectually, still stamped with the birth marks of the old society from whose womb it emerges." Therefore, before communism can achieve its full maturation ("from each according to his ability, to each according to his needs"), it will in some ways resemble that which it now negates. Hence Marx states,

> Accordingly, the individual producer receives back from society—after the deductions have been made—exactly what he gives to it. What he has given to it is his individual quantum of labor. . . . He receives a certificate from society that he has furnished such and such an amount of labor (after deducting his labour from the common funds), and with this certificate he draws from the social stock of means of consumption as much as costs the same amount of labour. The same amount of labour which he has given to society in one form he receives back in another.

While this notion seems structurally similar to earning wages under capitalism (hence the charge that such an arrangement is really only collective or "state" capitalism), Marx intends this to rest on the new premises of economic motivation and social merit that would be forged by the liberated workers themselves. Residues of attitudes embedded in human habits by capitalist economic production will linger and can even be used to advantage for a time, but Marx always understood that the transition to authentic communism would mean the radical reconfiguration of the way in which human beings think about labor and act upon their motivations. For Marx, while one might be given in the earliest manifestations of communism what is due according their work, ultimately a social paradise would spring forth dissolving all artifacts of capitalism, including incentives framed by old needs, wants, and fears. At that moment, for Marx, one freely gives as they choose, and receives only what is truly needed.

Related Entries
anarchism; communism; cost as the limit of price; from each according to his ability, to each according to his need; Marx, Karl; socialism

Suggested Reading
Marx, Karl, and Friedrich Engels. *The Marx-Engels Reader,* 2d ed., ed. Robert C. Tucker. New York: Norton, 1978.

fundamentalism
In general, the term fundamentalism can mean any movement or association that claims a special and therefore superior insight into the essential principles and practices of a given system of belief, particularly religious. In a sense, any religious, ideological, or political movement contains a core of fundamental ideas, and thus any number of interpretations of those core ideas can claim to be closer to the foundations than others. However, as the term is used by students of ideas, "fundamentalism" is generally regarded as containing at least the following elements: an exclusive claim to the truth

and the assertion of superior knowledge of the basic principles of a system of belief, a claim to purity of practice, a tendency toward literalism and legalism, a willingness to confront alternatives by impugning their interpretive integrity, and a proclivity to "recover" what is perceived to be a more authentic core of the faith regarded as lost or corrupted by modern deviations—using missionary zeal and/or resolute insularity.

The actual term "fundamentalist" can be traced not to ancient religious practices, but rather to a movement in modern evangelical Protestantism no older than the late nineteenth century. Fundamentalism in this sense is a movement that seeks a return to a more "Biblical" and morally clarified Christianity. This branch of Christianity is critical of many features of modern secular cultures as well as what are perceived by fundamentalist adherents to be corruptions of Christian practice in Catholicism and mainstream (i.e., historically older and institutionally developed) Protestantism. For this reason, fundamentalism is embraced by a certain wing of evangelical Christians as a positive revival of true Christianity but criticized by other branches of Christianity for disfiguring the inner essence of Christian theology and appropriating Christian ethics for a particular social agenda. Thus fundamentalist Christianity is seen as both a badge of honor by some and a troubling distortion by others. Either way, the emergence of fundamentalist Protestantism has held considerable social influence, visibly reaching into the political and ideological sphere and has become a topic of interest to students of political inquiry.

Fundamentalism, however, is not simply confined to a specific kind of Protestantism. In fact, a fundamentalist dynamic is present in nearly every religious tradition, and it is not unusual for this kind of impulse to exert its influence at various times. Catholic fundamentalism rejects the legitimacy of reforms instituted at the Second Vatican Council, even to the point of accusing every Pope since Pope John XXIII to be a false claimant to the Chair of St. Peter.

While decidedly on the margins of Catholic culture, the presence of such fundamentalists punctuates the fact that not all such movements are exclusively Protestant. Islamic fundamentalism, which is often depicted as a desire to return to the kind of Islam practiced by Muslims during the Middle Ages and associated with a decidedly aggressive and violent militant spirit, has caused considerable international upheaval in the past four to five decades. There are fundamentalist movements in Judaism (such as those led by the Orthodox and ardent nationalist Rabbi Meir Kahane) and Hinduism (such as those associated with Hindu nationalist movements and the Bharatiya Janata Party) as well, each bearing a militant tone not reticent to violence. Recently, a fundamentalist form of Buddhism has emerged in Bhutan, Myanmar (Burma) and Sri Lanka, claiming the superiority of Buddhism over other religious cultures and, as in the case of the Sri Lankan Sinhala Buddhist movement, resorting to violence in order to purge society of non-Buddhist elements. One might even identify a kind of atheist fundamentalism among individuals and groups who defiantly and even aggressively attack public displays of religion, all the while claiming the intellectual and ethical integrity of their principles and actions.

Fundamentalism as a general idea or practice can move enthusiasts and practitioners of any faith tradition or ideological system toward a greater sense of purity and authenticity. In this sense, fundamentalism can effectively serve as a renewal. On the other hand, in examining fundamentalist movements across all traditions, one can fairly detect dangerous tendencies to undercut the deepest principles of faith by grasping the criteria of truth and integrity with a narrow ardor incompatible with the inward essence of the great religions of the world.

Related Entry
ideology

Suggested Reading
Ruthven, Malise. *A Very Short Introduction to Fundamentalism*. Oxford: Oxford Univ. Press, 2007.

Also recommended is the 5-vol. *Fundamentalism Project* series sponsored by the Am. Academy of Arts and Science and ed. by Martin E. Marty and R. Scott Appleby, et al. Chicago: Univ. of Chicago Press, 1991–1995. *Fundamentalism and the State* (vol. 3 ; 1993, repr. 1996) is a good place for students of politics and religion to begin.

Funeral Oration of Pericles

The tradition of the wartime funeral oration honoring fallen warriors was an important feature in the Athenian *polis,* providing both a ritual for memorializing those who had died in service to their city and an opportunity to reaffirm the principal values of political life and commitment to the common good. The *Funeral Oration* of Pericles, as recounted by Thucydides (460 BC–c. 400 BC) in his *History of the Peloponnesian War,* is an outstanding example of this custom, and the oration is numbered among the exemplary speeches in the history of political rhetoric.

Pericles speaks of the relationship between Athens and her citizens in personal terms, celebrating the moment of Athens's glory and reminding the audience of the intimate connection between citizen and *polis.* As Pericles intones,

> I would have you day by day fix your eyes upon the greatness of Athens, until you become filled with the love of her; and when you are impressed by the spectacle of her glory, reflect that this empire has been acquired by men who knew their duty and had the courage to do it, who in the hour of conflict had the fear of dishonor always present to them, and who, if ever they failed in an enterprise, would not allow their virtues to be lost to their country, but freely gave their lives to her as the fairest offering which they could present at her feast.

In the virtues of citizenship, then, for Pericles, both the glory of the city and the meaning of the individual are brought together. The city supercedes all narrow interest, all vain ambition, and all other bonds of affection, and Athens becomes for Pericles the conduit wherein all citizens can embrace a common good and sacrifice their own abilities for the whole.

Pericles thus affirms the ideal of citizen/*polis* as an inextricable interrelationship. Such an ideal was familiar to the consciousness of the ancient Greeks, who conceived of the political as essential to the life of a flourishing person, a perspective not typical of modern attitudes. The virtue of the person, the activities of the person, and the aims of the person were deeply intertwined with the structure of the city and its ultimate fate in the mind of the ancient Greek, a notion beautifully embodied throughout Pericles's great speech. As Pericles asserts, those who are detached from the city (especially in the Athenian context) are useless, characters inimical to the interests of the common. Citizens, according to Pericles, must be actively committed to the city, engaged as far as possible, devoted to the growth of the city, and, equally, "sound judges" of her policies and goals. Faction and division are not salubrious to the security and prosperity of the city, and, indeed, must be prevented with firm resolve. This theme is drawn throughout Thucydides's larger work, emphasizing the necessity of drawing the bonds of harmony closer while discouraging defiance and insurrection.

As an Athenian statesman, Pericles celebrates the political and cultural primacy of his home. Athens is the epitome of the Greek political ideal, and ascends above all its rivals as the center of Greek culture. The ideal of a common political culture and shared dedication to the government of the city are best found in Athens, exceeding even Sparta, her greatest rival and contemporary enemy. In Athens, the many are preferred to the few, and the typical citizen is capable of a wide range of civic-minded activities. Culturally, Athens is the "school of Hellas," that is, the center of Greek thought, art, and life, and must be set as the guide to which the civilized communities can look to find their standard. Politically, Athens is the epitome of equal and just citizenship, blind interests there are transcended, and the people as a whole are free to seize upon and benefit from all opportunities. "Our constitution," Pericles announces,

> does not copy the laws of neighboring states; we are rather a pattern to others than imitators ourselves. Its administration favors the many instead of the few; this is why it is called democracy. If we look to the laws, they afford equal justice to all in their private differences; if to social standing, advancement in public life falls to reputation for capacity, class considerations not being allowed to interfere with merit; nor again poverty bar the way...The freedom which we enjoy in our government extends to our ordinary life.

To this day, the *Funeral Oration* of Pericles holds the highest regard not only among students of eloquence and grand rhetoric, but also among students of political ideas. In consulting Thucydides's rendition of this watershed speech, the aspirations of the past merge with the hopes of the present, and for this reason, the noble ideals of Athens at the summit of its power and yet on the precipice of its decline continue to endure through this remarkable speech.

Related Entries

democracy; Gettysburg Address; I have a dream

Suggested Reading

Thucydides, *The Peloponnesian War,* tr. Richard Crawley, rev. T.E. Wick. New York: Random House/Modern Library, 1982.

G

game theory

Game theory, an outgrowth of decision theory, entails the systematic examination of decisions committed by rational actors, with limited knowledge of pertinent variables, interacting with other rational actors while a specific goal is pursued that will serve to optimize the interest of the actors involved. Game theory attempts to demonstrate that our decisions as individuals are in most cases made with an awareness of the interests of others and an expectation of their decisions and reactions. While attempting to advance one's interests, one recognizes that the most attainable end is not always the best end, and thus game theory helps to demonstrate the importance of optimality in the formation of our decisions and commitments. As T.C. Schelling (1961) defined it, game theory is "the formal study of the rational, consistent expectations that participants can have about each other's choices." Due to its attempt to establish models for predictable behavior, game theory has held wide appeal in the social sciences, especially economics. Because politics tends to be understood in terms of contest and competition, it may also be useful to gain insight into the political motivations, decisions, and patterns of behavior of political actors through the use of the same patterns and behaviors that characterize games as well as certain types of economic decisions. Game theory is based on the premise that games themselves reveal the true inner workings of the decision processes of individuals and groups as they compete with other individuals and groups for possible advantages. Politics is regarded as like a game, and thus it is necessary to understand the dynamics behind situations and scenarios, strategy and tactics, competition, self-interest and self-promotion, scarcity, goal orientation (to win the game or to advance one's best interest), and optimal outcomes. In short, game theory is an attempt to logically study and anticipate behaviors of rational actors competing for advantage operating under a condition of scarcity wherein available benefits are won through competition. However, it should be noted that, while rational actors do compete for benefits, game theory does not preclude the possibility of cooperation, for it also illustrates that rational agents, while nonetheless competing to place their interests first, will often find that cooperation with potential competitors is required. Indeed, if one considers the nature of games, a common recognition of rules indicates that even in competitive situations a degree of cooperation is a precondition for success. Games such as chess, poker, fencing, and tennis provide clues into how actors make decisions under the stipulations set by mutually recognized rules, and by extrapolation, modes and patterns of thinking and reacting that are formed in the more complex relationships that are developed in social, economic, military, and political situations.

Game theory as a formal method can be traced as early as 1713 in a letter from James Waldegrave to Pierre Rémond de Montmort, who passed Waldegrave's early example of a maximin (maximized minimum) strategy to the Swiss mathematician Nicolas Bernoulli. Students of political inquiry have remarked on quasi-game scenarios discussed within political philosophy as early as Plato. Thomas Hobbes's political philosophy can be viewed as an early precursor to game theory, particularly if we focus on the manner in which rational actors choose civilization under a sovereign power over the state of nature under one's own self-governance. Utilitarianism, which can be traced to Hobbes but is more commonly associated with later thinkers, is also in some ways anticipatory of game theory, especially if we focus on the individual's interest in maximizing pleasure while minimizing pain and how decisions are calculated toward that end. This is a fair assessment, as game theory is interested in seeking maximum utility within a system of decisions and exchanges that operate toward equilibrium. These early forerunners aside, game theory as we know it nonetheless emerged out of mathematics in the 1940s, in particular through the work of Jon von Neumann and Oskar Morgenstern in their groundbreaking *Theory of Games and Economic Behavior* (1944), Herbert A. Simon (*Review of the Theory of Games and Economic Behavior,* 1945), and in the early 1950s in the work of John Nash, who was awarded the Nobel Prize in economics for his contribution to the formation of game theory. Merrill

M. Flood, Melvin Dresher, and Albert Tucker are noteworthy in their contribution in 1950, while working at RAND, of the widely influential "prisoner's dilemma" game, a behavioral model that would influence philosophy, political theory, and economic theory for the remainder of the century. Following the lead of these pioneers, a number of social scientists have embraced game theory since the mid-1950s and early 1960s. Anthony Downs (*An Economic Theory of Democracy,* 1957), T.C. Schelling (*The Strategy of Conflict,* 1960), William H. Riker (*The Theory of Political Coalitions,* 1962), A.O. Hirschman (*Exit, Voice and Loyalty,* 1970), John Rawls (*A Theory of Justice,* 1971), Steven J. Brams (*Game Theory and Politics,* 1975), Robert Axelrod (*The Evolution of Cooperation,* 1984), P.C. Ordershook (*Game Theory and Political Theory,* 1987), and mathematician Yisrael Robert John Aumann (cowinner with Schelling of the 2005 Nobel Prize in economics) provide notable examples of the influence of game theory in political inquiry. Rawls's *A Theory of Justice,* while too broad in its scope and influence to be regarded as a work in game theory, is nonetheless significant in that elements of Rawls's argument evince indebtedness to game theory methodology. Bernard Susser once remarked that "game theorists seek to specify what should be done in order to rationally maximize one's interests; they do not presume to tell us what those interests ought to be." Susser observed that "It is precisely the pristine clarity that the game possesses, the calculability and logic of its moves, and the simplicity of its objectives that inspired political scientists to envisage political contests in game-theoretical terms." These comments represent the tendency to think of game theory as value neutral, and thus disconnected from normative political theory. Nonetheless, with Rawls and his hypothetical original position, the relationship between game theory and normative political philosophy might, at least in some cases, be closer than normally admitted.

Five elements appear to be common to most games: (1) the assumption of the rationality of the actors involved or the practicality (or even prudence) of the "players of the game," (2) the existence of a state of contest (allowing various degrees of competition or cooperation throughout different scenarios) framed within preestablished rules, stipulations, and limitations, (3) an assumption of the need for equilibrium within a specific basic situation, (4) the awareness of a diverse matrix of strategies that enable the achievement of distinct ends (or the possible moves available to each participant), and (5) a set of possible outcomes (payoffs), some more desirable than others and some more attainable than others. These are not the only aspects of games, but they seem to be those that are comprehended in any given game situation. From this rudimentary foundation, several games can emerge, namely: "infinitely long games," symmetric or asymmetric, sequential or simultaneous, perfect or imperfect, and zero sum, cooperative, or noncooperative. Game theory in political science tends toward hybrids of these types, recognizing that most games in politics are more than "zero sum" (winner takes all) while less than fully and multilaterally cooperative (everyone wins all the time). The common theme throughout all the various game situations is a binding interdependency among the actors involved, which is one reason why game theory holds such an appeal for the social sciences. All decisions, even those arrived at in competition between actors with ostensibly incompatible goals, depend on the perceptions, needs and behaviors of other individuals; thus, even a zero-sum game is marked by mutual need and, to some extent, a reliance, however vague and attenuated, on cooperation. This common trait of game theory types and scenarios illustrates the communal and inter-relational nature of most of our important decisions, and even if we approach a situation to advance our own interests as in a game, the existential fact of reliance on others is inescapable. Whether or not this is a normative quality of game theory is debatable, but it does emphasize the connections between various interests within

the public sphere and how even the most ardently egoistic motive must be pursued as an attempt to optimize one's situation within conditions determined by others. Without doubt, if we regard the examination of choices set within the context of multiple interests, varying levels of information, and the tendency toward optimizing benefits across a decision matrix as germane to the dynamics of politics, policy, and public affairs, then game theory will remain an attractive tool in the analysis of interest-based individual interactions within finite communities.

Related Entries

prisoner's dilemma; Rawls, John; utilitarianism

Suggested Reading

Bram, S.J. *Game Theory and Politics*. New York: Free Press, 1975.

Ordershook, P.C. *Game Theory and Political Theory*. Cambridge, MA: Cambridge Univ. Press, 1987.

Schelling, T.C., *The Strategy of Conflict*. Cambridge, MA: Harvard Univ. Press, 1960.

general will (*volonte generale*)

In the political philosophy of Jean-Jacques Rousseau (1712–1778), the concept "general will" figures prominently. Rousseau's entire political theory rises or falls on his the assertion that free will is the defining essence of human nature, and thus any discussion of the will is central to establishing his views on the meaning and function of politics.

In his masterpiece, *The Social Contract,* Rousseau describes three types of will: particular will (or private will), the will of all, and general will. Particular will operates within individuals and groups adhering to similar interests and pursuing the same goals. Every person and every conscious association possesses a particular will, and exerts that will out of regard for self-interest, or for the parochial interest of a group, or in Rousseau's designation, "partial society." The will of all is described by Rousseau as the aggregate of all particular wills, or in other words, a compromise between partial societies that is arrived at through the assertion of the various wills of individuals and groups. The will of all, if broad enough in its provision for the interests of diverse groups, can resemble the general will and perhaps even approach it, but in the end, there is an important and enduring distinction between the will of all and the general will that lies at the center of Rousseau's project. As Rousseau explains it,

> There is often a great deal of difference between the will of all and the general will. The latter considers only the general interest, whereas the former considers the private interest and is merely the sum of private wills. But remove from these same wills the pluses and minuses that cancel each other out, and what remains as the sum of the differences is the general will.

Thus general will is always universal and detached from any private will. The will of all simply asserts private interest at a higher level, whereas the general will truly finds common accord. By eliminating those objects of will that are sought by private or partial interests, we can begin to discern that will which is in reality universally manifest in common interests held by each and all. Should any interest reflect any segment of society rather than the whole, it is an object of either particular will or the will of all. For the general will to be what it is, it must be just that—general; viz., universal, common, applicable in the same way to every member of society.

The general will operates directly on the individual. Given this, there is a constant tension between general will and particular or private will. Every person possesses their own will concerning their own affairs, which is somewhat akin to the natural liberty spoken of by Rousseau in the *Second Discourse on the Origins of Inequality*. Simultaneously, every person possesses a general will, which is manifest only within society and expressed only through laws and lawful conduct, and is related to Rousseau's moral or civil liberty as introduced in his *Social Contract*. The tension between these two wills has been imaginatively taught by Lee McDonald in the second volume of his *Western Political Theory*. "There are many helpful illustrations of the general will conceived as our better self," McDonald explains, to wit,

> [O]ur general will tells us that we ought to get up at seven A.M.; our particular will leads us to turn off the alarm and roll over. Our general will tells us that we need a strong army; our particular will wants to keep us out of the draft. The drunkard's general will tells him that he should have stopped drinking hours ago; his particular will gives him one more for the road. If the police throw him in jail; he is really throwing himself in jail. And he is free because his restraint is self-imposed.

In other words, the general will is the voice of our own moral agency, one that issues from our own individuality but can only become manifest in the process of doing our duty, of rising at seven A.M. to begin our day, of willingly submitting to public service just like everyone else does (or is supposed to do), and listening to the voice of conscience so that our actions will not violate the social terms that we have ourselves accepted.

General will is the purpose of political association, and is such because it is not actuated by private desire or partial interest. Hence for Rousseau, sovereignty is precisely defined as the "exercise of the general will." As the will is essential to our humanity, this sovereign will is never alienated (as one could argue that it is in Hobbes), but always dwells within the people as a whole, the collective sovereign as it were. As such, the sovereign general will is always driven toward the most general principles, always properly exerted from the assumption of its universality. Its only aim is that which is essentially common for all citizens. As Rousseau asserts, "only the general will can direct the forces of the state according to the purpose for which it was instituted, which is the common good." As he argues, private interest makes political society necessary, but common interest is the only thing that makes it possible. " [W]ere there no point of agreement among all these [private or particular] interests, no society could exist. For it is utterly on the basis of this common interest that society ought to be governed."

Some confusion about the exact numerical constitution of the general will is generated by apparently conflicting passages in *The Social Contract*. At one point, Rousseau states that the general will "is not so much the number of votes as the common interest that unites [the people]," yet later, in discussing the issue of legislation within "the people's assembly," Rousseau states, "what is asked of them is not precisely whether they approve or reject, but whether or not it conforms to the general will that is theirs." Here Rousseau seems to backpedal a bit on the relationship between the general will and popular voting, for he states that "Each man, in giving his vote, states his opinion on this matter, and the declaration of the general will is drawn from the counting of votes." To have voted in the minority only "proves merely that I was in error," Rousseau reflects, thus indicating that the general will is not as unanimous and universal as one might have anticipated given his earlier discussion. The general will, Rousseau adds elsewhere, is always right. Hence if I am outvoted, then one must ask if my will is in error, or, if in some way my will is more attuned to what the general will really is. The general will cannot err, but the people can be deceived as to what it really is, thus voting, this passage notwithstanding, cannot really be Rousseau's best measure of general will. Rousseau's deeper philosophical position insists on complete universality, detaching the general will from the process of voting *per se* and attaching the general will to the act of legislating, to that act which equally derives from all and equally operates upon all.

By definition, the general will is the will that is general or universal to all—each and every person and not simply a majority or even a consensus of society—and it is "only the general will [that] can direct the forces of the state according to the purpose for which it was instituted, which is the common good." If the general will and the common good toward which it aims is the remainder of the subtraction of all several interests that stem primarily from the particular wills, it must be a broad and somewhat abstract principle. According to Rousseau, "the greatest good of all consists [in] two principal objects, *liberty* and *equality*." These are interdependent concepts toward which every rational free agent aspires to embrace and apply, for no human person can renounce liberty, and no one would deliberately choose a condition of inequality. These are universal common interests and are thus, for Rousseau, the true objects of general will.

There are some difficulties that follow any attempt to define a universal principle in terms of the will, general or otherwise. The general will emerges when people act unanimously, but is this act sufficient by itself to establish a principle of right? In other words, is there something else about liberty and equality that makes them higher principles toward which the will aspires? What would happen if human beings chose other universal goals, would they be deceived in every case? Or, would they have changed the content of the general will? Or better still, does Rousseau really believe that the general will is an aspect of pure will? Can there be different kinds of general will operating within different communities? If so, would these different "general wills" still be accountable to an even greater general will? In the *Third Discourse on Political Economy,* Rousseau at one point casually equates general will with the law of nature, and thus in a way, detaches it from pure volition. Moreover, if the general will is always right but the people can confuse general will with the will of all, how are we to find the true general will within the will itself? Are liberty and equality teleological and thus not volitional as Rousseau understands it?

These and other, more profound questions set the discussion for further consideration of Rousseau's concept of the general will and, indeed, his entire political philosophy. General will continues to interest students of Rousseau, Kant, democratic and communitarian theory, and, perhaps above all, the moral dimensions of free societies. For these and other reasons,

Rousseau's legacy will remain tangible within the dialogue of political and moral philosophy.

Related Entries
Rousseau, Jean-Jacques; *The Social Contract*

Suggested Reading
Rousseau, Jean-Jacques, *The Social Contract*. trans. G.D.H. Cole. New York: E. P. Dutton, 1973.

Gettysburg Address

Abraham Lincoln's 1863 Gettysburg Address is not only his most famous speech, but it also in the voice of highest eloquence affirms the first principles and aspirations of democracy. Only his Second Inaugural can match both its oratorical artistry and its transcendent morality, and no speech other than Martin Luther King's 1963 "I Have a Dream" address resounds so profoundly in the American political psyche.

At Gettysburg, Lincoln managed to convey both the essential meaning of the American founding as well as the larger issue—the issue of slavery—driving the American civil war. In noting the republic as "conceived in liberty" and "dedicated to the proposition that all men are created equal," Lincoln grounded the great constitutional crisis that preceded the war in the faith pronounced within the Declaration of Independence. Liberty and equality are thus the twin foundations of the American republic and, indeed, the foundations for any society that aspires to promote "government of the people, by the people, for the people." (a phrase that, according to Gary Wills, closely resembles an earlier trope on the principles of democracy from Theodore Parker, to wit, "a government of all, for all, and by all")" The horrific war that led Americans to the slaughter at Gettysburg wherein the "last full measure of devotion" was nobly offered, was for Lincoln more than anything else, the battle for the full realization of those principles. Those principles, as Lincoln well understood them even long before Gettysburg, are radically opposed to the existence of slavery.

This full realization is what Lincoln meant by a "new birth of freedom," a freedom that would finally purge the tainted republic of its founding sin of slavery, and achieve the only just course available to Americans as well as to the rest of the world. While it has been argued, based on Lincoln's First Inaugural Address, that preserving the union was paramount for him even to the point of diminishing the importance of the slavery issue, the Gettysburg Address, along with other speeches and writings, reveal that in Lincoln's mind the union must be preserved as it is the only way to advance democratic government, a government of free and equal citizens. This meant, for Lincoln, a political rebirth, wrought in the tragic sacrifice of war and sealed in the meaning of the founding documents through the triumph of freedom over slavery. At Gettysburg, Lincoln himself supplies a new kind of founding document within the text of his laconic and yet illuminating affirmation, as provided here:

"Fourscore and seven years ago our fathers brought forth on this continent a new nation, conceived in liberty and dedicated to the proposition that all men are created equal. Now we are engaged in a great civil war, testing whether that nation or any nation so conceived and so dedicated can long endure. We are met on a great battlefield of that war. We have come to dedicate a portion of that field as a final resting-place for those who here gave their lives that that nation might live. It is altogether fitting and proper that we should do this. But in a larger sense, we cannot dedicate, we cannot consecrate, we cannot hallow this ground. The brave men, living and dead who struggled here have consecrated it far above our poor power to add or detract. The world will little note nor long remember what we say here, but it can never forget what they did here. It is for us the living rather to be dedicated here to the unfinished work which they who fought here have thus far so nobly advanced. It is rather for us to be here dedicated to the great task remaining before us—that from these honored dead we take increased devotion to that cause for which they gave the last full measure of devotion—that we here highly resolve that these dead shall not have died in vain, that this nation under God shall have a new birth of freedom, and that government of the people, by the people, for the people shall not perish from the earth."

Related Entries
Funeral Oration of Pericles; I have a dream

Suggested Reading
The Gettysburg Address is ubiquitous. For an excellent analysis of the speech, consult the following: Wills, Gary. *Lincoln at Gettysburg: The Words that Remade America.* New York: Simon and Schuster, 1992.

Gramsci, Antonio (1891–1926)

An Italian political theorist familiar to students of intellectual history for having suffered a long imprisonment in fascist Italy, Antonio Gramsci was a leading Marxist thinker critical of the more deterministic and positivistic strain of Marxism that had solidified as socialist orthodoxy in the early twentieth century. Gramsci regarded the "scientific" Marxism of Engels and Lenin as an intellectually simplistic and barren form of socialist theory, and thus sought to revive Marxian analysis and action through emphasizing its more humanistic and critical aspects.

To unravel the deterministic and uncritical aspects of the Leninist variant, Gramsci attempted to restore the dialectical nature of Marxian theory, which for Gramsci was not aptly understood as a law-like system as provided by the legacy of Engels. Gramsci did not conceive of the dialectic as operating independently in nature and history, as in the more positivistic approaches to Marx. Rather, the dialectic reveals the fundamental unity between freedom and natural dynamics, humanity as agent and history as context. Hence, while material forces are an important factor in shaping the social and political world, they do not do so with the kind of inevitability implied in the scientific notion of laws of nature. Economic determinism, then, which is a central feature of "scientific" Marxism, is not a realistic model for interpreting social struggle. Human agency is not so easily shaped or predicted, the human subject is not simply the conduit of irresistible historical and material forces. For Gramsci, cultural and political factors must also be regarded as equally influential and consequently equally important in the development of what he called the "philosophy of praxis," which is to say, the seamless blending of theory and action directed toward emancipatory ends. To deliver this philosophy of praxis, Gramsci argued that the communist party must be as a "new prince" (an allusion to Machiavelli), and exert its agency on a world that is far more contingent than "official" Marxism would ever allow.

From these premises, Gramsci developed his concept of cultural hegemony, affirming the importance of the role of culture in either the perpetuation of or resistance to dominant cultural structures. Culture is not simply the epiphenomena of the relations of material production, but rather the expression of subjective will within the context of objective conditions. To apply the philosophy of praxis requires the affirmation of "counter-hegemony," that is, of a new and oppositional consciousness that challenges the established order on the cultural level as well as through political and economic action. This demands that revolutionary action be critical and open, not rigid and closed as in the case of more deterministic types of Marxian ideology. The philosophy of praxis, while defined by the Marxian ideal of universal emancipation, must remain open to and in dialogue with other voices. Gramsci's openness to, for example, Catholicism, represents the dialogic nature of the Gramscian critique.

While Gramsci's ideas were never adopted by the Communist Party, his influence on what has been called "neo-Marxism" is formative. Few Marxian theorists in the twentieth century carry as much weight among critical Marxists in the West, and his writings continue to invite political theorists to engage in provocative dialogue.

Related Entries
communism; critical theory; Marx, Karl; neo-Marxism; socialism

Suggested Reading

Gramsci, Antonio. *Selections from the Prison Note-books,* ed. and trans. Quinton Hoare and Geoffrey Nowell Smith. New York: International, 1971.

Grotius, Hugo (Huigh or Hugeianus de Groot; 1583–1645)

Familiar to students of political thought as the author of *On the Law of War and Peace,* Hugo Grotius represents a change in the development of natural law theory that had been previously shaped throughout the Middle Ages, particularly in the works of St. Thomas Aquinas and the Salamanca school. It is not that Grotius substantively changes the concept of natural law but rather that he emphasizes it as a concept ultimately independent from the will of God. It is important to bear in mind that Aquinas also spoke of natural law as distinct from divine law, and thus promoted in line with church teaching a concept of nature that is independent of the divine while at the same time being a product of Creation. In other words, what Grotius attempts to do is not a radical departure from the Thomists, for they too recognized the need to be able to understand the world rationally, and to employ reason to discover natural moral principles independently of revelation. It might be accurate to say that Grotius, rather than effecting a complete break from the Medieval (Thomistic) conception of natural law, in actuality merely amplified one feature of it by insisting on the autonomy of natural law from the will of God. St. Thomas Aquinas, while noting the difference between divine and natural law, understood both to flow from the eternal law, which originates from the mind of God. In Grotius, there is an implied sense that such a law is completely detached from the purposes of the divine in a way that Aquinas could not accept. Ultimately, while Grotius holds some similarity to the Thomists, he reaches back not to St. Thomas Aquinas, but rather to Cicero.

Under the principles asserted by Grotius, natural law is treated as somehow preeminent to the will of God. Grotius muses that the natural law would remain as it is even without the existence of God. St. Thomas, by comparison, would agree with Grotius that the natural law bears a degree of independence, and thus the higher principles of nature can be discerned by reason alone, the ultimate source of all true law, natural or otherwise, is God, who cannot be removed from the conversation. Grotius postulates a natural law that is not only separate from revelation but is ultimately independent of divine agency. As Grotius states, "Just as even God, then, cannot cause that two times two should not make four, so He cannot cause that that which is intrinsically evil be not evil." Again, this is not a direct refutation of Thomism, for St. Thomas also held that God cannot make the evil good—but not because God is subject to a higher law than His own sovereignty, but because goodness is itself defined by God in a way that it cannot be changed. For Grotius, this means that it is possible to conceive of natural moral principles without relying on theological concepts. Grotius does not espouse a theory that rejects divine will, but only a concept of natural law that does not rely on such a will.

Additionally, and perhaps more significantly for the development of political theory as such, Grotius advances international law for the sake of governing actions that occur between independent nation-states. Grotius, like natural law theorists before him, understood the nature of man to be sociable, hence human beings will seek community at all levels of association, from the municipal to the international. Indeed, it is here that Grotius grounds his law of nature for he states that,

> The very nature of man, which even if we had no lack of anything would lead us into the mutual relations of society, is the mother of the law of nature.

In saying this, Grotius shifts the conceptual center to human sociability while not rejecting the transcendent source of natural law outright. And it is because this sociability applies to human beings as such that we can entertain the possibility of international law, a law based on that which human beings hold in common and which is equally willed by all nation-states. The emphasis on the role of human will and common interest is significant in Grotius, for here he resembles the tradition of the Roman jurist Gaius (110–180) in identifying the law of nations with the natural law, at least implicitly, through the explicit connection of international law to the "nature of man." Again, to contrast this with Aquinas, Grotius holds that the "law of nature" springs from the "nature of man"; Aquinas, on the other hand, holds that because of our innate dispositions, we are drawn toward the natural law.

Grotius's main concern was to establish viable international law equal to the task of governing the acts of nation-states. The welfare of all nations depends on common international law; hence Grotius devoted considerable effort to establish a perpetual legal agreement between states in order to ensure order between nations and thus secure and promote the natural "sociableness" of humanity.

To this end, Grotius was particularly interested in promulgating the laws of war. In his view, war can only justly be waged under the regulation of international laws, agreements, and good faith. In brief, wars must be waged for the right reasons and conducted through appropriate means. Again, Grotius does not depart radically from earlier theorists (just war theory was already firmly in place long before Grotius), but his importance is through his attempt to provide more detail into what is a just cause of war, and how wars can be rightly waged. In his desire for detail, Grotius attempts to apply the theory of just war with an eye to the many contingencies that may be involved as relations between nation-states turn belligerent.

In addition to his modification of both natural law and just war theory, Grotius is also of interest owing to his particular contribution to the development of a modern notion of right, one that certainly influenced Hobbes, and thus much of modern political thought, long after him. Medieval notions of right are dependent on a close relationship between right and moral law, and thus duties with regard to the political community in general and other persons in particular. It is significant that the Latin term *jus* is translated as both right and law. With Grotius, right involves power and entitlement, and is thus something to be possessed. It can also be dispossessed, or given away as with any other possession. This notion of the transferable nature of rights as possessions rests at the foundation of both modern notions of individual rights as well as the modern social contract. Hobbes and Locke in particular understood government by consent to originate in the transference of certain natural rights in order to more firmly secure other natural rights that remained in the possession of individuals in society.

While Grotius's influence on the development of political theory is substantial, his authority for the modern reader is secondary. Nonetheless, to gain a deeper understanding of the manner in which Hobbes represents an indisputable turning point in political philosophy, a reading of Grotius is beneficial, and one that sheds some light on the problems of right, law, and international conflict as it gripped the European continent during the sixteenth and seventeenth centuries.

Related Entries

Aquinas, Thomas; justice; natural law

Suggested Reading

Grotius, Hugo. *The Rights of War and Peace*, 3 vols., ed. Richard Tuck from the edition by Jean Barbeyrac. Indianapolis: Liberty Fund, Inc., 2005.

Habermas, Jürgen (b. 1929)

One of the truly seminal figures of contemporary political theory, and one of the more polyglot, Jürgen Habermas stands at the junction of a variety of theoretical movements. Initially indirectly associated with the Frankfurt School and a moving force in the early development of critical dialectical theory in the twentieth century, Habermas draws on numerous schools of thought and intellectual influences, ranging from the sociology of Max Weber to American pragmatism, from the critical Marxism of Theodore Adorno and Max Horkheimer to the moral theories developed in the psychology of Lawrence Kohlberg. Habermas has engaged in open dialogue with diverse intellectuals, ranging from Hans-Georg Gadamer to John Rawls, Michel Foucault to Cardinal Joseph Alois Ratzinger (who would become Pope Benedict XVI). All of this is not only evidence of Habermas's athletic intellect, but also illustrative of his principle of a thoroughly free and unrestricted exchange of ideas and the challenges that they bring.

Habermas's political thought, perhaps more than any thinker of his times, has experienced considerable change and modification throughout his intellectual career. Habermas's political theory is traced back to the influence of the Frankfurt School (of which Habermas was not technically a part, but with whom he is frequently and rightly associated) and the neo-Marxist critique of capitalism. Habermas embraced the basic critical analysis of capitalism generated within the Marxian tradition, but rejected the tendency among Marxists toward determinism and the insistence on the inevitability of revolution. Marxian dialectics often overlooks the intangible nuances of human interaction, and while correct in the perception that human beings are enslaved by alienation, the causes of this alienation are not wholly defined by the relations of production, nor is the solution necessarily or even preferably revolutionary. Human beings do seek emancipation, which is intimately tied to the relationship between knowledge and interest (which can be delineated as either technical, practical, or emancipatory in its focus and goals, the last seeking to overcome coercion and social control), but militant revolution as prescribed by most Marxists is actually counterproductive in Habermas's view. For Habermas, capitalism

and the liberal democratic state is constantly plagued by a variety of crises, in particular the crisis of legitimation, but it is not in the worker's party nor in the bureaucratic mechanisms of the state (liberal or socialist) that we can be assured of a solution. What Habermas seeks (especially in his earlier writings) is a deeper understanding of the relationship between knowledge and interest, and eventually, in his later works, a theory of political communication that can promote a truly critical, nonideological attitude.

Habermas's understanding of the relationship between knowledge and interest is influenced not only by Marx, but also by Kant and the American pragmatists and is thus less inclined to adhere to a strictly dialectical view of epistemology and its connection to human desires and activities. In going to Kant in particular, Habermas challenged the subjectivist "negative dialectics" of Adorno by again recognizing the value of objective principles, which were, for Habermas, affirmed through the consensus of free and rational thinkers in a way reminiscent of Kant's transcendental subject.

Hence, Habermas's historical and epistemological approach eventually developed with an emphasis on the communicative act. While the "linguistic turn" in Habermas's thought appears as a new direction in his overall philosophy, it is not necessarily a complete break, for there is something anticipatory about this turn in Habermas's understanding of Kant as well as in the constructivism of the pragmatists. Even though Habermas sets aside the old epistemological approach (largely in response to the antifoundationalist criticism of the postmoderns), his project is still somewhat colored by his earlier achievement. Habermas acknowledges the power of the postmodern incredulity toward metanarratives but nonetheless is unwilling to fully abandon a level of consensus regarding basic political and moral principles. Not wanting to rely on a transcendental objectivism, Habermas looks for universality in rational and authentically free consensus.

Through open, participatory, and discursive democracy, objective principles can be asserted without the need to depend on moral realism (the notion that moral principles are real, universal, and existing independently of the human subject). Truth, for Habermas, is not thoroughly contingent as the postmodernists would have it, nor is it an *a priori* reality toward which our ideas and certainties must correspond. Rather, truth becomes manifest through open and free democratic dialogue, a real consensus that is universally inclusive and thus able to arrive at common values held by all citizens. If discourse is inclusive, cosmopolitan, and open, and the political structure genuinely democratic and participatory, then our values and norms will bear an acceptable degree of objective truth without having to be justified by a transcendent ideal. Thus Habermas at once responds to both the postmodern rejection of dominant discourse while retaining residues of his early Kantianism.

Recently Habermas has undergone another change in direction through an increasing interest in the relationship between politics and religion, and in particular, Christianity. In 2005 Habermas engaged in a dialogue with Cardinal Ratzinger on the nature of the ancient connections between reason, faith, and society. In the course of the dialogue, Habermas recognized the importance of Christianity to the production of Western moral and political principles, particularly individual autonomy and moral agency, imagination and innovation in society, and a the tight relationship between individuals and the community. Much of what is valuable in Western moral and political thought originates in the Christian doctrine that human beings are created in the image of God, and thus bear a dignity that serves as the ground for just communities and responsible citizens. Typical of Habermas, he is willing to join in dialogue with all voices in pursuit of a deeper understanding of the human condition.

Related Entries
critical theory; dialectical theory

Suggested Reading

Habermas, Jürgen. *Knowledge and Human Interests,* trans. Jeremy Shapiro. 1968; repr. Boston: Beacon Press, 1971

Habermas, Jürgen. *Legitimation Crisis,* trans. Thomas McCarthy. Boston: Beacon Press, 1975.

Habermas, Jürgen. *The Philosophical Discourse of Modernity: Twelve Lectures,* trans. Frederick G. Lawrence. Cambridge, MA: MIT Press, 1995.

Habermas, Jürgen, and Joseph Ratzinger. *The Dialectics of Secularization: On Reason and Religion,* ed. and with a foreword by Florian Schuller, trans. Brian McNeil. San Francisco: Ignatius Press, 2006.

Hamilton, Alexander (c. 1755–1804)
Alexander Hamilton, coauthor with James Madison and John Jay of the series of essays that would eventually come to be known as the *Federalist Papers,* provides the most significant and consistent challenge to the Jeffersonian theory of politics. While both Jefferson and Hamilton believed in free government resting on popular sovereignty and buttressed by a notion of natural rights, Hamilton's overall vision for the emerging American republic was quite apart from that promoted by Jefferson and his followers. Hamilton did believe, with Jefferson, in government founded on consent of the governed and limited by constitutional principles and law, yet he departed from the Jeffersonian ideal by advocating what he would refer to as "energetic" government, a regime strong enough to produce domestic unity and a sense of national devotion as well as prepare for threats from ambitious powers abroad. Hamilton thus believed in a representative democracy protected from the caprice of the mob, and one that could secure the rule of law without impairing the liberties and opportunities of its citizens.

Thus, whereas Jefferson favored decentralized government, at least in theory, Hamilton advocated a strong national organ. Where Jefferson, again in theory, advocated a strong legislature and a milder executive, Hamilton called for a vigorous administration of the affairs of state, hoping that the office of the presidency could provide such qualities. Jefferson's ideal was agrarian, but Hamilton envisaged a republic invigorated by commerce and industry—a more urban republic that would not only generate opportunity for development, but that would also quickly emerge on the world stage as a major force. For Hamilton, government at all levels, but especially at the national level, should be allied with the interest of commerce in order to produce the prosperity requisite to becoming a great nation. Jefferson sought greatness through the extension of a vast agrarian republic, one that encouraged the pastoral virtues of the small farmer. As such, American political thought is often and rightly understood as a balancing between the Hamiltonian and Jeffersonian visions.

And yet, these disparate visions are nonetheless expressions of the same elemental political grammar, formed in the tradition of self-government and elevated toward the aspirations embodied in natural law and natural right. At this level, Jefferson and Hamilton come together in spite of their myriad differences and personal animosity, as evinced in the following passage from Hamilton's "The Farmer Refuted" (1775),

> The sacred rights of mankind are not to be rummaged for, among old parchments, or musty records. They are written, as with a sun beam, in the whole volume of human nature, by the hand of the divinity itself; and can never be erased or obscured by mortal power.

Related Entries

Federalist Papers; Jefferson, Thomas; Madison, James

Suggested Reading

Hamilton, Alexander, James Madison, and John Jay. *The Federalist Papers*, ed. Harold Syrett and Jacob Cooke. Vol. 1 of *The Papers of Alexander Hamilton*. New York: Columbia Univ. Press, 1961.

Harrington, James (1611–1677)

James Harrington stands as one of the more important political theorists of the seventeenth century, surpassed only by Hobbes and Locke in influence among his contemporaries. His greatest work, *Oceana*, provides a compelling response to Hobbes, and offers political principles that anticipate later developments in a way perhaps even more prescient than Locke. Thus, any student of political theory, and especially modern political thought, is well served by some exposure to his work.

In *Oceana*, Harrington framed his examination of politics within two principles, "internal, or goods of the mind, and external, or the goods of fortune." Intellect and virtue are the goods of the mind, which are both natural to a person and to some extent also acquired. Fortune refers above all to wealth, which is an external good. He also speaks of bodily goods such as health, beauty, and strength, but they are not the focus of politics. In politics, fortune is the foundation of power and empire, but the goods of the mind produce legitimate authority. Hence authority and power in Harrington's assessment of things are decidedly distinct, a direct rejection of the tendency of his contemporaries, and especially Hobbes, to confuse them. Authority is rooted in virtue and thus assumes a moral quality, whereas power is merely based on material advantage. This is a sharp contrast to Hobbes, who in essence reduces all authority to the power of the sovereign, and not to any clear conception of its virtue.

Harrington thoroughly embraced a republican model of government that owed much to the earlier ideas forwarded by Aristotle, Machiavelli, and the ancient example of republican Rome. Long before Montesquieu, Harrington prescribed a system of separated power (although without identifying a distinct judiciary as in Montesquieu), designed to prevent the absolutism that comes from the concentration of power into the hands of a monarch or group of oligarchs. Harrington advocated separating legislative power from the magistracy (or executive power), and further dividing the legislative branch into two separate bodies—an aristocratic senate (consisting of a natural aristocracy), which would debate laws and policies, and the popular assembly, which would approve or disapprove of the resolutions advanced by the aristocratic chamber. In addition to the important feature of dispersed power, so vital to republican government, Harrington proposed liberal use of popular elections, a secret ballot, mandatory rotation of offices, abolition of primogeniture, and public education.

The abolition of primogeniture reflects Harrington's understanding of the intimate connection between politics and economic power. Disparities in the holding of land is a direct cause of political inequalities and thus is incompatible with the republican ideal of equal citizenship. To address this, Harrington proposed a reform that he called the "Agrarian," or an agrarian law that guaranteed an even distribution of land throughout the commonwealth by "fixing the balance in land" throughout the commonwealth. For Harrington, this is how God intended property to be distributed, a common sharing of the fruits of the earth that would provide the foundation for social, legal, and political equality. "Equality of estates causes equality of power," Harrington advised, noting that inequities in wealth can only undermine political unity. In ancient Athens, the people who were poor fed off the few who were wealthy, and the reverse of this happened in ancient Rome. Only through the application of the agrarian could the economic equilibrium necessary for self-government be set into place.

While the agrarian reforms that Harrington proposed seem radical for his times, as a whole his political theory was received favorably by subsequent generations and in particular the American Founders, who saw in Harrington a thinker of some perspicacity.

Related Entry

Locke, John

Suggested Reading

Harrington, James. *The Commonwealth of Oceana* and *A System of Politics,* ed. J. G. A. Pocock. New York: Cambridge Univ. Press, 1992.

Hegel, Georg Wilhelm Friedrich
(1770–1831)

When we approach G. W. F. Hegel, we do so with the clear awareness that a thinker this complex and abstruse cannot be described or condensed in a few paragraphs. As Lee McDonald aptly stated, Hegel is "too systematic to summarize, too cumbersome to quote, and too influential to ignore." And so, attention must be given while painfully aware of the inadequacy of any summary treatment.

Premised on the notion that Spirit (*Geist*), or Mind, animates the whole of reality, and in so doing, seeks to reconcile itself with matter (ultimately, Spirit seeks to reconcile itself with itself, as matter is Spirit alienated from itself), Hegel's political theory is characterized as the manifestation of a larger, complex and interconnected manifold. Spirit is the unifying, dynamic totality that connects and develops throughout human history, culture, and institutions. As with Plato, the idea is a higher and deeper reality than the material and the apparent, but unlike Plato, Hegel understands this higher reality to itself be in motion (whereas Plato's Forms are eternally immutable). Furthermore, history itself is the unfolding of Spirit into the world of appearance; and thus every temporal act is somehow driven by forces and principles that are unseen in the moment. As Spirit is involved with idea, it is rational—a higher reason on which all of our external experiences and our internal reflections is grounded. As such, there is "reason in history," for the unfolding of Spirit into the visible world does not happen randomly or without purpose. Even the catastrophe of war conceals some rational principle; even the irrational convulsions that upend civilization from time to time are suffered for a reason. It is only in reflecting on the events that have preceded us that we can begin to understand the larger design of a rational order.

This order is not static. It moves from lower moments of development to higher moments. For humanity, this means that as Spirit unfolds itself into the world, it progresses from lower moments of consciousness to higher moments of consciousness and, more importantly, from lower moments of freedom to higher moments of freedom. This occurs on all levels of reality: from the individual psyche to the complex matrix of the state itself. Human history is the progress of reason and freedom; history is inherently rational in spite of outward appearance, and freedom is the one goal of human development, the one lodestar that fixes the human travail toward a greater end.

This process occurs dialectically. The term dialectic reaches back to the ancient Greeks, who understood the concept to involve the highest level of inquiry manifest through the dialogic form or, for Socrates, the critical interrogative method that winnows out error and ultimately leads to truth and the reality of things as they are. For Hegel, the dialectic involves both mind and matter, both idea and history, and depicts the manner in which Spirit reconciles itself with the world. For Hegel, all concepts and categories of thought are somehow connected, and similarly, all aspects of reality are intertwined and reflect each other in some way. The universal is reflected in the particular and vice versa, the negative is found in the positive and the reverse, and the dichotomy of essence/existence is ultimately illusory. Additionally, this interaction and interrelation occurs through contradiction and tension between the different facets within any given relationship. Borrowing more from Johann Gottlieb Fichte than Plato or Aristotle, Hegel posits a dialectic that sets every affirmation (thesis) in conflict with its own negation (antithesis). Every affirmation produces its own negation, and given Hegel's understanding of the process of reality, the conflictual dynamic that erupts between affirmation and negation cannot remain in stasis, but rather, must be resolved at another, still higher stage of reality. Hence the tension between affirmation and negation produces its own solution in what Hegel refers to as the negation of the negation (synthesis). For example, say being stands as the affirmation, nothingness would be the

negation produced by being—and becoming serves as the negation of the negation, the synthesis that simultaneously preserves (or absorbs), destroys, and transcends the realities of the affirmation and negation. In this way, nature and history—or the world in general—develop inexorably toward improved states of being. Ultimately for Hegel, this process is moving toward a final reconciliation of Spirit with its own externality (the world) in the climactic phase of Absolute Knowing.

Thus, reality on all levels is a struggle between interpenetrating contradictions. In the development of human history, this dialectical contest is epitomized in the existential struggle for recognition. We begin (historically and psychologically, universally and personally) with the conflict between independent consciousness—or consciousness that exists for itself—and dependent consciousness, i.e., consciousness for another, or consciousness that depends on the presence of the other for meaning. Independent consciousness, owing to its autonomy and sense of freedom, is prepared to always choose death rather than slavery, and understands the value of life only in terms of that freedom. Dependent consciousness, on the other hand, is unable to achieve freedom due to the unwillingness to risk death. Life for its own sake is the value embraced, even life under submission. This, for Hegel, is the defining relationship between what he calls the master/lord (*Herr*) and the slave/bondsman/ serf (*Knecht*). Because the master risks death for freedom, recognition is achieved; an affirmation of the quest for glory and the desire for esteem. The slave is not recognized but is rather defined only in terms of service to the master. However, as nothing in Hegel is static, this relationship must itself change. The slave, in serving the master, is forced to work with the material resources of the world to provide necessities. The master, in placing dignity as a value above life, is the manifestation of freedom; the slave, through immersion in the things that sustain life, manifests necessity and all its attendant burdens. But as the master becomes further removed from the realm of necessity, a new dependency emerges that inverts the old relationship. Whereas the slave was once dependent on the master for meaning, the master now depends on the slave for provision of needs. When the slave realizes this, a new awareness dawns, and self-consciousness enables the slave to find a new level of freedom that opens a higher stage of reality. But the struggle for recognition always pervades humanity, feeding our need for each other and our desire to overcome that need. Hence politics is driven by conflict and assertion; yet if one views the sum of human activity through a wider angle, the rational and yet normally imperceptible march toward freedom and knowing is revealed, but only after the fact of the events.

Hence history occurs in stages, and in broad strokes we can discern three primary stages that represent the advance of culture: what Hegel calls the Oriental stage wherein one person (the despot) is free, the Greek-Roman stage, wherein the idea of freedom emerges, but only a few can achieve it, and the Germanic-Christian stage, wherein the idea of freedom is universalized through the principles of Christianity and the heroic political affirmation of the German people, and in particularly, the Prussian state. It is in the Prussian state, a constitutional monarchy of a kind when Hegel lived and wrote, that we come to find Hegel's own paradigm of the best regime, or at least, the closest contemporary approximation to it.

Hegel's ideal regime, his theory of the state, is woven tightly with his dialectical understanding of the world and with the interconnection between politics and ethics. For Hegel, "the state is the actuality of the ethical Idea," the latter being the reconciliation (and transcendence) of abstract right (objective and legalist) and morality (subjective and interior, residing in the will). The state is at once "absolutely rational" and the "actuality of concrete freedom." That is to say, the state, as with the whole sweep of history, exists as it is for a reason, however inscrutable that reason might be.

The state is the manifestation of reason in history and the form of association wherein human beings can best exercise their freedom universally. This is not the individualistic freedom of Hobbes or J.S. Mill but rather a freedom that is a function of social development, a freedom defined in communal terms and closely allied to the notion of duty. Whereas the family represents emotional belonging, predetermined position, and dependency, and civil society represents the autonomy of the individual alone in the world, the state combines both a sense of interdependence and place with the freedom of the moral will. This is why the state is the embodiment of the Ethical Idea, the exertion of the human will at the level of the universal that combines the objective notion of right with the subjective nature of moral action (subjective in the sense that the moral will is interior and not an artifice of external laws and coercive methods to apply those laws). The state is the highest association, the one association that resolves all the conflict that occurs in lesser associations, such as families, guilds (corporations), and the many facets of civil society. In the state and through citizenship we become rational and free, no longer conflicted and vulnerable to contingency and need. The particular interest of the individual is raised to a new level of universality, the citizen (in contrast to isolated individuals or members of families) through duty "knows and wills the universal: they even recognize it as their own substantive mind." This is the philosopher-ruler of Plato's Form of the *polis* universalized and congealed in the Hegelian state, the complete fusion of private desire with public weal. It is only in and through the state that the conflicts that abide between esteem-seeking wills and moral principle find reconciliation. One element of Hegel's state, the bureaucracy or civil service, in some ways emulates the Platonic ideal of philosopher-rulers: a class utterly devoted to the common good, so much so that Hegel refers to the bureaucracy unabashedly as the "universal class," or that class which possesses no particular interest of its own but is somehow always directed to serve the good of all. For Plato, this is an intelligible paradigm to emulate, for Hegel it is materializing before us in the development of the modern state.

The image of the bureaucrat as modern hero might leave readers today cold and incredulous, but in fairness Hegel was not anticipating the sort of bureaucratic rationalism described later by Max Weber and experienced with some alienation by citizens of modern states in the twentieth century. Nonetheless, the image is hard to shake and certainly feeds into an overall criticism of the Hegelian state as a system for order and control rather than the manifestation of freedom that Hegel envisioned. Going further, Hegel's more insistent critics, rightly or wrongly, detect the stirrings of totalitarianism in Hegel's system. Indeed, R. Hartman has depicted the Battle of Stalingrad as the death struggle between the heirs of the right Hegelians (Nazi Germany) and the heirs of the left Hegelians (Soviet Marxism). Furthermore, the image of the state as the final reconciling totality of all lower forms of conflicted association does not lend itself to an easy rebuttal of such an observation, and indeed, if Hegel's state is about power, then such a conclusion is inescapable. Yet some students of Hegel also see more liberal elements in his political theory, and understand his notion of the state along more mystical lines, a transcendence of ordinary politics (again, loosely reminiscent of Plato).

To flesh this out, one needs to examine the structure of Hegel's paradigmatic regime in *The Philosophy of Right*. There, Hegel constructs a framework that depends on a kind of separation of powers, balanced together in a dialectical equilibrium. Furthermore, Hegel assumes, as a matter of course, freedom of the press and separation of church and state, features of the liberal polity. Moreover, even though Hegel expounds at murky length regarding his ideal state, he allows that, due to the rational process of history, every society and state possesses the constitution that is best fitted for its circumstances and conditions.

Hegel seeks an absolute ideal on the shifting flux of historicity, and comes out advocating both his own version of the political paradigm while still adhering to a Panglossian survey of the shape of things.

Still other aspects of Hegel's political philosophy stimulate controversy. Hegel speaks of manifestations of World Spirit, the very embodiment of the cunning of history at a particular moment. Napoleon, at least at one time and in either a moment of insight or weakness (depending on your point of view) served as one such example for Hegel of the passing of the World Spirit incarnate in one heroic personage. Hegel also tended to blend a complex, even ornate rationalism with the Romantic Great Man, a possibly volatile combination, some might argue, in the hands of ideologues and epigones. Hegel's admiration of the Prussian monarchy seems to be an idiosyncratic view for the Owl of Minerva's philosopher, and his inclusion of monarchy as an element in the equilibrium of power might be anachronistic, but then again, it might make sense dialectically, if the dialectic does indeed preserve as well as abolish. Perhaps one of Hegel's most controversial political doctrines is found in his view on war. Hegel argued that war at the right moment (and if we are to believe the overall logic of his system, whatever occurs must be occurring at the right moment) lends to the health of states, cleansing the international system of torpor and decay. War, Hegel muses, is vital to maintain the vigor of states and the "ethical health" of peoples. War purifies, "just as the blowing of the wind preserves the sea from the foulness which would be the result of prolonged calm, so also the corruption in nations would be the product of prolonged, let alone," in a passing swipe at Kant, "'perpetual peace'." There is reason in history, and war, being a part of history, happens for a reason.

Hegel's influence is pervasive. He directly influenced Marxism, Marx himself beginning his philosophical journey as a Young Hegelian and retaining much of the Hegelian conceptual structure throughout his work. Even *Capital*, as

Scott Warren once remarked, can be approached as a "concretization of *The Phenomenology of Spirit*." The connection to Marx is straightforward and for all to see, but other thinkers and schools of thought owe a debt to Hegel, for they either borrowed from his basic ideas, as in the case of Marx, or a good portion of their philosophy was a response and rebuttal, as in Kierkegaard. With Marxism, nationalism, phenomenology, existentialism, critical theory, structuralism, postmodernism, and even strains of both neo-conservatism and communitarian liberalism all owe a debt to Hegel's system. Finally, as some maintain, the fascistic impulses that led to twentieth-century totalitarianism are distant reverberations of Hegel's own quest for absolutism, a quest that some would regard as a Faustian bargain. If Hegel is right, the judgment of history will in the end serve as the only agent capable of resolving the debate over his legacy and his relevance.

Related Entries
dialectical theory; Kant, Immanuel

Suggested Reading

Avineri, Shlomo. *Hegel's Theory of the Modern State.* 1972; repr. New York: Cambridge Univ. Press, 1979.

Hegel, Georg Wilhelm Friedrich. *Hegel's Philosophy of Right,* trans. T.M. Knox. New York: Oxford Univ. Press, 1952.

McDonald, Lee. *Western Political Theory, Part Three: Nineteenth and Twentieth Centuries.* New York: Harcourt, Brace, Jovanovich, 1968.

Smith, Steven B. *Hegel's Critique of Liberalism: Rights in Context.* Chicago: Univ. Chicago Press, 1989.

Herzl, Theodor (1860–1904)

With his publication of *The Jewish State* in 1896, Theodor Herzl set into motion what would become the ideology of Zionism that itself contributed to the creation of modern Israel. Fully aware that anti-Semitism remained a perpetual threat against the people and culture of Judaism, Herzl championed the cause of a political homeland within which Jews could finally join the world stage as an independent national entity no longer scattered by the Diaspora or ghettoized in the midst of potential enemies. Cultural and religious identity had held the Jewish people together throughout the Diaspora, but what was now needed, Herzl emphasized, was a separate, secure and viable political entity for the promotion of Jewish interest and the survival of the Jews as a people.

While many of his contemporaries conceived of Zionism in cultural terms, Herzl, who recognized and embraced the value of Jewish culture, intended a further step, a more practical one informed by the *realpolitik* of his day. Anti-Semitism was too complex to unravel and too ingrained to excise; hence for Judaism to survive and thrive again, a physical place had to be won, a tangible homeland had to be built. "I consider," Herzl wrote,

> the Jewish question neither a social nor a religious one even though it sometimes takes these and other forms. It is a national question, and to solve it we must first of all establish it as an international political problem to be discussed and settled by the civilizations of the world in consent.

Herzl proposed a civilized, gradual relocation of the Jewish people and establishment of the state that would bear their culture and dignity. "The departure of the Jews," Herzl anticipated, "will leave no wake of economic disturbance, no crises, no persecutions... ...the outflow will be gradual, without any disturbance, and its very inception means the end of anti-Semitism. The Jews will leave as honored friends." This was critical for Herzl; only a gradual "exodus" and deliberate but measured construction of the Jewish state would succeed and, in the long term, benefit the Jewish community as well as the world at large. The first stage would involve the poorer classes, those who would lead the way to break ground, cultivate the soil, and erect the transportation and communication infrastructure, thereby preparing the economic foundations of the new state. With an economic matrix in place, the prospect of prosperity would attract other Jews who would recognize the potential for a life of freedom and affluence, motivated only by the promise of a new land rather than the demands of guarding the *status quo,* safe from the persecutions of the past, promising a new security in the immediate future. As Herzl announced,

> this is how it will go: precisely the poor and simple, who have no idea what power man already exercises over the forces of Nature, will have the staunchest faith in the new message. For these have never lost their hope of the Promised Land. Here you have it, Jews. Not fiction, nor yet fraud! Every man will carry over with him a portion of the Promised Land—one in his head, another in his arms, another in his acquired possessions.

Through a new homeland of their own, the Jews will rise again as the Macabees, to their benefit and to the benefit of the world community. A politically free Jewish people meant for Herzl a new era not only in the advance of Judaic culture and life, but also in the progress of the modern international order. A free and prosperous Jewish state means a more civilized humanity.

> We shall live at last as free men on our own soil, and in our own homes peacefully die. The world will be liberated by our freedom, enriched by our wealth, magnified by our greatness. And whatever attempt there for our own benefit will redound mightily and beneficially to the greatness of all mankind.

Related Entries
Buber, Martin; Zionism

Suggested Reading
Herzl, Theodor. *The Jews' State: A Critical English Translation,* trans. Henk Overberg. Lanham, MD: Jason Aronson, 1997.

Hobbes, Thomas (1588–1679)

Pessimist, absolutist, collectivist, relativist, secularist, and atheist—all of these have been popularly employed in efforts to concisely portray Thomas Hobbes, the Sage of Malmesbury. One might also choose to employ alternate adjectives such as realist, protoliberal, individualist, utilitarian, Erastian, and Calvinistic Anglican and evoke similar approval, or at the very least provoke lively disapproval. Such is the complexity, and at times controversy, surrounding the author of *Leviathan* and *On the Citizen (De Cive).* Indeed, irony can be experienced upon realizing the tension between, on the one hand, Hobbes's sincere desire to create a geometric logic of politics unburdened by what he saw to be the groundless assumptions and foolish errors of past thinkers, and on the other hand, the frequent and befuddling appearance of apparently irreconcilable contradictions scattered throughout the elements of his new civil philosophy. And yet, in spite of the contradictions that flaw his Euclidian method, there is a significantly consistent internal logic animating the heart of Hobbes's project.

One way, not necessarily the best way, to begin to understand Hobbes is through his conception of the relationship between felicity, scarcity, and power. One adjective that is used to describe Hobbes enjoys consensus: materialist. Hobbes's ontology conceives of the human person as a discrete material body, like any body in nature, perpetually in motion and impelled by appetites (desires—or what Hobbes names "motion toward") and aversions (motion "fromward," or away from something). Felicity, or the "continual progress of the desire," is the apparent engine that drives this corporeal dynamism. The individual, the basic unit of human association, is characterized as a restless, perpetually dissatisfied mass of desires, ever pursuing the elusive goal of felicity. Our appetites are endless, but the resources that we need to satisfy these appetites, however temporarily, are finite. For Hobbes, the world is essentially material, and thus finite—and such finitude can only produce scarcity when confronted by the inexhaustible desire of human appetites. This condition produces a "collision of wills," and a state of perpetual conflict. Therefore, in order to wrest from life at least a modest felicity, individuals are well served by power. "I put," Hobbes declaims, "for a general inclination of all mankind, a perpetual and restless desire for power after power, which ceaseth only in death," or, that is to say, only when our natural, interminable motion is finally suppressed once and for all. In sum, our insatiable appetites produce conflict with others in a finite material world, for there will always be instances wherein at least two individuals will "desire the same thing, which nevertheless they cannot both enjoy," forcing power into the equation in order to secure those goods of life necessary for a state of general felicity.

This is our natural condition. Hobbes develops the hypothetical device that we call the "state of nature" in order to more fully understand this aspect of humanity. By illustrating humanity in its most natural mode, Hobbes accomplishes two things: first, he rejects claims by classical thinkers that human beings are by nature political owing to our natural comity towards each other. Plato, Aristotle, St. Thomas Aquinas, and Richard Hooker, among others, all recognize friendship as both proof of our natural sociability *and* requisite to our participation in political life. For Hobbes, it is simply not the case that we are friends by nature, but rather we are, in reality, naturally enemies. Remove man from society, Hobbes argues, and our natural enmity—fueled by our diffidence toward one another and our limitless needs—quickly reemerges. Every person and every thing is either an obstacle or potential obstacle to our felicity, and the only way to surmount or remove obstacles is to increase our power. Absent the organizing power of formal society and the sustained institutions of law and politics, we slide into a state of nature that is nothing more than a "war of all against all," wherein natural life is "solitary, poor, nasty, brutish and short."

Hence power is both the principal object of our endeavors in nature and the only factor under which enduring political life is possible. As we are not by nature friends, power is employed to create an artificial condition wherein we can live, if not in a state of spontaneous amity, at least in a condition of comparative peace. Additionally, power is coupled with the concept of right, a conclusion arrived at by Hobbes that coincidentally echoes the remarks of Thrasymachus in Plato's *Republic*. According to Hobbes, even though the state of nature is a state of war, we do possess natural rights. Each individual is born with the natural right to self-preservation, or in essence, a natural right to life. Owing to the condition of perpetual war, with every man for himself, our natural right to life, which is summarized as a right to "by all means" defend oneself, is accompanied by the right to everything, "even to another's body." For Hobbes, in a state of nature, we must do what we can to survive and, if possible, secure as much happiness from the grim world as possible—hence we employ the power we have to assert our natural rights against all others. However, Hobbes also recognizes that human beings are by nature equal. We are not equal in the moral and/or theological sense as promoted by the ancient beliefs of Judaism, Christianity, and Stoicism. Rather, we are equal in the sense that we are equally mortal (every person dies) and equally vulnerable (even the "weakest" can destroy the "strongest" in nature). Right follows power, and in recognizing this hard fact, Hobbes realizes that our "natural right to everything" is only as good as our individual power to affirm it, but the power of the individual in nature is limited to the point of vanishing. Hobbes's logic leads, implicitly, to the conclusion that our natural right to everything, which depends solely on power, is in reality a right to nothing, power in nature being inconsiderable. What I have today because of my strength or wit will be gone tomorrow because of my lack of strength or wit relative to my unseen enemy. I have a natural right to what I possess that is neutralized by the right and the power of my adversary.

Uncertainty is concomitant to this condition of war of all against all. In a state of nature, there is no common notion of justice, nor is there any objective idea of good, evil, or bad. We only have our individual judgment, influenced by our appetites and aversions, interests and our fears, to determine what each of us deems good or bad. This moral uncertainty is perhaps the worst aspect of the state of nature, for there can be no arbiter of any kind to settle disputes without some common moral understanding of what is just and right. Our several and discrete impulses and needs alone determine what is good, "there being nothing by nature absolutely so." Faced with this, rational individuals are left only to their own emotions and devices in assigning what is right, and because every individual possesses the same claims to judge all actions, there is in effect, nothing in nature that is right or wrong, what remains is only what proves efficacious to self-preservation.

This depiction of natural humanity is the source of the charges of pessimism and relativism by Hobbes's critics. Conceding these threads in Hobbes's philosophy, it must also be noted that there is ample room for hope. Facile readings of Hobbes's work can prompt the conclusion that he considered humanity as naturally "evil,"—an assessment made by Rousseau in his *Second Discourse,* but nowhere does Hobbes explicitly make this claim. Nothing is naturally or absolutely good or evil, including human beings. Furthermore, Hobbes is clear that our actions in nature are "of themselves no sin," but only a consequence of the condition of war. We are by nature appetitive, emotive, self-interested, excessive, flawed beings, yes—but Hobbes attaches promise to the fact that we are also rational creatures capable of cooperation in spite of ourselves. As there is a natural right, there is also a natural law—indeed, there are a number of identifiable natural laws—based on the initial premise that through "right reason" (the same term employed by St. Thomas Aquinas and the Stoics before him) the human individual can discern the first and fundamental law of nature, which is to "seek peace and follow it." This is not mere "ratiocination," which is a calculative reasoning that allows us to make personal judgments about our immediate interests, but rather it is through reason as *logos,* engaged in through the interactive and interpersonal activity of

speech, that we become cognizant of this natural law of peace.

The first and fundamental law to "endeavor peace" establishes the grounds for the second law of nature prescribing natural humanity to "lay down" our individual right to everything, provided that this act is accomplished in reciprocity with others who also lay down this right. This renunciation of our natural right to everything must be voluntary and mutual, and it is through this cooperative decision that formal society in general and politics in particular is created. The second natural law is the origin, for Hobbes, of government by consent. Mutually and voluntarily renouncing our natural right to everything does not abolish that right, but only transfers it to a common power, hereafter known as the sovereign, which now possesses the sum of our individual wills. Through this transfer, our natural right to everything, which is only supported by our meager power in nature, is now embedded collectively in one sovereign. Our meager power in nature is now, in aggregate, formidable, capable of keeping "all in awe," and effectually rules by "terror thereof." The sovereign is thus known to Hobbes as the "generation of that great Leviathan," or "mortal god," that reigns with absolute authority over the state. Under the "immortal God," no human authority is greater than the sovereign. Once established, we can now determine justice and injustice, good and evil, and we can bind in the law what in nature existed in conscience only, viz., the various laws of nature from "gratitude to equity" that are obscured by ambiguity and raw self-interest in a stateless condition.

By definition, sovereign power is the highest human authority. If a ruler or rulers must acknowledge another authority, then by definition, the latter is sovereign, not the former. The matter or substance of all sovereignty is described as absolute (supreme), perpetual (transgenerational), and indivisible (unified and exclusive; power cannot be shared). These features lean toward monarchy, and it is evident that Hobbes preferred some form of royal government. Nonetheless, Hobbes allows for variation, recognizing that sovereignty can be held by one (monarchy), the few (aristocracy) or the many (democracy). In this way Hobbes follows the ancient typology established by Plato and Aristotle, but he departs from the old ancient philosophers by claiming that there are no deviant forms, that terms such as tyranny or oligarchy are relative complaints that apply only to governments disliked. A "tyrant" is only a king out of favor with his subjects; his power remains legitimate so long as the safety and "contentments" of the people are secured.

Hobbes does not advocate arbitrary or tyrannical government; he only recognizes the realities of it. Subjects are better served suffering a bad ruler than precipitating the state of nature. Hobbes writes to promote lawful government. Power remains central, but law is shown to be a decisive element for a successful sovereign. Hobbes endorses a system of limited laws designed to secure safety, establish property (propriety), encourage industry, and expand liberty. While natural man is accountable only to himself, his liberties are constricted by the condition of universal war. Awed by the sovereign, our liberties are effectively expanded, the sovereign being our only impediment as we employ our industry in the pursuit of a more certain felicity. We voluntarily submit to the sovereign will, and in the act of "submission consisteth both our obligation, and our liberty." Unfettered, illusory natural liberty is happily replaced with liberty under law, made secure by the sheer power of the "artificial person" that represents all authority within the polity.

And yet, Hobbes reminds us that sovereignty is a power above even the law, for it is the sovereign who legislates, executes, and judges. Indeed, Hobbes refer to sovereign power as "the rights of the sovereign by institution," contrasted with the liberties of the subject as the remainder of what is not prohibited by law. Legality, civil liberties, and justice are ever functions of sovereign will, politics the product of the transference of our natural right to everything into one body, and all the result of our mutual and unanimous consent to and authorship of Leviathan's irrevocable authority. Even the church must recognize the authority of the civil power, for it is only through the power of the sovereign that moral certainty and political justice can be established once and for all. The judges, while remaining beyond judgment, cannot, by definition, act illegally or unjustly. Only the subjects can be deemed lawful or lawless, just or unjust, the sovereign is the sole umpire of what is good and right. Rebellion, therefore, is technically an unjust defiance of that which is authored by all, and, *prima facie,* cannot be allowed. Some Hobbesian scholars, however, discern some implicit backpedaling in this regard, maintaining that Hobbes, in insisting that the sovereign is obliged to protect the subjects (the original reason for the contract) and maintaining that no one can surrender the right to life and thus always maintains the right to self-defense, tacitly and even esoterically leaves open the possibility for resistance to sovereign commands when protection is withdrawn and life is endangered.

The internal tension over the right to resistance in *Leviathan* is one example of several apparent contradictions within the Hobbesian system. Another contradiction in Hobbes that has drawn much attention revolves around his reliance on natural law corresponding with his clear affirmation of a kind of legal positivism. The laws of nature are described as both divine and yet only descriptive. If the former is the case, then there is a higher law that binds us beyond the sovereign, but if the latter is the case, then the "laws of nature" are only ways in which human beings describe the patterns of motion, not unlike those laws that Galileo spoke of, and that Sir Isaac Newton would later develop. In other words, in Hobbes's theory of law, natural law, and justice, there is a tension between first principles and human will, a tension that at times seems to undermine Hobbes's sincere desire to produce the first real logic of politics.

The complexities that strike us in Hobbes serve as useful reminders that every political theorist of any significance eventually encounters contradiction: it is in the nature of the questions raised within the Great Tradition. Thomas Hobbes, the logician of the *polis,* is no exception. Regardless, Hobbes remains a seminal figure in the development of modern political thought, and is numbered among the dozen or so most important thinkers in the history of political theory.

Related Entries

all other contentments; *bellum omnium contra omnes*; equality; justice; Leviathan; liberalism; Locke, John; three causes of quarrel; war of all against all

Suggested Reading

Hobbes, Thomas. *Leviathan,* ed. Edwin Curley. Indianapolis: Hackett, 1994.

Hobbes, Thomas. *On the Citizen,* ed. Richard Tuck and Michael Silverthorne. New York: Cambridge Univ. Press, 1998.

Hume, David (1711–1776)

A figure of considerable stature in the history of philosophy—especially in the fields of epistemology and moral theory, David Hume also holds a significant position in the history of political thought. Along with John Locke, James Harrington, and Baron de Montesquieu, Hume was highly regarded among the American Founders, and his influence can be detected in the political debates over the ratification of the Constitution. Hume is of particular interest owing to his tendency to hold both "liberal" and "conservative" principles, thus reflecting a tendency toward a moderate view of government and its role in the promotion of a just society.

Hume's "conservatism" stems from his appreciation of history as the best test for the value of an idea or political practice. Political liberties and the rule of law are the outcome of a long lineage of human development reaching into the dim past, providing the deep roots necessary for the achievement of a rational political order. It is the wisdom of the centuries more than anything else that has proven a doctrine or practice credible and worthy of retention, and not the more abstract, apparently ahistoric concepts of natural right in currency during Hume's time. Institutions that have endured over time are still in place for a reason, and that reason should be acknowledged. Hume objected to the presumption of both the social contract (we accept society out of habit, and no government is truly based on consent but rather on some distant act of coercion or usurpation; even a benevolent government can be traced to some act of force) and the claim to a right of revolution. The social contract is both false and pernicious, for it allows a single generation to discard from its own interest the legacy of past wisdom, well tested in the course time. This veneration of the past and the candid rejection of the social contract is evidence of both Hume's conservative understanding of the value of politics and his skeptical attitude about its origins and foundations.

However, Hume can also be seen as somewhat "liberal" (in a broad sense of that term) in his embrace of the social and economic revolutions of his time. Hume regarded the emerging commercial economy that would eventually evolve into industrial capitalism to be of great benefit, not only to the prosperity of the nation, but even in the moral improvement of society as a whole. The new economies encouraged industry, innovation, self-reliance, and investment in one's own affairs, all of which, for Hume, are hallmarks of a robust liberty worthy of human dignity. Hence, while Hume was politically conservative, his views toward economic growth and change were, at least compared to his contemporaries, anything but traditional.

Hume's belief in the advantages of combining republicanism with commerce may have influenced the American founding, particularly through the ideas of Alexander Hamilton and, later, the American System of Henry Clay. Moreover, Hume's distrust of "parties of principle" and the factional divisions that they draw to the detriment of political unity anticipate Madison and Washington. Hume's prudent skepticism regarding human nature are also features of certain strains within American thought, as well as his belief in the balancing effects of a mixed regime. It is in this latter facet of Hume's thought that his ideas evince a moderate tone, neither conservative nor liberal, and one echoing ancient themes running back to the classical theorists.

For Hume, human history has experienced an ongoing struggle between liberty and authority, an excess of one destructive to the benefits of the other. In order to arrive at a society that avoids the excesses of the extremes, Hume endorses a mixed regime, combining the right amount of liberty with a moderate authority. Through his theory of mixed regimes, Hume joins with Montesquieu, Harrington, and Locke in promoting a regime that seeks the equilibrium found between freedom and order. It is in Hume's moderation that we find his most enduring influence.

Related Entries

conservatism; *Federalist Papers*; Hamilton, Alexander; liberalism

Suggested Reading

Hume, David. *Essays Moral, Political and Literary,* ed. Eugene F. Miller. Indianapolis: Liberty Classics, 1987.

1

Ibn Khaldun (Abd al-Rahman Ibn Khaldun, 1332–1406)

A widely traveled scholar and public servant, Ibn Khaldun holds a particularly special place in the history of ideas as not only one of the more original voices among Islamic political thinkers but also for anticipating ideas that would later fix the attention of European political philosophers. His *Prolegomena* (*Muqaddimah*) to his larger text, *Universal History,* is regarded by scholars to be his principal work

and best summary of his overall thought. The *Prolegomena* illustrates the influence of Aristotle in the formation of his ideas, particularly in the manner in which he premises his study of politics from the affirmation of the political nature of humanity. But it does not stop there, as Ibn Khaldun also exhibits a more "modernist" turn throughout much of his work. Moreover, Ibn Khaldun saw himself as less reliant on Aristotle and Plato and more actively independent of any particular tradition or school of thought.

Universal History and the *Prolegomena* written as its introduction is noteworthy as an attempt to merge the methods of philosophy with those of history—the analytical rigors of the philosopher with the narrative talents of a good historian. Ibn Khaldun's project begins with a careful study of the nature of knowledge, which he conceived as divided into three basic types: essential (transphenomenal), material/natural/cultural, and moral. Of interest to modern students of political inquiry is how Ibn Khaldun contrasted knowledge of natural phenomena with "knowledge of civilization," or knowledge of political, social, and technological structures and applications. This can be seen as an anticipation of the Western discipline of sociology that emerged four to five centuries after Ibn Khaldun and certainly has been identified (by Anthony Black) as the first instance of a distinct awareness of "social knowledge," far in advance of Vico, as Black reminds us, and thinkers such as Max Weber and Karl Mannheim.

Perhaps the most important aspect of Ibn Khaldun's theoretical perspective stems from his recognition of the limits of human knowledge, regardless of the specific category under which a line of inquiry might fall. Philosophy, for all its value, is hardly without error. This awareness of the fallibility of reason and the arguments of philosophers has consequences for political thought, for we must always remind ourselves that error is inevitable within any system of thought. Owing to this, Ibn Khaldun suggested that philosophical system building is potentially dangerous for political theory and practice; rather, it is far more beneficial to carefully examine the case at hand rather than build unifying theories that presume to explain community in the abstract. One must take a practical approach, considering matters at hand without relying on generalized principles. This emphasis on prudence applied within given situations in some ways resembles modern pragmatism and holds a kinship with Machiavelli (however, Ibn Khaldun's theocentric orientation illustrates his common ground with a still more ancient political teaching far removed from Machiavelli). Those who study society must ground their investigations in social facts, which includes a serious study of history cleansed of folklore and myth, verified by reliable "reports" of past events. A solid knowledge of historical and social reality, things as they are and as they have truly been, will provide benefits to Islamic culture and, equally important, wisdom to the statesman.

Ibn Khaldun sought to promote a politics at once practical and moral. Rulers should seek to govern morally, both for its own sake but also because it is the only prudent course of action. Kings should be generous and kind as it is better for them as moral agents, but also good politics in that the people will be more likely to recognize their authority. Good moral conduct produces desirable effects. One can and should be both principled and practical.

Government, for the most part, regardless of its focus on realism and policy, must aim at benevolence. Care for the poor, for the widow and the orphan, are all responsibilities of public figures. Additionally, Ibn Khaldun understood economic regulation and management of public wealth a function of prudent government. Rulers must be devoted to ensuring opportunity and fairness for their citizens, and this requires a considerable level of government direction in the economic sphere. Property rights must be clarified and protected, the value of goods are drawn from labor invested (similar to John Locke and Adam Smith), labor must not be forced, and taxes must be minimal. In a word, Ibn Khaldun provides an early version of political economy, closely connecting the importance of public policy in encouraging economic prosperity.

In sum, Ibn Khaldun provides an exciting foreshadowing of a kind of social inquiry that would more fully emerge in the Western tradition centuries later, and his unfamiliarity to general readers should not be interpreted as diminished significance in the history of ideas. Concepts and approaches later applied by thinkers from Hobbes to Weber can be said to have been at least partially forwarded by this great and underappreciated scholar and public servant from fourteenth-century Tunis.

Related Entries
Alfarabi; Machiavelli, Niccolò

Suggested Reading
Ibn Khaldun, *The Muqaddimah: An Introduction to History,* trans. Franz Rosenthal, ed. and abr. N.J. Dawood, with a new introduction by Bruce B. Lawrence. 1969; repr. in abridged form. Princeton: Princeton Univ. Press, 2005.

ideology
Ideology is a variable concept, not always meaning the same thing for different readers (which is not in itself unusual for students of political inquiry). Fully aware of (and sympathetic to) Terry Eagleton's conclusion that nobody "has yet come up with a single adequate definition of ideology," it might nonetheless be helpful to float an incomplete description. Generally, an ideology is a system of fundamental beliefs animated by a few central principles regarding the nature of the political and social realm and marked by prescribed actions and policies for either political maintenance or reform. One might be tempted to broaden the definition to include cultural norms and configurations as well, but to do so would in some ways dilute the term "ideology" while approximating what would otherwise be described as a "worldview," or "*Weltanschauung.*"

Dante Germino, in his provocative work *Beyond Ideology,* defined ideology as

> a set of ideas about the ordering of society claiming the prestige of (phenomenal) science, based on an immanentist, reductionist epistemology, and aiming at the transformation of the world through making it conform to abstractions divorced from the reality of human existence in society.

Germino argues that ideology is not only different from philosophy and political theory, but it is actually a revolt against the grand tradition of theory that reaches back to the ancient Greeks, a deleterious rejection of philosophical openness. Ideology is reductionist to the extent of dangerous simplicity detached from a realistic and balanced conception of the political world and the aspirations of our humanity. Ideology, in this sense, coerces the conditions of the objective world into abstract interpretations of the world that can only produce folly, not wisdom. Germino argues for a return to the root of political inquiry through the openness of philosophy, abandoning the scientific pretensions of the ideologue.

An ideology is distinguished from a philosophy primarily through the attitude regarding certainty. By and large, philosophy retains a degree of uncertainty given the limitations of human knowledge, and thus remains open to further examination. This is not to say that philosophy denies the possibility of truth and real knowledge of things, but rather that there is always a need to reexamine certainties and to remain aware of new avenues to knowledge. Ideology is characterized by a higher degree of certainty regarding its basic principles and thus is less open to reexamination of its central ideas than a philosophical approach. In varying degrees, ideology is a closed system of ideas unreflectively presuming the incontrovertibility of its essential principles and the prescriptions consequent from their application, whereas philosophy, while still open to the possibility of incontrovertible truth (and in some cases affirming such truths) nonetheless operates from the assumption that human knowledge is limited regarding absolute certainty. Additionally, ideology is at once an expression of political aspiration, cultural supposition, and social interest, whereas philosophy, understood as a "love of wisdom," ultimately seeks to suspend supposition and exceed the self-imposed limits resulting from the exertion of an interest or desire. Owing to the connection of ideology to interest and its focus on politics and policies, ideology, unlike philosophy, is particularly enmeshed in the dynamics of power. In ideology, knowledge and power are combined, but in contrast to the Platonic ideal of power guided by reason, the truths asserted by ideology are inversely guided by the purposes of power. The ideologue is absolutely certain, and thus ideology is partially marked by a claim to omniscience in the understanding of the political order of things.

This is distinct from a religious belief, for while the faithful of a given religion admit the superiority of their theological concepts and core religious principles, all faiths recognize that the ultimate understanding of God remains beyond what Christian mystics have called the "cloud of unknowing." While religion can be politicized and succumb to ideological interests, in its essence religious belief and theological inquiry is detached from the quasi-omniscient claims of the ideologue. Any religion will reserve a sphere of Mystery; such a sphere is incompatible with ideological truth claims. In the twentieth and early twenty-first centuries, political movements animated by a central idea or set of principles that we can refer to as an "ideology" include, among others, liberalism, conservatism, socialism, Marxism, environmentalism, religious fundamentalism (including what is called "Islamism"), ultramontanism, feminism, fascism (including Nazism), anarchism, libertarianism, nationalism (vaguely), and various splintered sects and combinations of these general types. While each of these might be said to be informed by philosophical concepts and thus connected to elements of political theory, none of these are properly understood to be identical with a particular political theory, nor are they best understood as philosophical movements in themselves.

The term "ideology" was coined by the French thinker Destutt de Tracy to denote a "science of ideas" in 1796 during the gloaming of the French Enlightenment. An empiricist, de Tracy believed that all ideas and "ideological" systems were traceable to human sensory experience. De Tracy placed particular emphasis on the physiological aspects of sensation, and thus understood ideas to be a product of complex neurological activity. This stress on the material dimension of thought provoked some controversy, leading Napoleon to censor de Tracy's science of ideas in 1803. In the nineteenth century, the term ideology was freely used by Karl Marx, and in a pejorative sense. Ideologies were the intellectual and cultural tools of repression employed to justify and sustain the oppressive class, to reproduce the conditions of the power structure to the benefit of the dominant class and the culture that is thereby produced. For Marx, ideologies are but ideational manifestations within the political/social/cultural superstructure generated by the material base, a base that is organized by the ownership and control of the means of production. Political and cultural concepts and values are not in themselves objectively true but products of the socioeconomic alienation and oppression generated within the general system. Ideologies in the end, according to Marxian critique, are "false ideas," illusions concealing the hard realities of material exploitation that serve as their real source. Thus any ideas that are generated from this base reflect the exploitative manner in which production occurs, inevitably producing a "false consciousness" that legitimizes the base, its essential injustice notwithstanding. "The ideas of any age are the ideas of the ruling class," Marx asserted, and thus any ideology is but an extension of the consciousness of the masters. Therefore, while ideology, as a concept, was coined by de Tracy as a neutral descriptive term for scientific use, with both Napoleon and Marx

negative connotations were attached to it, the residue of which remains with us today. Karl Mannheim in his *Ideology and Utopia* recognized the existential power of Marx's historicist claims regarding the relationship between values and social systems but found Marx's analysis incomplete and his conclusions misguided. Like Marx, Mannheim understood ideology as a manifestation of the various relations within society as an interconnected system of ideas, practices, and institutions, but unlike Marx he did not regard ideology as necessarily driven by alienation alone (although ideologies can conceal exploitative dynamics within the structure). Ideologies, for the most part, sustain and, if successful in preserving legitimacy, strengthen the established social order. Mannheim contrasts this with what he refers to as "utopia," those principles and prescriptions for social reform or revolution that look forward to the reconfiguration or replacement of the status quo. As there are no objective truths or answers in the Platonic sense, any utopia will become an ideology over time, should it actually emerge as the prevailing ideational system in society.

Since the nineteenth and early twentieth centuries, the concept of ideology has undergone a variety of interpretations and thus experienced a diverse array of uses. Terry Eagleton has performed a useful service in identifying numerous definitions of ideology employed today, further emphasizing the diversity of approaches found in both the study and application of ideological norms and policies. "To indicate the variety of meaning," Eagleton offered in his *An Introduction to Ideology,* the following "more or less random [set of definitions] of ideology currently in circulation":

> (a) the process of production of meanings, signs, and values in social life;
> (b) a body of ideas characteristic of a particular social group or class;
> (c) ideas which help to legitimate a dominant political power;
> (d) false ideas which help to legitimate a dominant political power;

(e) systematically distorted communications;

(f) that which offers a position for a subject;

(g) forms of thought motivated by social interests;

(h) identity thinking;

(i) socially necessary illusion;

(j) the conjunction of discourse and power;

(k) the medium in which conscious social actors make sense of their world;

(l) action-oriented sets of beliefs;

(m) the confusion of linguistic and phenomenal reality;

(n) semiotic closure;

(o) the indispensable medium in which individuals live out their relations to the social structure;

(p) the process whereby social life is converted to a natural reality.

Illustrating the considerable multiplicity of definitions, not all compatible, Eagleton has provided a thorough and realistic analysis of a fundamentally misunderstood concept. Much of our understanding of ideology, according to Eagleton, rests on the perspective of individuals, often colored by the stubborn presuppositions of an interested party and refracted through a skeptical attitude regarding the credibility of alternative assertions, "There is no such thing as presuppositionless thought," remarked Eagleton in citing Martin Heidegger,

> and to this extent all of our thinking might be ideological. Perhaps *rigid* preconceptions make the difference: I presume that Paul McCartney has eaten in the last three months, which is not particularly ideological, whereas you presuppose that he is one of the forty thousand elect who will be saved on the Day of Judgment. But one person's rigidity is, notoriously, another's open-mindedness. His thought is redneck, yours is doctrinal, and mine is deliciously subtle.

Here Eagleton has perceptively charged us to an awareness of the power of our own interested perspective. Our ideological preconceptions will always influence our regard for the credibility of the utterances of others. This is a pervasive and enduring trait of all interest-oriented political knowledge (ideology), and thus a more critical eye is still needed to fully appreciate this relativist problem.

Nonetheless, if Germino and Eagleton are correct, any utterance, including that which is provided above, is suspect. Suffice it to say that, throughout political discourse, and especially in modernity, questions regarding the true nature of objective certainty and subjective interest have channelled and will likely continue to channel any serious debate over the nature of ideology and the possibility of political knowledge. An awareness of this tension is ancient. In Plato's *Republic* an important distinction is drawn between knowledge (which leads to wisdom) and "right opinion" which is the foundation of belief. In Plato's understanding, most human beings are capable of right opinion, but few if any are able to discern the nature of knowledge in itself. Plato's insight continues to draw our attention today, as students of politics and ideas attempt to sort the opinion from the right opinion, and the certainty that comes from one's convictions from the truth that is discovered in the nature of things.

Related Entries

anarchism; communism; conservatism; environmentalism; feminism; liberalism; socialism

Suggested Reading

Eagleton, Terry. *Ideology,* New York: Verso, 1991

Germino, Dante. *Beyond Ideology*. Chicago: Univ. Chicago Press, 1967.

McLellan, David. *Ideology*. Minneapolis: Univ. Minn. Press, 1995.

Vincent, Andrew. *Modern Political Ideologies*. Oxford: Blackwell, 1995.

I have a dream

Few speeches in American history are as timeless as Martin Luther King Jr.'s famous Lincoln Memorial Address on August 29, 1963. King's speech is numbered among the finest in the English language, along with Lincoln's Gettysburg Address and Second Inaugural, Franklin Roosevelt's First Inaugural, John F. Kennedy's First Inaugural, and speeches by Patrick Henry, Daniel Webster, and Frederick Douglass. It is from this speech we draw the phrase, "I have a dream," which has become so ubiquitous in popular culture and language that its initial power appears somewhat diminished, but a reflection on the message and its delivery soon brings the thoughtful reader back to a fuller understanding of the speech's importance in the development of American political culture.

King, an ardent integrationist, appealed to the founding principles of the United States in the advance of the cause of civil rights and social equality. In his Lincoln Memorial Address, he explicitly referred to "the magnificent words of the Constitution and the Declaration of Independence," which he described as a "promissory note to which every American was to fall heir," a promise that applied to all human beings, black and white. Yet, as King reminded his audience, "It is obvious that America has defaulted on this promissory note insofar as her citizens of color are concerned." Hence African Americans have been denied their rightful place as equals within the American vision of a just and dignified society of equals. Never one to mince words, King took the hypocrisy of American bigotry to task in no uncertain terms. Nonetheless, the speech emphasizes hope, and the refusal "to believe that the bank of justice is bankrupt," and the declaration that "Now is the time to make justice a reality for *all* God's children. [emphasis added]." It is in this way that King set the stage for a mesmerizing and transformative sequence of aspirations all generated by the dream of a promise fulfilled. Skillfully driving the speech toward a high pitch of eloquent and passionate idealism, Dr. King directed the vision of the American polity upward. "Let us not wallow in the valley of despair," the great orator began,

> I say to you, my friends, so even though we face the difficulties of today and tomorrow, I still have a dream. It is a dream deeply rooted in the American dream. I have a dream that one day this nation will rise up and live out the true meaning of its creed: "We hold these truths to be self-evident: that all men are created equal."

And so, in just a few, astonishing and evocative lines, King reached back to the American founding and stretched forward to the American future. Not since Lincoln's own Gettysburg Address, delivered 100 years prior, had any speech at once captured the meaning of the American founding, the reality of America's flaws, and the consequences of its inner shortcomings respective of those founding ideals, and simultaneously the endless hope for future generations that endure within those very ideals in spite of those practices that thwart their realization. From this point, King used the phrase "I have a dream," seven times to punctuate what he referred to as "our hope," and as "our faith." As the speech was drawn to its peroration, King employed another familiar phrase, "let freedom ring," to renew America's pledge for a truly just society, one that King knew to be far from realized, and yet one that he understood to be the only dream equal to the beauty of the human spirit.

Related Entries
the ballot or the bullet; content of their character

Suggested Reading
King's 1963 address before the Lincoln Memorial can be found in many sources, among them *A Testament of Hope: The Essential Writings and Speeches of Martin Luther King, Jr.,* ed. James M. Washington. San Francisco: HarperSanFrancisco, 1991, among numerous other sources.

immanentize the eschaton
To "immanentize the eschaton" is a phrase associated with the political philosopher Eric Voegelin (1901–1985) representing that attempt to "make heaven on earth," or to force the "end of days" and usher in a new reality. The term eschaton refers to the theological principle, prominent in Christianity as well as Islam, of an "end of days" or an "end of time" as we know it. Exactly what the end of days or end of time means is a matter of theological study and discussion, but for certain ideological movements, as Voegelin understands them, it represents the desire to abolish the current reality and replace it with a new one, presumably attaining the perfection that emulates the longing to establish "heaven on earth." For Voegelin, this is

essentially a dangerous doctrine, as those movements that seek to immanentize the eschaton claim a superior knowledge regarding the nature of reality (a kind of gnosticism) and believe that through the exertion of human will alone the eschaton can be forced, and the world cleansed of corruption, injustice, and oppression, and only then can it be thoroughly recreated. Voegelin argues that this is not only a dangerous conceit but ultimately a destructive principle as it regards the world we live in as both alien and dispensable.

According to Voegelin, modern movements that attempt to immanentize the eschaton are expressions of ancient gnosticism, renewed through Marxism, fascism, positivism, and certain strains of existentialism. In effect, the impulse to immanentize the eschaton is to substitute the inscrutable designs of God with the arrogant claims of human beings.

Related Entries
ideology; Voegelin, Eric

Suggested Reading
Voegelin, Eric. *The New Science of Politics.* 1952; repr. Chicago: Univ. Chicago Press, 1987.
Voegelin, Eric. *Science, Politics and Gnosticism.* Washington, DC: Regnery, 1997.

incredulity toward metanarratives
(incredulity toward grand narratives)
The central principle of postmodern theory, the phrase "incredulity toward metanarratives" was coined by Jean-François Lyotard as the principal term in his critique of transcendence, universality, and rationalism in the tradition of philosophy and political theory. Any "narrative" or set of concepts that attempts to promote an objectivist perspective or universalizing dynamic is to be considered askance. All phrases or approaches within a discourse that seek to forward a fixed conceptual foundation are suspect and, in the final analysis, repressive. As Lyotard explains in his *The Postmodern Condition* (as quoted by Honi Fern Haber),

I will use the term modern to designate any science that legitimizes itself with reference to

a metadiscourse of [the] kind [that makes an] appeal to some grand narrative, such as the dialectic of Spirit, the hermeneutics of meaning, the emancipation of the rational or working subject, or the creation of wealth. ... Simplifying to the extreme, I define *postmodern* as incredulity toward metanarratives.

No single narrative, or explanation of the world and how it works rooted in a false objectivity (and ultimately, for Lyotard, all objectivity is false), is legitimate. Hence Lyotard promotes the affirmation of "parologism," or a language and set of concepts that seeks to abolish current logical norms for the sake of fostering difference. In rejecting the grand or metanarrative, difference is promoted, which now replaces the old impulse toward uniformity and centrality with the liberation of repressed heterogeneity and a decentralized and multivocal community of diverse phrase regimens. Thus openness is introduced into human discourse, one that rebels against the "terror" of the metanarrative, a terror that destroys difference for the sake of coherence and uniformity. Grand narratives can only "totalize" our reality, and do so with the use of terror in various degrees. With the incredulity toward metanarratives, Lyotard calls for a deconstruction of accepted norms and assumptions, adopting the "politics of the pagan" that insists upon a notion of justice that is rooted in difference and no longer determined by a dominant, or "stronger voice." Operating from this premise, Lyotard and those influenced by his postmodern project propose a new politics and a new political theory that rejects first principles and eschews ideological attachments.

Related Entries
differend; Foucault, Michel; pagan politics; phrase regimen

Suggested Reading
Haber, Honi Fern. *Beyond Postmodern Politics.* New York: Routledge, 1995.
Lyotard, Jean-François. *The Postmodern Condition: A Report on Knowledge,* trans. Geoff Bennington and Brian Massumi, with a foreword by Fredric Jameson. Minneapolis: Univ. Minn. Press, 1984.

invisible hand

From Adam Smith's seminal *Wealth of Nations* (1776), the term *invisible hand* is employed to evoke an image of unseen and unexpected dynamics that convert the free pursuit of individual interest into the inadvertent but effective achievement of public benefit. Smith's specific example involves a rational choice by individuals operating in a free market from their own interest, preferring to support domestic industry over foreign trade. For Smith, this preference and the choices based on it are made through an individual's regard to his own security, and not from any other motivation such as a sense of duty, dedication to a common good, or sentiment of *patria*. In Smith's analysis, the consumer

> neither intends to promote the public interests, nor knows how much he is promoting it. By preferring the support of domestic to that of foreign industry, he intends only his own security; and by directing that industry in such a manner as its produce may be of the greatest value, he intends only his own gain, and he is in this, as in many other cases, led by an invisible hand to promote an end which was no part of his intention.

According to Smith, this is simply a realistic admission that human beings will always place their own interest first, because it is the only thing that they can see most clearly. Under the right conditions, that is, under a society that encourages free markets with comparatively little regulation of or influence by the power of the state, individuals will make choices for themselves that will ultimately improve society in general. Furthermore, to claim that one follows their rational choices and preferences out of motives detached from their own private gain is to be either disingenuous or misguided. Smith continues to explain,

> Nor is it always worse for society that it was no part of it. By pursuing his own interest, he frequently promotes that of the society more effectually than when he really intends to promote it. I have never known much good done by those who affected to trade for the public good. It is

an affectation, indeed, not very common among merchants, and very few words need be employed in dissuading them from it.

The "invisible hand" or innumerable private agents preferring their own interest and yet, when unfettered, producing a result amenable to all is the foundation of the principle of *laissez-faire* economics and has played an important role in the promotion of classical liberalism within the political sphere.

Related Entry
liberalism

Suggested Reading
Smith, Adam. *An Inquiry Into the Nature and Causes of the Wealth of Nations,* 2 vols., gen. eds., R.H. Campbell and A.S. Skinner, textual ed., W.B. Todd. Indianapolis: Liberty Classics, 1981.

iron cage of modernity

Sociologist Max Weber perceived the growing rationalization of human life in all aspects through the pervasive intrusion of bureaucracy, the hyper-intellectualism of the empirical sciences, and the entangling layers of legalism throughout political organizations. These, coupled with a general disenchantment of the world and a loss of political charisma and heroism, entraps us in a sterile world of detailed rules and constricted patterns of thought. The bureaucratic individual is thus a creature of reaction and impulse, unreflective and lacking imagination. Weber was not critical of reason itself nor social organization *per se,* as these are necessary elements of community, but only a certain kind of rationalism that produces emotionally truncated individuals and uninspired political and cultural leadership. This results in an increasingly formalized and mechanized world, an "iron cage" that forestalls the human imagination and sterilizes the human soul, setting the stage for what he would call the "icy night of polar darkness," a bleak future anticipated for the human race. Weber's concern over excessively rationalized bureaucracy represents one of the more compelling criticisms of modernity.

Related Entry
carceral society

Suggested Reading
Weber, Max. *The Vocation Lectures,* ed. David Owen
and Tracy Strong and trans. Rodney Livingston.
Indianapolis: Hackett, 2004.

iron law of oligarchy

One of the prominent founders of modern elite
theory, Robert Michels (1876–1936) perceived
perpetual dependency on concentrated leadership within any organization that always produces rule by a small minority. Even the most
radically egalitarian vision will, once applied,
produce a governing elite. Liberal democracies
and Marxist soviets are destined to the rule of
oligarchy, according to Michels, a political fact
that in his view was as ineluctable as Newton's
laws of physics. According to Michels, the elites
are ever motivated by the acquisition and
expansion of power, and in any organization,
whether it is socialist, liberal, conservative, or
otherwise, a small minority interested primarily
in power will emerge to govern the majority,
who are motivated by the desire for material
comfort and economic success. Indeed, Michels
goes further to assert that no society can

> exist without a "dominant" or "political" class,
> and the ruling class, whilst its elements are sub-
> ject to a frequent and partial renewal, never-
> theless constitutes the only factor of sufficiently
> durable efficacy in the history of human devel-
> opment. According to this view, the
> government...cannot be anything other than
> the organization of a minority.

Hence, democratic principles are not consistent
with the realities of power. Leaders are "necessary...in every form of social life," Michels
states, and this is neither to be judged by students of politics and political scientists as either
good or evil, but simply as the way of the
world. This is not a value judgment, according
to Michels, but merely a description of an
empirically based social law. "[E]very system
of leadership," Michels observes, "is incompatible with the most essential postulates of

democracy. We are now aware that the law of
the historic necessity of oligarchy is primarily
based on a series of facts of experience. Even
socialism, with its aspirations for a radically
egalitarian and classless society, is not immune
from the forces behind the law of oligarchy."
A "social revolution," Michels asserts, "would
not effect any real modification of the internal
structure of the mass. The socialist might conquer, but not socialism, which would perish in
the moment of its triumph." Oligarchy is an
"organic" inevitability. The principles and postulates motivating social change might say one
thing, and with sincerity, but the nature of the
social universe, characterized by the necessity
of leadership by a small elite, will always dominate that ideal. Oligarchies will vary to a small
degree, but in the end every organization of
any kind produces one.

Related Entry
circulation of elites

Suggested Reading
Michels, Robert. *Political Parties: A Sociological Study
of the Oligarchical Tendencies of Modern Democracy,*
trans. Eden Paul and Cedar Paul and with an
introduction by Seymour Martin Lipset. New
Brunswick, NJ: Transaction, 1999.

J

Jefferson, Thomas (1743–1826)

Thomas Jefferson's political ideas are essentially
Lockean. John Locke's notions of natural law,
natural right, popular sovereignty, limited
government, and resistance to tyranny are fully
manifest throughout Jefferson's writings about
politics. This is nowhere more evident than in
the *Declaration of Independence,* drafted by Jefferson with the assistance of Benjamin Franklin
and John Adams. For the most part, Jefferson
can be accurately and fairly described as borrowing heavily from Locke; nonetheless, as
Gary Wills has illustrated, a debt is also owed
to the ideas of the Scottish Enlightenment, in

particular the moral theories of thinkers such as Thomas Reid (1710–1796).

Even so, Jefferson's political ideas are primarily Lockean, with some modifications. Jefferson advocated localized government, proposing a system of "wards" or ward republics wherein the balance of government would be conducted. The wards would be essentially autonomous, allowing politics and governmental activity to be primarily decentralized. For Jefferson, this was an essential feature of his vision of an agrarian republic that relied on the development of American society as a vast community of yeoman farmers, all self-reliant property owners who essentially would govern themselves at the smallest possible level. Jefferson believed that the agrarian rural life cultivated human virtue to a noble degree, and is thus requisite to the success of an educated and morally sound republic. The urbanization and industrialization that he saw in Europe were, for Jefferson, anathema to both a virtuous citizenry and democratic principles. Mass society based on industry and commerce is not conducive to the kind of self-sufficiency and moral rectitude needed in a community that truly governs itself. Hence, for Jefferson, an agrarian economy combined with small, elementary republics or wards is the best possible regime for free men.

Jefferson did not oppose the maintenance of the state governments nor did he reject the establishment of a viable national government, but rather, only keeping their functions to a minimum. The federal government and the states play an important role in uniting and strengthening the new republic, but in the end, if free government is to be realized, it must be in the smallest units possible. Even traditional counties are too large for truly autonomous citizens; hence the basic ward is what is needed to ensure a political community of citizens rather than subjects. Thus Jefferson was a proponent of what is usually called "participatory democracy," a notion of democracy that not only allows a broader involvement of the citizenry, but in effect requires it. Every person should be involved in some way with the management of public affairs; hence direct participation in self-government for Jefferson was the only real possibility to forward the ideals of a democratic and egalitarian society.

Even though we can rightly call Jefferson egalitarian, he did believe, as did his friend and rival John Adams and other contemporaries, in a natural aristocracy of the intellect and moral virtues. There are those among us who through their own abilities and merit are suited to govern, but such an aristocracy could never be imposed arbitrarily or on any basis other than pure ability and moral character. Hence, for Jefferson, education is a vital factor in not only determining who belongs to the natural aristocracy, but also in ensuring that a participatory citizenry is truly equipped to govern itself by the light of reason and good judgment.

Much has also been made of Jefferson's apparent belief in frequent revolution. As with Thomas Paine, Jefferson expressed the need for citizens to renew their contract with society with each generation, even if this involved revolutionary action against the established power. However, Jefferson was no Trotskyite, and even though he was not as afraid of mass movements as some of his contemporaries (such as Adams and Alexander Hamilton), he was not inclined to encourage rebellion. Much has also been made of the conflict between Jefferson's egalitarianism and his ownership of slaves, a contradiction between theory and practice that merits consideration. To his credit, Jefferson did regard slavery as a social ill and essentially immoral, thus placing him at odds against the attitudes of most of his slave-owning contemporaries. Perhaps to his discredit (although this judgment is easily made from our more enlightened perspective), Jefferson kept his slaves at Monticello throughout the breadth of his life, thus enabling him to enjoy the life of a gentleman planter at the expense of the many slaves forced into servitude to support his refined tastes as well as at the cost of his own moral misgivings. Such comments are easily made in hindsight, and it is left to the reader to pursue this question with further research.

Related Entries
life, liberty and the pursuit of happiness; Locke, John

Suggested Reading
Jefferson, Thomas. *The Portable Thomas Jefferson,* ed. Merrill D. Peterson. New York: Penguin, 1975.

jihād (struggle, inner struggle, personal striving, Holy Striving, Holy War)
A concept within Islam of marked controversy within recent political currency, *jihād* has been variously interpreted as a struggle for inner piety, a nonviolent yet outward struggle against the temptations offered by the modern world, and a direct war against godlessness that can be drawn upon to justify violence on a number of levels and against any target deemed infidel. Given the political and cultural climate since the bombings of September 11, 2001, there has been a tendency to conflate the term *jihād* with the concept of Holy War, and in some respects this is not without justification. Nonetheless, within the Muslim tradition, the term *jihād* bears far more complex meaning than granted outside of Islam, and is not aptly understood as simply and exclusively open hostility against "unbelievers."

The term *jihād* is found in the *Koran,* the Holy Scriptures of the Islamic faith, wherein battle against nonbelievers is required. The question for interpretation involves the nature of this battle, should it be physically violent or does it mean to convey another kind of battle, a nonviolent struggle of the faith over the infidel? For example, in the *Koran* at Sura 22, verses 39 and 40, it states (rendered in English by N.J. Dawood) that "Allah will ward off evil from true believers. He does not love the treacherous and the thankless. Permission to take up arms is thereby given to those who are attacked, because they have been wronged." Hence the clearly defensive nature of Holy War is emphasized at this Sura. Elsewhere, at

Sura 9, verse 123, it reads, "Believers, make war on the infidels who dwell around you. Deal courteously with them. Know that Allah is with the righteous." Again, the passage lends itself to a variety of interpretations. At Sura 2, verse 190, it is translated as follows,

> Fight for the sake of Allah those that fight against you, but do not attack them first. Allah does not love the aggressor. Kill them wherever you find them. Drive them out of the places from which they drove you. Idolatry is worse than carnage. But do not fight them within the precincts of the Holy Mosque unless they attack you there; if they attack you put them to the sword. Thus shall the unbelievers be rewarded; but if they mend their ways, know that Allah is forgiving and merciful.

Thus the defensive nature of Holy War is clearly emphasized, but some would also assert a more offensive strategy, for as the verse continues,

> Fight against them until idolatry is no more and Allah's religion reigns supreme. But if they mend their ways, fight none except the evil-doers.

And elsewhere, in Sura 8, verse 12,

> Allah revealed His will to the angels, saying: "I shall be with you. Give courage to the believers. I shall cast terror into the hearts of the infidels. Strike off their heads, maim them in every limb." Thus We punished them because they defied Allah and His apostle [Muhammad]. He that defies Allah and His apostle shall be sternly punished. We said to them, "Feel Our scourge. Hell-fire awaits the unbelievers."

Before drawing conclusions from these selected passages, it is important to bear in mind that *jihād* has traditionally been understood in terms of *al-jihād al-akbar* (greater struggle) and *jihād al-asghar* (lesser struggle), the former referring primarily to the struggle within the heart and soul, the latter to the lesser struggle against external forces, a struggle that can but does not in every case lead to physical combat, struggle by the sword. As the struggle for the soul is undoubtedly more important, it is that type of *jihād* that is affirmed as the superior effort. Additionally, the juristic tradition within Islam has further identified four basic kinds of *jihād*: the struggle of the heart against the temptations of evil (identical to the greater struggle mentioned above), the struggle of the tongue to utter truth through the expressed support and teaching of the faith, the struggle of the hand in following righteousness and choosing justice over injustice, and the struggle of the sword in wielding arms against the infidel. It is this last type of *jihād* that has received the most scrutiny in recent years, and it is this type that is properly referred to as Holy War. Within the traditions of Islam, there is an important distinction between what is referred to as the House of Islamic Peace (those who declare and devoutly practice the Muslim faith supported by its five pillars) and the House of War—infidel humanity. There is a natural enmity between the House of Peace (Islam) and the unbelievers, hence a condition of Holy War always exist. For this reason, *jihād* has come to mean for so many (Muslim and non-Muslim alike) open, combative warfare. However, there is also a tradition within Islam that rejects a hostile posture to other faiths, and only allows physical, violent struggle in self-defense whenever the House of Islamic Peace is directly attacked.

Jihād as Holy War by and large means combat against non-Muslims. Nonetheless, Holy War has been waged by Muslims against other Muslims, and continues to be so in contemporary times. The more militant wing of Islam (which like most militant factions is a decided minority of the faithful) considers false Muslims to be equally infidel, and thus part of the House of War to be fought and defeated at all costs. Thus *jihād* is a concept that can hold severe consequences for Muslims themselves when distorted and applied by the more aggressive factions.

It is accurate to regard *jihād* as a broad and widely varied concept, with some considering it to be primarily a struggle of the soul and thus, when practiced as intended, nonviolent, with others considering it to be both of the soul as well as aimed at physical enemies, but only as a defensive measure, and with still others who regard it as a sixth pillar of Islam and thus a mandated and open war against all unbelief, questions of offense and defense ultimately rendered irrelevant. Whoever holds the deeper meaning of *jihād* (as open warfare or nonviolent striving) in terms of both theory and practice remains in dispute, but the current gravity of the term and its consequences is indisputable.

Related Entries
just war theory; Muslim Brethren

Suggested Reading
Black, Antony. *The History of Islamic Political Thought: From the Prophet to the Present.* New York: Routledge, 2001.

justice

Justice, according to Aristotle, is *the* political virtue, and indeed, it is also identified by Plato before him and St. Thomas Aquinas after him as one of the four cardinal virtues. For St. Thomas Aquinas, it is applied through the proper securing to a person what is fairly due, and requires the cultivation of the will and the fair discharge of our duties towards others. Most political theorists recognize the distinct difference between the principles of justice and the requirements of law; hence justice is in the main conceived as translegal as well as transpolitical. Throughout the balance of the history of ideas, justice has been understood by philosophers and laymen as somehow higher than mere law, and thus the standard by which all moral and legal activity can be measured. Conventionalist theories of justice, however, reject the notion of a higher justice that is the standard for moral and legal conduct, claiming instead that justice in the end is a function of political power or social and individual preference. Nonetheless, most political theorists over the course of history are convinced that justice is not to be equated with legal enactments, nor is it a function of power or interest but is rather some kind of principle independent of legality, power, and desire. This is understood in various ways, but for the most part it is clear that the majority of political thinkers are inclined to regard justice as different and apart from interest and power.

For Plato, justice is the virtue that emerges within a well-nurtured and balanced soul. It is defined by Socrates in *Republic* as "minding one's own" natural affairs or following one's inward purpose, but the definition that Plato offers through Socrates in *Republic* at 443d is more complete. "And in truth," Plato writes,

> justice is, it seems, something of this sort. However, it isn't concerned with someone's doing his own externally, but with what is inside him, with what is truly himself and his own. One who is just does not allow any part of himself to do the work of another part or allow the various classes within him to meddle with each other. He regulates well what is really his own and rules himself. He puts himself in order, is his own friend, and harmonizes the three parts of himself like three limiting notes in a musical scale—high, low, and middle. He binds together those parts and any others there may be in between, and from having been many things he becomes entirely one, moderate and harmonious. Only then does he act.

Hence, with Plato, justice is a matter of the soul as much as it is a matter of the *polis,* and the only political association that is worthy of the appellation "just" is one that is rooted in the essential character of the human person. Justice, therefore, is not framed within a set of rules or commands that determine our behavior but rather is a state of the soul that enables us to act for the sake of the Good. Plato's discussion of justice frames the concept for further examination, and the sense that justice involves more than commands and rules carries forward into the application of this essential principle.

In the fifth book of his *Nicomachean Ethics,* Aristotle states that "the just" is that which is at once "lawful and that which is equal and fair." (Thus, the unjust person tends to lawlessness and is consistently unfair, always undeservedly seeking the larger share, or exhibiting the vice of *pleonexia*.) As with Plato, Aristotle understands justice to be a virtue, indeed, a singular virtue in that it is oriented toward the good of others more than most other virtues. "This is why," according to Aristotle, "Justice is often thought to be the chief of the virtues, and more sublime," a "perfect virtue" because it is applied in consideration of what is fair to others, not simply what is good for the isolated self. With Aristotle and Plato, justice is thus a matter of the soul in community, and while it is a state of being, it is also a condition for right action and thus equally attached to the community as a whole.

Given this, Aristotle continues to examine justice in the particular, or special justice, as it is sometimes translated. Aristotle here identifies proportional (or distributive) justice directed at the fair apportionment of merit (and thus admits of a degree of inequality) and rectificatory (commutative, restorative, or corrective) that aims to restore a previous just arrangement that has somehow been violated, either voluntarily or involuntarily. As it is restorative, the special sense of rectificatory justice assumes a degree of equality between involved parties. It is to be understood that rectificatory or restorative justice is not retributive; it is not defined as a *quid pro quo.* The point of rectification in Aristotle's sense is simply to restore rather than to purely punish, although no doubt a rectificatory sense of justice involving the voluntary commission of injustice will contain an element of punishment. Both distributive and rectificatory types of justice are orientated toward the issue of desert, or what a person or persons deserve. Distributive justice conceives desert in terms of merit, rectificatory in terms of entitlement. Aristotle also identifies a third type of special justice, which he refers to as "political" and which is further subdivided into "natural" (*physikon*) and "legal (*nomikon*)," the former universally valid while the latter variable according to case. In this way Aristotle reaffirms his understanding of justice as based is some ways on universal principles that flow from our nature as human beings, but also with the recognition that different cities (or societies) will comprehend the conditions for just arrangements according to their own presuppositions, customs, traditions, and statutes. It is clear, for Aristotle, that political justice is established on certain (perhaps vague) principles that pertain to all human beings but that in the application of justice the legal structure of each polity and all that it implies must govern our understanding of what it means to act justly from case to case. We can speak of that which is just by nature while simultaneously realizing that what is just to some will be less just, or even unjust, to others. Both nature and convention, therefore, are to be considered in any thorough examination of justice.

Natural justice is not discussed in any detail by Aristotle, a reflection of the concept's detachment from any particular understanding. However, in defining justice as an intermediate (or mean) between committing injustice and suffering injustice, Aristotle provides us with a sketch of what justice is in every case, and again reaffirms the notion of justice as ultimately a virtue (for it is at the mean that we find the virtues). All told, Aristotle is with Plato and Sophocles, for example, in recognizing the universality of justice as translegal and transpolitical, while simultaneously acknowledging the innumerable declensions of justice and just action according to specific cases.

The notion of natural justice, which is both implicit and explicit in the writings of Sophocles (*Antigone*), Plato, and Aristotle, influenced the Stoic conception as well; a conception that itself would influence in turn the development of Roman law and jurisprudence. Natural justice and natural law are conceived as part of the higher principle of "right reason," which governs the universal order. The cosmos participates in a rational structure, and as such, humanity, being a part of this structure, is able to discern through the use of reason the natural law and the principles of universal justice. To act against this notion of natural justice is to defy morality itself, and in every case to be avoided. This idea is developed further within

Christianity. St. Augustine clearly understood there to be a higher principle of justice upon which laws were to be not only measured, but defined. A law that runs counter to justice (conceived as a higher independent principle) is in fact not a law. St. Thomas Aquinas elaborated upon this still further, drawing on not only St. Augustine, but also Aristotle, Cicero (or Tully), and the teachings of the church to define justice according to the relationships that exist among the four aspects of law: eternal, natural, divine (or revealed), and human (or positive, civil). Hence human law is just insofar as it is attuned with the eternal principles set in place by God through both the natural and the divine law. Human law, properly understood, is the particular application of the universal principles of natural justice as established by both reason (right reason) and revelation (in the Scripture and the teachings of the church). This notion was carried forward into the writings of the early modern thinkers, in particular, through the Salamanca school (Spanish Thomists who influenced modern notions of natural and international law), Hugo Grotius (who argued that even absent God, we would still be obliged to follow natural law owing to our rationality and inherent sociability) and John Locke (who argued that the state of nature is governed by a moral law to which all are obligated even absent a common power). Justice for all of these thinkers, and those like them, remained independent of legality, and the basis for legitimate legal enactments and fair judgment. Laws are thus just only insofar as they are grounded on principles over and above the law—the "law behind the law," as it were.

However, justice is not always conceived in these terms. While a good portion of political theory has advanced a notion of justice as a transcendent principle and as an independent measure of good laws, there remains a strain within political theory that regards justice to be defined under purely conventionalist terms, that is to say, according to social, political, and cultural conventions without any reference to a universal and objective principle. Such a conception of justice is invariably framed by interest and perspective (and thereby departing from the Aristotelian/Thomistic conception of justice as that virtue primarily involving the good of another). Hence a utilitarian position would define justice in terms of the maximization of utility (the greatest happiness for the greatest number), a Marxian view of justice would conceive it in terms of the interest of the oppressed class, a legal positivist view would rely on that which is supported by sovereign authority and/or social practices and expectations. This is not to say that a conventionalist view fails to aspire to objective standards—utilitarianism, Marxism, and legal positivism all recognize certain principles applicable to all cases. The main difference is in the positing of that standard in some act of human will or some interest formed by human preferences and shared desires. Ultimately, a conventionalist view examines justice in terms of interest rather than universal good (as in the case of Plato, Aristotle, and St. Thomas Aquinas, for example). Such a position might be gleaned from John Rawls, who sought a universal standard for justice as fairness based on the interests and preferences of rational actors within a position of equality, or Michael Walzer, who recognized the manner in which justice is differentiated according to various goods and ends.

Related Entries

advantage of the stronger; Aquinas, Thomas; Aristotle; difference principle; equality; equality of condition and equality of opportunity; freedom; Grotius, Hugo; natural law; Plato; Rawls, John; utilitarianism

Suggested Reading

Aristotle, *Nicomachean Ethics,* trans. H. Rackham. Cambridge, MA: Harvard Univ. Press/Loeb Classical Library, 1982.

Okin, Susan Moller, *Justice, Gender and the Family.* New York: Basic Books, 1989.

Plato, *Republic,* trans. G.M.A. Grube and C.D.C. Reeve. Indianapolis: Hackett, 2004.

Rawls, John. *A Theory of Justice.* Rawls, John. *A Theory of Justice.* 1971; repr. Cambridge, MA:

Harvard Univ. Press, 2005; new ed., Cambridge, Mass.: Harvard Univ. Press, 1999.

Sandel, Michael. *Liberalism and the Limits of Justice.* New York: Cambridge Univ. Press, 1998.

Walzer, Michael. *Spheres of Justice.* New York: Basic Books, 1983.

just war theory

Reaching back at least as far as the writings of St. Augustine, and for some scholars (such as James T. Johnson), further still to Plato, Aristotle, and especially Cicero, just war theory is a measure of both the legitimacy and the rectitude of military action given as a last resort. That is to say, ideally every effort is to be made to promote peace, using diplomacy as far as it will go to avoid belligerency. However, realistically, when war cannot be avoided or peaceful solutions are to no avail, just war theory requires that any martial action be engaged only on certain conditions and limited to narrow ends. In other words, there are specific conditions that justify war, and conventions that govern the just execution of war. Civilized nations are bound to prove that the conditions leave no alternative other than war, and once done, are further obligated to prosecute all military action within the moral and legal limits that define a just war.

While it is reasonable to trace just war theory to the classical tradition preceding the emergence of Christianity, just war theory primarily is associated with a tradition within the church as shaped by the ideas of both St. Augustine in his *Questions on the Heptateuch,* and St. Thomas Aquinas in his monumental *Summa Theologica.* The latter borrows from the former and provides the basic framework for modern just war theory. According to Aquinas, for a war to be just it must meet all three of the following criteria (quoted from *Summa Theologica*): (i) "that the ruler at whose command the war is to be waged have the lawful authority to do so," (ii) "there needs to be a just cause to wage war, namely, that the enemy deserves to have war waged against it because of some wrong the enemy has inflicted," and

(iii) "those waging war need to have a right intention, namely, an intention to promote good or avoid evil." All of these criteria must be met, for as Aquinas affirms, "*even if* legitimate authority declares war, and the cause is just, wars *may be unlawful* because they are waged with wicked intentions. [emphasis added]" In other words, the first precept of the law of nature, which is to always seek good and shun evil as discerned by St. Thomas Aquinas, governs all human relations, including those rare instances when warfare is no longer avoidable. Failing peace and the onset of war, only a just war can be fought. To abandon oneself to unjust or immoral actions, even during belligerency, is to violate the natural and divine law and the principles of morality contained therein.

Just war theory stems from the achievement of St. Thomas Aquinas and, further developed by thinkers such as Francesco de Vitoria, Francisco Suárez, Emerich Vattel, and Hugo Grotius, has become integral to modern theories of international relations, with contemporary political theorist Michael Walzer generally regarded as the preeminent commentator on just war theory. Even though the "fog of war" often militates against just conduct during combat, and even during preparations for combat, the community of nations nonetheless regards warfare as at once a last resort, which in itself is a modern criterion for just war, and governed by minimal standards of human decency. Given this, modern just war theory follows three general premises: (i) *jus ad bellum,* or the principle that requires a just cause, (ii) *jus in bello,* or the stipulation that once war has begun it must be conducted as justly as possible, and (iii) *jus post bellum,* or the requirement that any peace treaty that resolves the belligerent state of affairs is fair and just to all sides in the conflict. From these three general premises, modern just war theory is shaped by six criteria. The first three are based on the writings of St. Thomas Aquinas, namely, just cause, right intent, and legitimate authority. Added to this are the condition of last resort (already mentioned) as well as the notions of proportionality

and probability of success. Proportionality requires that the potential good gained from a commitment to war must be greater than the anticipated evils that might occur once combat is engaged. In other words, before declaring war, leaders are obligated to consider the possible goods secured against the cost of the unavoidable evils that will be produced. Such certainty is difficult; hence this one criterion by itself significantly limits the frequency of just war. The probability of success (which is not officially recognized in international law but is regarded as an important theoretical element) requires that a nation know beforehand that a commitment to war will likely result in a desirable change. A war of desperation, therefore, is unjust.

From these basic concepts and criteria, political theorists along with scholars of international relations and international law are able to examine more specific questions such as the fate of noncombatants, the use of certain weapons against soldiers and civilians alike, the treatment of prisoners of war, reasonable motivations and rational ends, consequences for other nations not directly invested in a war but are nonetheless involved, and just terms (including questions of reparations) of treaties or truces aimed at ceasing hostilities.

In sum, just war theory, unlike pacifism, recognizes that warfare is a political reality that cannot be avoided, And yet, similar to the moral principles that inspire pacifist movements, just war theory does affirm the need to encompass all human activity within a higher moral universe. Even warfare must be governed by universal standards of morality and conducted only under the reign of a sense of common human decency.

Related Entry
jihād

Suggested Reading
Elshtain, Jean Bethke. *Just War Theory.* New York: NY Univ. Press, 1991.
Kelsay, John, and James Turner Johnson, eds. *Just War and Jihad: Historical and Theoretical Perspectives*

on *War and Peace in Western and Islamic Traditions.* Westport, CT: Greenwood Press, 1991.

Walzer, Michael. *Just and Unjust Wars: A Moral Argument with Historical Illustrations.* 1977; repr. New York: Basic Books, 2000.

K

Kant, Immanuel (1724–1804)

Immanuel Kant is indisputably one of the more prominent and influential philosophers within the history of ideas; a groundbreaking thinker in epistemology and a compelling moral theorist, he has assumed his place with the most rarified of history's great minds. As a political theorist his influence, while considerable, is overshadowed by his larger philosophical system in the same way that St. Augustine's important contribution is secondary to his massive theological accomplishment. And while Kant's political theory may not match his stature as a philosopher in general, a few features are worth noting.

Kant's political thinking is an outgrowth of his moral system, emphasizing the rule of law and the recognition of one's duty through the exercise of the autonomous will for the sake of principle over inclination and self-interest. With Rousseau (whom Kant considered the Newton of moral theory), freedom is tantamount to the active submission to a self-legislated duty, or as Rousseau would more clearly state it, a law that we prescribe for ourselves. For Kant, this is the "Kingdom of Ends," or that realm of human action that is universal, transcendent of any specific context, and independent of particular interest. In the categorical imperative (act only in such a way that you would will your actions to become a universal law) and the practical imperative (always act in ways that treat others as ends in themselves and never as means to our own ends) the basic elements of duty are discovered and embraced by the good will that chooses to follow right even against the influence of one's immediate inclinations. For Kant, this moral system is the groundwork not only for the ethical conduct of individuals, but it is also the basis for the state. In the rule of law, which Kant regards as the first principle of any polity, the moral principles of the categorical and practical imperatives can be applied and practiced. Thus only republican governments (which are the only regimes truly premised on the rule of law rather than power) are legitimate regimes, framed within the institution of the separation of power, and based on the notion of popular sovereignty. Law is the essence of republics, not personal authority; hence the administration of the state should remain lean, the offices few. For with the expansion of officials, the ability of citizens to obey the law on their own accord is compromised. Kant's spare republic is not meant to be libertarian, but it is decidedly liberal and consistent with his emphasis on the autonomous will.

Republican governments are evidence of the inexorable progress of humankind, a belief that Kant held with most of his contemporaries and that anticipates the later confidence in human improvement exhibited by both G. W. F. Hegel and J. S. Mill. In addition, Kant advocates the erection of a more rational international order—guided by a law of nations and strengthened by a proliferation of international agreements as well as international commerce. More than anything, it is commerce in Kant's estimation that will draw nations closer to each other and that will produce the peace that has eluded humankind throughout the centuries.

Related Entries
Hegel, Georg Wilhelm Friedrich; Rousseau, Jean-Jacques

Suggested Reading
Kant, Immanuel. *Political Writings,* ed. Hans Reiss. New York: Cambridge Univ. Press, 1991.

knowledge is power

"Knowledge is power," a phrase coined by Sir Francis Bacon in the late sixteenth century (*Meditationes Sacrae,* 1597), is normally interpreted as advancing the notion that through the cultivation of learning, one's abilities will increase exponentially, and thus the accumulation of knowledge is itself a kind of power. Bacon regarded this relationship between knowledge and power in a constructive and positive light, recognizing that the more we can know about our humanity and the world around us, the more we are able to accomplish those things to which we set our purpose. This sentiment represents what would later become one of the principal beliefs of the eighteenth-century Enlightenment, the belief that the expansion of knowledge in itself generates the power needed to forward the progress of civilization. On a more cynical note, the connection of knowledge to power can also be perceived as a concession to the use of knowledge as a tool for manipulation, but this is not true to the context behind the maxim as initially conceived. Bacon was interested in the possibilities of the new experimental inductive science that he helped to construct and advance, and it is in this sense, the accumulation and rigorous analysis of data, that he understood the benefits of expansive knowledge. Our comprehension of the natural world must be deepened through methodical observation and experimentation, and it is from this that the elements of understanding will combine to shape our knowledge of the world and ourselves. This, in Bacon's view, was a powerful force in improving the human condition.

Additionally, Bacon believed, with nearly every major political thinker before him, that knowledge is directly linked to good government. "Sovereignty is married to counsel," he advised, and the "wisest princes need not think it any diminution of their greatness to rely upon counsel." Thus Bacon echoes the necessity of placing power under the guidance of reason, a concept that reaches back at least as far as Plato. Nonetheless, Bacon's opposition to common law jurists such as Sir Edward Coke indicates a notion of power that in some ways drifts closer to Hobbes, who, in chapter eleven of his *Leviathan,* remarked that "want of science," "ignorance of signification of words," and "ignorance of causes" undercut the prestige

and authority of those who hold, or seek to increase, their power. While Bacon's understanding of the connection between knowledge and power *both* recalls the classical belief in the rule of reason *and* anticipates the more instrumental uses of power advocated by modern students of politics, with Hobbes we seem to be fully immersed in the latter. This relationship is drawn even more tightly to the point of conflation through Michel Foucault's identification of power with knowledge, therefore concluding, following Nietzsche, that knowledge is ultimately either a product of power or refracted through it. This is not the intent of Bacon's famous phrase, but in certain quarters, its is the inherent outcome of the fullest application of the principle. However interpreted or applied, the assertion that "knowledge is power" remains an example of the efforts by students of political inquiry to examine the nature of the relationship between a certain kind of wisdom and political authority as well as the manner in which knowledge is properly acquired and applied to the benefit of prudent statesmanship.

Related Entries
Foucault, Michel; Hobbes, Thomas; Leviathan

Suggested Reading
Bacon, Francis. *Selected Writings.* New York: Modern Library, 1955.

L

Leviathan

Thomas Hobbes's masterpiece, *Leviathan, or the Matter, Forme, and Power of a Commonwealth Ecclesiasticall and Civil,* takes its name revealingly from the 41st chapter of the Book of Job. The Leviathan, the great sea beast of the Bible, is for Hobbes "the King of the Proud." "There is nothing on earth to be compared with him. He is made so as not to be afraid. He seeth every high thing below him, and is king of all the children of pride," Symbolically, the image of Leviathan conveys volumes—for pride and the attendant desires are the cause of much quarrel and a perpetual source of conflict throughout the human race. Leviathan stands over prideful humanity as a mortal god, preserving order and ensuring equity through the "awe" and "terror" of a common power capable of controlling our prideful inclinations.

From the beginning *Leviathan* provoked controversy in philosophy, politics, and theology, and to this day it remains one of the more challenging and provocative works ever produced by a political theorist. Written while in France during the turbulent 1640s, *Leviathan* was finished in April 1651 and initially published in England that very year; a Latin edition was produced on the Continent in 1668 and in England in 1676, the reprints of the English version having been prohibited. Interestingly, a handwritten copy was presented to Charles II in October 1651, shortly after his defeat at the hands of Cromwell. Hobbes's gesture earned his banishment from the royal court. *Leviathan's* notoriety also led to its burning, along with *De Cive* (*On the Citizen,* originally published in Latin in 1642), at Oxford University in 1683.

Composed as an exercise in political geometry, following an inspiration spurred by an encounter with Euclid's *Elements, Leviathan* is divided into four parts: "Of Man" (chapters 1–16), "Of Commonwealth" (chapters 17–31), "Of a Christian Commonwealth" (chapters 32–43), and "Of the Kingdom of Darkness" (chapters 44–47). The main body of the book is preceded by a dedication to friend and royalist Francis Godolphin along with an introduction and is drawn to a close by a separate "Review and Conclusion."

Part One, "Of Man," devotes the first 10 chapters to fleshing out Hobbes's ontological and epistemological worldview. Here Hobbes develops his empiricist view of knowledge, the origin (or "original") of all knowledge being "that which we call Sense;" his neo-Epicurean corporeal materialism, with discrete bodily matter being the substance of all things; his apparent determinism drawn out from his conclusion that

all "voluntary endeavor" is a reaction to our appetites and aversion; his nominalism, there being only universals in name only; his apparent relativism, there being nothing in nature absolutely good or evil; and his conclusions that human beings are deprived of contentment, haunted by " a constant fear of violent death," and incessantly enamored with power. It is also in Part One, chapter 13, that Hobbes pronounces his most famous statements on the human condition—that life without a common power to reign in our impulses is a "war of all against all," leading to a condition wherein "life in the state of nature is solitary, poor, nasty, brutish and short." In this one chapter Hobbes affirms our natural equality, emphasizes our inherent and universally mutual fear and enmity (the cause of the state of war in nature and the state of ongoing distrust within society), rejects original sin, denies that there is a natural right to property, refutes the notion that there is natural justice while expressing a positivist conflation of justice, law, and power, and premises our quest for peace on the passions of fear, desire, and hope, viz., the "fear of death," the "desire of . . . commodious living," and the "hope" that by our own "industry" we can acquire the comforts of life requisite to felicity.

Passion and impulse dominate the first 13 chapters, but a close reading of Hobbes also reveals his confidence in human reason. Ratiocination, or calculative reason, follows our impulses, but *logos,* a conflation by the Greeks of both reason and speech, collectively informs human beings in association of their truer interests, which is to escape the state of nature. Reason "suggesteth convenient articles of peace," and the first law of nature, to "endeavor peace," is identified as a "precept, or general rule of reason." Emotion and passion give way to right reason, and judgment and reason join appetite and aversion among those things that motivate human conduct. For this reason, students of Hobbes have been known to reconsider charges of determinism and fatalism, for if reason governs our escape from the state of nature, then not everything that we do is a reaction to desire and aversion. Nonetheless, Hobbes does define will as the "last appetite" in deliberation, a claim that by itself is a thorough rejection of classical and Medieval notions of the human soul.

Chapters 14 and 15 (Part One) are devoted to a reconstruction by Hobbes of the concepts of natural right and natural law. For Hobbes, natural right is defined wholly in terms of self-preservation, within a context of material struggle. Hobbes develops an economy of right that explains the transition from the self-preservationist state of right in nature to the granting of civil right by the sovereign once nature is abandoned for peace. Natural right includes what Hobbes claims to be a "right to everything;" viz., in a state of nature we can claim what we need in order to survive, and our claim to anything is as good as anyone else's claim to the same thing—regardless of possession or effort in production. But the right only extends as far as our power, and in the end the right to everything becomes tantamount to a right to nothing. We surrender this meaningless right to everything, and in so doing, transfer the force of our individual wills to the common power that will keep "all in awe" through a greater will, a will that now defines and grants civil rights for the parties in the contract, the subjects who pledge fidelity to the sovereign. Hence, from our individual right to everything the sovereign will is created, and whereas the individual wills in the state of nature were far too feeble to enforce their natural right to everything, the sum total of those wills concentrated in one common power possesses the will necessary to legislate true and binding law. The laws of nature, which are rooted in the first and fundamental law to "endeavor peace," are now given substance through the force of sovereign power.

After defining the first and second laws of nature in chapter 14 (the first law of nature being the command to seek peace, the second law of nature prescribes the mutual renunciation of the "right to all things"), Hobbes continues in chapter 15 to develop 17 "other laws of nature" that flow from the first two. Among these are the third law of nature, which is justice, or the keeping of covenants (Hobbes is clear in chapter 13 that there is no justice in a state of nature, and yet there remains a law of nature that objectively defines what justice is antecedent to political society), the fourth law, or gratitude, the ninth law, which proscribes pride (*pleonexia*), the 11th law, or equity, and the 17th law against subjective bias in judgments. Once these various natural laws are outlined, Hobbes asserts the notion that these laws, while always obliging in the conscience, even in a state of nature (which is a state of war), are only put into full effect where society, and particularly the sovereign, promises security. Yet Hobbes insists, at least in chapter 15, that these laws are "immutable and eternal," for those acts that breach the laws of nature, e.g., injustice, ingratitude, pride, etc., "can never be made lawful." Hence Hobbes seems to rely on an objectivist standard based on first principles of law, at least as prohibitive. Nonetheless, in almost the same breath Hobbes reaffirms his conclusion regarding moral principle first limned in chapter six, that "good and evil are names that signify our appetites and aversions," and thus the very heart of natural law, universal, moral judgment, depends on the relative and situational. This has puzzled modern readers of Hobbes. At one point Hobbes employs the term "law of nature" in a way that anticipates Sir Isaac Newton, these laws simply being descriptive patterns and tendencies operating within the universe. The laws of nature, while "eternal" and "immutable," nonetheless "oblige only to a desire and endeavor." "For the laws of nature," Hobbes explains, "in the condition of mere nature are not properly laws, but qualities that dispose men to peace and to obedience. When a commonwealth is settled, then are they actually laws." That is to say, only when a sovereign power is in place are the "laws of nature" binding in any real sense and only exist prior to the emergence of such power as patterns of reasonable behavior and not necessarily moral first principles. Here

Hobbes appears to reduce laws of nature to natural inclinations observable in the world, but not in themselves anything more than a description of certain qualities and tendencies in nature. And yet, elsewhere Hobbes explicitly equates natural law with the eternal, moral principles of Divine will, the law of nature undoubtedly being "God's law," and thus in every way compatible with the ethical injunctions of the Scripture. Natural laws "are those which have been laws from all eternity, and are called not only natural, but also moral laws." Hobbes even goes so far as to reduce the law of nature to the Golden Rule of the Gospel, thus closing the connection as tightly as the Thomists he derides. Even Hobbes's various "laws of nature" outlined in chapters 14 and 15 are moral precepts—particularly the natural laws regarding unequivocally ethical concerns such as justice and equity—and are understood to be recognized as such in the conscience, if not in the practical necessities of the state of nature. Hobbes is unable to resolve this tension without having his readers defend various interpretations over those less preferred. This tension, between the notion of natural law as objective and even divine in its source (chapter 26) on the one hand and the notion that moral first principles (the heart of any theory of natural law) are in reality subjectively dependent, is never fully resolved in *Leviathan* or elsewhere in Hobbes, clouding Hobbes's political geometry in ambiguity.

Part Two describes the "generation of the Great Leviathan," a mortal god that is by definition absolute in its authority, perpetual, indivisible, and created by mutual consent of those who renounce their claims to self-government and their natural right to everything. As Hobbes so provocatively demonstrates in Book One, human beings are by nature mutual enemies, each person being an enemy, either actually or potentially, to every other person. Only through the common recognition of this fact and the constant state of flux and disorder that it reveals are we able to renounce, on condition of reciprocity, our natural right to everything, transferring it to that "common power that will keep all in awe." This renunciation of the natural right to everything and the right to govern the self (which are inseparable) is the act that constructs the artificial man, or Leviathan, that through "terror thereof" is now able to establish domestic peace among those who are a party to (and the author of) its generation. Flowing from this elemental fact of the origin and nature of sovereignty (originating in our mutual renunciation of our claim to everything and essentially understood as now holding this universal claim to everything as the collective source of absolute power), twelve distinct rights of the sovereign (or sovereign powers) are enumerated in chapter 17. Included among these rights are claims against the forfeiture of sovereign power, protection of the sovereign from accusations of injustice, immunity for punishment by the subjects, the right to "judge of what opinions and doctrines are averse, and what conducing to, the common peace," the power to make law and judge law, and the "making of war and peace." Recognizing the considerable power of the sovereign, governing over all subjects by "terror thereof," Hobbes adds the disclaimer that there is nothing so dangerous than the want of such power, for without it civil war is risked, and the state of nature nigh.

The remainder of Part Two is devoted to examining the details of a political system premised on these notions. Ideas focusing on commonwealth, representation, office, administration, faction, and political communication are worked through with a greater sensitivity to a need for flexibility in the give and take of power and obligation, a sensitivity that belies the apparent absolutism of chapters 17 and 18. Chapter 26 is of interest as it returns again to the question of law, reflecting both a legalist-positivist tendency in Hobbes, laws being only commands of the commonwealth, and an older notion of natural law understood as "laws from all eternity" (and by definition antecedent to human judgment). In both chapters 14 and 26, Hobbes again summarizes the laws of nature by referring to the Golden Rule of the New Testament, hence giving a further nod to divine will. While Hobbes desires a notion of law as the command of the human sovereign, he seems not quite prepared to fully jettison more objectivist concepts.

Chapters 21–30 also restore the role of the subjects in the social covenant. The subject's right to life is affirmed as inviolate, the whole purpose of the generation of a common power being to protect this right, and subjects are even allowed a right against self-incrimination. Additionally, Hobbes unequivocally states that our obligation to the sovereign remains insofar as the sovereign protects us. Obedience is contingent on protection; remove one, and the other dissolves. Not only are we to be protected, but as stated in chapter 30 we are also entitled to the "contentments of life"—or those benefits of society described in chapter 13 as absent in the state of nature. Hence, while Hobbes does not advocate rebellion or dissent and never explicitly embraces revolution as a collective right, he tacitly allows it under dire circumstances .

Parts Three and Four attend to religion and are less familiar to students of Hobbes's political thought. Numerous doctrinal notions and scriptural commentary are advanced by Hobbes, including such conclusions that the age of miracles is over, replaced by devotion to Scripture, a discussion of spirit and body, the incomprehensibility of the nature of God (elsewhere Hobbes seems to tempt the heresy of God's materiality, but several passages in Part Three of *Leviathan* indicate a different state of mind), a discussion of prophets, the kingdom of heaven, the meaning of sacraments, the nature of Christ and the trinity (arousing concerns over Arian heresy among some readers of *Leviathan*) heaven, hell, and the "power ecclesiastical," which always remains inferior to the power of the sovereign. Hobbes understands true faith as beyond coercion, all religious authority deprived of the power of the sword. And yet, the sovereign can determine what is correct in the commonwealth, so even though faith is beyond the power of coercion, doctrine remains fully within the purview of the state. The ideas expressed in chapter 42 (Part Three), and the whole of Part Four, flow from Hobbes's Erastian position regarding the superiority of the civil authority even over the church. Part Four is a particularly severe attack on the Catholic church. But Hobbes is also critical of Presbyterian Protestantism, finding affinity between the priest and the presbyter, both challenging the authority of the civil power. Parts Three and Four are complex and difficult to follow, but they can be placed in context by referring to chapter 12 in Part One, where Hobbes asserts that "in the kingdom of God, the policy and laws civil are a part of religion; and therefore the distinction of temporal and spiritual domination hath there no place." A Christian commonwealth aims at reconciling the civil and the ecclesial, but there can only be one authority—and for Hobbes we cannot rely on the priest or the presbyter.

Leviathan appears as a turning point in political theory. The first principles of politics are subsumed under the natural mechanics of body in motion and are thus a necessary outcome of the procession of our appetites, aversions, and deliberations of the will. But, while the state is necessary for our survival, the polity is no longer regarded as essential to the human person. Political science assumes a new sense. With Hobbes, political inquiry becomes the science of consequences produced by the rights of sovereigns and the duties of subjects. In the end, it is revealing that Hobbes commits to a view that separates this science from the study of ethics and the study of what is just and unjust. After all is said and done, the artificial person that is the polity is a symbol for the dynamic of power.

Related Entries
Hobbes, Thomas; natural law; war of all against all

Suggested Reading
Editions of *Leviathan:* Curley (Hackett); Flathman and Johnston (Norton Critical Editions); Metternich (Broadview); and Oakeshott (Collier)

liberalism

The category "liberal" and term "liberalism" includes a varied and expansive set of ideas, movements, and policies. In a real sense, there is no one accurate definition of liberalism that adequately recognizes the complexities of liberal thought. Both the *laissez-faire* libertarianism of the nineteenth-century Manchester School and the New Deal state activism of the twentieth century have been denoted as "liberal," accompanied by variations on a theme in between these two conflicting methods. Liberalism in its development has been traced by some at least as far as St. Thomas Aquinas (described by Lord Acton as the "first liberal"), and has included an assorted and loosely connected set of thinkers including individuals as ostensibly distinct as Algernon Sidney, Thomas Hobbes, John Locke, Adam Smith, Benjamin Franklin, James Otis, Anders Chydenius, Thomas Paine, Thomas Jefferson, Jean-Jacques Rousseau (controversially), Mary Wollstonecraft, Immanuel Kant, Benjamin Constant, Jeremy Bentham, James and John Stuart Mill, William Gladstone, Alexis de Tocqueville, Wilhelm von Humboldt, James Fitzjames Stephens, Herbert Spencer, T. H. Green, John Dewey, Herbert Croly, Woodrow Wilson, both Theodore and Franklin Roosevelt, Konrad Adenauer, Isaiah Berlin, John Rawls, and an extensive, nearly innumerable array of thinkers and statesmen, particularly but not exclusively in the Anglo-American tradition. Given this diversity, we still generally speak of liberal political ideas with considerable ease and confidence; and in general use of the word "liberal" bears significant meaning for the modern citizen. In this sense, liberalism shares with conservatism a rich variety, revealing the complexity and nuance characteristic of these seemingly incongruent traditions.

Liberal political philosophy begins with the notion of the autonomous individual as the principal and governing category for political thought and the guiding touchstone for political activity. This is not to say that other philosophical or ideological movements posit a diminished concept of the individual, indeed, it is logically coherent to combine the prominence of the individual with a heightened awareness of communal relationships. That conceded, liberal political philosophy and its related ideological trends generally exhibit a particular sensitivity to the priority of the individual. This is expressed across all species of liberalism through the affirmation of two general principles: the sacrosanct liberty of the individual concurrent with an abiding belief in the fundamental equality of all human beings. These two principles are collaterally and famously expressed in such documents as Locke's *Second Treatise on Government,* the American Declaration of Independence, Abraham Lincoln's Gettysburg Address, and J. S. Mill's *On Liberty,* among many others. Liberty and equality, however varied and construed, serve as the dual founding stones of liberal thought and practice and reflect a theory of government that subordinates the needs of the state and its institutions to the goals and aspirations of any given body of citizens. It is in this commitment to the advancement of both of these concepts that liberalism draws its strength and yet at the same time experiences its deepest tension.

The liberty of the individual is, in liberal theory, defined in terms of individual rights. Rights, according to liberal philosophy, inhere in individuals by virtue of their humanity, and are not granted by government or created by the state. The rights of citizens are antecedent to the establishment of political institutions and the enactment of specific laws. Thus, the individual has priority over the state; the state's ultimate aim is to protect the rights of the individuals that exist independent of sovereignty. In this sense, the purpose of government is to serve its citizens by securing individual rights and promoting political institutions, and in some variations, social conditions, conducive to the happiness and full development of all. Locke's identification of the immutable natural rights of life, liberty, and property represent the bedrock of those rights that cannot be denied or abridged by society. This is not to say that these rights are in themselves absolute. One's liberty is circumscribed by one's duty to recognize the liberty of others. Our right to property —the protection of which is frequently referred to by Locke as the "chief end of government"—is bound by limitations of use (although the exact definition of this boundary has stimulated interpretation), and even our right to life is governed under a natural moral imperative prohibiting self-destruction. Nonetheless, for Locke and the liberal tradition that blossomed after him, the natural rights of the individual are the sole purpose for the construction of political, legal, and in some cases, social institutions. A fourth natural right, to dissolve government and erect it anew, is also generated within Locke's notion of sovereignty. In *On Liberty,* J.S. Mill identifies three freedoms central to the progress of a civilized society: freedom of thought and expression, freedom of tastes and preferences, and freedom to unite. Franklin Roosevelt, in his "Four Freedoms," Address (State of the Union Address, 1941), recognized freedom of speech, freedom of worship, freedom from fear and freedom from want as the universal constitutive features of a free society based in right and not driven by power. These rights affirmed by Locke, Mill, and Roosevelt along with the Lockean conception of natural rights in general epitomize the liberal mind and illuminate the significance of individual liberty within the several species of liberal theory and ideology.

Concomitant with the principle of liberty, the principle of equality serves as a central concept within the development of liberal political philosophy. All liberal theorists affirm a basic equality among human beings at some level, and include egalitarian policies and goals as an enduring pursuit within fair government. Citizens must be both free and equal in some sense, and it is here that liberal political thought encounters its own internal tension. To an extent "liberty implies equality," as L.T. Hobhouse once wrote in his survey of liberalism. That is, without the attainment of some degree of equality within a given polity, individual liberty cannot be effectively promoted. This is forthrightly recognized in Rawls's first principle of justice, wherein he states that in order to generate justice in society, each person must "have an equal right to the most extensive total system of equal basic liberties compatible with a similar liberty for all." Before Rawls, Rousseau argued in chapter 11 of the second book of The *Social Contract* that liberty "cannot subsist" without equality. This conceptual relationship notwithstanding, liberty and equality are often depicted as at once equally valued and essentially incompatible; expand one and risk contracting the other. Hence in order to protect liberty while addressing social inequalities, both the theory and practice of liberalism are constantly compelled to reconstrue the meaning of one or both.

All variant strains of liberalism regard individuals as equals in the moral, political, and legal sense. That is to say, all human beings are capable of acting as moral agents and thus possessing an essential dignity shared across the human community. This means that in political terms, each citizen is to be guaranteed uniform protection of rights, particularly those rights mentioned earlier as well as rights protecting and encouraging voluntary participation in the polity. Additionally, political equality in practice recognizes a mutual accountability between citizen and official. Equality in legal terms is expressed in the unequivocal view that the "law of the land" applies equally to all, and does so in a way that fortifies our rights rather than abridging them. Attached to equality under the law is an attendant sense of equal duty under the law, enjoining each element in society to the same relationship with the laws and institutions of the regime. The main factor in the generation of disparate varieties in liberal philosophy is found in different approaches to equality in other aspects of society, particularly and historically within the economic realm, but also social and cultural as well.

Liberal theory across the spectrum affirms the necessity for "equality of opportunity" within society, and especially involving economic activities. How this necessary principle is related to "equality of condition," or directed outcomes, shapes the type of liberalism promoted. Classical liberalism, typified by the Manchester School (or Manchester Liberals) of nineteenth-century Britain and presaged by the works of Adam Smith, held to a view that it is through free markets and a constitutionally restrained state that personal liberty is best exercised. Once rational actors are given a broader range of latitude in controlling their own choices, the correct degree of opportunity is produced, allowing all citizens an equal or nearly equal chance to improve their conditions according to their own lights. Rather than equality of outcome—for such equality is undesirable and unreasonable—classical liberalism stresses a diminished state hesitant to meddle with economic patterns and legally prevented from interfering with personal decisions regarding individual morals. The state plays a role, primarily one that keeps peace and prevents harm, but for the most part this notion is described as the policy of *laissez faire,* or to let go. This version of liberal theory is now almost universally described in contemporary terms as economic conservatism, following the example of Milton Friedman and associated with the political views of Herbert Hoover, Barry Goldwater, and Ronald Reagan, but in its intellectual and historic origins it began as a modality of liberalism. In its extreme expression, classical liberalism is associated with Social Darwinism, advocating a view that the state in almost every instance is a potential impediment to the natural development, and thus evolution, of both individuals and society. Hence the state must withdraw as far as possible from the direction of life and allow the "survival of the fittest" to promote the greater good of the community. This position tends to deemphasize equality to a vanishing point, and recasts liberty in terms of a struggle for the exertion of interest, potentially compromising the fair exercise of liberty for all citizens.

In contrast, an alternative version of liberal theory shaped itself along more activist lines. While complete equality of conditions is not within the liberal vision, statist liberalism does assert that equal opportunity alone is not sufficient to secure a society that is at once fair and prosperous across the entire citizenry. Thus the state, far from recoiling from economic direction, must rather devote considerable energy and focus to the implementation of policies that do influence economic activity and achieve a partially controlled distribution of wealth. Government is understood as responsible for a certain fairness of outcome, not thoroughly egalitarian as in socialist models, but the achievement of politically guided prosperity through concerted policies such as market regulation, progressive taxation, and redistribution of some wealth in the form of entitlements and other benefits. Equality of opportunity is thus augmented by policies that militate against excesses that often characterize unfettered acquisition, and economic stability is ensured through government involvement in the direction of the economy. Franklin Roosevelt's New Deal and Lyndon Johnson's Great Society programs are typical of this strain of liberalism, and for most students of politics today, it is this active, enlarged government that symbolizes the nature of liberal political thought and policy. As Hobhouse has stated, such measures are justified on the grounds that "prevention of suffering from the actual lack of adequate physical comforts is an essential element in the common good, an object in which all are bound to concern themselves, which all have the right to demand the duty to fulfil." Taken to its extreme (beyond Roosevelt and Johnson), activist statist liberalism does incorporate command economy strategies not unlike those expected from socialist arrangements. This might be rightly perceived as constriction of personal choice and thus individual liberty. If the extreme of classical, minimalist liberalism (economic conservatism) threatens equality, the statist liberalism commits the opposite risk, the potential constriction of the rational liberty of individuals.

More recently, and particularly in the last three or four decades, liberal notions of equality have been discussed in the context of group rights and communal identity. Race, ethnicity, religious values, sex, sexual orientation, and language are variables influencing discussions of equality and the related concept of social justice. Contemporary liberalism is thus shaped by an enduring concern for and sensitivity to marginalized groups who are unable to benefit fully from social, political, economic, and cultural opportunities afforded to other groups in society, or who are in some way openly deprived of the same guarantee of rights as enjoyed by other groups under the law. Here equality is couched not so much in individual terms (and thus not as overtly linked to liberty) but rather in terms of group interests and social fairness. Beyond equal opportunity, which remains important, this aspect of equality draws attention to cultural integrity as an important element in a more complete idea and practice of equality. Owing to this, liberal political principles and policies are now more inclined than most competing ideologies toward a multicultural awareness. Thus liberal political thought and activity is often cast as challenging more "traditional" norms within society as a whole.

Liberty and equality persist as the two vital components of liberal theory and practice. From these, other ideas and practices flow logically in support of these essential assumptions. Popular sovereignty grounded on constitutional principles is basic to all liberal thought. This arrangement combines the democratic impulse with the rule of law, forwards political opportunity and accountability, and maintains a tangible feature of sovereign authority restrained by strong legal and political institutions. Liberal democratic theory can advocate both representative (as in Mill, James Madison, et al.) and participatory (as in Paine and contemporary theorists such as Benjamin Barber, et al.) strains, but in either case, democratic practices are framed and supported within institutional matrixes. Participatory theories do advocate redefining current structures, particularly those features that centralize power or rely on governmental hierarchy and political elites, but for the most part both the representative model and the participatory model are compatible with the general liberal devotion to rule of law, constitutional frameworks, and broadly implemented suffrage.

Liberalism is also often identified with a particularly internationalist stance. Hobhouse employs Gladstone as an illustration of this attitude. According to Hobhouse, Gladstone " [proceeded] on the principle that reasons of State justify nothing that is not already justified by human conscience. [Thus t]he statesman . . . is a man charged with maintaining not only the material interests but the honor of his country. He is a citizen of the world in that he represents his nation, which is a member of the community of the world. He has to recognize rights and duties, as every representative of every other human organization has to recognize rights and duties." This international perspective is also represented in the work of Woodrow Wilson in the creation of the League of Nations and Konrad Adenauer in his reforming Germany in a way that intimately bound it to European destiny. One could argue with some credibility that the principles behind the formation and execution of the United Nations are in their essence liberal ideals. The Universal Declaration of Rights represents a set of values that, for the most part, concur with most types of liberal theory.

With the demise of the Soviet Union and its sphere of influence, many commentators, most notably political theorist Francis Fukuyama, concluded that liberalism as a political philosophy had emerged as not only definitive in Western political culture, but also as the dominating ideology spanning the globe. While there is some merit to this view, the accelerated growth of radical Islam as a political ideology, as well as the sustained presence of more communitarian movements, such as green parties in the West, indicate that liberalism, while a major intellectual and political force in the twenty-first century, is not yet the last word in political thought and practice.

Related Entries
conservatism; equality; freedom; ideology;
socialism

Suggested Reading
Gray, John. *Liberalism.* Minneapolis: Univ. Minn.
    Press, 1995.
Hobhouse, L.T. *Liberalism and Other Writings,*
    ed. James Meadowcraft. New York: Cambridge
    Univ. Press, 2000.
Manning, D.J. *Liberalism.* New York: St. Martin's
    Press, 1976.

libertarianism

Associated with both the *laissez-faire* liberalism
of the nineteenth century (particularly that
variety adopted by what Benjamin Disraeli
called the "Manchester School," which promoted a vigorous and uncompromising policy
of free trade) as well as antistatist conservatism
of the latter half of the twentieth century, libertarianism is less a coherent ideology and more a
requirement for a particular concept of the
meaning of the individual in the modern state.
Radical in its individualism and devoted to the
necessity of self-reliance, libertarianism holds
an appeal not only for nineteenth-century liberals and post–World War II conservatives,
but also for a prominent strain of anarchism.
In other words, libertarianism, perhaps by its
very nature, eschews a doctrinaire ethos as well
as a specifically focused ideological stance.
Rather, the libertarian seeks in every way to
expand the responsibilities of the individual for
her or his own happiness and well-being while
reducing the obligations, and thereby the
powers, of the state. Whether it is in the writings of Richard Cobden (a nineteenth-century
Manchester liberal) or Milton Friedman (a
twentieth-century free-market conservative),
or even the individualism advanced by still earlier thinkers such as John Locke (usually associated with liberalism) or William Godwin
(associated with anarchism), libertarianism
invests all faith in the ability of unfettered
rational individuals to choose the right course
of actions in governing their own lives. To do
this, the freedom of the person must be

expanded as the role and powers of the political
and legal spheres contract.

Hence, as Robert Nozick succinctly summarized the libertarian position in chapter
seven of his 1974 volume, *Anarchy, State and
Utopia,* "The minimal state is the most extensive state that can be justified. Any state more
extensive violates people's rights." Nozick further explains that even when states attempt to
increase their level of commitment to and
action within the distribution of social (especially economic) goods, the free agency of the
individual will eventually thwart such efforts.
"Liberty upsets patterns," Nozick concludes,
and the only way to fully implement and sustain
any governmentally directed distribution of
social benefits is through oppressive measures.
Given a free society, the activist state cannot
achieve its ends. Only through the unfettered
liberty of rational individual actors can substantive and just social change unfold.

Libertarianism is grounded in the premise
that the individual is and should be in full command of her or his own actions—a doctrine of
self-ownership that rejects the need for authority
beyond the conscience and choices of the person. For this reason one might characterize the
libertarian viewpoint as wholly invested in the
moral agency of individuals. Groups are incapable of acting morally, for groups lack either
the fixed interest of individuals or the opportunities to act morally that come with personal
conscience independent of coercion. The coercion that is imposed through political power,
legal institutions, or social pressures are viewed
from the libertarian perspective as debilitating
to the free agent, and must be reduced as far as
possible and, whenever feasible, abolished
altogether. Hence for the libertarian, the polity
and any attendant institutions or forces connected with it must be abridged to the barest
possible minimum. Government must be pared
and streamlined at every turn so that the individual is given full responsibility for choices made
and a wide range of options within which to
exert free will. Within this spirit, Henry David
Thoreau once wrote (*Civil Disobedience*),

I heartily accept the motto—"That government is best which governs least;" and I should like to see it acted up to more rapidly and systematically. Carried out, it finally amounts to this. . ." That government is best which governs not at all."

Thoreau's sentiment here, like Nozick's quote above, effectively represents the basis on which the libertarian commitment to individualism rests. Once government and the powers of society are diminished or eliminated, the full moral and intellectual development of the individual becomes a real possibility. Hence the goal of the libertarian is always to remove power from the state and invest power in free individuals; anything short of that tilts towards subjugation and the ultimate truncation of the person.

Libertarian political arguments are thus inclined to inveigh against the expansion of the modern state. The legacies of both welfare liberalism as well as moral conservatism are, for the libertarian, nothing less than the dwarfing of our humanity. As John Stuart Mill admonished in *On Liberty,*

> A government cannot have too much of the kind of activity which does not impede, but aids and stimulates, individual exertion and development. The mischief begins when, instead of calling forth the activity and powers of individuals and bodies, it substitutes its own activity for theirs, when, instead of informing, advising, and, upon occasion, denouncing, it makes them work in fetters, or bids them stand aside and does their work instead of them. The worth of a State, in the long run, is the worth of the individual interests composing it; . . . a State which dwarfs its men, in order that they may be more docile instruments in its hands even for beneficial purposes—will find that with small men no great things can really be accomplished.

This belief in the power of the individual agent and the necessity of its unfettered application is so strong in the libertarian mentality that it cannot be adequately identified with traditional ideologies framed along the somewhat limited left-wing–right-wing spectrum. A libertarian would agree with, for example, certain liberals who favor individual choice on moral issues such as abortion and gay marriage, but would be found more closely in line with a free-market conservative to the right of the traditional spectrum. The common feature here is the belief that, in both moral and economic decisions and activities, it is better to leave all choices to persons, leaving only a minimal political and legal structure in place to defend and help expand individual liberties. Any encroachment by the state on the liberties of individuals is one more step on what Friedrich Hayek called the "road to serfdom," who firmly asserted the "guiding principle that a policy of freedom for the individual is the only truly progressive policy that remains as true today as it was in the nineteenth century."

Related Entries
anarchism; liberalism; Locke, John

Suggested Reading
Boaz, David, ed. *The Libertarian Reader: Classic and Contemporary Readings from La Tzu to Milton Friedman.* New York: Free Press, 1997.
Boaz, David. *Libertarianism: A Primer.* New York: Free Press, 1997.
Nozick, Robert. *Anarchy, State and Utopia.* 1974; repr. Malden. MA: Blackwell, 2003.

liberty—*See* **freedom**

life, liberty and the pursuit of happiness
This famous line from the Declaration of Independence was penned by Virginian statesman Thomas Jefferson, borrowing directly from principles advanced by John Locke. Throughout Locke's *Second Treatise,* of which Jefferson was intimately familiar, the author refers to specific natural rights that he considers to be both inherent and fixed, that is to say, rights that would later be referred to as inalienable or unalienable. Specifically, Locke identifies three natural rights that cannot under any circumstances be estranged, to wit, life,

liberty, and property. This notion, coming out of the latter part of the seventeenth century, held great appeal to the American founders, in particular such thinker-statesmen as James Otis, Samuel Adams, Thomas Paine, and, significantly, Thomas Jefferson, among others. In the writing of the American Declaration of Independence in the summer of 1776, Jefferson (assisted by Benjamin Franklin and John Adams), steeped in Locke, stated that all men were "endowed by their Creator with certain unalienable rights; that among these are life, liberty and the pursuit of happiness." The natural right to property, while not explicitly stated in Jefferson's iteration is assumed to have been numbered among the features of the "pursuit of happiness." It is possible, and has been argued, that Jefferson's decision to replace property with the phrase "pursuit of happiness" is a demotion of the importance of this right, or perhaps even an indication that Jefferson did not consider property to be a natural right but only the offspring, albeit a necessary one, of social convention. Such an interpretation either depicts Jefferson as more radical than Locke (property is demoted, thus the perpetual acquisition of goods is not something that we are morally entitled to) or more conservative (property is not a natural right, and thus ownership is more dependent on the positive laws enacted by the sovereign, following Hobbes). More likely is the explanation that Jefferson, while unequivocally an ardent student of Locke's political theory, was nonetheless equally enamored with the more quasi-utilitarian bent of those thinkers associated with the "Scottish Enlightenment," in particular Thomas Reid and Adam Ferguson. A natural right to happiness is compatible with an ethic that is framed by the goal of promoting the "greatest happiness for the greatest number," a notion that does not find its way explicitly into the doctrine of the Declaration, but might account, at least partially, for the emphasis on the pursuit of happiness by rational and free citizens. Or, more likely still, would be the probable exposure of Jefferson to the writings

of Samuel Johnson, who actually coined the phrase, "pursuit of happiness," in 1759, seven years before the drafting of the Declaration. Finally, one might argue that the inclusion of happiness in place of property is a residual notion of a still older notion of natural rights that reaches back to the Thomistic conception developed in the High Middle Ages. Neither Jefferson nor Locke were Thomists, but as Charles Taylor has observed, the natural rights tradition behind the American founding owes more to the Middle Ages than appearances allow, and the emphasis on happiness may be better understood through a classical lens rather than a post-Hobbesian one.

Whatever Jefferson's reasons, the phrase "life, liberty and the pursuit of happiness" remains a stirring reminder of the obligation that governments hold in the protection of the inherent rights of the human person regardless of context or situation.

Related Entries
Jefferson, Thomas; Locke, John

Suggested Reading
The Declaration of Independence is widely available in print and online. For a reliable and comprehensive collection of major documents in American history, including the Declaration, consult the following: Commager, Henry Steele, and Milton Cantor, eds. *Documents of American History,* 2 vols., 10th ed. Englewood Cliffs, NJ: Prentice-Hall, 1988.

life, liberty, property

Life, liberty, and property are the three principal natural inalienable rights identified by John Locke (1632–1704) throughout his landmark *Second Treatise on Government*. All human beings, according to Locke, by virtue of their humanity as creatures of God, possess certain natural rights that cannot be renounced even by consent. Locke identifies three in particular: life, liberty, and estates (possessions, goods, property). While some of our natural rights (namely—the natural right to judge and execute the law of nature) must be surrendered and transferred to the government through the social contract that binds all equally, the natural rights of life, liberty, and property cannot be laid down or transferred, but are rather inalienable and can never be separated from the individual.

These rights are inalienable and thus can never be legitimately or justly abridged or denied by government or society. However, these rights are not absolute. Each of these rights is characterized in some sense by a natural limitation. The right to life is limited by the prohibition against self-destruction, for no one has a right to take his own life. Liberty is not absolute, even in a state of nature, for liberty is already, prior to the construction of "formal society" (i.e., political society), limited by the liberty of others. Liberty is not mere license, for Locke, but framed within the moral law of nature and our duties to respect the moral liberty and natural equality of other human beings. Indeed, for Locke we are duty bound to promote and preserve the good of others as long as such a promotion does not threaten our own liberty or well-being. The natural right to property is, in a state of nature, limited by the amount of property or goods that we can use without waste. Our right to property originates from the power of labor that is granted to each individual by the grace of God, but it is not meant to be absolute. We cannot claim a right to produce more than we can use; for Locke this is a critical factor of the justification of ownership in a state of nature. To violate the rule of use is to deprive others of their potential use of the property or goods in question, which would be a violation of the moral law of nature. Hence, even though all three of these most fundamental and vital natural rights are inalienable and sacrosanct in the Lockean view, they are not absolute principles that would justify any action in any situation. The upshot of this is the drawing of a clear and indissoluble connection between our natural rights and our moral duties, for each right indeed is accompanied by a concomitant duty.

Much has been made of Locke's inclusion of the natural right to property, not so much for its status as a part of the triad of essential and inviolable rights as for Locke's repeated insistence in his *Second Treatise* that preservation of the natural right to property is the "chief end" or highest purpose of the formation of government through the social contract. This apparent primacy of property has been both praised and criticized from a variety of quarters. One could argue that Locke's elevation of property is a healthy insight, recognizing the importance of private ownership as the premise for the security of the rights of life and liberty. In this vein, one's liberty is only guaranteed if one can claim ownership and command the use of one's goods according to one's own preferences, without interference from state or community. From the contrary perspective, one could argue with equal vigor that Locke's emphasis on property diminishes the value of liberty, and reduces our conception of free citizenship to one that depends on material acquisition and commercial ambition. Locke's notion of rights is thus attached to what C.B. Macpherson called a "possessive individualism" that renders liberty one-dimensional and actually encourages a situation wherein the acquisitive liberties of the commercial society militate against the natural equality that Locke also avers exists in a state of nature. Which of these positions is correct is left to students of Locke to sort out, but in either case, it is clear the Locke does invest great value in the natural right to own property.

It should be noted that, even though the natural right to property could be linked to permissible inequalities with the introduction of imperishable goods (specifically money), Locke never advocates a system of endless accumulation. The prohibition against waste and spoilage is still in place, only now modified in ways that are compatible with the sophisticated and variegated economies of modern society. As Locke clearly asserts in the *Second Treatise,* the moral law of nature (which defines and limits our natural rights) is drawn more tightly in society, thus the imperative against waste still holds. Thus the argument implicating

Locke's political theory as somehow supportive of an acquisitive society must be assessed with this in mind.

Related Entries
life, liberty and the pursuit of happiness; Locke, John; *Second Treatise on Government*

Suggested Reading
Locke. John. *Two Treatises of Government,* ed. Peter Laslett. New York: Cambridge Univ. Press, 1989.

Locke, John (1632–1704)

Few thinkers have enjoyed as much influence on the development of the modern political mind-set as the British philosopher John Locke. Regarded by many as one of the founders of liberal theory—and perhaps *the* true founder of liberal philosophy—Locke's influence is particularly pronounced in the political culture of both the United States and Locke's home country, and, as such, the reach of his ideas extends over a vast array of thinkers and statesmen. Among these is numbered Thomas Jefferson, who regarded Locke as one of the three greatest men of the modern era (the other two being Sir Francis Bacon and Sir Isaac Newton). Even a superficial reading of the Declaration of Independence reveals the prominent influence of the Lockean project, and it can also be argued that Locke's influence reaches into the United States Constitution as well. To the academic and professional philosopher Locke's ideas are as compelling as ever; to the citizen of western democracy, the political currents of popular government are more easily traversed owing to their having been charted by Locke well before the ascent of modern liberty.

Locke himself owed a considerable debt to those figures who directly influenced either his own thinking, or at least the tenor of the times in which he developed his ideas. Two close friends, Anthony Ashley Cooper (Lord Ashley, the First Earl of Shaftesbury) and James Tyrell, are said to be among his more important philosophical mentors, along with the scientist Robert Boyle, contemporary firebrand

Algernon Sidney, and Lady Damaris Cudworth Masham (the daughter of Cambridge Platonist Ralph Cudworth), with whom Locke was at one time romantically interested and with whom he sustained a friendship throughout his life. Above all, Shaftesbury and Tyrell held the strongest influence over Locke's own ideas, Shaftesbury directly influencing Locke's views on the supremacy of the legislative in government and religious toleration, such as it was in the seventeenth century. James Tyrell, through his friendship with Locke, is claimed to have had some influence over the development of his moral and political ideas, particularly with the claim that Tyrell shared with Locke (even prior to the writing of Locke's *Second Treatise*) a belief in a law of nature that governs human conduct absent society, thus commanding us to seek the common good, that all human beings are born both free and equal, that the importance of private property pointedly bears on political questions, and that there are important distinctions between different types of authority. These concepts are all affirmed in Locke's political masterpiece, *The Second Treatise on Government,* a work that seems to have been composed largely after Tyrell's *Patriarcha non Monarcha,* the treatise wherein most of Tyrell's elementary ideas are developed. The exact extent to which Locke borrows from Tyrell is uncertain, but that there is a relationship is clear. David Wooten, however, does draw a clear line of debt between the two thinkers, stating that "almost all the principles that we think of as being distinctly Lockean are in fact borrowed by Locke from Tyrell." Even so, Wooten elaborates certain differences between the two thinkers, especially on the issue of voluntary submission to authority and the emphasis on property, Wooten arguing that while both thinkers consider property a natural right in need of protection, Locke centralizes it even further within his own work.

Conceptually, however, the three philosophers whose influence appears most directly evident in Locke's writings are René Descartes, Thomas Hobbes, and Richard Hooker.

Descartes's influence is seen most clearly in Locke's embrace of the modern response to Aristotelianism that attracted so many thinkers of his age, in particular Thomas Hobbes before him. Hobbes, the titan of seventeenth-century political and moral thought, provided both the conceptual framework and political language in which Locke worked out his own ideas. While not referring to Hobbes explicitly in the *Second Treatise,* the shadowy presence of the Sage of Malmesbury is palpable. Hooker is directly quoted at length by Locke in the *Second Treatise* to notable effect, and to an extent the essence of Locke's own political philosophy rests on the foundations previously set down by Hooker. Because of Hooker's Anglicanism and the quest for the *Via Media* that distinguished Anglican theology and doctrine, it can be said without stretching incredulity that some of the ideas of Thomism are residual in Locke's writing, at least with regard to moral and political reasoning, but to pursue that connection would command more attention than can be afforded here.

Locke wrote extensively on politics and government, as well as in other areas of philosophy such as epistemology. His most famous and important political works are *The First Treatise of Government,* the *Second Treatise* mentioned above, and *A Letter Concerning Toleration.* Other writings and letters are also of interest, in particular his *Essays on the Law of Nature* and *An Essay Concerning Toleration.* Minor documents of interest include two early "tracts" on government, a proposed constitution for the colony of Carolina (the authorship of which has been a source of disagreement), and various journal entries, letters, and proposals. For the most part, the balance of Locke's political theory can be drawn from the two treatises, particularly the great *Second Treatise,* the *Letter Concerning Toleration,* and the *Essays on the Law of Nature,* number VIII. In these documents Locke advances those compelling ideas most commonly held as essential to liberal political philosophy, viz., natural law and right as the foundation of all

legitimate political society, natural equality and the inherent liberty of all human beings, the social contract manifest through both popular and limited sovereignty, the nature of representative government, distinct division of governmental function, and the legitimation of reasoned resistance to arbitrary power. This is not to claim that Locke invented each of these ideas; to the contrary, each of these concepts can all be identified in some form as having been advanced by previous thinkers. What Locke accomplished was a synthesis of these concepts into a new vision of politics that would resonate for generations throughout the progress of democratic theory.

Locke's *Letter Concerning Toleration* bridges politics and religion. Famous for its advocacy of religious freedom in an age of ubiquitous religious distrust, Locke observed "toleration to be the chief characteristical mark of the true Church." Central to Locke's argument in the *Letter* is the admonition against coercion by the state in matters of religion. "Civil interests," Locke defines, involve "life, liberty, health and indolency of body; and the possession of outward things." These are the proper concerns of the civil authority. The "care of souls," is separate from the political and always based on voluntary association. Thus the state cannot compel devotion to one religion. Nonetheless, Locke's toleration was directed mostly at the principal Protestant sects of his times. He harbored a dislike of Catholicism typical of his contemporaries, and he considered atheism to be beyond toleration. For the most part the *Letter* is significant for its spirit of separation between civil and ecclesial, even though the scope is narrower than our current sensibilities would allow.

In the *First Treatise* Locke devotes his energies to demolishing the divine right arguments of Sir Robert Filmer, who had previously argued that all power flows from God to kings through the lineage of Adam, the first man and first king. Locke argues that Filmer's use of Scripture to advance his position was in fact a cynical abuse of the ancient texts and builds an argument against Filmer by employing the same reliance on Holy Writ. Locke thus positions himself against the notion that political power is somehow legitimized by Divine sanction, and in so doing, prepares the way to develop an argument in the *Second Treatise* that advances the notion of legitimate government based on nothing more than the consent of free people. As Robert Goldwin aptly described it in his essay on Locke in the Strauss/Cropsey volume, the *First Treatise* is Locke's direct rejection of Filmer's claim that "no man is born free," while the *Second Treatise* advances the principle that all politics is to be premised on the one truth that "all men are born free." Ultimately, it is this premise that drives the central principles of Locke's overall political theory while firmly placing him at the foundations of liberal theory.

The basis of this statement is perhaps best understood by contrasting the essence of Lockean natural right with that of Hobbes. Locke understood natural right within the framework of a moral law of nature; Hobbes, by contrast, is less clear on the moral quality of the law of nature and decidedly inclined toward a notion of right—natural and conventional—as a function of power. Locke explicitly treats power and right as distinct concepts and distinct political facts. By unequivocally binding our liberties within the moral law of nature, Locke affirms the existence of natural rights prior to the emergence of "formal society" and its attendant political and juridical institutions, while simultaneously recognizing the limits to these rights. Even though each person, by nature, possesses rights independently of social convention or political assertion, these rights which are absolutely inherent are not in themselves absolute. That is to say, certain rights inhere by nature and universally and objectively belong to each human being, but no right is truly absolute. For example, the natural right to life is limited by the moral prohibition against self-destruction, the natural right to liberty is constrained by the moral law of nature which requires the recognition of the liberties of others, and the natural right to property is defined in terms of natural use. Social practice and the introduction of certain economic innovations modify the last, but as Locke states, the laws of nature are bound even more closely in society than they are in nature, the addition of commodities of exchange notwithstanding. In a word, where Hobbes grounds right in power owing to a claim of absolute right in nature (the right to everything), Locke denies the very existence of absolute rights, only limited rights that belong to the person absolutely.

This distinction is particularly pertinent to Locke's views on sovereignty and government. For both Hobbes and Locke, sovereignty rests on the consent of the governed, a consent that is generated by renouncing some of our natural rights to more fully secure other, still more fundamental rights. In Hobbes, the renunciation of an absolute right (the right to everything) produces absolute sovereign power as it is transferred away from the subject and deposited in the sovereign body. For Locke, no such absolute right exists (for the natural right to property extinguishes any such claim to everything); thus when the natural right to judge and execute the law of nature, which is already limited by the moral laws of natural justice, is renounced and transferred to a common umpire, a limited sovereignty results. Hobbes may or may not equivocate and backpedal a bit on the nature of sovereign power, but the initial act creating the Hobbesian sovereign allows, at least theoretically, for an absolute state, whether or not this is in line with Hobbes's intentions. Locke's sovereign is clearly limited; as the rights transferred to create sovereign power is itself limited. In this sense, the Lockean notion of natural rights, both retained and renounced, promotes the central tenet as noted by Goldwin above, that Locke's theory is derived from the principle that all human beings are born free, and the existence of both right and power must defer to that structuring principle.

Additionally, the prominence of the natural right to property is a distinctive feature of

Locke's political theory, and a further contrast to Hobbes. While both theorists recognize the importance of property for the stability of civilized society, Hobbes does not regard private property to be a natural right, but rather a convention dependent on the formation and authority of the common power. For Locke, the right to property is as natural as the rights to life and liberty, and important enough to command an entire chapter in his *Second Treatise*. For some commentators, Locke's theory of property represents a precursor to the emerging theories of capitalism in the eighteenth and early nineteenth centuries, and a philosophical justification for the economic consequences of acquisition and unstinted economic liberty. Others regard Locke's views on property as more complex, not necessarily promoting capitalism as an end in itself, and more closely connected to the notion of liberty as requiring a secure private sphere. Whether Locke is an apologist for free markets unimpaired by a minimal state as some would hold, or whether he is more concerned with reasoned ownership of property as a means to greater political liberty, property as a natural right holds a significant part in the ends of government. Indeed, Locke often refers to the preservation of this right as the chief or principle purpose of the social contract.

Locke's conception of government reveals a thinker devoted to the principle that the liberty of the person is the paramount charge of any type of political authority. The entire Lockean language of politics affirms the belief that government is created not to grant rights, but only to guarantee the security of those rights already possessed by all human beings simply by virtue of their humanity. Thus all political authority must be limited, and must be dedicated to the protection of our natural rights. Regardless of the type of government in place, it is understood to be of a limited kind and in service to the rights retained upon entering the social contract. As there is no absolute right in nature, there can be no absolute power in formal society. Therefore for Locke, all

political authority is conditional, viz., dependent on the fair execution of its initial charge in order for it to command the willing obedience of a given citizenry. In the Lockean conception of politics, political authority is a necessity and the rule of law is preferred to the lawlessness of the state of nature. As such, political order requires sustained deference to legitimate (i.e., consensual and limited) power. Still, all political power is subordinate to its initial purpose as set in the natural law. Even democracy is limited by the moral law of nature, and interference with individual rights is severely proscribed. It can be accurately said of Locke that his political theory includes popular sovereignty, but even the sovereignty of the people is limited by the law of nature and the social contract that has sprung from that law. According to Locke, what we today would call the inalienable rights of individuals supersede the powers of governmental authority. It is in this sense that Locke represents the high point of early modern thought and the platform for the further development of liberal theory in the Anglo-American tradition. Limited sovereignty, conditional authority, majority rule, legislative supremacy, and legitimate resistance to the abuse of power all come from the first principle that the rights of the citizens justify the powers of the government, and not the other way around as one might infer, rightly or wrongly, from Hobbes.

Yet like most great thinkers Locke is complex. In lesser writings Locke prescribes harsh measures against mendicants and vagabonds, his skewed view of toleration and his views on slavery appear mixed and, to twenty-first-century sensibilities, problematic. Some argue, as Leo Strauss does, that a close reading of Locke simply reveals a derivation of the ideas of Hobbes, thus lending credence to a notion of a Lockean politics characterized as resting fundamentally on self-interest. Nonetheless, an overemphasis on these idiosyncratic writings in Locke detract from his overall contribution to modern political thought, which is at root marked by a commitment to the rational government of free citizens dedicated to the rule of limited institutions by their own consent. From these elementary tenets a great portion of modern political theory has been advanced, including, many would concede, the central values of American democracy.

Related Entries
freedom; Hobbes, Thomas; Jefferson, Thomas; liberalism; Rawls, John

Suggested Reading
Locke, John. *Two Treatises of Government,* ed. Peter Laslett. New York: Cambridge Univ. Press, 1989.
Wooten, David, ed. *Political Writings of John Locke.* New York: Mentor Books, 1993.

logical positivism (logical empiricism, neopositivism)

Heir to the legacy of earlier attempts at radical empiricism (e.g., by Francis Bacon, David Hume) and positivism (by Claude Henri de St. Simon, Auguste Comte), logical positivism represents a renewed and vigorous attempt at realigning philosophical inquiry along conceptual and methodological patterns established by the physical sciences. Logical positivism goes a step further than its predecessor, classical positivism, in that it discards the quasi-religious aspirations of St. Simon and Comte. For the logical positivist, the enduring metaphysical questions of philosophy that deal with the nature of being and the ethical principles of moral conduct are irresolvable in any satisfactory manner, that is to say, in any manner that provides precision and certainty. The eternal verities that philosophers have sought since Socrates are at best opinions formed from bad questions, and are not properly the province of philosophical inquiry any more than they are of interest to a physicist or a chemist. Propositions of this nature are at best opinion and at worst meaningless doctrines about that which cannot be proved either way. True knowledge rests on the methodology of scientific experiential verification. Anything that cannot be verified through the scientific method cannot

be considered knowledge: opinion and belief, yes, but not knowledge. As A. J. Ayer (1910–1989), one of the leading proponents of logical positivism, wrote in *Language, Truth and Logic,* "The traditional disputes of philosophers are, for the most part, as unwarranted as they are unfruitful." What is now needed, according to Ayer, is a philosophy firmly fixed to the principle of verification, and the only real "function" of the philosopher "is to clarify the propositions of science by exhibiting their logical relationships, and by defining the symbols which occur in them." Or, as political theorist Lee McDonald has commented,

> In a striking reversal of Plato's distinction between knowledge and opinion, logical positivists hold that answers to these alleged questions [e.g., what is "the nature of the true, the beautiful, and the good?"] can never be more than opinion, for "meaningful propositions" the only basis of knowledge are those that can be verified by the methods of the natural sciences, that is, experimentation with data derived from direct sensory perception and/or logical inference from those data. Any statement, such has "God is love"—for which there is no possibility of refutation by appeal to specific empirical data is held to have no grounds for confirmation.

Logical positivism as a movement can be directly traced to the Moritz Schlick and the founding of the Vienna Circle, a group of philosophers and scientists who were active together from 1924 to 1936. Initially the Vienna Circle was influenced by the works of Ernst Mach (1838–1916), Gottlob Frege (1848–1925), Bertrand Russell (1872–1970), and most significantly by the early work of Ludwig Wittgenstein, specifically his 1922 publication, *Tractatus Logico-Philosophicus,* a work that has been described as essential to the development of logical positivism. Wittgenstein's philosophy would later move away from logical positivism, but the influence of the *Tractatus* remained seminal. Other philosophers, along with Ayer and the young Wittgenstein, who were important in the dissemination of logical positivism or a variant thereof, were the social scientist Otto Neurath (1882–1945) and philosophers Rudolph Carnap (1891–1970) and W.V.O. Quine (1908–2000), among others. The Vienna Circle, dedicated to the rubrics of radical empiricism and the scientific method, turned its attention to the possibility of a unified science wherein all the sciences, natural and social alike, would be governed by the same language and the same methodology. Neurath and Carnap, along with Russell, were particularly involved in this attempt, which was in many respects a revision of the encyclopedia movements spawned during the French Enlightenment. Neurath is particularly of interest to students of social and political inquiry for his role in spurring the Unity of Science movement as well as the introduction of Marxist elements to the methodology of logical positivism. Neurath understood Marxism in scientific terms, and regarded it as a rigorous method for rational and scientific social reform. Thus Neurath might reasonably be referred to as a "left" logical positivist, combining the desire for scientific rigor characteristic of logical positivism and behavioralism with the categories and goals of Marxism. In addition to his incorporation of Marx, Neurath was interested in the structure of language. For Neurath, certainty about any proposition must be pulled from the manner in which a sentence adheres to a complex of previously verified sentences and propositions. Truth is not a function of correspondence to the physical world, but rather a product of linguistic coherence. In this way, Neurath offers a coherence theory of certainty consistent with the analytical aspect of logical positivism. (Interestingly, Neurath was instrumental in designing the isotype pictogram, a nonverbal form of communication that has become common in the use of signs to communicate information without relying on verbal language.)

In addition to the influence of Neurath, the ramifications of positivism and logical positivism can be discerned through the works of such neopositivist/behavorialist thinkers as Charles Merriam (1874–1953), who is often referred to as one of the principal founders of behavioralism in political science, and a number of thinkers loosely grouped among the political behavioralists, including such luminaries as V.O. Key (1906–1963), Harold Lasswell (1902–1978), Heinz Eulau (1915–2004), Herbert A. Simon (1916–2001), Eugene Meehan (1923–2003), David Easton (1917–present) and, arguably for some, Robert Dahl (b. 1915). Further discussion of these thinkers and their contributions can be found under the entry for behavioralism.

Related Entries
behavioralism; positivism

Suggested Reading
Ayer, A.J. Language, Truth and Logic. 1946; repr. New York: Dover Books, 1952.
Richardson, Alan, and Thomas Uebel, eds. The Cambridge Companion to Logical Empiricism. New York: Cambridge Univ. Press, 2007.
Wittgenstein, Ludwig. Tractatus Logico-Philosophicus, trans. C.K. Ogden and with an introduction by Bertrand Russell. 1961; repr. London: Routledge & Kegan Paul, 1992.

M

Machiavelli, Niccolò (1469–1527)

Along with Karl Marx, Niccolò Machiavelli is one of the more controversial and yet influential thinkers in the history of political philosophy. Embraced by some as the first advocate of a "realistic" approach to the study and practice of politics, regarded by others as an inflated favor monger, and scorned by still others who discern in Machiavelli a perverse and diabolical teaching, Machiavelli is easily subject to more varied interpretations than any thinker of his stature. Ruthless, patriotic, manipulative, inventive, nefarious, honest, sacrilegious, patriotic, pandering, insightful, worldly-wise, wicked, humanistic, insincere, courageous, deceptive, democratic, autocratic, satirical, sagacious, calculating—all of these adjectives have been applied to Machiavelli. He has also been called a prudent advocate of the common good, a better psychologist than historian, a lucid and refreshing student of human nature, and an obscene subverter of Christian civilization. It is hard to imagine that all of these labels, or none of them, are right. Bernard Crick, in his introduction to Machiavelli's *Discourses,* identifies no less than sixteen disparate versions of Machiavelli, or the "many Machiavellis" as he calls it—the more famous among these are: the "teacher of evil" (Leo Strauss) and "doctor of the damned" (Jacques Maritain), "a cold technician" (Ernst Cassirer), "an elegant, balanced and patriotic Whig" (Lord Macaulay), "an American political scientist of the behavioral persuasion" (Max Lerner), a "preincarnation of Lenin" (Antonio Gramsci), a "ruthless and glorious nationalist" (J.G. Fichte and G.W.F. Hegel), a "funny kind of Christian" (Dante Germino), and, Crick continues, "either a pagan or an atheist to so many others; a toady of princes, or a democratic satirist... there is no end of it, nor will there ever be." To punctuate the point, Crick remarks in a footnote that Sir Isaiah Berlin claimed that "there are no fewer than twenty-five interpretations of *The Prince* alone," further affirming that the interpretation of Machiavelli appears to be a steady growth industry. Given the variety and disparity among the several interpretations of Machiavelli's project, one is drawn to conclude that Machiavelli must either be the most complicated thinker in the history of political ideas or that he is actually the simplest of thinkers who nonetheless provides a fertile medium highly productive of flights of fancy or, in at least one case (if Machiavelli is in the end simple), irresistible insight. Regardless of the conclusion so drawn, we can note with confidence Machiavelli's pivotal position in the history of political philosophy, and his continued attraction to the eager student who seeks to confront politics in its rawest manifestation.

Machiavelli was a prolific and diverse author, and a number of his works are related directly or indirectly to politics, but for the most part the balance of his political theory is contained within *The Prince* and the less famous but more comprehensive *Discourses on the First Ten Books of Titus Livius* (or just simply *Discourses*). Other works such as his *Art of War* are worth study, but for our purposes we will focus on his two principal writings, composed at about the same time, the former focusing on the dynamics of principalities and the latter republics, using republican Rome as a model. It is in *The Prince* that Machiavelli announces the central teaching of his political philosophy, viz.,

> I thought it sensible to go straight to a discussion of how things are in real life and not waste time with a discussion of an imaginary world....for the gap between how people actually behave and how they ought to behave is so great that anyone who ignores everyday reality in order to live up to an ideal will soon discover he has been taught how to destroy himself, not how to preserve himself....So, it is necessary for a ruler, if he wants to hold on to power, to learn how not to be good, and to know when it is and when it is not necessary to use this knowledge.

Whether or not he is sincere, it is here, at least in the text, wherein Machiavelli departs from all hitherto political theory, and in particular, the traditions as best represented by Plato, Aristotle, Cicero, and St. Thomas Aquinas. Since Socrates, political thought has focused on teaching ruler and ruled alike, but in particular those who rule, those principles through which a city and its citizens can become just, and in the end, good. In Machiavelli's *Prince,* as has been noted by many commentators of his work, a new exhortation to reject the ancient teaching is averred. Machiavelli breaks from Plato and turns himself in diametric opposition—those who rule must first learn how *not* to be good, and to understand the subtleties behind knowing when, and when not to use, this particular knowledge. The ideal that is represented in the paradigmatic polities (imaginary republics) of the past is far removed from the realities of human behavior, thus to repeat the ancient quest for the intelligible city of good men is no longer viable. This is a luxury that those who hold political power cannot afford. Rather, the "prince" (those who rule) must learn to "not be good," and to eschew the ideal of goodness as advocated by the likes of Plato or St. Thomas Aquinas. It is only in adopting this teaching that a state can be well governed and that a state's citizens can ensure both the glory of their country and the greatest possible freedom for themselves as individuals.

The lesson of "how not to be good" is central to Machiavelli's political teaching. Whether or not this is exhorting us to become evil is another question, but it is the decisive moment in which Machiavelli distinguishes himself from the thinkers of the past. Additionally, a second lesson is offered that for some is an indictment of Machiavelli's intentions, but for others serves as an example of Machiavelli's practicality. In politics, Machiavelli teaches us, appearance is everything. The reality behind the appearance is not as important as the appearance itself. Machiavelli concedes that there are certain "good qualities" that a prince should attempt to convey, viz., generosity, openhandedness, gentleness, reliability, sympathy, boldness, straightforwardness, and religiosity among others. These qualities are commendable, but it is difficult to acquire all these good qualities, and still more difficult to "always act in a praiseworthy fashion, for we do not live in an ideal world." A savvy prince, for Machiavelli, will attempt to appear to have these qualities, and to avoid the appearance of having their opposite, "evil qualities." In other words, a successful ruler is one who cultivates appearances, knowing what the people will admire, and polishing one's image to reflect those expectations. Indeed, if one truly has these good qualities, and one's actions are always based on the values therein, in the political sphere these virtues become "liabilities" that will actually cause a prince to suffer. Thus, one must really know how not to be good while simultaneously keeping up good appearances, for a "ruler need not have all the positive qualities…but he must seem to have

them." However, knowing the power of appearance, Machiavelli recognizes that for those who rule, one's reputation depends as much upon the ability to evoke fear as admiration. So, in addition to appearing to possess good qualities such as generosity and piety, one must also "not fear the reproach of being called cruel," for at times a leader will need to act without pity in order to secure a more merciful future in the long term.

Above all, a good prince must recognize that leadership requires the humane virtues of a civilized person in combination with the qualities of the beast—a model prince is like Achilles's tutor Chiron, "half beast and half man." Plato's philosopher ruler, Aristotle's serious person, Cicero's dutiful statesman, and the Christian rulers of the "mirror of princes" tradition are abandoned. What is really needed in a world full of fear and betrayal are governors who can muster the qualities of the animal, to imitate the lion and the fox, to be able to repel wolves with ferocity and to cunningly detect and avoid traps. Given this, those who have the responsibility of power must engender specific virtues that enable them to govern effectively. For Machiavelli, the prescriptions of those who find their model prince in the noble virtues of Christianity and classical theory are ineffective in this world. To be a lion and a fox a prince must follow a different credo, he must cultivate what Machiavelli referred to as *virtu,* variously translated as "skill, ingenuity, excellence" (Michael Morgan), grandeur of spirit, grandiosity, bold decisiveness, brave opportunism, manliness, martial valor, greatness of stature. These are the qualities of a successful prince. According to Machiavelli, the *virtu* of the ancient pagans was superior, at least in the realm of politics, to the moral virtues of classical theory or the compassionate values of Christianity.

Whether or not these prescriptions promote leaders like Lincoln or Churchill, or someone more like the fictional character Don Corleone, remains a topic of serious debate. *The Prince* confuses as much as it clarifies. At one point we find praise from Machiavelli for tyrants like Cesare Borgia (was it to curry the Borgia's favor, or at least to forestall their enmity, or was it a telling indicator of what Machiavelli really admired?) and at another point condemnation for the ancient Syracusian tyrant, Agathocles, for his brutality and inhumane cruelty. In the *Discourses* he praised Cincinnatus and criticized Caesar, yet he was able to justify the fratricidal murder of Remus by Romulus for the greater glory of Rome. Such apparent inconsistency conceals Machiavelli's motives, and fuels the discussion revolving around the morality of his political vision.

While Machiavelli's writings do unequivocally advocate a mastery of power politics apparently for its own sake, there is also a significant strain of pragmatic republicanism in his writings that indicates a second and, at times, seemingly disparate voice. While it would be misleading to characterize the *Discourses* as an alternative to *The Prince,* certain elements of the former lend a more complex and, for some, appealing texture to Machiavelli's overall political project. In the *Discourses* Machiavelli endorses republican Rome as the best model for founding and sustaining a state. It is likely significant that Machiavelli rejects imperial Rome for its republican predecessor. Machiavelli's interest in republicanism is an important ingredient toward a fuller understanding of Machiavelli's comprehensive political theory. In the *Discourses* Machiavelli inserts a discussion of types of regimes that closely follows Polybius and, to a lesser extent, Aristotle. Having identified three good (monarchy, aristocracy, democracy) and three bad (tyranny—which is called evil, oligarchy, and mob rule) regimes, Machiavelli asserts, along with Polybius and Cicero long before him, that the best regime is the one that successfully blends and encourages elements of the three good types in order to prevent deterioration into the three corrupt forms. More to the point, no "pure" regime serves as a practical model, for even the good regimes are inherently unsound. As Machiavelli wrote,

I conclude that all these forms of government are pestilential: The three good ones do not last long, and the three bad ones are evil. Those who know how to construct constitutions wisely have identified this problem and have avoided each one of these types of constitution in its pure form, constructing a constitution with elements of each. They have been convinced such a constitution would be more solid and stable, would be preserved by checks and balances, there being present in the one city a monarch, an aristocracy, and a democracy.

For Machiavelli, republican Rome and the Spartan constitution of Lycurgus are the models to consult in this proper blending of regimes. It is here, in mixed republican government, that Machiavelli saw the liberty of the people most secure, and the common good more readily advanced. Machiavelli thus spoke to the need to establish sturdy institutional foundations for a state, somewhat deemphasizing, at least in this instance, the skill of the leader (although skilled leaders remain worthy of admiration and emulation). Solid foundations and the rule of law are brought into the foreground in the *Discourses,* and through good laws the "more admirable qualities [*virtu*]" of the citizens can be found and trained. Lycurgus and Numa, founders and lawgivers, are praised in *Discourses,* as well as Moses, who is equally acclaimed in *The Prince.* Here is that voice in Machiavelli that, without rejecting the use of power as an important political instrument, nonetheless focuses upon a *raison d'état* framed within the vague notion of a common good.

Even so, Machiavelli holds a consistent view of human nature throughout all of his writings. The more appealing republicanism, at least to the modern reader, of the *Discourses* is offered with the same views of humanity that we find in *The Prince.* Human beings are driven by an "envious nature" and goaded by "insatiable appetites," a reality that forces the abandonment of the meek values of Christianity for the "more savage" example of the ancient pagans. Those who govern, whether in principalities or in republics, must act with the *virtu* of the pre-Christian warrior-king rather than follow the example of Plato's true navigator or the Medieval ideal of a Christian prince. Religion holds an important place for Machiavelli, but only as it provides tangible benefits to the state. It is in the uses of a religion that we measure its value for the state, and in Machiavelli's estimation, the otherworldliness of Christianity has proved deleterious to the civil sphere. Christianity may provide the true way to eternal salvation, but good Christians cannot run empires, nor can they inspire republics. These tasks are best left to a more ancient valor, one unafraid of standing forth as a law unto itself.

Perhaps the most effective way to encapsulate the elusive Machiavelli is to consider his conclusions regarding freedom. In this subject, Machiavelli resembles some of the writings of the Stoics. For Machiavelli, half of what we can accomplish in life is in our control, under the command of our free will—the remaining half is given by fate. Thus a good leader must recognize the irresistible forces of fate and anticipate the manner in which they bear upon events, and then employ that portion of free will left to us for the purposes of finding the best possible advantage within the conditions and circumstances set for us by destiny. "Fortune is a woman" Machiavelli asserts, one that must be subdued by a commanding leader. And yet, even a commanding leader must not presume to control fate. Rather, one's destiny, and the destiny of a city, is to be joined as one rides a wave, neither avoided nor changed. With bold leadership and intelligent anticipation of alternatives, rulers and citizens can turn possible hardship into triumph. We cannot prevent the "rising of flood waters," but we can divert their flow for our own advantage. It is perhaps in this facet of Machiavelli, that is to say, his understanding of the relationship between freedom and fate, combined with his views on power and political good, that the ambiguities within Machiavelli's project are lent at least a portion of clarity.

Related Entries
advice to princes; consequentialism

Suggested Reading

Machiavelli, Niccolò. *The Discourses,* ed. Bernard Crick, based on a translation by Fr. Leslie Walker. New York: Penguin, 1970.
Machiavelli, Niccolò. *The Prince,* trans. and ed. Angelo M. Codevilla. New Haven: Yale Univ. Press, 1997.

Madison, James (1751–1836)

James Madison is primarily known as one of the principal authors of the United States Constitution, and for this alone he deserves mention as a prominent student of politics. Additionally, his collaboration with Alexander Hamilton and, to a much lesser extent John Jay, in what would become known as the *Federalist Papers* is the outstanding treatise in political theory generated within the American context. Finally, his many letters and essays round out the picture of one of the more vigorous political minds of his age.

Madison's genius for republican government is easily evident in his role in the creation of the Constitution. While he alone is not in truth *the* "father of the Constitution," his hand is certainly the most pronounced in the process of its shaping. The principle of the rule of law, the wisdom of intricately dispersed and balanced power, a combination of belief in self-governing individuals and a distrust of self-promoting mobs, and his willingness to work compromise into consensus are all essential features of the constitutional order that Madison helped produce. In Madison, perhaps more than any American founder other than that august duo of Washington and Franklin, we find the voice of the moderate centrist. Human beings are prone to vice, Madison would concede, but they are also given to acts of virtue, and while they will ever consult their own self-interest as one can only expect, it is nonetheless true, for Madison, that liberty is the essence of politics, and justice is its animating purpose. In a desire for the promotion of liberty for all within a just and rational order, the self-interest that actuates all of us can be channeled to something more noble—and more worthy of a dignified humanity.

Madison's part in the *Federalist Papers* was substantial. While Hamilton wrote in greater volume, with a good number of his essays exhibiting an extraordinary eloquence and clarity, the very best of these writings come from Madison's pen. *Federalist* No. 10 is Madison's masterpiece—a single essay that exhibits the best qualities of sound political theory. Here Madison examines the nature of faction and its effects on republican government and in the end concludes that the only way to militate against the violence of faction is through the multiplication of factions so as to dilute their force. In so arguing, Madison deftly answers the charge of the Constitution's critics that a large republic is not possible without the sacrifice of freedom. For Madison, an extended republic under the rule of law and the institution of dispersed power not only solves the problem of division within society by using division against itself, but it also ensures the overall success of the new nation. Only republican government can manage faction, promote justice, and secure real liberty—and a republican regime, unlike a purely democratic, is best when it is extended and not constricted. In *Federalist* No. 39, Madison explains the nature of national and federal power contrasted against the consolidated power with which the Constitution had been accused. Madison argued that the Constitution would not consolidate power and further that its proposed nature was *both* national and federal, and as such, neither. Delineating certain features as national and others as federal, Madison again exhibited his tendency to express the moderate voice. In the *Federalist* Nos. 47–51, Madison, knowing that "men are not angels," expertly examines the proposed Constitution as a working example of the dispersal of power (separation of powers combined with checks and balances), concluding in No. 51 with the cogent Montesquieuian insight, "ambition must be made to counteract ambition." In No. 55, Madison perceptively and effectively analyzes the dynamics of representative government within the context of the question of the numerical configuration of a sound legislative body. Madison again seeks the moderate solution; a legislative body large enough to represent the disparate interests of an expansive republic and yet small enough to be able to conduct its affairs. For Madison, the size of the assembly does not guarantee sober deliberation, as he famously remarked, "Had every Athenian citizen been a Socrates, every Athenian assembly would still have been a mob."

While Madison was an ally of Hamilton's during the Ratification debates, he soon became a champion of Jefferson's vision of the agrarian republic. While not taking Jefferson's part on his more extreme views—Madison had no use for a revolution from time to time and did not embrace the model of the ward-republic, for the most part Madison sided with Jefferson in the conflict with the Hamiltonian faction. Madison, as was his practice, sought a middle ground between the grand nationalism of Hamilton and the Jeffersonian idyll of a republic of yeoman farmers, but in the end, he leaned toward Jefferson and together with his friend led the "republican" faction during the young nation's formative years.

Perhaps the best way to encapsulate Madison's aspirations for moderation are in the following assessment of human nature, "As there is a degree of depravity in mankind which requires a certain degree of circumspection and distrust, so there are other qualities in human nature which justify a certain portion of esteem and confidence. Republican government presupposes the existence of these qualities in a higher degree than any other form."

Related Entries

Federalist Papers; Jefferson, Thomas; Hamilton, Alexander

Suggested Reading

Hamilton, Alexander, James Madison, and John Jay. *The Federalist Papers,* ed. Clinton Rossiter and Charles Kesler. New York: Mentor Books, 1999.

Madison, James. *Notes of Debates in the Federal Convention of 1878 Reported by James Madison,* ed. Adrienne Koch. New York: Norton, 1966.

magister populi

In Latin, the "people's magistrate," or "people's master," a single person temporarily and legally invested with emergency power and full authority to govern in time of crisis. The *magister populi,* sometimes referred to as *Praetor Maximus* (Praetor Supreme or Highest Praetor), was also referred to as *dictatura* or the *dictator,* the "one who dictates" or commands with complete authority, and is the conceptual root of the term "dictator," although it is fundamentally distinct from the modern notion and usage. The *magister populi* was a legal institution employed under extraordinary circumstances and established in the early years of the Roman Republic as an occasional substitute for the monarchical power that had been previously abolished, but which was still necessary to draw upon in exigent circumstances. No dictator could be set into place without the determination of the Roman Senate; the dictator, who was initially to be drawn from the patrician class but, over time, became open to plebeians as well, was normally one who would have had previous experience as a consul or at least someone who enjoyed the endorsement of former consuls. The dictator acted independently of the Senate with impunity, and was able to impose measures typically against the law, such as the suspension of trials in cases of punishable offenses. Dictators were also able to change Roman law on their own authority, the changes remaining in place for the duration of the dictator's service. The dictator was limited to a maximum of six months in power, and it was customary for the *magister populi* to resign once it was certain that the crisis had abated. Two notable examples of dictators who did not follow this rule are Lucius Cornelius Sulla (appointed dictator in 82 BC), and Gaius Julius Caesar (initially appointed in 46 BC). Sulla held the office for just over two years before stepping down. Caesar, on the other hand,

managed to receive an initial appointment of one year, breaking the six-month precedent, followed by the Senate granting in advance nine consecutive one-year appointments, which guaranteed his status as dictator for a full decade. After one year, the Senate dispensed with the nine-year term and named Caesar *dictator perpetuus,* or dictator in perpetuity, which in effect made Caesar dictator for life. It was this act that led to his assassination.

Other notable Roman dictators from the era of the ancient republic, or men who held the office of *magister populi,* were Lucius Quinctius Cincinnatus (named dictator in 458 BC and again in 439 BC), the famed farmer-citizen-general (often compared to George Washington), and Fabius Maximus (dictator in 221 BC and again in 217 BC), the famed hero of the Second Punic War (to whom George Washington has also been compared).

Related Entry
dictator

Suggested Reading
Flower, Harriet I., ed., *The Cambridge Companion to the Roman Republic.* New York: Cambridge Univ. Press, 2004.

Maimonides, Moses (Moshe ben Maimon; 1135–1204)

Maimonides was one of the most important philosophers during the High Middles Ages, and he is indisputably the most important Jewish thinker to emerge within the Medieval world. He is to Judaic philosophy what St. Thomas Aquinas and St. Augustine were to Christian philosophy as well as what Alfarabi and Averroes were to Islamic thought. While he is most noted as a philosopher and theologian, much like St. Augustine, he did provide commentary about political issues and stands as an important influence in the conversation that is political theory. Maimonides's efforts develop from an already deep and ancient legacy of Talmudic scholarship, rooted firmly within the Torah and relevant to every aspect of life within the Jewish community, which, it must be remembered, was at this time defined by Diaspora and at various times and with fluctuating levels of severity either excluded from or assaulted by the prevailing cultural dynamics of its related Abrahamic faiths, Christianity and Islam. This makes the achievement of Maimonides and other Jewish thinkers in the Middle Ages all the more remarkable and admirable.

While he was influenced by the philosophic traditions of the ancient Greeks (especially Aristotle) as well as the writings of the Islamic thinker Alfarabi, the central principle for Maimonides is the existence of Divine Law, a Divine Law that has been revealed to us through the prophets of Israel. As with the ancient Greek and Roman thinkers before him, and St. Thomas Aquinas shortly after him, Maimonides held that human beings are essentially political creatures, law being the only reliable and rational means wherein we can construct political community and thereby ensure justice. Human beings are diverse but are also unified on a deeper level through the capacity to reason as well as through attention to revelation (as with St. Augustine, Alfarabi, and Aquinas). We are at once a multiplicity of individuals and a political and social unity, and it is through rational law that these two aspects of our humanity can be reconciled. For Maimonides, this requires two levels of law: law that is aimed at the perfection of the material realm and law aimed at the perfection of the soul. The former (the law of the material or the laws of the body, what he identifies as *nomos,* from the Greek) is directly political, dedicated to establishing order and harmony within a state, involved in the protection of all citizens, and invested in their moral education. *Nomos* guides the political and social activities of the community— preventing harm, establishing justice, securing public tranquility, and fostering virtue (an aim typical of classical and Medieval theorists). It is primarily about peace and justice within this world and does not address the higher metaphysical questions that are left to theologians.

The second and more important type of law seeks perfection beyond this realm and is therefore related to the soul itself. This law is Divine Law, and has been given to us through a series of revelations and embodied in the Law of ancient Scripture. The law of the body (material law or *nomos*) is necessary and must be well crafted and scrupulously observed, but it is only a precondition for the perfection of the human soul, which is the province of Divine Law. All that is revealed to humanity flows from the abundance that is God, and that revelation which is conveyed through legal promulgation is the highest expression of Divine will. For this reason, while all the prophets, being from God, are to be revered, it is Moses, the Lawgiver, who stands preeminent. Through the Mosaic Law, we are commanded to observe the laws of God through the community of believers and thus achieve perfectibility of soul as a people of the Law first and foremost.

The prophets of Israel, for Maimonides, were thus all somehow charged with this service to God and humanity, even though Moses stands as the greatest among their sacred rank. All prophecy is in some way the unification of rational and imaginative faculties. Hence the prophet is able not only to draw on the rational faculty as do the philosophers but also to add the imaginative faculty, which allows the prophet to act as a vessel of revealed wisdom and Divine admonition. Thus the prophet, in a way, is at once philosopher and statesman, legislator and mystic. It is in both its political and legislative capacities that prophecy provides insight into the leadership of the social body while being simultaneously attuned with the designs of the Divine mind.

Maimonides, as a Jewish thinker, also incorporated the belief in the promise of the Messiah into his views on politics. Indeed, the Messiah is decidedly political, the surest sign of the Messiah's appearance, for Maimonides, being the political liberation of the Jewish people and the end of the Diaspora. The Messiah is fundamentally a great king in the Davidic tradition, a warrior more than a prophet and is that figure who will secure a truly just political community for the Jewish people. Still, even though the Messiah in Maimonides's teaching is less miraculous than the prophet, the ultimate goal is the perfection of this world so that the perfection of the soul can follow thereafter. The Messiah holds the same aim as the Prophet Isaiah, the "peaceable kingdom" for all Creation as promised by God through the Covenant with Israel.

Related Entries

Alfarabi; Aquinas, Thomas; Augustine

Suggested Reading

Maimonides, Moses. *A Guide for the Perplexed,* trans. Chaim Rabin and ed. J. Guttman and D.H. Frank. Indianapolis: Hackett, 1995.

Marcuse, Herbert (1898–1979)

Herbert Marcuse served as an influential figure in the development of critical theory as it emerged out of the Frankfurt School and to the neo-Marxist movement in general. Marcuse's critique of society, strongly shaped by his reading of the writings of the young Marx in their Hegelian context, evolved into a syncretic fusion of elements from Freud, Nietzsche, Heidegger (for a time), the primary thinkers of the Frankfurt School (e.g., Max Horkheimer, Theodore Adorno and Leo Lowenthal) as well as his close friend, Barrington Moore Jr. As a critical theorist his primary influence was drawn from a humanistic reading of Marx, one that rejects the worldview upon which capitalism and liberal democracy rests while simultaneously discarding the vulgar, uncritical, and ultimately repressive Marxism as applied in the Soviet bloc. Marcuse believed that Marxian theory could be emancipatory if its Hegelian-dialectical roots were revived while incorporating ideas from other sources, especially Freud. In so doing, Marcuse's approach to radicalism is less driven by economic issues and more concerned with the transformation of consciousness through new forms of culture. A revolution that places the economic means of production into new hands without changing the manner in which we think about the purpose of such production

will, even if led by the proletariat, fail to liberate humanity. It is, in Marcuse's view, important to remember the economic and technological dimensions of oppression and liberation, but one cannot stop at that and rather must engage in a radical transformation at all levels of human interaction. Labor as a process is indubitably a principal factor in the affirmation of our humanity, and yet, other facets of human life are important and help us to more fully understand our condition. Marcuse, along with thinkers from the Frankfurt School, thus rebutted the more economically deterministic factions of Marxism who perceived history as forged by an interpretation of the dialectic more reminiscent of iron laws of nature and in its stead offered a vision of the dialectic as essentially open and contingent. Labor and the proletariat are certainly at the center of change, but it must be a change that is truly rational and multidimensional, a change not only in who holds power over the means of production, but a change in the purposes of production by reconstituting human needs. In meditating on the revolutionary shift in the control over the means of production, Marcuse, in his *Essay on Liberation* (1968) wrote,

> But we know now that neither their [the means of production and "technical and technological forces] rational use nor—and this is decisive—their collective control by the "immediate producers" (the workers) would by itself eliminate domination and exploitation: a bureaucratic welfare state would still be a state of repression which would continue even into the "second phase of socialism," when each is to receive "according to his needs."

For Marcuse, it is evident that a simple change in who controls the mechanisms of production and technology is required, but more essentially, a change in the very purposes of the productive act is also necessary. To alter the purposes of production, we must not only engage in a power shift that addresses economic exploitation, which is in effect a preliminary step that is rendered superficial if it is confused for the ultimate goal, but also transform the very needs that production serves in the first place.

> What is now at stake are the needs themselves. At this stage, the question is no longer: how can the individual satisfy his own needs without hurting others, but rather: how can he satisfy his own needs without hurting himself, without reproducing, through his own aspirations and satisfactions, his dependence on an exploitative apparatus which, in satisfying his needs, perpetuates his servitude? The advent of a free society would be characterized by the fact that the growth of well-being turns into an essentially new quality of life. This qualitative change must occur in the needs, in the infrastructure of man

Human liberation must not only involve seizing the controls that drive society but, rather, changing the controls themselves in a way that helps humanity recover its inward dignity. This amounts to the emancipation of the imagination and a reawakening of the aesthetic vision of humanity, one that is not an instrument of repression and social order but rather a vision that breaks repression and transgresses order. Prosperity alone, even if universalized, can produce a "cruel affluence" unless the needs that prosperity is committed to satisfy are altered radically, at the most basic level of life. This is why Marcuse turned to Freud as well as Marx and Hegel, for in this way the forces of necessity could be reshaped by the aspirations of a new kind of freedom.

Hence, following Freud, Marcuse recognized an inherent repression within the very concept of civilization. Civilization is on an ontological level antagonistic with the fulfillment of human happiness. Humanity is fundamentally the affirmation of life instincts, or what Freud referred to as *eros*. Freud, however, saw the conflict between individual need and repressive civilization as permanent. With Marcuse, human beings can be radically transformed even at the level of their instincts. Freud is right, in Marcuse's estimation, to connect the advance of civilization with the deepening of repression, but incorrect in that

he was unable to see the transformative power that human beings possess not only to release but to reconstruct the life instincts. This is where Marxism, with its emancipatory stance, supplies the defect of Freud's otherwise compelling vision. Changes in the structure of society—real changes and not simply shifts in power—can accelerate human growth by unleashing the life instinct. In so doing, death and necessity can be absorbed by the erotic (in the sense of *eros* as life instinct, not simply as sexuality) and propelled by and toward the aesthetic dimension. Even art itself, for Marcuse, would become meaningless in a society wherein universal and radical emancipation is effected, an emancipation that not only enables every person to fully immerse themselves in culture but also to define culture anew.

Marcuse called for a "new radicalism" that dissolves the need for social control and thus the elimination of the old politics centered around sovereignty, law, bureaucracy, and institutional controls (which are ultimately repressive regardless of who is at the helm). For this reason, Marcuse was embraced by the "New Left" of the 1960s and early 1970s—an embrace with which he himself was not always comfortable. In recent years, with the ascent of other attitudes within critical theory (particularly as influenced by postmodernism), Marcuse's *cachet* may have to some degree diminished, but his contribution to meaningful analysis of both the limits of modernity and the consequences of our own attachments to a certain species of rationalism maintain their persuasive force.

Related Entries
critical theory; Hegel, Georg Wilhelm Friedrich; Marx, Karl; neo-Marxism

Suggested Reading
Marcuse, Herbert. *Eros and Civilization*. Boston: Beacon Press, 1955.
Marcuse, Herbert. *One Dimensional Man*. Boston: Beacon Press, 1964.
Marcuse, Herbert. *An Essay on Liberation*. Boston: Beacon Press, 1968.
Marcuse, Herbert. *Counterrevolution and Revolt*. Boston: Beacon Press, 1972.

Maritain, Jacques (1882–1973)

A prominent neo-Thomist often associated with "Christian existentialism," Jacques Maritain provides an example of the convergence of the belief in transcendent principles and an ardent dedication to democracy. Like St. Thomas Aquinas, Maritain embraces the concept of an immutable transcendent law of nature that is the ground of both right and justice, and he regards the human community to be perfected through the application of the principles of nature through the acts of women and men. Democracy itself is justified by the natural law, which is itself a product of the wisdom and grace of God. Only in democracy will the natural law become manifest, and thus the democratic movement is fully compatible not only with natural justice, but ultimately with the higher spiritual goals of humankind as such.

This faith in the political community is intimately entwined with Maritain's conception of the person. Along with Emmanuel Mounier, Maritain advances a theory of personalism that distinguishes the ensouled person as a creature of infinite value from the material, physical individual driven by an incomplete understanding of immediate self-interest. It is as ensouled persons that human beings bear their dignity, and it is as persons that the human being is fully affirmed, both in temporal and spiritual terms. For Maritain, a "single human soul is of more worth than the whole universe of bodies and material goods. There is nothing above the human soul except for God." This is the essence of personalism, the notion that the ends of the person are not confined to the temporal but are rather an aspect of eternity itself. Thus the common good of persons is more than the administration of material concerns but involves the community of eternal souls. Because we are eternal, we are members of a community that reaches far beyond the narrow confines of material self-interest.

Yet Maritain is not a dualist. As with St. Thomas Aquinas, the material world is itself essentially good—although only a small facet of the infinite reality of which we are a part. But we exist in this world as bodies, and as such, we are enjoined to seek justice through our political activity. The political community is capable of perfection in the here and now to the extent that it serves the ends of persons. The state must therefore serve humankind and in so doing abandon the traditional notion of sovereignty in favor of a community of self-governing persons bearing rights and drawn toward a still more transcendent purpose.

Maritain's dedication to the dignity of human beings led him to become a participant in drafting the United Nations Declaration of Universal Rights. Today he remains one of the more important theorists in the neo-Thomist tradition and a clear advocate of a foundationalist approach to political valuation and meaning.

Related Entries

Catholic social teaching; Aquinas, Thomas

Suggested Reading

Maritain, Jacques. *Christianity and Democracy; and, The Rights of Man and Natural Law,* trans. Doris C. Anson and with an introduction by Donald Arthur Gallagher. San Francisco: Ignatius Press, 1986.

Maritain, Jacques. *Man and the State.* 1951; repr. Washington, DC: Catholic Univ. America Press, 1998.

Maritain, Jacques. *The Person and the Common Good,* trans. John J. Fitzgerald. 1947; repr. South Bend, IN: Univ. Notre Dame Press, 1966.

Marx, Karl (1818–1883)

One of the more controversial as well as more influential thinkers in the entire history of political theory, regarded as the founder of modern communism and the greatest of the socialist thinkers, a devoted champion of the oppressed and enslaved who envisioned a new Eden for all human beings yet a man not above mean-spiritedness in his writings and undercut by what appears to some as a self-loathing anti-Semitism, a figure of adulation for some and disdain for others,

Karl Marx remains relevant for us today as one of the more candid and systematic commentators on the nature of community considered within the context of the industrial and technological age. While most of Marx's immediate proposals for the radical reformation of humanity seem to have fallen into President Reagan's "ashbin of history," his overall analysis of the human community in modernity and, by extrapolation, postmodernity, continues to provide both insight and focal points for deeper examination.

As a young student of philosophy, Marx was drawn to the Hegelianism that had captivated much of the German academy, especially in Berlin where the young Marx undertook his more serious foray into academia after a brief period of study in Bonn. Hegel was the philosophical colossus of his age, and Marx was profoundly affected by the scope and depth of the Hegelian project. Nonetheless, Marx was also exposed to the ancients, having been impressed by the early materialists and devoting his dissertation to a study of Epicurus and Democritus, known for their materialism and atomistic view of reality. More importantly, the young Marx encountered the writings of the firebrand Ludwig Feuerbach, a leader of the Young Hegelians who had infused Hegelianism with both a commitment to radical political critique and a materialism that in effect abandoned the idealistic core of Hegelian thought. In a sense, Marx's dialectical materialism, as it would later be called, is a hybrid of the influence of both Hegel and Feuerbach, and one that would provide Marx with a philosophical base for the development of his comprehensive, radical critique. Nonetheless, as Lee McDonald reminds us, it is important to bear in mind that Marx himself did not produce the complex system of historicism and dialectical materialism that would come to be intimately associated with his ideas. As McDonald states, "the Marxian system was really built by those who followed, for Marx never worked out a complete, well-rounded theoretical 'system.'" Even so, we can trace the basic path of ideas from Hegel and Feuerbach to Marx in a way that reveals important elements of the overall Marxian worldview and the purpose behind his goal to revolutionize philosophy itself. "Hitherto philosophy has only interpreted the world in various ways"; Marx explains in his 11th Thesis on Feuerbach, "the point, however, is to change it." With this announcement, Marx intentionally marks his own project as a departure from the history of philosophy through Hegel. For Hegel, philosophy was purely reflective and analytical, but for Marx the philosopher must act in the world to promote emancipatory change.

Marx's political philosophy can be summarized through seven basic and frequently employed concepts: dialectical materialism, historical relativism, the primacy of labor, alienation, human malleability, revolution, and communism. According to Marx, the dialectical analysis employed by Hegel in his massive system is structurally correct. Hegel was right in his assertion that the whole of reality emerges from and develops through a complex dynamic of contradiction, tension, resolution, and progress. Expressed through the interaction of affirmation, negation, and negation of the negation (or more commonly, thesis, antithesis, and synthesis, respectively), Marx agreed that this is the key to understanding the nature of what is real and the pattern of movement and improvement throughout the course of human history. But for Marx, Hegel's dialectic was "standing on its head," primarily owing to its idealist orientation. Hegel saw the dialectic as evidence of Spirit unfolding into history, but for Marx this is an inversion of the process. With Feuerbachian precision, Marx argued that all concepts, ideas, beliefs, philosophies, religions, and principles are existentially the product of material production. Or, as it would be further developed, all elements of human society—political, philosophical/ideological, moral, religious, and cultural—are built on the material substructure of production, the economic base from which the superstructure of society and history is raised. In particular, this means that production and activity are antecedent to concepts and values and, still more specifically, that philosophy is in no uncertain terms a function of power. "The ideas of any epoch are the ideas of the ruling class," Marx proclaimed in the *Communist Manifesto,* a statement that not only demonstrates a serious departure from Hegel, but also one that thoroughly rejects the objectivism characteristic of most philosophers since the ancients. Truth is not discovered in the quest for first principles as in Plato, Aristotle, St. Thomas Aquinas, and others, but rather, truth is contingent on power. Wherever one finds the key to power, one finds the key to the certainties of a given age. As with Feuerbach before him, Marx regarded every idea, belief, and value as a product of the relations of production. Even God is but an expression of human activity, possessing no independence apart from those thoughts that are *produced* within a given socioeconomic system. "Life precedes consciousness," Marx observes in his *German Ideology,* and from this vantage point, he draws the conclusion that all thinking is rooted in material and phenomenal reality. There is no transcendent reality behind the veil as in Plato or St. Thomas Aquinas, or even Hegel by some interpretations, but only images of transcendence that are products of humanity's various exertions within the material world. Thus history has nothing to do with Hegel's *Geist* (Spirit), Plato's Forms (*eidos*), or St. Thomas Aquinas's vision of the Holy Trinity, but, rather, history is in reality the story of complex material development, particularly in terms of conflict regarding the use and command of material things. "The history of all hitherto existing society is the history of class struggle," Marx concludes,

> Freeman and slave, patrician and plebian, lord and serf, guild-master and journeyman, in a word, oppressor and oppressed, stood in constant opposition to one another, carried on an uninterrupted, now hidden, now open fight, a fight that each time ended, either in revolutionary re-constitution of society at large, or in the common ruin of the contending classes.

This class struggle progresses dialectically and in stages, that is, through the conflict between opposites, toward increasingly more liberated forms of community. Hence the oppression felt by the serfs of the Middle Ages leads to the conflict that stimulates a new revolutionary class, and thus a higher state of society. And, consequently, the truths embraced by the serf, and by those before him and those that come after him, are neither objective nor universal but rather are simply further products of the relations of power in that moment. Because of this, Marx's followers and critics alike have characterized his thought as both dialectical and historicist, dynamic on the one hand, and relativist on the other.

However, as with other great thinkers, Marx is a bit more complex than that. Marx's historicism is evident, and from this it can be reasonably argued that Marx is more relativist than objectivist, but there are clear objectivist elements in Marx's philosophy. He takes it as a leading premise that the dialectic, now standing upright after Marx's correction, is moving forward and upward, and that human history is marked by both struggle and inevitable progress. Additionally and perhaps more significantly, Marx does recognize that there are some facets of the human condition that abide perpetually and are thus not contingent on any given age or particular situation. Marx replaces Hegel's *Geist* with the activity of labor, or what he refers to as the "labor-process." This involves not only the labor of the industrial worker, but also any activity that produces or creates something of value to the world. For Marx, labor is so seminal to his analysis of society that it serves as an objective property of the human condition. It is not *Geist* that moves history but rather the labor-process. As Marx states in the first volume of *Capital* (*Das Kapital*), "The labor-process . . . is the necessary condition for effecting exchange of matter between man and Nature; is the everlasting Nature-imposed condition of human existence, and therefore is independent of every social phase of that existence, or rather, is common to every such phase." The contest over ownership of the means of production, that is, over who commands the labor-process, the "everlasting" element of the human condition, is the engine that drives the dialectic toward its conclusion. Therefore the power of labor is an objective and essential part of our humanity and it stands as the one category that enables us to scrutinize whether or not human beings are engaged with the world in any manner that would be deemed humane. Because of this, the primacy of labor is the hinge on which Marx's critique of modernity turns, and we see this fully developed in the concept of alienated labor proposed by the young Marx in his now familiar 1844 manuscripts.

Alienated labor is the principal problem with industrial capitalism and the liberal democratic institutions that support it, according to Marx. The estrangement of labor is - the root of our dehumanization, for that which is an abiding virtue of our humanity is to the modern worker a thing alien. Alienated labor is the consequence of private property and the true explanation of what the existence of that institution means to human beings and has meant to humanity since the emergence of bourgeois dominance after the economic and political revolutions of the sixteenth, seventeenth and eighteenth centuries. Marx recognizes four basic types of alienation within capitalist societies: alienation from the product of labor, from the process of labor, from man's "species-being," and from other human beings. The consequences of this alienation are grave in Marx's account. If our humanity is somehow defined by the fact that we are essentially laboring creatures, then any economic system and the state that supports or defends capital is fundamentally unjust. Therefore it is incumbent upon us—especially those engaged in social criticism, for the point of philosophy is to change the world—to challenge the established system and promote its abolition. As Marx would later write in *Capital,* "Labour is, in the first place, a process in which both man and Nature participate, and in which

man of his own accord starts, regulates, and controls the material re-actions between himself and Nature....By thus acting on the external world and changing it, he at the same time changes his own nature." In other words, it is imperative that human beings command their own labor power, for it is in and through labor that we both change the world external to us as well as change our own inward nature. Human nature is malleable for Marx, and it is altered at its core by the fact that we make ourselves in the very act of making the world. Once our own labor power becomes alien to us we are no longer capable of freely directing our own destiny or willingly choosing what it is we wish to make of ourselves. Under capitalism, where the ownership and operation of the means of production are at their most antipodal and contradictory, the ability to engage in authentic labor for the gratification of one's genuine needs is thoroughly stifled, and so the very essence of what it means to be human is truncated and suppressed.

Humanity, according to Marx, has historically suffered alienation in various degrees, a condition greatly intensified within the polarizing contradictions of life under capitalism. Nonetheless, Marx holds out hope that this historically pervasive problem will be surmounted, but it can only be surmounted through a change in human beings themselves. With the exception of the fact that human beings are essentially laboring animals, human character is radically mutable, and thus it is, for Marx, within our grasp to reconstruct society in such a way as to reconstitute human nature itself. This will occur for Marx through revolution.

Historically, revolution has been the predominant phenomenon of social and political change. Every epoch is initiated by some revolution resolving the tension between oppressors and oppressed, but, as is expected in the course of the dialectic, new tensions have ever emerged. Each revolution alters the structure of society and, in so doing, the definition of what it means to be human. Thus life in the

Middle Ages was dramatically different from life in the industrial age, and the actual individuals that experience each of these epochs are fundamentally different. The experiences that spin out of the relation between lord and serf, for example, are so different from the relations between capital and labor that the very persons themselves operating under these disparate relational systems are inherently distinct. An industrial worker in the nineteenth century is a different kind of being when compared to a Medieval serf or an ancient slave. Revolutions will continue to alter our humanity, and Marx is confident that the next revolution, which he regards as "necessary and inevitable," will not only alter humanity for the better but will actually "rehabilitate" humanity once and for all. The notion of "rehabilitation" does indicate for Marx that there still remains a fixed core within the human person that, while warped and buried by centuries of oppression and exploitation, is nonetheless inherently present within all human beings. Hence, again, Marx encounters ambiguity: human nature is only a concept that reflects the general character of persons in a given historical and cultural context, and yet, there remains a fixed capacity for labor power that defines humanity as such, one that has been perverted by alienation, and thus ripe for rehabilitation in a new and emancipatory world. In a word, human beings will become fully human, overcoming alienation and abolishing all exploitative relations, in and through communism.

In a word, communism is, for Marx, "the positive expression of annulled private property." But it is not that simple. Our popular perception of Marxian communism is influenced by old images of Stalinism and Maoism, and to an extent this is realistic, but Marx's understanding of the nature of communism is complex. It is unlikely that communism as envisioned by Marx in the nineteenth century was fulfilled, partly or completely, through the systems that emerged and fell in the twentieth century. Indeed,

Marx's own theory of the dialectical progress toward real communism held that a high stage of capitalism needed to occur prior to the revolution that would produce the truly classless society. A "dictatorship of the proletariat" would usher in the new society, but for the most part, the coercive techniques to build the new society would quickly dissipate. It is well known that Marx did not anticipate this happening anywhere other than the most politically and economically "advanced" countries, namely Great Britain, the United States, and the Netherlands. For Marx, these were the societies that would carve the way for revolution, and thus the very image that he held of communism was already somewhat defined within the scope of these sociopolitical systems. Marx did concede that a communist revolution could occur elsewhere, but for the most part, he was strongly convinced that the real event could only occur from within a highly developed capitalist system. The revolutionary class, the proletariat, needed to be fully developed and fully conscious of their immiseration and alienation before the true revolution could begin.

In his 1844 manuscripts, Marx identified two basic types of communism: what he refers to as "crude and unreflective communism," and what he simply refers to as "communism," or what can be aptly described as "essential" or positive communism. The former type, "crude communism," is a phenomenal form that alters the structure of society without changing human nature itself. Capitalism is abolished, but the categories of capitalism that govern human production are still in place. The community under crude communism is "only a community of labor, and an equality of wages paid out by the communal capital—the community as the universal capitalist." Thus their still remains the problem of alienation from one's labor-process, and thus the revolution that has produced such a condition is incomplete. Marx describes this crude communism as one that negates "the personality of man in every sphere," one that is "the consummation of this envy and leveling-down." In a sense, via extrapolation, one can imagine this type of communism as describing what transpired in places like the Soviet Union, where a revolution in Marx's name did occur, but one that produced what Marx seems to be warning against some 73 years before the fact. However, it is not clear in Marx's writing whether or not "crude communism" is a stage that must be endured; it is only clear that this stage is not the type of communism that Marx is hoping for the human race.

For Marx, real communism is the true abolition of the categories and characteristics of capitalist society, and thus requires a radical change in human nature, one that does not occur under crude communism. Indeed, this radical change is requisite to the successful achievement of the truly classless society. Without this change in human nature, communism will not supersede those attributes in capitalism that aggravate alienation. Marx is quite clear on what will lead to communist revolution, and why this revolution is necessary and imminent. But Marx cannot provide specific descriptions of what this type of communism will actually become. Rather, he relies on Hegelian abstractions or idyllic metaphor to convey a glimpse of an unknown future. Authentic communism is, for Marx, "the return of man himself as a social, i.e., really human, being, a complete and conscious return which assimilates all the wealth of previous development." Marx continues down the Hegelian road,

> It [communism] is the true solution of the conflict between existence and essence, between objectification and self-affirmation, between freedom and necessity, between individual and species. It is the solution to the riddle of history and knows itself to be this solution.

Additionally, in the *German Ideology,* Marx describes a quasi-utopian condition wherein human beings will no longer be defined by their role as industrial laborers, performing one task for the sake of another's needs. Communism is the pure gratification of one's own needs, one

that is accomplished only by a personality that is free to pursue multiple forms of activity. The new communist person is not a laborer *per se,* but rather a fisherman, hunter, poet, critical critic, and much more. The metaphorical image of the individual who is many things for his or her own purposes is powerful, and yet vague. Marx knows that a new age is coming, but he can only discern its outlines. While Marx does, in his *Civil War in France,* express his admiration for the Paris Commune, and thus points to it as a prelude to a broader communist revolution, the vision of authentic communism remains clouded. It is left to his followers to sketch in the details, and therein lies yet another tale.

Practical applications of Marxian ideas, some clearly deviations from Marx's purpose and others less so, have in many cases been no less than calamitous. For this reason few today would advocate unadulterated "Marxist" revolution, and still fewer would embrace its more perverted manifestations such as those that appeared under Lenin, Stalin, Mao, and their epigones. Nonetheless, as a student of the human condition, Marx arrived at compelling insights regarding the dynamics of modernity, and his genuine devotion to a just and humane community commands our attention regardless of the practicality of following his more specific prescriptions. In a word, as a practitioner of social revolution, Marx is rightly indicted for forwarding a vision incompatible with peaceable reform and social improvement, but as an observer of the complex dynamics of human society, particularly those aspects that reveal chronic oppression and exploitation within the human family, Marx remains a serious voice contributing insight and critical ardor within the Great Conversation.

Related Entries
communism; critical theory; dialectical theory; Hegel, Georg Wilhelm Friedrich; socialism

Suggested Reading
Avineri, Shlomo. *The Social and Political Thought of Karl Marx*. New York: Cambridge Univ. Press, 1988.

Marx, Karl, and Friedrich Engels. *The Marx-Engels Reader,* 2d ed., ed. Robert C. Tucker. New York: Norton, 1978.

McDonald, Lee. *Western Political Theory, Part 3: Nineteenth and Twentieth Centuries.* New York: Harcourt Brace Jovanovich, Inc., 1968.

Ollman, Bertell. *Alienation: Marx's Conception of Man in Capitalist Society.* New York: Cambridge Univ. Press, 1971.

Merleau-Ponty, Maurice (1908–1961)
More than any other continental thinker in the post–World War II era, Maurice Merleau-Ponty can be said to hold quietly an abiding influence on a variety of intellectual movements. Dialectical Marxism, existentialism, phenomenology, and postmodernism all to some degree owe at least part of their development to Merleau-Ponty, yet he remains one of the less familiar thinkers outside of academia. Despite this, his importance is likely to run even deeper than his erstwhile friend and more famous colleague, Jean-Paul Sartre, and his humanistic approach to hold more promise for political theory than the arid and remote meditations of Martin Heidegger. Merleau-Ponty, at least for the moment, lacks the notoriety of these thinkers, but his overall contribution to political theory may yet prove more enduring.

As a political thinker, Merleau-Ponty combines the more communitarian elements of dialectical Marxism (that is to say, a more open, humanistic understanding of Marx as contrasted against the statist and, at its worst, totalitarian applications of Marx exerted in the former Soviet Union) with a strong sense of communitarian purpose and the existentialist stance that is often more closely associated with Sartre. And yet, Merleau-Ponty, while drawing from both Marx and existentialism, cannot be fully described as either without considerable qualification. Merleau-Ponty firmly rejected deterministic strains in Marxist theory, emphasizing what he considered to be the intersubjective dynamic of Marxian thought inherited from Hegel. Marxism is philosophy in action and not simply the mindless forces of a fully deterministic and irresistible history. Marxism is a call to community, a return to the "flesh of history" in which human activity is embodied. Refusing the abstract Marxism of either Lenin or Sartre (a refusal that led him to break with Sartre over his friend's failure to denounce Stalinist oppression and Soviet aggression), Merleau-Ponty conceived of Marxism as a radical communitarianism not blindly driven by inexorable forces. As Scott Warren has explained in his *Emergence of Dialectical Theory,*

> For Merleau-Ponty...Marxism still retains its heuristic value and stands alone as an authentic attempt to unite theory and practice and to strive for universality over alienation and particularism. But the reification and canonization of Marx and Marxism, views as capable of possessing a truth applicable to all times and places, has transformed a living truth into a collection of ruins, a "classic," open to the archaeology of anyone.

As Warren explains, Merleau-Ponty sustained faith in the vision of community that he saw in the more critical and humane elements of Marx while thoroughly discarding the ossified and, in his view, unnatural attempt to reduce Marxian thought to materialist, even quasi-positivist laws and monolithic ideologies. Marxism, and politics as a whole, as Warren continues, are for Merleau-Ponty "action in the process of self-invention." "Action," in concurrence with the spirit of Marx's philosophy as a project directed at changing the world, and "self-invention" in full alliance with the existentialist philosophies of his own times—post–WWII France.

It should be noted that, even though Merleau-Ponty fell away from Sartre over the latter's unflinching apology for Stalinism, Merleau-Ponty himself once defended the severity of Soviet revolution and the persecution of counterrevolutionaries. His *Humanism and Terror* is a rococo twisting of radical idealism and revolutionary "justice." A failed rebuttal of Arthur Koestler's *Darkness at Noon,*

Merleau-Ponty's *Humanism and Terror* defends the irrational and cruel purges of Stalin through a particularly shocking notion of the "ends justifying the means." Such a position is incongruous with Merleau-Ponty's more insistent humanism, especially in his work following the break from Sartre, but incongruity aside, it remains a disturbing testament blemishing his otherwise humanistic vision.

It is through his theory of freedom that Merleau-Ponty's political ideas are clarified. Unlike in deterministic varieties of Marxism, we are not mere products of an unseen historical cunning or the concealed dynamics of deep structures and their complex of systems, nor are we "radically free" in the Sartrean understanding. We are never wholly determined nor completely free in Merleau-Ponty's estimation. We are neither exclusively material (and thus molded by our environment) as less critical voices in Marxism would assert, nor are we pure consciousness and thus absolutely free, as Sartre maintained. Rather we are a combination of both, consciousness embodied in the flesh and immersed in the word, finding meaning in perception and freely acting in response to those conditions that set our limits. As human beings we are both free and yet "situated," we are able to choose but our choices are finite as a function of our being bodies in the world. As a free agent, I cannot change the terrain of alternatives before me, but I can commit to those alternatives that I consider worthy of choice, and conduct myself in a manner that reflects my authentic self once my commitments are made. Our freedom is intertwined with the actions of others and the basic situation around us, and we can only act within this context of intersubjective activity rather than independently of it. "We are involved in the world and with others in an inextricable tangle," Merleau-Ponty observes in the final chapter of his *Phenomenology of Perception,* further remarking that

> The idea of situation rules out absolute freedom at the source of our commitments, and equally, indeed, at their terminus. No commitment, not even commitment in the Hegelian State, can make me leave behind all differences and free me for anything.

And reflecting further still on the realities of the embodied person immersed in the world of other people and commitments, physical terrain and objects,

> [T]here are these *things* which stand, irrefutable, there is before you this person whom you love, there are these men whose existence around you is that of slaves, and *your* freedom cannot be willed without leaving behind its singular relevance, and without willing freedom for all.[author's emphasis]

In the end, Merleau-Ponty might be described as a realistic communalist, a cautionary radical, and a tempered Marxist open to ideas beyond the materialist tradition. In this sense Merleau-Ponty is, for commentators such as Scott Warren, the epitome of a true dialectical philosopher. His overarching political project was to return humanity to an awareness of what it means to be human in the present, to act faithfully and hopefully within the given, to recognize that a person gives of themselves in exchange with others and that we are but a "network of relationships" in the larger view, and to embrace the moment as a possibility for change. As free agents radically embodied and interconnected, this change involves seeing the self in the other and knowing the other as part of the self.

Related Entries
critical theory; dialectical theory; existentialism; Hegel, Georg Wilhelm Friedrich; Marx, Karl

Suggested Reading
Baldwin, Thomas. *Maurice Merleau-Ponty: Basic Writings.* London: Routledge, 2004.
Merleau-Ponty, Maurice. *Sense and Non-Sense,* trans. Patricia Allen Dreyfus. 1964; repr. Chicago: Northwestern Univ. Press, 1992.
Warren, Scott. *The Emergence of Dialectical Theory.* Chicago: Univ. Chicago Press, 1984.

Whiteside, Kerry H. *Merleau-Ponty and the Founda-tions of an Existential Politics.* Princeton: Princeton Univ. Press, 1988.

Mill, John Stuart (1806–1873)

Along with Jeremy Bentham, John Stuart Mill is regarded as one of the principal philosophers in the utilitarian tradition. Mill's great work, *Utilitarianism,* is at once an extension of Ben-tham's work and a substantive modification of it. In spite of Mill's emphasis that he remains a utilitarian (reaffirming the "Greatest Happiness Principle" as the only valid lynchpin for human moral action), one could argue that his modifi-cations of Bentham's utilitarianism in effect amounts to a distinct departure from the doctrine of utility.

Mill's support of Bentham begins and ends with his insistence that the Greatest Happiness Principle is not only an accurate description of the way things work, but also the only truly moral foundation of any school of thought or belief. Mill even goes so far as to redefine the Golden Rule of the Gospel as an example of the Greatest Happiness Principle. This makes sense to Mill in light of his considerable over-haul of Bentham's hedonistic calculus. Mill agrees with Bentham that happiness depends on the maximization of pleasure, but he rejects the quantitative reduction of all pleasures to the same level. Bentham holds that all pleasures are equal, and what matters therefore is the quan-tity of pleasure experienced—it is thus in the expanded volume of pleasure that happiness can be asserted. But for Mill (echoing Plato and Aristotle as well as the Stoics and Epicurus), all pleasures are decidedly *not* equal, and a per-son must seek those pleasures of the higher fac-ulties (intellect and virtue). "It is better to be a human being dissatisfied than a pig satisfied," Mill proclaims, "better to be Socrates dissatis-fied than a fool satisfied." Thus pure pleasure and even simple happiness are not enough for Mill. What he sought was an elevated happi-ness, one that ennobled the human spirit through the right kind of pleasures, similar to the views held by Plato and in conflict with

his great mentor. Mill fully understood that one cannot force a person to pursue the nobler pleasures, but we must nonetheless recognize that they are both real and preferable to lesser choices.

Like Bentham, Mill's political theory is essentially egoistic—but again with some important qualifications. Mill joined Bentham and his father, James Mill, in promoting democracy as the best form of government (the only kind of government that will enable human beings to act as autonomous agents). However, with his friend Alexis de Tocqueville, he perceived dangers lurking within democratic force. Not only does democracy tempt the tyranny of the majority, but even more ominously, democracy is accompanied by an insidious "social tyranny" that reaches into the human soul itself and imposes an undesirable level of conformity at the expense of individual creativity and moral autonomy. To militate against this social tyr-anny, Mill forwards a notion of individual sov-ereignty over all self-regarding interests (the problem emerges in determining just what actions are truly and exclusively self-regarding), and thus the coercive power of the state, or any other element or instrument of society and its institutions, must be prevented from intruding on the individual's freedom of thought and expression, preferences, and free association with other members of society. The state (and society in general) can only inhibit the actions of an individual to prevent harm to others, this "no harm" principle being the only legitimate directive guiding the coer-cive abilities of the community. One's overall happiness or good is under the sovereignty of the individual. The state and society can entreat, persuade, or reason with an individual regarding what is good, but a person can never be coerced to accept a good that is not deter-mined by their own judgment of self-interest.

Mill's individualism is real but is not one-dimensional. While Mill does advocate a minimal state (it is an evil to add too much power to the state, turning citizens into docile dependents), he nonetheless recognizes the importance of government. Given Mill's notion of the sovereignty of the individual, one would expect a *laissez-faire* attitude toward the state in its relation with the market. But Mill sees trade as a "social act" (an other-regarding interest that falls under the rule of the "no harm" principle), and thus the state is obligated to regulate markets to protect consumers. Additionally, Mill, while allowing that individuals must be left to conduct their lives as they deem fit, nonetheless argues that the state plays a paramount role in ensuring the education necessary to encourage the right kinds of choices that will foster human improvement. Mill does not advocate liberty for its own sake, but rather liberty for the sake of human progress. This is a vital element to understand Mill's overall vision of the democratic state.

To complicate matters further still, Mill, a sincere advocate of democracy, nonetheless perceives the need to employ specific measures to prevent a vulgar mass democracy that will impose the social tyranny that he fears. Thus, while Mill advocates universal suffrage (including the franchise to women, placing Mill ahead of his time in this regard), he supports a system of weighted votes (a plurality of votes) for those who are more educated or skilled. This will at once secure a greater voice to the minority of the intelligent and virtuous and ensure that democracy is elevated above the passions and impulses of the crowd. Additionally, while Mill believes in a representative system accountable to the people as a whole, he argues that the balance of governmental work should be conceived and administered by experts—civil servants who hold office on merit and are able to apply the skills needed to practice the art of governing. Elected representatives would supervise and approve the actions of the administration, thus keeping institutions and their leaders accountable to the broader electorate, but the actual practice of governing would be managed by the experts. In a real sense, Mill emulates (inadvertently) the

proposal by Plato, found in his *Republic,* that envisions a class of wise rulers who know the higher principles of governing and are thus the only ones capable of leading the state toward justice.

In sum, Mill enthusiastically embraces the utilitarian principle, but in terms that are so altered as to push Mill toward a real alternative to the utilitarianism of Bentham and his father James Mill. At times Mill espouses a political vision closer to the classical views of Plato and Aristotle, and while never directly rejecting the utilitarian ethic, he nonetheless incorporates sufficient themes from other thinkers to place him at a critical distance from the rudimentary Benthamite principle of the greatest happiness for the greatest number.

Related Entries
Bentham, Jeremy; consequentialism; utilitarianism

Suggested Reading
Mill, John Stuart. *On Liberty and Other Essays,* ed. JohnGray. New York: Oxford Univ. Press, 1991.

monarchomachs (*Monarchomaques,* "king killers")
During the religious wars between the Catholic and Protestant branches dividing Christianity on the European continent during the sixteenth century, a group of Huguenot (French Calvinist) political polemicist emerged advocating policies of defiance and resistance to "tyrannical" rulers who oppressed the new religious sects. Pejoratively deemed "monarchomachs" from the Greek meaning "warriors against monarchy," or "killers of kings" in 1600 by William Barclay, the monarchomachs adopted political views that fueled the growing support among intellectuals behind early notions of popular sovereignty in the sixteenth and seventeenth centuries. With the tragedy of the St. Bartholemew's Day massacre (wherein Huguenots were attacked and killed in Paris and throughout Protestant strongholds in provincial France), a series of fiery revolutionary tracts were composed advocating open resistance to

kings who had become tyrants, even to the point of regicide (or tyrannicide as the case may be). François Hotman and Theodore Beza of France and Switzerland, Nicholas Barnaud and Hubert Languet of France, Switzerland and Holland, Phillip de Mornay of France, and George Buchanan of Scotland are among the more familiar of the monarchomachs. Hotman's *Franco-Gallia* asserted a notion of sovereignty that placed the "welfare of the people" above the authority of the king. Another highly influential tract that was publish anonymously (probably written by either de Mornay or Languet) under the pseudonym "Stephanus Brutus" and titled *Vindiciae contra tyrannos* provided a justification for resistance to monarchs who had committed the error of issuing decrees against the Law of God as well as those kings who had acted in such a way as to oppress a polity in a manner that leads to its destruction. The *Vindiciae* is equally known as an early expression of modern social contract theory, wherein two contracts exist within the state: one contract between God and sovereign and a second between God and the people as a whole. If the king offends God and His law, the people are no longer bound to follow him, for the king has violated the contract between God and sovereign. Moreover, a people that does not resist such a king *qua* tyrant in effect "make the fault of their king their own transgression." Or, more precisely, the people's representatives (ephors, or those who monitor the behavior of kings) must resist such a king, for the author of the *Vindiciae,* unlike fellow monarchomach Buchanan, did not advocate a mass uprising, but rather relied on others who hold public authority within a kingdom. The author of the *Vindiciae* embraced the rule of law, and while taking a militant stance against king's who violate God's law, nonetheless insisted upon not only lawful restraint of established authorities, but also lawful action against such authorities only when they defy God.

The monarchomachs actively contributed to a reorientation of the concept of sovereignty and the right of resistance in the development of early modern political thought. They inadvertently join certain Catholic counterparts (such as Mariana, Suárez, and Cardinal Bellarmine) in their insistence on the strict accountability of all who hold political power and the sovereign authority of the people, or representatives of the people, to openly resist and even replace a monarch who presumes to defy Divine Law.

Related Entry
Politiques

Suggested Reading

McDonald, Lee. *Western Political Theory, Part 2: From Machiavelli to Burke.* New York: Harcourt, Brace and Jovanovich, 1962
O'Donovan, Oliver, and Joan Lockwood O'Donovan. *From Irenaeus to Grotius: A Sourcebook in Christian Political Thought, 100–1625,* Grand Rapids, MI: Eerdmans, 1999.

monarchy

Plato and Aristotle both defined monarchy as legitimate rule of the one for the good of the *polis*. In other words, for both thinkers, a monarchy is an acceptable (and in some ways preferable) type of government that is beneficial to the promotion of a common good. Aristotle is careful to illustrate an important contrast between a monarch (*basileus*) and a tyrant (*tyrannos*): the former rules over free citizens according to a legitimate basis for power and limited by the governing rule of law (for both Plato and Aristotle, kings could not rule absolutely, but could only govern according to the rule of law or at least under the guidance of some transcendent principles of justice), while the latter commands subjects according to the personal caprice of the tyrant.

Monarchy, or kingship, in Medieval thought was influenced by this distinction. Kings and princes held authority and were to govern as "first among equals" within the noble class. John of Salisbury's notion of the king as serving his subjects rather than dominating them by force of will was the accepted notion of kingship—regardless of the extent to which a king realized the ideal. Kings, like bishops and priests, were regarded as holding legitimacy through Divine will, and thus were to "minister" to the people as John of Salisbury held in his *Policraticus*. Should a monarch renounce this obligation or somehow manipulate power for private gain, then the authority of the monarch is no longer clear, and the leader in question risks slipping into the role of a tyrant. In the strict sense, monarchy represents a legitimate government under the rule of law, sanctioned by God, and, in the end, supported by the consent of either the nobility (directly) or the people as a whole (indirectly).

Related Entries

aristocracy; despotism; two-swords doctrine; tyranny

Suggested Reading

Myers, Henry. *Medieval Kingship*. Chicago: Nelson-Hall, 1982.
Sabine, George H. *A History of Political Theory*. 1937; repr. New York: Dryden Press, 1973.

Montesquieu, Charles-Louis de Secondat Baron de la Brede et de la (1689–1755)

Montesquieu is known to students of the history of ideas as the great advocate of the doctrine of the separation of powers and checks and balances, and while the general notion of dispersed and balanced power predates Montesquieu (traced back at least as far as Plato's *Laws*), it is in his *Spirit of the Laws* that it receives its clearest annunciation.

Montesquieu works from the premise that "power always tends to abuse," and that no regime is invulnerable to the caprice of arbitrary power. Liberty can only be realized in moderate regimes, and even in moderate mixed regimes it is not guaranteed. To achieve a greater liberty under the law (as opposed to mere license or a vulgar self-interested independence) it is necessary, according to Montesquieu, to divide power and check it against itself. The checking of power by power is the essence of the notion of power balanced in equilibrium, using its own force to keep itself in check. Montesquieu

envisions a dispersal of power across three branches: legislative, executive, and judicial, all set in balance against each other in a way so as to prevent any one segment of the government from gaining preeminence. As long as power is kept in check against itself, Montesquieu explains, its tendency toward corruption will be diminished. Thus it is easy to see why Montesquieu was referred to as the great "oracle" for the American founders. Regardless of partisan affiliation, the American theorists and statesmen that designed, debated, and eventually ratified the Constitution were in agreement on the authority of Montesquieu.

In addition to the doctrine of checks and balances, Montesquieu is well known for his attempt to combine a belief in universal principles of natural law with sensitivity to the various conditions that cause laws to be quite different from place to place. There is indeed, for Montesquieu, a universal natural law that is fully rational and common to all human beings, but, for the most part, the laws that govern us are functions of the culture and society in which we live. Hence, in assessing the "spirit" of laws, we must look to the many conditions from which they spring. Montesquieu is not a relativist or contextualist, but he does recognize the fact of diversity in laws and political institutions as an organic outgrowth of the deeper social, cultural, economic, and even geographic forces that generate a national consciousness. To promote the best possible laws within the most effective political design, we must examine the myriad facets of a society; for this reason, Montesquieu is sometimes considered a forerunner of modern sociology.

Montesquieu was also interested, as was Plato long before him, in the relationship between the type of regime and the virtues of its citizens. Monarchy requires honor, aristocratic republics moderation, and democratic republics a general virtue and love of laws and country. Power is the only principle behind despotism, and despotism is ensured when the various functions of government (legislative, executive, and judicial) are blended into one body. Thus for Montesquieu, the dispersal of power balanced in equipoise, combined with the rule of law and the virtues of a law-abiding citizen, is the most certain safeguard against despotism as well as the best medium from within which liberty can be realized in its fullest sense.

Related Entries

checks and balances; *Federalist Papers*; Locke, John; Madison, James

Suggested Reading

Montesquieu, Charles-Louis de Secondat Baron de la Brede et de la. *Persian Letters,* trans. C.J. Betts. New York: Penguin, 1973.

Montesquieu, Charles-Louis de Secondat Baron de la Brede et de la. *The Spirit of the Laws,* ed. Anne Cohler, et al. New York: Cambridge Univ. Press, 1989.

Muslim Brethren (Society of Muslim Brethren)

Initiated in 1928 by the Egyptian activist Hasan al-Banna, the Society of Muslim Brethren devoted itself to recovering the ancient vision of Islam as encompassing all aspects of life, political, economic, social, military, cultural, as well as religious. For the Muslim Brethren, there is no distinction between religious practice and political commitment; the House of Islam combines all human endeavors under one community of believers. Given this, al-Banna and the Muslim Brethren sought the restoration of the Caliphate (the institution of the Caliph, or *kalifa,* once regarded as a successor of Muhammad by Sunni Muslims and serving as a single religious leader for the universal Islamic community) and the fusion of political duty to religious devotion.

Al-Banna adopted a view challenging the cultural and political eminence claimed by the West. A newly unified Islam must reject the influence of Western ideas, attitudes, and practices, and mine the traditions of the Islamic past for the promotion of a just and pious society. Al-Banna was willing to concede the more humanistic dimensions of Western liberalism, but found the tendency toward materialism and secularization troubling and was particularly repulsed by the atheistic materialism associated with Western communism. Islamic renewal need not be violent, but it must be aggressive in its rooting out what was perceived to be the rot of Western imperialism.

Doubtless owing to al-Banna's homeland, the Muslim Brethren were particularly dedicated to building a new Islamic state in Egypt, one purged of secularism and all European vestiges. Additionally, the Muslim Brethren were early advocates of a separate Palestinian state. Even so, their focus on Egypt and Palestine did not attenuate their commitment to the House of Islam as a universal reality. Modernity must be challenged everywhere, and a new, stronger and purer Islamic community vigorously advanced. A righteous godly state must replace the corrupt nation-state of Western liberalism while resisting the vulgar atheism of Marxism. To this end, the power of politics and government must be brought to bear on behalf of the faith—there can be no separation between mosque and state. Islam is not only an expression of devotion to the Divine, but also a community identical with righteousness.

The movement toward a renewal of Islam cleansed of Western influences was also shared by Wahhabism as well as thinkers such as Abu'l-A'la al-Mawdudi and Sayyid Qutb. All would agree that only through a return to the fundamentals of Islamic faith and social organization can the House of Islam submit to God's will on earth. Failing a complete reimmersion in the teachings of Muhammad in every facet of life, the House of Islam will always be at risk from the encroachments of infidel cultures without as well as from faithlessness within.

Related Entries

Qutb, Sayyid; Wahhabism

Suggested Reading

Bergesen, Albert, ed. *The Sayyid Qutb Reader.* New York: Routledge, 2007.

Black, Antony. *The History of Islamic Political Thought: From the Prophet to the Present.* New York: Routledge, 2001.

N

nationalism

The concept of the nation, the origin of which is unclear but rooted in the ancient notion of a unified people, is much older than the ideological impulse of nationalism, which is driven by the desire to fuse the cultural sentiments and loyalties of nations with the tangible political framework of the state. By combining the nation and the state, nationalism channels the powerful energies that bind a sense of national unity with the political and legal institutions of states.

Nationalism can work as a positive force binding a people together through a love of country and even a quasi-spiritual devotion to a higher ideal of unity and fraternity. In this sense of national devotion, the private and narrow interests that human beings pursue in the ordinary course of their affairs is drawn into perspective when a larger cause suddenly presses the moment. While this often occurs as a confrontation with an external threat, it is not necessarily a military crisis that can stir the spirit of a nation. A connection to one's nation and the people and culture that the idea of the nation symbolizes can manifest in a number of ways, whether it is in a collective effort to improve the social fabric, to engage in a challenging struggle, or to prosecute a war in defense of one's land and ideals, the nation can serve as a point of unity and strength urging a people onward to meet the challenge at hand. Nationalism so conceived, or rather, expressed, places the interest of the whole above the many and conflicting interests of partisans, and the ego defers to the needs and aspirations of the *patria* (fatherland) or the motherland.

That said, nationalism also contains a potentially destructive force. Authoritarianism, chauvinism, imperialism, xenophobia, and even racism and fascism can be blended with a more aggressive manifestation of nationalism. The attachments of a people to their homeland and their culture can be manipulated into a sense of superiority over aliens, or into a defensive paranoia anxious over the preservation of the purity of the folk. Patriotism, which in its more positive expressions can stir a sense of pride of place and affection for country and one's fellow citizens, when warped by ambition or a zealous triumphalism can indeed be a "refuge for scoundrels" (as Samuel Johnson is reported to have said). Both Franklin Roosevelt and Adolf Hitler were ardently devoted to their respective nations, and in that comparison, a clarifying contrast reveals the stark differences between the various ways in which nationalism can affect those who live and die by it and the world in which they act.

Related Entry
ideology

Suggested Reading
Hobsbawm, Eric J. *Nations and Nationalism since 1780: Programme, Myth, Reality,* 2d ed. New York: Cambridge Univ. Press, 1992.
Hutchinson, John, and Anthony D. Smith. *Nationalism: A Reader.* New York: Oxford Univ. Press, 1994.
Smith, Anthony D. *Nationalism: Theory, Ideology, History.* New York: Polity, 2002.

natural law

Natural law in the classic and Medieval tradition of political theory represents a set of objective, universal principles, values, procedures and moral standards that govern the actions and institutions of all human beings. Natural law in this sense is the absolute measure of all human law and the only true ground of justice. There are innumerable kinds of human law, but the justice of these diverse enactments and practices can be discerned with an intelligent appeal to the natural law. The concept is clearly evident as early as Sophocles's *Antigone* (442 BC) in the affirmation of a higher law that governs even the gods, and it is compatible with the similar position taken by both Plato and Aristotle (and presumably Socrates) that there are transcendent principles that do govern the moral and political actions of all human beings. Aristotle specifically speaks of *dikaiosyne physis,* meaning the justice of nature (or the moral principles of nature) and is thus closely associated with the notion of a natural law. With the Stoic philosophers, and especially Cicero (106 BC–43 BC), natural law (*jus naturalis*) is further shaped and defined. Natural law, for Cicero, is nothing less than "right reason;" thus every human being holds the capacity to discover the moral principles that guide the actions of all human beings toward the right kind of living through the ability of their own intellect.

Natural law continued to influence the development of political and moral principles in the Middle Ages. The most important Medieval commentator on natural law is St. Thomas Aquinas (1225–1274), who understood the natural law to be that part of the eternal law of God that is accessible to human reason. Following Cicero (who he referred to as "Tully"), Aquinas identified natural law with the rational faculty. Through reason the moral principles of nature can be known and then applied. However, he added that the natural principles of morality were also related to his notion of *synderesis,* or a natural inclination to do the good inherent in all human beings. Thus the "first precept of the law of nature," for St. Thomas Aquinas, which is to do good and shun evil, is consonant with both "right reason" and with our truly natural disposition. For Aquinas, rational natural law is wholly compatible with the revealed divine law, hence the natural law discovered by reason through philosophy and announced by God through revelation flow from the same source, the eternal law that governs the entire breadth of creation.

For centuries natural law was accepted as a real, objective and universal standard for the human polity and its juridical affairs. With the emergence of modernity, the notion of natural law underwent modification and ultimately attempts at refutation. Hugo Grotius, while still embracing the concept of natural law, attempted to emphasize its rationalistic properties but detach it from reliance on the divine law of St. Thomas Aquinas. Thomas Hobbes,

more than any political theorist, demonstrates the internal conflict over the conceptual structure of natural law. Hobbes understands natural law in two ways. First, he adopts a more scientific understanding of the natural law, that is to say, the "laws of nature" that explain the operation of the world, the repeatable patterns within nature that reveal a predictable tendency in things. This notion of natural law is purely descriptive, and closer to the "laws of nature" posited by natural science. Second, Hobbes still speaks of the natural law in moral terms, attaching it to reason and even refers to it as generated by divine command. The laws of nature that he specifies are in fact moral principles, and evince at least a partial debt to his forerunners.

With John Locke, the law of nature is both rational and moral. He is much clearer on this point than Hobbes, there being in his estimation a moral law of nature that governs the conduct of all human beings whether in nature or society. Locke's theory of natural law, while regarded as a modern conception, still exhibits a strong debt to the Thomistic view that had ostensibly been rejected by Grotius and Hobbes. But the influence of St. Thomas Aquinas, whether direct, indirect, or absent in Locke, clearly was sustained through the natural law theories of the Salamanca Thomists who preserved the Stoic-Medieval lineage through the Renaissance and into the early decades of modernity. Moreover, even in the eighteenth century, the great English jurist William Blackstone affirmed that the natural law is "coeval with" all of humankind and promulgated by God himself. The Declaration of Independence speaks of the laws of nature and Nature's God, thus reemphasizing the foundational connection between the universal moral law of nature and what Cicero once called the "very Mind of God." It is only in the nineteenth century that the notion of the law of nature was either rejected out of hand or modified to solely mean the scientific laws descriptive of the hidden mechanisms of the material universe rather than prescriptive of the inner conscience of the human soul. But even the utilitarians, who rejected outright the existence of natural law, could not quite escape objective foundations. Jeremy Bentham grounds human behavior in a universal natural condition (pain and pleasure), and concedes that all of our actions are governed by these two states of mind. Bentham rejects natural law as "non-sense on stilts," but only as conceived as a transcendent principle. There still remains a natural ground for the measure and application of ethical values.

Natural law has historically been inextricably intertwined with a notion of natural rights, in spite of Hobbes's efforts to sever their connection. The very term *ius,* from the Latin, can mean not only justice, but also both right and law. *Lex* is also a Latin root for modern law, but it bears a different connotation that has more to do with legitimacy of the actions and enactments of rulers than the objective moral law. Hence the foundation of natural right is the natural law. In other words, natural right, according the classical and Medieval tradition of natural law, is essentially the ground of human dignity as shaped by the natural and divine law of God. We bear rights because of our status as creatures of God, and thus it is in this fact that we possess a degree of dignity on the one hand and moral obligation on the other. As political theory moved into modernity, natural rights increasingly were considered as fundamental and inalienable claims protecting individual liberties against the power of the sovereign. The emphasis shifted to the inherent and irrevocable rights (such as life, liberty, property) of the human agent perceived as the sacrosanct limits to state power. This notion does not, however, sever itself from the deeper principle of natural law but only shifts the emphasis away from the community of equal souls sharing equal moral obligations to each other (classical and Medieval theory) and to the specific claims of the individual against the encroaching power of the modern state. These are not incompatible as Hobbes tried (and failed) to argue, but rather different facets of

the principle that there remains a translegal and transpolitical standard for both the moral obligations of persons and the legitimate authority of political bodies.

In the nineteenth and through most of the twentieth century, natural law lost its compelling influence in both political and legal thought, but in recent years scholars have begun to reconsider its validity as a concept and its benefits as a directive influence in society. Thinkers as diverse as John Finnis and Ronald Dworkin have challenged the assumptions of legal positivism and recommended a return to a naturalist, objective and hence moral ground for the continuing development of rational law. While natural law theory is not likely to become the dominant voice in legal theory any time soon, it is again being taken seriously by a small but growing number of political theorists.

Related Entries
Aquinas, Thomas; Grotius, Hugo; Hobbes, Thomas; Locke, John; Suárez, Francisco

Suggested Reading
Finnis, John. *Natural Law and Natural Rights.* New York: Oxford Univ. Press, 1980.
McLean, Edward. *Common Truths: New Perspectives on Natural Law.* Wilmington, DE.: ISI Books, 2000.
Sigmund, Paul E. *Natural Law in Political Thought.* 1971; repr. Lanham, MD: Univ. Press America, 1982.

negative and positive liberty

In Isaiah Berlin's 1958 essay, "Two Concepts of Liberty," a distinction is drawn between what is deemed "negative liberty" and "positive liberty." The first, negative liberty, is a notion of freedom framed in terms of the latitude of individual autonomy. Negative liberty is a function of one's ability to act with minimal interference from the state or other individuals or groups within society. Both the liberty of individuals and groups can be understood in this sense. As Berlin defined it, liberty in the "negative sense is involved in the answer to the question 'What is the area within which the subject—a person or group of persons—is or should be left to do or be what he is able to do or be, without interference by other persons?" As Berlin further observed,

> I am normally said to be free to the degree to which no man or body of men interferes with my activity. Political liberty in this sense is simply the area within which a man can act unobstructed by others. If I am prevented by others from doing what I could otherwise do, I am to that degree unfree.

Berlin's notion of negative liberty, which he himself associated with "such libertarians as Locke and J.S. Mill in England, and Constant and Tocqueville in France," is reminiscent of the Hobbesian definition of liberty as "the absence of impediment," or "the absence of opposition," a conception of individual autonomy that is frequently identified with the classical liberal approach to the relationship between individual and community. As Berlin explained, "there ought to exist a certain minimum area of personal freedom which must on no account be violated." This type of liberty is often seen in conflict with the pursuit of equality, for the only way to establish a more egalitarian society through the actions of the state requires an involuntary contraction of a person's individual liberty. Moreover, we cannot justify the pursuit of one ideal, such as justice or equality, for the sake of liberty, for according to Berlin this is to confuse disparate values. "Everything is what it is: liberty is liberty, not equality or fairness or justice or culture, or human happiness or a quiet conscience." Hence Berlin found unpersuasive the view that the overall liberties of individuals can be somehow enhanced through attempts to establish the reality of other values; a more egalitarian society will not improve freedom, it might accomplish other goals, but it can only be won at the expense of the basic liberty of individuals and groups.

Positive liberty is, for Berlin, couched in a different terminology, promoting a "freedom to" in contrast to the "freedom from" intrusion that characterizes negative liberty. It is defined specifically by Berlin as the "wish of the individual to be his own master." This in itself is not so very far from negative liberty, but it is a self-mastery that requires an appeal to an abstract notion of a "higher self," a concept that Berlin finds unreliable at best and at the worst potentially dangerous. This higher self is associated with a "true self," a self that affirms a higher freedom in line with a particular vision of society. The quest for the higher, true self, according to Berlin, justifies social and political coercion to direct individuals toward self-realization, and thus toward a more just community for all that embraces a superior kind of freedom, not the negative freedom that is associated with the simple absence of opposition. In the worst possible case, a well-intentioned paternalism that "knows better than us" will impose policies and manipulate behaviors that will redefine our humanity according to some remote ideal. Hence idealistic "social reformers" who understand our true nature and only what is best for us unintentionally precipitate through social engineering a totalitarian nightmare.

> [T]o manipulate men, to propel them towards goals which [the] social reformer [sees]...is to deny their human essence, to treat them as objects without wills of their own and therefore degrade them.

Such reformist visions that aim at changing human nature so that a higher nature and thus an "authentic" freedom can be constructed are bound to produce the opposite of what they intend, which is the "very antithesis of freedom." Epictetus, Berlin mused, may "feel freer" than his master, but he remains a slave all the same. "Quiet conscience" may be a legitimate goal of humankind, as are many other values such as equality, justice, ascetic denial, and universal love. But we are again reminded by Berlin that these are not liberty, and an ideology that claims to combine these ideals into a notion of a higher and truer freedom commits the error of redefining freedom into nonfreedom.

A 1979 essay by Charles Taylor provides perhaps the most substantive response to Berlin's influential analysis. While Taylor acknowledged the value of liberty conceived along these lines (negative and positive), he took issue with the manner in which Berlin tended to focus on the extremes, a focus that in Taylor's mind leads to an inaccurate caricature of both concepts. Yes, Taylor concedes, positive liberty taken to its extreme is potentially dangerous, but it is an "absurd caricature" to merely think of positive liberty as a possibility *only* at the extreme. Positive liberty, according to Taylor, need not result in statist social engineering or totalitarianism, but rather, actually includes a wide range of political traditions, including the ancient and viable ideal of civic republicanism. Moreover, negative liberty is equally caricatured by Berlin, depicting it solely in its "tough-minded version going back to Hobbes [and Bentham]...which sees freedom simply as the absence of external physical or legal obstacles." Taylor does not reject the distinction between negative and positive liberty; he only rejects drawing a polarized dichotomy between the two based on exaggerated degrees of each. Additionally, Taylor proposes that we can think of freedom in terms not fixed on the negative-positive distinction, but also with regard to what he calls concepts of "exercise" and "opportunity." The former is defined as that kind of freedom that "involves essentially the exercising of control over one's life," whereas the latter conceives a type of liberty "where being free is a matter of what we can do, of what is open to us, whether or not we do anything to exercise these options." Positive freedom is grounded in the exercise concept, and is thus concerned with a notion of self-direction that allows for a degree of self-realization that separates human potential from simple opportunity. Opportunities might be multiplied under a strictly negative conception of freedom, but is every opportunity to be pursued, is every want to be indulged? An exercise concept of freedom, in Taylor's estimation, relies on a free agent who will discriminate between choices, and who will seek to realize the self rather than gratify any set of wants. For Taylor, the exercise concept legitimizes that aspect of positive liberty that seeks a qualitatively superior freedom and not a freedom to follow the impulses of our immediate wants, to "do as one lists" in the language of the early modern thinkers.

There are goals and purposes in our lives that help us define who we are, and this requires a distinction between different kinds of activity. There is, according to Taylor, a higher senses of self that cannot be served by the negative conception (opportunity concept) of liberty alone. Not all wants are valuable, and indeed, it is not the case that every subject knows his true wants all the time. Berlin found this position untenable, inviting paternalism and coercive social engineering. But Taylor held that this is also a reality, that human beings can be both deceived as to the degree of freedom they really enjoy as well as to which goods and activities substantively advance their higher purposes. "Freedom is no longer," Taylor observed,

> just the absence of external obstacle *tout court*, but the absence of external obstacle to significant action, to what is important to man. There are discriminations to be made; some are utterly trivial. About many, there is of course controversy. But what the judgment turns on is some sense of what is significant for human life.

Negative liberty alone does not recognize that we can be "hemmed in" by internal impediments that inhibit our motivation to do more than simply pursue our appetites, resulting in an "impoverished freedom." As Taylor concludes,

> [F]reedom now involves my being able to recognize adequately my more important purposes, and my being able to overcome or at least neutralize my motivational fetters, as well as my way being free of external obstacles.

The dialogue examining the nature of freedom in positive and negative terms continues.

Readers are encouraged to seek out commentary by other scholars on this issue, particularly Gerald MacCallum (1967), arguing against Berlin's dichotomy and asserting that there is really only one fundamental concept of freedom variously interpreted. Freedom involves both the ability to "do" certain things (which is the basic claim of Berlin's negative freedom) and "become" certain things (which is the concern of those who adhere to "positive" freedom) More recently, John Christman (1991), while rejecting the viability of negative liberty as endorsed by Berlin, has attempted to recast positive freedom in light of Berlin's criticisms. Positive liberty, for Christman, is really about how our desires emerge; whether or not they are formed and pursued rationally or are the effects of social and cultural pressures, ignorance, or direct manipulation and coercion. The actual content of desire is not as significant as the way in which those desires are formed. In this way, Christman believes we can avoid the dangers that Berlin feared, that is, the potential threat against freedom that stems from the assertion that there is only one solution to achieving the true self, only one way toward a noble society. There are nobler ideals, but they must be discerned and embraced in multiple ways by free agents not subject to manipulation or pressure from external force.

In the final analysis, both conceptions of freedom are beneficial to students of political inquiry, offering a basic vocabulary in which to consider the basic elements of a free society from the essential nature of a free agent. Whether or not the debate over the nature of true liberty is resolved is less important than the continued examination of the important political question, "what does it mean to be free?" And, perhaps even more crucially, "why is freedom central to political life?"

Related Entries
equality; freedom; justice; liberalism

Suggested Reading
Berlin, Isaiah. *Four Essays on Liberty*. New York: Oxford Univ. Press, 1969.

Goodin, Robert E., and Philip Pettit, eds. *Contemporary Political Philosophy: An Anthology,* 2d ed. Malden, MA: Blackwell 2006.
Ryan, Alan. *The Idea of Freedom.* New York: Oxford Univ. Press, 1979.

neo-Marxism

As early Marxism became more doctrinaire and less dialectical during the first two decades of the twentieth century, and in particular, as the Soviet Union exhibited repressive elements little different from the Czarist past (and in some cases, worse), a number of scholars in the West sympathetic to the basic principles of Marx's philosophical foundations began to construct a more critical, less doctrinaire socialist analysis. Loosely described as "neo-Marxist," these authors—typified by such thinkers as Antonio Gramsci, the intellectuals of the critical Frankfurt School, Jürgen Habermas (although he defies accurate description with any label), Erich Fromm, and Herbert Marcuse—based much of their social interpretation on Marx (with special emphasis on his early, more humanistic writings) while weaving other, non-Marxian ideas into their general worldview. Along with Marx, the neo-Marxists incorporated ideas and analytical approaches from Hegel, Nietzsche, Weber, Freud, pragmatism, and existentialism, among others. In so doing, neo-Marxian authors remained committed to the basic principles of analysis established by Marx, such as alienation, exploitation, class consciousness, and revolutionary action, but they resisted the tendency to ossify these concepts into a rigid, systematic, and closed ideological system. By incorporating other types of analysis and schools of thought, neo-Marxism retains its emancipatory vision while rejecting the more "vulgar" elements of ideological, "scientific" Marxism as adopted by figures such as Lenin and Mao. In this way, neo-Marxism is an attempt to detach itself from the repressive methods of Soviet socialism as well as from the uncritical guerilla Marxism of its Maoist variant, and restore Marxian analysis to its initial position as a branch of theoretical inquiry. For this reason, neo-Marxist critique is more likely to remain an academic hermeneutic than an activist movement, owing primarily to its disaffection from the image of the Marxian revolutionary associated with Bolshevism and its imitators.

Related Entries
communism; Marx, Karl; socialism

Suggested Reading

Gorman, Robert A. *Neomarxism: The Meaning of Modern Radicalism.* Westport, CT: Greenwood Press, 1982.

Kolakowsi, Leszek. *The Breakdown,* vol. 3 of *Main Currents of Marxism,* trans. P.S. Falla. New York: Oxford Univ. Press, 1981.

Marcuse, Herbert. *Essay on Liberation.* Boston: Beacon Press, 1968.

Warren, Scott. *The Emergence of Dialectical Theory.* Chicago: Univ. Chicago Press, 1984.

neo-positivism—*See* logical positivism

neo-Thomism (neo-Scholasticism)

During the nineteenth century, a renewed interest in the writings of St. Thomas Aquinas drew the attention of a number of Catholic thinkers (beginning with Italian scholars but spreading to other parts of Europe and even to Asia) interested in applying the general principles of his philosophical legacy—pared of its more Medieval components—to modern questions. In 1879, with his papal encyclical *Aeterni Patris,* Pope Leo XIII affirmed the reinvigoration of Catholic social teaching through a reemphasis of basic Thomistic principles regarding the nature of law (and the relationship between higher law and civil law), virtue, political association, and the human person. Pope Leo XIII regarded both capitalism and communism critically, advocating a middle way to avoid their excesses. By mining the more philosophically enriching ideas of classical and Thomistic theory, a more human and compassionate world can be shaped to serve the dignity of the person, rather than promote the many interests that are asserted through worldly power.

In the twentieth century, thinkers such as Jacques Maritain, Étienne Gilson, and Emmanuel Mounier, along with Pope John XXIII and Pope John Paul II, further expanded the neo-Thomist critique of modernity that was initiated in the previous century. Modern philosophy, and thus modern political thought, can be elevated by a reconsideration of Thomistic principles such as natural law, the reality of the soul, and the immaterial basis of all human dignity and, in so doing, pushed beyond the narrow confines of materialism and historicism. In the case of thinkers such as Maritain and Pope John Paul II, elements of phenomenology and existentialism are incorporated into the essentialist approach of Thomism. In this way, the neo-Thomist restores the Thomistic foundationalist base of analysis while providing a critical methodological framework more sympathetic to modern readers who are inclined to think of social and political life in more contingent terms. Hence the neo-Thomists provide an alternative to a number of competing modern theories, one that reaffirms the quest for absolutes while recognizing the existential contingencies faced by humanity influenced by the strains and stresses of modern society.

Above all, neo-Thomism embraces the infinite value of the human person, and as such, rejects both the dehumanizing tendencies of certain kinds of collectivism as well as theories that conceive of the individual in atomized, materialist, and hedonistic terms. The natural law serves the good of humankind, and in order to fully comprehend what this means, the neo-Thomists regard as critical and central the restoration of the soul in modern political thought. Materialism, whether collectivist or individualist, is both insufficient in providing the best analysis of the human condition and, as such, doomed to fail in its attempts to provide systematic prescriptions for a better political life. Only in beginning with the soul, as did the classic theorists and the Scholastics, can we begin to fashion our political world to serve not only human freedom, but to also affirm humanity oriented toward the good.

Related Entries

Aquinas, Thomas; Maritain, Jacques

Suggested Reading

Cessario, Romanus. *A Short History of Thomism.* Washington, DC: Catholic Univ. of America Press, 2005.

Hittinger, John P. *Liberty, Wisdom, and Grace: Thomism and Democratic Political Theory.* Lanham, MD: Lexington Books, 2002.

Kerr, Fergus. *After Aquinas: Versions of Thomism.* Oxford: Blackwell, 2002.

Niebuhr, Reinhold (1892–1971)

As with his Catholic contemporary, Jacques Maritain, Protestant theologian Reinhold Niebuhr's political thought begins and ends with his Christian faith. Referring to himself as a "Christian realist," Niebuhr believed that the spiritual values of Christianity could supply the moral deficiencies attendant upon the hyper-rationalism of the twentieth century. Like Maritain, Niebuhr adopted the view that reason and faith are more compatible than conflictual, but he was convinced that reason alone could lead to knowledge without purpose, a meaninglessness that can be corrected by the values of religion. At best reason can preserve us or at worst lead us to nothingness, but it is in the combination of reason and spiritual faith that we can affirm a transcendent self.

Politically, Niebuhr drew his attention to the problem of finding a suitable moral ethic within the tumultuous dynamics of the human community. Niebuhr observed that only individuals are capable of moral action; it is in the group that we begin to fall away from our ethical values and principles. This is not to say that individuals are without their own corruptible aspects—as a Christian Niebuhr well understood the problem of sin. But it is in the group that immorality inevitably gains the advantage over our better selves. Immoral action increases in direct correlation to the size of a given group—the larger the crowd, the higher the odds for immoral conduct. The moral "children of light" tend to be overshadowed by the selfish, grasping "children of darkness" as the groups become crowds and crowds the masses; collective pride, irrationality, and blind loyalty to the group replace the liberal and tolerant altruism of individual agents. Niebuhr did not regard politics as hopeless, but he did see it as limited. Without the consistent reminder of the need to renew moral discourse within a democracy, the impulses of the egoistic crowd will destroy the purpose of free government by the sheer force of its own aggressive will.

For Niebuhr, this requires a return to the Christian principle of *agape,* the selfless love of all human beings. While it is a personal state that only individuals can achieve, it is also the rudimentary ingredient of an ethic that will challenge the selfishness of the ego in the crowd. *Agape* is the transcendent principle upon which we can establish an authentic justice that is more than the justice of simple reason, but one that is both rational and spiritual.

Niebuhr, in spite of an ardent distrust of the crowd, was far from an individualist. The community is that realm wherein the individual can attain the height of her or his promise. The community is a given for us, and to a large extent we are dependent on it for our very identity. We are part of the social, or collective, and we are thus only able to truly stimulate our individual vitality through our commitment to the community as such.

Niebuhr accepted democracy as the most compatible with his vision of a just community defined by its commitment to *agape,* but he was less optimistic about it than Maritain. Materialism, self-interest, and vanity all plague modern societies, and especially democratic ones. Love is the highest and best norm for humankind, but the power of selfish love, what St. Augustine called *amor sui,* will always warp our higher aspirations and pervert our visions of ourselves. Thus Niebuhr defined his Christian realism: the belief in the basic principles established in the Gospel tempered by the shortcomings of democratic society. This project is an ancient one, that is, the desire to strike a balance between the highest ideals that stem from human hope and the many frustrations felt when faced with the irrational and blind pressures of mass society. As a Christian thinker, Niebuhr had to find faith and hope in society; as a realist he had to remind himself of the dangers of hope without judgment. Perhaps the best way to summarize and conclude Niebuhr's modern Augustinianism is through his own statement regarding the nature of and need for democracy, "Man's capacity for justice makes democracy possible; but man's inclination to injustice makes democracy necessary."

Related Entry
Maritain, Jacques

Suggested Reading

Niebuhr, Reinhold. *The Children of Light and the Children of Darkness*. New York: Scribner's, 1972.

Niebuhr, Reinhold. *Moral Man and Immoral Society*, with an introduction by Langdon B. Gilkey. Louisville: Westminster John Knox Press, 2001.

Nietzsche, Friedrich (1844–1900)

Perhaps the most volatile philosopher of his or any age, Friedrich Nietzsche was one of the most influential of the thinkers who shaped the intellectual terrain of the past century. Known for his provocative (some would say blasphemous) challenge to the entire religious, philosophical, political, and cultural traditions of the West, Nietzsche is received either as the prophet of a new dawn for humanity or as a shrill and self-indulgent madman. Either way, Nietzsche stimulates discussion, and his writings at their best provide revealing insights often overlooked by previous thinkers. Adored or despised, Nietzsche must be addressed, if not to embrace his sweeping criticisms at least to acknowledge their sheer power and, for some, allure.

Lack of space prevents a thorough review of his general philosophical ideas. Our concentration here is upon his contribution to the dialogue that is political theory. This is not because Nietzsche is necessarily more profound or complex than other great thinkers, but only due to the unfamiliarity and idiosyncratic quality of his claims. That said, none of Nietzsche's ideas are fully understood without some basic foreknowledge of his larger project. Thus we will summarize (hoping to avoid bowdlerizing) certain key elements that emerged in Nietzsche's brief career. Those elements that will be mentioned here (and incompletely) are the teaching of the Eternal Return of the Same (or the Eternal Recurrence), the Overman (*übermensch*, also translated as Superman), the "transvaluation" of all values," the "death" of God, will to power, perspectivism, and the fundamental irrationality that underlies our culture at every level, even our ostensibly more rational ideas and refined moral principles. These are not the only important principles in Nietzsche, but they are those that will speak most directly to his views on politics.

Nietzsche's critique of Western culture in all its manifestations rests on his assertion that all values and truths are at root expressions of life instincts. There are no eternal verities, no Platonic Forms or Divine Commandments, only the manifestation of our instincts masked as rational concepts or moral principles. It is in a study of the irrational and emotive that we can come to understand this; only by reexamining the relationship between the "Dionysian frenzy" and the "Apollonian balance" will we be able to more honestly understand the spring of our art and the aspirations that it conveys. Life at its barest is simply exertion of instinct, a fact for Nietzsche that is hidden by our own refinements and our own pretensions and self-induced delusions. Once we realize the flux behind the order that we ourselves impose upon things, we can more candidly confront our hopes and our potential to see them to their realization. In his *On the Genealogy of Morals,* Nietzsche opens with the statement that "we are unknown to ourselves, we men of knowledge," and hopes to explore the inward prerational, even irrational, core of our humanity to reveal what is behind the façade of our ideals and conceits. For Nietzsche, too few have admitted that our rationality and our ethical attitudes are the accretions of nonrational drives, and it is his hope that he will uncover the animate nature behind the form and structure of our conceptual and cultural frameworks. There is nothing civilized that is not somehow the result of the instinctive drives of irrationality.

Given this, Nietzsche claims that all truths are simply the certainties meaningful to particular perspectives. Objectivism is simply another mask, all truth is produced by a point of view specific within a cultural context, there is no absolute or transcendent truth that exists independently of our own desires, the ornamentation placed around such certainties notwithstanding. Ultimately, truth is not discerned by detached reason, or even discovered through philosophic dialogue, but rather, our truths are willed; it is in the will that truth finds relevance for any given culture within its own age.

Will is the key to all culture and values in Nietzsche's philosophy. Indeed, will is at bottom the essence (a term that would cause Nietzsche himself to balk) of life. All life is "will to power," and values and certainties are but extensions of life. Hence Nietzsche has been described as subscribing to a kind of *lebensphilosophie*, that is, a philosophy of life that focuses on the sheer energy of life as the source of our knowledge, principles, and any wisdom that we might chance upon in our drive to live. Power in Nietzsche, as commentators have remarked, can mean the drive to dominate— thus depicting life as a contest for supremacy and a will to exceed others. For some readers, this can only lead to unpleasant conclusions if the logic of such an idea is fully developed. However, other commentators recognize that the will to power also means the will to the affirmation of life in the highest possible degree, hence domination is not in itself a goal, but only a consequence of the dynamic that produces higher types, or those few who realize this affirmation. One seeks to affirm life; domination is not a goal, but only the by-product, if you will, of a state wherein one has exerted the will in extraordinary ways. Fundamentally will to power is a psychological instinct, a drive to

live on one's own terms that is natural to all life. However, one cannot stop there, for will to power is also expressed in groups as well as in individuals, and in both the higher type as well as the lower type. Everything is somehow a result of the will, even submission is nothing more than a will to submit, ignoble in Nietzsche's estimation, but a type of will all the same.

Life is will to power; hence all that is deemed beautiful, valuable and moral are so regarded owing to the intent of the will. Even our religious beliefs are the product of a certain will for Nietzsche, and reflect the inward drive of those who adhere to it. The ancient pagans are admired by Nietzsche for the pure will to power exerted through their customs, values, rituals, and articles of faith. As with Machiavelli and Rousseau before him, Nietzsche casts a critical eye toward Christianity. But with Machiavelli and Rousseau, Christianity is challenged for its incompatibility (and in some cases hostility) toward the uses of worldly power and the primacy of civil life. Nietzsche's critique is, on the other hand, contemptuous. Christianity, in Nietzsche's condemnation, promotes the ethic of the slave and the herd; indeed, it is in his mind a "slave revolt" against all that is noble, cheerful, and free. In the end Christianity is but "Platonism for the masses," an expression of the will to power of the weak against the strong, marked by resentment and illusory devotion. Christianity, along with the rationalism that characterizes philosophy since Socrates (whose value system supersedes the Dionysian-Apollonian synthesis), has corrupted a once strong European culture, leading to decadence and pettiness. In Nietzsche's assessment, Europe must return to a philosophy of life, not a Christian-Platonist search for transcendent answers but rather a devotion to all that is earthly and bold.

Along these lines, Nietzsche perceives the nadir of Judeo-Christian ethics and theology in what he refers to as the "death of God," perhaps the one concept for which Nietzsche is known to the general public (along with the catchy epigram from *Twilight of the Idols,* often quoted even in the movies, "that which does not kill me makes me stronger."). Nietzsche does not mean that God as a being once lived and is now dead, but rather, that God as a life-affirming principle no longer serves the exertion of a strong vigorous will and the culture that it seeks. All absolutes are wiped away, for Nietzsche, exposing the emptiness of reality and the illusion of the divine. But Nietzsche does not celebrate this momentous event—an event that we have brought upon ourselves—for he recognizes the hard significance of such a reality. If God is dead, as Nietzsche asserts, then we are cut adrift in the cold and empty gulf of darkened space. There is no Truth to guide us or Providence to steer us toward meaning and salvation, but rather the abyss and our own shuddering as we hang over the precipice. For Nietzsche God is "dead," but the consequences of such a cultural event are shattering. Either we remain shattered, or we affirm our will to new values and ideals and aspirations that in Nietzsche's eyes can take us still higher. We are "spinning through space with "no up or down;" thus if we are to affirm ourselves anew, we must "seek new tablets," new concepts of reality and new values that will reorient us toward a new brighter joy, absent the old prejudices and the image of God behind them, but this is a dangerous undertaking and "crossing over."

All values are thus to be "transvalued." The old distinction between "good and evil" rested on the resentment of the weak and decadent against the superior types, and was advanced by the spirit of Platonism and Christianity, the dual foundations of Western civilization, and the chief corrupting influences in contributing to its decay. What is needed now are new values, values that affirm life while rejecting self-abnegation, values that celebrate the song and dance of Dionysus and not the cool rationalism of Socrates and Plato, values true to the earth and indifferent to otherworldly aspirations and hopes, values that seek distance from the mercenary, the comfortable, the priest, and the democrat. These values are epitomized in the rejection of the "human all-too-human" and in the truth of the earth, the "Overman."

The Overman is what Nietzsche refers to as the "highest hope," as distinct from man as man is to the ape, or even "the worm." This is more than a "higher type," the leaders and artists of our times; it is a new avatar of will to power and a way of being beyond humanity itself, and as indifferent to our humanity and the questions that are raised by our existence as we are indifferent to what we regard as the lowest of life forms. This is more than a "master race" (as one can easily be tempted to surmise)—it is a state of being, far removed from us, and yet our only real hope now that the old tablets and their god have been declared invalid. The Overman is heralded by higher types, but exceeds them still, and in ways that diminish even the best among us today. It is the Overman who is capable of saying "yes" to the earth, to laugh when confronting the abyss, to know the deepest secrets of our world without fear or nausea.

This last secret—what Nietzsche suffers as the most unutterable and yet the most truthful of all—is the Eternal Return of the Same (or Eternal Recurrence). This is actually a freshly recast exposition of the ancient, pre-Christian cycle of being, a principle that all that there is fades and then returns just as it was, or rather, just as it is eternally. Every moment of the world and thus every part of our lives has happened before and will happen endlessly again. For Nietzsche's Zarathustra (*Thus Spake Zarathustra*) this is the lesson that he cannot confront, that he cannot bear to pronounce and thus relies on his animal companions (the eagle who represents the Overman and the snake who, in its uroboric shape, represents the Eternal Return) to fully and finally announce. This notion induces a state of paralyzing nausea in Zarathustra, as he realizes that not only will the great and brilliant return eternally, but, equally so, will the small and petty return eternally. It is this latter prospect that forces Zarathustra to withhold his final teaching, but once it is sung by the animals, he becomes resigned to its depth and accepts it in all its contours.

Now what has this to do with politics? Nietzsche's philosophy seems to be aimed at cultural, social, moral, even ontological and epistemological questions more than political ones, but in the final analysis, the aforementioned concepts, and others that remain unexamined here, hold considerable implications for political ideas as well as for intellectual and political movements. The very idea of the ''death of God'' by itself suggests a type of political ethic completely fixated upon a new kind of worldly attitude, and his general low opinion of "the herd" and the "crowd" speaks for itself. Nietzsche regarded modern politics, dominated by democrats and socialists, liberals and philanthropists, English utilitarians and Continental Cartesians to be a politics of the *untermensch,* or the ''under human'' (lesser human) or lower type, a politics that seeks comfort, safety, self-control, and devotion rather than danger, risk, frenzy, and iconoclastic assertion—the latter characteristics among those associated with higher types and those who really affirm life, and not simply accept their lot in it. Nietzsche thus responded to the politics of his day—or at least what was taken to be its most progressive movements, with contempt. Nietzsche believed that the only good use for politics—for the state itself—was the production of high culture and the promotion of new and vigorous ambitions, to cultivate the noble and to placate the base without letting the latter assert itself, through the power of sheer numbers, over the truly noble, who are in Nietzsche's perspective, the only ones who can value what is good. Nietzsche thus embraced a *Grosse Politik* (Great Politics, power politics) that would involve the rule of the true aristocrats, the highest types who point to the Overman, and who are primarily concerned with great achievement. While one can easily conclude that these higher types would be disposed to tyranny (as Plato certainly so concluded), Nietzsche believed that the noble would command the lesser benignly, the truly noble not being concerned with controlling the small, but only with seizing and holding

what is glorious. This is not to be expressed in empire building or in aggressive nationalism, the true will to power exerted by the noble is aimed at the construction of a culture worthy of our participation, and in the end the only reason for the institution of any political establishment. But democracy, liberalism, socialism, and Christianity humble humanity and force an equality that is driven more by resentment rather than a love of justice, ultimately spilling forth egotism, self-contentment, and the governance of the appetites at the expense of greatness. In the end, the noble are not political leaders, or if they are such, they are only as an afterthought. Nor is the Overman a political figure, but rather the cultural and ethical ideal toward which the noblest human can only aspire. The Great Politics in the end compares, not without some irony, to Marxism—as both Marx and Nietzsche foresaw a future wherein politics as we have known it throughout history will fade and be replaced with something new, and something that will reshape human nature itself.

One can easily see how Nietzsche could be appropriated by more pernicious ideologies such as Nazism, and, indeed, the Nazis regarded Nietzsche as an important philosopher and an influence on their movement. Whether or not Nazis actually read Nietzsche, or read him carefully, is another question, but he was embraced within Nazism as a precursor to their own ideals. Much of this is largely unfair to Nietzsche himself, and a good deal of the blame for it has been placed with his sister, Elizabeth Förster-Nietzsche, who admired Mussolini and was infatuated with Hitler. She knew both men and deliberately cultivated a relationship with them, through correspondence with Mussolini and actually meeting Hitler and flattering him by drawing a comparison between the Führer and the Overman. Owing to this association, Nietzsche for a time was regarded as the ideologue of totalitarianism, a proponent of the kind of herd mentality that he himself frequently denounced. More recent Nietzsche scholarship, spearheaded by

Walter Kaufmann in the 1950s and 1960s, offered an alternative to this scandal that is received by many as a corrective to the older misconception, and thus rescuing Nietzsche from his Hitlerian captivity. For the most part, this is a fair and necessary task, for the whole of Nietzsche's philosophy, if read carefully and within context, is in many ways as equally anti-totalitarian as it is antidemocratic. If anything, Nietzsche may be said to have inadvertently promoted a kind of "aristocratic anarchism" through his Great Politics, a politics so ennobled that it no longer needs itself to affirm its inward desires. Nonetheless, while Nietzsche may be exonerated from the efforts of his sister and the usual self-interested interpretations, one cannot but pause with some hesitation when reading Nietzsche's musings over the Blond Beast or the decadence of liberal democracy, or references to himself as the Anti-Christ breaking old tablets and hewing newer more vigorous values worthy of the ancient Pagan warriors. Still more to the point, Nietzsche's admission to an understanding of life, and thus political life, as ultimately reduced to the will is a theme that is central to the fascistic mentality. Indeed, recent criticism has led to a reexamination of the older charge against Nietzsche as a precursor to fascistic impulses. More recently, Steven Aschheim reconsiders Nietzsche's relationship to Nazism and argues, against Kaufmann, that the philosopher does indeed provide a conceptual medium generative of fascistic ideology, however inadvertent or unforeseen. In the final assessment, it is clear that Nietzsche's intent was far from the mass movements of fascism and National Socialism, which would be in Nietzsche's view another variation of small politics, the politics of crowds and herds. However, the connection between Nietzsche and Hitler, while perhaps based on distortion, falsehood, poor schooling, and bad relatives, well illustrates the importance of ideas and, at times, their dangerous consequences, however intentional or inadvertent. Nietzsche is not to be blamed for National Socialism any more than Marx can be blamed for the worst excesses of Stalinism, but the responsibility of the author is considered in the very raising of the question.

Related Entries
existentialism; Foucault, Michel

Suggested Reading

Nietzsche, Friedrich. *Beyond Good and Evil,* trans. Walter Kaufmann. 1966; repr. New York: Vintage Books, 1989.

Nietzsche, Friedrich. *On the Genealogy of Morals,* trans. Walter Kaufmann and R.J. Hollingdale. New York: Vintage Books, 1969.

Nietzsche, Friedrich. *Ecce Homo,* trans. and ed. Walter Kaufmann. New York: Vintage Books, 1969.

Nietzsche, Friedrich. *Thus Spoke Zarathustra: A Book for All and None,* trans. Walter Kaufmann. 1954; repr. New York: Modern Library, 1995.

Nietzsche, Friedrich. *Human, All Too Human,* trans. Marion Faber with Stephen Lehmann, with an introduction by Marion Faber and a new introduction by Arthur C. Danto. Lincoln, NE: Univ. Nebraska Press, 1996.

nonsense on stilts

"Natural rights is simple nonsense: natural and imprescriptible rights, rhetorical nonsense,—nonsense upon stilts," so wrote Jeremy Bentham in his *Anarchical Fallacies,* (an analysis of the French Declaration of Rights written between 1791 and 1795, published in 1816.) Bentham rejected any moral or legal principle incompatible with the doctrine of utility. All values are to be traced back to the expansion of pleasure and the reduction of pain, and their real social utility can only be measured to the extent that this is accomplished across society (the greatest happiness for the greatest number). Natural right is an ambiguous and figurative metaphysical doctrine that, from sheer sentimentality, claims a ground for our values transcendent to simple utility. Rights, Bentham asserts, are in reality the product of positive law, which in turn are nothing more than the commands of the sovereign. There can be no moral principle separate from utility, and there can be no legal principal antecedent to government. Thus to say that a right is natural is to commit oneself to fallacious, nonsensical, and even dangerous reasoning.

Additionally, Bentham argues that the idea of rights as natural is essentially anarchic because it posits a claim to rights by nature as prior to law and thus legitimate authority. If individuals sincerely ground their actions on such claims, law is in danger of becoming subordinate to unrestrained freedom, consequently militating against social order and undermining governmental authority.

"Nonsense on stilts," more generally, refers to faulty or even ludicrous reasoning, an attitude that Bentham assumed in considering any philosophical concept that denied its true utilitarian basis.

Related Entries
Bentham, Jeremy; utilitarianism

Suggested Reading
Bentham, Jeremy. Vol. 2 of *The Works of Jeremy Bentham: Published under the Superintendence of His Executor, John Bowring,* 11 vols. 1843; facs. repr. Edinburgh: Adamant Media Corp., 2005.
Bentham, Jeremy. *Rights, Representation, and Reform: Nonsense upon Stilts and Other Writings on the French Revolution,* ed. Philip Schofield et al. New York: Oxford Univ. Press, 2002.

objectivism—*See* absolutes

ochlocracy
From the Greek, *ochlocratia,* or rule of the mob, is usually associated, as in Polybius, with the "savage and violent rule of the crowd." Ochlocracy is in essence a term employed to depict democratic impulses at their worst. For Polybius, democracy, or rule of the many, while in itself good, contains a flaw within it that, if left unchecked, will decay into the violence of a disorganized mob. This danger can be averted through institutional devices such as the distribution of power and the rule of law.

Warnings against ochlocracy as a deviation from democracy pervade political theory as well as constitutional thought, and continue to remind the advocate of unrestricted direct democracy of the imperfections characteristic of and inherent dangers latent within any pure regime.

Related Entries
anarchism; democracy

Suggested Reading
Polybius, *The Histories,* Vol. III, Books 5–8, trans. R. W. Paton. 1923; repr. Cambridge, MA: Harvard Univ. Press/Loeb Classical Library, 1979.

open-ended distributive principle
"*No social good x should be distributed to men and women who possess some other good y merely because they possess y and without regard to the meaning of x.*" This dictum, conceived by political theorist Michael Walzer in his *Spheres of Justice,* is a shorthand summary of his thesis that the notion of complex equality, while admitting inequality within some spheres of social and cultural activity, disallows the domination of all political, social, and cultural spheres across society as such. That is, while a monopoly of distribution of rewards might apply to certain specific spheres of human endeavor, holding such a monopoly in one sphere does not entitle similar influence in other spheres. Hence, a person who has exceeded others in one sphere (such as the acquisition of wealth or a reputation for artistic skill, for example) would not be entitled to convert that power or influence to another sphere, even if said power or influence is justly earned. Walzer's distinction between monopoly and dominance provides the axis for what he believes to be a more nuanced analysis of the just distribution of social goods within liberal societies.

Related Entries
complex equality; difference principle; Rawls, John; Wilt Chamberlain argument

Suggested Reading
Walzer, Michael. *Spheres of Justice: A Defense of Pluralism and Equality.* New York: Basic Books, 1983.

organicism (Medieval organicism)

Medieval organicism describes the premise of a tangible and close interdependency and mutuality held by political thinkers in the Middle Ages. Rulers and ruled were knit together in a bond of mutual support and obligation that resembled an organic creature, analogous to the human body in both shape and function. If the church was considered to be the Body of Christ within Medieval culture, the polity was a social body, each part depending upon the other for survival, direction, and prosperity.

In his *Policraticus,* twelfth-century political thinker, cleric, and companion of St. Thomas Becket, John of Salisbury, provides perhaps the most succinct account of the organic analogy of state and human body,

> The place of the head in the body of the commonwealth is filled by the prince, who is subject only to God and to those who exercise His office and represent Him on earth, even as in the human body the head is quickened by the soul. The place of the heart is filled by the Senate, from which proceeds initiation of good works and ill. The duties of eyes, ears, and tongue are claimed by the judges and the governors of provinces. Officials and soldiers correspond to the hands. Those who always attend upon the prince are likened to sides. Financial officers may be compared with the stomach and intestines...The husbandmen correspond to the feet, which always cleave to the soil, and need more especially the care and foresight of the head, since while they walk upon the earth doing service with their bodies, they meet the more often with stones and stumbling, and therefore deserve aid and protection, and move forward the weight of the entire body.

Hence for John of Salisbury, every portion of society has its responsibility, and every part depends on the other. The head (prince) while ruling, must serve the good of all in the same way as the mind of an individual would attend upon the whole body with equal care. Hence, while the organicism of thinkers such as John of Salisbury admits to a natural hierarchy, it is one of mutual service, and one that posits a type of rule that, as John of Salisbury himself asserts, is closer to the ministry of the priest than the command of the despot.

Related Entries

Aquinas, Thomas; circle of power; two-swords doctrine

Suggested Reading

John of Salisbury. *Policraticus,* ed. Cary J. Nederman. Cambridge, UK: Univ. Cambridge Books, 1992.

owl of Minerva

In the preface to his *Philosophy of Right,* the German philosopher G. W. F. Hegel (1770–1831), observed that philosophy is a purely speculative enterprise, that it achieves wisdom in reflecting on events as they have already occurred, in the same way as the "owl of Minerva" takes flight at dusk, Minerva being the goddess of wisdom and the Roman equivalent of Athena, and the owl, the goddess's companion, the symbol of wisdom itself. Philosophy analyzes, but it does not act; it prescribes and understands but does not vivify: it does not compel history forward. Rather, philosophers, like Hegel himself, stand at the end of history as it has evolved to any given point, able to see the expanse of all events behind it and to discern the meaning of it all through a wide-angle view of the totality of all that has passed. Hegel draws his preface to a conclusion by musing on the question of what ought to be done to promote the human good. Hegel, whose analysis of the nature of history and the structure of political reality rests on the assumption that "what is rational is actual, and what is actual is rational," (or, "what is rational is real and what is real is rational"), which is also quoted in the preface, asserts that

> One word more about giving instructions as to what the world ought to be. Philosophy in any case always comes on the scene too late to give it. As the thought of the world, it appears only when actuality is already there cut and dried after its process of formation has been completed....When philosophy paints its grey in grey, then has a shape of life grown old. By philosophy's grey in grey it cannot be rejuvenated

but only understood. The Owl of Minerva spreads its wings only with the falling of dusk.

Hence, Hegel punctuates the point that the meaning of world history is only revealed in the culmination of its forces, and philosophy does not itself act upon it but only provides that comprehension necessary for human beings to sort through any sense of it.

This position by Hegel is often referred to as an example of Hegel's conservatism, as well as a tangible indication of a deep fatalism operating within the Hegelian system. However, Hegel's overall philosophy, while at times appearing conservative, is far too expansive to be pinned to one ideology and exhibits perhaps in equal proportions elements of liberalism and even radicalism, depending on one's interpretation. However, the fatalism in the owl of Minerva passage is more difficult to escape, and it stands as a sharp contrast to those voices that reject the notion that the destiny of the human race is foreordained, or beyond the efforts of humanity to influence before the fact. Here Hegel exhibits an *amor fati* reminiscent of the Stoics and anticipatory to Nietzsche.

Finally, Hegel's owl of Minerva is commonly contrasted to Marx's 11th thesis on Feuerbach, wherein Marx argues that true philosophy does act upon the world, rather than merely interpret it. Additionally, one might compare Hegel's sentiment to other philosophers' as well. Socrates, for example, understood philosophy to be a way of life, and thus a prescription for a certain kind of action. Aristotle, while still valuing the contemplative life as the highest life, nonetheless recognized the importance of philosophy as informing practical, namely, political activity. Hence the image of the owl of Minerva, at least as Hegel understood and used it, revolves around an enduring issue in the conversation that is political theory: what is, in truth, the proper relationship between theory and practice, between knowledge of and knowledge for political change.

Related Entries
Hegel, Georg Wilhelm Friedrich; Marx, Karl

Suggested Reading
Hegel, Georg Wilhelm Friedrich. *Hegel's Philosophy of Right,* trans. and ed. T. M. Knox. New York: Oxford Univ. Press, 1977.

P

pagan politics

A concept spawned by the postmodern politics of Jean-François Lyotard, the "pagan" ideal serves as an alternative to what Lyotard calls "totality," or the elimination of heterogeneity and, by extension, dissent. In Lyotard's nomenclature, the "pagan" is identified with multiplicity of voices, with the necessary fragmentation of discourse toward heterogeneity in opposition to homogenizing consensus or objectivist "phrases." In Lyotard, as long as political discourse is differentiated and open to change the pagan ideal is sustained. This includes the opening of innumerable "phrase regimens" (basic vehicles of communication) that encourage the expression of a diverse and ever-expanding array of perspectives. The pagan ideal celebrates a radical pluralism that by its very nature resists normativity in discourse. Once normativity and objective principle are established, the pagan voice is denied, and the loss of possibility in politics endangers just political arrangements.

Lyotard's pagan politics is inflected through an aesthetic sensibility that values multivocality and the perpetual testing of institutions. For some the ideal that Lyotard embraces in the pagan is a liberating moment; for others of a more traditional orientation, Lyotard's singular vocabulary that develops his pagan critique is insurmountably incoherent. But that is, in part, Lyotard's point—for reliance on coherence automatically narrows the variety of possible phrases. It is this concern of Lyotard's that is found within the heart of the postmodern critique.

Related Entry
incredulity toward metanarratives

Suggested Reading

Haber, Honi Fern. *Beyond Postmodern Politics*. New York: Routledge, 1994.

Lyotard, Jean-François. *Just Gaming*, trans. Wlad Godzich. Minneapolis: Univ. Minn. Press, 1985.

Lyotard, Jean-François. *The Postmodern Condition*, trans. Geoff Bennington and Brian Massumi. Minneapolis: Univ. Minn. Press, 1984.

panopticon

A term coined by English utilitarian thinker Jeremy Bentham, "panopticon" (all-seeing) was an innovative design for a new type of prison, itself an outgrowth of Bentham's interest in penal reform. Bentham also referred to his panopticon design as an "Inspection-House" or "the Elaboratory," a prison structure that would enable efficient and effective monitoring and control of prisoners with minimum effort. With the use of a circular structure located around a single tower or guardhouse that in effect is the radial center of the complex, a single guard could observe, or at least give to the prisoners the perception of being constantly observed (what Bentham referred to as the "apparent omnipresence of the inspector"), the entire compound from one station. "The essence" of the panopticon, Bentham claimed, "consists, then, in the centrality of the inspector's situation, combined with the well-known and most effectual contrivances for seeing without being seen." Bentham also saw additional uses for his design, ranging from "guarding the insane" to "employing the idle" along with its uses for penal institutions. The idea is to maintain a constant impression on those being observed of perpetual monitoring of behavior.

While Bentham's model has indeed been applied, especially as a design for prisons, the idea of the panopticon is, for the student of power within modern political communities, a symbol of the virtual omnipresence of the state. Michel Foucault, in particular, has employed the imagery of the panopticon to describe the manner in which the lives of individuals are under constant scrutiny from the anonymous, and indeed, diffused, forces of power within modern societies. For Foucault, the degree of surveillance to which human beings are exposed within our times has in effect produced an expanded panopticon. This panopticon is not one that singles out and scrutinizes a particular group such as legal inmates of an institution but is rather a condition of monitoring that renders each citizen an inmate and thus every individual an object of examination at any given time.

Related Entries

Bentham, Jeremy; carceral society; Foucault, Michel

Suggested Reading

Bentham, Jeremy. *The Panopticon Writings*, ed. Miran Bozovic. London: Verso, 1995.

Foucault, Michel. *The Foucault Reader*, ed. Paul Rabinow. New York: Pantheon Books, 1984.

Pareto optimality (Pareto ophelimity, Pareto efficiency, Pareto preference or preferability)

Conceived by Italian sociologist/economist Vilfredo Pareto (1848–1923), Pareto optimality describes a socioeconomic state or set of conditions wherein no other arrangement can improve the current status quo without harming at least one individual. In other words, the optimal condition for all within a given community is reached when there is no alternative that improves the basic situation in everyone's favor. Should any attempt at improvement militate against the interest of any one individual within the given set, then the Pareto optimal would be violated. Any general improvement must not diminish the status of any one person. If such a condition is reached, it is optimal and, in general, cannot be improved upon. In Pareto's words,

> We will say that the members of a collectivity enjoy *maximum ophelimity* in a certain position when it is impossible to find a way of moving from that position very slightly in such a manner that the ophelimity enjoyed by each of the individuals of that collectivity increases or decreases. That is to say, any small displacement in departing from that position necessarily has the effect of increasing the ophelimity which

certain individuals enjoy, and decreasing that which others enjoy, of being agreeable to some, and disagreeable to others.

Thus Pareto argued that the optimal conditions are met when a given system cannot be improved without deleterious effects to at least one person under that system.

Pareto optimality is primarily associated with economics and game theory, but it does appear in political theory. For example, John Rawls relies on the Pareto optimal as a useful tool in shaping the difference principle in his *Theory of Justice*.

Related Entries
difference principle; game theory; Rawls, John

Suggested Reading
Pareto, Vilfredo. *Manual of Political Economy*. New York: Augustus M. Kelley Publishers, 1906.
Rawls, John. *A Theory of Justice*. 1971; repr. Cambridge, MA: Harvard Univ. Press, 2005; new ed., Cambridge, MA: Harvard Univ. Press, 1999.

Pareto's Law (Pareto Principle, Law of the Vital Few, the 80–20 rule, Juran's Principle)
Pareto's Law, or the 80–20 Rule, describes the proposition that in any given system directed by any particular operation, 80 percent of the effects can be traced to only 20 percent of the causal factors within the universe of discourse. In other words, Pareto's Law holds that most of what happens is caused by a comparatively low number of actors within the populations under examination. The principle is traced to an observation made by elite theorist Vilfredo Pareto, who once observed that 80 percent of the land in Italy was owned and managed by 20 percent of the population. The "law" was actually developed by managerial theorist Joseph Juran, who inspired by Pareto, postulated the 20–80 ratio, arguing that the "vital few" actually direct all operations within society, followed by the "useful many," who represent 80 percent of the population.

Pareto's Law (or Juran's Principle) is familiar to students of economics and managerial

sciences, but given its association with Pareto, there are connections to political and social inquiry. Elite theory, of which Pareto was a principal proponent, informs the notion of the vital few, holding that any given social system, political or nonpolitical, is inevitably governed by an active and talented minority.

Related Entry
circulation of elites

Suggested Reading
Pareto, Vilfredo, "The New Theories of Economics." *Journal of Political Economy* 1897, 5: 485–502.

Paris was well worth a Mass
Attributed to French monarch Henry IV (Henry of Navarre), the phrase "Paris was well worth a Mass" is said to have been uttered by the king after his conversion to Catholicism had secured for him the French throne. Formerly a Huguenot (French Calvinist), Henry is said to have converted to the Catholic faith as a means to secure his title as rightful heir to the Bourbon monarchy. Hence the aforementioned quotation is employed as an example of political cynicism, even one's religious convictions being susceptible to substantive alteration when the object is political power.

Nonetheless, historical records tracing the quotation to a specific episode or utterance cannot be identified, and thus it may be that Henry of Navarre never actually made such a statement. Additionally, while some commentators regard Henry's conversion as an attempt to regain political leverage, others conclude that there was in fact sincerity behind the king's actions. Henry is know to have taken keen interest in theological debates between Catholics and Protestants (especially the debate at Mantes in 1593), resulting, according to some accounts, of a change of heart regarding Catholic beliefs. Thus the phrase "Paris was well worth a Mass" may not be historically accurate. Even so, it is still employed as an example of political expediency extended to the point of a shameless cynicism, regardless of Henry of Navarre's true motivations.

Suggested Reading

Holt, Mack P. *The French Wars of Religion, 1562–1629*. New York: Cambridge Univ. Press, 2005.

Princes, N.M.*Politics and Religion, 1547–1589*. London: Hambledon Press, 1984.

personalism

Personalism is a philosophical, moral, and political framework wherein the human as person is regarded as unique, inviolate, absolutely valuable, and categorically an end in itself. The end of society and the reason for politics is to affirm the person as the only true purpose of the community and to produce an environment wherein free persons, acting on their own will, are able to fulfill their potential. Given this, it is critical to the philosophy of personalism to remember that, while the person is absolutely valuable, the person is not absolute. Personalism is conceived within a theistic worldview, recognizing the person as a creature of God and thus understanding both person and community as given meaning from this transcendent source. Hence the person is not god-like, as in some forms of individualism, but rather, the person's dignity and value stem from the fact of holding the status of creature. The person is in truth an embodied soul and, as such, is more valuable, as Jacques Maritain once stated, than the entire universe of matter. Still, the person cannot be said to be equal to or above God, and in this sense personalism recognizes at once the remarkable singularity of humanity as well as the place of the human race, and thus the human person, within a greater community of souls.

For this reason, personalism, while regarding the person as the end of society, is not a radical individualism. Because we are persons, we are only fulfilled in our relationship with God and with other human beings. To be a person is to be for others and to benefit from the mutuality of this shared personhood. Hence, for the personalist perspective, a person is a fundamentally social and political being, echoing the tradition of Plato, Aristotle, and St. Thomas Aquinas, and adopting the view that the free agency of all persons is somehow guided by a desire toward goodness in service of both self and others. The human person can only be understood in this communal context, one that emphasizes the natural interconnection of human beings as well as the ontological connection to God.

While personalist ideas and attitudes can be traced, as mentioned above, to classical political theory, as a formal school of thought it is usually identified with Maritain and Emmanuel Mounier, who in turn were influenced by thinkers such as Søren Kierkegaard, Max Scheler, Nicolas Berdyaev, Charles Renouvier (whom Mounier identified as having, along with the poet Walt Whitman, coined the term), Bordon Parker Bowne, Gabriel Marcel, and Karl Jaspers. In addition, personalism influenced the principles and actions of Martin Luther King Jr. and Pope John Paul II. It remains today a viable alternative to radical individualism and extreme collectivism.

Related Entries

Catholic social teaching; I have a dream; Maritain, Jacques

Suggested Reading

Maritain, Jacques. *The Person and the Common Good*. 1966; repr. Notre Dame, IN: Univ. Notre Dame Press, 1985.

Mounier, Emmanuel. *Personalism*. 1952; repr. Notre Dame, IN: Univ. Notre Dame Press, 2004.

Wojtyla, Karol (Pope John Paul II). *The Acting Person*. 1969; repr. Dordrecht, Holland: D. Reidel, 1979.

the personal is political

A phrase that first emerged in the late 1960s describing the recommendation from within the feminist movement for a reexamination and eventually a reshaping of the boundaries of formal power and individual privacy, the "personal is political" is attributed to a 1969 essay penned by feminist activist Carol Hanisch and included in an anthology edited by Shulamith Firestone and Anne Koedt. However, Hanisch herself has credited the phrase to her editors, who gave her essay the title, "The Personal Is Political."

Hanisch's article addresses the need for the women's movement to go beyond "navel-gazing" and "personal therapy" and become more actively engaged in the direct challenge of coercion within all aspects of society, not just the political. She observed that the real purpose of such therapeutic methods is to uncover political dynamics within what is regarded traditionally as personal aspects of life, particularly the lives of women. Mainstream politics (including liberal feminism) insists in a sharp division between personal concerns and political issues. But for Hanisch and the more radical voice within feminism, the personal concerns of oppressed groups (and especially women) *are* political, for they have been effectively shaped by political and economic pressures originating from within patriarchal power structures and modern capitalism. For example, abortion and reproduction are more than merely private matters, they are, within the matrix of patriarchal capitalism, political issues. To separate them is to repress real problems that are far more immediate to women than to their opponents supportive of the repressive status quo. To say that the personal is one thing and the political another is to sustain male supremacy while simultaneously silencing the voice of women. Dismissing women's issues as "private" is to depoliticize important social questions and thus deprive women of any access to meaningful political power. It is not enough for radical feminists to gather to share their complaints; it may be therapeutic, but it deflects the movement from necessary collective action. As Hanisch elaborated,

> So the reason I participate in these meetings is not to solve any personal problem. One of the first things we discover in these groups is that personal problems are political problems. There are no personal solutions at this time. There is only collective action for a collective solution. I went, and I continue to go to these meetings because I have gotten a political understanding which all my reading, all my "political discussions," all my "political action," all my four-odd years in the movement never gave me. I've been forced to take off the rose-colored glasses and face the awful truth about how grim my life really is as a woman. I am getting a gut understanding of everything as opposed to the esoteric, intellectual understandings and noblesse oblige feelings I had in "other people's" struggles. This is not to deny that these sessions have at least two aspects that are therapeutic. I prefer to call even this aspect "political therapy" as opposed to personal therapy.

"The personal is political" is now firmly ensconced in the feminist lexicon, although its origins remain virtually unknown to the general public. It continues to express the abiding concern for a consideration of the political as a way to improve the lives of all citizens, and especially women or other traditionally oppressed or disadvantaged groups throughout all facets of their lives. Then a radical manifesto, now a popular slogan, it continues to affirm the need to think of politics as somehow involved in more than public policy, but equally in the pursuit of personal liberation.

Related Entry
feminism

Suggested Reading
Hanisch, Carol. "The Personal Is Political." Alexander Street Press, 2006; http://scholar.alexanderstreet.com/pages/viewpage.action?pageId=2259.

phrase regimen

"Phrase regimen" is a term defined by Jean-François Lyotard in his *Differend: Phrases in Dispute* to signify the normalization of phrases within a communicative dynamic. All meaning is conveyed through the intermediary of language, thus the social world, the communicative world, is a universe of heterogeneous phrases. No phrase is "first," that is to say, there cannot be a metaphrase that serves as the standard of all phrasing or the arch phrase that governs all meaning. Phrases just happen without design. The regimen is the rule that governs the phrase, but in so doing, it inevitably militates against heterogeneity, as the rule of the phrase regimen no longer recognizes difference. Phrase regimens silence other phrases.

This produces the *differend*, or that phrase which is silenced or remains to be phrased.

For Lyotard, all truth, including political truth, must come to grips with this fact, and realize that discourse, if it is to be free, creative, and truly just (not just according to one phrase regimen, or even free and creative for that matter, according to one phrase regimen), the *differend* must find expression and do so as a legitimate voice. If there are no real "grand narratives," then we are left with multiple phrases, the heterogeneity of meaning and non-meaning. Hence Lyotard's concept serves as a starting point for the postmodern project of deconstruction and liberation.

Related Entries

differend; Foucault, Michel

Suggested Reading

Lyotard, Jean-François. *The Differend: Phrases in Dispute,* trans. Georges Van Den Abbeele. Minneapolis: Univ. Minn. Press, 1988.

Plato (427 BC–347 BC)

Political philosophy owes an immeasurable debt to Plato, who, along with Aristotle, built the foundation of all subsequent political theory in the Western tradition. Plato stands at the pinnacle of political thought, one of the few true masters whose work remains canonical without dispute. It is not an exaggeration to say that Plato's political and moral philosophy in some way, direct or indirect, anticipated the concepts and controversies of all following schools of thoughts and, in so doing, stands as the logical beginning of every serious study of the history of political and moral ideas. The famous and nearly ubiquitous quote from Alfred North Whitehead, "All philosophy is a footnote to Plato," still remains the most effective way to encapsulate Plato's enduring pre-eminence. A summary of Plato's ideas and his contributions to political philosophy and the entire lexicon of political theory is admittedly impossible within the confined space of an encyclopedia. But there are a few key aspects of Plato's thought that can be shared given

limited space, and must be shared owing to Plato's importance.

Any understanding of Plato's philosophy in general and his political theory in particular begins with a discussion of Socrates (469 BC–399 BC). The life and mission of Socrates, which comes to us primarily through Plato, is nothing less than the pivot of Western philosophy. With Socrates, the pursuit of knowledge, already highly valued throughout the ancient Mediterranean world, and especially in Athens, was turned toward the examination of the inner self above all else. Knowledge for its own sake, while important and worthwhile for Socrates, ultimately serves a higher purpose: the improvement of the soul. It is in the examination of one's life and the larger questions that draw us upward toward self-improvement; it is in service to goodness that the intellect achieves its real purpose. To know many things is necessary and admirable, but to know how the many kinds of knowledge draw us toward goodness is the mark of a true lover of wisdom. All knowledge must in the end serve to ennoble the soul; otherwise it becomes coarsened by vanity and pride.

Spurred by the Oracle of Delphi to embrace the life of the philosopher, which literally means a "lover of wisdom," Socrates soon discovered that the Oracle's claim that he was the wisest of all the Greeks hinges on one small difference between Socrates and his contemporaries. That is to say, Socrates concluded that the only characteristic that produces wisdom in him as opposed to those who claim wisdom for themselves stems from his recognition that he does not claim to know what he does not know, while others hold the opposite claim, presuming to know what they in the end really can't fully understand. In a sense, Socrates teaches us that the beginning of wisdom is in our admission of ignorance, an ignorance that will soon vanish as we seek truth, but an ignorance nonetheless. Moreover, and perhaps more significantly, Socrates recognized that the Oracle, in declaring Socrates the wisest of men, may have meant to convey the poverty of human knowledge when contrasted with the divine. It is here that Socrates reminds us of our mortal limitations, and challenges us to re-examine the true depth of our own knowledge of self and world.

For Plato, Socrates is the very embodiment of the philosophical spirit; a lover of wisdom in every sense of the word, combining endless self-examination with a quest for truths that will enlighten the souls of his friends and fellows. Beginning from a position of the suspension of certainty, Socrates's only aim is at a transcendent certainty that is liberated from the blinders of subjective perceptions, particular interests, and conventional prejudices. Plato reveals a Socrates courageously and relentlessly resisting the superficialities that pass for learning and, in so doing, attempting to awaken his fellow seekers to the true requirements of the soul led to virtue. It is in the life and teachings of Socrates that Plato witnesses the good in action.

The example of the life of Socrates and the motivation behind his quest for wisdom is the impetus that animates Plato's own philosophical activity. The nature of the Good, and the question of how the Good must be put into action, holds a central position in the philosophy of Plato. The many aspects of Plato's philosophy radiate from this central idea of the primacy of the Good, and therefore also serves as the starting point to understand his political theory. Politics consists of many elements and facets, including themes and issues that one would expect to find in any political theory— themes such as the nature of power, the meaning of the political sphere and the person's relationship within it, the purpose of law, the nature of the best regime, the interrelationship between authority and obligation. These are important questions for the discussion of politics, but they are secondary to the principle that the best city is directed above all by justice, and in being just, the final aim of all political activity is to discover the Good and promote its realization in the actions of human beings. For Plato, the meaning and highest purpose of all true politics is to guide human beings to goodness. Less noble tendencies within politics are recognized as well, but these are only meaningful if they are in service to what is admirable, just, and good by nature. This is more than the "common good" of general consensus or popular mores and social habits, this is the Good as eternal measure for all virtue, whether we are speaking of the activities of persons or the ambitions of states.

Thus the quest for wisdom about political activity and the proper constitution of those regimes wherein it can manifest requires a deeper understanding of the nature of the human soul. Indeed, Plato goes so far as to draw a direct identity between the nature of the soul and the character that it bears within the city as a whole. To understand the city, one must look at the souls of its citizens, and to understand the soul of each person, one must view the person in the wider context of the city. Soul and city are isomorphic (bearing the same shape); this is an essential feature throughout Plato's discussion of political life. The Good is the locus of all virtuous action, whether in the individual soul or throughout the community writ large. Furthermore, the structure of the city enables the development of a certain kind of soul, one that reflects the city around the person as well as representing its constituent and generative parts. For this reason, the political question is intimately entwined within the larger and more elusive question of human virtue, the moral questions that help to shape the admirable kind of soul that acts for the sake of the Good. Thus it does not suffice to study Athenian politics or Spartan politics on their own terms, and it follows that scrutiny directed at the character of citizens from Corinth and Argos is little more than the satisfaction of a curiosity. To truly comprehend the nature of the polis, we must uncover the nature of nothing less than the human soul itself—not the Athenian character or the Spartan demeanor, but the souls of human beings as human beings, and the *polis* as it is meant to be by the internal dynamics of its singular nature. Plato thus does not point to Athens or

Sparta as his ideal, however admirable they might be. They are not even the baseline from which we can begin a comparison of better and best regimes. They might enter conversation as examples or cases, but they are neither the beginning nor the end of authentic political wisdom. We must, according to Plato, discover the concept of political meaning through the gateway of human nature, and this can only mean, for Plato, the very thing that Socrates firmly sought—the careful study of the soul.

Plato's quest for the harmony that aligns elements of the good soul, and the good soul with the good city, is an intellectual travail of the highest difficulty. Adding greatly to this difficulty is Plato's awareness that there is an unseen divide separating the realm of things as they appear to us from the reality behind the manifold of phenomena. We cannot rely on our experiences and perceptions of phenomenal appearance, for what we sense and perceive is but a fragment of the totality of things, only a shadow of what is truly real. Any examination of life in the *polis* will be immediately thwarted if we remain at the surface, or if we allow ourselves to be entrapped by the "evidence" before us. True understanding of the nature of humanity, which is requisite to a fuller understanding of the nature and purpose of politics, requires engagement in an upward journey of the intellect, which is simultaneously an aspect of the education of the soul for the sake of becoming better. This demands of us a suspension of the belief that the political realm in which we live is the only medium through which we can discern and analyze the patterns and principles of political life. In Plato's view, political reality is only obscured by what passes for political practice in the temporal realm. If we are to arrive at the truth about the essence of politics, and thus uncover what is truly real about politics, we must engage the greater questions independently of the particular manifestations of political experience.

This does not mean that Plato is unrealistic about the nature of politics as it is usually practiced. Plato's discussion of political types and the tendencies of political actors exhibit a striking familiarity with the concrete side of politics and the daily administration of cities and the human characteristics that are associated with the exercise of power. Throughout his dialogues Plato displays a keen understanding of politics as it is. Still, Plato never abandons his quest for the ideal, and he always sustains his belief that the ultimate realities of political life are only penetrated once we transcend the reigning confusion that we experience through our immediate and daily political encounters. At best these encounters expose us to one aspect of politics, and usually superficially. To reach the truth about anything, including the apparently practical things of politics, we must employ the intellect, detached from the dependent ways of thinking that emerge within a particular environment, and elevated to an examination of political questions against the context of the larger questions of the nature of justice and the Good.

Plato's political theory is primarily but not exclusively drawn from *Crito, Gorgias, Republic, Statesman,* and *Laws.* Other dialogues also turn to political questions to various degrees, but it is in these five that the essence of Plato's political thought is represented, with particular emphasis in the last three. *Crito* is among those dialogues often categorized as providing an account of the last days of Socrates and thus of interest to readers who are seeking a more developed portrait of Socrates's character as he confronts his fate. Politically, *Crito* raises the question of the relationship between the formal authority of the state with the obligations and responsibilities of citizens, particularly when it is clear that a citizen is being treated unfairly or unjustly. In *Crito* Socrates never wavers from his stance, already established in the *Apology,* that he is far from being guilty of any charges brought against him. Given this, Socrates's friends—and in this dialogue Crito in particular—encourage him to escape and slip quietly into exile, it being apparent that the authorities and those who work for them would not be disappointed by such a result. Socrates refuses on two grounds. First, he reminds Crito that, even though he is wronged by Athens, he still owes an allegiance to the city in which he has spent the sum of his days and for which he has dutifully and diligently served. He has always accepted the laws of the city and for him to reject the rule of law now, even though his fellow citizens are using law to commit an injustice, would be to selfishly taint his life of principle and devotion to his home. While this might be interpreted as an act of blind obedience to the state, a better and more accurate interpretation is offered through the second reason for his decision to face his sentence. Socrates has always taught that it is wrong to exchange injustice for injustice. Hence, even though he has been unjustly indicted, convicted, and sentenced, he will not return the injustice by flaunting the obligations which his city requires of him. In an argument that anticipates the response of Socrates to Polemarchus in *Republic,* a tranquil Socrates reminds his student that to return injustice for injustice is never right. His life may be taken, but his principles prevail.

Gorgias is a longer and far more complex work. It involves Socrates engaged in dialogue with three figures, the sophist Gorgias who is a teacher of rhetoric of some distinction, his younger friend and loyal follower Polus, and the true antagonist of the dialogue, an irreverent, provocative, and decidedly arrogant figure named Callicles. The first part of the dialogue is driven by Socrates's inquiry into the nature of Gorgias's vocation, one that leads Socrates to assert that the esteemed sophist is not really teaching anything of value, but only instructing his students in the uses of a knack for flattery that does not lead to real education, but only to persuasion for the sake of winning arguments. Here Plato draws a distinction familiar throughout his dialogues. First, there are those intellectuals whose teachings are no better than opinions of various degrees and who are more concerned with seeming to be intelligent and thus capable of persuading people to their point

of view but who, in truth, have only a shallow understanding of the things they purport to know. Second, there are those lovers of wisdom, the true philosophers, who seek to know things and to use persuasion not simply to convince others that one is right, but to educate others through the pursuit of real knowledge and not mere opinion alone. Gorgias recognizes that a person must know things to be successful in life, but in the end, he maintains his position that the art of persuasion is alone the most important and useful thing to know if a person wants to exert influence upon the city. Polus continues the argument on behalf of his teacher, which evolves into a moral debate about whether it is better to commit wrong or to suffer wrong, there being no other option available in the moment. Socrates firmly believes that, while one should avoid both, if given no other choice, it is better to suffer the injustice than to commit it. Even though Polus is initially incredulous, Socrates pushes his point, and even goes further in his assertion that should a person choose to commit a wrong, it is in their best interest to welcome correction. Better to be caught in the wrongdoing and penalized than to get away with some malfeasance. Hence not only should one always try to avoid wrongdoing (even if it means choosing to be a victim of wrongdoing), but if one does an injustice, one should not try to hide it, but to be openly accountable and accept the discipline of the laws. While Polus eventually concedes to Socrates, Callicles brazenly and flippantly enters the discussion, rejecting the notion as an inversion of reality and admonishing Socrates for his shameful immaturity. He insults Socrates, scolding him for his decision to consort with philosophy rather than assuming a position of responsibility in the city, and warns him that unless he learns the art of rhetoric, such as taught by Gorgias, he will not be able to protect himself when his indiscretions force him to defend himself before a court of law.

Callicles claims that Socrates is arguing on behalf of an inferior, conventional species of morality that undermines the natural order of things. In so doing, Callicles advances what he describes as natural law, but in this sense, it is the law of the stronger, or truly superior person, over the weaker, the latter using traditional conventions and mores to keep their natural betters in check. Those who are superior are right to rule, and they should not be cowed by the popular morals and laws of the many who are weak. Criticizing Socrates for his admiration of the virtue of temperance (*sophrosyne*—self-mastery), Callicles asserts that a person who is naturally superior should not contain the appetites the way a slave would, but rather enlarge the appetites, and take what life offers without stint. This is nature's way; it is only the weak who adopt self-control, only the slavish who allow themselves to be harnessed. Socrates responds with his analogy of two jars, illustrating the manner in which such shameless campaigning for indiscipline only leads to the worst kind of servility. Callicles is still unmoved by Socrates, who in the end attempts to reverse the warning of Callicles by stating that Callicles himself will find that he is incapable of self-protection before the judges of the dead in the afterlife.

Republic, one of Plato's more famous and arguably his most significant work will be treated at length in another entry (see **Republic, The** (*Politeia*). To summarize for our purposes here, there are essentially two fundamental questions that together form the axis around which this complex, multilayered, and beautiful dialogue turns. First, Socrates and his companions inquire into the nature of justice, attempting to provide a definition that adequately describes justice in it essence. But the dialogue is soon redirected toward a second and more compelling question regarding the nature of the better life for a human being with regard to the question of justice in particular and virtue in general. The Sophist Thrasymachus claims that a life of injustice—and especially the life of the greatest and most successful injustice, tyranny—is in fact a finer and more admirable life to pursue than the life of justice. In making this claim, Thrasymachus

challenges Socrates not only to define justice but also to defend the just life, and in so doing, to examine not only the just soul, but also the just city. When Glaucon enters the conversation in the role of Devil's Advocate against his friend Socrates in Book II, the life of injustice has been convincingly endorsed, and it is left to Socrates to now produce a truly viable response against such a monstrous doctrine. The remainder of the *Republic* is that response.

In the course of this response, Plato has Socrates imagine his ideal city, explore the nature of the soul and the dimensions of virtue, define justice and champion the just life while recognizing its limitations given the practicalities that face us in the world as it is, advance the rule of philosophy, develop a theory of education and describe the soul's upward journey toward wisdom, announce the theory of Forms and teach the centrality of the Good, sound the depths of being and chart the topography of knowing, analyze the imperfections of politics in its basic types, demolish the claim that tyranny is the best sort of life, and speculate on the journey that awaits all of us upon passage into the afterlife. Emerging from this array of ideas and inexhaustible insight is a theory of politics that remains compelling, one that, simply put, rejects the view that the political merely can be reduced to raw power and unabashed self-interest, and promotes the teaching that the essence of the *polis* is truly discovered in the examination of justice and goodness in soul and city. Not blind to the foibles of humanity, Plato explicitly reminds us that these are ideals that lead us to perfection, but are likely to elude our attempts to realize them even in part. The political world is corrupted by power at every turn, regardless of the nature of the regime and the quality of its leaders. Nonetheless, it is in the approximation of the ideal that we can exercise a decent regard for the good of all, and it is through a close study of the features of the ideal city that the person can come to know what is required of the best soul. Plato's *Republic* is as much about becoming a good human being as it is about the quest for the best possible city.

In spite of his skepticism regarding the extent to which politics and politicians can lead us to justice, Plato remains convinced throughout his writings that he has discerned the Form of the *polis* and thus the essence of a just and good state. Ideally, political activity should always be separated from private interests as far as possible, power should be held only by those who are truly inwardly the best regardless of superficial differences (such as those between men and women), and that reason should ever guide power (this is the meaning of the seemingly outlandish prescription for the rule of philosophy). This is the Form of the *polis,* and it holds throughout time as the highest possible standard and only real model for all political regimes within our experience. Later works such as *Statesman* and *Laws* will offer further commentary on the meaning of politics and the aspiration for the ideal, but Plato's theory of the Form of the *polis* never changes in its essence but is only further illuminated by the modifications to the conversation that Plato offers in these later works.

The *Statesman* is a conversation that is actually part three of a dialogic trilogy (including *Theatetus* and *Sophist*) in which, atypically, Socrates does not play a principal role. *Statesman* examines the art of political leadership, an activity that is regarded as neither purely contemplative nor simply practical. It is a kind of science, informed by reason but oriented also toward a species of action that is aimed at the direction of the state. The early part of the dialogue is fixated on a lengthy discourse on division and classification of various activities and objects of study, eventually turning to a meditation on a time when Cronus managed human affairs in such a way that political constitutions were not necessary. Human beings were supplied with ample resources, yet they were unable to care for themselves. When the ubiquitous management of the gods was withdrawn, humanity needed certain gifts (fire from Prometheus, crafts from Hephaestus, for example) in order to attend to their affairs under kingly, not godly rule, that is to say, under a type of human rule now aimed at communal self-sufficiency under political constitutions rather than pastoral care under divine nourishment. After some interesting remarks regarding weaving as a model for the political art and considerations regarding the nature of measurement, Plato has the Eleatic Visitor (occupying the principal role vacated by Socrates) announce a doctrine of the mean that anticipates Aristotle. Additionally, the Eleatic Visitor sketches a typology of regimes that is not only different from *Republic* but also anticipatory in detail of Aristotle's *Politics.* The art of statesmanship depends on proportion and measure and thus is an expertise that must not become superficial. A city of "wise and good rulers" exceeds in justice even a city under the rule of law; hence the art of the statesman must be carefully fostered, distinct from both the omnipresent management of god-like herdsmen as well as the inflexibility of a fallible code of laws. The ideal polity in *Statesman* resembles the City of Speech in *Republic* insofar as it is the rule of expertise, yet Plato again recognizes the improbability of instituting such an office and mustering the true experts needed to hold it, therefore that polity which approximates this ideal most closely is a monarchy limited by and bound to the rule of law. The worst possible regime is, as in the *Republic,* the lawless rule of one that we call tyranny. The Visitor now prescribes the rule of law, knowing that the "wise and good ruler" is utterly elusive. As with weaving, kingship requires the ability to intertwine the virtues so as to dissolve any contradictions. Those parts of the soul that appear to conflict are woven together through education and training under the guidance of good laws, and in this way the statesman knits the divine with the worldly. The courageous and the contemplative are reconciled, the mean is struck, and the state is steered toward the middle and best course. Through *Statesman,* Plato considers again the improbability of the rule of the philosophers. As desirable as it is, it is at odds with the manner in which most human beings are capable of living, and thus the political constitution itself must replace, as far as humanly possible, the rule of the wise. Noteworthy among the features of *Statesman* are certain elements that prefigure Aristotle, particularly his treatment of the importance of the measure of the mean, and the offering of a typology of regimes that anticipates (and likely inspired) that which is provided in greater detail in Book III of Aristotle's *Politics*.

Laws is Plato's last work, and perhaps the one dialogue that is the most explicitly and consistently political throughout its parts. It also happens to be Plato's longest dialogue, and like *Statesman,* the principal role usually held by Socrates is now assumed by another anonymous figure, this time the "Athenian Stranger." In some ways *Laws* is still more complex than *Republic,* and is not easily summarized in a few short paragraphs. Suffice it to say that in this work Plato returns again to the method of imagining an ideal city, but in this case, it is the "second-best city" ("Magnesia") that approximates the Form of the *polis* as described in *Republic.* Philosopher rulers are not conscripted to govern; rather, wisdom rules through the laws, which for the Stranger are—if they are in fact true laws and not the commands of self-interested politicians—imbued with qualities of the divine. Law rules in the absence of philosophy, and yet the love of wisdom remains a presence throughout the dialogue in the mentoring of the young dictator/founder by a mature sage, the emphasis on education and the importance of the Ministry of Education as a high office of notable influence, and the institution of a Nocturnal Council charged with examining the effectiveness of the laws in both following and promoting moral virtue.

Moral virtue remains the focal point. The function of laws and the duties of the legislators that enact them is nothing less than the promotion of complete virtue within the citizenry. The cardinal virtues examined in *Republic* reappear with slight modification as good judgment, temperance, justice, and courage, ranked in that order of importance and all necessary for the operation of good cities and the cultivation of healthy souls. Laws, if they are true, are ultimately divine; therefore persons and cities who adhere to lawful government will in some way participate in divinity. Even though the philosophers are not in power, the purpose of *Republic's* philosopher-ruler remains—the government of reason over the passions, and the guidance of limited power by wisdom, only this time found in laws and not in persons.

The second-best city, guided by reason through law, is structured through a combination of "two mother regimes": democracy, which provides freedom and friendship, and monarchy, which offers order and vigor. Plato's second-best city is thus a mixed regime, one that initiates an advocacy of blended government that would run from the elder Plato to Aristotle and from there throughout the entire history of political ideas. Plato's mixed regime is one that elaborately combines authority and liberty and moves toward an equilibrium and balance that militates against the extremes of his time. Additionally, the city is further balanced by the introduction of a class system that allows mild inequity in the distribution of private property and yet prevents the gross disparities that result in less moderated regimes. The wealthiest property class is to hold no more than four times that which is owned by the lowest economic group. Thus Plato reintroduces private property, even among the rulers, in the second-best city, but suggests a way of dampening its effects on social hierarchy and thus political deliberation. Plato's city is also further divided into twelve tribes, each of which shares equally in the responsibilities of the city. Power is divided among these classes and tribes, and further separated and deposited in a great council (360 members, four from each property class), a magistracy consisting of 37 "guardians of the law," each tribe contributing three members with one member selected from "at large." A variety of administrative offices, each charged with a specialized function, would serve a regulative role, and the Nocturnal Council would act as the final assessor of the strength of the city's first principles and their realization in the laws and codes that govern the citizenry in their daily lives. A small city of precisely 5,040 citizens and many opportunities to participate in the public sphere, Magnesia features democratic institutions and practices in close combination with institutions and offices more commonly associated with autocratic regimes. In its detail it appears to break from the principles of the Form of the *polis* discovered by Socrates in *Republic,* but when one examines the whole of it and not just its multiple parts, the approximation of the City of Speech is revealed.

Political theory is inconceivable without Plato. Aristotle is rightly credited for having shaped political inquiry as a methodological science and his contribution certainly is of the same league as his great teacher. But it is with Plato, more than any thinker in the tradition of political philosophy, West or East, that the foundation of the theoretical study of politics begins, and it is often toward Plato that we are again drawn for those answers that will produce within us a level of wisdom far beyond our poor imaginings.

Related Entries
advantage of the stronger; allegory of the cave; analogy of the jars; Aristotle; *Republic, The (Politeia);* Socrates; Xenophon

Suggested Reading
Klosko, George. *The Development of Plato's Political Theory.* New York: Oxford Univ. Press, 2006.

Plato. *Complete Works,* ed. John M. Cooper. Indianapolis: Hackett, 1997.

Schofield, Malcolm. *Plato.* New York: Oxford Univ. Press, 2006.

Taylor, A.E. *Plato: The Man and His Work.* 1926; repr. New York: Harper & Row, 1978.

Vlastos, Gregory, ed. *Plato: A Collection of Critical Essays,* Vol. II, *Ethics, Politics and Philosophy of Art and Religion.* Notre Dame, IN: Univ. Notre Dame Press, 1971.

pleonexia

The term *pleonexia* is from the ancient Greek and can variously mean having more than one's share, to "outdo," "outdoing" (*pleonektein*), an insatiable desire to exceed others in everything, the prideful effort to surpass all others for the sake of popular acclaim or to overwhelm and outshine, greed, avarice, grasping, unnatural acquisitiveness, and to greedily beat down the competition. *Pleonexia* is a persistent problem in political life that commands considerable attention in Plato's *Republic.* Injustice (*adikia*) and the unjust life are, for Plato, largely the result of the endless, need to "outdo others and get more and more." This irrational state of mind is further illustrated in *Gorgias,* through the analogy of the two jars. The unjust person constantly strives to outdo everyone, but does so without ever experiencing gratification, always chasing after more of everything—power, wealth, pleasure, esteem—at the expense of others. Ultimately the wages of lust and greed warp the soul, turning even the most successful tyrant into a misshapen slave to unbridled appetite. The term is also employed in the Greek New Testament, appearing in both the Gospel as well as in St. Paul's epistles.

While the notion of *pleonexia* is associated with classical political philosophy, it has been noted by later thinkers as well. In chapter fifteen of *Leviathan,* for example, Thomas Hobbes links *pleonexia,* or "a desire of more than their share," to "arrogant men" in breach of the natural law of equity. *Pleonexia* is also evident, as a problem in human nature, in such concepts as Machiavelli's *virtu,* John Adams's "passion for distinction," Rousseau's *amour propre,* and Hegel's observations regarding the desire for recognition. More recently, Francis Fukuyama's discussion of excessive pride and the fixation on achieving public superiority (or *megalothymia*), perspicuously illustrates the tensions forced by *pleonexia* throughout political life

Alternatively, thinkers such as Herbert Spencer or Friedrich Nietzsche would be disposed to view *pleonexia* as a natural instinct that, if repressed or constrained, would defeat the spirit of the more talented and impose on the whole of human culture an unnatural mediocrity. This line of thinking is explored, and rejected, by Plato through the exchange between Thrasymachus and Socrates in the *Republic* and the debate between Callicles and Socrates in *Gorgias*.

Related Entries
amour de soi/amour propre; analogy of the jars; *Republic, The (Politeia)*; tyranny

Suggested Reading
Hobbes, Thomas. *Leviathan,* ed. Edwin Curley. Indianapolis: Hackett, 1994.
Plato. *Republic,* in *Complete Works,* ed. John M. Cooper. Indianapolis: Hackett, 1997.

Plymouth Rock landed on us

"We didn't land on Plymouth Rock, Plymouth Rock landed on us!" is a quote of uncertain origin attributed to Malcolm X expressing in a richly symbolic and dramatic manner the long history of oppression felt by the African American community since the early Colonial period. Plymouth Rock, the traditional landing site of the Pilgrims in 1620 and a symbol of hope and opportunity, came to represent for Malcolm X the twin hypocrisies of American inequality and racism. The image of the Pilgrims, themselves striking out on adventure in flight from persecution and finding great promise in the New World, is a particularly meaningful one in the American cultural *mythos*. Yet, for Malcolm X, the image masks the fact that, from the beginning, this *mythos* included not only the hope and unity of purpose of a new world and a symbol of American national pride but also quite the reverse, hopelessness and exclusion for millions of citizens of African descent who have been victimized by the legacy of colonialism and slavery. As Malcolm X averred in his famous "The Ballot or the Bullet" speech (1964),

> No, I'm not an American. I'm one of the 22 million black people who are the victims of Americanism. One of the 22 million black people who are the victims of democracy, nothing but disguised hypocrisy. So, I'm not standing here speaking to you as an American, or a patriot, or a flag-saluter, or a flag waver—no, not I. I'm speaking as a victim of this American system. And I see America through the eyes of the victim. I don't see any American dream; I see an American nightmare.

The phrase, "Plymouth Rock landed on us" has also been quoted by Native American activists to emphasize their plight in the confrontation with the European movement westward. The phrase is a potent reminder of the complexities of democratic promise when drawn into tension with disaffected or alienated groups. Few speakers could match Malcolm X's ability to phrase this disaffection so concisely and effectively.

Related Entries
Afrocentrism; the ballot or the bullet; I have a dream

Suggested Reading
Conyers, James L., and Andrew P. Smallwood, eds., *Malcolm X: A Historical Reader*. Durham, NC: Carolina Academic Press, 2008.
Malcolm X, "The Ballot or the Bullet," Address delivered April 12, 1964.
Malcolm X. *A Malcolm X Reader,* ed. David Gallen. New York: Carroll & Graf 1994.

political animal—*See zoon politikon*

Politics

If any text has earned an undisputed position in the "canon" of Western political theory, it is the *Politics* of Aristotle, which, along with Plato's *Republic* and *Laws* stands at the very foundations of political thought. Much of our current terminology and conceptual grammar regarding politics can be traced in some way to either or both Plato and Aristotle, and an enduring intellectual debt is owed in particular to the achievement of Aristotle's *Politics*.

The *Politics* is actually the second half of a larger project that begins with the *Nicomachean Ethics* and is framed within the larger context of Aristotle's general philosophy, especially his

Metaphysics. While the work does stand alone, it is best understood with at least some exposure to the *Ethics* (in particular Aristotle's principle of the mean) and the notion of the four causes in the *Metaphysics.* This is so because Aristotle, in Book I of *Politics,* regards the *polis,* or the sphere of politics and public affairs, to be natural to our humanity. As it is natural, we are perfected through political association, a perfection that involves our mutual self-sufficiency that is solely achieved through the partnership of the *polis.* All things aim at an end (or *telos,* which is one of the four causes or explanatory factors discussed in *Metaphysics*), and thus all associations (partnerships, communities) aim at an end—which is for Aristotle the *polis,* the most complete association that encompasses all other forms of partnership (from the family to the village). The *polis,* being the end of all association, is thus *essentially* (not chronologically or physically) prior to the individual, and prior to all other forms of association which are themselves encompassed by the political sphere. Hence, we cannot be human separate from political society, for only gods (who are immortal and thus wholly self-sufficient) and beasts (who are able to sustain themselves through necessity alone) can live outside the city. Our very humanity is partially defined by the fact that we are political creatures, what Aristotle describes as *zoon politikon.* The *polis* thus begins with the need to live, but it aims at living well, something that human beings cannot do without each other. A human being outside the *polis* or beyond law and justice is the most savage of all creatures. But, with justice, which is only possible in the *polis,* humanity is at the pinnacle of creation, the "best of animals." It is the good for human beings (defined by Aristotle in *Ethics* as *eudaimonia,* or happiness understood as flourishing) that the *polis* seeks, that of a life well lived in mutual self-sufficiency and justice in the most perfect of human communities (the *polis*).

Having established that the aim of the *polis* is to live well (which for Aristotle involves a life of noble flourishing habituated by the virtues found at the intermediate), Aristotle launches into a comparison of the private sphere (the household, which is the sphere of *oeconomia:* economics, household management, domestic acquisition and production) and the *polis,* the former being concerned with living (necessity) and the latter with living well (action). However, even though the private sphere manages what is necessary, its aim is the same as that of the *polis*—the good life. But as the household is concerned with necessity in a way that the *polis* is not, Aristotle focuses on three issues that are encompassed only within the private sphere: acquisition, slavery, and the rule of the family.

According to Aristotle, in order to live a good life, some degree of prosperity is required, although it should be confined to a modest and well-ordered affluence that is aimed at still higher ends. Here Aristotle draws his famous distinction between limited and unlimited acquisition that is subordinate to immaterial ends, and unlimited acquisition that elevates material needs and wants to directive ends, but does so perversely. Wealth acquired for the sake of *eudaimonia* (noble flourishing, happiness) is necessary and worthwhile, but wealth that is acquired for its own sake undermines the higher immaterial ends of the household and thus undercuts the still higher aim of the city. Aristotle's distinction between limited and unlimited acquisition is explained in terms of use and exchange value—those goods acquired as limited wealth are used for other ends, whereas unlimited wealth is driven by a constant exchange of wealth as good in itself—thus employing categories that anticipate far in advance Adam Smith and Karl Marx.

Aristotle's discussion of slavery is alien to the modern reader, but nonetheless revealing. Here another division is drawn between those who are slaves by nature (a person who is unable to govern himself, or to "be his own person") and conventional slaves (slaves owing to conquest or other events unnatural). Aristotle does not justify conventional slavery, and in this sense he places himself at odds with his contemporaries. However, he does claim that some are by nature slaves, and thus places himself at odds with modern readers. His point, however, must be kept in view: political rule is different from other types of rule—such as a master over a slave or a parent over the household, for the former is government over citizens who act, whereas the latter two are direction (and in the case of slavery, mastery) over those who provide or serve. In this same context Aristotle also discusses the family, wherein he not only reviews the kind of rule that it is (as distinct from the political), but also reasserts his preference for patriarchy. Again, the modern reader rightly finds such a concept foreign, but for Aristotle, the point is that the statesman is not a husband, father, or master—but a governor over citizens (who are, Aristotle assumes, all male).

Turning back to the *polis* in Book II, Aristotle examines the nature of the ideal state, beginning with a thorough critique of Plato's notion of the perfect city of speech outlined in *Republic* as well as the second-best city of *Laws,* while also examining and rejecting the ideal arrangements advocated by the lesser figures of Phaleus and Hippodamus along with actual cities (Athens, Sparta, and Carthage) and the theories of a handful of jurists. It is the critique of Plato that is the most revealing for a study of Aristotle. While Aristotle still seeks the best city for all human beings (as stated in Book V of *Ethics*), he rejects the form of the *polis* forwarded by Plato in *Republic.* Plato's ideal political community is, for Aristotle, in actuality not political at all. The emphasis that Socrates places on unity in the city is contrary to the necessity of plurality in Aristotle's view. A city, while centered on a common good and unified to an extent, relies on multiplicity. Plato's city of speech seeks a unity that approaches that of a family, or even an individual, and is thus not truly political. Moreover, the community of common families and property is contrary to nature, blurring the boundaries between private and public and imposing false solidarity that inadvertently leads to neglect of both things and persons. Above all, the guardians are incapable of happiness, which implicitly means for Aristotle that they lead a deficient

life—the consequences for the *polis* in Aristotle's view are obvious. On this point Plato can be defended on the grounds that philosophers pursue a different kind of happiness, but Aristotle seeks the best regime available to most people, and in his view the city of speech as limned by Socrates in *Republic* produces a contrary model.

Aristotle's critique of *Laws* is basically an extension of his critique of *Republic,* and less compelling and less central to an understanding of Aristotle's essential views. He takes Phaleus to task for advocating the equality of property, emphasizing the importance of tempering the appetites through education and philosophy rather than any coercive scheme of property distribution. His critique of Hippodamus is unremarkable save for his reiteration of the notion that laws can only be employed to gradually change habits over time in the pursuit of stronger character for the citizenry, and thus law must only be introduced and modified with caution and not in the expectation of immediate reform. Aristotle's examination of actual states is designed to demonstrate the need for moderate and balanced government—Sparta in particular receiving criticism for overemphasizing martial valor. However, the Cretan constitution is inferior still to that of Sparta, being but a pale imitation of it. Aristotle views Carthage more favorably as it seems at least in principle, if not in practice, to approximate the ideals of equilibrium between the classes that Aristotle admired. But even Carthage falls short, corrupted by deviations from its basic patterns.

Having treated ideal and actual cities, Aristotle focuses anew on the nature of the *polis* and its citizens, moving us into Book III and what might be the critical segment of the *Politics.* Book III is certainly one of the more famous passages from Aristotle's works, and perhaps the most influential in the further development of political theory as a discipline. Here Aristotle begins with an extended examination of citizenship, choosing to define it as a means toward a greater understanding of the true nature of the political community. Citizenship, for Aristotle, is an activity, one that involves some degree of participation in the administration of the city and the judgment of fellow citizens, with varying levels of participation corresponding to the type of regime to which a citizen belongs. While Aristotle admits that his definition of citizenship more closely resembles some kind of democracy, all cities, if they are to be administered politically, must involve all citizens to some extent. In essence, a citizen is one who is capable of *both* ruling and being ruled, of governing and being governed—and it is only in the *polis* that government can occur. Hence the very definition of a political community for Aristotle is shaped by the act of statesmen governing free citizens, in contrast to leaders commanding subjects or mastering slaves.

Given this, Aristotle typically recognizes many different cases of citizenship—and concludes that what makes a good citizen is relative to the kind of regime within which a citizen participates. Democracies and oligarchies, for instance, require different qualities of their citizens, thus those who might be good citizens in the one will not necessarily be good in the other. Still, for Aristotle, there is only one standard for the good man, for the good man is always the same regardless of the political community in which he lives. One might be a good citizen, and yet not be a good man, Aristotle observes. Furthermore, it is difficult to be both a good man and a good citizen, and in most cities the qualities of both are usually combined only in the statesman, or one who governs with maturity over free citizens, virtuously regarding only the common good. And yet, for Aristotle the best regime is that regime wherein good citizens *are* good men, thus it is possible with the right constitution and education to realize a political community of good citizens who are absolutely good.

From this point, Aristotle directs his attention to the types of regimes that are, and in so doing, perhaps discovers the kind of regime that will enable the good person to be a good citizen. Much of what Aristotle writes in Book III at this point bears a strong resemblance to an earlier typology already established by the Eleatic Visitor in Plato's *Statesman* (*Politicus*). Aristotle begins his classification of regimes by first looking at the quantitative feature, dividing cities based on the rule of the one, the few, and the many. From the quantitative he then further classifies regimes based on the quality of rule, that is, those regimes that lawfully govern free citizens for the common advantage, and those regimes that lawlessly rule over subjects for the private advantage of those in power. Monarchy (or kingship), aristocracy (rule by the few who are the best in terms of virtue and excellence), and the constitutional polity (rule by the many which is best) are the types of the one, few, and many that govern for the common good, that is—lawfully and correctly. Tyranny (the worst possible regime), oligarchy (rule by the few who are not the best for the sake of wealth), and democracy (rule by the many who are poor) are deviations of the three correct types, respectively, and represent political communities that have succumbed to selfish interests and lawlessness.

In chapters xi and xiii of Book III, Aristotle shares two compelling and to some apparently conflicting observations. In chapter xi he argues, contrary to Plato (as well as to some of his own observations elsewhere, particularly in *Ethics*), that under the right conditions (free and educated citizens guided by law) the many can act with wisdom, perhaps exceeding even that of a philosopher. Thus Aristotle here seems to tilt toward a vague type of popular rule. In chapter xiii, though, Aristotle raises the possibility of a statesman so noble and eminently good that he by all rights should govern as king perpetually, sovereign even over the laws. Hence on the one hand Aristotle suggests the possibility of wise rule involving the public, and then on the other he promotes the permanent kingship of a "god among men." While this might not be a contradiction given the teleological purposes behind these ideal types (that is, the common good), it does demonstrate Aristotle's flexibility. The fact that Aristotle devotes the remainder of Book III to discussing kingship while insisting, in a familiar passage, that the dispassionate rule of law is always superior to the impassioned rule of even the best human beings is clear evidence of his commitment to just rule. Aristotle affirms the principle that

> He that therefore recommends that the law shall govern seems to recommend that God and reason alone shall govern, but he that would have man govern adds a wild animal also; for appetite is like a wild animal, and also passion warps the rule even of the best men. Therefore the law is wisdom without desire.

Book III establishes a useful typology that enables us to study politics in its rich variety, yet it returns to the Platonic quest for that regime that is aimed at absolute justice, and can be described as truly right and good. As Aristotle states,

> It is clear that those constitutions which aim at the common advantage are in effect rightly framed in accordance with absolute justice, while those that aim at the rulers' own advantage only are faulty, and are all of them deviations from the right constitutions; for they have an element of despotism, whereas a city is a partnership of free men.

The remainder of *Politics* elaborates and expands on much of what has been taught in Book III. The types of regimes introduced in Book III are examined in greater detail and further variety, there being four types of oligarchy and four of democracy (five types of kingship were discussed in the previous chapter), three of tyranny and a vague reference to the declension of aristocracy. That which is aristocratic in the true sense, that is, government by the few who are really the best in terms of virtue and intellect, is said to be that regime wherein the good man and the good citizen are combined into the same person without qualification. This would imply that, by definition, aristocracy is for Aristotle the absolutely best regime. However, political inquiry must also seek that regime which is best for most human beings, one that can be achieved by most people and sustained in most situations. This regime is the "most practicable regime," a regime that is known as the correct rule of the many, or the constitutional polity.

In essence, the polity is that regime that is found at the mean, or intermediate, and in that sense is "also best," for virtue is always found at the mean. A polity is a mixture of features from oligarchy and democracy, both incorrect regimes given to vice, with the polity as a virtuous mean between their two extremes. As such, the war between the classes that Aristotle identifies (the rich contemptuously disregarding the poor, and the poor harboring envy of the rich) in other regimes is abated by the introduction of an extended middle class in the polity, that middling regime that reduces conflict between factions. Additionally, as a polity is a mixture of rule by the few and rule by the many, it will be characterized by a sharing of power between the classes. From here Aristotle moves to an examination of the different functions of power (deliberative, executive, and judicial) which appear to anticipate, at least for the modern reader, later theories of the strict separation of powers. Aristotle's conception is not quite along those lines, but it is fair to say that Aristotle understood power to be best managed when divided.

Book V examines states as they decline and slide into instability, and in modern terms, revolution. The cause of decline and instability is, for Aristotle, those perceptions regarding inequality and unfairness that, while certainly involving economic concerns, are driven more by moral considerations of honor and dignity. Aristotle saw class conflict framed by envy and contempt, but he was not Karl Marx—the inequalities felt are those that speak to one's character and esteem in the city. Most of Book V is a discussion of how the several types of regime slide into dissolution. Significantly, and evincing the influence of Plato, Aristotle warns both against extreme democracy and its warping of liberty into a license to do anything and also against tyranny (the worst of all regimes) and its domination of all aspects of life that turns citizens into strangers to each other.

Book VI appears to be less significant and incomplete compared to the other books of the *Politics*. Much of what is offered here is a repetition of or expansion on topics previously covered. However, Aristotle does share more observations on democracy that are of interest, particularly as he has established democracy as a kind of incorrect regime (albeit the least incorrect). He states in Book VI that democracy does work best within an agrarian population. Not only will the pastoral conditions within which the citizens live keep them from becoming an urban crowd given over to their passions, but Aristotle argues that under an agrarian democracy only the best will find themselves holding office. Hence Aristotle notes with some admiration a kind of democracy that is not necessarily his constitutional polity.

Books VII and VIII turn to more practical and policy-oriented concerns, such as the ideal size of a state, territorial arrangements, economy, defense, and, most importantly, education. Yet philosophical considerations remain, such as the nature of the relationship between the happy *polis* and the happy man, which, in the end, turn out to be the same. The proper relationship between the life of contemplation and the life of action are also weighed, and the conclusion that both are necessary and interrelated is once again drawn. Additionally, in Book VII Aristotle restates his belief that human beings are meant to be free by nature, and thus the *polis* that governs free citizens is justified on no other grounds but that of nature itself. Book VIII is particularly devoted to education for, as with Plato, the best citizens can only become the best people through education. Aristotle discerns three methods toward a well-educated and flourishing citizenry: nature, reason, and habit. Throughout Book VIII, Aristotle considers the proper elements for this kind of education, one that resembles the previous observations of Plato before him without producing the philosopher-ruler.

In the end, Aristotle's *Politics* is a marvel of perception and insight. It is small wonder that this work continues to serve as a part of the foundations of political theory, its place in the canon firmly fixed, its value for future students of political inquiry well secured. Almost every major political thinker will at some point turn to Aristotle and Plato, and in so doing, uncover new insights mined from the rich veins of Aristotle's *Politics*.

Related Entries
Aquinas, Thomas; Aristotle; Plato; *Republic, The (Politeia)*

Suggested Reading
Aristotle. *Politics,* trans. H. Rackham. 1932; repr. Cambridge, Mass.: Harvard Univ. Press/Loeb Classical Library, 1977. There are a number of additional fine translations of Aristotle's *Politics* in print. Barker (Oxford), Everson (Cambridge), Lord (Univ. Chicago), Sinclair/Saunders (Penguin), and Jowett (available in *The Complete Works of Aristotle,* ed. Jonathan Barnes, vol. 2. Princeton: Princeton Univ. Press, 1984; Bollingen series) are all embraced within the academic community.

politics of presence, politics of ideas

A "politics of ideas," according to political theorist Anne Phillips, is insufficient to forward our understanding of a society defined by the fact of diversity and difference. One component of liberal political theory and practice is the aspiration for inclusion of all citizens within the political processes of the state regardless of particular affiliations and characteristics. Liberalism thus posits a notion of the individual as citizen acting among equals within the political sphere to realize goals based on interests and public values common to all. For Phillips, this notion of the universality of equal citizens is premised on an artificially imposed equality of "sameness," one that adopts an image of citizens as void of any attachment to a particular identity. Moreover, this generalized and uniform citizen is in fact the product of a particular dominant social and political voice, primarily male, and operating under the assumption of a false universality. Hence the liberal notion of the politics of ideas involves an "abstract individualism that ignores its own gendered content," one that produces "homogenizing ideals of equality that require us to become the same." Difference and diversity, which are valued by the rhetoric of liberal thought, are in the end inadvertently erased by a conceptual discourse that assumes a false commonality. In the perception of liberalism, differences of opinion and belief are the province of political discourse and the resolution of any conflict between opposing interests is framed conceptually by ideas and their various policy applications, all operating under the premise of one common interest associated with the artificial image of the universalized citizen. Such a notion of difference neglects problems of political exclusion that run more deeply than ideological belief or disparate perceptions of interest.

Phillips proposes that a "politics of presence" is needed to more fully remedy the problem of exclusion in pluralist societies. Not only ideas, but group identities orbiting "shared experiences" are necessary to ensure a more genuine inclusion of difference within the political sphere. "Shared experience," Phillips writes,

> here takes precedence over shared ideas, more precisely, no amount of thought or sympathy, no matter how careful or honest, can jump the barriers of experience.

Ideas are still necessary for political action, and they indeed serve an important function in understanding and promoting the principles of right and justice. The politics of presence is not to be set in opposition to ideas, but only to supply the deficiency of political principles that are otherwise detached from the power of social identities. Phillips remarks that

> when the politics of ideas is taken in isolation from the politics of presence, it does not deal adequately with the experiences of those social groups who by virtue of their race or ethnicity or religion or gender have felt themselves excluded from the democratic process. Political exclusion is increasingly . . . viewed in terms that can only be met by political presence.

Ideas and principles alone cannot guarantee inclusion. Indeed, a dominant ideational voice can produce a privileged worldview that imposes an artificial unity at the expense of a diversity of voices. The politics of presence seeks to encourage more than tolerance of the other voice, but recognition of it—to foster a democracy engaged with difference informed by the vision that comes from high ideals.

Related Entries
equality; feminism; justice; liberalism

Suggested Reading
Phillips, Anne. "Dealing with Difference: A Politics of Ideas or a Politics of Presence?" *Constellations* I (1994), pp. 74–91. (Also in Goodin, Robert E., and Philip Pettit, eds. *Contemporary Political Philosophy*. Oxford: Blackwell, 1997).

Politiques

A loose association of French intellectuals, primarily Catholic, who advocated a more tolerant response to the Calvinist presence within France as it appeared in the sixteenth century. The *Politiques* regarded toleration as a political necessity, the sectarian divisions in Christianity apparently being permanent, and promoted the public power of the state as the only secure means to unify society given the religious conflicts of the previous generation. Tolerance, independence of the state, and the embrace of private conscience in religious matters were all features of the *Politiques,* who were led primarily by Michel de l'Hôpital (technically a forerunner to the *Politiques* proper), François de Montmorency, Pierre Gregoire, and above all, the great French political theorist Jean Bodin, whose work would to a great extent shape the mind of modern political thought by laying the foundations for the theories of the seventeenth and eighteenth centuries. Caught between the militant extremes of Catholic ultramontanism and the Protestant monarchomachs, the *Politiques* insisted on holding a moderate position, working actively to foster a peaceful resolution to the political differences between Catholic and Huguenot interests. The *Politiques* are also associated with Gallicanism, a movement in France that sought the independence of the monarchy from Papal influence without provoking a break from the Pope's ecclesial authority as the Vicar of Christ.

In the overall treatment of the state, the *Politiques* believed that the civil power of the monarchy was the only instrument that could reestablish peace. Thus the office of the king was treated as the center of reconciliation and national unity. The *Politiques* recognized the importance of religion but insisted that religious differences needed to be tolerated for the sake of civil harmony and that the only way to promote this would be through the office of a monarch whose only interest was the strength and cohesion of the nation as a whole.

Related Entries
Bodin, Jean; Catholic League; monarchomachs

Suggested Reading
Allen, J. W. *Political Thought in the Sixteenth Century.* 1928; repr. New York: Rowman and Littlefield, 1977.
Church, William Farr. *Constitutional Thought in Sixteenth-Century France.* Cambridge, MA: Harvard Univ. Press, 1941.
Holt, Mack P. *The French Wars of Religion, 1562–1629,* 2d ed. New York: Cambridge Univ. Press, 2005.

positivism

Emerging in the nineteenth century with Auguste Comte, positivism is a philosophical attitude that seeks to acquire certainty while focusing on empirically observed and conceived reality. Marked by a rejection of any philosophical system that incorporates metaphysics, positivism emulates the natural sciences with its emphasis on systematic observation and its goal of employing empirical, scientific methods to understand human behavior and, in so doing, reform society. Knowledge, for the positivist, is limited by observation and experience, and only in applying the methods of science can we arrive at any certainty about social or political reality. Metaphysical and traditional approaches to ethics are insufficient. We can only understand what we should do by first arriving at what is, and the reality of "what is" can only be revealed by observing and studying the phenomenal. Thus positivism turns to math and natural science as the only valid key to the social sciences, and concerns itself primarily with developing a systematic theory of reality based on what is observable. Certainty about anything, including human relations, is grounded in the empirically verifiable; this is the first rule of the positivist method.

While positivism is identified as an outgrowth of the nineteenth-century post-Enlightenment scientism, particularly as represented by Comte and his followers, one can recognize earlier adumbrations. In the ancient world, the Skeptics, particularly beginning with Sextus Empiricus (second century, AD) but influenced by Pyrrho of Elis (360 BC–270 BC), attempted to define certainty in terms that approximate modern empiricism, thus adhering to a view of knowledge as basically *a posteriori.* Modern philosophers such as Sir Francis Bacon (1561–1626), Thomas Hobbes (1588–1679), and David Hume (1711–1776), among others, argued in various degrees for an approach to knowledge rooted in empiricist epistemology. Hobbes in particular desired to develop a "civil philosophy" following the model that was provided by his contemporaries who were reshaping the way in which the natural world was to be understood. For Hobbes, all knowledge is grounded in experience. Because of this, the only knowledge of the social and political upon which certainty can be constructed is empirically supported. The Hobbesian rejection of Scholasticism implies a reliance on the new science, and the careful study of history and observable political tendencies can lead us to an awareness of general predictable rules of human behavior. Thus the "laws of nature," for Hobbes, are not "properly laws," as in the Thomistic understanding, but "qualities that dispose men to peace and obedience." Hobbes's reexamination of the laws of nature reflects the mood of his times and anticipates the later work of Sir Isaac Newton. Natural laws are not so much first principles as phenomenal tendencies. Nonetheless, as scholars of

Hobbes have indicated, Hobbes also speaks of natural law in ways that are reminiscent of earlier concepts. This apparent contradiction indicates for most readers that Hobbes is not in every sense a precursor to positivism, although elements of a new, more "scientific" approach to human problems are evident in his political philosophy.

Francis Bacon, while not technically a positivist, provides the conceptual foundations of a scientific approach to the study of society through the method that he helped to invent. Bacon's attempt to develop a purely inductive method aligns him with the earliest proponents of a new science, and positions him as a figure as influential as Galileo and Newton in the restructuring of natural philosophy into modern science. David Hume is significant in that he supplies the most thoroughgoing, influential and philosophically provocative empiricism available to the emerging modern mind of the enlightenment and post-Enlightenment periods. While Hume cannot be accurately described as a positivist, his exhaustive treatment of knowledge as experiential provides the epistemological framework from within which later empiricists would have to operate, or at least to which most serious philosophers of any epistemological orientation would have to respond. Hobbes, Bacon, and Hume are crucial figures in the promotion of a new "scientific," empirically driven study of politics, and it is in these three thinkers that the deeper conceptual foundations of positivism are to be found.

Thinkers from the Enlightenment period such as Claude Adrien Helvetius (1715–1771), Paul-Henri Thiry (Baron) d'Holbach (1723–1789), Jacques Turgot (1727–1781), Marie Jean Antoine Nicolas de Caritat, marquis de Condorcet (1743–1794), and, later and still more directly, Claude Henri de St. Simon (1760–1825; an erstwhile mentor for Comte), all focused in various ways on the empirical source of certainty and were profoundly influenced by the methods of modern science and mathematics. Additionally, these thinkers posited a

theory of human progress that drew a distinction between the more primitive forms of knowledge (usually associated with religion and metaphysics of some kind) and the more advanced form of knowledge identified with the scientific achievements of the seventeenth and eighteenth centuries (especially as exemplified by Galileo and Newton). Even more than Hobbes, Bacon, or Hume, these thinkers represent the immediate forerunners of classical positivism.

St. Simon in particular conceived of a new science of human society that he hoped would accomplish the same thing for our understanding of politics that Newton accomplished for our understanding of nature. This is a logical extension of the study of nature, for humanity is nothing but a part of nature, and thus any laws that operate in the natural world also operate, in the same way, in the social world. Hence St. Simon spoke of a "social physiology" that would establish the science of man on a "positive basis," the same ground on which chemistry, physics, and astronomy had already been planted. Borrowing heavily from St. Simon, without openly admitting it, Comte brought positivism to its fullest form. As early as 1819, Comte spoke of the need for politics to be "transformed into a positive science," which is to say that political inquiry and government, like any other field of investigation and application of theory, must be guided by a close study of the phenomenal laws of nature, in this specific case the laws of political activity. Comte clearly campaigned for a method of political and social investigation worthy of the appellation "science," and saw in this mission the ushering of a new age that would surpass the superstitions of theology and the abstractions of metaphysics (two forms of belief and inquiry that define the more primitive stages of history). For this reason Comte is often seen as a seminal figure in the movement toward behavioralism as well as a kind of protosociologist. A new science of politics will allow a new kind of government, one that, while responsive and accountable to the masses in general, will be nonetheless directed by science in pursuit of the common good. This new science of political direction would be wedded to economics, for in Comte's vision; the grand utopia of positivism would depend on the guidance of a committee of three bankers in determining and implementing industrial, agricultural, and commercial activities. For Comte, modern science and modern commerce join to lead the modern community into a new order, one that finally overcomes the abstractions and superstitions attached to previous forms of religion, philosophy, and patriotism.

However, Comte's desire for a rigorous scientific rationalist approach to politics was not without internal contradiction. Comte's ardent attempt to ground knowledge in experience is combined with a return to a new metaphysics, one ostensibly based on science yet containing elements deliberately emulative of religious concepts. For Comte, positivism is based on science but is in fact a new "religion of humanity," with its own materialist "trinity," dogma, sacraments, and scientific priesthood. Following the lead of his mentor St. Simon—who admired Christianity in its essential principles—Comte ultimately recognized the value of religion in the proper ordering of even the most rational society, and attempted to create his religion of humanity to replace traditional Christianity as the spiritual wave of the new age that he himself was to midwife. Comte coined a new motto for the positivist age: "Love, then, is our principle; Order our basis, and Progress our end." Comte goes on to explain that "Such is the essential character of the system of life which Positivism offers for the definite acceptance of society." Comte, as with St. Simon before him, reached for a more scientific and rationalistic philosophy to understand human nature but emulated religion, and in particular Christianity as he interpreted it, to further his personal vision of what human beings should become. Thus, positivism, which represents the rejection of first principles, metaphysical systems, and teleological ends in favor of the rigors of modern scientific methods, is accompanied by the grand vision of reality that only a transcendent perspective, such as Christianity, can provide. For this reason it is left to later outgrowths such as logical positivism and behavioralism to fully effect the turn away from metaphysics and the embrace of materialism that represent today the imitation of the hard sciences in the study of human action.

Comte's positivism left disciples, notably Emil Litree (1801–1881), who endorsed the scientific aspects of Comte's thought while rejecting the neo-religious aspirations, and Pierre Laffitte (1823–1903), who is seen as most closely following the whole of Comte's doctrine. Ernst Mach (1838–1916), physicist and philosopher of science, is also a notable follower of positivism, and as with Litree, he embraced that part of positivism that focuses on rigorous science, abandoning the more metaphysical elements found in Comte. Mach would serve as a bridge between "classical" positivism and the logical positivism (or neopositivism) of the twentieth century. For a time the great British political theorist John Stuart Mill was drawn to Comte's system, but was eventually disappointed by Comte's attempt at creating a new religious system. While Mill eventually dropped positivism, it did hold some appeal among a minority of scholars and activists in the British Isles. Richard Congreve (1818–1899), for example, helped to establish a London Positivist Society, a philosophical circle dedicated to the application of positivism to the solution of contemporary political problems. Miguel Lemos (1854–1917) and Raymond Teixeira Mendez (1855–1927) are notable in their efforts to establish a positivist religion in Brazil, with a Temple of Humanity as its center. Mendez in particular was influential for a time in Brazilian politics, and it is to him and Lemos that the Brazilian flag owes its motto, *Ordem e Progresso* (Order and Progress). Positivism's legacy, while somewhat checkered, can still be detected in the desire among social scientists of various disciplines to arrive at a factual, verifiable, or falsifiable methodology for the rigorous study of human behavior. Absent the religious pretensions of both St. Simon and Comte, this is the unfulfilled quest of classical positivism.

Related Entries
behavioralism; logical positivism

Suggested Reading
Comte, Auguste. *Auguste Comte and Positivism: The Essential Writings,* ed. Gertrud Lenzer. 1975; repr. Chicago: Univ. Chicago Press 1983.

potestas

From the Latin for power, initially a description of the coercive power held by leaders of the Roman Republic, bearing a close similarity to the more tangible power of military leaders and asserted through the enactment, promulgation and enforcement of laws (as opposed to military orders or edicts). In the Middle Ages, *potestas* (power) was distinguished from *auctoritas* (authority) and framed within the balance of influence between civil and ecclesial communities. The pope was said to have authority, while the Holy Roman Emperor was to hold power (*potestas*). However, within the Roman Catholic Church, the pope holds *plenitudo potestatis* (power in its fullness, or plenitude) and thus is a figure comparable to the secular emperor. In the growing controversies brewing in the Middle Ages between proper provinces of church and state, the influence of the pope directly challenged that of civil leaders, and thus the distinction between authority and power became blurred. In modern terms, the notion of popular sovereignty situates power within the government and authority within the citizenry. Rousseau's separation of power (held by magistrates or princes) and will (inherent in the people as sovereign) is analogous to the ancient distinction between *potestas* and *auctoritas*.

Related Entry
auctoritas

Suggested Reading
Curtis, Michael. *The Great Political Theories,* Vol. 1. New York: Avon Books, 1981.

Power tends to corrupt, and absolute power corrupts absolutely

Also known as Lord Acton's dictum, the phrase "power tends to corrupt, and absolute power corrupts absolutely" has become one of the more famous and revealing epigrams in our political lexicon. The phrase, penned by Lord Acton, was included within a letter addressed to Bishop Mandell Creighton in April 1877 in response to the First Vatican Council's 1870 promulgation under Pope Pius IX clarifying the doctrine of papal infallibility. Lord Acton, a devout Roman Catholic, expressed his disagreement with the doctrine in no uncertain terms. "Power tends to corrupt," the great man observed, "and absolute power corrupts absolutely. Great men are almost always bad men." In spite of Lord Acton's criticisms, he remained loyal to the church, affirming his full devotion to Catholic theology even though he often questioned its leadership.

Observations regarding the tendency of human beings to abuse power precede Lord Acton's dictum, and are native to the conversation of political theory. Aristotle in his *Politics* noted well the necessity of rule under law rather than men, for even the best of men will be warped to wickedness by power. Baron de Montesquieu's teaching regarding the inevitability of the abuse of power is nearly as famous as Acton's, and the American founders as a rule distrusted the accumulation of power, regardless of their philosophical orientations and their more immediate political affiliations and personal loyalties. The Elder Pitt, long before the discussion of the suspect character of power in the American Constitutional debates, averred in a speech before the House of Lords in January 1770, "Unlimited power is apt to corrupt the minds of those who possess it." Hence, long before Acton's maxim, students of the human condition have shared the sentiment that power is by its very nature deleterious to the integrity of those who seek it, and even to those who have it thrust upon them. But no phrase is as effective in communicating this basic truth as the one Lord Acton coined as a caution against our ambitions and our pride.

Related Entries
Federalist Papers; Montesquieu, Charles-Louis de Secondat Baron de la Brede et de la

Suggested Reading
Lord Acton. *Essays in Religion, Politics and Morality: Selected Writings of Lord Acton, Vol. III,* ed. J. Rufus Fears. Indianapolis: Liberty Classics, 1985.

pragmatic maxim

The pragmatic maxim, first sketched by C.S Peirce (1839–1914) in 1878 as follows: "Consider what effects, which might conceivably have practical bearings, we conceive the object of our conception to have. Then, our conception of these effects is the whole of our conception of the object." In other words, only the "practical bearings" and effects of a notion are the notion itself, the concept is equated with its consequence. This notion is the basic premise for the pragmatist school of thought, epitomized in the voluminous writings and extensive influence of John Dewey, who embraced Peirce's dictum as one of the key features of his own approach to knowledge and its relationship with the social and political world.

Related Entries
consequentialism; Dewey, John

Suggested Reading
Peirce, Charles S. "How to Make Our Ideas Clear," in *Values in a Universe of Chance: Selected Writings of C. S. Peirce,* ed. Philip Weiner. Garden City, NY: Doubleday Anchor, 1958.

prisoner's dilemma

A hypothetical scenario used to illustrate the deliberative processes of rational and self-interested individuals faced with a critical decision, the "prisoner's dilemma" has entered into the lexicon of contemporary political inquiry, particularly within the United States. In short, the dilemma is presented as follows. Imagine two criminals who, in the commission of a crime are apprehended, booked and under interrogation having been separated by the police in their attempt to increase their chances of obtaining a confession from at least one of them. Even though the police strongly suspect guilt, they lack sufficient evidence to press the kind of charges they feel appropriate to the offense and are thus relying on confession. They proceed, therefore, to offer a deal to each prisoner, separately and without either prisoner knowing what is happening in the interrogation of their partner. The police promise, separately to both prisoners without their knowledge of the statements and action of the other, that if the one confesses without a confession from the other, the prison sentence will be guaranteed at only one year in prison, while the partner will be required to serve twenty years. Each prisoner is now aware that the reverse is true—in either case, one prisoner (the confessing prisoner) will receive a lenient one-year sentence while the other prisoner (who remains silent) will be tried, convicted, and sentenced to 20 years without clemency. The police go further, claiming that if neither prisoner confesses, they will still prosecute their case on lesser charges guaranteeing a conviction followed by a sentence of three years in prison to both of them. If both confess to the more serious charges that the police desire to pursue, then each prisoner will receive a 10-year sentence. Hence the dilemma: a unilateral confession guarantees but one year, and yet if both confess then the prisoners are facing ten. Remaining silent could secure the second-best result—a three-year sentence, but only if the partner is also silent, otherwise one prisoner is facing the worst possible sentence of 20 years. If both confess, which is tempting owing to the possibility of only one year in the slammer if the confession is unilateral, both prisoners will serve 10 years—half of the worst case scenario but seven years longer than the second-best scenario, the one wherein they both remain silent.

For political theory, and social inquiry in general, the prisoner's dilemma illustrates the tension between acting solely in one's own self-interest and acting with an awareness of the interests (and simultaneous actions) of other individuals. To act in one's own self-interest (take the deal and confess immediately) without regard for the other (whose actions are unseen) can secure the highest reward (only one year in prison) but also result in the second-worst situation, a 10-year sentence should both independently follow the same course (acting egotistically). Refusing to rat out the partner could at best result in a three-year sentence (the second best), but also carries the highest possible risk (a full 20-year sentence). Thus the individual is caught between doing what is in one's immediate self-interest and the risks attendant on that decision, or doing what is in the interest of both (operating under the belief that the partner will make the same decision) and facing the most severe punishment if he or she wrongly anticipates the partner's actions. Thus every decision of any consequence that individuals must face within the context of a society of rational, self-interested actors will always bear a high degree of uncertainty, and often force us to abandon our designs for the best outcome in order to avoid suffering the worst outcome. Acting out of purely egoistic motives for the advance of one's narrow self-interest, while in some cases potentially producing the highest rewards, will in other cases lead to undesirable consequences. And, acting with a view to the common interest against one's self-interest, while potentially beneficial and even rewarding, could produce misery in a world populated by rational, self-interested agents. Individuals must constantly weigh their interests and their ability to gratify them against commitment to the larger interests and the risks of subordinating one's own best interest to that of the greater good. Hence the dilemma, and hence the value of this exercise for understanding the behavior of free agents within the social and political sphere.

As a hypothetical scenario, or game, the prisoner's dilemma originated at RAND in the 1950s through a series of conundrums developed by Merrill M. Flood and Melvin Dresher. These scenarios were attempts at developing strategies for thermonuclear warfare, but were eventually broadened to include other problems. The prisoner/confession angle was introduced by Albert Tucker who is attributed with having given the puzzle its name and emphasis on individual rational actors. Political theorists such as David Gauthier, Robert Nozick, Gregory Kavka, Philip Pettit, and Edwin Curley, among others, regard the prisoner's dilemma to be particularly beneficial in examining rational moral decisions as well as in understanding social contract theory, particularly as advanced by Thomas Hobbes and in certain elements of rational choice situations hinted at by David Hume. Robert Axelrod, in his *The Evolution of Cooperation,* has provided an informative overview of the prisoner's dilemma as it has evolved to greater complexity through various additional scenarios and situations. An amazingly diverse number of puzzles involving a variety of actors and moves have sprung from the prisoner's dilemma, games with compelling names such as Asymmetry, Centipede Finite, Stag Hunt, Infinite and Finite Iterations, Haystack, and several others. The prisoner's dilemma can also be compared with John Rawls's notion of the maximin, although Rawls himself did not draw this connection.

Related Entries
difference principle; game theory; Rawls, John

Suggested Reading
Davis, Morton D. *Game Theory: A Nontechnical Introduction,* rev. ed., with a foreword by Oskar Morgenstern. 1983; repr. New York: Dover Publications, 1997.
Poundstone, William. *Prisoner's Dilemma.* New York: Anchor Books, 1993.

procedural republic
According to political theorist Michael Sandel, the procedural republic is the result of philosophical and historical developments that have fused the liberal principles of individual autonomy, limited power, and decentralized self-government with the nationalist vision of a large centralized republic. Originally

diametrically opposed, these two political projects—liberalism and nationalism—are brought together in the Progressive movement of the latter nineteenth and early twentieth centuries and culminating with the New Deal and its progeny, the Great Society. In Sandel's estimation, this fusion of liberalism and the "national idea" succeeded during a time of immense crisis (the Depression and World War II), but has in recent times failed to sustain itself. Such a synthesis is, in Sandel's view, unable to cultivate the social awareness needed for a sense of real community on a scale as vast as the American polity. The era of New Deal liberalism, and the kind of liberal theory advocated by a diverse group of thinkers ranging from Herbert Croly to John Rawls, is behind us, leaving in its wake a

> gradual shift from a public philosophy of common purposes to one of fair procedures, from a politics of good to a politics of right, from the national republic to the procedural republic.

A sense of common purpose, or a devotion toward a common good (as found in the early republic) is no longer available to us: our interests are too diverse, our attitude toward the political too detached. We are a nation dependent on government in a variety of ways, but not engaged in its political life—we are at once detached and entangled—detached in the sense that we do not identify our good with a common interest nor general good and thus do not engage in public life from a sense of civic responsibility, and, entangled in the sense that we are ever increasingly dependent on the services of the state, in spite of our disinterest in the political dimension. Such a condition is, for Sandel, a manifestation of the priority of right over the good, thereby illustrating the flaw in the Rawlesian conception of the relationship between the right and the good. We live in a republic that cannot embrace a single vision of the good, and thus can only offer procedural, rights-based safeguards to guarantee that citizens will enjoy the pursuit of their own particular vision of the good unimpeded. Common

purpose is now replaced by procedural fairness, and the notion of individual rights that "trump" the common good is elevated to primacy. The procedural republic does not commit itself to a single good, its only task being the defense, through a system of rights, of each citizen to define and seek their own good. Procedural rights precede these varied conceptions of the good, and manages conflict between state and citizen as well as between citizen and citizen through the procedural rules of legal systems and electoral politics.

The procedural republic in its attempt to guarantee rights of individuals against the possible intrusions of the community requires centralized power, and as such, unintentionally undercuts the principles of self-government traditionally associated with liberal theory. "Liberty in the procedural republic is defined in opposition to democracy," that is, in opposition to the interests of the civic sphere in the conflict between individual rights and majority will. In the end, the procedural republic fails to promote the kind of liberty associated with the liberalism from which it developed. According to Sandel, this is a consequence of positing the procedural defense of right in the national organ, which in effect fuses the pursuit of individual liberties with the realities of centralized power. As Sandel asserts,

> Insofar as I have a right, whether to free speech or minimum income, its provision cannot be left to the vagaries of local preferences but must be assured at the most comprehensive level of political association. It cannot be one thing in New York and another in Alabama. As rights and entitlements expand, politics is therefore displaced from small forms of association and relocated at the most universal form—in our case the nation.

It is in this transfer of the ordered protections of our rights from the self-governing localities to the centralized national power of the procedural republic that we find the conflict with democratic government. In Sandel's view, this creates the arrangement wherein we are at once excessively dependent on the power of the national arm and simultaneously disengaged. In the procedural republic, we are immersed in the many activities provided by government, but we are no longer invested in its vision.

Related Entries

democracy; Kant, Immanuel; liberalism; Rawls, John

Suggested Reading

Sandel, Michael J. "The Procedural Republic and the Unencumbered Self." *Political Theory* 12 (February 1984).

propaganda of the deed

The concept of the "propaganda of the deed" expresses the old chestnut, "actions speak louder than words," with the qualifier that the action in question is usually violent or disruptive and aimed in particular at the rapid achievement of a specific political goal; or, perhaps more simply, the action uses antipolitical and dramatic tactics, usually violent, toward political ends. Associated primarily with militant anarchism, the propaganda of the deed is also rightly descriptive of any act of terrorism regardless of long-term political objectives or underlying ideologies.

Central to the propaganda of the deed is the notion that one violent act by itself can provoke a shift in public thinking. Additionally, the commitment of certain types of disruptive and violent deeds can provoke political authorities to respond repressively and in force, thus exposing the tyrannical nature of the established government. It is in the deed that the will of the militant or terrorist is exerted for the greater cause, a deed that will compel both governments and publics to change their ways and worldviews.

Nineteenth-century anarchism and revolutionary tactics serve as the source for the violent prescription encapsulated in the phrase. Italian revolutionary Carlo Pisacane (1818–1857) held that deeds generate ideas, rather than ideas provoking one to action. During the Paris Commune of 1871, French anarchist

Paul Brousse (1844–1912) exhorted his comrades to emulate Italian revolutionaries by engaging in what he specifically called "the propaganda of the deed." A year prior to the Paris uprising, anarchist firebrand Mikhail Bakunin (1814–1876) announced that "we must spread our principles, not with words but with deeds, for this is the most popular, the most potent, and the most irresistible form of propaganda." Petr Kropotkin (1842–1921) argued that "A single deed is better propaganda than a thousand pamphlets." Direct, defiant, and astonishing acts must be committed to embarrass governments and expose the hypocrisy of traditional political, legal, religious, and cultural institutions and the wickedness of the socioeconomic status quo, to "excite hate for all the exploiters, to ridicule the Rulers, to show us their weakness and above all and always to awaken the spirit of revolt." The ideas of Max Stirner, Georges Sorel, and Frantz Fanon can also be said to justify, in different ways, the means of the propaganda of the deed and the anarchistic or socialist ends toward which they are directed. The German-American anarchist, Johann Most (1846–1906) in particular was associated with the open advocacy of the violent deed.

Political assassinations, bombings targeted at public institutions and gathering places, incitement to riot, prison breakouts, monkey-wrenching, and more militant forms of the general strike are examples of the propaganda of the deed. For the most part, as indicated above, the propaganda of the deed is a tactic employed mostly by extreme anarchists, although radical socialists have also been known to advocate tactics of this nature. The popular image of the anarchist as bomb-throwing assassin has, rightly or wrongly, been formed primarily because of the propaganda of the deed. While certain variants of anarchism are open about the deliberate and necessary uses of violence, it must be remembered that not every anarchist group engages in this way. The propaganda of the deed is widely perceived as nothing less than terrorism, although for the militant anarchist, violent means for a just cause cannot be properly so called. From either perspective both the means and the goals of the propaganda of the deed reduces all political activity to the shock of destruction and the remorseless threat of imminent death.

Related Entry
anarchism

Suggested Reading
Ward, Colin. *Anarchism (A Very Short Introduction).* Oxford: Oxford University Press, 2004.

Protestant Reformation and political thought

What we today call the Reformation includes far more than we normally attribute to it. Church reform, both from within the priesthood and religious orders of the ancient church as well as from those who, like John Wycliffe and Jan Hus, challenged the church in ways that set them against the established traditions, was well underway prior to Martin Luther (1483–1546) and John Calvin (1509–1564) and would not be confined to those sects that pulled away from Rome to become known as the Protestant denominations. To summarize, the Reformation was a Christian phenomenon, involving both Protestant and Catholic movements, and culminating in the division of Christianity into three main bodies: Orthodox (from a division that preceded the Reformation by five centuries), Roman Catholic, and the various Protestant confessions.

The actual details of this story involve a prolonged study of both theological and philosophical disagreements on one hand and political machination (and, alas, the sacrifice of religious principle for political interest on all sides) on the other, and cannot be covered in this entry. For our part, we turn to the central features of Protestant political thought as it influenced the development of modern political theory. It is interesting to note that, while the term Protestant represents a variety of theological positions distinct from Catholicism, the actual word does have a connection to the political struggles between crown and miter. The word Protestant comes from the Latin *protestation* (declaration), and was first employed in 1529 (eight years after the Diet of Worms) by six German princes along with representatives from fourteen independent cities who, in supporting Martin Luther's break from Rome, issued a "letter of protestation" to the Reichstag of Speyer challenging the ban against Luther and his teachings.

More than any other idea, Luther's principle of the "priesthood of all believers" is regarded as emphasizing the autonomy of individuals in new ways. This is not to say that individual autonomy and individualism were created with Lutheranism out of whole cloth, but it is to observe that the religious notion of the priesthood of all believers stimulated new ways of thinking about individuals in society. In effect, the priesthood of all believers represents the rejection of the need for the traditional priesthood and the attendant revision of the sacramental life. This pushed the sacraments and good works out of the salvific plan, leaving room only for Divine grace—it is grace alone (*sola fides*) that provides redemption, a grace that does not require, for Luther, the priesthood as conceived in the ancient church. Attendant upon this, the cosmic order, intricate and mysterious, which characterized the Medieval world, was reconstituted into a vision of the world less complex and more accessible to the understanding of the ordinary believer. The structure of the universe is more plainly presented to the Reformation mind, and thus the political realm far simpler than previously accepted. Just as the priesthood of all believers dispenses with the old priesthood, the membership in the political order is recast as less structured, but not necessarily less hierarchical. Luther himself recognized the need for a strong monarchy and in some ways endorsed forms of authority more absolutist than his Catholic counterparts. Indeed, Luther supported the use of state power to preserve religious doctrine, and was not averse to using the power of the sword against both political and religious dissent. But, the new understanding of individual grace that Luther promoted would encourage a political counterpart that fostered a notion of individual participation in the polity that was not part of the Medieval vision. For the most part, Luther's contribution to political theory consists in his departure from the Thomistic worldview, which in itself was heavily influenced by Aristotle. While it is simplistic to attribute "individualism" to Luther and the Reformation in contrast to the more "communitarian" worldview of the Thomistic system supported by Catholicism, it is accurate to remark on the dramatic shift in how the relationship between person and society was viewed in light of Luther's "priesthood of all believers."

The early Protestant movement ramified rapidly into four main branches: Lutheran, Anabaptist, Calvinist, and Anglican. Lutheranism and Anglicanism were, at least initially, among these early Protestant sects the closest to the Roman Church in matters of theological doctrine. Calvinism and the Anabaptist movements were viewed as more distinct breaks from the ancient church, both theologically as well as culturally. In terms of political beliefs, the Calvinists were more receptive to the newer modes of social and economic interaction that had been emerging since the latter decades of the High Middle Ages. Calvinists rejected the old manorial economic system that Luther still found comfortable and right. In so doing, the Calvinist wing of Protestantism encouraged a "work ethic" that helped to justify the growth of new attitudes toward industry and commerce—attitudes that, as the sociologist Max Weber observed, were in full support of the growth of capitalism in the West. While this argument might be overstated and misunderstood (Calvinists were not capitalist by any real sense of the term), it is fair to say that Calvinism, even more so than Lutheranism, aggressively rejected the vestiges of the Medieval world, whether speaking of religious institutions such as the Papacy and priesthood or economic arrangements such as the custom of setting a "just price" for marketable goods under the advice of the local clergy. By and large, Calvinist political notions urged on the one hand the need for state power to protect the purity of the church, even though Calvinism understood that the ecclesial and civil spheres should be separate. Even so, it is with Calvin that we are more quick to associate the notion of Christian theocracy, and while it is clear that state and church are separate, it is evident from the efforts of early Calvinists that religion is at the center of political activity. Additionally, Calvinism tended to promote the notion of government by consent, which in itself is not a Calvinist innovation, but when combined with a distrust of ecclesial hierarchy, fostered a practice of local governance—first within congregations and, by extension, within the province of civil government. More radical expressions of Calvinism (such as those found in England during the civil war of the mid-seventeenth century) were still more insistent on the notion of a social compact as the legitimate basis for all government and, when coupled with a strong instinct for egalitarianism among the more radicalized Puritan sects, pointed unequivocally to political attitudes and arrangements more familiar to the modern mind. Anabaptists were equally committed to the practices of social and political egalitarianism, comparatively speaking, and were still more ready to resist hierarchy and centralization than even their Calvinist counterparts. For this reason (along with differences in religious doctrine), Anabaptists were often persecuted by whatever church happened to be in the majority in the region where they were active. Calvinist, Lutheran, Anglican, and Catholic authorities all considered the Anabaptist movement a serious threat to social order and religious integrity.

In sum and in brief, it can be said with some generalization that Protestantism contributed to (i) a new view of the individual and the relationship between individuals and community, one that is accompanied by (ii) a sense that the individual alone can arrive at, through their own lights and without the mediation of priest and sacraments, their comprehension of what it means to have faith (a notion that inspires a new understanding of individual conviction), (iii) the growth of the autonomous nation-states and, inadvertently, the strengthening of centralized government in Europe, (iv) political equality and a suspicion of hierarchy (which was often undermined by the centralization of government in the nation-state system), (v) a stronger notion of the separation of church and state (which was not necessarily an innovation as the ecclesial and civil spheres had already been viewed as separate since the origins of Christianity and was an idea reinforced by several leaders in the Catholic church) that was in some cases compromised by theocratic tendencies, (vi) a more aggressive resistance to ''tyrannical'' authority (although Luther himself criticized rebellion), (vii) a trend toward a more secular culture based on the Protestant principle that religious views are primarily private (even though early Protestant communities were more willing to foster a public religious confession toward the end of protecting religious doctrine through the authority of civil office and social expectation), and (viii) rejection of the Thomistic worldview that had dominated the High Middle Ages. No doubt other distinctions can be added, but suffice it to say that these are general consequences of the Protestant impetus toward the formation of a new worldview in the sixteenth and early seventeenth centuries that would develop into what we today refer to as the modernist perspective.

Related Entries
Catholic social teaching; liberalism; Social Gospel movement

Suggested Reading
Harrison, E. Harris. *The Age of Reformation.* Ithaca, NY: Cornell Univ. Press, 1955.

O'Donovan, Oliver, and Joan Lockwood O'Donovan. *From Irenaeus to Grotius: A Sourcebook in Christian Political Thought, 100–1625.* Grand Rapids, MI: Eerdmans Publishing Co., 1999.

Weber, Max. *The Protestant Ethic and the Spirit of Capitalism,* trans. Talcott Parsons with an introduction by Anthony Giddens New York: Routledge 2001.

Pufendorf, Samuel, Baron von (1632–1694)

Samuel Pufendorf is numbered among those political theorists of the late sixteenth through the seventeenth century that helped to reshape the concept of sovereignty in a way that separates the modern understanding of political power from that of the classical and Medieval theorists. Along with Thomas Hobbes, John Locke, François Hotman, James Harrington, Baruch Spinoza, and Johannes Althusius (among others), Pufendorf contributed his voice to the construction of the modern political mind and influenced the institutions of the nation-state. While his influence and reach is not as extensive as most of the other names in the aforementioned list, he is still a theorist of note, and important enough to grab the attention of the American Founders.

Pufendorf understood human nature to be essentially sociable. He criticizes Hobbes for his ''clever deduction'' from natural law to the conclusion that human beings are solely concerned with their own welfare, and thus apprehend natural law through their own self-interest. While it is obvious to Pufendorf that all human beings are concerned with their own preservation and those goods needed to secure it, in the end he concludes that we cannot really understand our interest apart from others. Pufendorf rejects both altruism and egotism as the main impetus of our actions. Rather, we are sociable in such a way as to simultaneously promote our ends as well as the ends of others. As Pufendorf states,

> Indeed, reason is also quite insistent that one who has his own welfare and preservation at heart cannot renounce the care of others. For since our safety and happiness depend for a large part on the benevolence and help of others, and indeed men's nature is such that they wish to be repaid in kind for their good deeds, and when this does not happen they put aside the spirit of beneficence, surely no sane person can set his own preservation as a goal for himself in such a way as to divest himself of all regard for others.

Pufendorf thus considers Hobbes's depiction of human nature as relentlessly self-interested, detrimental, and benighted. And while he does not embrace a Lockean notion of a natural impulse toward fellowship or communion, he does recognize that human nature is for the most part "meant for sociality." Human beings are, as both Hobbes and Locke maintained, driven to self-preservation. While we are impelled by a strong desire for fellowship as in Hooker and Locke, we see that our interests are best promoted and preserved in society, wherein we enjoy mutual assistance and a more firm support of our private good.

Humanity's social nature is related to Pufendorf's conception of natural law. Without disputing the truth of sacred Scripture or its compatibility with reason, Pufendorf allow that the natural law can "nonetheless be investigated and firmly demonstrated even without that assistance through the rational powers which the Creator has granted to and still preserves in us." Through reason alone we realize the inherent social nature of humanity, one that is defined by a natural freedom and equality. "And so," Pufendorf concludes,

> the fundamental law of nature will be this: "Any man must, inasmuch as he can, cultivate and maintain toward others a peaceable sociality that is consistent with the native character and end of humankind in general." For sociality... [means] a kind of disposition whereby a man is understood to be joined to every other man by ties of benevolence, peace and charity, and therefore by mutual obligation.

Pufendorf makes it clear in this passage that this sociality is directed toward that which is good for moral beings living together in community, it being "utterly false to claim that the sociality we are introducing is indifferent to whether a society is good or evil."

Significantly, natural equality, or "equal freedom," is implicated with Pufendorf's conception of natural law and the society that it supports. There is a universal human nature, in Pufendorf's estimation, one that requires

mutual acknowledgment (not unlike Hobbes's ninth law of nature in chapter 15 of his *Leviathan*.) Social living depends on this equality and its mutual recognition, and thus it is a "precept of natural law that 'Everyone must esteem and treat other men as his natural equals, or as men in the same sense as he'." Upon both the common desire for mutual benevolence and the recognition of universal equality Pufendorf's political community must rest if it is to be aligned with the rational law of nature.

In addition to his discussion of natural law and the social nature of humanity, Pufendorf offered an alternative to theories of sovereignty, developed through Jean Bodin, Hobbes, and Spinoza, that posited a notion of political power as concentrated and, with some qualifications, absolute. Rather than insist on the ultimate authority of an absolute sovereign, Pufendorf identified two aspects of sovereignty, both absolute and restricted. Sovereign power is, as Hobbes had understood, absolute in the cases "when its acts cannot be rendered void" by a separate authority. Additionally, absolute sovereignty requires unconditional obedience; there is no appeal to right when confronting sovereignty in this sense. Restricted sovereignty, on the other hand, is formed when one or both of these features are removed. That is to say, if there is a separate authority to which the sovereign itself is bound and/or if citizens can legitimately and effectively claim rights unimpeded by sovereignty, then the alternative restricted sense is adopted. Pufendorf recognized that absolute sovereignty is a reality and can be legitimate, but, more to the point, he asserted that citizens in the act of consenting to the social contract can install restrictions to the effect that certain potential commands by the sovereign are not options. Natural freedom is consistent with the notion of restrictive sovereignty, but even these restrictions must not attenuate the power of sovereigns to pursue the public interest.

A characteristic of Pufendorf's writing appears to be a desire for balance between a strong sovereignty and a free citizenry as well as between the rational pursuit of self-interest with the recognition of a legitimate and beneficial public good. This might be why the American founders were attracted to some of Pufendorf's writings, for while his influence is not as pronounced in American theory as Locke, Montesquieu, David Hume, Algernon Sidney, or Harrington, the framers were familiar with his writings and occasionally referred to his work. Political power is a necessity, and thus citizens must retain their loyalty and respect for legitimate authority. Obedience is required of citizens, and a good citizen recognizes that the "safety and security [of the state] is his dearest wish," and in preserving both, to offer freely "his life, wealth and fortune." Conversely, Pufendorf follows the common law tradition as well as thinkers such as Hotman in reminding us that ultimately "The welfare of the people is supreme law (*salus populi suprema lex est*)." The public good and private interests must ever be intertwined with one another.

Finally, Pufendorf is regarded as an early influence in the promotion of international law, along with Hugo Grotius before him and Emerich Vattel after him. Natural law is the foundation of international relations, and thus nations are obligated to seek a greater peace in their various interactions through legal institutions rather than through the caprice of war.

Related Entries
Althusius, Johannes; Grotius, Hugo; Hobbes, Thomas

Suggested Reading
Pufendorf, Samuel. *The Political Writings of Samuel Pufendorf*, ed. Craig Carr and trans. Michael J. Seidler. New York: Oxford Univ. Press, 1994.

Q

Qutb, Sayyid (1906–1966)

Poet, teacher, editor, bureaucrat, and dissenter, the Egyptian Sayyid Qutb emerged in the 1950s as one of the seminal thinkers in the resurgence of Islamic fundamentalism in the post–World War II era. Owing to his position in the Egyptian Ministry of Education, Qutb was dispatched to the United States in 1948 with the charge of conducting research on the American educational system. Qutb spent time at Wilson Teachers College in the District of Columbia (later to be folded into what would eventually become the University of the District of Columbia) and the University of Northern Colorado, earning a master's degree at the latter school before returning home to Egypt in 1950. While in the United States, Qutb was duly impressed by the economic, industrial, and technological achievement of America in particular and Western civilization in general, but he was disturbed by his encounter with American and Western materialism, promiscuity, and racism. America demonstrated economic might and dazzling innovation, but in Qutb's view this was rendered meaningless by a lack of civility and a loss of moral direction. Having returned to Egypt just prior to the rise of Nasser, Qutb resolved to stand against Western influence in the Islamic world. He joined the Muslim Brethren toward this end, while simultaneously working for Nasser's early regime, but his antimodernist sentiments led to a break with Nasser, one that would lead to nine years of imprisonment and torture. During his imprisonment, he encountered the writings of Alexis Carrel, a French anatomist who collaborated with the Vichy regime until his death in 1944. Carrel's attack against the false progress of western materialism fortified Qutb's own position and provided him with an example of an internal dissent against what he perceived to be the dehumanizing values of Western democracy and liberalism. Finding a sympathetic ear in Qutb, Carrel's prescription for a new elite of ascetic mystics to cure the decadence of the West would thus inadvertently contribute ideas to the development of Islamic fundamentalism in the near and middle east.

Qutb thus comprehended the world as divided by two parties: the Party of God (*hizb Allah*) and the party of the devil. These two parties are grappling for control in a war of ideas and values, the Party of God composed of faithful Muslims, the party of the devil nearly everyone else. Judaism in particular is an active enemy of the Party of God, for Qutb claimed that it is the aim of the Jewish people to conquer and control the entire world. Christianity and Communism are also accused in Qutb's indictment, but the Zionists represent the greatest threat to the establishment of divine government in his estimation.

Antony Black identifies four basic elements in Qutb's ideology. First, he avers the belief that the *Qur'ān* (*Koran*) is the only legitimate source of knowledge available to humanity. Nothing from the West can be incorporated into Qur'anic scripture, for all Western values are inherently decadent or impious. Islam is both "comprehensive" and self-sufficient, and capable of solving all earthly problems if left untainted by outside (namely, Western) corruption. Second, while Islam offers the solution to perfection, it is not ossified, but rather adaptable. Qutb was not a literalist; the *Qur'ān* is to be read poetically, allusively, intuitively. To bind the *Qur'ān* to archaic commentary would be to actually impede the vitality of Islam. Third, it is not through law alone, but through "conscience" and openness to revelation that Islamic wisdom is discovered. Through conscience alone, Qutb argued, the human person can understand the meaning of the divinely ordered universe. A dependency on the Islamic juristic tradition interferes with the cultivation of this independent pathway to the order of things. Therefore, and finally, once the devices of oppression (law, secular government, Westernization, materialism) are broken, the human person is liberated and subject only to the government of God as proclaimed through the Prophet. For Qutb, all of these elements draw inevitably to the conclusion that a complete rejection of modern political structures is necessary; to be replaced by religiously governed societies absent any vestiges of secular politics or Western political and legal ideas or institutions.

Ultimately, Qutb advocates a *jihād* against all ideas contrary to the correct Muslim faith and predicts the eventual universal triumph of fundamental Islam. Qutb endorsed the idea of a clandestine loyalist who would lead his revolution. Peaceful means would be employed if met with tolerance, but, if faced with reaction or suppression, violence becomes a legitimate recourse. Such declarations remain influential to this day, as Islam continues to respond to his claims and legacies.

Related Entries
jihād; Muslim Brethren

Suggested Reading

Black, Antony. *The History of Islamic Political Thought: From the Prophet to the Present.* New York: Routledge 2001.

Qutb, Sayyid. *Milestones (or, Signposts along the Way),* rev. ed. Cedar Rapids, IA: Unity, [1981–1985].

Qutb, Sayyid, *Sayyid Qutb and Islamic Activism: a Translation and Critical Analysis of Social Justice in Islam,* trans. William E. Shepard. Boston: E.J. Brill, 1996.

Qutb, Sayyid. *The Sayyid Qutb Reader: Selected Writings on Politics, Religion, and Society,* ed. Albert J. Bergesen. New York: Routledge 2007.

R

raison d'état (reason of the state)

Operating under the principle of the "reason of the state," political actors emphasize the preservation of the political order and the promotion of the common good as the foremost consideration of public life. All citizens, and especially leaders, are bound by duty to serve the "reasons of the state" above their own private interests, even to the point of calling for a suspension of scruples of private conscience under times of crisis. Hence, acts that would normally be regarded askance might be regrettably permitted during exigent circumstances, for the "reasons of the state," assuming that those reasons are understood rationally and that any acts so engaged are last resorts.

One of the best discussions of the principle of *raison d'état* is succinctly provided by Lee McDonald in the second volume of his *Western Political Theory*. McDonald emphasizes the notion of the "reason of the state" as an alternative to the modern natural law theories contemporary to it. According to McDonald, the "doctrine of the reason of the state...postulates a rational standard for political action in the interests of the state." It is not in adherence to natural law or some other extra-political principle on which we are to base our decisions or our actions, but rather in the rationally conceived interests of the state, a forerunner of the notion of acting on the "national interests" in contrast to more transcendent (and thus more abstract) ideals that are detached from the practical demands of ordinary politics. Leaders have a responsibility to place the interest of the state first, and cannot afford the luxury of appealing to any other standard, transcendent or otherwise. McDonald traces this notion to the sixteenth century, particularly in the writings of Francesco Guicciardini and Giovanni Botero, although Niccolò Machiavelli's political realism certainly provides the most exhaustive and compelling theoretical foundation for *raison d'état,* and many students of political theory identify Machiavelli as the main proponent of reason of the state prescriptions. Thinkers such as Botero were, in McDonald's estimation, following the "nonethical or Machiavellian lines" already established in the early part of the sixteenth century. In any event, the epitome of the practice of *rasion d'état* is perceived by McDonald in the beliefs and action of the eighteenth-century French monarch Louis XIV. To illustrate the apex of *raison d'état* politics, McDonald quotes from the Sun King's memoirs,

> It is always worse for the public to control the government than to support even a bad government which is directed by Kings from whom God alone can judge....Those acts of Kings that are in seeming violations of the rights of their subjects are based upon reasons of state—the most fundamental of all motives, as everyone will admit, but often misunderstood by those who do not rule.

While Louis XIV's inflated and self-aggrandizing justification of a politics of *raison d'état* is distasteful, especially to modern democratic and secular sensibilities, more moderated interpretations of reasons of the state are often recognized as valid, even if begrudgingly. In the contest between nations, or in the need to sustain domestic peace, political leaders even in democracies are allowed some latitude in times of crisis, thus recognizing that the "letter of the law" does not apply in every case. The demands of action under exigent circumstances might justify some decisions by political leaders that would otherwise be regarded as above the law in the ordinary course of things. Abraham Lincoln's wartime decisions regarding *habeas corpus,* for example, can be regarded as a rational application of *raison d'état* and one that can be justified on constitutional grounds. President Franklin Roosevelt's deployment of the navy against Nazi wolf packs in the North Atlantic prior to a declaration of war might also qualify as a rational application of the principle. However, students of politics are hesitant, for good reasons, in embracing the notion of *raison d'état* as a general rule, as the abuses of power will often imperil the ends of just societies even when their rulers are men and women of conscience and sincerity.

Related Entry
Machiavelli, Niccolò

Suggested Readings

McDonald, Lee. *Western Political Theory, Part 2: Machiavelli to Burke.* New York: Harcourt, Brace, Jovanovich, 1968.

Meinecke, Friedrich. *Machiavellism: The Doctrine of Raison d'Etat and Its Place in Modern History,* trans. Douglas Scott with an introduction by W. Stark. Boulder, CO: Westview, 1984.

Rawls, John (1921–2002)

John Rawls is one of the more innovative and influential thinkers in contemporary political theory. His *Theory of Justice* (1971) initiated a wave of political inquiry that at once renewed the basic principles of the social contract theory and the Kantian quest for a nontranscendent objectivism with the precision of modern analytical philosophy and the imaginative speculation of game theory. With Rawls the ancient question regarding the nature of justice, raised by Plato in *Republic* over two millennia ago, was once again brought forward as the central issue of political theory.

Rawls's notion of justice as fairness springs from his concern over the predominance of utilitarianism within the discipline of political theory in particular and the social sciences in general. The maxim that promotes the "greatest happiness for the greatest number" is not a sufficient aspiration for a society that seeks the improvement of the lives of all citizens. Thus Rawls returns to the social contract, but now raised to a "higher level of abstraction," in order to arrive at an operable principle of justice as fairness. Employing the mind game of the original position behind a veil of ignorance (see **veil of ignorance**), Rawls concludes that two principles of justice would be embraced by all rational individuals deliberating from an initial situation of absolute equality: (i) "each person is to have an equal right to the most extensive total system of equal basic liberties compatible with a similar system of liberty for all," and (ii) any social and economic inequalities within society "are to be arranged so that they are to the benefit of the least advantaged" (the difference principle) and "attached to offices and positions open to all" under equal opportunity. According to Rawls, if we are to choose from a true position of equality, one that occurs behind a "veil of ignorance that actually establishes a state of genuine objectivity" about the most fair distribution of social goods in any given society, we can create a social and political order that merits being called just.

Concomitant to this notion is Rawls's position that, in order to ensure that the just society is achieved and sustained, the concept of right must be prior to the good. Or, that is to say, the rights of individuals must be established so that they are free to choose for themselves, within the set of choices framed by the principles of justice, their own conception of the good. Rights are therefore universal and can be affirmed by the political community as such, but the many goods that individuals seek are particular, and must be left to the person to decide. Should a person be accorded an equal amount of liberty as the rest, and should the rights that orbit this portion of liberty be general for all, then the many goods that are sought and adopted are those that are compatible with a person's genuine self-interest. We should not seek the greatest good for the greatest number, according to Rawls, but rather we must guarantee the same rights for all so that the goods selected and the values embraced will be so by free and equal citizens working to affirm their own interest while simultaneously guaranteeing the best possible good for the entire community, and not for any given number other than the whole itself.

Related Entries
difference principle; game theory; Locke, John; Pareto optimality; utilitarianism; veil of ignorance; Wilt Chamberlain argument

Suggested Reading
Rawls, John. *A Theory of Justice.* 1971; repr. Cambridge, MA: Harvard Univ. Press, 2005; new ed., Cambridge, Mass.: Harvard Univ. Press, 1999.
Rawls, John. *Political Liberalism.* New York: Columbia Univ. Press, 1993.
Rawls, John. *Lectures on the History of Philosophy,* ed. Samuel Freeman. Cambridge, MA: Harvard Univ. Press/Belknap Press, 2007.

republic (*res publica, civitas,* things public, things political, commonwealth, common weal)

From the Latin, rooted in the ancient principles of government that emerged out of

Rome and influenced by Greek political theory, the concept of "republic" encapsulates several features that constitute a regime dedicated, at least ideally, to the common good. By and large, these features include the rule of law, free citizenry (and the promotion of basic liberties both guaranteed and defined under the law), some degree of equality among free citizens, constitutionalism, some form of representative government (usually a mixed or composite form of government blending elements of other kinds of regimes such as monarchy, aristocracy, and democracy, thus producing a dispersal of power), accountability of governing officials to the populous, partisan politics, and some sense of the importance of the political participation of a virtuous citizenry. A republic is a direct contrast to more personal and arbitrary forms of power, such as autocracy or, in the extreme case, despotism. Republican principles are thus, to a large extent, understood by what they oppose, to wit—the irrational and excessive ambitions of those who seek to rule for their own gain. Republicanism, to the contrary, is the pursuit of a kind of government independent of the domination of private influences, as far as humanly possible. A republic is literally the "things that are public," or even "the property of the people," in contrast to res privata, or "private things." Hence republican government, regardless of its actual structure (whether the government is largely elected and guided by the legislative body, or whether it includes a ruling elite or even a constitutional monarchy), must be actuated by the common interest and guided by the rule of law, which is itself sovereign. It is, as James Harrington wrote in his *Commonwealth of Oceana,* "an empire of laws, not of men," a sentiment later rephrased by John Adams as a "government of laws, not of men." This idea is ancient. In Plato's *Laws* it is affirmed that those who govern must do so as "slaves to the law," and in Aristotle's *Politics* as well as the *Nicomachean Ethics,* the rule of law is clearly adopted as in every sense preferable to the rule of men, regardless of their abilities. Following Harrington, modern thinkers such as Rousseau reiterated the importance of this premise. As Rousseau states in his *Social Contract,*

> I therefore call every state ruled by laws a republic, regardless of the form its administration may take. For only then does the public interest govern, and only then is the "public thing" [in Latin: *res publica*] something real. Every legitimate government is republican.

While some students of the history of ideas see in the ancient Greek concept of *politiea* the direct ancestor of republics (and indeed, Aristotle's constitutional polity as described in his *Politics* resembles what we would today call a republic), the term itself does come from the Latin and is evident in the writings of Polybius and Cicero. In his *De Re Publica (Republic)* Cicero writes,

> [A] commonwealth is the property of the people. But a people is not any collection of human beings brought together in any sort of way, but an assemblage of people in large numbers associated in an agreement with respect to justice and a partnership for the common good. The first cause of such an association is not so much the weakness of the individual as a certain social spirit which nature has implanted in man.

Cicero's definition aptly summarizes the essence of republicanism: the belief in the political community as natural and salubrious to human life, the notion that society is a partnership among fellows, the respect for justice under the law, and the sense of a common good that both encompasses and exceeds private ambition. This interpretation from Cicero provides a theoretical base for subsequent understanding of the principles of republican government. It is not the rule of the one or the few or the many, but rather the sovereignty of just law aimed at the affirmation of a body of citizens free, equal (at least in the political and legal sense), and committed to a common purpose. Republican government is not designed to eradicate private affairs, but rather to enable the freedom of private activities by preserving a common space wherein no particular group or individual influence can dominate. This same precept is asserted by Machiavelli in the second book of his *Discourses,* wherein he states that "for it is not the well-being of individuals that makes cities great, but the well-being of the community; and it is beyond question that it is only in republics that the common good is looked to properly in that all that promotes it is carried out."

Montesquieu, in his monumental *Spirit of the Laws,* included "republics" within his typology of regimes, along with two species of autocracy, "monarchy" and "despotism." For Montesquieu, a republic is distinguished from these other types in that it is to a large extent animated by virtue. Republics may be aristocratic or democratic, and it is in the latter that virtue, understood as a love of law and country among the citizenry as a whole, is most fully realized. In democratic republics, the "preference for public interest" is the "source" of all private interests, a preference that stems from this love of laws and country that is "peculiar to democracies." Thus with Montesquieu, the principle of democratic virtue is critical to at least one major type of republican government. Moreover, while it is common to remind ourselves of the difference between a democracy and a republic, something which was uppermost in the mind of the American founders (such as James Madison in his Federalist No. 10); it is a distinction that is really of a technical nature. Nonetheless, regardless of the structure of any given republic, some element of democracy is contained therein, however diluted or balanced against the potential excesses of direct and uninhibited democratic forces. While some republics might include vestiges of autocracy (such as a constitutional monarchy), no republic is without a democratic component. Hence, there has always existed a strong affinity between republican principles and democratic aspirations, an affinity that is likely to become still more pronounced as more regimes cultivate some variety of democratic practice.

Related Entries

Aristotle; Cicero, Marcus Tullius; democracy; Harrington, James; liberalism; Machiavelli, Niccolò; Madison, James; *Republic, The* (*Politeia*); Rousseau, Jean-Jacques

Suggested Reading

Cicero, *De Re Publica* and *De Legibus,* trans. C. W. Keyes. 1928; repr. Cambridge, MA: Harvard Univ. Press/Loeb Classical Library, 1977.

Harrington, James. *The Commonwealth of Oceana* and *A System of Politics,* ed. J. G. A. Pocock. 1992; repr., New York: Cambridge Univ. Press, 1996.

Machiavelli, Niccolò, *The Discourses,* ed. Bernard Crick; trans. Leslie J. Walker, rev. Brian Richardson. 1970; repr. New York: Penguin, 1979.

Rahe, Paul A. *Republics Ancient and Modern,* 3 vols. Chapel Hill, NC: Univ. North Carolina Press, 1994.

Rousseau, Jean-Jacques. *On the Social Contract,* trans. Donald A. Cress. Indianapolis: Hackett, 1987.

Republic, **The** (*Politeia*)

Plato's *Republic* may be the single most important text in the history of political thought, although other candidates might include Aristotle's *Politics,* Hobbes's *Leviathan,* and Locke's *Second Treatise.* Even should we concede that these other texts match the influence of Plato's *Republic,* none of them combine the comprehensive sweep of the *Republic,* which is a masterpiece not only in political thought but also as a preeminent text in metaphysics and epistemology, ethical theory, theories of education, the apotheosis of metaphor, and the nature of the philosophic life. Moreover, there is no other single text in the canon of political and moral philosophy that achieves the literary height and sheer aesthetic beauty of *Republic,* although other works by Plato approximate it. Whether or not one accepts Plato's primary lessons in *Republic* or agrees with his conclusions, reading the great work is an undertaking ensuring a significant reward for the student of the history of ideas. Western political theory traces its foundation to Plato, and his *Republic* is at the heart of this foundation.

Politeia is the title of the *Republic* in Plato's original Greek, a word that connotes the whole of the political sphere and public affairs within the ancient community. The word *politeia* can also mean simply "constitution" (in the broad sense) or political structure, even regime or the association of public things. This last sense is translated into Latin as *res publica* (literally "things public" or "common weal,"—commonwealth), and thus comes to us as *Republic.* While some complain that this is a poor translation of *Politeia,* the name is, as Robin Waterfield has remarked, irremovable. While it must be conceded that the book is not about a republic in the modern understanding, in a sense the title is apt if understood in the ancient way—an examination of the "things public," a study of political things as they are and as they ought to be. But as stated above, perhaps no title could appropriately encapsulate the entire meaning of the book, for *Republic* is both about politics and about far more than politics. In fact, the breadth of the work renders a just summary nearly impossible, so with that in mind we move forward in the full admission that what follows is inevitably and lamentably incomplete.

Republic is traditionally divided into ten "books," although this division is not Plato's own, but rather the consequence of later methods of compiling and printing the work that would overlay Plato's original text. Nonetheless, it is useful to follow this division as an efficient means toward synopsis.

Book I opens with Socrates and his traveling companion, Glaucon (Plato's brother) being persuaded to interrupt their journey back to Athens after attending a new religious festival in the Piraeus (the port of Athens) that was dedicated to the goddess Bendis. Invited to join a gathering at the home of Cephalus, Socrates and Glaucon agree to attend and are soon in the presence of several friends and acquaintances, which include Adeimantus (another of Plato's brothers), Cephalus (the patriarch), his sons Polemarchus and Lysias along with Euthydemus, Charmantides, Cleitophon, and,

significantly, Thrasymachus (a renowned sophist), and a handful of other guests. After what appears to be a routine exchange of pleasantries between Socrates and Cephalus, Plato has his characters raise a question regarding the nature of justice (*dikaiosyne*—which can also be translated as morality, or righteousness, or correct living), and a conversation ensues regarding its proper definition. Cephalus and Polemarchus each present a definition that Socrates easily dismisses. Socrates actually helps draw out a definition from Cephalus based on certain claims that he has freely announced to the company, a definition holding justice to be speaking honestly and paying one's debts. Socrates finds this to be incomplete, for such actions, while they may be admirable, cannot be the whole of the definition of justice, and admit too readily of exceptions. Once Socrates has rejected this definition, the patriarch Cephalus promptly exits, explaining that he must now attend to his devotion to the gods through their propitiation. Polemarchus inherits his father's argument, and offers a revision: just acts (or moral conduct) are acts that benefit one's friends and harm one's enemies. Socrates also rebuts this definition with ease, for it is more than simply incomplete but rather is quite obviously wrong for two reasons. First, this definition assumes a kind of knowledge that is beyond us, for we do not always really know who our true friends are, and moreover, we might be misled into friendship with people who are bad, and thus our friendship with them would be to the benefit of unjust people. Additionally, and more importantly, Socrates points out that, regardless of the character of our associates, a just person does not commit injustice, hence it is wrong even to harm one's enemies, or at least it is not an act that we can call just or moral. As in *Crito,* Socrates teaches that to be a person of just principles, one does not exchange wrong for wrong, nor treat the unjust with injustice. To do so would only add to the injustice, and would do nothing to promote the cause of justice for any party involved.

In challenging these definitions of justice, Socrates opposes the conventional wisdom of his day. Most of his contemporaries would define justice in similar ways. But they cannot be definitions of justice itself, as they rely too much on how a person is related to others externally—they are oriented toward particular situations and do not really reflect any quality of our character. Socrates affirms that justice is really a function of the soul, a virtue of the person, and cannot be defined solely in terms of specific cases that are made to fit particular scenarios. Justice is at once internal and universal, this is why a just person either is just or is not just—creditors, friends, and enemies notwithstanding.

Having effortlessly demolished the situational ethics of the family of Cephalus, Socrates appears to have made his point, but he is now challenged by an irascible and skeptical Thrasymachus; the famous sophist who is depicted by Plato as an impatient, aggressive, and derisive debater. With a degree of haughtiness, Thrasymachus claims to know what justice is and announces it to be nothing more than "the advantage of the stronger," thus arguing that justice is in fact a function of power, and thus completely conditional on who holds political advantage within a city. It has nothing to do with the soul or virtue, and everything to do with interest and power. At this point, Socrates and Thrasymachus offer two diametrically opposed conceptions of politics, both in conflict with the popular norms of the times. For Thrasymachus, the political sphere and the principles that are associated with it (such as justice) are in every instance a question of power and will. For Socrates, politics is at once an art (comparable to medicine) and in its essence an act of service. Furthermore, in the "good city" if such a city existed, citizens would only compete against each other to avoid having to govern, whereas in the image of politics advanced by Thrasymachus, citizens are in constant competition to gain the advantage and rule over others. Thrasymachus adopts as his model for political conduct the quest to "outdo" others in every activity, to have more than one's ordinary share—a notion denoted by the Greek term *pleonexia.* Indeed, in his argument for surpassing all others, Thrasymachus unabashedly asserts that the most advantageous life is one in which all others are outdone, and to have more than all others is the surest way to the most beneficial life. For Thrasymachus, it is the tyrant who more than anyone else leads such a life, and in concluding this, Thrasymachus radically alters the conversation from a discussion of the definition of justice to an assertion that injustice is actually the only choice for a superior life, and especially the injustice that comes from tyranny. Hence the second major question is raised: which life is more advantageous, the life of the just person or the life of injustice. The remainder of the book will attempt to prove that a just life is the only course for a rational and virtuous person, a principle that Socrates must go through some effort to prove.

After Thrasymachus and Socrates have argued past each other, Socrates appears to have prevailed as the first book draws to a close. But Book II opens with the "spirited" Glaucon dissatisfied with the results of Socrates's exchange with Thrasymachus. Glaucon believes Socrates to be right but finds his argument weak and states that he wants to truly "know" what justice is and why it is better to live a life of justice rather than injustice. Hence he revives and strengthens Thrasymachus's fundamental principle, that a life of injustice with impunity is the most beneficial through argument and analogy (the myth of the Ring of Gyges), holding that no one is willingly just and that it is better to live tyrannically if one can maintain a good reputation than to live justly while losing all esteem in the eyes of the public. Even though the inner premise is the same, Glaucon's argument is superior to Thrasymachus's, compelling Socrates to now engage in a long discussion that brings the political dimension to the foreground (although in a way Thrasymachus has already done this in his discussion of tyranny as the best possible life). Stating that we must look at justice not only in the soul, but also in the city, Socrates begins to examine the origins and nature of the city, noting that in so doing we also can understand the nature of the soul, given the isomorphism between the two. Hence Socrates widens his angle of view to illuminate the essence of a just society and prove that it is always better to be just. Socrates creates a city in theory, or city in speech (*kallipolis,* the beautiful or fine city), for if we are going to discover justice as it is, we must examine the city as it is, not using examples (such as Athens or Sparta) in order to discover the nature of justice and not simply situational justice (as offered by Cephalus, Polemarchus, and perversely, Thrasymachus). This city springs from necessity and aims at self-sufficiency and moderation, accomplished through the assignment of necessary tasks in line with the innate talents of the diverse citizens. Glaucon objects that Socrates's city is only concerned with bare necessity, fit for pigs but not for human beings. Human desire is expansive, and cannot nor should not be so easily moderated. While not conceding this point, Socrates agrees to Glaucon's terms, for the fever that Glaucon gives to the city through the insertion of "luxuries" might be useful in discerning not only justice, but the nature of justice as well. Socrates never rejects his initial attempt, and still refers to it as the "true city."

Guardians are now recognized as necessary to the city of speech as modified by Glaucon's qualifications, and Socrates focuses on the notion that only those of the best natures (philosophic, spirited, strong, and agile) should govern, but they must be carefully educated to love the city as a watchdog loves the flock if they are to serve rather than oppress their charges. Hence Plato has Socrates devote considerable time to the proper education of the guardians so that the right natures can be properly nurtured to the proper state of mind. Those who are to be given the responsibility to rule the city must be schooled in the right forms of music and poetry as well as gymnastics and other subjects of education. Above all, they must not be misguided by false stories about the gods and heroes. In so arguing, Socrates critiques the culture of his day by rejecting the reliance on stories from iconic figures such as Homer and Hesiod. Children are malleable like wax, and should not be exposed to untruth or indecency. To become both capable leaders and gentle ones, the young must understand the true nature of divine and heroic things.

Socrates further develops the structure of the ideal city of speech through three reforms that must sustain "waves of criticism": the common sharing of property, spouses and children, the inclusion of women as guardians equally with men, and the rule of the philosophers. Each of these reforms, respectively, represents a feature of the ideal city, or the form of the polis, that provides a lesson toward which all cities may approximate: that public good and private interest be separated, that only essential qualities are legitimate grounds for who rules rather than superficial differences, and that reason should always guide power.

It is this last reform—the rule of philosophers or that reason should guide power—that is in Plato's estimation the most controversial, and he has Socrates go to great lengths to prove the truth behind this principle. The philosopher is compared to a true captain or navigator of a ship who happens to be the only one who knows how to practice the art of sailing, but he is ridiculed and persecuted while the crew, none of whom admits that there is an art of navigation (that is, the art of ruling cities) compete, plot, and employ fraud and coercion to take the helm. The one person who is qualified to do so is denied the position of captain, while others put the ship at risk through their misplaced presumption to command, or for the simple lust for power. Most cities are in this situation, according to Plato, thus even though the rule of reason is ever the ideal, it is seldom even approximated in practice throughout the cities of our experience.

Socrates's discussion of the ideal of rule by philosophers leads into a compelling examination of the nature of knowledge itself, and how true knowledge is distinct from right opinion and ignorance. As we move further into Plato's theory of knowledge, we also move into his ontology—or his basic theory of being, of what is essentially real. For Plato, it is in the discovery of the intelligible Forms (*eidos*) that we find the highest and surest reality. The Forms are the essence of being, eternal and immutable, and for this reason they are more real than the material things that at best reflect or participate in them. It is only through thought that we can know the Forms, once we turn to the phenomenal, we can only perceive certain aspects of the Forms, and even then incompletely and vaguely. Socrates's analysis of true knowledge and true being culminates with his sublime allegory of the cave in Book VII.

The allegory of the cave is discussed further in a separate entry (see **allegory of the cave**), but for our purposes here suffice it to say that with this allegory *Republic* reaches its zenith. The allegory illustrates several aspects of Plato's philosophy: being and becoming, knowing and perspective, the education of the soul, the guiding principle of reason in the ideal state, and, above all, the centrality of the Good. Even before Socrates shares the allegory, he has established the Good as the highest principle of being—or "that which is most prized." Analogous to the sun, the Good is to the soul as the sun is to the eye. Without the sun the eye would be deprived of sight, and so it is with the Good, for it is the Good that makes it possible for the soul to come to know. Hence the Good is the highest of all the Forms, the one thing that stands apart at the pinnacle of being and knowing. The Good is prior to even justice, which was the initial topic of the dialogue, but as we move deeper into Plato's teaching, we discern the Good as the only first principle behind being and knowing, and thus the ultimate aim of the *polis.* Justice, truth, and beauty are all "good-like," but they are not to be identified as *the* Good, it is only in and through the Good that we arrive at a Form (*eidos*) that is unqualified and complete. It is

the universal principle upon which all values and all acts are grounded and through which they gain meaning.

Only the city of speech is a city of "good men," wherein the form of the *polis* is established from the love of wisdom in the pursuit of true justice for the sake of the Good itself. The city of speech is the form of the *polis,* and is thus more real than any city in our experience (such as Athens, Sparta or Corinth); but to set its principles into actual operation is nearly impossible. Even if such a city were achieved in the visible (phenomenal) realm, it would not endure, as everything that enters into the world is subject to change. A perfect city applied in experience could only change for the worse, and it is here, in Book VIII, that Plato discusses his imperfect regimes. Socrates demonstrates the relationship between regime and the character of its citizens, once again emphasizing the isomorphism between city and soul. The least imperfect city of *Republic* (not to be confused with his "second-best city" in *Laws*) is what he names "timocracy," wherein the rational lovers of wisdom are replaced by the spirited lovers of honor and virtue. Timocracy further degenerates into oligarchy owing to the secret desire for material gain (which begins to replace honor), or rule of the few who are not the best, and moreover, who are motivated by wealth. Plato's oligarchy is what we would call a "plutocracy," the rule of the wealthy for the sake of wealth. Whereas the timocrat was spirited, the oligarch is an appetitive individual who subdues reason and spiritedness, ruling over the better parts of the soul through the lesser part. Oligarchy intensifies class division, creating a gulf between the rich who look down on the poor with contempt and the poor who regard the rich with envy. Eventually the many who are poor triumph, leading to the next step in the descent into imperfect regimes—democracy.

The democratic city and the democratic character are the same: indisciplined, fickle, chaotic, unstable, erratic, self-absorbed, and self-indulgent. As with oligarchy, it is a city wherein the appetites govern, no longer fixed on wealth alone but on a variety of pleasures that number wealth as only one desire among many. The democratic person values unrestrained liberty and pleasure for its own sake. The nature of the pleasure is unimportant so long as the democrat can enjoy it. This is the greatest injustice in the democratic city for Plato, that all pleasures, both the necessary and the unnecessary ones, are available to be indulged, and furthermore, that all of these pleasures are considered equal. It matters not to the democratic person if one leads a life of quiet asceticism or of insatiable hedonism. The democrat rejects the truth that some things are to be loved and some things are to be despised. Rather, in a democracy, anything that is pleasurable is to be enjoyed, and the pleasures and liberties that secure them are all equivalent in their value. This, for Plato, is the gravest problem in democracy, and the engine of its slide into tyranny.

As Socrates enters the tyrannical city, that city which Thrasymachus claims is the finest city supporting the most admirable man, the question regarding the advantages of justice is finally answered. The tyrant and his city are motivated by lust and haunted by fear, thus even though they may appear to have surpassed everyone (*pleonexia*) through that most "commendable" achievement praised by Thrasymachus as extensive and thoroughgoing injustice, the tyrannical city is a city with but one master and many slaves, and indeed, because of insatiate lust and the constant nettle of fear, the tyrant actually is the most complete slave of all, regardless of his appearance as the master of the city. The soul of the tyrant is the most enslaved, and thus the least happy. Hence, Socrates in Book IX finally answers the claim of Thrasymachus as refined and fortified by Glaucon—it is better to lead a just life, even if it means suffering for the just person than to live with complete injustice, impunity notwithstanding. The state of the soul is the paramount consideration, so it is possible that we have been speaking of the soul the whole time. Even

so, much has been said about the nature of justice and politics in service to goodness, and thus Plato has Socrates draw more tightly the intimate bond between the constitution of a city (*politeia*) and the structure of one's soul.

The *Republic* ends in Book X with a discussion of the afterlife that continues to clarify the various ways in which the imagination imitates true knowledge. The book concludes with another story, the Myth of Er that dwells on Plato's belief in the transmigration of souls, speculation on the structure of the universe, and the notion of knowledge as recollection.

As cautioned above, it is impossible to summarize the *Republic* in the space allowed here, and difficult enough within the limits of an entire book. Plato's great achievement is worth a careful and extended examination by any genuine student of political theory and philosophy, and its continued prominence at the core of the philosophical canon is assured as long as copies of *Republic* are drawn from the bookshelves of sincere students of political inquiry.

Related Entries
allegory of the cave; Plato

Suggested Reading
There are numerous translations of Plato's *Republic* in print, well over a dozen of which are held in high regard. For our purposes, we recommend: Plato. *Republic,* in *Complete Works,* ed. John M. Cooper. Indianapolis: Hackett, 1997.
See also: Annas, Julia. *An Introduction to Plato's Republic.* New York: Oxford Univ. Press, 1981; Brann, Eva T.H. *The Music of the Republic.* Philadelphia: Paul Dry Books, 2004; and Rice, Daryl H. *A Guide to Plato's Republic.* New York: Oxford Univ. Press, 1998.

rights
The concept of rights is a seminal principle in the definition and establishment of a just polity, and yet in many ways it remains vague and abstractly understood. Citizens of democracies, and even citizens of regimes oriented more toward autocracy, intuitively understand what

it means to have rights, such as a right to life, the right to liberty, the right to property, the right to the pursuit of happiness, the right of *habeas corpus,* the right to be represented, the right of free expression, and the right to worship according to one's own conscience. Nonetheless, just what each of these means and the source from which they are derived remains a subject of ongoing dialogue and, in some cases, conflict. In the course of such discussions and debates, questions are raised about the nature and extent of rights. Are rights entitlements? How is right linked to interest? Is right defined by the moral law of nature? Or, is right the product of social consensus? Are rights absolute? Are rights properly conceived by an order of rank? If so, which rights are superior? (For example, is the right of free speech superior to the right to counsel beforehand when one is arraigned before a court?) If not, are all rights, then, of equal importance (the right to life is equal to the right to vote, or the right to marry, for example). Political theorists, philosophers, and jurists continue to examine the origin, nature, and scope of the concept of right, with the promise of a definitive set of answers always in question. And yet, few concepts are as important to the promotion of a just society as the principle that human beings do possess rights.

While it is common to think of rights as a modern legacy of the Anglo-American political movements and the various philosophies of the eighteenth-century Enlightenment, the principle of rights is far older, traceable at least as far as the ancient Judaic notion that protects the rights of the "widow and the orphan" and holds the community accountable for their treatment. In both Judaism and Christianity, as well as in the ancient notions of citizenship in the Athenian *polis* as described by Pericles in his *Funeral Oration* and theoretically developed by Plato and Aristotle, the dignity of the human person is advanced, providing the ground for the affirmation of rights. When questions such as justice and fairness are raised, as they were in the most ancient political theories, the

inquiry is directed at what is right, not in terms of mere want or desire, but in terms of some standard principle that applies to each individual in the same way. Hence the concept of right draws on the dignity of persons, the fairness of actions, the justice of laws, and the equal treatment of citizens. For the Roman jurists, the notion of right was intrinsically linked to the notion of natural law, for the term *jus* was employed both as law and implied to apply to the rights of persons. Dometius Ulpianus (Ulpian), for example, argued that justice is understood in terms of what is right for each person, and thus is promoted when all are given what is properly their due. Hence, long before the development of modern notions of rights, the principle of rights was in full operation within the moral system of Judaism and Christianity, the theoretical writings of Plato, Aristotle, and the Stoics, and the legal tracts of the Roman jurists.

With the emergence of newer political attitudes and structures in the European context of the sixteenth and seventeenth centuries as well as the American contributions of the eighteenth and early nineteenth centuries, the notion of rights has become at once more tangible in that political and legal systems are largely shaped by the principle of rights and at the same time and in some ways more conceptually vague. Thomas Hobbes, John Locke, Alexander Hamilton, and Thomas Jefferson all recognized what we call today "inalienable" rights, that is, certain aspects of our person over which we retain self-government. Yet each of these thinkers conceives of these rights in different ways. For Hobbes, natural rights are thoroughly distinct from natural law (a departure from the Stoic and Thomistic approach that understood the dignity of the person as inextricably linked to the natural and divine law), and are, at least in a state of nature, concurrent with power. Additionally, for Hobbes the natural rights held in nature, part of which are transferred to the sovereign, are absolute, thus the absolute rights renounced and transferred are the basis for the power of the sovereign, which in turn may be seen as absolute (with qualifications). Locke regarded rights to be real and essential to the person, but all natural rights were limited by the moral law of nature, hence when some rights are renounced and transferred to a common authority, that authority remains clearly limited. Hamilton's and Jefferson's language of natural rights carry the Lockean tradition forward, recognizing that right is not a function of power, but rather "endowed" by a transcendent source that affirms an objective principle for the claims of human dignity. This concept is drawn to its logical conclusion in John Stuart Mill, who stated that the individual must be sovereign over his own body and mind, that "the only freedom which deserves the name, is that of pursuing our own good in our own way," and furthermore, that "If all mankind minus one were of one opinion, mankind would be no more justified in silencing that one person than he, if he had the power, would be in silencing mankind." As Ronald Dworkin in following this same vein once wrote, rights are "trumps" that establish the proper province of individual liberty as prior to the aims of society in general, and especially of government. For H.L.A. Hart, if there is any one natural right, it is "the equal right of all men to be free," which again affirms the primacy of the free agent. It is this sense of rights, as developed by Locke, the American founders, and Mill, that is closer to the principles that most people have come to embrace. Hence rights are by their very nature distinct from both power and interest, and conceptually interwoven with justice, fairness, dignity, and some level of equality (with notable variations). Right is ever distinguishable from might; perhaps this is the initial premise that is the foundation of any rational examination of the concept. Not only this, but also the idea that a right held by a person is always morally prior to a claim made by a government, or even by a group. It is in this sense that the concept of rights is surely guarded from the ambitions of power.

Related Entry
Funeral Oration of Pericles

Suggested Reading
Brett, Annabel S. *Liberty, Right, and Nature.* New York: Cambridge Univ. Press, 1997.

Feinberg, Joel. *Rights, Justice, and the Bounds of Liberty.* Princeton: Princeton Univ. Press, 1980.

Finnis, John, *Natural Law and Natural Right,* New York: Oxford Univ. Press, 1980.

Hart, H.L.A. *The Concept of Law,* 2d ed., with a postscript ed. Penelope A. Bulloch and Joseph Raz. New York: Oxford Univ. Press, 1994.

Hohfeld, Wesley N. *Fundamental Legal Conceptions,* ed. Walter W. Cook, with a new foreword by Arthur L. Corbin. 1964; repr. Union, NJ: Lawbook Exchange, 2000.

Strauss, Leo. *Natural Right and History.* 1952; repr. Chicago: Univ. Chicago Press, 1971.

Rorty, Richard (1931–2007)

A major figure in twentieth-century philosophy, Richard Rorty is also a key figure in the development of what can be called postmodern political theory. As a philosopher, Rorty can loosely be described as a perspectivist in the tradition of Friedrich Nietzsche, a pragmatist following, with some modification, the ideas of John Dewey, a constructivist and antiessentialist (and a confirmed anti-Platonist) and, for lack of a better term, historicist. For Rorty, there are no objective truths or essential aspects of nature; at least that we can confidently know. Rather, truth, value, and meaning are functions of language within a given social context, and there are no absolute, ahistorical political truths or eternal values that reflect an essential human nature. Absolutes and first principles are themselves derived from social perspective and linguistic interaction, and are never objects or elements of being that can be known in themselves. Language and meaning do not represent any reality beyond the context of language itself within a particular social and historic structure.

This perspectivist stance influences Rorty's political ideas. For the most part, Rorty recommends a combination of pragmatism and pluralism, while rejecting the pursuit of transcendent concepts and higher principles. For Rorty, such pursuits are philosophically untenable and potentially harmful as there is nothing that is objectively good in itself, nor any concept or idea that represents reality as it is. It is human discourse and human need that generates reality and good. Thus, in political life, principles and values are in competition with each other as means to address the needs and wants of a given community within a specific cultural and linguistic context. Ideas and political positions are adopted not because they are true, but because they address needs and lend meaning. Should an idea prove beneficial, it is sustained as a frame of theoretical reference; otherwise it is abandoned as human beings seek out new ideas for the implementation of practical policies and contextually sensible themes. There are no enduring foundations upon which the best kind of political life can be built for human beings transhistorically and transculturally, but rather, only those ideas and practices that are accepted at a given time by the consensus of a particular community for the achievement of specific sets of goals. Hence ideologies and theoretical approaches are equal competitors in the arena of human discourse; there is no objective standard to which we can appeal. In a sense, Rorty argues that whatever works for the satisfaction of particular human needs within a cultural set of meanings is what becomes true and good for those humans within that culture. Political life is characterized by a plurality of ideas and interests, none intrinsically better than the other, and those ideas that emerge as acceptable to the broader consensus, which is itself always in flux given the pluralistic nature of society, are regarded with a pragmatic sentiment and adopted to the satisfaction of immediate needs. As nothing is permanent, no verities eternal, or foundations real, consensuses form and dissolve, and as such, so do truths and values. What is true and valuable is only so because of use, and thus we are to expect change and adaptation, understood in somewhat Darwinian terms, in the development and adoption of political principles.

While Rorty holds that all ideas and values are on some level equal (due to the reality that there are no objective standards by which to measure them, no language, political or otherwise, that represents reality outside of social context), he clearly recognizes that there are certain ways of thinking about the world that are preferable. Rorty seeks a sort of liberal irony in the political, not the liberalism of, say John Locke or Thomas Jefferson that is framed by an objectivist certitude (for example, "We hold these truths to be self-evident"), but a liberalism that seeks irony and play in the social realm, and in so doing, challenges given structure and arbitrary authority, regardless of its source. As there are no objective truths, it is in the engagement of the ironist that we can fully dismantle arbitrary authority and playfully affirm a life of creative spontaneity. Here the influence of Nietzsche is brought forward, for Rorty's views on political engagement are focused on the triumph of the aesthetic dimension, the return of the poetic to both philosophy and politics, and in the end, a reshaping of the language of community in ways that value difference and imagination. The ironist will not seek out a system to understand and then frame the political, but rather, the liberal as ironist will constantly promote social change and disruption of dominant discourses. In rejecting first principles, the ironist cannot generate a theory in the traditional sense, but can only provide an aesthetic within which the political can be transformed through the creative energies of human agents.

Even though Rorty can be described as a kind of relativist (a term that he argued only made sense given an objectivist context), he nonetheless finds certain objective markers that prevent him from slipping into nihilism. While Rorty rejects affirming eternal political truths, he does argue that the liberal ironist can promote a just society by affirming human solidarity (political truths and meaning are, after all, selected by consensus) and diligently working to eliminate cruelty. While we cannot say that certain ideologies or theories are inherently better than others, we can say without equivocation that cruelty is always to be resisted. In this way Rorty is able to discern between political consensus that is playful (such as that of the liberal ironist or the Nietzschean Overman) and those that are cruel (the imagination does not need to be stretched here). In this way Rorty does find an orientation; a polity is well-served in advancing human dignity and creativity and must guard against the emergence of cruel practices. It is here that Rorty lands, and here that he finds a principle that can be embraced transcontextually.

Related Entry
pragmatic maxim

Suggested Reading
Rorty, Richard. *Contingency, Irony, and Solidarity.* 1989; repr. New York: Cambridge Univ. Press, 1996.

Rousseau, Jean-Jacques (1712–1778)

A thinker who lived thoroughly immersed in the French Enlightenment and yet whose ideas are emphatically not of the Enlightenment, Jean-Jacques Rousseau poses a particular set of problems for his readers and interpreters. The unusual details of his biography aside, Rousseau's political theory is enigmatic on many levels. For some, his ideas are undercut by contradictions, reducing his status as a thinker, yet for others Rousseau arrived at numerous insights that have either influenced or anticipated the balance of all subsequent political theory and therefore is a figure of primary standing in the history of ideas. Only Machiavelli has provoked more debate, only Marx has garnered more controversy. A "dreamer of democracy" to some, a protofascistic "enemy of the open society" for others, Rousseau is nothing if not a puzzle, and whichever conclusion one draws about the sum of his work, he is on all accounts idiosyncratic and intriguing.

Rousseau's political thought can be framed inside two basic assumptions: that the only essential property of human beings is free will, and that, following from the first assumption,

the only purpose of the state is to produce moral citizens. Additionally, a recurring theme throughout the whole of Rousseau's work animates these assumptions, viz., the notion that human intellect alone, and the civilization that it has produced, is not sufficient to secure the improvement of the human person, and, more to the point, has for the most part led to the corruption of human nature. Contrary to the tenor of his times, Rousseau was not enamored with the notion of human progress. Instead, Rousseau concluded that our vaunted capacity for reasoning, while both necessary and even admirable on some levels, has in the final analysis promoted the ascent of egotism and the descent of our natural innocence. It is not in our rationality that we are elevated, but only through our moral character, and thus it is not reason that causes us to be distinctively human, but rather, our free will, the fact that we are free agents capable of choice. All animals, Rousseau maintains, are capable of forming ideas on some level. Human reason is superior, but only in such a way as it causes human beings to be different in degree, not in kind. Only free will makes us different in kind from the rest of nature, and only that will which pursues a moral life ennobles our humanity. But when our natural innocence is lost, our capacity for action is enfeebled, our civilization corrupt. What is needed, according to Rousseau, is to understand humanity in its barest state, and in so doing, to reconstruct a form of association that, while not returning us to this state, nonetheless rehabilitates what is best in our nature, and thus, that which defines our true humanity.

Following Hobbes and Locke, Rousseau begins his political philosophy with a discussion of human nature. This requires us to conceive of human beings in a completely natural state, absent any features or residues of society. In Rousseau's estimation, this is a radical enterprise, concluding with the image of a human creature in nature, isolated and disinterested in fellow members of the species. To understand human beings in nature otherwise would be to inject elements of society, and thus the artifice of convention, into the analysis. Humanity in the state of nature is alone, independent, innocent, and self-sufficient, capable of providing for all needs and content to live without any attachments to person or place. Humans live in a state of freedom and equality as in both Locke and Hobbes, but it is a freedom faced with few needs and an equality that is enjoyed unaware. Rousseau's state of nature is not determined by conflict stemming from insatiability within scarcity, as in Hobbes, owing to the level of desire experienced by Rousseau's natural person being low in the comparison. Few needs and still fewer wants amount to fewer causes of quarrel, or, in the purest state of nature, no occasion for quarrel at all. The human person in the state of nature is both robust and simple; robust enough to thrive in even harsh environments, simple enough never to need more than what is within the reach of one's hands. It is not so much that nature is abundant as it is that our natural desires are finite. Hence Rousseau reverses the Hobbesian state of nature from a condition wherein limitless desire is frustrated by finite resources and becomes a situation wherein finite desire is satisfied by any given set of resources. Being self-sufficient and easily satisfied, a life of independence and solitude is neither brutish nor blissful, it just is.

A person living in such a state, in Rousseau's eyes, is superior to those who are corrupted by the appetites that have multiplied within society. Rousseau has but to compare his Parisian contemporaries to the natives of America, the former, while sophisticated, are in effect effete and without substance, and could never survive under conditions in which the latter thrive and live happily in their rusticity. All the more is the case for those in a true state of nature, without any sustained contact with others, completely left to drift through life as the wind and stream. Such a person, compared to the denizen of the world's great cities, is a brilliant triumph of nature. In a sense, Rousseau's state of nature describes in metaphor what it means to be a human stripped of the luxuries and temptations of society that have corrupted us, a person so free in their lack of attachments and needs that they are able to give themselves over to the commands of nature without resistance. The choice, therefore, is still that of a free agent, but in this case, the choice is to succumb to nature, not to set oneself against it.

Yet, for Rousseau, such a condition, if it ever existed (for Rousseau admits that it is pure speculation), is only a concept for the measure of humanity within society, a measure that finds humankind falling short of the natural independence and innocence that would characterize us if cast outside of society—a measure and nothing more. The state of nature itself is forever lost, but what it symbolizes (that is, our original nature), remains hidden deep within us, covered over and obscured by the overwhelming sediments of history and culture. It is because we are also by nature reasoning creatures that this condition has befallen us, or to put it more simply, that which separates us from the rest of nature by degree (reason) has initiated a circumstance wherein that which separates us from the rest of nature in kind (our capacity for free will) is repressed or warped. In short, according to Rousseau, reasoning leads to comparison, and comparison leads to wanting to be compared with others— to look at and to want to be looked at—which, in effect, is the origin of the desire for self-esteem, or the drive for recognition. This produces the first fixed attachment for human beings, the need for the acclaim of others. What Rousseau refers to as a natural love of self (*amour de soi*) is perverted into an artificial and needy vain love of one's own (*amour propre*) the former is a mark of independence and self-sufficiency, the latter the consequence of our desire for the judgment of others. Once such a desire emerges, what Rousseau calls "trivial inequalities" gain significance and are exaggerated to such an extent that our natural equality is overshadowed and forgotten. Needs and wants multiply, possession is introduced, conflict appears, and the lust for power as the surest way to command the respect of others and control over the environment emerges, resulting in the enslavement of humanity by its own devices. Society is now characterized by inequality and marred by corruption, a state of being that we have fled to on our own accord, ultimately driving us toward a future wherein power becomes the only force in society, controlled by one, and wherein we are all once again equal, but "equally nothing" as we are equally slaves.

The fall from nature is one in which there is no recovery. Yet recover our humanity we must; this means, for Rousseau, that we must in some way restore what was lost in the decline from nature into society. This requires a restoration of our natural freedom without reverting to a state of nature; a reconstruction of human free will in and through society. To do this, we must abandon our lust for power and domination over others as well as those slavish tendencies that drive us into submission, and thus dehumanize us—"to renounce liberty," Rousseau asserts, "is to renounce being a man, to surrender the rights of humanity and even its duties." To regain our freedom and thus our humanity within political society we must reassert our will, that is, our ability to choose, but no longer a will detached from the interests of others, but one that works to strengthen freedom against submission while through the choice to, at least on some level, submit. Rousseau raises the question, "How will the individual in society manage to engage one's "own force and liberty" without causing harm to himself?" Rousseau further develops his question in the following way, thus inquiring as to how we can

> find a form of association which defends and protects with all common forces the person and goods of each associate, and by means of which each one, while uniting with all, nevertheless obeys only himself and remains as free as before? This is the fundamental problem for which the social contract provides the solution.

That choice that has been lost in the abandonment of our natural liberty reappears collectively through this social contract, the basic consent to be governed without capitulating to arbitrary power. In the social contract, society is transformed from curse into a potential blessing allowing humanity the chance not only to act as free agents once again but also to act now as free and moral creatures and thus become still nobler in comparison to the simpler character of our original nature. In the renunciation of power as the basis for political control and the advancement of rights as the only foundation for legitimate political authority, the person is now able to act as a being capable of moral choice, and thus the freedom enjoyed under a social contract within the perimeter of a legitimate state is in effect superior to the liberty of the state of nature. In nature, we are free to follow our appetites, but in the last analysis for Rousseau, just as with Plato (with whom some have compared Rousseau) this amounts to a "slavish" kind of liberty. Moral liberty is that which is enjoyed by citizens, and therefore the social contract that creates a state of free human beings is not only restorative, but also redemptive. We are now free to truly act either for or against the impulses of nature, and hence the freedom that was enjoyed in a state of nature was only an adumbration of the true freedom that can only be exercised in society.

Through the social contract, members of a society act as both collectively sovereign and as individually subject. In this way Rousseau recalls the ancient definition of citizenship, viz., those who are capable of ruling and being ruled. The social contract only exists between citizens, who are simultaneously subjects and sovereign, government being mandated as only an intermediary between the citizens themselves. Hence for Rousseau, unlike Hobbes (who regards sovereign and subject as wholly disparate) and Locke (who states that sovereign power, while always belonging to the people, can be deposited in the legislature as a fiduciary), the people are always sovereign, for to surrender permanently (Hobbes) or transfer conditionally (Locke) the sovereign power is tantamount to renouncing one's free will. Power can be transferred, and thus power is the province of those who govern in our behalf. But the will cannot be transferred without eradicating our freedom, and thus as stated above, our very humanity. Therefore Rousseau's social contract and this theory of sovereignty depend on a purely democratic foundation, one wherein each gives himself to all and in effect "gives himself to no one."

The retention of sovereignty in the people means for Rousseau that the people themselves, acting in their capacity as sovereign, are the only legitimate legislative authority. Magistrates (governments, princes) enforce the laws approved by the people and issue orders and decrees pursuant to that end, but technically lawmaking is always a task of the people. This does not mean that the people meet as a body of legislators to enact law, rather, it means that any resolution by the people's representatives is not law until the people themselves assent to it. Additionally, it can also be interpreted to mean that the fundamental constitutional principles of a state represent the law as the people affirm or consent to it; all other statutes are given legitimacy owing to these principles. Rousseau recognizes the need for the people to concede the operation of government, including statutory craft, to its deputies. His point is to illustrate the true role of the government vis à vis the people. The government is granted authority to govern citizens, but it can only do so in accordance with the general will of the people, a general will that is manifest through the laws that universally apply to all in the same way. In this sense, Rousseau understands that law must be truly objective, and that any legitimate government must apply those laws, which are the will of the people whether the people write them or not, in a manner that is fair to each and all.

Rousseau draws tight connections between popular sovereignty, the rule of law, general will and the affirmation of a moral liberty. Liberty is, for Rousseau, "obedience to a law that we prescribe for ourselves," a definition that anticipates the theories of freedom later to be developed by Kant and Hegel. It is through this self-prescription that our freedom is both recovered and ennobled. For natural liberty is a lawless, amoral condition. Rousseau laments its loss in his *Second Discourse on the Origins of Inequality,* but he in the end recognizes its insufficiency in the *Social Contract.* In Rousseau the moral and political converge in a manner reminiscent of the classical theorists, and especially Plato, and it is through this convergence that the redemptive qualities of society become clarified. No longer a curse, political society under the social contract and guided by the general will is the only sure path to a moral freedom that supersedes natural liberty, which in effect, is now seen as a shallow false freedom. But one must be careful not to understate the importance of lawful government established by consent and charged with securing the rights of its members. Any government that abandons the rule of law, one that refuses to reconcile right and justice on the one hand with interest and utility on the other, is no longer legitimate. The general will in a sense is the fusion of right and interest, justice and utility, and it is expressed in republican regimes defined by the rule of law. When such a political culture is established, citizens will respond to the government out of a sense of duty, they "fly to the assemblies," for they know that the general will is affirmed therein. However, if disaffection descends upon the citizenry, if the general will no longer finds expression, then citizens withdraw their sense of duty, regard their political institutions with indifference, and considered the state to be lost.

A deep commitment to republican values resides in Rousseau's writing. Still, visible elements of Rousseau's work that appear antirepublican and antidemocratic cause confusion among his readers, and even provoke charges of authoritarianism. While the general will is meant to express popular sovereignty and the pursuit of the common (universal) interest, it also appears to be on the one hand a simple majoritarian principle (not in itself authoritarian, but potentially so) and, on the other hand, the potentially repressive power of mass conformity. Additionally, Rousseau recommends censorship (again, not in itself authoritarian, but always accompanied with that risk if not applied with reserved care), banishment, a civilly engineered religion that replaces Christianity, and dictatorship during times of crisis, measures which tilt toward authoritarian rule. More ominously, Rousseau almost flippantly recommends the need to pressure dissent into conformity, to force freedom upon those who differ from the apparent general will, thus mustering a sentiment that for some critics anticipates Orwellian double-speak. There is some credence to such a concern, for the concept "forced to be free" defies Rousseau's own ontological assumptions about the nature of humanity, and his ethical ideals for the best regime. This is a side of Rousseau that even the most optimistic reader must confront before drawing a final conclusion, and before one can properly place Rousseau in the tradition of democratic theory.

In any case, however, Rousseau continues to fascinate and to frustrate, and as with Machiavelli before him and Marx after him, he provides fertile ground for serious conversation about the nature of free societies. Above all, Rousseau represents an attempt to bridge the modern love of democracy with the ancient call of virtue, whether or not he succeeds in this endeavor continues to command the attention of today's student of political thought.

Related Entries
general will; *Social Contract, The*

Suggested Reading

Cullen, Daniel E. *Freedom in Rousseau's Political Philosophy.* DeKalb, IL: Northern Illinois Univ. Press, 1993.

Rousseau, Jean-Jacques. *The Social Contract and the Discourses,* trans. G.D.H. Cole, rev. J.H. Brumfitt and John C. Hall and with an introduction by Alan Ryan. New York: Knopf 1993

Shklar, Judith N. *Men and Citizens: A Study of Rousseau's Social Theory.* 1969; repr. New York: Cambridge Univ. Press, 1985)

Strong, Tracy B. *Jean-Jacques Rousseau: The Politics of the Ordinary.* Thousand Oaks, CA: Sage Publications, 1994.

S

***Salus populi suprema lex est—See*Welfare of the people is the supreme law.**

satyagraha

The term *satyagraha* is a principle advanced by Mohandas Gandhi (or Mahatma Gandhi, the Great Soul). It is from the Sanskrit word *satya* meaning "truth," which is in turn derived from *sat,* meaning "being," and *agraha* meaning "to embrace, to grasp"; also known as "love-force," "soul force," "truth-force," or "silent force." Gandhi used it to represent his ideal of nonviolent action against oppression. Or as Gandhi explained, "Its [*Satyagraha*] root meaning is 'holding on to truth,' hence 'Truth-force.' I have also called it 'Love-force' or 'Soul-force.'" By embracing truth and love above power, power is exposed for what it is, and the humanity of the way of peace is forwarded through determined yet nonviolent resistance to injustice. For Gandhi, the way of satyagraha could be employed to oppose subjugation and violence on the larger scale (as in his political movements in South Africa and, later, in his homeland on the Indian subcontinent) as well as on a much smaller scale, in the very lives of individuals who seek righteousness in their personal lives and relationships with others. Gandhi wrote,

> *Satyagraha* is not physical force. A *satyagrahi* [practitioner of satyagraha] does not inflict pain on the adversary. A *satyagrahi* does not seek the adversary's destruction. . . . In the use of *satyagraha,* there is no ill will whatsoever.

Satyagraha, in its essence, refuses to meet violence with violence, but rather, in resisting the injuries and insults of the aggressor, the well-being of all is taken into account. That is to say, even the well-being of the aggressor is regarded as valuable, and the practitioner of the satyagraha doctrine will care for the safety of the perpetrators of violence. As it has often been noted, even by Gandhi himself, the principle of satyagraha, while directly emerging from within the Hindu-Buddhist-Jain ethic of *ahimsa* (to avoid all violence, to harm no living being), is identical to the teachings of the Sermon on the Mount: to love one's enemies, to resist not evil, to offer the other cheek. Hence satyagraha is a principle quite close to Leo Tolstoy's understanding of an uncompromisingly nonviolent Christianity as expounded in his *The Kingdom of God is Within You.* Additionally, a connection has been drawn between Thoreau's notion of civil disobedience and Gandhi, as well as with the activism of Martin Luther King Jr., who acknowledged the influence of Gandhi's teachings in his own application to nonviolent resistance. In other words, satyagraha is a universal principle, drawn from all faiths and philosophies, and directed at the whole of creation itself. As Gandhi explained,

> Complete non-violence is complete absence of ill will against all that lives. It therefore embraces even sub-human life not excluding noxious insects or beasts. They have not been created to feed our destructive propensities. If we only knew the mind of the Creator, we should find their proper place in God's creation. Nonviolence is therefore, in its active form, goodwill toward all life. It is pure Love. I read it in the Hindu scriptures, in the Bible, in the Koran.

Satyagraha is also notable for its rejection of the separation of means and ends. The old Machiavellian formula, for Gandhi, violates the principle of just social action. For that reason, it is impossible to employ unjust means to achieve a just end. Rather, one must see the end already in the means, and thus act accordingly. In this sense, the notion of satyagraha bears a close resemblance to arguments found in Plato's *Republic* and *Crito.* For Gandhi, nonviolent resistance must always respect the dignity of every

human being, even (and perhaps especially) the aggressors. One cannot be just and be aggressive, one cannot be truthful through anger, and one cannot be humane through retaliation and revenge. Those who apply the principle of satyagraha must suffer the insults and aggression of the oppressors without responding in kind. For in the end, it was Gandhi's belief, the tyrant will see the inhumanity of his own actions, and recognize his humanity in the sufferings of those he subjugates. Nonviolence is, as Gandhi understood it, ultimately indestructible. It is, as he states, "the very law of the human race. It is infinitely greater than and superior to brute force," and for this reason, will always triumph.

Related Entries
Republic; Machiavelli, Niccolò

Suggested Reading
Gandhi, Mohandas. *Satyagraha,* ed. Bharatan Kumarappa. 1951; repr. Mineola, NY: Dover, 2001.
Juergensmeyer, Mark. *Gandhi's Way: A Handbook of Conflict Resolution,* updated ed. Berkeley: Univ. California Press, 2005.
Power, Paul F., ed. *The Meanings of Gandhi.* Honolulu: Univ. Press Hawaii, 1971.

second principle of justice (Rawls)—*See* difference principle

Second Treatise on Government
John Locke's *Second Treatise on Government* comprehensively represents his mature political philosophy. A masterpiece in the great tradition of political theory, Locke's *Second Treatise* stands as one of the five or six most important books in the history of political ideas. Often associated with Great Britain's Glorious Revolution, it clearly resonates with the principles of the American Revolution. Few books offer a fuller account of the centrality of the rights of human beings, the significance of the rational law of nature, the true source of legitimate power in the consent of the governed, the reality of popular sovereignty, the necessity of representative and limited government, and the right of resistance. Primarily written

between 1679 and 1680, revised in 1681, and possibly modified between 1682 and 1683 with evident further modifications in 1689 (the extent of which remains uncertain), the *Second Treatise* reflects the mood of the times that eventually led to the Glorious Revolution, while not itself being the product of or a direct justification for that revolution as it is commonly perceived. In terms of the times, the *Second Treatise* definitely owes a great deal to the common mood that brewed after the Restoration. Intellectually, in terms of the influence of other thinkers, Locke explicitly relied on Richard Hooker and implicitly on his friends and fellow theorists James Tyrrell and Anthony Ashley Cooper (Lord Ashley, the First Earl of Shaftesbury) and, quite likely, Algernon Sidney. Locke directly responds to Sir Robert Filmer, and the entire treatise can be read as a deep response to Hobbes, although Hobbes's name is noticeably absent.

The *Second Treatise* is divided into 19 chapters of various lengths, and further subdivided into a total of 243 sections, some of which are but a paragraph or two in length. Chapter one draws the connection between the *Second Treatise* and the *First Treatise,* which was in essence an effective rebuttal of Sir Robert Filmer's convoluted apology for the notion of the Divine right of kings. In Chapter one Locke reasserts the implausibility of Filmer's position, observing that we "must of necessity find out another rise of government, another original of political power," than the Divine lineage traced back to Adam that Filmer had previously claimed. For Locke, political power, which can only involve the public good and is defined in terms of rightful legislation, proper enforcement of laws by the "force of the community," and defense from foreign enemies, cannot be understood in the same terms as other expressions of power (such as father and child, master and slave, etc.), but rather rests on both a different source and is held together by a different structure. To understand the origin and structure of legitimate government, one must first posit a state of nature, which is

the subject primarily of chapter two as well as a prominent concept in the arguments of chapters three through five and chapters seven through nine.

In chapter two, Locke recognizes a basic premise developed earlier by Hobbes: human beings are by their nature free and equal. But Locke quickly departs from Hobbes in the manner in which he understands natural liberty and natural equality. For Locke, natural equality is evident in that all human beings are born to all the same advantages of nature. This primal condition is not "a war of all against all," as in Hobbes, a position that Locke clearly announces in chapter three when he distinguishes the state of nature from the state of war. Rather, following from Hooker, not Hobbes, "This equality of men by nature . . . [is] the foundation of that obligation to mutual love amongst men on which he builds the duties they owe one another." Thus, a state of nature is not a constant collision of wills, although conflict can indeed arise in such a condition (the state of nature is not an Edenic paradise for Locke; it does contain real dangers). Instead, human beings are naturally drawn together in "communion and fellowship," as Locke quotes Hooker, thereby indicating that, for Locke, human beings are not inherently solitary, isolated competitors and combatants, but by nature harbor a need for each other that springs from an instinctive affection and is fortified by a sense of duty to common interests. This suggestion by Locke is further strengthened by his conclusion that liberty is not "license," the right to whatever one pleases within one's power. Human beings are born to a "perfect freedom" to self-command, but this freedom is delimited by the moral law of nature, which precludes the Hobbesian "right to everything." While one is obliged to place one's self-interest first and thus defend oneself and one's possessions, one is also obligated to the moral law of nature. "And reason," Locke explains, "which is that law, teaches all mankind who will but consult it, that being all equal and independent, no one ought to harm another in his life, health, liberty, or possessions." This is directly antithetical to Hobbes's claim that in a state of nature, everyone holds a right to everything, "even to another's body." Such an absolute right is absent in Locke. Indeed, Locke even goes so far as to propose that in a state of nature, one ought "as much as he can, preserve the rest of mankind. . . [preserving] the life, liberty, health, limbs or goods of another."

These passages and others like them illustrate the unambiguous break from Hobbes. Even though the state of nature is a state of "inconvenience" containing real dangers, it is not without governing principles. The rights of human beings are formed by the moral law of nature, which is equated with right reason (as Hobbes at times recognizes) and detached from the dynamics of power (a position that Hobbes cannot approach).

Additionally and significantly, for Locke as discussed in chapter two, human beings, while not possessing the Hobbesian right to everything, nonetheless do possess a natural right to judge and execute the law of nature. But, owing to a natural tendency to be biased in our own interest (a tendency shared by all, even among the most reasonable and objective, to be partial to one's own case out of a natural self-love), the enforcement of the natural law by private individuals causes this inconvenient state and provokes injustice. Thus, in order to ensure that some of our natural rights (life, liberty, property, among others) are secured, the natural right to judge and execute the law of nature must be renounced and transferred to a common umpire. This is the true "original" of government, made legitimate by the commission of a unanimous and voluntary act among those who are willing parties to the contract. As Locke summarizes in chapter seven, "Wherever, therefore any number of men are so united into one society as to quit every one his executive power of the law of nature and to resign it to the public, there and there only is a political or civil society." Such a government is decidedly distinct from other forms of power such as paternal, which is only held over those who are neither rational enough or free enough to govern their own actions (as discussed at length in chapter six). Consent to surrender the right to judge and execute the law of nature is the act of the rational and the free, and the only real foundation of political authority of any kind.

Chapter five contains Locke's seminal discussion of the natural right to property. Unlike Hobbes, the right to property is held under the moral law of nature, and is to be respected even in a state of nature (although human foible renders this uncertain). Locke explains that the world is given in common to all human beings, and so long as it remains in common no one's claim is above another's. Each human being, as a creature of God, is given, within limits (i.e., no one has a right to destroy oneself), full and free possession of his own person, to command his own labor as is necessary. As one labors, the act of mixing one's labor with the materials of nature "excludes" any claim by others, and thus private property originates from one's power of labor as it is productively joined to the world. Thus our labor power is the source of the natural right to property and the ultimate measure of its value. But as with all natural rights discerned by Locke; the right to property is limited. No one can claim the right to deliberately spoil or waste the materials of nature, even those things that have been produced by one's labor. Thus the right to property is limited in its scope by the degree to which property can be used. In a state of nature, within a rudimentary economy, one can only possess as much as one can use. Thus even one's labor power is not sufficient to determine what is owned by right.

Given this, Locke further examines the manner in which exchange value—first emerging from the ability to acquire and store more durable goods such as nuts (in contrast to fruits which perish quickly), and then developing through an attraction to still more permanent objects bearing no obvious intrinsic use (such as a pleasing sea shell or colorful stone, or "little piece of shiny metal," to wit—gold and silver), and culminating in the abstract agreement that is the basis for modern currency—further complicates the rights to property once settled society is firmly and finally established. In a state of nature operating under a rudimentary barter system, disparity in wealth would be minimal, for even the more industrious can only produce what they can use. But as exchange value (whether based in precious metals or in abstract concepts such as paper currency) becomes more prominent, the disparities in wealth that are universal to all societies are expected, and even justified. For some, this admission by Locke is a defense of economic inequality, allowed in society in spite of the natural equality of all human beings. Others might argue that Locke simply recognizes that equality will not manifest in all dimensions of society, thus political and legal equality does not require social and economic equality. Others still might remind us that Locke's prohibitions against waste and spoilage are still in place (the laws of nature are "always binding," and even more so in formal society), but only to be redefined as civilizations enjoy a greater and more variegated prosperity. In any case, regardless of one's favored interpretation, chapter five's theory of property is probably the most important discussion of the relationship between politics and economics since Aristotle.

Chapters 10–14 develop Locke's ideas regarding the different kinds of political power and the indispensable functions of government. It is here that Locke advances a notion of the separation of powers that anticipates later developments by Montesquieu. In chapter 12, for example, Locke states explicitly that "well-ordered" commonwealths are characterized by the crucial separation of the legislative and executive functions. "Human frailty" demands it of us, and human reason recognizes the wisdom of limited and dispersed power. Chapter 12 identifies three principal functions present in any ordered commonwealth: the legislative and executive, to which Locke

devotes considerable thought, and what he refers to as the "federative" power, which for Locke entails those functions stemming from international affairs. Locke is not necessarily speaking here of three branches, but rather three functions divided under normal conditions into two separate spheres of government, for the executive and federative are, in Locke's observation, "always (almost) united."

The preceding chapter (chapter 11) presents Locke's views on the legislative, and in so doing, affirms many of his basic political tenets. As the first and fundamental law of nature, for Locke, is the preservation of society and of every person in society, so the first and fundamental positive law of all commonwealths, having been formally created from the mutual and unanimous consent of the governed and perpetuated by the rule of law and the deliberations of the majority, is the establishing of a legislative power. According to Locke, the legislative power is by definition limited, with arbitrary power being impossible for Locke in a true commonwealth, for "nobody can transfer to another more power than he has in himself; and nobody has an absolute arbitrary power over himself, or over any other, to destroy his own life, or take away the life or property of another." On this principle, Locke explicitly limits the power of the legislative in four ways: first, laws must be established, promulgated, and applicable to all in the same way (rich and poor alike); second, all laws must aim at the good of the people; third, the natural right of property prohibits the seizure of that property by any power without the consent of the governed—in particular, taxes cannot be raised without the consent of the people through their designated deputies (adumbrating the principle, "no taxation without representation" adhered to by the American colonists over the Stamp Act crisis in the mid-1760s); and fourth, the legislative power cannot be transferred to any other power unless by an act of the people as a whole. In these four proscriptions, Locke emphasizes the role of the legislative body in terms of the common good understood as deference to natural rights the protection of which government is charged to secure. Failure to protect these rights and to exert arbitrary power, Locke unequivocally and deliberately asserts, would place a government's citizens in a condition markedly worse than the state of nature, an apparent broadside against the unnamed author of *Leviathan*.

Chapter 14, or "Of Prerogative," refers to those powers exercised by the executive "according to discretion for the public good." While Locke, overall, maintains a consistent advocacy of the supremacy of the legislative power, in this chapter he does assert that executive power is nonetheless substantial, and when the legislative is not in session, can act with considerable scope, even against the will of the lawmaking body ("without the prescription of law, and sometimes even against it"). This prerogative power is not intended to aggrandize the power of the executive, but only to ensure that, where the public good requires it, an executive authority can act even against the immediate directives of the legislative. While this can be read in a way that might arouse distrust of Locke's republican credentials owing to the expansion of executive power, it is understood that the exercise of such power is extraordinary, only executed against laws that violate the public interest, and is thus always a "power in the hands of the prince to provide for the common good" (as he writes in the preceding chapter), and in clear recognition of the need at times to act on behalf of the commonwealth and its citizens in cases where the law is silent. In a sense, the prerogative power of Locke's executive anticipates the evolution of the American presidency, although it must be admitted that this is not necessarily what Locke intends. In any event, whether or not Locke's views on executive power foreshadows the office of the American president, it is to be remembered that, even though the power of the prerogative is significant, the executive is always "visibly subordinate" to the legislative.

Chapter 13 is critical, particularly sections 149–151 and 156–158. In this chapter Locke discusses both legislative and executive power, but it is more notable for the theory of sovereignty that emerges in the first two sections. Here Locke reasserts that the legislative is always the supreme power within a rational commonwealth, but he illustrates that this power is only "held as a fiduciary," or in trust, the supreme power always belonging the people themselves. Under the original social contract, each person consents to renouncing certain natural rights, surrendering those rights to a "common umpire" now charged with the responsibilities of protecting all other natural rights retained by the people. This renunciation of rights is conditioned on the good faith performance of the "common umpire," or the government in the pursuit of its basic duty to the security of the inalienable rights of the citizenry. Should that trust be violated, the people retain the right to remove or alter the legislative body. Hence the people, while agreeing to obey the laws and follow the commands of the government, act as a sovereign body over that government in that they possess all rights to act on their own should a government forfeit their trust, or fail in their duties as fiduciary. Hence Locke clarifies what was less clear in Hobbes: there is a distinction between sovereign and government, and within the Lockean view, the former, being the superior authority, is ultimately posited in the people themselves. This is the heart of the relationship between government and citizen in the *Second Treatise,* and the foundation of the American principle of sovereignty as advanced in its founding documents.

This notion is the conceptual root of Locke's theory of the natural right to resistance, or the right of revolution, more extensively treated in chapters 18 and 19. For Locke, a government that fails to preserve the natural rights retained by the people actually places itself in a state of war against the commonwealth, and technically, it is the government that is in rebellion, the initial violator of the social contract. This idea is somewhat reminiscent of the notion in St. Thomas Aquinas, wherein he argues that, while sedition is a mortal sin, tyrants commit sedition against the people, and thus it is not a seditious act for the people to depose a tyrant, but rather, the mortal sin has been committed by those who exercise tyrannical authority. While this approach is Thomistic, the Lockean approach is similar. The people do not in fact rebel against tyrants (defined in Aristotelian/Thomistic terms in chapter 18), the rebellion was set into motion by the tyrant. Thus the people, acting as true sovereigns, are right in withdrawing their support of an arbitrary power and erecting a new legislature (anarchy not being an option). Not given to incendiary prescriptions, Locke cautions against such resistance. With words that anticipate Jefferson, arbitrary and even unjust power is to be suffered to a point, "Great mistakes in the ruling part, many wrong and inconvenient laws, and all the slips of human frailty will be born by the people without mutiny or murmur. But if a long train of abuses, prevarications, and artifices all tending the same way" persist, as Locke affirms, then the people must "rouse themselves" and, in their capacities as true sovereigns, rectify the situation. This chapter concludes his treatise, the final paragraph reaffirming Locke's principle that power must revert to the people once the trust formed in the consent of the governed is forfeited by the fiduciary power.

Locke's political theory is certainly not confined to this great treatise. Readers of Locke would benefit from an exposure to the *First Treatise* and his *Letter on Toleration,* as well as lesser known works in the form of various essays, papers and letters. But perhaps more than most political theorists, Locke's overall philosophy of politics is encapsulated in this one work to great effect, and to the benefit of nearly every student of politics who approaches its pages. It stands as one of a handful of classics that have contributed to the shaping of modern political theory; its influence is broad and its relevance sustained even to this day.

Related Entries
liberalism; Locke, John

Suggested Reading

Ashcraft, Richard. *Locke's Two Treatises of Government.* Boston: Allen & Unwin, 1987.

Grant, Ruth W. *John Locke's Liberalism.* Chicago: Univ. Chicago Press, 1987.

Locke, John. *Two Treatises of Government,* ed. Peter Laslett. New York: Cambridge Univ. Press, 1988. (There are a number of other fine editions of this text in print.)

Seneca, Lucius Annaeus (c. 3 BC–65 AD)
The writings of Seneca represent in part the ideas of what is normally called "Middle Stoicism," known for its more political orientation compared to the earlier Stoics. Historically and conceptually Seneca's writings sit on the cusp between the socially conscious Middle Stoics and the more quietist views of the Late Stoics.

Seneca's writings exhibit the ascetic renunciations accented with the language of fatalistic resignation characteristic throughout the historical arc of Stoicism but less pronounced in the writings of Middle Stoics such as Cicero. "We are all chained to Fortune [Fate]," Seneca muses, reminding us that the whole of life is essentially slavery regardless of our social status. The wise person copes with this inevitability through trained forbearance and an existential dispassion. Through a disciplined mind "the hard can be softened, the narrow widened," and all that is heavy made light. To find the peace of wisdom the soul must resolve to withdraw inwardly and learn self-mastery, for that is the only way to truly deal with hardships such as poverty, loss, disease, and injustice.

In this way, at least a large portion of Seneca's philosophy is apolitical. It is not through the actions of legislator, judges, rulers, and public action that we achieve tranquility in life, but only through tempering the passions of the soul. "Self-sufficiency and abiding tranquility" are the virtues of the wisest soul, and not participation in the life of the polity. Wise men will never rest well in any commonwealth—even Athens was an inferior habitation for Socrates and Aristotle, the latter driven into exile, the former unjustly condemned.

Yet Seneca lived in a highly charged political world. He knew Caligula and Claudius, was tutor to the young Nero, and for a time was himself a personage of some status and influence. He was surrounded by tyrants and degenerates, a situation guaranteed to challenge personal forbearance and stoic indifference in even the most resolute souls. Politics as a subject, therefore, found its way into Seneca's broader philosophy. Exposed to the mad excesses of Roman tyrants, Seneca nonetheless resigned himself to the abolition of the republic and the destiny of Rome as a monarchy. Whereas earlier Stoics ardently embraced republicanism, Seneca simply assumed monarchy as a foregone conclusion. His commentary on politics was therefore expressed within the framework erected by the Caesars.

In his work, *On Mercy,* an early example of the "mirror of princes" literature dedicated to his pupil Nero, Seneca held that the human being is a "social animal, born for the common good," in spite of his abiding pessimism about the goodness of commonwealths. As the common good is natural to the community, so the mild statesman (typified by the "deified Caesar Augustus," perceived by Seneca to be a "mild prince") governs benevolently. Seneca illustrates this through a discussion of the "patterns of authority." Parents and children, officer and soldier, teacher and student, are all better served when authority is gentle and severity eschewed. Even nature supports gentle authority. As proof, Seneca discusses the example of the gentle rule among the tiniest of social creatures; the beehive. The "king" bee (classical and Medieval authors notoriously mistook the queen bee for a male) possesses no stinger and apparently no weapons for coercive purposes, and yet the entire hive eagerly submits to "his" mastery. Following the examples of nature and the various dyads involving the

mild exercise of human authority, the wise ruler comes to appreciate that both the honor and safety of a ruler is secure through the practice of mercy.

Alas, such mercy was not to redound upon Seneca. Feeling slighted by his old teacher, the insane Nero ordered Seneca, in retirement and fully withdrawn from court politics, to commit suicide. Whatever one wishes to say about the authenticity of Seneca's stoicism as practiced through his life, it is noteworthy that in his last act, Seneca indifferently met his duty, and without hesitation or complaint embraced his final renunciation of the world.

Related Entry
Cicero, Marcus Tullius

Suggested Reading
Fitch, John G., ed. *Seneca.* New York: Oxford Univ. Press 2008.
Seneca. *Seneca: Moral and Political Essays,* ed. John M. Cooper and J. F. Procopé. New York: Cambridge Univ. Press, 1995.

shari'a (or *seriat*)
The term *shari'a* can be translated as the way to the watering place, the way, religious law, rectitude, righteous code. Muslims consider the shari'a as a higher law that is revealed through the *Qur'ān* (*Koran*) and fortified by the *Hadith* or *Sunnah* (Reports, or extra-Quranic teachings of Muhammad), reasoning by analogy and the following of precedent (not unlike English common law), *fatwas* (religious edicts or pronouncements of learned clerics), as well as the consensus of the broader community of believers within the House of Islam. Shari'a guides human activity publicly and privately, politically and morally, encompassing an expansive range of human activities from politics and economics to personal hygiene, diet, and familial relationships. For the Muslim, the shari'a comes from God, and thus ordains a standard of legal and moral conduct for all believers. It is at once a set of ethical and behavioral codes serving as a legal structure for the government of society.

For Muslims, shari'a opens an enlightened path of conduct that is inspired by divine truth and aimed at aligning personal conduct to God's will. For non-Muslims it appears to be a severe and antiquated code that militates against personal liberty and may often employ repressive measures. Perhaps these disparate perceptions are the product of varied interpretation, a feature attendant on any endeavor to align ordinary law and codes of conduct to higher law divinely revealed as embraced by any faith. Traditionally there are four basic interpretations of shari'a developed within Sunni Islam and advanced by different juristic perspectives known as the Law Schools: Hanafi, Maliki, Shafi'i, and Hanbali. The Hanafi school, which is the oldest variation of shari'a, adopts a rationalist approach and is perceived by modern commentators as comparatively liberal. The Hanbali variation can be seen as critical of the dependence on rationalism, and seeks a more literalist and some would say conservative adherence to the explicit teachings of *Qur'ān* and *Hadith*. Hanbali is at once rigorously moral and populist, constricting the limits of personal conduct while appealing to the people as a whole in its criticism of elitist rationalism. Reason alone is always insufficient; we thus must rely completely on the revelation of the *Qur'ān,* which because it is the direct and uncreated expression of God, is perfection itself. Shafi'i attempts to draw on both the rationalism of Hanafi with a more literal approach to Scripture, and Maliki emphasizes consensus while depending less on *Hadith* without diminishing Muslim reverence held for Muhammad's Reports as an important source for the tradition.

Ja'fari, a fifth school, emerging from clerical traditions within Shi'a Islam, focuses more on the practice of the *fatwas,* particularly those of the ancient Muslim jurists represented by the Shi'a imams. This school of law is heavily reliant on the pronouncement of the jurists themselves, who are less bound by precedent and more free to modify earlier edicts. Nonetheless, this flexibility is more apparent than substantive

among more conservative interpreters of the shari'a, and as the Ja'fari approach is particularly rooted in the lessons of the *Hadith,* there is a temptation to adhere to a literalism not found in schools such as the Hanafi.

The concept and practice of shari'a reaches back to the earliest decades of Islam, but it has assumed new relevance in contemporary political issues. For some, shari'a provides another valuable source for the measuring of human legislation against the first principles of objective moral values, while for others reliance on shari'a transgresses well-guarded boundaries established to preserve state and faith within their proper spheres. Just how shari'a will be viewed and adopted in the future depends a great deal on which Law School's distinct understanding of higher law becomes more pervasive.

Related Entries
circle of power; *dhimmi*; natural law

Suggested Reading
Hallaq, Wael B. *A History of Islamic Legal Theories: An Introduction to Sunnī uṣūl al-fiqh.* New York: Cambridge Univ. Press, 1999.

Si guarda al fini

"*Si guarda al fini,*" is the Renaissance Italian phrase employed by Niccolò Machiavelli in chapter 18 of *The Prince* and often translated as or associated with the English expression, "the end justifies the means." Whether or not this is the meaning, in English, that Machiavelli intended or not is a matter of some dispute. Luigi Ricci's translation does in fact render "*si guarda al fini*" as "the end justifies the means," but other translators offer a slightly different rendition of the phrase. Leo Paul S. deAlvarez translates the term as "one looks to the end," while Robert Adams and Angelo Codevilla render the phrase as "we must always look to the end" and "one looks to the results," respectively. David Wooten and George Bull, respectively, prefer "judge by the outcome" and "one judges by the results," while Peter Bondanella and Mark Musa prefer "consider the final result." For Alan Gilbert, the phrase "people think of the outcome" is the best translation of Machiavelli's Italian. It is perhaps noteworthy that there is an Italian proverb, "*Il fine giustifica i mezze,*" that is also rendered as "the end justifies the means."

"The end justifies the means" is a depiction of the essence of Machiavelli's new way of thinking about politics (his "new modes and orders") that is critiqued by Leo Strauss, who, in his work *Thoughts on Machiavelli,* states, "contemporary tyranny has its roots in Machiavelli's thought, in the Machiavellian principle that the good end justifies every means." Whether or not these various translations offer different meanings of the phrase is open to reflection and debate. Does "consider the final result," for example, mean the same thing as "end justifies the means?" If so, then the observations of Strauss are irresistibly compelling. However, if there is a real distinction between the translations that exceeds nuance, then the question remains less certain but no less important.

Related Entries
Machiavelli, Niccolò; Strauss, Leo

Suggested Reading
Machiavelli, Niccolò. *The Prince,* trans. and ed. Angelo M. Codevilla. New Haven: Yale Univ. Press, 1997.

The Social Contract

With its famous opening remark declaring that "man is born free and everywhere he is in chains," *The Social Contract* is Jean-Jacques Rousseau's political masterpiece, a work that to this day is widely read and discussed among students of political ideas. While the *Discourses on the Origin of Inequality* (Rousseau's *Second Discourse*) contains Rousseau's theory of human nature and the story of the social corruption of our original state of innocence, *The Social Contract* offers Rousseau's political views in their maturity. It can be said that in some aspects *The Social Contract* departs from the *Second Discourse* significantly enough that it illuminates

the concepts of the earlier work in a new light. It does not do so in a way that makes the *Social Contract* stand alone and distant from the *Second Discourse,* but it can be said that the *Second Discourse* depends more upon the *Social Contract* than the reverse.

The *Social Contract* is divided into "four books," each "book" further segmented in to short chapters focusing on a specific subtopic. Book One, which consists of nine chapters, opens with a prefatory remark stating the general purpose of the book: the reconciliation of "what right permits with what interest prescribes, so that justice and utility do not find themselves at odds with one another." This is the charge of what Rousseau refers to as the social compact, that arrangement wherein the individual "in giving himself to all, each person gives himself to no one. And since there is no associate over whom he does not acquire the same right, he gains the equivalent of what he loses, along with a greater amount of force to preserve what he has." What we surrender is the unabated self-interest characteristic of our radically individualistic natural liberty; what is gained is the moral liberty of the communal interest as asserted by the general, or universal, will. Since we only surrender what others equally surrender, we only gain what others equally gain. This is the heart of the contract, and what is gained equally by all is a new and superior kind of freedom that allows human beings to act as moral agents, and not simply as creatures of self-interest. Thus each party to the contract, meaning each citizen, "finds himself under a twofold commitment: namely as a member of the sovereign to private individuals, and as a member of the state towards the sovereign." This contract and any terms or features that flow from it rests on the mutual and universal consent of all individuals involved. Thus all political authority must be an act of consent, expressing the universal will and aimed at the establishment of rights, raw force being a false origin of authority and the ground of slavery, and hence, for Rousseau, the loss of our humanity. All authority, and in reality all right (in particular the individual right to property, which is always subordinate to the community), are the products of convention for Rousseau, there being no authority in nature to rule over one's fellow human beings. Thus the ends of the social contract are to reaffirm the liberty that makes them human, and in so doing, to ground political authority in a conception of right that negates any coerced power in its attempt to subjugate or enslave. This "first book" emphasizes the new, "civil state of moral liberty, which alone makes man truly the master of himself," a moral liberty that encourages duty over impulse, and that in the end "forces" us to be free in a nobler way. Additionally, our natural equality is replaced with a "moral and legitimate equality" through the social contract, eliminating the importance of any naturally imposed inequalities, and providing the foundation for social equality by "convention and right."

In the second book (consisting of 12 chapters), Rousseau turns his attention to a more detailed examination of sovereignty (earlier broached in the first book), the general will, law and the act of legislation, the concept of the "legislator," and his understanding of the "people." For Rousseau, sovereignty always remains a collective right of the people that is produced by the social contract; hence it is incorrect to speak of any authority other than the people themselves as sovereign. The sovereign is nothing more than the expression of the general will, which is viewed as that will which alone aims at the common good (not just a majority, nor even a consensus, but a will that is truly universal). Here Rousseau compares this general will (which is identical to the sovereign will) to the private wills of individuals and groups and the sum of the private wills that he refers to as the "will of all." Rousseau claims that if the general (sovereign) will is to be truly "articulated," there "should be no partial society in the state," or, that is to say, there should be no factions or particular interests militating against the common good. There is only the general will and the individual citizen who is

to "make up his own mind" to follow that general will. Not parties, factions or partial associations should distract individuals from consulting and following the general will. In a statement reminiscent of Hobbes, the "body politic [possesses] an absolute power over all its members," but it is important to bear in mind that the "commitments that bind us to the body politic are obligatory only because they are mutual, and their nature is such that in fulfilling them one cannot work for someone else without also working for oneself." In other words, if the true general will, which is inerrant, is actualized and expressed without distraction, then we become sovereign as a collective association, harmonized by "one common interest that unites them," and sanctified by the unanimity of the social compact and the moral freedom that it has exerted.

Chapter six of Book Two is central to arguments in *The Social Contract* as well as to a fuller understanding of Rousseau's general political theory. It is here that Rousseau clarifies the relationship between popular sovereignty, general will, law, and government. There is no general will in relation to a particular object, and from this, there is no law aimed at a particular party to the exclusion of others, for the law is nothing more than the act of general will. Law is always general in the sense that it is enacted by all and it effects all in the same way. That which involves a particular interest or object is simply a decree issued by official authorities, but without the force of law. This is important for Rousseau, as it asserts again the distinction between sovereignty (held collectively by the people and expressed through the infallible general will) and government (those who hold authority—a relationship that is further clarified in Book Three). All legitimate government is ruled by law, a regime referred to as republican, from the Latin *res publica* (public thing). Thus, it follows that every legitimate government is republican "regardless of the form its administration may take." Later, in Book Three, Rousseau relies on the ancient typology of regimes (monarchy, aristocracy, democracy) and concedes that each of them is beneficial according to circumstances, but it is clear that they must be "republican," that is, they must always submit to the rule of law, and in so doing, submit to the general will.

Rousseau concludes chapter six of book two by reasserting the purity of the general will, but allowing that the "judgment that guides it is not always enlightened" and indeed, is susceptible to seduction. The concept of the "legislator," the topic of chapter seven, is introduced here as a necessary preventive to popular deception. The "legislator is in every respect an extraordinary man in the state," a "superior intelligence" who serves as the framer of the laws. Such a person, being so remarkable, must not embrace power, but only establish principles upon which a republic should be governed. Ultimately, only the general will and the people who express it are true legislators, but the extraordinary man who is a legislator is needed to provide the good judgment required to assist the populace in following its own will. The legislator is only to submit possible laws for the approval of the sovereign people. Additionally, the legislator leads by way of good example, teaching the populace the art of citizenship. Indeed, the legislator is regarded by Rousseau as magnificent, so extraordinary that he somehow speaks with the authority of the divine. Rightly or wrongly, Rousseau points to Lycurgus and John Calvin—or at least the legends that surround them—as examples of this archetype. In chapter nine, while discussing the necessity of framing laws appropriate to the character of a people at a given stage of development, Rousseau withholds such praise from Peter the Great for he lacked the wisdom to build Russian character before imposing the laws needed for civilization. In this sense Rousseau focuses on enacting laws that are good relative to a people's culture and in this way resembling a conventionalist approach. Nonetheless, in chapter 11, Rousseau commits to a standard for all laws that is found "precisely wherein the greatest good of all consists, which should be the purpose of every system of legislations." Given Rousseau's logic, it is here that we can begin to clarify the objects of the general will, for as stated above, true law is the expression of the general will, which for Rousseau, "boils down to the two principal objects, *liberty and equality.*" In this way, Rousseau reconnects his discussion of situational requirements for founding and law-making the objective principles of legitimate government, which is always republican, and thus always under the rule of law, and, as such, aims at the essential objects of the general will, identified, however vaguely, by Rousseau as liberty and equality.

Book Three opens with a discussion of "government in general," wherein Rousseau provides more detail explaining his views on the relationship between sovereignty and government. Rousseau begins with a discussion comparing the "two causes" of free action: one moral, the other physical. Moral causes are associated with the will, whereas physical causes involve power. Will and power are aspects of human action, and similarly, they are manifest in the body politic, where they are associated with the legislative function, which is produced by the will, and the executive function, which is the vehicle for the exercise of power. "Nothing is done, or ought to be done," Rousseau avers, "without their concurrence." Concurrence may be essential, but separation is necessary. If Rousseau is to remain consistent with his notion of popular sovereignty, the "legislative power belongs to the people," for the people can never relinquish their own will. The executive power, on the other hand, cannot remain with the people since it is always directed to particular cases (whereas law is by definition universal, coming from all and applying to all equally), and is therefore deposited in the government, which for Rousseau, is "an intermediate body established between the subjects and the sovereign for their mutual communication." Hence the people, as sovereign, possess the will that allows them to "legislate" (loosely understood), and the government is commissioned with the authority to execute the laws. There is no social contract between the people as legislators and the government as executors; rather there is one contract between the people who are collectively sovereign and individual subjects who agree to obey themselves, and in so doing, recognize the authority that has been commissioned to administer the laws. Citizens are those who rule collectively as sovereign and are ruled individually as subjects, a principle that imitates the definition of citizenship offered by Plato and Aristotle. Rousseau explains further that under these conditions, ideally, the sovereign will of the people (general will) will always prevail over private interests. "In a perfect act of legislation, the private or individual will should be non-existent; the corporate will proper to the government should be very subordinate, and consequently, the general or sovereign will should always be dominant and the unique rule of all the others."

Having established the fundamentals, Rousseau explores the varieties of government and their relationship to social and geographic conditions. Here Rousseau not only borrows from the ancients, but he specifically acknowledges in chapter eight his indebtedness to Montesquieu. All three pure forms (monarchy, aristocracy, and democracy) are only suited to certain conditions. Each type possesses admirable qualities, but each type depends on specific elements for success. Specifically, Rousseau praises "elective aristocracy" as "the best" (whether he means this to be the best subtype of aristocracy or the "best" government *per se* is unclear), as well as monarchy if set within the proper environment and governed by those who are devoted to the public weal. Democracy is described by Rousseau as the most perfect and the one requiring the most virtue. Indeed, several conditions are requisite to democracy, each of them reflecting Rousseau's preference for a moral state, and revealing the difficulties inherent in democratic government. Democracies must be small enough for all the people to "gather together and where each citizen can easily know all the others," simple, homogeneous, marked by "little to no luxury"

and minimal disparity in "ranks and fortunes." Such conditions are rare, perhaps nonexistent, leading Rousseau to conclude that "Were there a people of gods, it would govern itself democratically. So perfect a government is not suited to men." As with Plato's city of speech in his *Republic,* the perfect regime in Rousseau's theory is a divine standard beyond human reach. Ultimately, Rousseau concedes that none of these simple types of government exist, and following his predecessors, recognizes the qualities of mixed government. Simple government may be the ideal, but mixed regimes are better equipped to balance the relationship between executive authority and legislative will. However, curiously, Rousseau devotes little space to mixed regimes, even though he concedes that there is "no such thing as a simple form of government."

Ultimately, Rousseau insists that the true sign of a sound government is its pursuit of the common interest, understood morally, and realized through the sense of duty held by its citizens. Private interests, commerce, the arts, "softness and the love of amenities." all enervate the body politic, which depends on the virtue of its citizens more than on their talents. This virtue produces devotion to the state, the only real sign of a good government.

> The better a state is constituted, the more public business takes precedence over private business in the minds of the citizens."...In a well run city everyone flies to the assemblies; under a bad government no on wants to take a step to get to them, since no one takes an interest in what happens there, for it is predictable that the general will will not predominate. . . Once someone says *what do I care?* about the affairs of the state, the state should be considered lost.

Rousseau concludes Book Three with his observations about the dissolution of government. With Locke, he recognizes that the people retain the right to "revoke" the social contract, reminding his readers that those who hold governmental power do so as "trustees of the executive power," language reminiscent of the *Second Treatise*. And, with Locke, Rousseau tempers his argument by cautioning against revolution by popular caprice, "[I]t is impossible to be too careful" Rousseau admonishes, "about observing all the formalities required in order to distinguish a regular and legitimate act from a seditious tumult, and the will of an entire people from the clamor of faction." The citizens retain the right to break the compact (by "common agreement"), but with Locke, Rousseau is careful to ensure that this is an act both grave and rare.

Rousseau attracts the greatest controversy in Book Four, which begins with a return to a discussion of general will (wherein he reasserts that it is the indestructible and pure will of each and every member of the state) and the need for a simple system of legislation to express it, and then elides into a discussion of voting. Here Rousseau causes confusion by identifying the general will with the "counting of votes," an entirely different proposition from the notion that the general will is purely universal and expressed only through true law, and is thus independent of electoral politics wherein the will of all often predominates. In chapter two of Book Four, Rousseau seems to reduce the general will to the power of the vote, and those who vote against a proposal are quickly proven to be at odds with the common good, "When, therefore, the opinion contrary to mine prevails, this proves merely that I was in error, and that what I took to be the general will was not so." Rousseau attempts to clarify this by asserting that the majority formed is done under the presupposition of a body of free citizens, which is in accord with the notion that the general will aims at liberty and equality. Nonetheless, this position is confusing, particularly when compared to earlier statements noting the difference between general will and the accumulation of votes. Additionally, Rousseau causes further confusion in his admiration of sortition for the selection of magistrates. Arguing that the election of officers is a function of government and not of sovereignty, sortition, or selection by lot, does not violate the need

to sustain harmony with the general will. Whether this is an inconsistency or an idiosyncrasy is not clear, but it is at odds with certain principles of popular choice that must be manifest should the general will prevail.

From this point, Book Four explores at length the model of republican Rome, which Rousseau, like Machiavelli, Cicero, and Polybius, regards with esteem. It is here that Rousseau supports dictatorship in times of emergency, censorship for the maintenance of mores, the "reunification" of the civil and ecclesial spheres (citing Hobbes's Erastianism), and the replacement of Christianity with a civil religion reminiscent of Machiavelli's *Discourses*. As with Machiavelli, Christianity is excessively otherworldly and essentially incompatible with the cultivation of a political ethic. Political society must be a society of the worldly, and in a decidedly Machiavellian moment, Rousseau associates the triumph of Christianity with the loss of those virtues requisite to political and military success, "And when the cross expelled the eagle," Rousseau scolds, "all Roman valor disappeared." Such a civil religion should be simple and mandatory; those who refuse it risk banishment. Rousseau does soften the severity of this prospect with a nod to tolerance, provided the dogmas of one's beliefs are compatible with the characteristics of good citizenship. He then exhibits his personal perception of such tolerance with a broadside against Catholicism, a religion he describes as "bizzare" and "ruinous," whose adherents should be "expelled from the state."

The Social Contract is marked by hyperbole and contradiction, and yet it remains for the most part a formidable exercise in the project that is political theory. At times its observations exhibit a brilliant thinker in service to the cause of free government, at other times, perplexing phrases and astonishing ideas spring forth that provoke criticism from even the most sympathetic reader. That said, *The Social Contract* has proven its worth in the test of time, and should continue to perplex and provoke for generations to come.

Related Entries
general will; Rousseau, Jean-Jacques

Suggested Reading
Gildin, Hilail. *Rousseau's Social Contract: The Design and Argument*. Chicago: Univ. Chicago Press, 1983.
Rousseau, Jean-Jacques. *The Social Contract,* trans. Donald Cress. Indianapolis: Hackett, 1987. There are a number of other excellent translations available, from Cambridge Univ. Press, Penguin, and Bedford/St. Martin's, among other publishers.

social Darwinism

Social Darwinism is an attempt to apply the observations of Darwin's theories of evolution through natural selection to the social and political realm. Human beings and the societies in which they live are subject to the same laws of nature and the same organic interactions that we find in a study of the animal world, and thus the best way to understand political, social, and even moral questions is to apply the laws of evolution to reach a more profound understanding of the nature of human development as well as to prescribe a rational course of action to ensure a more reasonable social order. The leading proponents of social Darwinism were Herbert Spencer (1820–1903), William Graham Sumner (1840–1910), and Lester Frank Ward (1841–1913). Spencer and Sumner understood social development in terms of the "survival of the fittest" (a term actually coined by Spencer, not by Darwin himself), and thus advocated political activity and governmental policies that allowed individuals the maximum amount of freedom in order to ensure their survival. Life is a contest, and it is to the benefit of all society if individuals are allowed to compete for success and dominance. Hence the state must refrain from interfering with the natural order of things. Nature's "stern discipline" is the only way to encourage the best individuals to direct society. The "feeble minded," incompetent, and morally defective must not be allowed to sustain themselves, hence the state should not intercede on their behalf out of an excessive sentimentalism or false sense of compassion. For Spencer, it is preferable to allow a little cruelty now against the less fit than to promote their perpetuation, for to do so would actually in the long term cause still further misery for generations to come. Let the self-reliant and talented succeed, the dependent and incapable fail, and the fittest will indeed survive to the great benefit of society as a whole.

Whereas Spencer and Sumner advocated an aggressively competitive and egoistic social Darwinism that endorsed only the minimal state, Ward argued that evolution occurred on the level of the mind as well as in the more material aspects of society. The rational community is thus also a product of evolution, and therefore rather than a competitive struggle for survival, human society has evolved because of and toward greater degrees of cooperation. Thus from the same premise, Spencer and Sumner on one hand, and Ward on the other, drew different conclusions about the role of politics. For the egoistic Darwinist (Spencer and Sumner) the state must always forebear from public assistance, and promote a *laissez-faire* approach. For Ward, a rationalist and cooperative community *is* a product of evolution, and to thwart the common efforts of human beings working with the same purpose is to run counter to those instincts that have elevated humanity beyond the rudimentary survival of the fittest individuals. For the most part, the Spencerian strain of social Darwinism became the most influential, but it is noteworthy that not all social Darwinists were persuaded by Spencer's principles of the "stern discipline" of nature.

Related Entry
liberalism

Suggested Reading
Spencer, Herbert. *The Man v. the State*. Indianapolis: Liberty Classics, 1982.
Spencer, Herbert. *Social Statics*. Baltimore: Robert Schalkenbach Foundation, 1995.
Sumner, William Graham. *On Liberty, Society and Politics: The Essential Essays of William Graham*

Sumner, ed. Robert C. Bannister. Indianapolis: Liberty Classics, 1992.

Sumner, William Graham. *What Social Classes Owe Each Other.* New Haven: Yale Univ. Press, 2003.

Social Gospel movement

Devoted to applying the ethical principles and concerns of Christianity to social issues and problems, the Social Gospel movement was set into motion in the latter half of the nineteenth century as a response by diverse Protestant theologians and activists to various social ills such as poverty, injustice, inequality, inadequate public education, racism, labor reform, alcohol abuse, and urban congestion marked by the expansion of slums. As with the principles and practices associated with Catholic social teaching, the Protestant Social Gospel movement represents a concerted effort to realize the ideals of Christianity within the reality of social and political life.

Perhaps the most famous theologian associated with the birth and development of the Social Gospel is Walter Rauschenbusch (1861–1918), who more than any single figure defined and promoted the ideals of the movement. Rauschenbusch understood love to be the central and defining fact of Christianity, and, given this, he affirmed the commission to turn one's love for God toward the improvement of humanity as a whole, to love both God and one's neighbor as commanded in the Scripture. From the Scripture it can be read that the Kingdom of God is here, Rauschenbusch would remind his followers and critics, and thus we should direct our spiritual energies to spreading justice and mercy in this world rather than focusing solely on the world after. Rejecting what he perceived to be the apolitical attitudes of mainstream Protestantism in his time, Rauschenbusch insisted that Christianity can only fulfill the charge given to it by Christ through perpetual engagement with society— to uplift the poor, illuminate the ignorant, liberate the oppressed, and temper the profligate.

According to Rauschenbusch, Christ died to redeem us for our sins, but not in a personal sense. Rather, the redemption spoken of in the Gospel is a social one, which is certainly intertwined with the lives of all persons, but nonetheless more concretely involving humanity as a totality. It was sin that forced Christ to the Cross, but not the petty sins of each individual, rather the sins of society as a whole. In particular, according to Rauschenbusch, we can identify six social or public sins for which Christ suffered and died, namely, religious bigotry, class hatred, justice corrupted, the madness of the mob, political graft among the powerful, and the violence of militarism. These public sins were carried by Christ, not in a symbolic way, but as a reality, assaulting Jesus in both body and divine soul. In this way Christ died for all the sins of humanity, not for the most specific transgressions of individuals, but rather for the great social ills that have plagued every society throughout history.

In addition to Rauschenbusch, other famous Social Gospel activists included workers advocate Washington Gladden (1836–1918) along with the champion of the poor and founder of Hull House, Jane Addams (1860–1935). Josiah Strong is also associated with the movement, but in significant ways turned away from its core principles through his embrace of social Darwinism and his advocacy of Anglo-Saxon exceptionalism, a modification directly contrary to the critique of racism found in the writings of Rauschenbusch as well as in the inclusive spirit of Hull House. And yet, outliers such as Strong aside, the Social Gospel movement is more closely related to the progressivism of the latter nineteenth and early twentieth century and clearly holds an affinity with the programs and goals of the New Deal. More recently, the influence of Rauschenbusch in particular is evident in the civil-rights movement, as he served as a source of inspiration for Martin Luther King Jr. as well as other Christian activists, both Protestant and Catholic.

Related Entries

Catholic social teaching; equality; justice

Suggested Reading

Rauschenbusch, Walter. *Christianity and Social Crisis in the Twenty-first Century,* ed. Paul Rauschenbusch, with essays by Tony Campolo et al. New York: HarperOne 2007.

socialism

Socialism, while characterized by a varied and complex history, is an ideological orientation that in general embraces the following fundamental principles and attitudes. First, socialism embraces values of strong communitarianism or social solidarity, elevating the community itself to a level of normative preeminence that in some variants exceeds that of the individual. This value is epitomized in Karl Marx's assertion that "man is a species-being," a term forwarded by Marx from a reading of Ludwig Feuerbach, and "a universal and consequently free being." That is to say, each human being is the "ensemble of social relations," and thus what we are is defined by the society in which we live. Even our level of freedom is a "consequence" of our status as social beings. The relations and structures that inhere within the community, or within society itself, precede and determine the formation of the individual. There is no inherent individuality independent of social relations and systems. Rather, our individuality is a reflection of the properties, dynamics, and institutions that occur and exist within society as such. This is not to say that the individual is unimportant, but rather to affirm the idea that even our individuality and its attendant attributes are rooted in and spring from the complex social manifold.

Second, socialism by and large does not recognize a sharp delineation between the political and juristic aspects of a given community and society in general. Political activity is not isolated nor excluded from the private sphere or from the realm of the social. Thus political direction does and should extend into areas of life that are perceived as distinct from the power of government or the organizing practices of politics. For most socialists, the social dimension of life, which included economic production and distribution, has always been associated with politics and the coercive power of the state. The aim of socialism is to transform this relationship from an instrument of domination by those who command economic and social power for their own benefit while reducing the state to an instrument of oppression and into a positive force for the equal and "free development of all." There being no real distinction between public and private, political and social, state and economy, the goal of socialism is to reconstruct a society in which these spheres are thoroughly reconciled for the sake of the good of the community as a solidified whole. Ultimately, as in the case of Marxian communism, politics itself is rendered unnecessary, as the need for the coercive power of the government dissipates upon the approach toward a society that renders class structures and distinctions obsolete.

Third, and following less abstractly from the principles above, socialism is defined by a pronounced direction of economic activity by political agents or state institutions, a level of direction that exceeds even the more activist variants of twentieth-century liberalism. Economic direction of this nature ranges from sustained political steering of the economy through extensive regulation of economic activities and the application of policies measured at redistributing wealth to actual state ownership and command of the means of production. Indeed, control over the means of production, particularly vital industries, is often regarded as the *sine qua non* of socialist practice. This could mean, in some cases, governmental redistribution of wealth through confiscatory taxation coupled with an active regulation of the balance of all economic activity, or in other cases, this could mean nothing less than the direct state ownership of all industry, transportation, and communication. In either case, the goal of socialist policy is to obviate the volatility of capitalist systems while simultaneously, and more importantly, eliminating the exploitative and inegalitarian tendencies regarded as persistent within the acquisitive, alienating, and chaotic nature of capitalist systems.

Fourth, socialism is generally regarded as an attempt to abolish those historically produced distinctions within the human community that have led not only to exploitation of the oppressed by the oppressor, but that have also produced a deeper alienation within society that has ultimately produced a general dehumanization of the individual. While socialism has tended to focus on the economic causes of alienation, estrangement in other dimensions of society, such as race and sex, has in the last five to six decades become a theme of concern for socialist thinkers and activists. This is usually characterized by a desire to at once celebrate difference while simultaneously transcending it. The goal of socialism in general is to empower all groups (particularly those that have historically suffered some form of marginalization or direct exploitation) on an equal basis, protecting the multiple interests of a variety of associations through the assertion of group rights while remaining true to the universalism of a society that will eventually and inevitably promote the equal interests and claims of all human beings without regard to other affiliation.

As the quotes selected above clearly demonstrate, the German philosopher Karl Marx (1818–1883) is universally and rightly regarded as the single most important figure in the development of socialism as both a philosophical and ideological approach to the world and as a vehicle for revolutionary social transformation. Even more than John Locke, Thomas Jefferson, and J. S. Mill for liberalism and Edmund Burke for conservatism, Marx is *the* great, singular intellectual figure and force behind the formation of modern socialism and its offspring, Marxian communism. The basic ideas behind socialism, however, can be traced further back. The word "socialism" bears the same root as the word "society," derived from the Latin *socius* and meaning "association, to share together, partnership, or to combine." One notes the difference between the Greek term *polis,* which is closer to the Latin *res publica,* and *socius,* as the latter encompasses a broader range of common activities extending beyond the province of distinctly political action. Hannah Arendt, in her landmark study *The Human Condition,* commented extensively on the "rise of the social" and the concomitant blurring, and ultimately destruction, of the margin that separates the political and public realm from the nonpolitical and private realm. If Arendt is correct, modernity can be partially marked by the ascent of a new notion of society that regards a more extensive collective control of human activity in contrast to the narrower and clearly demarcated sphere of the *polis* that shaped the classical, Medieval, and early modern view of politics. In other words, one of the marks of the onset of modernity is the introduction of a more expansive view of central control over the different spheres of life within the community. Politics becomes increasingly more enmeshed in the social-economic activities of the community even to the point of, in Arendt's view, the absorption of politics into the activities of the private sphere. However, this conclusion might be slightly exaggerated, as we know from historical record that political activity as the Greeks knew it at times involved direction of economic activities. Nonetheless, Arendt's main point is noteworthy, particularly in our attempt to understand the origins of socialist philosophy and practice. Once the margins separating public action from private activity are reshaped, the distinctions traditionally drawn between political direction and economic distribution are reformed or, in some cases, distorted.

Historically, modern socialism can be traced to a point sometime between the appearance of the Latin understanding of *societus* (shared community, association) as distinct from *res publica* (things public) and the political, social, and cultural upheavals that occurred in Europe during the seventeenth and eighteenth centuries as a result of a confluence of events (the Reformation, the Renaissance, early colonialism that followed the "age of discovery," the rise of the nation-state, and the cultural effects of the Scottish and French Enlightenment as well as the

German *Aufklarung*). Some commentators, such as Tom Bottomore, identify the emergent radicalism in the English Civil War in the activities of the Diggers (1640s and early 1650s) as a precursor to the more systematic and sustained development of socialist ideas that would emerge later. Others, such as Norman Cohn and Ernst Bloch, seem to regard the varied and often violent millenarian movements of the Middle Ages and early Renaissance (typified by the activities of Thomas Munster and similar peasant revolts inspired by chiliastic aspirations) as the roots of modern socialism and communism. French radical François Noel (Gracchus) Babeuf (1760–1797) principal leader of a conspiratorial organization known as the "Society of Equals," envisioned a society of pure equality on every level and advocated militant and dictatorial measures as the only means toward that end. In a sense, Babeuf was the first of the truly modern militant socialists, his influence reaching into the nascent socialism of early nineteenth-century France (Louis Blanqui, Étienne Cabet) and even, according to some historians, influencing the early stages of Russian socialism through the Russian Populists of the latter part of the nineteenth century.

While tempting, it is a mistake to regard the communalist prescriptions of earlier philosophers such as Plato and St. Thomas More as genuine blueprints for a socialist or communist utopia. The same can be said for the communalistic arrangements of Christian monasticism or the Anabaptist communitarian patterns that arose in the early Reformation. While resembling later socialist or communist schemes, neither serves as adequate examples of early forerunners to socialism. Suffice it to say that, for the most part, the evolution of socialism appears to reach back before Marx and the nineteenth century into movements that assumed a more radical position toward the modern concept of equality and its political-social applications. The Diggers of the seventeenth century and the Society of Equals in the eighteenth century, along with the utopian

communities that materialized in Britain and America (Robert Owen's New Lanark in Scotland and New Harmony in America as well as the Brook Farm experiment in New England) during the first half of the nineteenth century and the populist Chartist movement that sprang to life in Britain during the 1830s are all more convincing adumbrations of modern socialism. Additionally, the ambitious social engineering designs of the French writers Claude Henri de St. Simon (1760–1825) and Auguste Comte (1798–1857), the founder of positivism, are clear expressions of a type of hyper-industrial socialism built and directed by a managing technocratic elite. Charles Fourier (1772–1837), perhaps more than anyone, typifies the concept of "utopian socialism." Fourier envisioned a society of small, centrally directed communities based on a complicated lattice of individual specialization, all derived from personality types and ultimately aimed at reconciling the activity of manual labor with the joy of play. Fourier, Owen, St. Simon, and Comte, among others, were all stridently criticized by Marx himself as merely "utopian socialists," but in any event, they unequivocally represent early strains of socialist thinking that would influence ideological debate well into the latter part of the nineteenth century. However, it was Marx who would come to symbolize the essence of the socialist ideal.

Marx's acute critique of nineteenth-century industrial capitalism, his dialectical and materialist theory of history combined with his approach to philosophy as an engine of change, his analysis of the inter-relational connections between material base and immaterial superstructure, and his conviction in the inevitability of a classless and truly egalitarian society generated by a transformative revolution all established the language and conceptual framework of modern socialism. Beginning with the first publication of the *Manifesto of the Communist Party* in 1848 and running through the decline of the Soviet Union, what is loosely called Marxism has been regarded as the most systematic and influential form of socialist ideology. Upon Marx's death, his legacy quickly ramified into a number of ideologically divided schools and movements, all claiming a kind of orthodoxy, and none conceding variety of interpretation. Karl Kautsky (1854–1938), Georgi Plekhanov (1856–1918), August Bebel (1840–1913), Eduard Bernstein, Jean Juares, and Rosa Luxemburg were representative of those earliest thinkers who devoted considerable effort toward building more fully on the legacy of Marx and Engels. With the success of the Bolsheviks in Russia, Vladimir Lenin (1870–1924) emerged as the voice of Marxist "orthodoxy," becoming so prominent that his name would be semantically attached to the great founder's through the ideology of Marxist-Leninism. Lenin's militant, elite-driven centralized and internationalist approach would be contrasted against Plekhanov's more traditionally partisan and nationalist approach as well as Bernstein's more compromising evolutionary and parliamentary strategy, a distinction that would mark an early division among Marxian theorists along the lines of revolution or reform. But even within the dominant orthodoxy of Marxist-Leninism, sects arose and divided allegiances were formed. Ultimately, Marxism as a political philosophy spun into a variety of ideological threads, ranging from the humanistic Marxism of postwar Western Europe to virulent totalitarianism under Stalin, Mao, and various imitators.

Marx himself appears to have preferred the term communism to "scientific socialism" as his own thought matured, but the common distinction between these terms is not always instructive. Communism, which is often interpreted as either a more primitive, naturalistic and apolitical communalism or as a more radical and exhaustive form of organized collectivism in comparison to socialism, is in the end a shorthand for a kind of revolutionary and uncompromising socialism specifically associated with or closely related to Marxism. In any event, the conceptual lines between what we call communism and socialism are sufficiently blurred as to render them inadequate to the task of fostering a sensitive understanding of Marxism in particular and socialism in general. Still, rightly or wrongly, the popular perception holds, often associating socialism with a more moderate, reformist, and even parliamentary approach and communism with militant, revolutionary, and transformative collectivism.

It is important to bear in mind that, while Marx remains the colossus of socialist thought, socialism includes numerous non-Marxists variants. British labor movements such as Fabianism, initiated by Sydney and Beatrice Webb and supported by intellectuals such as H. G. Wells, Graham Wallas, and George Bernard Shaw, and Guild Socialism (promoted by, among others, Fabian socialists Arthur Penty and G.D.H. Cole), a libertarian strain celebrating the worker as artisan and recalling the old Medieval guilds, were both decidedly non-Marxist and each committed to a meliorist reformism aimed at empowering democratically directed worker control over their own productive activity. Fabian socialism did resemble Marxism in its attempt to advance a "scientific socialism," but social Darwinist and positivist threads weaved into Fabianism are markedly distinct. Socialism has also been associated with religion. Christian socialism bases its political project on the notions of universal love and social justice as taught by Christ in the New Testament. Thinkers such as Charles Kingsley (1819–1875), Conrad Noel (1886–1942), R. H. Tawney (1880–1962), Reinhold Niebuhr (1892–1971), and Dorothy Day (1897–1980) drew a deep connection between Christian ethical values and socialism. Tawney, in particular, perceived in capitalism a system of distribution wholly incompatible with the requirements of Christian principles, and some argue that he identified socialism as the only alternative following from Christian values. In the twentieth century, Liberation Theology grew out of movements in Latin America that attempted to fuse Catholic social justice concerns with the revolutionary worldview of Marxism. Similarly, Buddhist socialism advances the principle that a socialist or communalist political structure is the most compatible with an ethic of compassion and an awareness of the natural basis of socialist and communalist organization. Thailand's Buddhadasa Bhikku (1906–1993), for example, advocated a melding of Buddhist moral teaching with Western political egalitarianism. The kibbutzim (rural communal settlements) established in modern Israel are based on democratic, cooperative models that are distinctly socialist and yet non-Marxist in both theory and application. The kibbutz movement grew out of Labor Zionism, which fuses Jewish religious and moral values with the cooperative model of communal living. Kibbutzim have not always adhered to rural, socialist models, and thus have in some cases moved toward the more market-oriented systems that typify most of Israel's economy. Islamic socialism, a term associated with the Muslim Brethren, Pakistan's Prime Minister Zulfikar Ali Bhutto (1928–1979) and Libya's Muammar al-Quaddafi (b. 1942), advanced the notion that social distribution of resources following Western socialist models were in line with the basic ethic of Islam. Quaddafi's *Green Book* proposes the melding of Islamic values with socialist practice.

Other examples of non-Marxian socialism have emerged within the latter part of the twentieth century. Arab socialism, represented by the figures such as Egyptian leader Gamal Abdel Nasser (1918–1970) and groups such as the Baath Party attempted to develop ideas of social control of the means of production through nationalization of heavy industry while retaining some features of private enterprise on a smaller scale. The main goal of Arab socialism was to replace the vestiges of Western influence in the Arab world with a sense of Arab unity and commitment to social and economic reform. Eco-socialism is inspired by a worldview that adopts an ethic of the land, placing the environment and its protection at the center of its values, and encouraging a socialism that places the community within the larger context of the ecological system around it. While somewhat influenced by Marxism, eco-socialism rejects the basic economic assumptions that underlie Marxian thought and advocate a new approach to economic development that emphasizes not so much production and command of one's environment as sustainability and recognition of one's place in a larger ecological system. Eco-socialism is anti-statist and generally skeptical of the benefits of traditional political organizations, and thus is also associated with a type of libertarian anarchism redefined in terms of environmental commitment. Additionally, beginning in the late 1960s and early 1970s, certain strains of feminism radicalized, and in so doing, abandoned the liberal roots of feminist theory and action and embraced notions decidedly socialist and at best only tangentially Marxian. Class struggle, while remaining important, for the radical feminist is ultimately an extension of a deeper patriarchal oppression and androcentric domination. A new collectivism would, for radical feminism, go beyond control of the means of production and rest on a reconfiguration of interpersonal relationships between men and women.

Socialism remains an important concept in global politics today, as there are parties and movements especially outside of the United States that aspire toward the achievement of some socialist goals. Within the United States, socialism remains outside of traditional political discourse, yet still attracts both the disaffected and the visionary idealist. In a sense, and by way of conclusion, socialism has always represented for some the end of freedom and the abolition of the individual, while for others it is the only viable launching point for the creation of a new order dedicated to the construction of a more humane world. Whether one adopts the former or the latter view, socialism as a general approach to politics continues to provoke exercised debate from both proponents and opponents.

Related Entries
communism; ideology; liberalism; Marx, Karl

Suggested Reading

Fried, Albert, and Ronald Sanders, eds. *Socialist Thought: A Documentary History,* rev. ed. New York: Columbia Univ. Press, 1992.

Marx, Karl, and Friedrich Engels. *The Marx-Engels Reader,* 2d ed., ed. Robert C. Tucker. New York: Norton, 1978.

Newman, Michael. *Socialism: A Very Short Introduction.* New York: Oxford Univ. Press, 2005.

Vincent, Andrew. *Modern Political Ideologies,* 2d ed. Cambridge, MA: Blackwell, 1995.

Socrates (469 BC–399 BC)

Socrates is the only human personage in the history of ideas who is regarded as the pivot point in the development of philosophical inquiry. Philosophy and, in truth, Western culture, was so changed by the life and death of Socrates that we regard all Western philosophers predating Socrates as the "pre-Socratics." There was philosophy before Socrates, and quite a bit of it, and most of philosophy's history follows him—but that is just the point, it is Socrates who stands at the center of the great community, antecedent and subsequent to him, of those who love wisdom.

For all this, little is really known about the life and personality of Socrates. Most of what we know of him comes to us directly through Plato, a philosopher of major magnitude in his own right. Xenophon mostly rounds out the picture, with some fragmentary references here and there, a spoof by Aristophanes, and some interesting "second generation" comments from Aristotle, who knew Plato but not Socrates himself. Thus Socrates is one of the rare figures whose importance to human civilization is incalculable and cannot be overstated, yet of whom we have only a fragment of real knowledge.

That Socrates influenced Plato is enough to regard him as a person of immeasurable profundity and influence. Socrates is, by and large, the virtuous and wise hero found at the center of most of Plato's dialogues, and while Plato no doubt embellishes, we have no reason to believe that his presentation of Socrates is simply for his own purposes. For Plato, Socrates is the only true "lover of wisdom," the only real thinker who engages in philosophy in the right way, for the sake of truth and in service to the goodness of human souls. Indeed, Plato treats Socrates as the very embodiment of philosophy. He loves philosophy as no one else, and in so doing, he exemplifies the true nature of the life of the intellect, and ultimately, of the life of the good person. While Socrates considers knowledge for its own sake a fine thing to embrace, he nonetheless judges it as secondary to the good of the soul. It is right to want to know as much as possible about the world and the human beings who live in it, but this desire to know is always a means to the higher end of improving the soul. Hence Socrates engages the city, exhorting those who speak with him to learn as much as they can about the real nature of things for the sake of becoming good people, for the sake of the essential harmony of the soul. Hence we do not learn to prove our worth to others, and we do not argue merely to win the debate or to display one's rhetorical agility; rather, we converse together as companions on the upward journey of truth, a journey with the ultimate purpose of doing what is good and becoming like goodness. Plato perceived Socrates as one who consorts in the proper way with the divine, and in so doing shows us how the philosopher comes to emulate the divine as far as a person can within the limited abilities of a human being. Socrates is not perfect, nor does Plato refer to him as divine—hence the popular comparisons of Socrates and Plato to Christ and St. Paul, respectively, are only superficial. However, through his genuine "erotic" love of wisdom, Socrates comes to intuitively know the nature of the divine in a way that most human beings could never approximate, yet, he remains in humility fully aware that all human knowledge is but a poor thing.

By seeking out (under the divine inspiration of the Oracle at Delphi) those who have a reputation for wisdom and asking them questions—thus engaging in the Socratic interrogative method of the *elenchus*—Socrates's quest was to unravel the riddle of the oracle. Frustrated by the realization that a reputation for or claim to wisdom usually conceals only conceit, Socrates concluded that the Oracle was right, he is the wisest man in Greece, but only because he recognizes the limits of his own knowledge when others refuse to recognize their own lack of true understanding. Socrates is the wiser, but only in one respect: he does not claim to know what he does not know, or, he knows but one thing with any certainty, and that is that he does not really know. As the only intellect to arrive at and then admit this conclusion, he is identified by Plato as the one and only true lover of wisdom in Athens. Moreover, Socrates reflected that, when compared to divine wisdom, the human claim to wisdom reveals its own inadequacy. Hence Socrates, who regarded the faculty of reason as the ruling part of the soul and the love of wisdom as the most virtuous life, came to realize that the secret to human wisdom, and by extension (and more importantly) the secret to human goodness, begins with the humble recognition of the real limits imposed on our ability to really know and understand the world.

However, Socrates was not without hope. While the beginning of wisdom may indeed be the admission of our own ignorance and thus the suspension of our own assumptions (beginning with the conceit that we can know all that there is to know), we can through arduous dedication and sustained inquiry arrive at the truth of things as they are. Vital to Plato's understanding of Socrates, the philosopher is the one person who seeks to discover the reality of things and not dwell on their appearance. For Socrates, we begin by admitting that we do not know, and that we are uncertain about truth, but we cannot remain in such a condition. For there are absolute principles that are real and certain; and it is the philosopher who desires to enter the company of the True, the Beautiful, and the Good. We begin as far away as possible from these absolutes, but if our journey is undertaken with authentic care for the souls of human beings—a journey that must begin first and foremost with our own inward self-examination—we will arrive at the highest principles of being, and, in coming to know the good, we are good.

Whether or not Socrates achieved this can only be known to Socrates himself. Yet, his innumerable companions along the eternal journey need only to remember his calm acceptance of his fate at the end of his life. Rather than inveigh against the injustice committed against him in his final days, Socrates exhibits a humble courage scarcely observed in the annals of the story of human dignity. In the way he faced death, Socrates teaches his friends the meaning of virtue in his actions. Plato knew this well, for the Good is ultimately beyond the power of words, but within the soul of the person.

Related Entries
advantage of the stronger; allegory of the cave; analogy of the jars; Plato; *Republic, The (Politeia)*

Suggested Reading
Brickhouse, Thomas C., and Nicholas D. Smith. *Socrates*. New York: Oxford Univ. Press, 1996.
Guthrie, William Keith Chambers. *Socrates,* part 2 of *The Fifth-Century Enlightenment* (1972), vol. 3 of *A History of Greek Philosophy,* 6 vols. New York: Cambridge Univ. Press, 1962–1981.
Plato. *Complete Works,* ed. John M. Cooper. Indianapolis: Hackett, 1997.
Vlastos, Gregory. *Socrates: Ironist and Moral Philosopher.* Ithaca, NY: Cornell Univ. Press, 1991.

sortition (allotment)
Sortition is the selection of public officials or the drawing of citizens for service by lot or by chance. Rather than appoint or elect, sortition relies entirely on the allotment of offices through a chance drawing, such as a lottery, or by some other indeterminate means. Used infrequently today, sortition was a familiar practice during the apex of Athenian democracy, and was held in esteem by some modern political theorists, viz., Montesquieu and Rousseau. For the Athenians, sortition was a way to fully realize its democratic ideals. Elections are prone to manipulation and

corruption, and reliance on a segment of the population with the influence of skills necessary to successfully achieve office through election or patronage. Sortition is intended to eliminate those features of democracy while still advancing its basic principles, particularly those principles that seek a high degree of equality among citizens as well as cultivating a pervasive sense of shared duty. However, sortition does not necessarily guarantee democratic government. Selection by lot could result in the representation of interests angular to the mores and consensus of its citizenry taken as a whole, perhaps even to the point of subversion. Additionally, sortition, while procedurally fairer than elections and politically driven appointments, fails to guarantee competence and thus substantively undercuts responsible government.

Sortition is still practiced in the drawing of jury pools, but for the most part is a democratic practice that has fallen into disuse.

Related Entry
democracy

Suggested Reading
Manin, Bernard. *The Principles of Representative Government.* Cambridge: Cambridge University Press, 1997.

sovereignty

Sovereignty refers to the highest political authority within a polity or political community, it is, as Lee McDonald defined it, "the fact of a determinate center of governmental power in every society." Sovereignty implies the final word in political power and legal obligation, the organization of all formal political institutions into a coordinated collective directed by a specified central authority, however abstract, as well as full state autonomy relative to other nation-states defined by their own sovereign authority.

Political authority is as old as the *polis* itself; hence in the abstract the principle of authority that is central to the idea of sovereignty reaches back to the most ancient cities. However,

political theorists and students of the history of ideas tend to regard sovereignty *per se* as a more modern concept, with roots reaching into the High Middle Ages and perhaps even earlier, but in the final analysis a different, less personal and less mystical, as it were, understanding of the sources of political power. For Ernst Kantorowicz, sovereignty as a modern phenomenon can be traced to theological beliefs that developed within the Medieval church. Within the church, according to Kantorowicz, the Body of Christ was gradually understood as manifested in two ways: *corpus naturale* (the consecrated host at Mass) and *corpus mysticum*—the social "body" of the church, which includes both clerics and laity. In Kantorowicz's analysis, the *corpus mysticum* was eventually infused into the polity, the "body politic" sharing the same kind of mystical substance as the ecclesial community. By the time Shakespeare wrote Richard II, the notion of the *corpus mysticum* qua body politic had become fully entrenched in the political consciousness of the West. The person of the king will die, but the mystical person of kingship is perpetual—indeed, there is a supernatural aspect to kingship that ensures immortality, not only of the memory of the descent of kings, but also the idea of the king as something that never dies, something that indeed is long-lived beyond the limits of mortality. The king is the mystical embodiment of the dignity, power, grace, and justice of the body politic and, like the *corpus mysticum* of the church, is imperishable.

While kings are no longer requisite to identify sovereignty, the notion of a central, commanding, and mystical power remains in the modern state. Thomas Hobbes's *Leviathan* is an easily identifiable example of the evolution of sovereign power from personal king to "that mortal god" that serves "under the immortal God" as a "common power to keep all in awe." While Hobbes did incline toward a preference for monarchy, he understood that sovereignty simply means ultimate authority and power, and it can exist within one man or "an assembly of men." Before Hobbes, Jean Bodin understood the sovereign to be "absolutely seized of his power" an authority so preeminent that it exceeds even the civil law (albeit still bound to God and the natural law). While Bodin and Hobbes argued that sovereign power was translegal, Locke insisted otherwise, and affirmed a notion of limited sovereignty that was only held within the governing body as a "fiduciary," the people still holding on to the ultimate authority. Even so, for Locke, that "ultimate authority," whether held by a government in trust or returned to the people, is by definition limited under the rule of law and guided by the moral law of nature. In Rousseau's definition, sovereignty is the deposit of will and identical to the people as collective agent possessing will but relinquishing power. Hence Rousseau, building on a foundation established by Locke, Hobbes, and Bodin, among others, distinguishes sovereign will from governmental authority. Governments, under this view, serve the sovereign while exerting authority over subjects. In the end, for Rousseau, it is the attribute of being at once sovereign and subject that we are citizens, both above and below the authority of the government. Ultimately, as a concept, sovereignty gradually detached itself from the person and grew into an abstraction of power beyond reproach. Thus the modern state is born, an abstract unity, as viewed by Hegel, for example, which reconciles and harmonizes all particular associations and interests. It is not located in any one place (although for Hegel it is symbolically represented by the monarch, whose power is limited and shared with a legislature and civil service), yet it is the only certain foundation for a just and dignified political order.

Historically, the modern concept of national sovereignty defined by exclusive authority over a specific territory under the centralized authority of an identifiable political entity has been traced to the Treaty of Westphalia (1648). While this is not universally recognized as the demarcation between Medieval and early modern structures of authority and modern sovereignty, it is often identified as the watershed moment in the European production of the sovereign nation-state. With Westphalia, the power of the Holy Roman Empire was curtailed, the temporal (i.e., political) influence of the ancient church was significantly reduced, the European wars over religion by and large terminated, and the territorial integrity and consolidation of distinct polities were firmly established, at least in legal terms. Obviously, this did not eliminate political and military conflict over disputed territory, but with Westphalia the modern European nation-state configuration was in place. In other words, it is with Westphalia that we see the precursor to the respect for territorial integrity eventually embraced in international law and asserted in the United Nations Charter.

While much of modern political theory has been developed with sovereignty as a key principle, some theorists have either considered it dated or even regarded it askance. Jacques Maritain, as an example of the latter, considered sovereignty to be a fundamental error in modern theories of the state, a concept that is, for Maritain, "intrinsically wrong." Maritain cautions that sovereignty and political absolutism are conjoined, and should be together "scrapped." No temporal authority can hold sovereign authority, and the only true source of political right, and therefore obligation, for Maritain, is the natural law. Indeed, for Maritain, it is not the state that claims sovereignty over persons, but God. Michel Foucault serves as an example of the former proposition, that sovereignty is antiquated, and thus we must abandon models of power based on the Hobbesian Leviathan, lop off the kings head, and examine power as "the study of the techniques and tactics of domination" given the ubiquity of power diffused throughout society and no longer visibly located in any one institution or office.

While the principle of sovereignty is unlikely to vanish, it is being recast as the international order is influenced by transnational, extra-political and nonsovereign actors of considerable influence. While sovereignty will remain a viable concept, its role as a political force will continue to be modified. Even so, questions regarding the proper scope and responsibilities of political authority, however conceived, will continue to animate discussions over the nature of power within the political community.

Related Entries

Bodin, Jean; Foucault, Michel; Leviathan; republic

Suggested Reading

Jackson, Robert. *Sovereignty: The Evolution of an Idea.* Cambridge: Polity, 2007.

Kantorowicz, Ernst H. *The King's Two Bodies: A Study in Medieval Political Theology.* 1957; repr. Princeton, NJ: Princeton Univ. Press, 1997.

Maritain, Jacques. *Man and the State.* 1951; repr. Washington, DC: Catholic Univ. Press, 1998.

McDonald, Lee. *Western Political Theory, Part 2: From Machiavelli to Burke.* New York: Harcourt Brace Jovanovich, 1968.

Spinoza, Baruch (Benedictus de Spinoza, 1632–1677)

One of the founders of modern philosophy (along with René Descartes and Gottfried Leibniz), Spinoza was also a major contributor to the reshaping of political theory that occurred during the sixteenth through eighteenth centuries. While he is often overlooked today, his impact was considerable in his own time, and his influence is still detected in contemporary attitudes regarding individual motivation and the power of the state. Similarly to Hobbes, from whom a clear influence is discernable, Spinoza went to great lengths to develop a systematic philosophy aimed at a thorough explanation of the universe and humanity's place within it. And, like both Hobbes and Machiavelli, Spinoza's attempt at exposing the political strata of human community relies considerably and unabashedly on a candid view of the nature and centrality of power. Indeed, power, its waxing and waning throughout the various attributes and modalities of the universe, is a primary explanatory factor throughout the whole range of things,

from finite human emotion to the infinite cause of all things itself.

In Spinoza's metaphysics, God is equated with nature. This is more than a comparison, but an authentic expression of identity: God is Nature. In effect, God is all that there is; the universe itself. "God, or Nature," is the only substance that exists; everything else is an attribute or a finite mode of this universal, natural substance. The laws of nature are thus manifestations of the operation of God's power. We cannot properly speak of transcendence, for God is immanent throughout the whole of the natural world. This philosophy of immanence holds that the world is all that there is— and thus God is the world itself. Such ideas drew Spinoza into conflict with his Jewish community, leading to his excommunication (by "writ of *cherem*") by the rabbinical leadership of his native Amsterdam. Hence Spinoza's ontology of immanence placed him in opposition to both Judaism and Christianity, causing him considerable isolation throughout his brief life.

This notion held implications for his political theory as well. All power flows from God, which is immanent and identified with nature itself. Hence every mode of existence, including human being, is a manifestation of power. Furthermore, what human beings do is ultimately produced by some action undertaken by the universal immanence that is God—for human passion, thought, and action are but exertions of the ubiquitous power of God operating throughout the whole of nature. By this Spinoza does not mean to argue that God is personally involved in our affairs, but rather, that God, as infinite substance, is the direct cause of all that occurs within the compass of our reality and awareness. This means that our moral actions (the things that we should do) are one and the same with our natural actions (the things that we do). When we appear to act immorally, we do so only through a diminution of power, which in itself is traced back to the expression of the power of nature. Thus Spinoza, even more than Hobbes, establishes a matrix of being, acting, and power that leads directly to a deterministic dynamic. We act a certain way because it is the power of nature/God working through us. For this reason we cannot act against nature and its laws. Unlike previous natural law theorists, Spinoza posited that we cannot break the natural law, for God wills that what we do is according to the principles of nature, and how we act is as we ought to act. We can proceed with our lives, both private and public, ignorantly, but we cannot properly be said to defy the law of nature (and by extension, morality), for the law of nature is as God, fully immanent.

In Spinoza's vision, what we call "free will" is essentially awareness of our acts, or consciousness. Ultimately, we are not the true cause of our actions, for the universe itself, which is identical to God, is the only efficient source of motion and change, the only true cause of action. We can, however, experience a kind of freedom that comes with a true awareness of the nature of things and one's position in the world. Freedom is an illusion if we think that we have command of our actions without regard to the ultimate source of will, which is found in the concept of immanence. The only true sense of freedom is the consequence of the formation of "adequate ideas," which opens our consciousness to a deeper understanding and awareness of our passions. One cannot alter the course of reality, but in knowing the nature of it and our position therein, we can experience a sense of calm that is in itself a kind of liberation, even if it ultimately means that our will is neither the cause of nor a product of our own free agency. This inward calm that comes from adequate ideas has been compared to similar notions in the ancient Stoics. Both Spinoza and the Stoics understood God as immanent and pervasive throughout nature, and both embraced a kind of freedom that in the end is a rational state of quietude. In other words, Spinoza conflates the notion of freedom with the peace of mind that is only made possible through adequate ideas.

This metaphysical system is the ground for Spinoza's view on the nature of right. "Nature," Spinoza explains,

> has the sovereign right to do anything she can; in other words, her right is co-extensive with her power. The power of nature is the power of God, which has sovereign right over all things.

Here Spinoza conceives of right as a function of power, much in the same way as Hobbes previously asserted. For the individual, Spinoza concludes that rights "extend to the limits" of a person's power. Furthermore, in Spinoza's view, individuals are primarily motivated to self-preservation, and must always seek to secure it, placing their own regard above all else. Given that rights are a function of power and humans are motivated first and foremost by self-preservation without recognized limits, Spinoza concludes that the "natural right of the individual man is thus determined not by sound reason, but by desire and power."

Initially, Spinoza adhered to a concept of the social contract reminiscent of Hobbes in explaining the origins of government. As such, he emphasized the role of rationality in the consensual act, in this way emphasizing reason more than Hobbes does in his notion of the generation of the great Leviathan. However, shortly before his death he altered his position, seemingly abandoning the rationalist social contract for a more naturalistic explanation. The social contract, after all, depends on reason and the ability to make a free and rational choice, and even in the Hobbesian analysis of political origins it is reason that discerns the first and fundamental law of nature that guides human beings away from the state of nature and under the protection of a common power. For Spinoza, by contrast, human beings are always led by passion (whereas even Hobbes allows for the role of detached reason as crucial for the original agreement that forms society) and the passion for self-preservation leads us to political community not through reason or deliberate choice (as would be required in a true social contract), but through "some common passion—that is, . . .

common hope, or fear, or the desire to avenge some common hurt." For this reason, the nature of sovereignty is not shaped by an act of will nor by consent, but as a natural development in the overall course of things.

Yet, even though passion and emotion are preeminent in the universe that Spinoza constructs, reason is vital to the affirmation of human power. To be free is to live according to reason, not the "right reason" of Locke and St. Thomas Aquinas but rather reason understood as "adequate idea" of the totality of things. To be free is to have formed adequate ideas and to know that the root of our emotions is in the increase or decrease of our power, and that pleasure, pain, good, and evil are the inevitable conclusions drawn about things as they relate to the preservation of the self and the assertion of our power. In a very real sense, in knowing that the cause of all things, as well as the principles of all value, are immanent, we in effect are able to grasp, through the adequate ideas of this reality, the nature of the infinite substance (God) as far as humanly possible. It is in this way that we uncover the truth of right (an extension of power) and natural law (an immanent attribute of God or Nature) and know the relationship of our individual interest to the greater whole.

Thus Spinoza, due to his emphasis on right as an extension of individual power and the view that freedom is achieved through adequate ideas, embraced democracy as the ideal regime, a conclusion that might come as a surprise given the Hobbesian leanings of his notion of sovereignty. As individuals are concerned above all with self-preservation and the promotion of their interests as they judge them, liberty must be the premium value of any rational political system. And, it is in democracy, under the rule of law, that the passions of human beings can be channeled toward rational decisions made in such as way as to bring private judgment about what is good in accord with common interests in peace and social harmony.

Owing to this, Spinoza endorses a political community that encourages free thought, unrestricted expression in the criticism of government (short of blatant sedition), and toleration, likely a result of his own experiences (confronting his own Jewish community) and the experiences of his Iberian parents (who fled Portugal to elude the Inquisition). However, it is interesting to note that Spinoza advocated insertion of political sovereignty into questions regarding religious affiliation. The sovereign, Spinoza concludes, should be granted the power to enact "whatever laws about religion that it decides," thus echoing the subordination of religion to politics found in Thomas Hobbes, who himself was following the views of Thomasus Erastus (Thomas Lieber). On the other hand, Spinoza still considered the separation of religion and politics, and at other points in his system reasserted the need for religious toleration. Spinoza seems torn between two impulses: the desire to achieve the level of social harmony requisite to internal peace (which is vital to the enjoyment of freedom) and the recognition that adequate ideas that lead to rationality (and thus true freedom) can only be formed in an environment that encourages the intellectual and critical pursuits. For the sake of the former the sovereign can legislate in matters of religion, for the sake of the latter toleration of divergent religions must be promoted.

Spinoza's influence is felt most deeply in his study of power, his notion of the immanence of God, his emphasis on self-preservation/self-interest, the ethical relativism of his understanding of the connection between value and pleasure, and his advocacy of democracy as the preferred regime for a free society. In the history of ideas, political or otherwise, Spinoza's formidable project requires our consideration and challenges the intellectually complacent among us.

Related Entries
Hobbes, Thomas; natural law

Suggested Reading
Spinoza, Benedict. *Complete Works,* trans. Samuel Shirley and ed. Michael L. Morgan. Indianapolis: Hackett, 2002.

Strauss, Leo (1899–1973)

Few thinkers in recent years have provoked as much controversy as Leo Strauss. While Strauss has always been an enigmatic figure susceptible to misinterpretation and thus a ready target for criticism from many quarters, his name has currently been attached to a militaristic neoconservatism that is at best simplistic and at worst unjustified. In truth, Leo Strauss stands among a handful of twentieth-century intellectuals (along with Hannah Arendt, Eric Voegelin, John Rawls, Jürgen Habermas, and Isaiah Berlin) who are largely responsible for reviving the tradition of political inquiry after it narrowly missed being relegated to irrelevance. Strauss understood political inquiry to begin with the classics, and in a close reading of the classics, not only can we better understand the works themselves but we also open ourselves to the discovery of enduring and objective truths about politics emerging from the particular contexts of the time in which they arose. It is largely because of Strauss's admiration for the Greeks and his willingness to take seriously their criticisms of democracy that causes him to be grouped rather casually with conservatism. While it is true that much of what Strauss wrote is conservative in its approach, it is inaccurate to define Strauss as a conservative ideologue, or even a conservative thinker. Like Arendt and Voegelin, Strauss defies easy definition, and he certainly is not well understood—if understood at all—in association with a narrow strain of any one ideology. Even the "Straussian" school of political theory is not easily categorized or described by one set of ideas or principles, other than the belief that a careful and thorough reading of the great texts will reveal meaningful insights for the contemporary student of political activity.

Strauss reconsiders the ancient authors—Plato and Aristotle in particular—in order to mine answers to help resolve the "crisis of modernity." In Strauss's assessment, political and moral thought in the West is in decline owing to a tendency toward relativism and historicism, and through reexamining the ancient ideas of the past as they were originally conceived we can gain a greater understanding of the foundations upon which the edifice of Western political ideas and statesmanship still rest, in spite of our contemporary tendency to ignore or reject them outright. This involves at least in part, for Strauss, a rejection of the notion that political thought is identical to interest-driven ideology, but, rather, properly practiced it is a form of philosophical inquiry. Additionally, Strauss and the Straussians all seek to cut through the conceptual fragmentation in contemporary thought wrought by the relatively recent separation of facts from values. The "fact-value" dichotomy, especially as it is applied to political investigation, is for Strauss one of the leading errors of our times, and a way of looking at political questions that was quite foreign to the classical thinkers who established the original principles of political inquiry. Political philosophy is neither value-neutral nor conventionalist; it is a quest for objective order, one upon which we can rest the principles of right, justice, and goodness on a bedrock of reality rather than the sifting sands of contingency. In this sense, Strauss is with Voegelin in affirming the reality of truth as given rather than constructed.

Strauss thus teaches openness to reading the great works of the past, and especially the premodern thinkers, with diligent effort. One must avoid reading anachronistic ideas into the ancients, but rather try to absorb their teaching with an awareness of their own context. The context is not, however, a boundary that encloses the reader in a specific cultural language—for the great thinkers, the true lovers of wisdom, are able to ascend beyond their context and speak to the twenty-first century in the same way that they spoke to the ancient world. Obviously this is not to say that everything written by the classics is immediately relevant to us today, but rather to say that from within their own context, against the background of their own experiences (not ours), the philosophers of the first rank discover meaning and in turn share teaching that reaches beyond their own culture and situations. This requires the discipline not to read the ancient texts as we want them read in order to understand the lessons of the authors as they wanted us to understand them.

One method (but certainly not the only one) of uncovering meaning for Strauss and his followers is to seek the esoteric teaching behind the exoteric writing. All great authors wrote on two levels and often to more than one audience. Read superficially, the exoteric meaning is readily absorbed, but the fuller sense of what the author sought to accomplish remains concealed. A more careful reading is one that examines every part of the context of the work, the choice of words and how they are used, what is said where and why, and perhaps more importantly, what is not said when one would expect it, or what is said when one would not expect it, the location of phrasing and the meaning of silence orbited by allusion—all important clues to the esoteric lesson that an author seeks to convey. This is not to claim that the great writers conspired to pass along a gnostic teaching, but rather that the author, both in seeking protection from persecution and in plumbing more nuanced depth, writes on two levels, for the casual reader who will carry away one thing, and the serious reader who will carry away something else, and something better. It is with this method that Strauss famously examines Machiavelli and concludes that he is a teacher of evil, a position that challenges the very heart of political writing, whether one agrees with its conclusions or not.

Perhaps the most important part of Strauss's political theory is his belief that we really can speak of things that are good and things that are not. For Strauss, just as there cannot be a value-neutral social science, there cannot be a value-tolerant politics. If politics is about improving the human condition, then it stands to reason that we can speak of something better as well as something worse, and in so doing, we speak of a good that is independent of any particular measure. Therefore, perhaps it is the real purpose of Strauss to advance this single

proposition and nothing more. But the cagey author remains the sphinx both to his supporters and detractors, and one is always left wondering whether or not the alleged cageyness of Strauss is a result of his own spirited prose, or the consequence of our own preconceptions in approaching his work. *Thoughts on Machiavelli* will ever evoke thoughts and second thoughts on Strauss.

Related Entry
teacher of evil

Suggested Reading

Strauss, Leo. *The City and Man,* new ed. Chicago: Univ. Chicago Press 1978.

Strauss, Leo. *Natural Right and History.* 1950; repr. Chicago: Univ. Chicago Press, 1999.

Strauss, Leo. *On Tyranny, including the Strauss-Kojève Correspondence,* rev. ed., ed. Victor Gourevitch and Michael S. Roth. Chicago: Univ. Chicago Press, 2000.

Strauss, Leo. *Thoughts on Machiavelli.* 1958; repr. Chicago: Univ. Chicago Press, 1978.

Strauss, Leo. *What Is Political Philosophy?* 1959; repr. Univ. Chicago Press, 1988.

Suárez, Francisco (1548–1617)

Francisco Suárez, *Doctor Eximius* and a major Jesuit theologian, is generally considered to be one of the most important thinkers within the Thomistic movement centered around the Salamanca School during the sixteenth and early seventeenth centuries. As a major Thomistic philosopher, Suárez's works are voluminous and primarily theological. Even so, Suárez did write about politics and law, and a sufficient political theory emerges from his works to warrant some attention by students of political ideas, particularly those interested in or inclined toward the further development of Thomistic thought. Suárez was perhaps the most important political theorist to carry forward the legacy of St. Thomas Aquinas. Additionally, his ideas influenced the writings of Hugo Grotius, and as such, have a relationship to the origins of modern international law. In his time, Suárez was important enough to draw considerable spleen from Thomas

Hobbes, an indication of his prestige among his contemporaries.

Following St. Thomas Aquinas and Aristotle, Suárez premises his political account on the idea that "man is a social animal," and desires to live with others fully immersed in community. With Aquinas, Suárez regards human society to be an aspect of our original nature as created beings, and not the result of our corruption as in St. Augustine. Politics is a part of our humanity, and therefore is necessary for human beings to live a life of fullness and justice. Indeed, politics is society in its perfection, especially when compared to the imperfect societies of the domestic (private) sphere. Even were we to have remained in a state of innocence, we would seek community and need direction within that community; this is the source of political power for Suárez, wholly natural and thoroughly legitimate. Illegitimate power does exist, but it is imposed by force or some other violent or deceptive method. True political power is natural and deposited within the human race collectively.

Suárez goes further still. As we are created to be free, which means for Suárez that we need the political realm as a means to cultivate this freedom, the true sovereign of all is God himself who has placed freedom within the human soul. Thus those who rule, those who enact laws, and those who obey rulers and the laws so enacted, are in the end obligated first and foremost to God. As Suárez affirms, "[M]an is by nature free and subject to no one, save only to the Creator, so that human sovereignty is contrary to the order of nature and involves tyranny." The human community is a moral association, and only free citizens can act within this community. Thus government based solely on coercion or some other foundations cannot be justified. The human community is a fellowship of equal and free agents, directed through politics toward a common purpose as sanctioned by the will of God. Political power is a product of God's creation, and thus does not stem from any other source in nature or through convention. Nonetheless,

even though political power is a gift of God, it is also dependent on the fact that we are creatures of free will. Therefore, not only is politics and political power a feature of God's design, it is also defined in terms of consent. Suárez does not choose a divine right approach; he does not see political power as something claimed by any particular group or individual, nor does it reside only within a particular form of government. It stems from God, but is manifest through the people themselves from the fact of their natural freedom. In other words, God created political power, and it is held by the people as a collective, and authority of rulers is dependent on the intentional willingness of the people to be ruled. Human beings give their consent because it is natural for them to do so, and not out of any other motivation, such as self-interest or fear. All political power therefore stems from two sources, our nature, which is characterized as essentially political, and our consent, which is the proper foundation of any sovereign authority regardless of the type of government through which it is claimed and exercised.

Should tyranny occur, the people acting as a whole are entitled to resist and reconstruct tyrannical force as political rule based on consent. Suárez was not militant in this position, but he was clear. For the most part, a Christian republic should be one that abides by law, but if a tyrant does usurp power, then any obligation to obey the tyrant dissolves, and resistance, particularly if collective, is allowed. With St. Thomas Aquinas and others before him, the laws of states and actions of rulers are subject to the higher law of nature, which is the law of God. Tyranny by definition resists natural law, and debilitates natural community. Therefore, when forced into the choice to either obey the tyrant or the natural law, the only moral option is obvious to Suárez.

As a Jesuit theologian, Suárez was interested in clarifying the appropriate relationship between ecclesial and civil authorities. For the most part, Suárez argued for separation, each authority properly acting within its own sphere. The church therefore, save for the Papal States, does not possess any legitimate political power. However, like St. Thomas Aquinas and other Christian theorists (both Catholic and Protestant), Suárez held that the church is not without influence. Because of its higher purpose, the church is greater than the state. It may not have the power of the sword over the state, but it possesses true moral authority over rulers and ruled alike. By and large this authority is not set in motion, but when confronted with tyrannical rulers and the evil they can produce, the church, and in particular the pope, is obligated to assert its supremacy. The pope, because of his moral office and salvific charge, is required to bring immoral government back into harmony with the moral laws of God. As Suárez writes, "[T]he Pope...is also able to coerce and to punish those princes who disobey his just commands," and further, the "pope may correct and reform, or may even fittingly punish, a rebellious prince." Punishment involves both spiritual and temporal means, excommunication in the case of the former and removal from power in the case of the latter.

Additionally, the pope is given authority in the determination of just war. War is inherently sinful, but following St. Thomas Aquinas and St. Augustine, war can, in rare cases, be necessary and thus such wars must be justly waged. Toward this end, the pope is entitled to intercede in order to consider the justice of the cause of war, and in particular, holds moral authority when wars occur between Christian states.

In sum, Suárez's importance to political thought is illustrated through his considerations of the proper source of political power, the importance of the rule of law (to which he extensively wrote as a follower of St. Thomas Aquinas), the distinction between church and state qualified by the important role held by the former when moral questions are raised, and the right of resistance held by the people and directed in extreme cases by the pope against the abuses of tyranny. From these observations, it is easily observed that Suárez—like other Thomists, such as Francesco de Vitoria and Juan de Mariana—acts as a bridge between the High Middle Ages and the initial foray into modernity, and, significantly, Suárez provides an example of how political thought can at times confidently wade into the cultural complexities that constitute the modern world while remaining fast to the ancient principles first discerned by classical political theory.

Related Entries
Aquinas, Thomas; Catholic social teaching

Suggested Reading
Suárez, Francisco. *A Treatise on Laws and God the Lawgiver,* in *Selections from Three Works of Francisco Suárez, S.J.,* trans. Gwldys L. Williams, et al., 2 vols. 1944; repr. Buffalo, NY: W. S. Hein, 1995. Facs. Latin texts with English translation; orig. ed. is No. 20 of the Classics of International Law, Publications of the Carnegie Endowment for International Peace.

subsidiarity

Subsidiarity is essentially a doctrine affirming the desirability and necessity for placing political and governmental responsibility, as far as possible, into local institutions and groups. Political and governmental organization should be based on the principles of simplicity and local control. Most political activity is better conducted in this way and for the most part is at best needlessly complicated and at worst thoroughly undermined when larger and more remote actors become involved in matters that could be managed by smaller and more localized groups. In the end, small, simple, and efficient government is not only more effective in achieving its immediate goals but also more compatible with the values of personal freedom and equality.

Subsidiarity is a central political prescription within the tradition of Catholic social teaching. In the early 1990s, His Holiness Pope John Paul II warned against the continued expansion of the large, centralized, and intrusive state, endorsing instead the transference of responsibility to local associations and institutions. This notion is also deeply connected to the philosophy of personalism, which is also identified with Catholic political thought. Even though subsidiarity is, as stated above, a tenet of Catholic social action, it is fully compatible with non-Catholic and nonreligious views regarding participatory government. Thomas Jefferson's vision of small republics, or "wards," for example, while not identified as subsidiarity or associated with any set of religious values, is nonetheless a fair example of the structure of the idea implemented through a different set of assumptions. Other types of participatory democracy that emphasize the need for small, local control are, at least in spirit, in line with the principle of subsidiarity.

Related Entries
Catholic social teaching; personalism

Suggested Reading
Pope John Paul II. *On the Hundredth Anniversary of Rerum Novarum: Encyclical Letter Centesimus Annus of the Supreme Pontiff* Boston: St. Paul Books & Media, 1991.

synderesis (*synteresis, synteresin, scintilla conscientiae,* habitus)

Neither a faculty of the intellect nor the exertion of the will, synderesis is generally described by philosophers within the natural law tradition as that part of one's nature that inclines a human being toward the good. The concept's origin is specifically traced to a passage in the *Commentary on Ezekiel* by St. Jerome (c. 340–420), wherein the eagle in Ezekiel's vision of four creatures (along with the human, the lion, and the ox) is compared to that part of the soul that is somehow above and perhaps directive of its companion elements. From this passage Peter Lombard (c. 1100–c. 1160) and other Medieval thinkers discovered a quality of the person that is by nature oriented toward that which is good and thus instinctively repelled by an innate sense of what is bad. Neither rational (represented by the human) nor the irascible and concupiscent (the lion and ox,

respectively), synderesis is an aspect of the soul that inclines the person toward goodness—an inclination that is not a function of pure reason, nor will, nor simple desire. Hence the soul has a natural capacity toward doing good, one that is not defined or initiated by reason nor compelled by the assertion of will, but rather it is a tendency that inhabits our very soul independent of intellect and volition. Synderesis, therefore, is that part of our nature through which we are capable of knowing goodness at a precognitive level and of being good without relying on the exertion of an often imperfect will. Within Christian theology, such a principle stems from a belief that Creation is inherently good; thus in spite of the Fall, a spark of goodness remains within the human person.

St. Thomas Aquinas (1225–1274), for example, in his *Summa Theologica,* speaks of our "natural participation" in "God's wisdom" through a noncognitive awareness of the "general principles" of the natural law, which is itself an extension of the eternal law. This natural participation is identified by Aquinas as *synderesis,* a faculty of the human person that enables one to share in the "eternal plan" of God through inherent inclinations that direct us toward our own end, which is, in essence, to follow the first precept of the law of nature, viz., to "seek good and avoid evil." For Aquinas this is not a product of rational deliberation (although reason can and should aid in our full understanding of the good) nor a function of will (although free will is requisite to performing good acts), but rather a disposition independent of intellect and volition that inheres in us by virtue of the fact that we are creatures of God. Our capacity for goodness is certainly aided and augmented by will and reason, but it is possible owing to a quality of the human self that is naturally disposed toward good things and moral action. Hence our capacity for discerning and following the law of nature exists independently of reason and will, and is simply a natural part of the human constitution. For Aquinas, it is the fact of Creation and the goodness that defines it in and of itself that is both necessary and sufficient toward the disposition of human moral activity. Reason and will still play a role, but neither one is the key factor in drawing us toward true goodness. Conscience is rooted in the rational faculty, which can be mistaken and is thus not in itself sufficient to know the good without error. We are good by nature; this fact, for Aquinas, is beyond our own self-determination. It is thus, synderesis, or our natural disposition to goodness, and not the conscience alone, that "incite[s] to good" and causes us to "murmur at evil."

Nonetheless, St. Thomas Aquinas does associate synderesis more closely with the intellect than do other natural law theorists. St. Bonaventure, by contrast, regards synderesis as more emotive. For both thinkers, conscience and synderesis are different dimensions of the soul, but for Aquinas, it is affiliated with the virtue of prudence, which is related to the notion of practical reason (phronesis) as discussed by Aristotle. Still, Aquinas appears to depart somewhat from Aristotle in his understanding of synderesis, and through his very use of the term synderesis he is more closely located to Plato, the Stoics, and the church Fathers. With St. Bonaventure, the distinction between synderesis and conscience is more pronounced, as these two elements seem to occupy different parts of the soul, with synderesis possessing decidedly more affective attributes. In either case, though, the role of a noncognitive, nonvolitional faculty in the moral development and activity of the person is evident. For both St. Thomas Aquinas and St. Bonaventure, human beings are capable of following the moral law of nature simply because they are naturally inclined to do so. Reason and will are important for understanding and choice, but moral action is not dependent on or rooted in either one. For Christian natural law theory, such as that developed by St. Thomas Aquinas, we act according to the good because we are, ultimately, created for the sake of all that is good. Hence the human person can learn through prereflective habit the kinds of activities that will cultivate the elevated measure of our nature.

For Thomistic theory and similar or related schools of thought, synderesis is important to natural law theory as it disabuses us from the perception that the natural law is equated with reason alone, or that natural law is simply another variation of the self-prescribed command of the will. If natural law is real, according to the Thomistic view, then it must be at once relevant and accessible to us while at the same time independent of our own influence or interpretation. Thomistic theory still maintains that natural law is accessible to reason (following the Stoic notion of "right reason") and yet recognizes that even prior to the participation of reason the human soul is disposed, by virtue of our status as creatures, toward the good. Hence the concept remains meaningful to those strains of political thought open to the possibility of transcendent law and the application of that law to political and ethical questions.

Related Entries
Aquinas, Thomas; Aristotle

Suggested Reading
Aquinas, Thomas. *On Law, Morality and Politics,* trans. Richard J. Regan and ed. William P. Baumgarth and Richard J. Regan. Indianapolis: Hackett, 2002.
Budziszewski, J. *Written in the Heart: The Case for Natural Law.* Downers Grove, IL: Intervarsity Press, 1997.
Copleston, Frederick, S.J., *Late Medieval and Renaissance Philosophy,* vol. 3 of *A History of Philosophy,* 9 vols. 1946–1975; vol. 3, under the title *Ockham to Suárez,* 1963; repr. New York: Doubleday, 1993).

synteresis—*See* **synderesis**

T

teacher of evil

In Leo Strauss's provocative book, *Thoughts on Machiavelli,* he opens his introduction with the proposal,

We shall not shock anyone, we shall merely expose ourselves to good-natured or at any rate harmless ridicule, if we profess ourselves inclined to the old-fashioned and simple opinion according to which Machiavelli was a teacher of evil.

From this admission, Strauss carefully examines, in his own inimitable style, the manner in which Machiavelli's ideas amount to a promotion of evil. What was once negatively represented by Callicles and Thrasymachus in Plato's writings as examples of the unjust and evil became, for Strauss, the ideal toward which Machiavelli rests his entire system of political thought. "He," Strauss avers in reference to Machiavelli, "says in his own name shocking things which ancient writers had said through the mouths of characters. Machiavelli alone has dared to utter the evil doctrine in a book in his own name." From this point, Strauss offers an analysis of Machiavelli that also serves to indict certain cultural tendencies and ideological proclivities in the study and practice of modern politics, offering Machiavelli not only as the turning point in the history of political thought but also as the origin of our descent from the classical virtues as taught by Plato, Aristotle, Maimonides, and St. Thomas Aquinas. Strauss's argument is based on a thorough examination of the Machiavellian *oeuvre,* and not only confined to a study of *The Prince* as one might expect. Given the exhaustive nature of his account, Strauss has provided a compelling question for consideration, and has thus influenced much of the scholarship on Machiavelli since the publication of his work. To this day, Strauss's followers and detractors comb through the evidence offered, thus sustaining a debate that is not likely to find resolution any time soon.

Related Entries
Machiavelli, Niccolò; Strauss, Leo

Suggested Reading

Pangle, Thomas. *Leo Strauss: An Introduction to His Thought and Intellectual Legacy.* Baltimore: Johns Hopkins Univ. Press, 2006.
Sorensen, Kim A. *Discourses on Strauss: Revelation and Reason in Leo Strauss and His Critical Study of Machiavelli.* Notre Dame, IN: Univ. Notre Dame Press, 2006.
Strauss, Leo. *Thoughts on Machiavelli.* 1958; repr. Chicago: Univ. Chicago Press, 1978.

three causes of quarrel

In chapter thirteen of his *Leviathan,* Thomas Hobbes identifies "three principal causes of quarrel," competition, diffidence and glory. These are enduring factors that stem from human nature itself and are connected to Hobbes's conception of the state of nature as a "war of all against all" as well as Hobbes's understanding of political realities.

Human beings are, according to Hobbes, naturally competitive, always seeking to follow the appetites in the acquisition of more for the sake of individual felicity. Competition, Hobbes observed, "maketh men invade for gain," a natural propensity that if left unconstrained fuels our natural enmity. Additionally, individuals are naturally diffident, or timid (lacking confidence) in a world of general scarcity, distrust, and comparative equality. When we invade for gain (caused by competition), Hobbes continues, we employ violence to subdue and gain mastery over "men's persons; wives, children and cattle." Diffidence causes human beings to "invade" or preemptively attack others for the sake of safety, our fear and distrust compelling us to oppress others before they can oppress us, for oppress us they will. Thus we invade others to prevent such oppression and to preserve what we have, which has likely been acquired at someone else's expense. Finally, as reputation is an aspect of power, the desire for glory, the extreme of public acclaim, is sought as an enhancement of the felicific life. Reputation, or glory, causes us to invade others as evidence of our power, and goes before us as a shield of intimidation to those who might challenge us for what we possess. Because of the power behind reputation, we will invade or attack others for the sake of a "trifle, as a word, a smile, a different opinion," or anything that causes another to "undervalue" ourselves. Glory insures that we will not be undervalued in even the most abstract or intangible ways and thus will persist as a particularly arbitrary cause of quarrel and conflict. The causes of quarrel are manifestations of the state of nature and in nature constantly prod us into conflict. Within formal society these propensities are checked and channeled, but they do not disappear, for it is in our nature to strive, fear, and want for the sake of our material interests, personal security, and emotional well-being in the judgment of others.

Related Entries

Hobbes, Thomas; Leviathan; war of all against all

Suggested Reading

Hobbes, Thomas. *Leviathan,* ed. Edwin Curley. Indianapolis: Hackett, 1994.

tikkun olam

From the Hebrew meaning to "repair" or "restore" the world, the ethical principle of *tikkun olam* stems from ancient Jewish mystical writings describing a cosmic fragmentation of an illuminated, primal, and divine unity that held all the values of goodness together in an indescribably ecstatic harmony. Having been shattered by a cosmic catastrophe before the beginning of time, the shards of goodness and light are scattered throughout the void, to be found, reclaimed, and reconstructed by human souls (each soul itself being also fragmented and in need of repair). Everything and everyone we encounter is in some way a small spark of this incomprehensible and infinitely good divine light, and thus it is our responsibility as human beings to try to find that small light within each of us and liberate it from the opaque prisons that are suffering and pain.

In political and social terms, the Jewish principle of *tikkun olam,* or repairing the world, bears much in common with Catholic social teaching, the Protestant Social Gospel, and socially engaged mindfulness in Buddhist traditions. In the way of *tikkun olam,* we must at

every opportunity help the disadvantaged, the vulnerable, and the victimized. In so doing, we help to find and liberate another spark of divine light, which in itself is a small but real step toward our final reconciliation with God, with each other, and thus with all that is good in the universe.

Related Entries

Catholic social teaching; Social Gospel movement

Suggested Reading

Jacobs, Louis. *The Concise Companion to the Jewish Religion,* abridged and updated ed. New York: Oxford Univ. Press, 1999.

Shatz, David, et al., eds. *Tikkun Olam: Social Responsibility in Jewish Thought and Law.* New York: Jason Aronson Publishers, 1997.

Tocqueville, Alexis de (1805–1859)

Tocqueville is one of the most important students of democracy within the tradition of political theory, and his book *Democracy in America* serves as both an important window revealing the world of Jacksonian America as well as a perspicuous commentary on the nature of democracy itself.

Tocqueville, a French aristocrat, recognized that democracy's triumph in France and elsewhere was irresistible. Neither endorsing nor opposing the movement of democracy, Tocqueville undertook the study of it for the sake of ensuring that its eventual emergence as the dominant social order would benefit humanity, or at least not work to its detriment. Democracy, which rests on the premise of individual liberty and self-government, is capable of degenerating into a form of tyranny—a tyranny of the majority, to be sure, but also the tyrannical force of conformity. Contrary to the claims of individual free expression, Tocqueville discerned in democracy the erosion of free thought. Subtle social pressures force citizens to repress their individuality, and the emphasis on equality over other political ideals in Tocqueville's estimation actually stifles creative liberty and the ability to accomplish worthwhile goals to the betterment of all. Democracy, for Tocqueville, while managing to create a condition of universal fairness before the law and in the political arena, eventually advances a herd society, one that is excessively absorbed in material comfort and the power of "public opinion" in the shaping of the attitudes and beliefs of democratic individuals. In a word, the individualism of democracy actually abolishes true individuality, replacing it instead with a banal shade of the human person.

What is needed, in Tocqueville's assessment, is the "education" of democracy, a way to refine it so as not to completely reshape the social order as we know it. Equality is the central principle of democracy, centralization its more troubling outcome, and mediocrity its unavoidable product. For Tocqueville, the severity of these trends can be partially reduced by fostering decentralized administration and localized self-government, private associations, the security of property, a free press, and a freedom of religion that promotes sincere moral values—through these measures the inexorable victory of democracy can become a positive force, even though the nobility and virtues of the old order would largely be lost. Democracy's tendency to induce dull conformity and a benign complacency cannot be fully prevented, but in the more libertarian impulses of democratic political culture and the self-reliance of the frontier spirit epitomized in America, the strength of democracy's bland egalitarianism can be mitigated.

It is by examining and applying the lessons of the American model that the future of democracy in Europe can be directed toward an overall improvement of society. The greatness of the past might be forever lost, but the new society ahead need not be that of the directionless masses under the sway of their own social tyranny. With his friend, John Stuart Mill, the lowered sights of egalitarian society need not defeat the spirit of liberty and opportunity in democratic man, but in order for that spirit to be encouraged and sustained, the dispersal of political power and administration, along with the encouragement of diversity of thought, are absolutely vital. Absent these, the insidious tyranny of a mindless mob is the fate of the democratic nations yet to be born.

Related Entries
democracy; Mill, John Stuart

Suggested Reading

Tocqueville, Alexis de. *Democracy in America,* trans. and ed. Harvey C. Mansfield and Delba Winthrop. Chicago: Univ. Chicago Press, 2000.

Tocqueville, Alexis de. *The Old Régime and the French Revolution,* trans. Stuart Gilbert. 1955; repr. New York: Doubleday/Anchor Books, 1983.

Welch, Cheryl. *De Tocqueville.* New York: Oxford Univ. Press, 2001.

Wolin, Sheldon. *Tocqueville between Two Worlds: The Making of a Political and Theoretical Life.* 2001; repr. Princeton: Princeton Univ. Press, 2003.

totalitarianism

The most virulent and destructive species of authoritarianism, totalitarianism is in effect a social arrangement wherein all elements of politics are completely destroyed. Totalitarianism describes the complete control of all aspects of human life, and the manipulation of every institution by the forces of fear and paranoia. Under totalitarianism, the distinction between public and private are completely eradicated, and as such, there being no sphere for the engagement of private activity, the behavior of every individual is vulnerable to the machinations and manipulations of power. In effect, the political state is abolished, replaced by raw power, total surveillance and control, and a constant state of fear bordering on mass paranoia.

Totalitarianism, while emphasizing the will of the collective, is in reality the destruction of the community. It is not in the generation of a common collective mind that totalitarianism is produced, but rather in the complete severing of all moral and juridical connections between individuals. The legal institutions of the state evaporate under totalitarian power, and the moral conscience of men and women is perverted by the violent disconnection of the individual from any authentic sense of community. Culture is artificially reshaped for the uses of power. Barbarism is embraced at the expense of civilization. Religions are either banned or seized and then manipulated for even greater social control. Enemies are invented both within society and from without. The media becomes the mouthpiece of power, the courts irrelevant, and the military a refuge for the criminal and the insane. The family itself is dissolved by the withering totalitarian gaze; no one can be trusted; everyone is to be feared.

While it is tempting to refer to authoritarian regimes as totalitarian, such a conflation of terms is in fact inaccurate. Few regimes in history have actually been totalitarian, and for the most part, it is only in the twentieth century that the barbarity of totalitarianism thrust itself fully on the world stage. Hitler's Nazis, Stalin's Soviet Union, the tyrannies of Mao in China, Pol Pot in Cambodia, and the legacy of Stalinism in Albania and (currently) North Korea are generally regarded as true totalitarian systems. Regimes under Lenin, Mussolini, and Castro are also strong candidates for the classification of totalitarian. Other dictatorships, while authoritarian and certainly pernicious in many cases, are not necessarily totalitarian in the strict sense, although it must be allowed that any pervasive abuse of power accompanied with comprehensive social control within a given state either borders on the totalitarian or initiates its appearance.

Related Entries

Arendt, Hannah; authoritarianism; fascism; tyranny

Suggested Reading

Arendt, Hannah. *On the Origins of Totalitarianism,* with an introduction by Samantha Power. New York: Schocken Books, 2004.
Halberstam, Michael. *Totalitarianism and the Modern Conception of Politics.* New Haven.: Yale Univ. Press, 2000.

two-swords doctrine

The separation between church and state is not simply a modern issue; rather, it can be traced to the early centuries of Christianity, having initially been given voice and definition by Pope St. Gelasius I toward the end of the fifth century. St. Gelasius taught that there are two realms, *sacerdotium* (the sacred, the ecclesial) and *regnum* (the regal, the civil, or political), and each is to have authority over the other in its own sphere. The church, led by the pope and his bishops, is to guide the state in matters spiritual and moral, while the state is to have authority in all other areas. Thus princes defer to bishops on religious and theological matters, and bishops recognize the full authority of princes in governing the polity. Thus, as early as the last decade of the fifth century, a statement on the relationship between church and state is offered by the leader of what was at that time a unified Christendom.

Since St. Gelasius's pronouncement, the actual configuration of this relationship—distinct and yet somehow not entirely separate—has been the subject of much debate, even into the twenty-first century. While St. Gelasius appears to have regarded these spheres as equal in influence, later figures would assert the primacy of one over the other. Pope St. Gregory VII, for example, recognized the independent authority of the state as did his predecessor, yet he affirmed the principle of papal supremacy. For St. Gregory VII, the prince (state) is to the pope (church) as the moon is to the sun, both are luminescent objects of the heavens and thus worthy of reverence, but the brilliance (and hence importance) of the sun, or church, far exceeds that of the lesser object, the state (compared with the moon). Other Medieval figures such as John of Salisbury and Giles of Rome hewed closely to this line of reasoning. However, thinkers such as Marsiglio of Padua and Dante Alighieri regarded the temporal power as independent of the power of the church. For the latter, that power is equally inspired by the Divine. Later figures such as Thomasus Erastus argued for the primacy of the state, a position that Thomas Hobbes famously adopts in his *Leviathan*. Finally, the notion of "two-swords" finds its way into the "wall of separation" between church and state commonly associated with the American founding, to this day yielding a harvest of diverse interpretations.

Related Entries
Aquinas, Thomas; Augustine; circle of power; Hobbes, Thomas; organicism

Suggested Reading
Hallowell, John H., and Jean Porter. *Political Philosophy: The Search for Humanity and Order*. Englewood Cliffs, NJ: Prentice Hall, 1997.

tyranny (*tyrannos*)
Originally, a tyrant was viewed by the archaic Greeks as simply a strong leader, who, in seizing power, was able to exert his will to the end of establishing a degree of order and stability, especially in response to a crisis or general state of disorganization brought on by a loss of political will. Hence the term *tyrant* was in its origins a neutral one—a successful tyrant could prove beneficial to a city-state in need of direction. It is with Plato and Aristotle that the term *tyrannos* is drawn as a contrast to a monarch, or to any form of legitimate political rule. A tyrant, for both Plato and Aristotle, governed lawlessly for his own advantage, and was ultimately the kind of person who preferred a vicious life to a virtuous one and thus caused vice to grow in the *polis* to the detriment of morality. For Plato in particular, a tyrant was the direct opposite of the philosopher, the latter a lover of wisdom in pursuit of the just and Good, the former driven by lust and fear. This tradition, that of regarding the tyrant as a vicious ruler, has been the model for Western political thought since Aristotle. It is seen in the Middle Ages, for example, in John of Salisbury's description of tyrants as being the "very likeness of the Devil," and continues today in our image of tyranny as in all cases intolerable. This is not to reject all forms of autocratic rule (even a despot can be "benevolent"), but only

to remind us that all power must be limited and restrained by moral principles of some kind. It is in tyranny that we see unrestrained and immoral abuses of power. Tyranny is, for both Plato and Aristotle, the abolition of politics, replacing the public sphere with the rule of one master over a multitude of slaves. But as Plato reminds us, in a tyranny, it is the tyrant who is the worst slave of all.

Related Entries
authoritarianism; despot, despotism; dictator

Suggested Reading
Strauss, Leo. *On Tyranny, Including the Strauss-Kojève Correspondence,* rev. ed., ed. Victor Gourevitch and Michael S. Roth. Chicago: Univ. of Chicago Press, 2000.

U

unencumbered self

Political theorist Michael Sandel, in his reassessment of the original position conceived by John Rawls, has defined the imaginary person choosing principles of justice in advance from a hypothetical original position as an "unencumbered self." For Sandel, the unencumbered self is Rawls's renewal of the concept of Kant's transcendental subject, revived by Rawls for the purpose of discerning the foundations of the just distribution of social goods and modified so as to resituate persons within a practical context more tangible than the vague ideal of Kant's "kingdom of ends."

Michael Sandel has described the unencumbered self as the "self understood as prior to and independent of purposes and ends." This is a conception of the self that separates one's values and character traits from one's existence as a living being, an exercise that in Sandel's estimation is untenable. For Sandel, the unencumbered self, stripped of all traits, interests, and values, is an anonymous indistinct specter "standing behind" the characteristics, ambitions and purposes that truly define the person.

This notion of selfhood that Rawls conceives as the main component of the original position is absent experiences and attitudes and is now only defined in terms of the "capacity to choose" values, and not by the values themselves. The unencumbered self, according to Sandel, "rules out constitutive ends," that is to say, it artificially suspends the various ideals and goods that truly constitute or define who we are and in its place leaves an incomplete deliberator attempting to sort out preferences and potential future interests in an intellectual vacuum. Thus the principle in Rawls that proposes the priority of right over good is premised on a basic misunderstanding of what it means to be a person and how that meaning influences the choice of our values. As Sandel asserts,

> Only if the self is prior to its ends can the right be prior to the good. Only if my identity is never tied to the aims and interests I may have at any moment can I think of myself as a free and independent agent, capable of choice.

Sandel concludes that the self in the original position as conceived by Rawls (the unencumbered self) is capable of joining communities based on cooperation, which is a benefit, but lacks the kind of communal membership and sense of belonging that is associated with what Sandel calls "constitutive." A constitutive community "would engage the identity as well as the interests of the participants, and so implicate its members in a citizenship more thoroughgoing than the unencumbered self can know."

Sandel's critique of Rawls is often described as "communitarian" and contrasted against what is deemed Rawls's atomistic liberalism. Whether or not these descriptions are accurate (and they are likely not completely adequate to the task of describing their political theories), the impression remains that for Sandel, Rawls's basic misstep is in his attempt to denude the person of personhood—even a hypothetical exercise that undertakes this process is not a realistic or beneficial premise for the understanding of the inextricable relationship between identity and interest in the political realm, particularly when considering the just distribution of social goods.

Related Entries
Kant, Immanuel; procedural republic; Rawls, John

Suggested Reading
Sandel, Michael J. "The Procedural Republic and the Unencumbered Self." *Political Theory* 12 (February 1984).

utilitarianism

Utilitarianism is essentially a moral theory adopting the view that all values, both moral and political, are to be measured and assessed in terms of their utility, or the extent to which they produce "the greatest good (or happiness) for the greatest number." Happiness in turn is measured in terms of the maximization of pleasure and minimization of pain. Utilitarianism is thus grounded on the premise of the pursuit of rational self-interest, human beings knowing no other way to deliberate with regard to their own good. Thus utilitarianism is basically egoistic in its assessment of value and dependent on the assumption that in the end it is the individual ego that is best equipped to identify her or his best interest.

For Jeremy Bentham, considered to be the greatest of the utilitarian theorists, all human conduct is fundamentally determined by the attempt to expand pleasure and contract or eliminate pain: it is in the expansion of pleasure that happiness is secured. This not only describes the way human beings think and choose, but it also prescribes the way we ought to think and choose. Thus Bentham argued that the calculus of felicity is the actual manner in which human beings make their decisions in the hope of increasing their pleasure (and thus happiness) as well as the only legitimate ground upon which we can prescribe our actions according to a moral principle. This "principle of utility," while based on a radical empiricism and individualism, is nonetheless the foundation for all human conduct (moral, political, or otherwise), and is thus the substantive core within our concepts, values, and relationships.

Utilitarianism's political form is associated with the promotion of democratic institutions, a species of legalism that rejects natural law as the foundation of justice and posits the ground of law and justice in the sovereign, rejection of both the social contract tradition and the classical view of the political community as natural, and a preference for a minimal state. The doctrine of utility (or the "greatest happiness principle") is essentially consequentialist; thus the best measure of the value of an act, individual or otherwise, is by examining the consequences or results. If a policy, law, or governmental act results in a greater good for the largest possible number of citizens, then it can be said to be of value. Failing this, there is no other measure to determine the moral legitimacy and political efficacy of an act or policy. In a sense, utilitarianism is the epitome of the consequentialist ethic—it is only in the effects of an act or decision that we are able to truly judge the merits of it; it is only in the increase of the general happiness that we can determine the value of a regime.

As stated above, utilitarianism is generally identified with Bentham, who, more than any other thinker, is the major thinker in developing its basic principles. Before Bentham we can detect ideas and approaches to politics that adumbrate the utilitarian ethic. The voice of utility can be heard as far back as Thomas Hobbes, albeit implicit, and some (including J. S. Mill) trace utilitarianism explicitly as far back as Epicurus, who held that pleasure is the highest good (although he was careful to emphasize the higher pleasures of the virtues and the intellect). Immediate precursors to nineteenth-century utilitarianism can be found in the political writings of Joseph Priestley, and more directly still, the French Enlightenment *philosophe* Claude Adrien Helvetius. David Hume has also been so associated, but his moral and political thought is too complex to fit into the utilitarian mold. It is Bentham, however, who, along with James Mill, formally founded British

utilitarianism and gave it a coherent and systematic doctrine centered on the principle of the greatest good for the greatest number. John Stuart Mill (son of James Mill) and Henry Sidgwick are also regarded as primary utilitarian authors; their modifications to Bentham's overall vision are significant—particularly those of the younger Mill, whose own ideas about the greatest happiness principle in some ways set him at odds against the Benthamite system.

Related Entries
Bentham, Jeremy; Mill, John Stuart

Suggested Reading
Sen, Amartya, and Bernard Williams, eds. *Utilitarianism and Beyond.* New York: Cambridge Univ. Press, 1982.

Smart, J.C.C., and Bernard Williams. *Utilitarianism: For and Against.* 1973; repr. New York: Cambridge Univ. Press, 1998.

Troyer, John, ed. *The Classical Utilitarians: Bentham and Mill.* Indianapolis: Hackett, 2003.

veil of ignorance

In his *Theory of Justice* (1971), philosopher John Rawls employs the "veil of ignorance" as a means to arrive at those principles of justice that would universally be chosen by rational actors from an original position of equality. The "veil of ignorance" is an imaginary suspension of one's self-knowledge aimed at a consideration of what principles of justice would be most acceptable to a person unaware of their own basic situation within the larger social structure. The veil of ignorance is a purely imaginative exercise that forces the thinking agent to consider the various conditions of life that might be confronted within a given social order, and thus the a broader understanding of a distribution of social goods that would be just in any given case. Hence behind the veil of ignorance a person is to arrive at principles of justice that would be beneficial even if one finds oneself to be the least advantaged within society. The veil of ignorance invites us to suspend any knowledge about oneself or one's attributes so as to consider the myriad possibilities that a person might face in society once the "veil" is lifted, so to speak. One does not know one's economic class or natural abilities, one is ignorant of all the variables in life that shape a personality, or even a "conception of the good." From behind this veil, the rational agent, knowing that others are equally ignorant of their own situation and abilities, would arrive at the same general principles of justice—namely, a society wherein the most extensive amount of liberty will be realized compatible with an equal liberty for all, and a distribution of social goods that are to the benefit of even the least advantaged. According to Rawls, if we really could engage in this kind of thought exercise or game, each one of us would choose those principles of justice that would advance equal liberty and secure benefits to all within the bounds of what he calls a "permissible inequality."

In a real sense, the "veil of ignorance" is not so much an attempt to wipe away awareness as to open it—to compel rational actors to consider the best possible system of justice regardless of one's own personal limitations and social status. In this way it can be fairly said that Rawls's veil of ignorance is really a "lens of awareness" that helps us to understand the notion of justice as fairness in the context of the best possible distribution of social goods across society as a whole.

Related Entry
Rawls, John

Suggested Reading
Rawls, John. *A Theory of Justice.* 1971; repr. Cambridge, Mass.: Harvard Univ. Press, 2005; new ed., Cambridge, MA: Harvard Univ. Press, 1999.

virtu

In his study of the nature of politics and the requirements of power, Niccolò Machiavelli concluded that the traditional moral virtues of Christianity are fundamentally and irreconcilably incompatible with the values of good citizenship. The otherworldliness of Christianity teaches humility and self-abnegation, along with a level of mercy and compassion that prescribes even the love of one's enemies, which, for Machiavelli, is a liability in the competitive and often aggressive world of politics. Hence Machiavelli proposes reviving another standard for action, one that emulates the virtues of the ancient heroic ideal of Rome and the pre-Socratic Greeks. Machiavelli employed the term *virtu* to summarize the kind of character needed to become a ruler of skill and gravity, a term that is often left in the original language by Machiavelli's interpreters as a way to underscore his departure from ancient moral ideals.

In short, *virtu* encapsulates a number of qualities. Grandeur of spirit, boldness, "manliness," and heroic daring are included as parts of *virtu*. Michael Morgan, in his introduction to Machiavelli in his anthology *Classics of Moral and Political Theory,* has defined *virtu* as "skill, ingenuity, excellence." This runs close to the ancient notion of *arete* held by the Greeks, but Plato and Aristotle construed this concept in moral terms framed by the concepts of wisdom, courage, justice, and temperance, all orbiting an objective and transcendent Good. For Machiavelli, the skill and excellence that he speaks of is success in politics, in the acquisition, maintenance, and expansion of power and the preservation of the liberties and prosperity of one's subjects or citizens. The measure of *virtu* is ultimately a worldly, and for Machiavelli's critics (rightly or wrongly), a relativistic one.

Virtu is aptly described in *The Prince* through the metaphor of the "lion and the fox." A successful prince must develop the traits of both animals; the lion as it possesses the sheer power and ferocity to frighten away ravenous wolves (of which there are many in this world), and the fox as it is expert at sniffing out and evading all traps that a lion might miss. This combination of strength and ferocity in the lion and the clever instinct of the fox is an effective analogue for *virtu,* and provides the best example of what Machiavelli in truth seeks in the pursuit of practical leadership.

In sum, *virtu* is that set of qualities that provide what political leadership needs to govern effectively. It is not the elevated moral virtues of Plato or St. Thomas Aquinas, but for Machiavelli, such traits are regrettably inconsonant with the practicalities of a world shaped by the ambitions of envious and aggressive men. As Machiavelli reminds us, those rulers who always attempt to be good will ultimately bring about their own ruin. It is only by training oneself toward *virtu* that enemies of the city's common interest will not thwart the designs of an able leader.

Related Entry
Machiavelli, Niccolò

Suggested Reading
Machiavelli, Niccolò. *The Prince,* trans. and ed. Angelo M. Codevilla. New Haven: Yale Univ. Press, 1997.
Parel, Anthony, ed. *The Political Calculus; Essays on Machiavelli's Philosophy.* Toronto: Univ. Toronto Press, 1972.

Vitoria, Francisco de (c. 1485–1546)

Students of the history of ideas recognize that it is not Hugo Grotius, but Francisco de Vitoria, who has the best claim to the title of the modern "father of international law." A leading Thomist of the Salamanca school, Vitoria applied the principles of St. Thomas Aquinas and the Stoic philosophers to the question of political conflict between kingdoms in the nascent international order. While much of Vitoria's political thought draws heavily from Aquinas, he is especially notable for his emphasis on the equation of the law of nature with the law of nations (a view similar to that of the great Roman jurist Gaius, 110–180). The moral principles of the natural law are the binding force of the international order and thus must be so applied. Nation-states must not be driven by consideration of power alone, but are obliged to act first on moral principles.

In defining international law as natural law was, for Vitoria, the driving concept behind his theory of just war. Influenced by St. Augustine and St. Thomas Aquinas, Vitoria contributed to the development of just war theory. For Vitoria, wars cannot be waged as a means for expansion alone, nor are they justly prosecuted in the name of a religion. Vitoria wavered somewhat on this position upon reflecting on Spain's extensive encroachment into the New World—an inconsistency not lost on the modern reader. However, Vitoria was, along with Bartoleme de Las Casas (1484–1566), an open critic of the treatment of the natives in the New World. For Vitoria, the rights that stem from the natural law (and thus law of nations), applies equally to all, including the natives who were being subjugated by the Spanish conquests. The natural law is universal and all human beings are guided by its principles and protected by natural right against subjugation. Hence the treatment of the natives was, in Vitoria's judgment, a case of the violation of this law.

Vitoria, with Grotius after him, provides the basic conceptual structure within which modern international law would eventually be constructed. But for Vitoria, that construction was executed with the law of nature as the only real blueprint.

Related Entries
Grotius, Hugo; Suárez, Francisco

Suggested Reading
Vitoria, Francisco. *Political Writings,* ed. Anthony Pagden and Jeremy Lawrance. New York: Cambridge Univ. Press, 1991.

Voegelin, Eric (1901–1985)

Eric Voegelin is a major actor in the recovery of political theory in the twentieth century, a political thinker occupying that rarefied rank of twentieth-century theorists along with Jacques Maritain, Reinhold Niebuhr, Leo Strauss, Hannah Arendt, Jürgen Habermas, Michael Oakeschott, Michel Foucault, and John Rawls. These are the thinkers that would most likely be mentioned in any list of principal influences on the recovery and advance of political theory in the twentieth century, and of these mentioned in this list, Voegelin is perhaps the most difficult to characterize (although Strauss and Arendt can be equally elusive). Voegelin is a complex thinker able to draw on an inexhaustible knowledge of human civilization, and his prolific writings provide a rich ground for exploration and reflection. In some ways Voegelin offers a challenge as immense as Hegel, and for the same reason, he is as difficult to condense into a few short encyclopedic paragraphs.

Dante Germino lends assistance in this endeavor through his observation, "The starting point of Voegelin's explorations is the empirical fact of the human person in his awareness of the finiteness of his existence." This awareness of finitude is formed against the background of the reality of a transcendent and infinite reality. Voegelin grounded his political theory on objective truths, or moral absolutes, from which all values, including those of the *polis,* are derived. The beginning of this awareness is an inward illumination (*nous*) that leads to the realization that the human person is not a world of its own but is rather immersed in a world with others. Owing to our finitude and constricted intellect, we can only know transcendence at best in part, and we can only express it and reflect upon it imperfectly, symbolically, analogically. Political thinking, as with anything else, is ultimately informed by the ground of being beyond experience, hence this too, must be understood, however imperfectly, as related back to the ineffable and the principles of being therein. Ultimately, Voegelin merges reason and faith, considering them to be necessarily linked and recognizing that any grasp of the transcendent is inevitably the result of faith. But it is not an isolated faith that trumps reason, rather, as with St. Augustine and St. Thomas Aquinas, they are allies of the human spirit in their quest for higher truth. Political truth must be so attuned, and for Voegelin, no real political knowledge

can begin without at first coming to terms with transcendent principles. All theory, in Voegelin's terms, is initiated by a kind of faith.

The fullest understanding of this reality is impossible. We can experience through faith the transcendent, but we can never gain absolute knowing of it any more than we can give it full expression. And yet much of the history of philosophy in general and political ideas in particular is marked by such efforts, which are taken still further in an attempt to bring the transcendent into time, and thus to "immanentize the eschaton," that is, to force the transcending hope of salvation into the phenomenal realm of social experience. For Voegelin a particular strain of human consciousness regards the world as alien, and the self as somehow perfectible even against the corruption of the earthly realm. This strain of thought reaches back to the ancient Gnostics, who saw the material world as essentially corrupt, even evil, and thus the human spirit's seeking awareness as alien to the profane realm of the phenomenal. Unlike the revelation of Judaism and Christianity, which speaks of the world as essentially good in spite of human tendencies to corrupt it due to Original Sin, the Gnostic regards the world and everything of the world as essentially evil. For Voegelin, this same strain of thought is present in modern political theory in the notion that the world is essentially estranged from the human subject; thus we are detached manipulators (positivism) or "estranged" (Hegel and Marx) on an ontological level from the world around us, or "disenchanted" (Weber) or "thrown" (Heidegger) and existentially alone within the world. For Voegelin this is the return of the Gnostic rejection of matter, and thus a rebellion against the structure of existence. The Gnostic claims to possess precise knowledge of the whole of reality, rejecting the limits of human thought and the boundaries of human action. We can know the world in its totality, and can use that knowledge to will its purification and thus achieve on our own, without relying on God or rational nature, our own perfection on our own terms. This is the Gnostic *hubris* that Voegelin sees beyond all mass movements that seek to storm the gates of Paradise, forcing a reentrance; or to bring the structure of salvation to earth by our own hands, to immanentize the eschaton. This, in effect, is the attempt to make literally heaven on earth—for Voegelin, this is nothing less than the usurpation by human beings of what is in reality the provenance of the Divine. This is accomplished through a claim to a critical insight, and set into motion through the construction of a system of knowledge that will enable the human mind both to know the whole of reality and then to use that knowledge to reform the real according to the structure of the system. For Voegelin, this is a Procrustean crime that leads not to liberation but to deformation of the human subject. It involves both the "murder of God" and the reduction of all values to power, a reduction that for Voegelin can only produce totalitarian systems—evidence of which is exposed in the inward dynamics of National Socialism and Stalinist Marxism, but also pervasive in less horrific forms through much of modernity.

Voegelin cautioned the political inquirer against the kind of system building that forces our examination of the human agent and the human condition into a fixed pattern of analysis that can at best only reveal particular, disconnected dimensions of human life. Against both the materialist empiricism of his times as well as the utopian speculations of the modern gnosis, Voegelin proposes a revival of the ancient *episteme politike,* a science of politics as a function of the philosopher's quest. Such a quest is attuned to the essence of what is objectively and, for Voegelin, transcendentally real, and not shaped on our terms alone or constructed from within the limitations of context and situation. As Socrates affirmed long ago, such a quest begins with the admission of the limitations of human knowledge and is aimed at the love of being. Socrates was never an alien in the world, even though the world was frequently at odds with Socrates. This is the model

for Voegelin, the best one that can be offered in comparison to the philodoxers who claim unlimited access to a hidden gnosis revelatory of the alien nature of the world. For Voegelin, the recovery of *episteme politike* begins not in alienation, but in openness to the essence of being as it is.

Related Entry
immanentize the eschaton

Suggested Reading
Sandoz, Ellis. *Eric Voegelin's Significance for the Modern Mind.* Baton Rouge: Louisiana State Univ. Press, 1991.
Voegelin, Eric. *The New Science of Politics.* 1952; repr. With a foreword by Dante Germino. Chicago: Univ. Chicago Press, 1987.
Voegelin, Eric. *Order and History,* 5 vols. 1956–1987; repr. Columbia, MO: Univ. Mo. Press, 2001.

Wahhabism (wahabism, wahabi Islam)
Named for its founder, Muhammad ibn Abd al-Wahhab (d. 1792) Wahhabism is a conservative strain of Islam that espouses a rejection of all innovations within Islam since the middle part of the tenth century. Since then, Islam has fallen away from the fundamental teachings of its founder Muhammad (d. 632), succumbing to numerous additions that have violated the principle of simplicity and piety as established in the religion's earliest decades. Beyond that, any commentary in Islam, especially after the tenth century, is suspect. A strict adherence to the purity of the faith as Muhammad envisioned it is the only true form of Islam, all other variations are in fact false and are to be spurned.

Wahhabism is associated today with Islamic extremism, particularly in its most violent form. For the wahhabi, it is permissible to kill a non-Muslim, and because only those who practice Islam as Muhammad and the first few generations practiced it are true Muslims, then it is permitted to use violence against all innovators and infidels. For this reason, most Muslims regard Wahhabism, which is the ideological base for terrorists such as al-Qaida, as a distortion of their faith. But the wahhabi would have it the other way around, refusing to acknowledge other forms of Islam, and insisting on a purity of doctrine that in their view is close to its source. For the wahhabi, only a return to Islam as practiced during its first two centuries will restore the faith to its pristine doctrine and requirements.

Related Entries
fundamentalism; *jihād*

Suggested Reading
Algar, Hamid. *Wahhabism: A Critical Essay*. Oneonta, NY: Islamic Publications International, 2002.

war of all against all

In describing the state of nature, Thomas Hobbes, in chapter 13 of *Leviathan* (1651), writes, "Hereby it is manifest that during the time men live without a common power to keep them all in awe, they are in that condition which is called war, and such a war as is of every man against every man." (*Bellum omnium contra omnes* in the Latin edition of *Leviathan*.) Further into the same chapter, Hobbes punctuates his observation by stating that "to this war of every man against every man, this is also consequent: that nothing can be unjust." In the following chapter, Hobbes reiterates the claim that the condition of man "is a condition of war of everyone against everyone," the justification for the natural right to everything as long as human beings remain in nature. Later in chapter 14 Hobbes repeats that the condition of nature, which is specifically equated with war, is a war of every man against every man (duplicated in chapter 19), and in chapter thirty Hobbes reminds us that, should the "essential rights of sovereignty" be revoked, the return to the "condition and calamity of a war with every other man (which is the greatest evil that can happen in this life)" is inevitable. In *On the Citizen* (*De Cive*), published in 1642 (Latin version), Hobbes anticipates this teaching through his observation that human beings have a "natural tendency [to] exasperate each other," caused by the passions and, when added to the "right of all men to all things," creates a natural condition of "war of every man against every man." Given natural equality, there is no victor in such a war and thus no end to it as long as human beings live in nature.

This "miserable condition of war" abolishes all the benefits of society: industry, culture of the earth and its produce, navigation and the commodities imported across the sea, commodious building, machines, knowledge of geography, time, arts, letters, and society in general. Perpetual fear and danger of violent death haunt the denizens of the state of nature—there is no enduring formal society, only a situation in which every person is obliged to attend only to their own interests in a constant state of colliding wills. All associations that do emerge are transitory and evaporate once self-interest is no longer served by what little cooperation might be wrung from such a state of affairs. For Hobbes, this is the sole reason why subjects must obey even bad rulers, for there is no tyrant so oppressive as to render the state of nature, which is identical to a state of ubiquitous war, preferable to our appetites and interests.

The war of all against all is not necessarily a state of constant combat. "For War," Hobbes elaborates, "consisteth not in battle only, or the act of fighting, but in a tract of time wherein the will to contend by battle is sufficiently known." The state of nature is thus a duration wherein individuals know that violence may be employed against them at any given moment. Hence the appetite for reputation (especially of one's power) becomes important during such a time, for if one can, through a reputation for cunning or ferocity, hold potential invaders at bay, then one can more readily sustain security against the encroachments of others. But even reputation is not enough to abate the war of all against all, for Hobbes remarks that no one is completely secure because we are all vulnerable to death at the hands of anyone around us, even the weakest among us being able to dispatch the strongest. This diffidence leads to a relentless uncertainty—we never know for certain if our person and our possessions are really secure, now or in the future, and above all (and more significantly), we are never certain if our actions in defense of or on behalf of our interests are incontrovertibly right. Uncertainty of body, things, and judgment is the worst aspect of life without a common power.

Hobbes does not attempt to prove a historical state of nature, his point, rather, is to remind us that human beings—creatures of passion—will place their interests first, and without the restraint of society, we would brook no quarter in the preservation of our lives and the pursuit of our security and pleasure. Hobbes punctuates this by observing, in chapter 13 of *Leviathan,* that we never fully transcend our natural enmity and distrust of others, for even in formal society with good laws and effective police, we lock our doors and chests wherein our valuables are stored. In so doing, we "accuse mankind" by our actions even in lawful society, and even in high civilization we retain aspects of our natural condition that are far more than simply echoes or atavistic reflexes of the past. The state of war is in our marrow; only rational submission to sovereign law allows us to carve out felicity in this world.

Related Entries
Hobbes, Thomas; Leviathan; *pleonexia*

Suggested Reading
Hobbes, Thomas. *Leviathan,* ed. Edwin Curley. Indianapolis: Hackett, 1994.

Welfare of the people is the supreme law

"*Salus populi suprema lex est*" is a phrase coined by Cicero in his *De Legibus.* This is a principle further developed out of the English common law tradition and affirmed by political theorists such as François Hotman, Samuel Pufendorf, and John Locke. Operating under this principle, governments and their citizens are obligated to put the interests of the whole above

that of governmental power or private interests. In a word, it is neither government nor citizenry that bear the sovereign will, but rather that will is located solely within the common good—it is the welfare of the people as a whole that reigns as sovereign above any office or institution, or any body, political or private. To engage otherwise is to commit an act of usurpation.

Related Entry
Cicero, Marcus Tullius

Suggested Reading
Cicero, *De Re Publica, De Legibus,* trans. C.W. Keyes. 1928; repr. Cambridge, MA: Harvard Univ. Press/Loeb Classical Library, 1977.
Franklin, Julian H., ed. *Constitutionalism and Resistance in the Sixteenth Century: Three Treatises by Hotman, Beza and Mornay.* New York: Pegasus Press, 1969.

What is conservatism?

Addressing the issue of slavery and its incompatibility with the American founding in his Cooper Union Address of 1860, Abraham Lincoln responded to his critics by drawing a distinction between "conservative" and "revolutionary." "But you say you are conservative—eminently conservative," Lincoln observed,

> while we are revolutionary, destructive, or something of the sort. What is conservatism? Is it not adherence to the old and tried, against the new and untried? We stick to, contend for, the identical old policy on the point in controversy which was adopted by "our fathers who framed the Government under which we live;" while you with one accord reject, and scoff, and spit upon that old policy, and insist upon substituting something new.

For Lincoln, the evidence for controlling slavery according to the intentions of the founders was clear; thus he viewed his own policy in this regard as "conservative," and therefore not radical, a charge made against him by pro-slavery apologists. Lincoln's statement is also of interest to those who seek a concise definition of what it means to be conservative—"adherence to the old and tried," a notion compatible with the sentiment of conservatism throughout its many variations. As a political thinker, Lincoln himself has been variously described as conservative, liberal, centrist, and revolutionary.

Related Entry
conservatism

Suggested Reading
Lincoln, Abraham. "Cooper Union Address," New York City, February 27, 1860. The text is available in many editions of Lincoln's works, including vol. 2 of the 2-vol. Library of America edition, *Speeches and Writings, 1859–1865,* ed. Don E. Fehrenbacher. New York: Literary Classics of the United States, 1989.

What is rational is real, and what is real is rational

In the preface to G.W.F. Hegel's *Philosophy of Right* (1821), the author states that "What is rational is real and what is real is rational," sometimes translated, as in the case of the widely read T.M. Knox version, "What is rational is actual and what is actual is rational." Hegel continues, "On this conviction the plain man like the philosopher takes his stand, and from it philosophy starts in its study of the universe of mind as well as the universe of nature." For Hegel, all historical events, political and legal institutions, social traditions and cultural expressions exist for a reason, and are thus in themselves inherently rational, even though the minds of human individuals cannot always comprehend the rationality of the current order. In Hegel's view, the world develops not out of chance, or even from the exertion of human will alone, but rather from some ineffable purpose that will become increasingly more evident as humanity inexorably progresses from the primitive to the more civilized. There is "reason in history," and therefore everything that is, in spite of its appearance, bears some rational purpose that will become evident with greater objectivity. Thus what actually exists can be said to be an expression of what is rational, for if reason does order history and culture, then nothing that is inherently irrational can emerge. It is only irrational from our inadequate perspective, but even that perspective will eventually come to know over time the fundamental rationality of history.

Hegel connects this principle with his theory of the state, which is to be fleshed out in full through the following pages of his *Philosophy of Right*. If the rational is actual, then the state, which is the highest form of political association, must therefore be rational as well. "This book," Hegel writes of his *Philosophy of Right*, "then, containing as it does the science of the state, is to be nothing other than the endeavor to apprehend and portray the state as something inherently rational." In other words, in Hegel's estimation, the state is as it should be, and in describing the state as it is, a prescription for the further development of the state is irrelevant, for the state in its current manifestation is a rational thing. "As a work of philosophy, it [*Philosophy of Right*] must be poles apart from an attempt to construct a state as it ought to be...it can only show how the state, the ethical universe, is to be understood." At this point, Hegel asserts another famous statement, "*Hic Rhodus, hic saltus*" (Here is the rose, here we dance), to punctuate his affirmation of the embrace of history as it has emerged to this point.

One can interpret Hegel's approach as a kind of realism, and yet that would work contrary to his fundamental idealist position. One might also discern in Hegel a sense of Stoic fatalism, a conclusion that might be fair enough, yet the complexity of Hegel's theory of progress and his reliance upon the concept of freedom as the goal of history might not be a perfect fit with the more deterministic strains of Stoic thought. In any interpretation offered, Hegel's central point is sustained; the history of the human race and the institutions and practices that have materialized and persisted in time are consonant with a higher purpose, one that is not immediately comprehended by the human intellect but one that is fully explained in terms of a deeper rationality in all things.

Related Entry
Hegel, Georg Wilhelm Friedrich

Suggested Reading
Hegel, Georg Wilhelm Friedrich. *Hegel's Philosophy of Right,* trans. T.M. Knox. New York: Oxford Univ. Press, 1977.

While power resides in the people, authority rests with the Senate

The aphorism "While power resides in the people, authority rests with the Senate" ("*Cum potestas in populo auctoritas in senatu sit*"), according to the philosopher Cicero, encapsulates the relationship between the formal authority of the government and its attendant institutions on the one hand and the legitimizing source of that authority, the people as a whole, on the other. While a government acts on its own authority in its official capacity, the ultimate power resides in the citizenry. Hence, as Cicero would say elsewhere (and others, such as St. Augustine, reiterate), the commonwealth is the "public's affair," and thus officialdom, while claiming its own right to act, must always defer to the public weal when properly understood and expressed. This notion was further developed within modern concepts of popular sovereignty, such as those advanced by John Locke and Jean-Jacques Rousseau.

Related Entry
Cicero, Marcus Tullius

Suggested Reading
Zetzel, James E.G. (trans.), *Cicero: On the Commonwealth and the Laws.* Cambridge: Cambridge University Press, 1999.

Wilt Chamberlain argument

Premised on the notion that "liberty upsets patterns," philosopher Robert Nozick developed the "Wilt Chamberlain" argument to illustrate the manner in which the voluntary actions of individuals freely making the most of their talents and opportunities will always alter any organized attempt to distribute social goods through the power of the state or even through the ideological preferences of a specific social

consensus. Chamberlain, a dominating basketball player in the 1960s and one of the preeminent professional athletes of his day, became the exemplary instrument of Nozick's critique of both welfare liberalism and more radical forms of redistribution as proposed or implemented within socialist systems.

Nozick's theory of just distribution is rooted in his notion of entitlements defined in terms of "just holding," or social goods and economic benefits that are acquired and transferred by free agents. Such an arrangement, Nozick contends, would be preferred by any group of rational individuals provided they are not coerced. To prove this premise, Nozick invites the reader to "suppose a distribution favored by [a] non-entitlement" pattern. Consider introducing an individual, like Wilt Chamberlain, whose gifts at his chosen profession put his services in high demand. Chamberlain's abilities are so superior to his fellow basketball players that he is able to arrange a special contract for himself wherein he will receive a quarter for each ticket sold to games in which he participates, the money allotted to Chamberlain to be placed in a separate box at the gate. Fans are eager to pay this separate charge as Chamberlain on the court is worth seeing for its own sake. Consequently, Chamberlain's annual salary far surpasses the average earnings of the rest of the league, which was initially regulated under the established nonentitlement pattern. This was the result of voluntary transactions. No one had to attend the games, nor were they forced to drop additional change into Chamberlain's box. Nozick muses that they "could have spent it on going to the movies, or on candy bars, or on copies of *Dissent* or *Monthly Review,*" but of their own volition the fans chose to accept Chamberlain's contract and freely rewarded his talents in a manner different from the established pattern regulating the rest of the league. Additionally, Chamberlain works overtime, exhibiting his talents outside of league games and on his own time, earning still more than his basketball comrades. Fan response to Chamberlain's talents and his initiative to rewrite the rules result in a shift from the old engineered pattern of distribution to an entirely new arrangement spontaneously generated by free individuals acting on their own rational decisions. "Liberty upsets patterns," concludes Nozick, thereby providing a substantively challenging critique of the activist state and theorists, such as John Rawls, who support it.

Related Entries
entitlement theory; Rawls, John

Suggested Reading
Nozick, Robert. *Anarchy, State and Utopia*. 1974; repr. Malden. MA: Blackwell, 2003.

worst form of government, except for all the others

Sir Winston Churchill described democracy as the worst form of government except for all the others in a speech delivered in his inimitable style to the House of Commons on November 11, 1947. The actual quotation from that speech is as follows: "Many forms of Government have been tried and will be tried in this world of sin and woe. No one pretends that democracy is perfect or all wise. Indeed, it has been said that democracy is the worst form of Government except all those other forms that have been tried from time to time."

Epigrammatically, Churchill insightfully reminds us that, even though democracy with its many flaws and tendency to produce political miasma, is generally a more amenable form of government than most other regimes. More deeply, Churchill's comment reminds us of the reality of human limitations. No government is ideal, and even that government that might be embraced as the best by a sizeable portion of the world is at best the "worst form except for all the others," and far from the perfection that human beings expect without possessing the ability to realize.

More recently (1999), political scientists Richard Rose, William Mishler, and Christian Haerpfer have called this famous dictum the "Churchill Hypothesis," and have claimed that it is actually a hypothesis that can be tested to demonstrate the relationship of democracy to other types of regimes. If a given population has been governed by both democratic and nondemocratic regimes, and if they have suffered the worst that can be offered from both categories, then it is possible to test whether or not people in general would prefer the disadvantages of democracy to those of nondemocratic regimes. In this way, Churchill's potent epigram can be examined and analyzed using the rigorous methods of social science.

Regardless of the results of any study, Churchill's dictum still stirs an important reminder in the psyche of even the most uncompromising critic of democratic government and politics. For all its many foibles and in some real cases, dangers, democracy at its worst is still a regime that people in general regard with some, even if begrudging, admiration.

Related Entries
conservatism; democracy; Plato

Selected Reading
Jasiewicz, Krzysztof. "The Churchill Hypothesis." "Books in Review," *Journal of Democracy* 10:3 (1999), 169–173.
Rose, Richard, William Mishler, and Christian Haerpfer. *Democracy and Its Alternatives: Understanding Post-Communist Societies*. 1998; repr. Baltimore: Johns Hopkins Univ. Press, 2000.

X

Xenophon (430 BC–350 BC)
Xenophon presents students of philosophy with another source for the life of Socrates, one that supplements Plato's more famous treatment without deviating from the basic image of the great master. While Plato's depiction of Socrates appears more complete and in most cases is more compelling, Xenophon's account is worth examining as a means toward a still fuller picture of the manner in which Socrates was perceived in his time.

Xenophon's writings accentuate Socrates as a person of admirable moral resolve and irreproachable piety (a swipe at Socrates's accusers), presenting him as more practically oriented when compared to Plato's Socrates (although not in a way that provokes tension between the two accounts), focused on immediately useful definitions of concepts (a marked difference from Socrates as Plato usually portrays him) and committed to the pursuit of truth through the cultivation of *elenchus,* or critical questioning and conversational inquiry. For the most part, Xenophon's Socrates is presented as interested in the utility of his teachings and in the manner in which those teachings can be easily set into motion through practice. Interestingly, Xenophon does not introduce the Forms in his Socratic conversations, a crucial difference setting him apart from Plato.

Admired by Machiavelli and well regarded in the eighteenth century by prominent intellectuals such as the Earl of Shaftesbury, Xenophon today wields considerably diminished influence. Nonetheless, Leo Strauss and Alexandre Kojeve significantly center their discussion of tyranny on Xenophon's dialogue *Hiero,* and in so doing, helped to reignite interest in Xenophon and reconsideration of his proper place in the traditional canon of political ideas.

Related Entries

Plato; Socrates; Strauss, Leo

Suggested Reading

Xenophon. *Memorabilia, Oeconomicus, Symposium, Apology,* trans. E.C. Marchant and O.J. Todd. 1923; repr. Cambridge, MA: Harvard Univ. Press/Loeb Classical Library, 1992.

Z

Zionism

Initially coined by Nathan Birnbaum in 1891, the term *Zionism* encompasses a variety of ideals and strategies all centered around the cohesion and future survival of the Jewish people as a nation. Partly motivated by the resurgence of anti-Semitism across Europe in the latter half of the nineteenth century and in part a product of the larger movement of nationalism that marked the *fin de siècle,* Zionism provided an ideological framework wherein Jews could advance both a sense of unity within and their interests as a distinctive people among the broad community of nations. In a fuller sense the notion of Jewish distinctiveness is traced to Biblical times, and the hope of returning to the Holy Land as old as the Diaspora, but it is really within the age of ideology that characterizes the nineteenth century that Zionism became a focused theoretical position as well as a political movement.

For the most part, Zionism is understood in two general ways: cultural/spiritual Zionism focusing on Judaism as a religious identity and the Jewish people as a cultural community and political Zionism directed at the founding of an actual Jewish state. The writings and activities of Theodor Herzl, often attributed as the founder of modern Zionism, represent the latter, while Jewish existentialist Martin Buber is usually associated with the former. Prior to Herzl, socialist author Moses Hess advocated a sense of Jewish nationalism not unlike that underway in Italy at the time. Additionally, Jewish immigration (or *aliya,* "going up) to the Holy Land increased in the latter decades of the nineteenth century as part of an overall design to restore a significant Jewish presence in the homeland. The revival of Hebrew as a practical language further reaffirmed the cultural aspects of Zionism, effectively renewing a sense of Jewish culture independent of European influences. A second wave of immigration (or second *aliya*) was influenced by socialist practices, launching the *kibbutz* movement that would continue into the foundation and growth of the state of Israel. From the kibbutz a new type of Zionism, known as "labor Zionism," contributed a new voice to the promotion of Jewish cultural freedom and political autonomy. David Ben-Gurion, Israel's first prime minister, was drawn to the socialist idealism of the labor wing of Zionism and helped to promote the *kibbutz* movement as an important element of the settlement and development of the new Israel. Chaim Weizman, Israel's first president, viewed labor Zionism and political Zionism as two strategies advancing the same goal, and sought to merge their disparate methods through a "synthetic Zionism" that adopted a broad political and economic agenda. Critical of labor Zionism for its perceived fixation on a Jewish working class, "revisionist Zionism" sought to emphasize the need for Jewish self-defense along with a more rapid and assertive immigration to the Holy Land (rejecting the gradualist approach favored by Herzl) and elevated the notion of the Jewish nation above economic concerns or more bland political objectives. "Post-Zionists" represent a fairly recent approach to Jewish nationhood, seeking to reduce the fervor for an exclusively Jewish nation in response to the ongoing tensions between Jews and Arabs in the Middle East and hoping to restructure the image of Israel as a multinational state.

Zionism encapsulates a positive affirmation of Jewish identity, politically, economically, and culturally. Nonetheless, critics of Israel as well as contemporary anti-Semites prefer to use the terms "Zionism" and "Zionist" as pejoratives. Nonetheless, Zionism has primarily meant a general movement for the promotion of the Jewish people, particularly in the aftermath of the Holocaust, and containing specific approaches to and conceptions of what it means to be a "light unto all nations."

Related Entries
anti-Semitism; Buber, Martin; Herzl, Theodor; ideology; nationalism

Suggested Reading
Herzl, Theodor. *The Jews' State: A Critical English Translation,* trans. Henk Overberg. Lanham, MD: Jason Aronson, 1997.

Laqueur, Walter. *A History of Zionism: From the French Revolution to the Establishment of the State of Israel.* New York: Schocken Books, 2003.

zoon politikon

The "political animal" in the ancient Greek; *zoon politikon* is a phrase from Aristotle's *Politics* employed as a way to punctuate the principle that the human person is by nature a political being, and thus our humanity cannot be fully appreciated without a consideration of the political sphere as an ontological necessity. Only beasts and gods are capable of habitation outside the *polis;* for human beings, the city is vital for the achievement of self-sufficiency through the mutual cooperation of citizens within the larger community. Self-sufficiency, which is beyond the isolated person, and flourishing, which is the consequence of the public person, are both secured within the institutions and practices of political life, the life of the *politeas* (citizen). The city is the ground for the enactment of law, the affirmation of justice, and the development of friendship. Each of these ennobles the human animal, and each of these is in some way dependent on the commitment to a political and public existence. Indeed, each of these is a part of our potential nature and is only actualized within the *polis,* which is itself indispensable for our humanity. Hence for Aristotle as well as for Plato before him, the creature that is the human person is also a political person. One cannot be less and remain human, nor can one become more without consorting with the divine.

Related Entry
Politics

Suggested Reading
Aristotle. *Politics,* trans. H. Rackham. 1932; repr. Cambridge, MA: Harvard Univ. Press/Loeb Classical Library, 1977.

SELECTED BIBLIOGRAPHY

This bibliography is provided to supplement those "suggested readings" already supplied within this text. It is not meant to be comprehensive, but only as a signpost of other works that are more likely to interest students of political theory and the objective study of ideology. From these works, additional bibliographies can be consulted and the adventure that is political thought pressed forward still further. Moreover, a good portion of the works enumerated below have influenced the writing of this text, perhaps in ways that are unrealized even by the author, who acknowledges innumerable debts to teachers and students of political inquiry across the discipline. Finally, it would be impossible to provide a complete list of recommended sources for the simple reason that political theory as a discipline of study is growing at an unprecedented pace. The moment this bibliography emerges in print, it will already be dated. Hence, what is offered here is a sample of works that the author believes will remain timeless, as well as more recent works that promise to hold merit well into the future.

A NOTE ABOUT PRIMARY TEXTS

All students of political ideas must read through the primary texts of the Great Tradition, from the ancient Greeks forward to the finest works of the past century. There is not space available to provide a proper bibliography of these great works in this volume; however, it will be easy to locate these texts as the ageless canon is readily available in print. In particular, certain publishing houses generously concentrate their considerable resources to supply the public with the great books. Some of the publishers that can be recommended due to their commitment to this endeavor are as follows: Harvard's Loeb Classical Library, Hackett Publishing Company, Penguin Classics, Mentor Books, Cambridge Texts in the History of Political Thought, Oxford World Classics, W. W. Norton, Liberty Classics, Modern Library, Focus Publishing, Broadview Publishing, and Gateway Books. These and other publishing houses are dedicated to the dissemination of principal works in political thought, each offering extensive and diverse catalogs.

Additionally, there are some excellent anthologies in circulation, provided by Hackett Publishers, Oxford, Blackwell, St. Martin's, Broadview, Avon Books, Modern Library, Penguin and Norton.

ENCYCLOPEDIAS AND DICTIONARIES

This is not the first encyclopedic overview of political thought. There are many fine volumes that cover general philosophy that will provide additional information and insight to help launch students of political inquiry toward still more serious study. Among these previously published works are those cited below.

Multivolume Sets

Craig, Edward. *Routledge Encyclopedia of Philosophy*. New York: Routledge, 1998.
This set ambitiously runs to ten volumes, and includes philosophical traditions drawn from Eastern as well as Western thought. By any standards it is a useful reference source for any scholar or general reader who is searching for a comprehensive guide.

Edwards, Paul, et al. *The Encyclopedia of Philosophy*. New York: Macmillan and Free Press, 1967.
   A classic among specialized encyclopedias, this four-volume set remains one of the more reliable sources for students in search of substantive introductions to thinkers, themes and topics within general philosophy. The entries range from brief to extensive, and the writing is generally clear and efficient.

Single-Volume Works

Angelis, Peter. *The Harper Collins Dictionary of Philosophy*. New York: HarperCollins, 1992.
   This volume provides readers with a quick and accessible introduction to the field of philosophy as a whole. It holds a strong appeal to serious and casual students alike.
Blackburn, Simon. *The Oxford Dictionary of Philosophy*. New York: Oxford, 2007.
   A nice introduction to a variety of philosophical ideas and the thinkers who developed them, this volume includes entries effectively describing both Western and Eastern philosophy. The entries are brief and well written, and will stimulate readers to continue their exploration.
Craig, Edward. *Concise Routledge Encyclopedia of Philosophy*. New York: Routledge, 1999.
   This is a refreshingly inclusive volume. As in the Blackburn text, the entries are fairly short, but this text's concision allows a wider variety of thinkers and ideas than one will find in other editions.
Honderich, Ted. *The Oxford Companion to Philosophy*. New York: Oxford, 1995.
   This Oxford volume is an impressive effort covering general philosophical ideas and thinkers in one exhaustive volume. The entries are both lively and engaging. The longer entries are pleasantly thorough, while the shorter entries manage to convey the central themes and points with both brevity and clarity. This volume also makes a solid effort at representing the diversity of philosophical movements, and there are a fair amount of entries from Eastern traditions as well as those more familiar to readers steeped in Western approaches.
Mauntern, Thomas. *The Penguin Dictionary of Philosophy*. New York: Penguin Reference, 2005; and Mauntern, Th. *The Penguin Dictionary of Critical Theory*. New York: Penguin Reference, 2002.
   The Penguin tradition of promoting the study of great ideas continues in these compact but substantively loaded volumes. The *Dictionary of Philosophy* supplies readers with a firm exposure to the full range of Western philosophy. The *Dictionary of Critical Theory* is the only volume of its kind offering a systematic summary of key ideas and thinkers in the critical theory movement of the twentieth century.

On-Line References

By and large, serious scholars must be wary of the Internet universe, as there is much chaff among the wheat. However, there are a few excellent encyclopedic sources on-line, and there is considerable potential for cyberspace as a conveyor of knowledge, given the right guidance and assurance of quality. There are three sources on-line that can be confidently recommended.
Dictionary of the History of Ideas. http://etext.virginia.edu/DicHist/dict.html
   An on-line reprinting of an older series, the *Dictionary of the History of Ideas* allows students to browse through a broad variety of concepts and themes in the discipline of intellectual history, many of which have a direct bearing on political and social thought.
The Internet Encyclopedia of Philosophy. http://www.iep.utm.edu/
   This is a carefully produced resource that always succeeds in offering solid overviews of any given topic in general philosophy. It is peer-reviewed and thus the information contained on this site accurate and well-managed.
Stanford Encyclopedia of Philosophy. http://plato.stanford.edu/
   This is the best on-line reference for general philosophy. The entries are all expertly written and informative. For the most trustworthy on-line introduction to a given topic in philosophy, a dedicated student will be satisfied by what is offered on the Stanford site.

Histories and Analytical Surveys

Students of philosophical and political ideas should begin with primary texts, but are nonetheless well-served by consulting good historical surveys that help explain complex theories within the historical context. Among the better volumes you will find those offered here.

Black, Antony. *The History of Islamic Political Thought: From the Prophet to the Present.* New York: Routledge, 2001. This is the only volume of its kind, and it is to our great fortune that it is an excellent one. Black's treatment of the history of Islamic political thought is meticulous and stimulating, going beyond the expectations of most introductory texts.

Copleston, Frederick, S.J. *A History of Philosophy.* New York: Doubleday, 1946. Brilliant, accessible and exhaustive, Copleston's nine volume *opus* is a required reference in the library of any serious lover of wisdom.

Eatwell, Roger and Wright, Anthony. *Contemporary Political Ideologies.* London and New York: A Casell Imprint, 1993. Eatwell and Wright have gathered and edited select essays exploring the major ideologies prominent in the world today. Each essay is tightly written and useful, and the volume is prefaced with a basic discussion of the nature of ideology as such.

Germino, Dante. *Beyond Ideology: The Revival of Political Theory.* Chicago: The University of Chicago Press, 1967. Germino's slim volume is the best discussion of the relationship between political theory and ideology available. It serves as an exciting introduction to political theory as well as an irresistible critique of ideological thinking.

Hallowell, John H. and Porter, Jean M. *Political Philosophy: The Search for Humanity and Order.* Englewood Cliffs, NJ: Prentice Hall, 1997. This highly recommended single-volume study of political theory covers the tradition from the Pre-Socratics through the nineteenth century in an intelligent and engaging manner. Complex ideas are explained with ease, making this one of the more accessible texts for new readers while remaining a helpful review and refresher for more experienced scholars.

Klosko, George. *History of Political Theory.* New York: Harcourt Brace, 1993 and 1995. Klosko's two-volume introduction to political theory is well worth the attention of students at all levels of political study. Here is provided a solid frame of reference within which students can find a reliable supplement as they endeavor to orient themselves in their exploration of the classics in the Great Tradition.

McDonald, Lee. *Western Political Theory.* New York: Harcourt, Brace, Jovanovich, Inc., 1968. This three-volume set is the finest overview of the Great Conversation of political theory available. McDonald's discussion is always insightful and evenhanded, and his scope far more comprehensive than most texts of its kind. As with that of Copleston, McDonald's text is essential.

Passmore, John. *The Perfectibility of Man.* Indianapolis: Liberty Classics, 2000. Passmore's thematic overview of the history of political ideas is compelling and worth reading. The running examination of perfectibility successfully introduces students to important dimensions of political theory.

Sabine, George H. *A History of Political Theory.* New York: Holt, Rinehart, and Winston, 1937. Sabine's historical treatment is a reliable and astonishingly thorough overview of the history of political ideas. For those who are seeking their first exposure to political theory as well as for those who require a quick review, Sabine's volume remains solid.

Schall, James V. *Roman Catholic Political Philosophy.* Lanham, MD: Lexington Books, 2004. Schall's book provides a superior discussion of the contribution of Catholicism to the exploration of political ideas and the promotion of higher principles. It will provide serious and casual readers alike with important perspectives on the great and enduring questions that mark the adventure of political theory.

Skinner, Quentin. *The Foundations of Modern Political Thought.* New York: Cambridge University Press, 1978. Skinner's two-volume introduction to modern theory is extensive and compelling and unlike any of its kind in scope and depth. For students of modern theory, this is an excellent entrée into the universe of political thought from the Renaissance forward.

Strauss, Leo and Cropsey, Joseph. *History of Political Philosophy.* Chicago: University of Chicago Press, 1963, 1972, and 1987.

342 SELECTED BIBLIOGRAPHY

There is no better selection of essays on the major thinkers than the familiar Strauss-Cropsey text. Each essay, devoted to a seminal figure within the canon, is in itself a modern classic of scholarly commentary. As with Copleston's and McDonald's contributions, this is an essential requirement for the scholar's library.

Vincent, Andrew. *Modern Political Ideologies*. Oxford: Blackwell Press, 1992.

In this volume students will find an excellent summary of main ideological currents. For those who are now beginning to explore the nature and history of ideology, Vincent's work is an effective launching point.

Voegelin, Eric. *Order and History*. Baton Rouge: Louisiana State University Press, 1956.

This epic achievement is divided into five volumes: *Israel and Revelation, The World of the Polis, Plato and Aristotle, The Ecumenic Age,* and *In Search of Order.* Not for the casual reader, but thoroughly engaging to the serious student. While this work requires some effort, it is rewarded by Voegelin's incomparable insight into the meaning and purpose of ideas about politics and the human condition.

Wolin, Sheldon. *Politics and Vision*. Princeton: Princeton University Press, 1960, 2004.

Wolin is familiar to all students of political thought primarily through this erudite and compelling study of the history of political ideas. While it serves as an introduction to the history of political ideas, it has in itself become an indispensable work of modern political commentary.

In addition to the volumes mentioned above, the Cambridge series in the history of political thought (Cambridge University Press) is an enriching investment of one's time and energy. The series is divided into six remarkably comprehensive volumes: *Greek and Roman Political Thought,* edited by Christopher Rowe and Malcolm Schofield, *Medieval Political Thought,* edited by J.H. Burns, *Political Thought, 1450–1700,* edited by J.H. Burns and Mark Goodie, *Eighteenth Century Political Thought,* edited by Mark Goldie and Robert Wokler, *Nineteenth Century Political Thought,* edited by G.S. Jones and G. Claeys, and *Twentieth Century Political Thought,* edited by Terrence Ball and Richard Bellamy. The contributions to this series are superior, and any student of the history of ideas would benefit from the inclusion of this resource in their personal library. Additionally, Cambridge University Press publishes a companion series that focuses on recent writings devoted to a specific thinker within the tradition, ranging from Plato through Habermas and offering students the opportunity to explore academically sound secondary literature examining further the ideas of the classics.

Selected Recommended Commentaries and Critical Overviews

Adler, Mortimer J. *Six Great Ideas*. New York: Touchstone Books, 1997; and *Ten Philosophical Mistakes*. New York: Touchstone Books, 1985.

For any student attempting to sort through the essential issues, any of Adler's books will serve as both introduction and encouragement to a more profound understanding. These two are mentioned for their relevance to the Great Conversation, but any of Adler's text will compel curious minds.

Arendt, Hannah. *The Human Condition*. Chicago: University of Chicago Press, 1958.

Few books are as compelling and enduring as this one. Not for the light reader, *The Human Condition* affords all serious students of politics and philosophy ample inspiration to more deeply engage the issues of our time.

Berlin, Isaiah. *Four Essays on Liberty*. New York: Oxford University Press, 1969.

Berlin's four texts on liberty are seminal reading in the history of ideas, and will prompt debate among more attentive readers.

Bernstein, Richard J. *Beyond Objectivism and Relativism*. University Park, PA: University of Pennsylvania Press, 1983.

Bernstein's work bridges several contemporary schools of thought and thus provides readers with one of the better discussions of the more recent developments in intellectual history.

Brunschwig, J. and Lloyd, G. (with Catherine Porter), *Greek Thought: A Guide to Classical Knowledge*. Cambridge, MA: Harvard/Belknap, 2000.

This is one of the better single-volume studies of the ancient foundations of political theory, covering the full scope of Greek ideas and culture from the Pre-Socratics through the Hellenistic schools. It is a solid introduction to the history of ideas.

Eagleton, Terry. *Ideology: An Introduction*. New York: Verso, 1991.

Erudite, insightful, and often witty, Eagleton's critique of ideology provokes thought and seeks reflection while sharing valuable insights on the meaning of ideology and the character of ideological movements.

Elshtain, Jean Bethke. *Public Man, Private Woman*. Princeton: Princeton University Press, 1981.
An early voice in the reconsideration of classic texts through feminist interpretations, Elshtain's thoughtful book will encourage further study into the many dimensions of political inquiry.

Finnis, John. *Natural Law and Natural Rights*. Oxford: Clarendon Press, 1980.
For students interested in exploring the dimensions of natural law, right, and objective principles, Finnis's ample volume will direct serious readers to the higher questions while integrating theorists, past and present, drawn from numerous fields of study. Finnis is well grounded in classical and Medieval thought but is also quite familiar with modern and contemporary issues and movements.

Germino, Dante. *Political Philosophy and the Open Society*. Baton Rouge: Louisiana State University Press, 1982.
Germino's work is an exhilarating exploration of the transcendent nature of political thought, weaving themes at once philosophical and theological with the great questions raised through open political inquiry. It is through the spirit of openness that political theory is advanced, and Germino understands that openness as leading us beyond the mundane experiences of ordinary discourse and into the realm of the divine.

Gilson, Étienne. *The Spirit of Medieval Philosophy*. Notre Dame, IN: University of Notre Dame Press, 1936.
This is a powerful treatment of the development of ideas throughout the Middle Ages, one that carefully emphasizes the nexus between faith and reason that marks Medieval culture at its height.

Jay, Martin. *The Dialectical Imagination*. Boston: Little Brown and Company, 1973.
This is the best history available of the Frankfurt School and the origins of critical theory. Along with Scott Warren's book (also listed here), this serves as an effective springboard into the study of dialectical theory in its more open form.

Jung, Hwa Yol. *Rethinking Political Theory: Essays in Phenomenology and the Study of Politics*. Athens, OH: Ohio University Press, 1993.
Jung's ten essays offer exciting and provocative portals into the exploration of contemporary theory and thus serve in total as one of the better texts for students who are of a mind to engage in more recent developments in political inquiry.

Kirk, Russell. *The Conservative Mind*. Lake Bluff, IL: Regnary Books/Gateway Editions, 1986.
This is the best introduction to conservative political thought, and should offer much to any student of the history of ideas regardless of personal persuasion.

MacIntyre, Alistair. *After Virtue*. Notre Dame, IN: University of Notre Dame Press, 1981.
A serious study of moral philosophy past and present with important implications to political inquiry, this volume serves to draw readers into a deeper level of analysis. MacIntyre's work, both in this volume and elsewhere, remains compelling and increasingly relevant.

Nussbaum. Martha C. *The Fragility of Goodness*. New York: Cambridge University Press, 1986, 2001.
For students seeking a stimulating exposition of ancient political theory, Nussbaum's writings are excellent for readers at all levels of study. Here she engages in the relationship between ancient philosophy and tragedy, with an eye to the political realm.

Oakeshott, Michael. *Rationalism in Politics and Other Essays*. Indianapolis: Liberty Classics, 1962.
A monumental achievement, worth devoting one's energy to in the careful reconsideration of the Great Conversation, Oakeshott's essays provide insight and probity without fail.

Okin, Susan Moller. *Women in Western Political Thought*. Princeton: Princeton University Press, 1979.
Okin's volume is a landmark achievement, focusing on the question of women in political theory through the lens of classic thinkers.

Rorty, Richard. *Contingency, Irony, Solidarity*. New York: Cambridge University Press, 1989.
Rorty's work is perhaps the best introduction to the postmodern mood and supplies ample assertion to provoke debate. For students who are interested in the nature of certainty and its relationship to political action, this volume will serve well regardless of how one responds to it.

Searle, John. *The Construction of Social Reality*. New York: The Free Press, 1997.
Always lucid, Searle explores the nature of social thought and practice in a refreshingly candid manner.

Strauss, Leo. *City and Man*. Chicago: University of Chicago Press, 1964; *Studies in Platonic Political Philosophy,* University of Chicago Press, 1983; and *What is Political Philosophy? And Other Studies,* University of Chicago Press, 1959.

Strauss is one of the more important figures in the study of political theory, and the essays in these three volumes provide a fine introduction into the world of this subtle and often misunderstood student of ideas. Further reading in Strauss is also recommended, but for beginners these works will supply abundant opportunity for reflection.

Warren, Scott. *The Emergence of Dialectical Theory*. Chicago: University of Chicago Press, 1984, 2008.

Recently reissued, Warren's discussion of dialectical theory is essential to the student of modern and contemporary thought. It offers a far more comprehensive view than most treatments of dialectical thought, pulling in ideas and approaches from existentialism and phenomenology as well as critical theory. Warren's prose never fails to stir readers onward in pursuit of further knowledge and engagement with the ideas presented.

INDEX